Dictionary of British Portraiture

IN FOUR VOLUMES

EDITED BY RICHARD ORMOND AND MALCOLM ROGERS

WITH A FOREWORD BY JOHN HAYES
DIRECTOR OF THE NATIONAL PORTRAIT GALLERY

VOLUME

2

Later Georgians and Early Victorians · historical figures born between 1700 *and* 1800

COMPILED BY ELAINE KILMURRAY

B.T.BATSFORD LIMITED · *LONDON*
IN ASSOCIATION WITH
THE NATIONAL PORTRAIT GALLERY · *LONDON*

© *National Portrait Gallery* 1979
ISBN 07134 1470 7

Filmset in 'Monophoto' Bembo by
Servis Filmsetting Ltd, Manchester
Printed in Great Britain by
The Anchor Press Ltd,
Tiptree, Essex
for the publishers
B.T. Batsford Ltd,
4 Fitzhardinge Street
London W1H 0AH

Foreword

This four-volume *Dictionary of British Portraiture*, of which the first two volumes are now published, was the idea of Sam Carr, Director of Batsford. He was correct in his view that there exists no comprehensive handbook to the portraits of famous British men and women. Specialized surveys and studies there are, but no compact work to which the researcher or layman can turn easily for information about the likeness of this or that individual. The present dictionary cannot claim to be a complete or exhaustive study; inevitably there has to be a degree of selection in the people represented, and the portraits that have been listed. This is explained in the introduction. But within these limitations it does offer a reliable guide to the portraiture of a wide range of eminent British men and women from the Medieval period to the present day.

The dictionary relates directly to the purposes for which the National Portrait Gallery was founded in 1856: the collection, preservation and study of historical portraits. It has been compiled mainly from the Gallery's own immense archive, and I am delighted that its resources should be made available in this way. The information in the archive has been gathered slowly over the course of the last century or so by many devoted scholars and members of staff, and I think it is only right that I should first record our debt to them. Without their labours such a dictionary could never have been compiled. I would also like to pay a special tribute to the staff of the Guthrie Room, who maintain the archive, add to its holdings, and answer so many questions so patiently and efficiently. The work of editorial supervision has been handled most competently by my colleagues, Richard Ormond and Malcolm Rogers, who originally discussed the project with Sam Carr, and have now guided the first two volumes through the press. To Sam Carr himself we are grateful for his continuing enthusiasm and support, without which the project would never have materialised. Mrs Underwood undertook the task of typing the entries with her usual thoroughness and accuracy. Finally, I must thank our two hard-working and dedicated compilers, who took on the daunting job of recording and researching the thousands of portraits listed here. It is a tribute both to their enthusiasm and to their composure in the face of sometimes inadequate, sometimes confusing records, that the work has been completed so expeditiously. We are deeply grateful to them for the skill and accuracy with which they have carried out their task.

JOHN HAYES

Introduction

The aim of the present dictionary is to provide a listing of the portraits of famous figures in British history that are either in galleries and institutions, or in collections accessible to the public. It is intended for the general researcher and student who needs a reliable guide to portraits on public view of which illustrations can be obtained relatively easily. It is not concerned with the intricacies of iconography, though decisions have had to be taken about the likely authenticity of particular images, nor is it comprehensive. The decision to exclude portraits in private collections was dictated by the need to limit the scope of the work, by the difficulty of obtaining permission from owners to use their names, and by the impossibility of directing readers to the specific location of privately-owned works. In a few entries it has been indicated that a privately-owned portrait is the only known likeness, or the most significant likeness, of a particular person.

The series of detailed National Portrait Gallery catalogues have provided invaluable information for those sitters included in them. They are as follows:

Roy Strong *Tudor and Jacobean Portraits* (2 vols), 1969
David Piper *Seventeenth Century Portraits*, 1963
John Kerslake *Early Georgian Portraits* (2 vols), 1977
Richard Ormond *Early Victorian Portraits* (2 vols), 1973
Richard Walker *Regency Portraits*, forthcoming

Extensive use has also been made of Freeman O'Donoghue and Henry Hake, *Catalogue of Engraved British Portraits . . . in the British Museum* (6 vols), 1908–25.

Each volume of this dictionary covers a different historical period. Though there were arguments in favour of dividing the dictionary alphabetically, it was decided on balance that it would be more useful to make each volume self-contained. The chronological dividing-lines are inevitably arbitrary, and will mean that certain figures, whose contemporaries appear in one volume, are by accident of birth in another. But provided that the reader knows the birth date of his or her chosen subject, there should be no problem in turning to the correct volume.

The question of selection was a thorny one. We have relied heavily, though not exclusively, on the *Dictionary of National Biography*. A number of minor figures listed there are omitted in this work, and others who are excluded, but whom we felt to be important, appear in this dictionary. Readers will no doubt be disappointed by some omissions, but it is important to remember that the non-appearance of a particular figure may simply reflect the fact that no authentic portrait of him or her is known.

This is especially true of the earlier periods from which so few portraits survive.

The entries themselves are cast in a condensed form, but we hope they will be comprehensible once the format has been mastered.

The arrangement of the entries is as follows:

> Surname of the sitter, with Christian names (peers are listed under their titles)
> Birth and death dates, where known
> Profession or occupation
> Known portraits, recorded under:

P	Paintings	SC	Sculpture
D	Drawings	T	Tapestry
M	Miniatures	W	Stained-glass windows
MS	Manuscripts	PR	Prints
SL	Silhouettes	C	Caricatures
G	Groups	PH	Photographs

> Within each category portraits are listed chronologically, and then alphabetically by name of artist where known.

> Information on individual portraits is arranged as follows:

> name of artist
> date of portrait where known
> size (ie half length, whole length, etc)
> other distinguishing features (with Garter, in a landscape, etc)
> medium, in the case of drawings, groups, prints and caricatures
> location, with accession number in the case of national galleries and museums

> For further details see abbreviations opposite.

The absence of illustrations will be a cause of complaint. But the only possible solution would have been to illustrate everything (a selection would have satisfied few), and that would have made the series prohibitively large and expensive. In any case the dictionary has been conceived as a reference work and not a picture book, and it is as such that it must stand or fall.

RICHARD ORMOND

MALCOLM ROGERS

Abbreviations

A

ABBOT, Charles (1757-1829), see 1st Baron Colchester.

ABBOT, William (1789-1843) actor and dramatist.
PR UNKNOWN, hl, mezz, BM, NPG. Several theatrical prints, BM, NPG.

ABBOTT, Charles (1762-1832), see 1st Baron Tenterden.

ABBOTT, Lemuel (1760-1803) portrait painter.
PR V.GREEN, after L.Abbott, hl with crayon and print of Lord Nelson, mezz, pub 1800, BM, NPG.

ABEL, Carl Friedrich (1725-1787) musician.
P THOMAS GAINSBOROUGH, RA 1777, wl seated with viola da gamba, Huntington Library and Art Gallery, San Marino, USA. C.J.ROBINEAU, 1780, hl seated at harpsichord, Royal Coll. Attrib TEEDS, called Abel, hl, Faculty of Music, Oxford.
D THOMAS GAINSBOROUGH, c1763, tql seated, chalk, NPG 5081.
C JOHN NIXON, 1787, tql seated profile, playing, ink wash over chalk, NPG 5178.

ABERCORN, James Hamilton, 8th Earl of (1712-1789) representative peer of Scotland.
P THOMAS GAINSBOROUGH, 1778, wl in peer's robes, Alte Pinacothek, Munich.

ABERCROMBIE, John (1726-1806) writer on horticulture.
PR UNKNOWN, wl with spade, in garden, line, for *Every Man His Own Gardener*, pub 1800, BM, NPG.

ABERCROMBIE, John (1780-1844) physician.
PR F.CROLL, hs profile, medallion, line, for *Hogg's Weekly Instructor*, NPG.

ABERCROMBY, Alexander Abercromby, Lord (1745-1795) judge.
P SIR HENRY RAEBURN, 1788-1789, hl, Faculty of Advocates, Parliament House, Edinburgh.
SC JAMES TASSIE, 1791, paste medallion, SNPG 1257.

ABERCROMBY, James (1776-1858), see 1st Baron Dunfermline.

ABERCROMBY, Sir Ralph (1734-1801) general.
P JOHN HOPPNER, hl, SNPG 989; version, NPG 1538. COLVIN SMITH, after Hoppner, wl, SNPG 250.
G THOMAS STOTHARD, 'Sir Ralph Abercromby at the Battle of Alexandria, 1801', scene of his mortal wounding, oil, Royal Coll.
SC G.F.PIDGEON, 1801, silver medal, SNPG 1549. UNKNOWN, 1801, copper medal, SNPG 765. SIR RICHARD WESTMACOTT, equestrian figure on monument, St Paul's Cathedral, London.
PR Several popular prints, BM, NPG.
C J.KAY, 1801, 'Giving the word of command', etch, and 'Viewing the Army', etch, BM.

ABERDEEN, George Hamilton Gordon, 4th Earl of (1784-1860) prime-minister.
P M.HEALY, after Sir Thomas Lawrence of 1808, hl, Musée de Versailles, France. SIR MARTIN ARCHER SHEE, c1839, hs with ribbon and star, SNPG 1482. JOHN PARTRIDGE, c1847, tql seated, related to figure in NPG 342, NPG 750.
G P.C.WONDER, wl with Lord Farnborough and Sir Abraham Hume, pencil and oil, c1826, study for a large group, NPG 793.

SIR GEORGE HAYTER, 'The House of Commons, 1833', oil, NPG 54. SIR DAVID WILKIE, 'Queen Victoria Presiding over her First Council, 1837', oil, Royal Coll. SIR GEORGE HAYTER, 'Christening of the Prince of Wales', oil, 1842, Royal Coll. F.X.WINTERHALTER, 'Queen Victoria Receiving Louis Philippe at Windsor', oil, 1844, Palais de Versailles; version, Royal Coll. JOHN PARTRIDGE, 'The Fine Arts Commissioners, 1846', NPG 342, 3. E.M.WARD, 'Queen Victoria Investing Napoleon III with the order of the Garter', oil, 1855, Royal Coll.
SC WILLIAM THEED jun, c1865, plaster bust, possibly after Nollekens of c1814, Royal Military Academy, Sandhurst, Camberley, Surrey. MATTHEW NOBLE, 1874, bust, Westminster Abbey, London. SIR J.E.BOEHM, effigy, Great Stanmore Church, Middx.
PR S.COUSINS, after T.Lawrence, tql with seal of office, mezz, pub 1831, BM, NPG. T.WOOLNOTH, after A.Wivell, hl, for Jerdan's *Nat Portrait Gallery*, 1831, BM. E.DESMAISONS, tql seated, lith, pub 1843, BM, NPG. E.BURTON, after Sir John Watson-Gordon, wl in uniform, mezz, pub 1853, BM.

ABERNETHY, John (1764-1831) surgeon.
P SIR THOMAS LAWRENCE, 1820, tql, St Bartholomew's Hospital, London. C.W.PEGLER, 1828, tql seated, St Bartholomew's Hospital.
D GEORGE DANCE, 1793, hl profile, pencil, NPG 1253.
SC R.W.SIEVIER, 1828, marble bust, St Bartholomew's Hospital. SIR FRANCIS CHANTREY, 1833, marble bust, Royal College of Surgeons, London. WILLIAM GROVES, 1837, marble bust, St Bartholomew's Hospital.
PR J.THOMSON, after J.Partridge, hl profile, stipple, for *European Mag*, 1819, BM, NPG. R.COOPER, after C.Penny, tql, stipple, pub 1825, BM.

ABERSHAW, Louis Jeremiah, see Avershawe.

ABINGDON, Willoughby Bertie, 4th Earl of (1740-1799) politician.
PR M.BENEDETTI, after J.F.Rigaud, wl seated with his music-master playing the lute, stipple, pub 1800, BM, NPG.

ABINGER, James Scarlett, 1st Baron (1769-1844) chief baron of the exchequer.
PR B.HOLL, after C.Penny, hl, stipple, pub 1824, BM, NPG. H.COUSINS, after M.A.Shee, hl in old age, mezz, pub 1837, BM, NPG.
C J.DOYLE, 1829, wl 'A Joinder in the Pleas', pencil, BM. 'BENTIVOGLIO', tql profile, entitled 'A Bit of Scarlet', etch, BM, NPG.

ABINGTON, Frances, née Barton (1737-1815) actress.
P SIR JOSHUA REYNOLDS, 1764-65, wl as *The Comic Muse*, Waddesdon Manor (NT), Bucks. JOHAN ZOFFANY, 1768, wl in *The Way to Keep Him*, Petworth (NT), W.Sussex. SIR JOSHUA REYNOLDS, RA 1771, hs as Miss Prue in *Love for Love*, Yale Center for British Art, New Haven, USA. THOMAS HICKEY, 1775, wl as Lady Bab Lardoon in *The Maid of the Oaks*, Garrick Club, London.
D JAMES ROBERTS, several drgs in character, BM. ROBERT WEST, hs, chalk, oval, Garrick Club.
G JAMES ROBERTS, as Lady Teazle in a scene from *The School for*

Scandal, oil, RA 1779, Garrick Club.
PR Various theatrical prints, BM, NPG.
 C J.SAYERS, wl as Scrub in Farquhar's *Beaux Stratagem*, etch, pub 1786, NPG.

ACCUM, Frederick or **Friedrich Christian (1769-1838)** chemist.
PR J.THOMSON, after S.Drummond, hl, stipple, for *European Mag*, 1820, BM, NPG.
 C THOMAS ROWLANDSON, lecturing at the Surrey Institution, 1809, pen, pencil and w/c, Museum of London.

ACHESON, Sir Archibald, see 2nd Earl of Gosford.

ACLAND, Lady Christian Henrietta Caroline (1750-1815) wife of John Dyke Acland.
PR J.CHAPMAN, hs profile, stipple, oval, pub 1796, NPG. RIDLEY, after Rivers, hs profile, stipple, oval, pub 1800, NPG. S.W.REYNOLDS, after J.Reynolds, tql seated, mezz, pub 1820, BM, NPG.

ACLAND, John Dyke (d1778) soldier and politician.
PR S.W.REYNOLDS, after J.Reynolds, tql, mezz, pub 1820, BM, NPG.

ACLAND, Sir Thomas Dyke, 10th Bart (1787-1871) politician and philanthropist.
 P JAMES RAMSAY, hl, Ugbrooke Park, Devon.
 D SIR FRANCIS CHANTREY, hs profile, pencil, NPG 316a(1).
SC E.B.STEPHENS, 1861, statue, Exeter.
PR S.W.REYNOLDS, after W.Owen, wl in landscape, mezz, BM, NPG. F.C.LEWIS, after J.Slater, hs, stipple, one of 'Grillion's Club' series, BM, NPG.
PH HILL & SAUNDERS, tql seated, carte, NPG Francis Album.

A'COURT, William, see Baron Heytesbury.

ACTON, Sir John Francis Edward, Bart (1736-1811) prime minister of Naples.
 P G.M.GRIFFONI, hl, Coughton Court (NT), Warwicks.
 M P.E.STRÖHLING, hl, NPG 4982.
PR F.BARTOLOZZI, after C.Marsili, tql, stipple, NPG.

ADAIR, James (d1798) recorder of London, and king's serjeant.
PR C.H.HODGES, after G.Romney, tql, mezz, pub 1789, BM, NPG.

ADAIR, Robert (1711-1790) surgeon-general to the army, 'Robin Adair'.
PR J.JONES, after L.Abbott, hl, mezz, pub 1791, BM.

ADAIR, Sir Robert (1763-1855) diplomatist.
 P THOMAS GAINSBOROUGH, mid 1780s, hs, Baltimore Museum of Fine Art, USA.
 D SIR GEORGE HAYTER, head, pen and ink, BM.

ADAM, Alexander (1741-1809) writer on Roman antiquities.
 P SIR HENRY RAEBURN, tql seated, SNPG 2038.

ADAM, Sir Charles (1780-1853) admiral.
 G SIR GEORGE HAYTER, 'The House of Commons, 1833', oil, NPG 54.

ADAM, Sir Frederick (1781-1853) general.
 P WILLIAM SALTER, tql study for 'Waterloo Banquet', NPG 3689.
 G W.SALTER, 'The Waterloo Banquet at Apsley House', oil, 1836, Wellington Museum, Apsley House, London.
SC PAOLO PROSELENDIS, c1835, bronze statue, Corfu.

ADAM, James (d1794) architect to George III.
 P Attrib ALLAN RAMSAY, c1754, tql, Laing Art Gallery, Newcastle upon Tyne.

ADAM, John (1721-1792) architect, eldest of the Adam brothers.
SC JAMES TASSIE, 1791, medallion, NPG 4612.

ADAM, Robert (1728-1792) architect.
 P Attrib GEORGE WILLISON, c1773, tql, NPG 2953.
SC JAMES TASSIE, 1792, paste medallion, SNPG 262. JAMES TASSIE, paste medallion, SNPG 201.

ADAM, William (1751-1839) politician.
 P COLVIN SMITH, Kinross County Council.
SC UNKNOWN, bust, Abbotsford House, Borders region, Scotland.
PR S.W.REYNOLDS, after J.Opie, wl seated, mezz, pub 1804, BM, NPG. J.P.QUILLEY, after Colvin Smith, wl, mezz, pub 1833, NPG.

ADAMS, John (1764-1829) one of the mutineers of the *Bounty*.
PR J.A.VINTER, after R.Beechey, hl, lith, BM.

ADAMS, William (1706-1789) divine.
 P After JOHN OPIE, hl, Pembroke College, Oxford.

ADAMS, William (1772-1851) lawyer.
 D SIR GEORGE HAYTER, tql study for NPG 999, NPG 1695 h.
 G SIR GEORGE HAYTER, 'The Trial of Queen Caroline, 1820', NPG 999.

ADDINGTON, Anthony (1713-1790) physician.
 P JOHN ROWELL of Reading, c1750, hs, on glass, Royal College of Physicians, London.
SC THOMAS BANKS, 1791, marble bust, V & A; related bust, Royal College of Physicians.

ADDINGTON, Henry (1757-1844), see 1st Viscount Sidmouth.

ADDINGTON, Stephen (1729-1796) independent minister.
PR UNKNOWN, hs, line, oval, for *Protestant Dissenters' Mag*, 1796, BM, NPG.

ADDISON, John (1766?-1844) musician.
PR R.COOPER, after J.Slater, hl, stipple, pub 1819, BM, NPG.

ADDISON, Thomas (1793-1860) physician.
SC ALFRED HONE, 1838, marble bust, Royal College of Physicians, London. JOSEPH TOWNE, 1852, bust, Guy's Hospital, London.

ADELAIDE Amelia Louisa Theresa Caroline of Saxe-Coburg Meningen (1792-1849) Queen of William IV.
 P SIR WILLIAM BEECHEY, RA 1831, wl, Trinity House, London; related hl version, NPG 1533. JOHN SIMPSON, c1832, Brighton Art Gallery. SIR DAVID WILKIE, c1833, wl equestrian, SNPG 956. SIR DAVID WILKIE, c1835–38, wl, Examination Schools, Oxford. SIR MARTIN ARCHER SHEE, RA 1837, wl, Royal Coll. F.X.WINTERHALTER, c1849, hl seated, Royal Coll.
 D SIR DAVID WILKIE, c1833, with William IV, w/c study, TATE 1942. JOHN LUCAS, 1844, hs, pencil, BM.
 M MRS JAMES GREEN, probably c1821, tql seated, Royal Coll. SIR W.C.ROSS, 1844, Royal Coll.
 G HENRY ROOM, 'Queen Adelaide Receiving Malagissy Ambassadors', oil, 1837, Queen's Palace Museum, Madagascar. SIR GEORGE HAYTER, 'Marriage of Queen Victoria and Prince Albert', oil, 1840, Royal Coll. C.R.LESLIE, 'Christening of the Princess Royal', oil, 1841, Royal Coll.
SC G.BOUL, marble bust, Royal Coll. SIR FRANCIS CHANTREY, stone medallion, Ashmolean Museum, Oxford.
PR S.W.REYNOLDS, after A.Grahl, hl, mezz, pub 1833, BM. J.THOMSON, after J.Lucas, tql seated, stipple, pub 1845, BM, NPG. J.THOMSON, after G.Richmond, hs, stipple, pub 1845, BM, NPG. Various popular prints, BM, NPG.
 C Various caricature prints, BM, NPG.

ADOLPHUS Frederick, Duke of Cambridge (1774-1850) seventh son of George III.
 P THOMAS GAINSBOROUGH, 1782, hs in uniform, oval, Royal Coll. SIR THOMAS LAWRENCE, 1818, wl in uniform, with stars of Garter and of Black Eagle of Prussia, Royal Coll. By or after SIR

WILLIAM BEECHEY, tql in Garter robes, Yale Center for British Art, New Haven, USA. E.GUSTAVE GIRARDOT, 1845–47, wl, Army and Navy Club, London.
D HENRY EDRIDGE, wl, Royal Coll.
M SIR WILLIAM CHARLES ROSS, hl, Royal Coll.
G BENJAMIN WEST, wl with Princess Mary and Princess Sophia, oil, 1778, Royal Coll. BENJAMIN WEST, three family groups, the children of George III, oil, Royal Coll. GEORGE JAMES, 'The Banquet at the Coronation of George IV, 1821', oil, Royal Coll.
SC LAWRENCE MACDONALD, 1846, marble bust, Royal Coll. G.G.ADAMS, 1866, marble bust, Royal Coll.
PR D.CHODOWIECKI, aged 6, hs, medallion, etch, for *Lauenburg Calendar* for 1782, BM. UNKNOWN, hl in uniform, stipple, oval, pub 1806, BM, NPG. W.SKELTON, after W.Beechey, hl with star, line, pub 1808, BM. J.GODBY, after F.Rehberg, hs, stipple, oval, pub 1814, BM, NPG.
C JOHN DOYLE, equestrian, pencil, BM.

ADOLPHUS, John (1768-1845) barrister and historical writer.
PR W.RIDLEY, after Allingham, hl, stipple, oval, for *Monthly Mirror*, 1803, BM, NPG. V.GREEN, after T.Walker, hl, mezz, pub 1804, BM, NPG.

AFFLECK, Philip (1726-1799) admiral.
P EDWARD PENNY, c1767–74, wl seated, NMM, Greenwich. L.F.ABBOTT, hs, NPG 1579. UNKNOWN, after a portrait of c1793–95, hl, NMM, Greenwich.

AGAR, John Samuel (1770-1858) engraver.
D Self-portrait, head, profile, pencil, NPG 2560.

AGNEW, Sir Andrew, Bart (1793-1849) sabbatarian.
G SIR GEORGE HAYTER, 'The House of Commons, 1833', oil, NPG 54.
PR J.TALFOURD SMYTH, after Sir J.Watson-Gordon, hl, line, 1850, NPG.

AICKIN, Francis (d1805) actor.
PR C.GRIGNION, after R.Dighton, wl as Bolingbroke in Richard III, line, for Bell's ed of *Shakespeare*, 1776, BM, NPG.

AICKIN, James (1740-1803) actor.
P Attrib SAMUEL DE WILDE, hs, Garrick Club, London.
D UNKNOWN, hs, gouache, Garrick Club.
PR Several theatrical prints, BM, NPG.

AIKENHEAD, Mary (1787-1858) founder of the Irish Sisters of Charity.
P N.J.CROWLEY, RA 1845, seated, watching Miss Jane Bellew being received as a nun by Archbishop Murray, St Vincent's Hospital, Dublin.

AIKIN, Arthur (1773-1854) chemist and geologist.
D WILLIAM BROCKEDON, 1826, hs, chalk, NPG 2515 (9).
PR J.THOMSON, after S.Drummond, hs, stipple, for *European Mag*, 1819, BM, NPG.

AIKIN, John (1747-1822) physician and author.
G N.BRANWHITE, after S.Medley, 'Institutors of the Medical Society of London', stipple, pub 1801, BM.
PR C.KNIGHT, after J.Donaldson, hl, stipple, oval, BM.

AINSLIE, George Robert (1776-1839) general, governor of Dominica.
PR J.T.WEDGWOOD, after C.Hayter, hl in uniform, line, oval, BM.
C B.W.CROMBIE, 1838, wl, coloured etch, reprinted in *Modern Athenians*, 1882, NPG.

AIRLIE, David Ogilvy, Lord, 6th titular Earl of (1725-1803) Jacobite.
P COSMO ALEXANDER, 175?, hl, Airlie Castle, Tayside region,

Scotland. DAVID MARTIN, hl, Airlie Castle. After ALLAN RAMSAY, hl, wearing tartan, oval, Airlie Castle.

AITKEN, James (1752-1777) called 'John the Painter', executed for setting fire to Portsmouth Dockyard.
PR UNKNOWN, after W.Cave, wl in fetters, in Winchester gaol, line, pub 1777, BM, NPG. UNKNOWN, in the dock at his trial, line, BM, NPG.

AITKEN, John (1793-1833) editor of *Constable's Miscellany*.
PR W.H.LIZARS, after J.Chisholm, hl, line, NPG.

AITKIN, John (1747-1822), see AIKIN.

AITON, William (1731-1793) botanist.
P Attrib JOHAN ZOFFANY, hl, Royal Botanic Gardens, Kew.
M? GEORGE ENGLEHEART, hl, Royal Botanic Gardens, Kew.

AITON, William Townsend (1766-1849) botanist.
PR L.POYOT, 1829, hl, Royal Botanic Gardens, Kew.

AKENSIDE, Mark (1721-1770) physician and poet.
PR E.FISHER, after A.Pond, hl semi-profile, aged 35, mezz, for his *Poems*, 1772, BM, NPG.

ALBANY, Louisa of Stolberg-Gedern, Countess of (1753-1824) wife of Prince Charles Edward Stuart.
P UNKNOWN, c1772, hl with guitar, Stonyhurst College, Lancs. UNKNOWN, hs, SNPG 1520. Attrib H.D.HAMILTON, c1785, hl, called Countess of Albany, NPG 377. F.X.FABRE, tql seated, Uffizi Gallery, Florence.
D Attrib H.D.HAMILTON, hs, pastel, Musée Fabre, Montpellier.
M OZIAS HUMPHRY, c1772, hs, Burghley House, Northants. UNKNOWN, Edinburgh Castle.
PR A.GIARDONI, after C.Marsigli, tql with rose, line, oval, pub 1773, BM.

ALBEMARLE, George Keppel, 3rd Earl of (1724-1772) general.
P GEORGE ROMNEY, tql with Garter star, Goodwood, W.Sussex.
PR E.FISHER, after J.Reynolds, hl, mezz, BM, NPG.

ALBEMARLE, George Thomas Keppel, 6th Earl of (1799-1891) soldier and politician.
PR UNKNOWN, after a daguerreotype by Claudet, hs, woodcut, for *Illust London News*, 1852, NPG.

ALBEMARLE, William Anne Keppel, 2nd Earl of (1702-1754) general and diplomatist.
PR J.SMITH, after G.Kneller, as a child seated on a cushion, mezz, BM, NPG. J.FABER jun, after J.Fournier, tql, mezz, pub 1751, BM, NPG.

ALBEMARLE, William Charles Keppel, 4th Earl of (1772-1849) Master of the Horse.
G SIR GEORGE HAYTER, 'The Trial of Queen Caroline, 1820', oil, NPG 999. SIR DAVID WILKIE, 'The First Council of Queen Victoria', oil, 1837, Royal Coll.
PR C.TURNER, after M.A.Shee, wl, mezz, pub 1820, BM. UNKNOWN, wl with his groom, lith, BM, NPG.

ALCOCK, John (1715-1806) organist of Lichfield Cathedral.
PR W.NEWMAN, after R.Cooper, hl in robes, stipple, oval, for *Monthly Mirror*, 1797, BM, NPG.

ALCOCK, Thomas (1784-1833) surgeon.
P B.R.HAYDON, c1825, hs, Royal College of Surgeons, London.

ALDBOROUGH, Edward Augustus Stratford, 2nd Earl of (d1801) politician.
P Attrib MATHER BROWN, Oriental Club, London.
G FRANCIS WHEATLEY, 'The Irish House of Commons, 1780', oil, Leeds City Art Galleries, Lotherton Hall, W.Yorks. FRANCIS WHEATLEY, reviewing volunteers at Belan House, County Kildare, oil, Waddesdon Manor (NT), Bucks.

SC After JAMES TASSIE, plaster medallion, SNPG 483.
PR S.EINSLIE, after Thomas Gainsborough, hl in peer's robes, mezz, BM.

ALDERSON, Amelia, see Opie.

ALDERSON, Sir Edward Hall (1787-1857) baron of the exchequer.
P H.P.BRIGGS, tql in robes, Inner Temple, London. UNKNOWN, Caius College, Cambridge.

ALDERSON, John (1757-1829) physician.
P UNKNOWN, Wilberforce House, Hull.
SC SIR RICHARD WESTMACOTT, 1833, stone statue, Old Hull Royal Infirmary.

ALDIS, Sir Charles (1775?-1863) surgeon.
PR T.WAGEMAN, hs, stipple, for *European Mag*, 1817, BM, NPG.

ALDRIDGE, William (1737-1797) nonconformist minister.
PR POLLARD, hs profile, line, oval, NPG.

ALEMOOR, Andrew Pringle, Lord (d1776) judge.
P Attrib WILLIAM MILLAR, hl in robes, Faculty of Advocates, Parliament Hall, Edinburgh.

ALEXANDER, Daniel Asher (1768-1846) architect.
P Attrib JOHN PARTRIDGE, c1818, tql, NPG 4827.
D SIR FRANCIS CHANTREY, c1818, hs profile, pencil, V & A.

ALEXANDER, Michael Solomon (1799-1845) first Anglican bishop of Jerusalem.
PR J.W.COOK, after E.Fancourt, hl, stipple, pub 1843, NPG.

ALEXANDER, William (1767-1816) artist and first keeper of prints and drawings at the British Museum.
D Self-portrait, 179?, hl, pencil and ink, BM. SAMUEL COUSINS, 1815, hs, pencil, BM.
PR C.PICART, after H.Edridge, hs, aged 41, stipple, BM, NPG.

ALISON, Archibald (1757-1839) prebendary of Salisbury and writer.
SC JOHN HENNING, 1802, porcelain medallion, SNPG 529. SAMUEL JOSEPH, 1841, marble bust, SNPG 1219.
PR W.H.LIZARS, after 'P.Morris', tql seated, etch, for Lockhart's *Peter's Letters to his Kinsfolk*, 1819, BM, NPG. W.WALKER, after H.Raeburn, hl, stipple, pub 1823, BM, NPG.

ALISON, Sir Archibald, Bart (1792-1867) historian.
P ROBERT SCOTT LAUDER, two portraits, SNPG 323 and L285.
SC PATRIC PARK, marble bust, SNPG 1291.
PR L.GHÉMAR, hl, lith, BM. D.J.POUND, after Werge, tql seated, stipple and line, NPG.
PH MAULL and POLYBLANK, tql seated, NPG 'Photographs-Portraits' Album 44. Two cartes, NPG.

ALISON, William Pulteney (1790-1859) physician.
PR H.ROBINSON, after G.Richmond, hs, stipple, pub 1849, BM, NPG.

ALLAN, David (1744-1796) Scottish painter.
P Self-portrait, 1770, wl seated, SNPG L227. DOMENICO CORVI, 1774, hs, SNPG 731. JOHN MEDINA, after David Allan, hl, SNPG 325.
SC JAMES TASSIE, 1781, paste medallion, SNPG 261.

ALLAN, George (1736-1800) antiquary and topographer.
D UNKNOWN, hs, pastel, NPG 4307.
PR J.COLLYER, after J.Hay, tql seated with William Hutchinson, line, for Nichols's *Literary Anecdotes*, vol IX, 1814, BM, NPG.

ALLAN, Sir William (1782-1850) painter.
P WILLIAM NICHOLSON, hl, SNPG 1022. Self-portrait, 1835, hl, Royal Scottish Academy. SIR JOHN WATSON-GORDON, hl, Royal Academy, London.

D WILLIAM BEWICK, 1824, hs, chalk, SNPG 1048.
PR A.GEDDES, wl as a Circassian warrior, etch, BM.
PH D.O.HILL and ROBERT ADAMSON, three hl calotypes, NPG P 6 (9, 35, 55).

ALLARDICE, Robert Barclay (1779-1854) pedestrian.
PR WILLIAMS, wl on Newmarket Heath performing his feat of walking 1,000 miles in 1,000 hours, coloured aquatint, pub 1809, BM, NPG. UNKNOWN, wl walking, line, pub 1813, BM. R.M.HODGETTS, after J.Giles, tql, mezz, pub 1843, NPG.
C R.DIGHTON, wl, coloured etch, pub 1809, NPG.

ALLEN, John (1771-1843) historian.
P SIR EDWIN LANDSEER, 1836, tql seated, NPG 384.

ALLEN, William (1770-1843) chemist and philanthropist.
P H.P.BRIGGS, tql seated, Pharmaceutical Society, London.
G B.R.HAYDON, 'The Anti-Slavery Society Convention, 1840', oil, NPG 599.
PR C.BAUGNIET, after T.F.Dicksee, tql seated, lith, NPG.

ALLEN, William (1793-1864) rear-admiral.
D WILLIAM BROCKEDON, 1834, hs, chalk, NPG 2515 (68).
PR G.COOK, after W.Barclay, hl in uniform, line and stipple, for his *Narrative of the Expedition to the Niger in 1841*, 1848, BM, NPG.

ALLINGHAM, John Till (fl 1799-1810) dramatist.
PR W.RIDLEY, after S. de Wilde, hs, stipple, oval, for *Monthly Mirror*, 1804, BM, NPG.

ALLOWAY, David Cathcart, Lord (d1829) lord justiciary in Scotland.
P COLVIN SMITH, tql seated in robes, Faculty of Advocates, Parliament Hall, Edinburgh.

ALTEN, Sir Charles, Count von (1764-1840) general.
P G.F.REICHMANN, 1836, wl with orders, Royal Coll.
D THOMAS HEAPHY, 1813-14, hl, w/c, NPG 1914(1).
G J.W.PIENEMAN, 'The Battle of Waterloo', oil, Rijksmuseum, Amsterdam.

ALTHORP, Viscount John Charles, see 3rd Earl Spencer.

ALVANLEY, Richard Pepper Arden, 1st Baron (1744-1804) master of the rolls.
G K.A.HICKEL, 'The House of Commons, 1793', oil, NPG 745.
PR UNKNOWN, tql seated in judicial robes, coloured lith, BM, NPG.
C Two etchings by Dighton and Gilray, NPG.

AMELIA, Princess (1783-1810) 6th daughter of George III.
P Several paintings in Royal Coll: JOHN HOPPNER, RA 1785, wl seated with drum and spaniel; SIR THOMAS LAWRENCE, RA 1790, hl with roses, oval; SIR WILLIAM BEECHEY, RA 1797, hl seated; P.E.STROEHLING, c1805, wl leaning on sofa; P.E.STROEHLING, 1807, wl in landscape, with lyre.
D Several drgs in Royal Coll: JAMES ROBERTS, 1793, hl as a child, pencil and w/c, oval; HENRY EDRIDGE, wl, pencil and wash; JOSIAH SLATER, hl, pencil and wash.
M RICHARD COSWAY, 1802, hs?, V & A. RICHARD COSWAY, hs, Royal Coll. ANDREW ROBERTSON, 1811, hs, Royal Coll.
G JOHN SINGLETON COPLEY, 'The Three Youngest Daughters of George III', oil, RA 1785, Royal Coll.
PR J.S.AGAR, after Anne Mee, tql, a memorial print, stipple, pub 1811, BM, NPG.

AMELIA Sophia Eleanora, Princess (1711-1786) second daughter of George II.
P MARTIN MAINGAUD, 1718, wl with her sister Anne, in landscape, Royal Coll. PHILIP MERCIER, 1728, wl, Shire Hall, Hertford. Attrib J.B.VANLOO, c1738, tql in robe of state with coronet, Royal Coll. UNKNOWN, c1740, hs in robe, oval, Royal Coll. UNKNOWN, c1755, wl on horseback in park, Royal Coll.

DOROTHY, COUNTESS OF BURLINGTON, hs profile, Chatsworth, Derbys.

G MARTIN MAINGAUD, hl with Princesses Anne and Caroline, oil, 1721, Royal Coll. WILLIAM HOGARTH, 'The Family of George II', oil, c1731–32, Royal Coll; version, NGI 126. PHILIP MERCIER, 'The Music Party', Frederick, Prince of Wales, with his three sisters, oil, 1733, NPG 1556; version, Royal Coll.

SC JOHN SIGISMUND TANNER, medal, as a girl, BM. L.F.ROUBILIAC, bust, Fitzwilliam Museum, Cambridge.

PR J.SIMON, after Maingo, aged 9, tql with flowers, mezz, BM. UNKNOWN, after J.Amiconi, tql seated with coronet, line, BM, NPG. J.FABER jun, after H.Hysing, tql with cornet, mezz, BM.

AMESBURY, Charles Dundas, Baron (1751-1822) politician.

PR W.SAY, after W.Beechey, tql seated, mezz, BM, NPG.

AMHERST, Jeffrey Amherst, 1st Baron (1717-1797) field-marshal.

P By or after SIR JOSHUA REYNOLDS, 1765, tql in armour, with Bath star, Amherst College, Amherst, Mass, USA. Attrib THOMAS LAWRANSON, previously attrib Reynolds, c1785?, hs with Bath star, National Gallery of Canada, Ottawa. THOMAS GAINSBOROUGH, hl with Bath star, Amherst College; version, NPG 150.

G FRANCIS HAYMAN, 'The Clemency of General Amherst', oil, c1760, The Beaverbrook Art Gallery, Fredericton, Canada. M.F.QUADAL, 'George III at a Review', oil, 1772, Royal Coll. JOHN SINGLETON COPLEY, 'The Collapse of the Earl of Chatham in the House of Lords, 7 July 1778', oil, TATE 100, on loan to NPG.

SC After JAMES TASSIE, plaster medallion, SNPG 456.

PR S.W.REYNOLDS, after J.Reynolds, on horseback, in armour, mezz, pub 1820, BM.

C J.SAYERS, wl, etch, pub 1782, NPG.

AMHERST of Arracan, William Pitt Amherst, 1st Earl (1773-1857) statesman, governor-general of India.

P SIR THOMAS LAWRENCE, 1821, wl in peer's robes, Toledo Museum of Art, Ohio, USA. After A.W.DEVIS, wl in uniform, NPG 1546. F.R.SAY, tql in peer's robe, Christ Church, Oxford.

G SIR GEORGE HAYTER, 'The Trial of Queen Caroline, 1820', oil, NPG 999.

PR J.POSSELWHITE, after H.L.Smith, tql seated with star, stipple, BM, NPG.

AMORY, Thomas (1701-1774) dissenting tutor.

P UNKNOWN, hl, Dr Williams's Library, London.

PR J.WOODING, hs profile, line, oval, pub 1789, NPG. J.HOPWOOD, after Baxter, hl, stipple, BM, NPG.

AMOS, Andrew (1791-1860) lawyer.

P? UNKNOWN, Downing College, Cambridge.

PR J.H.LYNCH, after S.Laurence, tql, lith, NPG.

AMYOT, Thomas (1775-1850) treasurer of the Society of Antiquaries.

PR S.FREEMAN, after T.C.Wageman of 1836, tql, stipple, for Gent Mag, 1851, BM, NPG.

ANDERSON, Adam (d1846) physicist.

P? UNKNOWN, University of St Andrews, Scotland.

ANDERSON, Christopher (1782-1852) theological writer.

PR J.HORSBURGH, after a daguerreotype, tql, line, NPG.

ANDERSON, Sir George William (1791-1857) governor of Mauritius.

P UNKNOWN, Town Hall, Port Louis, Mauritius.

ANDERSON, James (1739-1808) economist.

SC After JAMES TASSIE, 1793, plaster medallion, SNPG 370.

PR B.PASTORINI, hs, stipple, pub 1795, BM. S.FREEMAN, after J.Anderson, tql seated, stipple, for Gent Mag, 1809, BM, NPG.

ANDERSON, James (d1809) botanist, physician-general of East India Company, Madras.

SC SIR FRANCIS CHANTREY, RA 1819, seated statue, Madras; model, Ashmolean Museum, Oxford. SIR FRANCIS CHANTREY, marble bust, Galleria d'Arte Moderna, Palazzo Pitti, Florence; model, Ashmolean Museum.

PR L.SCHIAVONETTI, after a miniature by J.Smart, hs, stipple, oval, BM, NPG.

ANDERSON, John (1726-1796) scientist.

P UNKNOWN, hs, SNPG 327. UNKNOWN, Royal Technical College, Glasgow.

SC After JAMES TASSIE, plaster medallion, SNPG 371.

PR SWAN, hl seated, line, pub 1825, NPG. W.HOLL, hl, stipple, for Chambers's Dict of Eminent Scotsmen, BM, NPG.

ANDERSON, Lucy (1790-1878) pianist.

PR R.J.LANE, after J.Notz, hl, lith, pub 1833, NPG.

ANDERSON, Robert (1750-1830) writer, editor of the Edinburgh Magazine.

SC UNKNOWN, wax medallion, SNPG 436.

PR W.H.LIZARS, hl seated, line, NPG.

ANDRÉ, John (1751-1780) major.

D Self-portrait, hl seated, pen and ink, sketch, Yale University, New Haven, USA.

SC VAN GELDER?, relief scene on monument, Westminster Abbey, London.

PR J.K.SHERWIN, after Major André, hs, stipple, oval, pub 1784, NPG. COOK, after Dodd, wl, line, for Raymond's Hist of England, BM, NPG. UNKNOWN, wl, line, BM.

ANDREWES, Gerrard Thomas (1750-1825) dean of Canterbury.

P Attrib SIR THOMAS LAWRENCE, hl, The Deanery, Canterbury.

PR R.DUNKARTON, after J.Pocock, tql, mezz, pub 1807, BM, NPG. S.W.REYNOLDS sen, after S.W.Reynolds jun, hl, mezz, pub 1834, BM, NPG.

ANDREWS, Henry (1743-1820) astronomical calculator.

PR T.BLOOD, after J.Watson, hs, stipple, pub 1820, NPG.

ANDREWS, James Pettit (1737?-1797) antiquary.

P School of REYNOLDS, hl, Society of Antiquaries, London.

PR J.CHAPMAN, after S.Drummond, hs, stipple, oval, for European Mag, 1796, BM, NPG.

ANDREWS, Miles Peter (d1814) dramatist.

PR W.RIDLEY, after P.Jean, hs, stipple, oval, for Monthly Mirror, 1797, BM, NPG.

ANDREWS, William Eusebius (1773-1837) journalist.

PR E.SCRIVEN, after T.Overton, hl, stipple, pub 1820, NPG.

ANGELO, Henry (c1755-1835?) fencing-master.

P SAMUEL DE WILDE, wl as Mrs Cole in The Minor, Garrick Club, London.

PR W.BOND, after W.Childe, hs, line, for his Reminiscences, 1828, BM. B.F.SCOTT, after J.R.Smith, hl, mezz, BM.

ANGERSTEIN, John Julius (1735-1823) merchant and picture collector.

P SIR JOSHUA REYNOLDS, RA 1765, hl in Vandyck dress, City Art Museum, St Louis, USA. SIR THOMAS LAWRENCE, three portraits: c1800, hl, NG 6370; c1810–15, tql seated, Metropolitan Museum of Art, New York, USA; after his portrait of c1816, hl, NG 129.

D GEORGE DANCE, 1795, hs, pencil, BM.

G SIR THOMAS LAWRENCE, wl with his wife Emily, oil, RA 1792,

Louvre, Paris.

PR J.G.WALKER, after T.Stothard, head, profile, line, pub 1824, BM, NPG.

C JAMES GILLRAY, several sketches for 'Connoisseurs examining a collection of George Morland's', chalk and ink, V & A.

ANGLESEY, Henry William Paget, 1st Marquess of (1768-1854) field-marshal.

P JOHN HOPPNER and SAWREY GILPIN, 1798, wl standing in uniform by his horse, Plas Newydd (NT), Gwynedd. SIR THOMAS LAWRENCE, 1817, wl standing in uniform, Plas Newydd. UNKNOWN, formerly attrib Sir William Beechey, 1817, hl in uniform, NPG 1581. J.W.PIENEMAN, 1821, hs sketch for 'The Battle of Waterloo', Wellington Museum, Apsley House, London. Attrib P.E.STRÖHLING, 1826, wl in uniform, riding a grey charger, National Army Museum, London. R.B.DAVIS, 1829–30, wl on horseback, with his dog, shooting a blackcock at Cannock Chase, Plas Newydd. WILLIAM SALTER, c1835, tql study for 'The Waterloo Banquet at Apsley House', NPG 3693. M.A.SHEE, 1836, wl in uniform, Royal Coll. F.X.WINTERHALTER, c1840, hs in uniform and orders, Plas Newydd.

D RICHARD DIGHTON jun, 1806, wl in uniform, w/c, Royal Coll. HENRY EDRIDGE, 1808, wl in uniform, w/c, NPG 313. DENIS DIGHTON, 1815, w/c, Royal Coll. SIR FRANCIS CHANTREY, 1818, two drgs, hs, pencil, V & A. JAMES STEPHANOFF, 1821, as Lord High Steward, carrying the crown of St Edward at the Coronation of George IV, V & A. LORD CLARENCE PAGET, 1840, with Wellington at Uxbridge House, w/c, Plas Newydd. COUNT A.D'ORSAY, 1843, pencil, Plas Newydd. HENRY GRAVES, 1848, wl pencil, NPG. SIR WILLIAM BEECHEY, chalk, Goodwood, W.Sussex.

G SIR GEORGE HAYTER, 'The Trial of Queen Caroline, 1820', oil, NPG 999. J.W.PIENEMAN, 'The Battle of Waterloo', oil, 1824, Rijksmuseum, Amsterdam. GEORGE JONES, 'The Catholic Emancipation Act', a House of Lords group, oil, 1829, on loan to the House of Lords. SIR GEORGE HAYTER, 'The House of Commons, 1833', oil, NPG 54. SIR DAVID WILKIE, 'The First Council of Queen Victoria', oil, 1837, Royal Coll.

SC SIR FRANCIS CHANTREY, 1816, marble bust, Ashmolean Museum, Oxford. W.HACKWOOD, 1821, Wedgwood medallion, after Beechey portrait of 1815, City Museum and Art Gallery, Stoke-on-Trent. PETER TURNERELLI, 1828, marble bust, Royal Coll. WILLIAM THEED jun, c1830, bronze statuette, Plas Newydd. R.C.LUCAS, 1851, wax relief, National Museum of Wales, Cardiff. MATTHEW NOBLE, 1854, marble bust, Royal Coll.

ANNE, Princess Royal (1709-1759) daughter of George II; princess of Orange.

P MARTIN MAINGAUD, 1718, wl with her sister Amelia, in landscape, Royal Coll. PHILIP MERCIER, 1728, wl, Shire Hall, Hertford. JACOPO AMIGONI, c1734, wl in robe, Royal Coll; version, DoE (Wrest Park, Beds). D.KOCK?, 1736, hl, Gripsholm, Stockholm.

D J.AMIGONI, tql, wash, Museum Boymans-van Beuningen Rotterdam. THOMAS WORLIDGE, hl, chalk, Royal Coll.

M CHRISTIAN FRIEDRICH ZINCKE, hl, enamel, Mauritshuis, The Hague.

G MARTIN MAINGAUD, hl with Princesses Amelia and Caroline, oil, 1721, Royal Coll. WILLIAM HOGARTH, 'The Family of George II', oil, c1731–32, Royal Coll; version, NGI 126. PHILIP MERCIER, 'The Music Party', Frederick, Prince of Wales with his three sisters, oil, 1733, NPG 1556; version, Royal Coll.

SC JEAN BAPTISTE XAVERY, 1736, marble bust, Mauritshuis, The Hague. Various medals, BM.

PR JOHN SMITH, after G.Kneller, tql aged 10, with wreath, mezz, pub 1720, BM, NPG. J.FABER jun, after H.Hysing, tql with coronet, mezz, BM. J.FABER jun, after P.Mercier, hl profile, mezz, 1734, BM, NPG. J.FABER jun, after P.v.Dyk, tql seated with Prince of Orange, mezz, BM.

ANNESLEY, James (1715-1760) claimant.

PR KINGS, after Bickham, 1744, hl, line, NPG.

ANSON, George (1797-1857) general.

D J.S.COTMAN, 1820, pencil, V & A. UNKNOWN, chalk, SNPG 2291.

G SIR GEORGE HAYTER, 'The Trial of Queen Caroline, 1820', oil, NPG 999. SIR G.HAYTER, 'The House of Commons, 1833', oil, NPG 54.

PR R.J.LANE, after A.d'Orsay, hl seated, profile, lith, pub 1840, BM, NPG.

ANSPACH, Elizabeth, née Berkeley, Margravine of (1750-1828) dramatist.

P Attrib THOMAS BEACH, c1767–76, wl with harp, John Paul Getty Museum, California, USA. GEORGE ROMNEY, 1778, hs, TATE 1669. SIR JOSHUA REYNOLDS, RA 1781, called the sitter, tql with her son, Petworth (NT), W.Sussex. OZIAS HUMPHRY, c1780–83, hs, TATE T 756. GEORGE ROMNEY, 1797, wl, Fishmongers' Hall, London.

D RICHARD COSWAY, wl as Elia, Royal Coll.

PR W.RIDLEY, after J.Reynolds, hl, stipple, oval, for *Monthly Mirror*, 1801, BM, NPG.

ANSTEY, Christopher (1724-1805) poet.

P Attrib WILLIAM HOARE, Victoria Art Gallery, Bath. WILLIAM HOARE, hl seated, with child holding up doll, NPG 3084. THOMAS BEACH, hl, King's College, Cambridge.

PR W.BOND, after T.Lawrence, hl seated, stipple, pub 1807, BM. F.ENGLEHEART, after J.Thurston, tql seated, line, for *Effigies Poeticae*, 1826, BM, NPG. W.HOARE, hs profile, etch, BM.

ANSTRUTHER, Sir John, Bart (1753-1811) chief justice of Bengal.

D GEORGE DANCE, 1797, hs profile, pencil, SNPG 589.

APPERLEY, Charles James (1779-1843) sports writer.

D DANIEL MACLISE, wl, pencil, V & A.

PR E.FINDEN, after D.Maclise, hl, stipple, pub 1837, NPG. UNKNOWN, hs, woodcut, for *Illust London News*, 1842–43, NPG. UNKNOWN, wl seated, lith, BM. UNKNOWN, wl seated, line, NPG.

APSLEY, Henry Bathurst, 1st Baron, see 2nd Earl Bathurst.

ARAM, Eugene (1704-1759) scholar and criminal.

PR UNKNOWN, hs, etch, for Caulfield's *Remarkable Persons*, 1819, BM. Several popular prints, NPG.

ARBUTHNOT, Charles (1767-1850) diplomat.

G SIR GEORGE HAYTER, 'The Trial of Queen Caroline, 1820', oil, NPG 999.

ARBUTHNOT, Marriot (1711?-1794) admiral.

PR C.H.HODGES, after J.Rising, hl in uniform, mezz, pub 1794, BM.

ARCHER, Edward (1717-1789) physician.

P R.E.PINE, 1782, wl, Royal College of Physicians, London.

PR H.KINGSBURY, after R.E.Pine, hl, stipple, oval, for Woodville's *Hist of Inoculation*, 1796, BM.

ARCHER, James (fl 1820) catholic preacher.

PR J.MURPHY, hs, mezz, pub 1791, NPG. C.TURNER, after J.Ramsay, hl seated, mezz, pub 1826, BM, NPG.

ARDEN, Richard Pepper, see Baron Alvanley.

ARGYLL, Elizabeth Gunning, Duchess of Hamilton and, see HAMILTON.

ARKWRIGHT, Sir Richard (1732-1792) engineer and

inventor.

P MATHER BROWN, 1790, tql seated, New British Museum of American Art, Conn, USA. JOSEPH WRIGHT of Derby, c1790, hl, NPG 136.

PR T.O.BARLOW, after Gainsborough, hl, mezz, oval, one of set of *Portraits of Inventors*, 1862, BM. UNKNOWN, tql seated, stipple, BM.

ARMSTRONG, John (1709-1779) physician and poet.

P SIR JOSHUA REYNOLDS, RA 1767, hl, Art Gallery of South Australia, Adelaide, Australia.

PR W.RIDLEY, after W.H.Brown, hs, stipple, oval, for Cooke's *Select Poets*, BM.

ARNE, Thomas Augustine (1710-1778) composer.

D THOMAS WORLIDGE, 1764, head, profile, Plymouth City Museum and Art Gallery. FRANCESCO BARTOLOZZI, hl profile, pencil, Royal Coll.

PR W.HUMPHREY, after R.Dunkarton, hl with music, mezz, oval, pub 1778, BM. After BARTOLOZZI, tql profile, coloured etch, NPG 1130.

C W.N.GARDINER, after J.Nixon, profile, playing the organ, etch, BM.

ARNISTON, Robert Dundas, Lord (1713-1787) judge.

P Attrib W.MOSMAN, hl as a boy, with bow, Arniston House, Lothian region, Scotland. ANDREA SOLDI, 1757, tql, Faculty of Advocates, Parliament House, Edinburgh. SIR HENRY RAEBURN, tql seated in robes, Arniston House; copy, Parliament Hall, Edinburgh.

ARNOLD, Benedict (1741-1801) general.

PR UNKNOWN, after du Similier, hs, line, oval, for *European Mag*, 1783, NPG. W.GRAINGER, after D.Montague, hs profile, stipple, oval, BM, NPG. UNKNOWN, hl, line, oval, for *The Universal Mag*, BM, NPG.

ARNOLD, John (1736?-1799) chronometer maker.

G ROBERT DAVY, with his family, Science Museum, London.

PR S.E.REID, after R.Davy, tql seated with chronometer, mezz, BM.

ARNOLD, Samuel (1740-1802) musician.

P UNKNOWN, c1780, tql, Royal College of Music, London.

D GEORGE DANCE, 1795, hl profile, pencil, NPG 1135.

PR UNKNOWN, after J.Russell, hl, stipple, oval, pub 1790, BM, NPG. T.HARDY, hl in academic robes, stipple, pub 1797, BM. W.RIDLEY, after S.J.Arnold, hl, stipple, oval, for *Monthly Mirror*, 1803, BM.

ARNOLD, Samuel James (1774-1852) dramatist.

P JAMES LONSDALE, hs, Garrick Club, London.

ARNOLD, Thomas (1742-1816) physician.

PR F.LEGAT, after G.Ralph of 1793, hl, line, oval, pub 1806, NPG.

ARNOLD, Thomas (1795-1842) headmaster of Rugby School.

P THOMAS PHILLIPS, 1839, tql seated, NPG 1998.

SC WILLIAM BEHNES, 1849, marble bust, NPG 168. SIR ALFRED GILBERT, bust, Rugby School, Warwicks. JOHN THOMAS, recumbent effigy, Rugby School.

ARNOT, Hugo (1749-1786) Scottish advocate.

C Several JOHN KAY etchings, BM, NPG.

ARNOTT, Neil (1788-1874) physician and scientist.

PR UNKNOWN, after a daguerreotype by Jabez Hogg, hs, woodcut, NPG.

ARROWSMITH, Aaron (1750-1823) cartographer.

PR T.A.DEAN, after H.W.Pickersgill, tql seated with compasses, stipple, pub 1825, BM, NPG.

ARROWSMITH, John (1790-1873) map-maker.

P H.W.PICKERSGILL, c1820, hl, NMM, Greenwich.

ARTAUD, William (1763-1823) portrait painter.

P Self-portrait, hl, Dr Williams's Library, London.

D Self-portrait, hs, pastel, oval, NPG 4862. Self-portrait, hs with sketch of two children, pencil, NPG 4863.

ARTHUR, Sir George (1784-1854) lieutenant-general.

PR R.J.LANE, 1842, hs, lith, NPG.

ARUNDELL, Francis Vyvyan Jago (1780-1846) traveller and antiquary.

D WILLIAM BROCKEDON, 1829, hs, chalk, NPG 2515(36).

ASBURY, Francis (1745-1816) Wesleyan bishop.

PR R.M.MEADOWS, hs, stipple, NPG.

ASGILL, Sir Charles, Bart (1763-1823) general.

G UNKNOWN, after P.Sandby, 'Sketches taken at Print Sales', line, pub 1798, BM.

PR UNKNOWN, hs profile, line, oval, for Andrews' *History of the war with America, France, Spain and Holland*, 1786, BM, NPG. C.TURNER, after T.Phillips, tql in uniform, mezz, pub 1822, BM.

ASH, John (1723-1798) physician at Birmingham.

P SIR JOSHUA REYNOLDS, RA 1788, wl seated, Birmingham General Hospital.

ASHBURTON, Alexander Baring, 1st Baron (1774-1848) financier and statesman.

P G.P.A.HEALY, hl, New York Historical Society, USA.

G SIR GEORGE HAYTER, 'The House of Commons, 1833', oil, NPG 54. JOHN PARTRIDGE, 'The Fine Arts Commissioners, 1846', NPG 342,3.

PR C.E.WAGSTAFF, after T.Lawrence, tql, mezz, pub 1837, BM, NPG.

ASHBURTON, John Dunning, 1st Baron (1731-1783) solicitor-general.

P Studio of REYNOLDS, 1768–73, hl, NPG 102. SIR JOSHUA REYNOLDS, c1782–83, tql seated in robes of chancellor of the Duchy of Lancaster, with Lady Ashburton, TATE 6244.

D JOHN DOWNMAN, 1782, hl profile, chalk, oval, BM.

G J.WARD, after J.Reynolds, with Lord Lansdowne and Col Isaac Barré, mezz, BM.

PR F.BARTOLOZZI, after J.Reynolds, hl in counsellor's dress, stipple, oval, pub 1787, BM, NPG.

C C.BRETHERTON jun, profile head, entitled 'Orator Hum', 1782, BM. J.SAYERS, 'Razor's Levée', etch, 1783, BM, NPG.

ASHBURTON, William Bingham Baring, 2nd Baron (1799-1864) statesman.

G SIR GEORGE HAYTER, 'The House of Commons, 1833', oil, NPG 54.

PR F.C.LEWIS, after G.Richmond, hs, stipple, one of 'Grillion's Club' series, BM, NPG. UNKNOWN, after a bust by A.Munro, hs, woodcut, for *Illust London News*, April 9th 1864, NPG.

ASHBY, Harry (1744-1818) writing engraver.

PR HOLL, after Borckhardt, hl, stipple, oval, pub 1803, BM.

ASHFORD, William (1746-1824) landscape painter.

P WILLIAM CUMING, hl seated, Royal Hibernian Academy, Dublin.

PR T.NUGENT, after J.Comerford, hs, stipple, pub 1803, BM, NPG.

ASHLEY, Charles Jane (1773-1843) performer on violoncello.

P UNKNOWN, hl with violoncello, Royal Society of Musicians, London.

ASHTON, Thomas (1716-1775) divine.

P SIR JOSHUA REYNOLDS, 1756, hl, King's College, Cambridge.

PR J.McARDELL, after Gainsborough, hl, mezz, oval, BM, NPG.

ASHURST, Sir William Henry (1725-1807) judge.
PR J.JONES, after J.Plott, tql seated in robes, stipple, pub 1796, BM, NPG.

ASHWORTH, Henry (1794-1880) opponent of corn-laws.
G S.BELLIN, after J.Herbert, 'The Anti Corn Law League', mixed engr, pub 1850, BM, NPG.
PR S.W.REYNOLDS jun, after C.A.Duval, hl, mezz, pub 1844, BM, NPG.

ASKEW, Anthony (1722-1774?) physician, scholar and book collector.
P ALLAN RAMSAY, 1750, tql in robes, Emmanuel College, Cambridge.
SC CHITQUA, c1770, polychrome statuette, Royal College of Physicians, London.

ASPLAND, Robert (1782-1845) unitarian minister and writer.
PR H.MEYER, after J.Partridge, hl seated, mezz, BM.

ASTELL, William (1774-1847) chairman of the East India Company.
PR G.R.WARD, after F.R.Say, tql seated, mezz, BM, NPG.

ASTLE, Thomas (1735-1803) antiquary and palaeographer.
G JOHAN ZOFFANY, 'The Towneley Gallery', oil, 1781-83, Burnley Art Gallery.
PR W.RIDLEY, hl seated, stipple, oval, for *European Mag*, 1802, BM, NPG. W.SKELTON, after H.Howard, hl seated, line, pub 1803, BM, NPG. R.STANIER, hl, stipple, oval, BM.

ASTLEY, Philip (1742-1814) equestrian performer.
G HILL, after Pugin and Rowlandson, 'Astley's Amphitheatre', coloured aquatint, pub 1808, NPG.
PR J.SMITH, hl profile, silhouette, line, oval, BM, NPG.

ATHERTON, William (1776-1850) Wesleyan minister.
PR J.THOMSON, after W.Gush, hl, stipple, for *Methodist Mag*, BM.

ATHOLL, John Murray, 3rd Duke of (1729-1774) peer.
G JOHAN ZOFFANY, wl with his family, oil, 1765-67, Blair Castle, Tayside region, Scotland.
SC JOHN KIRK, 1774, silver medal, SNPG 702.
PR UNKNOWN, hs, profile, etch, BM.

ATKINSON, James (1759-1839) surgeon bibliographer and portraitist.
P WILLIAM ETTY, hl, York City Art Gallery.

ATKINSON, James (1780-1852) army surgeon, oriental scholar and amateur artist.
P Self-portrait, c1845, hl, NPG 930.
M MRS MARIA BELLETT BROWNE, hl, as a young man, SNPG 435.

ATKINSON, Miles (1741-1811) minister at Leeds.
PR W.HOLL, after J.Russell, hs, stipple, for Whitaker's *Hist of Leeds*, 1816, BM, NPG.

ATKINSON, Peter (1776-1842) architect.
P Attrib SIR MARTIN ARCHER SHEE, hl with plan, York City Art Gallery.

ATMORE, Charles (1759-1826) Wesleyan minister.
P Attrib JOHN JACKSON, hl, Methodist Publishing House, London.

ATTWOOD, Thomas (1765-1838) musician.
P UNKNOWN, hl, Royal College of Music, London.

ATTWOOD, Thomas (1783-1856) political reformer.
D B.R.HAYDON, 1832, hs, chalk, Birmingham Reference Library.
G SIR GEORGE HAYTER, 'The House of Commons, 1833', oil, NPG 54.

SC JOHN THOMAS, marble statue, Calthorpe Park, Wolverhampton.
PR J.MILLS, hs, lith, pub 1831, NPG. J.B.ALLEN, after W.Green, hs profile, line, pub 1832, BM, NPG. C.TURNER, after G.Sharples, tql seated, mezz, pub 1832, BM. UNKNOWN, hl, seated, stipple, NPG.

AUBERT, Alexander (1730-1805) astronomer.
PR J.CHAPMAN, after S.Drummond, hs, stipple, oval, for *European Mag*, 1798, BM, NPG.

AUCHINLECK, Alexander Boswell, Lord (1706-1782) Scottish judge.
P By or after ALLAN RAMSAY, tql seated in robes, Yale Center for British Art, New Haven, USA.

AUCHMUTY, Sir Samuel, Bart (1756-1822) general.
P SIR THOMAS LAWRENCE, 1815, Government House, Madras.
G A.W.WARREN, after H.Corbould, 'The Storming of Monte Vidio', line, pub 1809, NPG.
SC THOMAS KIRK, bust on monument, Christ Church Cathedral, Dublin.
PR A.CARDON, after L.Abbott, hl in uniform, stipple, oval, pub 1808, BM, NPG.

AUCKLAND, George Eden, 1st Earl of (1784-1849) governor-general of India.
G SIR GEORGE HAYTER, 'The Trial of Queen Caroline, 1820', oil, NPG 999.
PR J.THOMSON, after L.Dickinson, tql, lith, pub 1850, NPG, similar engr by G.Stodart, stipple, NPG.

AUCKLAND, William Eden, 1st Baron (1744-1814) statesman.
P SIR THOMAS LAWRENCE, 1792, tql seated, Christ Church, Oxford.
D HENRY EDRIDGE, 1809, hl seated, w/c, NPG 122.
SC E.G.MOUNTSTEPHEN, c1789, Wedgwood medallion, BM.
PR J.BROWN, engr as after N.Dance, wl seated with dog, stipple and line, pub 1860, NPG.
C J.SAYERS, 'Concerto Coalitionale', etch, pub 1785, BM, NPG.

AUGUSTA, Princess of Wales (1719-1772) mother of George III.
P CHARLES PHILIPS, c1736, tql, NPG 2093; similar portrait, attrib William Hogarth, wl in robes of state, with spaniel, Royal Coll. CHARLES PHILIPS, 1737, wl seated in robes with her baby daughter and a spaniel, Warwick Castle. J.B.VANLOO, 1742, wl in robes of state, with roses, Royal Coll. THOMAS HUDSON, wl, Cliveden (NT), Bucks. Studio of ALLAN RAMSAY, wl in garden wearing black lace shawl, with parasol, Royal Coll. Attrib ALLAN RAMSAY, hl, Museo de la Fundación Lázaro Galdiano, Madrid.
D J.E.LIOTARD, 1754, hl, pastel, Royal Coll.
G J.B.VANLOO, with members of her family and household, oil, 1739?, Royal Coll. GEORGE KNAPTON, 'The family of Frederick, Prince of Wales', oil, 1751, Royal Coll. SIR JOSHUA REYNOLDS, 'The Marriage of George III, 1761', oil, Royal Coll.
SC JOHN KIRK, medal, BM. ISAAC GOSSET, after Kirk, Wedgwood medallion, Royal Coll.
PR J.FABER jun, after T.Hudson, hl, mezz, oval, BM. J.JOHNSON, after F.Huysman, tql in robes with coronet, mezz, BM, NPG.

AUGUSTA Sophia, Princess (1768-1840) second daughter of George III.
P THOMAS GAINSBOROUGH, 1782, hs, oval, Royal Coll. SIR WILLIAM BEECHEY, RA 1797, tql seated with sketchbook and classical bust, Royal Coll. SIR WILLIAM BEECHEY, RA 1802, wl, Royal Coll. P.E.STROEHLING, 1807, wl in robe, with musical instruments, Royal Coll. After SIR WILLIAM BEECHEY of c1815, hl, Royal Coll. SIR WILLIAM BEECHEY, probably RA 1819, tql in

landscape, Museum of Fine Art, Baltimore, USA.
D HENRY EDRIDGE, several drgs, Royal Coll.
M ANDREW ROBERTSON, hl, Royal Coll.
G Several family groups by SIR BENJAMIN WEST and three family groups by JOHAN ZOFFANY, Royal Coll. THOMAS GAINSBOROUGH, 'The Three Eldest Princesses', oil, 1784, Royal Coll.
PR R.J.LANE, after W.C.Ross, hl seated in cap, lith, pub 1840, BM, NPG.

AUGUSTUS Frederick (1773-1843), see Duke of Sussex.

AUSTEN, Jane (1775-1817) novelist.
M CASSANDRA AUSTEN (her sister), c1810, hl seated, pencil and w/c, NPG 3630.
SL Attrib MRS COLLINS, c1801, hs profile, called Jane Austen, NPG 3181.

AUSTIN, John (1717-1784) Irish jesuit.
PR H.BROCAS, after J.Petrie, hl, line, oval, pub 1792, BM, NPG.

AUSTIN, John (fl 1820) Scottish inventor.
PR J.KAY, 1802? or 1812?, hs, etch, NPG.

AUSTIN, Sarah, née Taylor (1793-1867) translator.
P LADY ARTHUR RUSSELL, c1867, hs, NPG 598.
D JOHN LINNELL, 1834, h! seated, chalk, NPG 672.
PR W.TAYLOR, after H.P.Briggs, tql seated, lith, pub 1835, BM, NPG.

AUSTIN, William (1721-1820) drawing master and engraver.
G UNKNOWN, after P.Sandby, 'Sketches taken at Print Sales', line, pub 1798, BM.

PR J.GODBY, after E.Scott, tql seated, stipple, pub 1809, BM, NPG.

AVERSHAWE, Louis Jeremiah or **Jerry (1773?-1795)** highwayman.
PR J.CHAPMAN, hs, stipple, pub 1804, NPG.

AVONMORE, Barry Yelverton, 1st Viscount (1736-1805) Irish politician.
P H.D.HAMILTON, King's Inns, Dublin. G.F.JOSEPH, posthumous, wl seated in robes of the baron of the exchequer, Trinity College, Dublin.
G FRANCIS WHEATLEY, 'The Irish House of Commons, 1780', oil, Leeds City Art Galleries, Lotherton Hall, W.Yorks.

AYSCOUGH, Francis (1700-1763) dean of Bristol, tutor to George III.
G RICHARD WILSON, c1749-50, wl with the Prince of Wales and his brother Edward Augustus, oil, NPG 1165.

AYSCOUGH, George Edward (d1779) dramatist and traveller.
PR S.HARDING, after G.Dance, hl profile, stipple, pub 1794, BM, NPG.

AYSCOUGH, Samuel (1745-1804) librarian and index maker.
PR J.BASIRE, hl, line, for Nichols's *Literary Anecdotes*, 1804, BM, NPG.

AYTON, Richard (1786-1823) dramatist and miscellaneous writer.
PR F.C.LEWIS, after R.Westall, hs profile, stipple, for his *Essays*, 1825, BM, NPG.

B

BABBAGE, Charles (1792-1871) mathematician.
P SAMUEL LAURENCE, 1845, tql, NPG 414.
D WILLIAM BROCKEDON, 1840, hs, chalk, NPG 2515(33).
PR J.LINNELL, after M.R.S., tql seated, profile, stipple, pub 1833, BM, NPG.
PH ANTOINE CLAUDET, hl seated, daguerreotype, NPG P28. HENRI CLAUDET, hs, carte, NPG Cunnington Coll.

BABER, Henry Hervey (1775-1869) philologist and keeper of Printed Books in the British Museum.
P UNKNOWN, c1830, hs, NPG 591.
PR HENRY CORBOULD, hs profile, lith, 1836, BM.

BABINGTON, Benjamin Guy (1794-1866) physician and linguist.
SC C.A.RIVERS, 1867, based on a death mask, wax statuette, Royal College of Physicians, London.

BABINGTON, William (1756-1833) physician.
G N.BRANWHITE, after S.Medley, 'Institutors of the Medical Society of London', stipple, pub 1801, BM.
SC WILLIAM BEHNES, 1833?, marble bust, Royal College of Physicians, London. JOSEPH TOWNE, 1834, bust, Guy's Hospital, London. WILLIAM BEHNES, 1837, statue on monument, St Paul's Cathedral, London.
PR W.T.FRY, after J.Tannock, hl seated, stipple, BM, NPG.

BACHE, Sarah (1771?-1844) hymn-writer.
PR T.GARNER, after F.Cruikshank, hl, line, NPG.

BACK, Sir George (1796-1878) admiral.
P UNKNOWN, hs, McCord Museum, McGill University, Canada.
D WILLIAM BROCKEDON, 1833, hs, chalk, NPG 2515(46).
G STEPHEN PEARCE, 'The Arctic Council planning a search for Sir John Franklin', oil, 1851, NPG 1208.
PR E.FINDEN, after R.Woodman, hl, stipple, pub 1828, NPG. W.DRUMMOND, hs, lith, *Athenaeum Portraits*, No 50, BM.
PH ERNEST EDWARDS, wl seated, for *Men of Eminence*, ed L.Reeve, 1865, vol III, NPG.

BACON, Sir James (1798-1895) judge.
SC SIR J.E.BOEHM, 1879, marble statue, Lincoln's Inn, London.
PR UNKNOWN, hs, woodcut, for *Illust London News*, 1870, NPG.
PH London Stereoscopic Company, hs, carte, NPG. UNKNOWN, hs, NPG Photographs of Legal Celebrities.

BACON, John (1740-1799) sculptor.
D WILLIAM BROCKEDON, after a bust by Bacon's son, sepia, BM. GEORGE DANCE, hs profile, Royal Academy, London. JOHN RUSSELL, hs with marble head, pastel, V & A.
M WILLIAM BATE, after Mason Chamberlin of 1785, hs, NPG L152(27).
G HENRY SINGLETON, 'Royal Academicians, 1793', oil, Royal Academy.
PR UNKNOWN, hl, line, oval, for *European Mag*, 1790, BM, NPG.

BACON, John (1777-1859) sculptor.
PR T.BLOOD, after J.Russell, hl profile, stipple, for *European Mag*, 1815, BM, NPG.

BADDELEY, Robert (1733-1794) actor.
P JOHAN ZOFFANY, 1777, wl as Moses in *School for Scandal*, Lady Lever Art Gallery, Port Sunlight. SAMUEL DE WILDE, wl as Sir Harry Gubbin in *The Tender Husband*, Garrick Club, London. Attrib THOMAS HARDY, hs, Garrick Club.
D THOMAS PARKINSON, wl as Trinculo in *The Tempest*, ink and w/c, BM.
M After RICHARD COSWAY, in profile, as Canton in *The Clandestine Marriage*, Garrick Club.
G JOHAN ZOFFANY, in a scene from *The Clandestine Marriage*, oil, Garrick Club.
PR Various theatrical prints, BM, NPG.

BADDELEY, Sophia, née Snow (1745-1786) actress and singer.
G JOHAN ZOFFANY, in a scene from *The Clandestine Marriage*, oil, Garrick Club, London.
PR E.WELSH, after J.Reynolds, hl with cat, mezz, oval, pub 1772, BM. R.LAURIE, after J.Zoffany, hs, mezz, oval, pub 1772, BM. NPG. Several theatrical prints, BM, NPG.

BAGOT, Sir Charles (1781-1843) governor-general of Canada.
P H.W.PICKERSGILL, RA 1835, tql in Bath robes, Christ Church, Oxford.

BAGOT, Lewis (1740-1802) bishop of St Asaph.
P JOHN HOPPNER, RA 1794, tql seated, Christ Church, Oxford.
SC SIR FRANCIS CHANTREY, 1829, marble bust, Christ Church, Oxford.

BAGOT, Richard (1782-1854) bishop.
P SIR FRANCIS GRANT, 1846, tql seated in robes with Garter badge, The Deanery, Canterbury. H.W.PICKERSGILL, hl seated with Garter badge, All Souls College, Oxford. UNKNOWN, Blithfield Hall, Staffs.

BAGOT, William Bagot, 2nd Baron (1773-1856) landowner and agriculturist.
D WILLIAM BRADLEY, c1838, two sketches, head, pencil, Manchester City Art Gallery.
G SIR GEORGE HAYTER, 'The Trial of Queen Caroline, 1820', oil, NPG 999.
PR G.CLINT, after J.Hoppner, tql in peer's robes, mezz, BM.

BAGSTER, Samuel (1772-1851) publisher of polyglot Bibles and other aids to the Scriptures.
D JOHN LINNELL, c1850, hs, pencil and chalk, NPG 1816.

BAILLIE, Joanna (1762-1851) dramatist and poet.
D MARY ANN KNIGHT, pencil and w/c, SNPG 2036. SIR W.J.NEWTON, hs, w/c, SNPG.
M J.C.D.ENGLEHEART, after Sir W.J.Newton, hs, Royal College of Physicians, London.
PR H.ROBINSON, after J.J.Masquerier, tql seated, stipple, NPG.

BAILLIE, John (1772-1833) orientalist and Indian administrator.
PR J.COCHRAN, after A.Wivell, hl, stipple, pub 1823, BM, NPG.

BAILLIE, Matthew (1761-1823) anatomist.
P SIR THOMAS LAWRENCE, c1806?, hl, Royal College of Physicians, London. JOHN HOPPNER, before 1809, hl seated, Royal College of Physicians. WILLIAM OWEN, 1817, tql seated, Balliol College, Oxford. UNKNOWN, hl, Royal College of

Physicians.

SC JOSEPH NOLLEKENS, 1812, marble bust, Royal College of Surgeons, London; marble copy by Sir Francis Chantrey, 1824, Royal College of Physicians. SIR FRANCIS CHANTREY, c1823, bust on monument, Westminster Abbey, London.

C THOMAS ROWLANDSON, 'The Dissecting Room', pencil, Royal College of Surgeons.

BAILLIE, Thomas (c1725-1802) naval captain.

P NATHANIEL HONE, 1779, hl seated, NMM, Greenwich.

BAILLIE, William (1723-1810) connoisseur and artist.

R W.BAILLIE, after N.Hone, hl, stipple, oval, BM, NPG.

C J.GILLRAY, several sketches for 'Connoisseurs examining a Collection of George Morland's', V & A.

BAILLIE, William (d1816), see Lord Polkemmet.

BAILY, Edward Hodges (1788-1867) sculptor.

D C.H.LEAR, c1846, hs, profile, pencil and chalk, NPG 1456 (1).

SC A.B.WYON, bronze medallion, NPG.

R J.SMYTH, after T.Bridgeford, tql seated, line, for Art Union, 1847, BM, NPG. MISS TURNER, after W.Beechey, hs, lith, BM, NPG.

H Several photographs, NPG.

BAILY, Francis (1774-1844) president of the Royal Astronomical Society.

P THOMAS PHILLIPS, RA 1839, tql, Royal Astronomical Society, London.

G J.F.SKILL, J.GILBERT, W. and E.WALKER, 'Men of Science Living in 1807-08', pencil and wash, NPG 1075.

SC E.H.BAILY, 1848, marble bust, Royal Astronomical Society.

BAINE, James (1710-1790) minister of the Relief Congregation, Edinburgh.

C J.KAY, hs profile, etch, oval, 1789, BM, NPG.

BAINES, Edward (1774-1848) journalist.

SC WILLIAM BEHNES, 1858, stone statue, Leeds City Art Galleries.

R J.COCHRAN, after T.Hargraves, hl, stipple, for Jerdan's Nat Portrait Gallery, 1834, BM, NPG.

BAINES, Matthew Talbot (1799-1860) politician.

R W.UNDERWOOD, after a daguerreotype by Kilburn, tql, lith, pub 1854, NPG. D.J.POUND, after a photograph by Mayall, tql seated, stipple and line, presented with Illust News of the World, NPG.

BAIRD, Sir David, Bart (1757-1829) general.

P SIR HENRY RAEBURN, RA 1814, wl with horse, Lennoxlove, Lothian region, Scotland. Attrib SIR JOHN WATSON-GORDON, 1820, tql, NPG 2195.

D THOMAS HICKEY, 1799, two hs sketches, charcoal and chalk, Stratfield Saye, Hants. SIR DAVID WILKIE, c1834, hs, w/c, NPG 1825.

G SIR DAVID WILKIE, discovering the body of Tipoo Sahib, oil, 1834-39, on loan to Edinburgh Castle; various studies, Fitzwilliam Museum, Cambridge, Ashmolean Museum, Oxford, Royal Scottish Academy, BM, V & A; oil sketch, SNPG 644. SIR FRANCIS GRANT, 'The Melton Hunt', oil, RA 1839, Stratfield Saye.

SC J.B.PHILIP, 1870, statue, Calcutta.

R A.CARDON, after A.J.Oliver, hl in uniform, stipple, oval, pub 1806, BM, NPG.

BAIRD, George Husband (1761-1840) principal of Edinburgh University.

P After ANDREW GEDDES, tql, Edinburgh University.

R W.WARD, after A.Geddes, tql seated, mezz, pub 1817, BM.

C J.KAY, wl with Thomas Elder, entitled 'Friendship', etch, 1793, BM, NPG.

BAKER, David Erskine (1730-1767) compiler of the Biographia Dramatica.

PR H.R.COOK, after S.Harding, hl, stipple, for Harding's Biographical Mirror, 1810, BM, NPG.

BAKER, Sir George, Bart (1722-1809) physician.

P OZIAS HUMPHRY, 1794, hs, Royal College of Physicians, London.

BAKER, George (1781-1851) historian of Northamptonshire.

PR MISS TURNER, after N.C.Branwhite, hl seated, lith, BM, NPG.

BAKEWELL, Robert (1725-1795) grazier.

P JOHN BOULTBEE, wl on a bay horse, Leicester Museum and Art Gallery.

PR F.ENGLEHEART, hl, line, pub 1842, NPG.

BALGUY, Thomas (1716-1795) divine.

P UNKNOWN, hs, St John's College, Cambridge.

BALL, Sir Alexander John (1757-1809) admiral.

P H.W.PICKERSGILL, tql, posthumous, NMM, Greenwich.

BALL, Edward (1792-1873), see Fitzball.

BALLANTYNE, James (1772-1833) printer of Sir Walter Scott's works.

D JOHN BALLANTYNE, hs, pencil and wash, NGS D 2694.

BALLANTYNE, John (1774-1821) publisher.

P UNKNOWN, c1810, hl, SNPG 1142.

D UNKNOWN, pencil, ink and w/c, SNPG 1673.

BALMER, Robert (1787-1844) minister.

PR F.SCHENCK, after a painting from memory by M.Burton, hs, lith, NPG.

BALMUTO, Claud Irvine Boswell, Lord (1742-1824) Scottish judge.

C J.KAY, seated on the bench, etch, oval, 1799, BM, NPG.

BALTIMORE, Frederick Calvert, 6th Baron (1731-1771) rake.

PR J.MILLER, hs, stipple and line, oval, NPG.

BAMPFYLDE, John Codrington Warwick (1754-c1796) poet.

P SIR JOSHUA REYNOLDS, 1777-79, tql with George Huddesford, TATE 754.

BANCROFT, Edward (1744-1821) naturalist and chemist.

G N.BRANWHITE, after S.Medley, 'Institutors of the Medical Society of London', stipple, pub 1801, BM.

BANDINEL, Bulkeley (1781-1861) librarian of the Bodleian.

P THOMAS KIRKBY, 1825, hl seated, Bodleian Library, Oxford.

M UNKNOWN, hs, Bodleian Library.

BANDINEL, James (1783-1849) clerk in foreign office.

PR R.J.LANE, after J.C.Horsley of 1850, from memory, hl, lith, NPG. C.BAUGNIET, after a sketch from memory, tql, lith, NPG.

BANIM, John (1798-1842) novelist.

P G.F.MULVANY, hl, NGI 208.

BANIM, Michael (1796-1874) novelist.

P T.C.THOMPSON, hl, NGI 320.

BANKES, William John (d1855) traveller in the East.

G SIR GEORGE HAYTER, 'The House of Commons, 1833', oil, NPG 54.

BANKS, Sir Edward (1769?-1835) builder.

P WILLIAM or GEORGE PATTEN, hl seated, Guildhall Art Gallery, London.

SC THOMAS SMITH, c1835, bust on monument, St Margaret's Church, Chipstead, Surrey.

BANKS, Sir Joseph, Bart (1743-1820) explorer and botanist.
P SIR JOSHUA REYNOLDS, RA 1773, tql seated, Parham Park, West Sussex. SIR THOMAS LAWRENCE, RA 1806, hl, BM. THOMAS PHILLIPS, 1810, hl seated, NPG 885. THOMAS PHILLIPS, 1815, hl as President of the Royal Society with mace and Bath ribbon and star, Royal Society, London. THOMAS PHILLIPS, tql seated, Guildhall, Boston, Lincs.
D SIR THOMAS LAWRENCE, hl, pencil, NPG 853. THOMAS HEARNE, hs, pencil, BM. JAMES SHARPLES, hs, pastel, Bristol City Art Gallery.
G WILLIAM PARRY, with Omai and Dr Daniel Solander, oil, 1776, Parham Park. SIR JOSHUA REYNOLDS, 'The Society of Dilettanti', oil, 1777–79, Society of Dilettanti, Brooks's Club, London.
SC By or attrib JOHN FLAXMAN, three Wedgwood medallions, Wedgwood Museum, Barlaston, Staffs. PETER TURNERELLI, c1814, marble bust, Royal College of Surgeons, London. Several busts by SIR FRANCIS CHANTREY: 1818, National Gallery of Victoria, Melbourne, Australia; 1818, Royal Society; 1822, Linnean Society. SIR FRANCIS CHANTREY, 1826, marble statue, BM (Natural History).
PR J.R.SMITH, after B.West, wl in Otaheitan mantle, mezz, pub 1773, BM.
C J.GILLRAY, 'The great South Sea Caterpillar, transform'd into a Bath Butterfly', etch, pub 1795, NPG.

BANKS, Sarah Sophia (1744-1818) collector.
P ANGELICA KAUFFMANN, tql, Maidstone County Hall, Kent.
M NATHANIEL HONE, 1768, hs, oval, NGI.
PR After J.RUSSELL, hl, process block, BM.

BANKS, Thomas (1735-1805) sculptor.
D GEORGE DANCE, 1793, hl profile, Royal Academy, London. G.DANCE, 1794, hl profile, BM. RICHARD COSWAY, hs profile, pencil, oval, BM.
G HENRY SINGLETON, 'Royal Academicians, 1793', oil, Royal Academy, London.
PR J.CONDÉ, after a bust by T.Banks, stipple, oval, for European Mag, 1791, BM, NPG. W.BLENKINSOP, after J.Northcote, hl with a bust, stipple, pub 1802, BM. W.C.EDWARDS, after J.Flaxman, hs profile, line, for Cunningham's Lives, 1830, BM, NPG.

BANNATYNE, Sir William Macleod (1743-1833) Scottish judge.
P SIR HENRY RAEBURN, hl, Polesden Lacey (NT), Surrey.
C J.KAY, 1799, hl profile, etch, oval, NPG.

BANNISTER, Charles (1738?-1804) actor and singer.
P Attrib JOHAN ZOFFANY, wl, Garrick Club, London. THOMAS or CHARLES PYE, hl, as Steady in The Quaker, Garrick Club.
D MISS BANNISTER, hs profile, pencil, Garrick Club. UNKNOWN, hs profile, gouache, Garrick Club.
PR Several theatrical and satirical prints, BM, NPG.

BANNISTER, Elizabeth, née Harpur (1752-1844) singer.
D JOHN RUSSELL, 1799, hl, pastel, NPG 1770.
PR Several theatrical prints, BM, NPG.

BANNISTER, John (1760-1836) comedy actor.
P SAMUEL DE WILDE, 1797, as Sylvester Daggerwood in New Hay at the Old Market, with Suett as Fustian, Garrick Club, London. JOHAN ZOFFANY, wl as Scout in The Village Lawyer, with Parsons as Sheepface, Garrick Club.
D JOHN RUSSELL, 1799, hl, pastel, NPG 1769. GEORGE DANCE, 1800, hl profile, pencil, NPG 1136. JOHN RUSSELL, 1802, as Lenitive in The Prize, pastel, Garrick Club. JOHN VARLEY, 1816, head, pencil, Garrick Club. Three undated drgs by de Wilde, Condé and an unknown artist, Garrick Club.
G SAMUEL DE WILDE, in a scene from The Village Lawyer, oil, RA

1793, Garrick Club.
PR Various theatrical prints, BM, NPG.
C THOMAS ROWLANDSON, 1783, tql seated in his dressing room Drury Lane, pen and wash, Yale Center for British Art, New Haven, USA.

BANNISTER, Saxe (1790-1877) pamphleteer.
G B.R.HAYDON, 'The Anti-Slavery Society Convention, 1840' oil, NPG 599.

BARBAULD, Anna Letitia (1743-1825) poet and writer.
G RICHARD SAMUEL, 'The Nine Living Muses of Great Britain' oil, exhib 1779, NPG 4905.
SC After JOACHIM SMITH of 1775, Wedgwood medallion, Wedgwood Museum, Barlaston, Staffs.
PR T.HOLLOWAY, hs profile medallion, line, for European Mag, 1785, BM, NPG. CHAPMAN, hs, stipple, oval, pub 1798, NPG. H.MEYER, hs profile, stipple, pub 1822, BM, NPG.

BARBER Beaumont, John Thomas, see BEAUMONT.

BARCLAY, John (1758-1826) anatomist.
P JOHN SYME, 1816, hl, oil, NPG.
C J.KAY, 'The Craft in Danger', etch, NPG.

BARCLAY, Robert (1774-1811) lieutenant-colonel.
PR J.BLOOD, after Dillon, hs in uniform, stipple, oval, for European Mag, 1811, BM, NPG.

BARCLAY, Robert (1779-1854), see Allardice.

BARDSLEY, Samuel Argent (1764-1851) physician.
PR J.THOMSON, after C.A.Duval, tql seated, stipple, pub 1848, NPG.

BARETTI, Giuseppe Marc' Antonio (1719-1789) writer.
P After SIR JOSHUA REYNOLDS of 1774, hl, John Herron Art Museum, Indianapolis, USA.
D Attrib SIR JOSHUA REYNOLDS, hl, chalk, NPG 3024.
SC THOMAS BANKS, relief bust?, St Mary's Parish Church, Marylebone, London.
PR J.WATTS, after J.Reynolds, hl, seated reading, mezz, pub 1780, BM, NPG.

BARHAM, Charles Middleton, 1st Baron (1726-1813) admiral.
P UNKNOWN, hl, posthumous, NMM, Greenwich.
PR MISS M.BOURLIER, after J.Downman, hl in peer's robes, stipple, for Contemporary Portraits, 1809, BM, NPG.

BARHAM, Richard Harris (1788-1845) author of Ingoldsby Legends.
P UNKNOWN, c1794, wl with dog, Royal Museum, Canterbury. UNKNOWN, 1820, hs, Corporation of Canterbury.
D R.J.LANE, c1842-3, hs, pencil, NPG 2922. CHARLES MARTIN, 1845, wl, bm.
PR H.GRIFFITHS, after Rev D.Barham of c1840, wl seated, stipple, for Bentley's Miscellany, 1847, NPG. UNKNOWN, after G.Cruikshank, hl seated, writing, surrounded by some of his characters, etch, for The Ingoldsby Legends, 1870, NPG.

BARING, Alexander, see 1st Baron Ashburton.

BARING, Sir Francis, Bart (1740-1810) merchant banker.
P CHARLES MUSS, after Lawrence, wl seated, on enamel, NPG 1250.
D HENRY BONE, after Benjamin West, tql, pencil, NPG Bone Drawings.
G J.WARD, after T.Lawrence, 'The Baring Family', mezz, BM, NPG.
PR W.EVANS, after T.Lawrence of 1807, hs profile, stipple, NPG.

BARING, Sir Francis Thornhill, see 1st Baron Northbrook.

BARING, Thomas (1799-1873) financier.
P UNKNOWN, tql, Hughenden (NT), Bucks.

R W.HOLL, after G.Richmond, hs, stipple, one of 'Grillion's Club' series, BM, NPG. D.J.POUND, after a photograph by J. & C.Watkins, tql seated, stipple and line, NPG.

BARING, William Bingham, see 2nd Baron Ashburton.

BARKER, Robert (1739-1806) painter of panoramas.
R J.FLIGHT, after C.Allingham, hl, mezz, BM, NPG. J.SINGLETON, after C.Ralph, hs, stipple and aquatint, oval, pub 1802, NPG.

BARKER, Thomas (1769-1847) painter.
P Self-portrait, c1793, hl at easel, Holburne of Menstrie Museum, Bath. Self-portrait, c1796, TATE 5044. Self-portrait, tql seated at easel, with Charles Spackman, Victoria Art Gallery, Bath.

BARLOW, Sir George Hilaro, Bart (1762-1846) governor-general of India.
P UNKNOWN, c1840, wl seated, NPG 4988. GEORGE WATSON, wl, Government House, Madras.
C BERTEL THORVALDSEN, 1828, bust, Thorvaldsen Museum, Copenhagen.

BARLOW, Peter (1776-1862) mathematician, physicist and optician.
R MISS TURNER, after T.Fielding, hs, lith, 1835, BM, NPG. S.COUSINS, after W.Boxall, tql seated, mezz, BM, NPG.

BARNARD, Sir Andrew Francis (1773-1855) general.
P GEORGE JONES, head, sketch, NPG 982a. WILLIAM SALTER, tql study for 'Waterloo Banquet', NPG 3695.
D COUNT ALFRED D'ORSAY, 1845, hl profile, pencil and chalk, NPG 4026(3).
G W.SALTER, 'Waterloo Banquet at Apsley House', oil, 1836, Wellington Museum, Apsley House, London.
R UNKNOWN, after J.P.Knight, wl seated, woodcut, for *Illust London News*, 1852, NPG.

BARNARD, Lady Anne, née Lindsay (1750-1825) writer.
D UNKNOWN, wash, SNPG 1674.

BARNARD, Thomas (1728-1806) bishop of Limerick.
R W.DANIELL, after G.Dance of 1793, hl seated, profile, soft-ground etch, pub 1812, BM, NPG.

BARNARDISTON, Thomas (d1752) serjeant-at-law and legal reporter.
R G.BICKMAN jun, hl, line, oval, BM, NPG.

BARNES, Sir Edward (1776-1838) lieutenant-general.
P GEORGE DAWE, hs, Wellington Museum, Apsley House, London. WILLIAM SALTER, tql study for 'Waterloo Banquet', NPG 3696. JOHN WOOD, Army and Navy Club, London.
D THOMAS HICKEY, two hs drgs, w/c, NPG 1914 (2, 3).
G W.SALTER, 'Waterloo Banquet at Apsley House', oil, 1836, Wellington Museum, Apsley House.
C HENRY WEEKES, 1846, statue, Colombo, Ceylon.

BARNES, Thomas (1747-1810) unitarian minister.
R E.SCRIVEN, after J.Allen, hl, stipple, pub 1811, BM, NPG.

BARNES, Thomas (1785-1841) editor of *The Times*.
M SIR GEORGE HAYTER, c1820, related to figure in NPG 999, The Times Newspapers Ltd, London. SIR WILLIAM NEWTON, 1832, The Times Newspapers Ltd.
G SIR GEORGE HAYTER, 'The Trial of Queen Caroline, 1820', oil, NPG 999.

BARON, John (1786-1851) physician.
P HENRY ROOM, c1838, Royal College of Physicians, London.
D UNKNOWN, hs, chalk, NPG 4548.

BARRÉ, Isaac (1726-1802) soldier and politician.
P GILBERT STUART, 1785, hl seated, Brooklyn Museum, New York. GILBERT STUART, c1785, hl, NPG 1191.

G J.WARD, after J.Reynolds, with Baron Ashburton and Lord Lansdowne, mezz, BM.
PR R.HOUSTON, after H.D.Hamilton, hl profile, mezz, oval, pub 1771, BM, NPG.
C J.SAYERS, wl, etch, pub 1782, NPG. J.SAYERS, 'Date obolum Belisario', etch, pub 1782, NPG. J.GILLRAY, 'Ancient Music', etch, pub 1787, NPG.

BARRET, George (1728?-1784) landscape painter.
D JOHN GREENWOOD, head profile, pen and pencil, BM.
G JOHAN ZOFFANY, 'Royal Academicians, 1772', oil, Royal Coll.

BARRET, George (1774-1842) painter.
P Self-portrait, tql, NGI 415.

BARRETT, John (1753-1821) divine.
P G.F.JOSEPH, 1820-21, hl seated, Trinity College, Dublin.

BARRETT, William (1733-1789) surgeon and antiquary.
PR W.WALKER, after Rymsdick, hl aged 31, stipple, NPG.

BARRINGTON, Daines (1727-1800) justice of Chester and antiquary.
PR W.BROMLEY, after S.Drummond, hs, line, oval, for *European Mag*, 1795, BM, NPG. C.KNIGHT, after J.Slater, tql seated, stipple, for 5th ed of his *Observations on the Statutes*, 1796, BM, NPG.

BARRINGTON, George (1755-1804) pickpocket and author.
D I.R.CRUIKSHANK, two ink and w/c drgs, V & A.
PR UNKNOWN, hl seated, stipple, pub 1803, BM. J.CHAPMAN, hs, stipple, pub 1804, NPG. Several popular prints, BM, NPG.

BARRINGTON, Sir Jonah (1760-1834) judge of the court of admiralty in Ireland.
PR J.HEATH, after J.Comerford, head, stipple, for his *Historic Memoirs*, BM, NPG.

BARRINGTON, Samuel (1729-1800) admiral.
P Attrib NATHANIEL DANCE, c1770, hl, NMM, Greenwich. SIR JOSHUA REYNOLDS, RA 1779, hl, NMM. GILBERT STUART, 1786, Saltram (NT), Devon. SIR JOSHUA REYNOLDS, c1788, head, Royal Coll. UNKNOWN, hs, NPG 740.
PR R.EARLOM, after B.Wilson, hl, mezz, pub 1779, BM, NPG. J.COLLYER, after P.Jean, hl, line, oval, pub 1790, BM, NPG. W.SHARP, after J.S.Copley, hl, line, pub 1810, BM.

BARRINGTON, Shute (1734-1826) bishop of Durham.
P GEORGE ROMNEY, 1784-86, tql with Garter insignia and Chancellor's purse, Christ Church, Oxford. Attrib JOHN OPIE, c1800-10, hl, The Bodleian Library, Oxford. SIR THOMAS LAWRENCE, RA 1816, tql seated, Bishop Auckland Palace, Durham. EDWARD HASTINGS, 1821, tql seated, Balliol College, Oxford. WILLIAM OWEN, hs, Balliol College, Oxford.
D SIR FRANCIS CHANTREY, hs and hs profile, pencil, NPG 316a (3, 4).
G SIR GEORGE HAYTER, 'The Trial of Queen Caroline, 1820', oil, NPG 999.
SC SIR FRANCIS CHANTREY, marble statue, Durham Cathedral.
PR C.PICART, after H.Edridge, hl seated, stipple, for *Contemporary Portraits*, 1810, BM, NPG.

BARRINGTON, William Wildman Barrington, 2nd Viscount (1717-1793) statesman.
PR C.KNIGHT, after T.Lawrence, hl, stipple, BM, NPG. W.A.RAINGER, after J.Reynolds, hl, mezz, oval, BM, NPG.

BARROW, Sir John, Bart (1764-1848) founder of the Royal Geographical Society.
P Attrib JOHN JACKSON, c1810, hl, NPG 886. JOHN LUCAS, 1846, hl, DoE (Admiralty House, London).
D T. (or J.) MACDONALD, 1844, wl, w/c and chalk, Royal

Geographical Society, London.

M UNKNOWN, hs, NPG 769.

G STEPHEN PEARCE, 'The Arctic Council planning a search for Sir John Franklin', oil, 1851, NPG 1208.

SC THOMAS MILNES, relief portrait on memorial tablet, Ulverston Parish Church, Cumbria.

BARRY, Mrs Ann Spranger, née Street (1734-1801) actress.

P Attrib JAMES ROBERTS, c1775, wl as Gertrude, with Spranger Barry as Hamlet, Garrick Club, London.

PR Various theatrical prints, BM, NPG.

BARRY, Sir Charles (1795-1860) architect.

P H.W.PICKERSGILL, RA 1849, tql, Palace of Westminster, London. J.P.KNIGHT, c1851, tql, NPG 1272. LOWES DICKINSON, RIBA, London.

G JOHN PARTRIDGE, 'The Fine Arts Commissioners, 1846', NPG 342, 3. H.W.PHILLIPS, 'The Royal Commissioners for the Great Exhibition', oil, V & A.

SC PATRIC PARK, 1848, marble bust, Reform Club, London. J.H.FOLEY, 1865, statue, Palace of Westminster.

PR T.W.HARLAND, hl seated, stipple and line, NPG.

PH JOHN WATKINS, hs, carte, NPG Album of Artists vol I.

BARRY, Edward (1759-1822) religious and medical writer.

PR J.JONES, after M.Brown, hl, stipple, pub 1789, BM, NPG.

BARRY, Henry (1750-1822) colonel.

PR W.NUTTER, after S.Shelley, hl in uniform, stipple, oval, BM, NPG.

BARRY, James (1741-1806) painter.

P Several self-portraits: c1767, hl with Paine and Lefevre in background, NPG 213; c1780-1804, hl as Timanthes with portrait of a sleeping cyclops, NGI 971; c1800, hs, V & A; hl with brushes and palette, Royal Society of Arts, London. JOHN OPIE, hl, NGI 614.

D GEORGE DANCE, hl profile, Royal Academy, London. WILLIAM EVANS, hl profile, chalk, NPG 441. JAMES NORTHCOTE, hl seated in church, pencil, NGI 2585. Self-portrait, c1800, hs, chalk, pen and wash, Ashmolean Museum, Oxford. Self-portrait, c1802, hs, pen and ink, Royal Society of Arts.

G HENRY SINGLETON, 'Royal Academicians, 1793', oil, Royal Academy. JAMES BARRY, 'The Society for the Encouragement of the Arts', oil, Royal Society of Arts.

C NATHANIEL DANCE, wl, pencil, BM.

BARRY, James (1795-1865) woman who lived as a man, soldier.

M UNKNOWN, hs, RAMC, London.

C EDWARD LEAR, wl, ink, RAMC.

PH UNKNOWN, tql, RAMC.

BARRY, Spranger (1719-1777) actor.

P FRANCIS HAYMAN, c1751-54, as Hamlet with Mrs Elmy(?) as Gertrude, Garrick Club, London. Attrib JAMES ROBERTS, c1775, wl as Hamlet, with his wife as Gertrude, Garrick Club. UNKNOWN, hs, Garrick Club.

PR Various theatrical prints, BM, NPG.

BARTLEMAN, James (1769-1821) singer.

M THOMAS HARGREAVES, hs, V & A.

PR J.THOMSON, after T.Hargreaves, hl, stipple, pub 1830, BM, NPG. W.H.WORTHINGTON, hs silhouette, line, oval, NPG.

BARTLEY, George (1782?-1858) comedian.

P SAMUEL LANE, Dulwich College Picture Gallery, London. ISAAC POCOCK, hl as Hamlet, Garrick Club, London.

PR Several theatrical prints, NPG.

BARTLEY, Sarah (1783-1850) actress.

P SAMUEL LANE, Dulwich College Picture Gallery, London.

D SAMUEL DE WILDE, playing lute, w/c, Garrick Club, London.

PR Several theatrical prints, BM, NPG.

BARTOLOZZI, Francesco (1727-1815) engraver.

P SIR JOSHUA REYNOLDS, 1771-73, hl, Saltram (NT), Devon. JOHN OPIE, c1785, hl, NPG 222. DOMENICO PELLEGRINI, c1795, hl, Galleria dell' Accademia, Venice.

D G.B.CIPRIANI, Bartolozzi asleep in a chair, pencil, Royal Coll. GEORGE DANCE, hl profile, Royal Academy, London. HENRY EDRIDGE, tql seated, pencil, BM.

G JOHAN ZOFFANY, 'Royal Academicians, 1772', oil, Royal Coll. J.F.RIGAUD, tql with Giovanni Battista Cipriani and Agostino Carlini, oil, 1777, NPG 3186. HENRY SINGLETON, 'Royal Academicians, 1793', oil, Royal Academy.

PR R.MENAGEOT, hs profile, pub 1778, BM. PASTORINI and P.W.TOMKINS, after W.Artaud, tql seated, with crayon, stipple, pub 1803, BM, NPG. J.ROMNEY, after F.Bartolozzi, wl seated, line and etch, BM, pub 1817, NPG.

C THOMAS ROWLANDSON, c1815, hs, pen, w/c and pencil, Yale Center for British Art, New Haven, USA.

BARTOLOZZI, Gaetano Stefano (1757-1821) engraver.

SC J.PLUM, 1782?, wax medallion, V & A.

BARTON, Bernard (1784-1849) quaker poet.

P R.MENDHAM, hl, Christchurch Mansion, Ipswich.

PR R.COOPER, hl, stipple, BM, NPG. J.H.LYNCH, after S.Laurence of 1847, hs, semi-profile, lith, NPG. UNKNOWN, hl, stipple, NPG.

BARWELL, Richard (1741-1804) member of the supreme council in India.

P GILBERT STUART, hl, Luton Hoo, Beds.

PR W.DICKINSON, after J.Reynolds, wl seated in library, with his son, mezz, BM.

BASEVI, George (1794-1845) architect.

SC UNKNOWN, probably based on a life mask by Mazzotti, plaster bust, Fitzwilliam Museum, Cambridge.

BASIRE, James (1730-1802) engraver.

PR UNKNOWN, hs, line, oval, for Nichols's *Literary Anecdotes*, 1815 BM, NPG.

BASKERVILLE, John (1706-1775) printer and designer of type.

P JAMES MILLAR, 1774, hl seated, City Museum and Art Gallery, Birmingham; version, NPG 1394.

M SAMUEL RAVEN, after Millar, hs, City Museum and Art Gallery Birmingham.

BASS, Michael Thomas (1799-1884) brewer.

SC SIR J.E.BOEHM, bronze statue, The Wardwick, Derby.

PR C.PELLEGRINI (Ape), wl, chromo lith, for *Vanity Fair*, 20 May 1871, NPG.

BASSET, Francis, see DE DUNSTANVILLE.

BASTARD, John Pollexfen (1756-1816) politician.

PR S.W.REYNOLDS, after J.Northcote, tql with his brother Edmund, mezz, pub 1795, BM. W.RADDON, hs, line, pub 1817 NPG.

BATE Dudley, Sir Henry, see DUDLEY.

BATES, Joah (1741-1799) musician.

PR W.DANIELL, after G.Dance of 1794, hs profile, soft-ground etch, pub 1809, BM, NPG.

C J.GILLRAY, 'Ancient Music', etch, pub 1787, NPG.

BATES, Joshua (1788-1864) financier.

SC WILLIAM BEHNES, bust, Public Library, Boston, USA.

BATES, Sarah, née Harrop (d1811) singer.

D OZIAS HUMPHRY, hl, pastel, Knole (NT), Kent.
PR DELALTRÉ, after A.Kauffman?, tql, stipple, NPG.

BATH, Thomas Thynne, 1st Marquess of (1734-1796)
statesman.
P SIR THOMAS LAWRENCE, RA 1796, tql seated in peer's robes, Longleat, Wilts.

BATH, Thomas Thynne, 2nd Marquess of (1765-1837)
politician.
P J.SALISBURY, hs as a young man, oval, Longleat, Wilts. JOHN HOPPNER, tql, Longleat.
G SIR GEORGE HAYTER, 'The Trial of Queen Caroline, 1820', oil, NPG 999.
PR W.J.WARD, after H.W.Pickersgill, wl in Garter robes, mezz, pub 1834, BM, NPG.

BATHER, Edward (1779-1847) archdeacon of Salop.
PR S.COUSINS, after W.Etty, hl, mezz, NPG.

BATHURST, Henry (1744-1837) bishop of Norwich.
P SIR MARTIN ARCHER SHEE, 1818, tql seated, King Edward VI's School, Norwich. THOMAS KIRKBY, 1826, tql, New College, Oxford.
D SIR GEORGE HAYTER, c1816, hl seated, pencil, NPG 883(1).
SL AUGUSTIN EDOUART, 1829, wl, Castle Museum, Norwich.
SC SIR FRANCIS CHANTREY, 1841, marble statue, Norwich Cathedral.
PR T.A.DEAN, after M.Sharp, hl, stipple, for Jerdan's *Nat Portrait Gallery*, 1830, BM, NPG.

BATHURST, Henry Bathurst, 2nd Earl (1714-1794) lord chancellor.
P NATHANIEL DANCE, hl in chancellor's robes, Lincoln's Inn, London. DAVID MARTIN, wl, in chancellor's robes with mace and purse, Balliol College, Oxford.
G JOHN SINGLETON COPLEY, 'The Collapse of the Earl of Chatham in the House of Lords, 7 July 1778', oil, TATE 100, on loan to NPG.
SC JOSEPH NOLLEKENS: 1776, bust, Palace of Westminster, London; bust on monument, Church of St John the Baptist, Cirencester.
PR R.HOUSTON, tql seated in chancellor's robes, 1773, mezz, BM.
C J.SAYERS, wl, etch, pub 1782, NPG.

BATHURST, Henry Bathurst, 3rd Earl (1762-1834) statesman.
P SIR THOMAS LAWRENCE: c1818, hl, Wellington Museum, Apsley House, London; 1820–23, tql seated with Garter star, Royal Coll. WILLIAM SALTER, 1834, tql study for 'Waterloo Banquet', NPG 3697.
G SIR GEORGE HAYTER, 'The Trial of Queen Caroline, 1820', oil, NPG 999. GEORGE JONES, 'Catholic Emancipation Act 1829', oil, on loan to Palace of Westminster, London. W.SALTER, 'Waterloo Banquet at Apsley House', oil, 1836, Wellington Museum, Apsley House.
PR T.WATSON, after N.Dance, wl as a boy, with his brother Apsley, mezz, pub 1776, BM. H.MEYER, after T.Phillips, hl, stipple, for *Contemporary Portraits*, 1810, BM, NPG.

BATTIE, William (1704-1776) physician.
P UNKNOWN, tql, Royal College of Physicians, London.

BATTISHILL, Jonathan (1738-1801) composer.
PR S.HARDING, after a miniature by L.Sullivan, 1765, hs, stipple, oval, pub 1803, BM, NPG. J.CHAPMAN, after Drummond, hl, stipple, pub 1805, NPG.

BATTY, Robert (1763-1849) physician.
D Attrib GEORGE DANCE, 1799, hl profile, pencil, Royal College of Physicians, London, engr W.Daniell, soft-ground etch, pub 1810, BM, NPG. W.H.CLIFT, hs, pencil and w/c, BM.

BAXTER, Sir David (1793-1872) manufacturer and benefactor.
P SIR JOHN WATSON-GORDON, tql, Edinburgh University.
SC SIR JOHN STEELL, 1873, statue, Dundee.

BAYLEY, Sir John, Bart (1763-1841) judge.
P WILLIAM RUSSELL, c1808, tql seated in robes, NPG 457.
SC E.B.STEPHENS, RA 1849, marble bust, St John's Church, Meopham, Kent. E.B.STEPHENS, 1850, marble bust, Eton College, Berks.
PR S.TOPHAM, after W.Robinson, hl, line, NPG.

BAYLEY, William Butterworth (1782-1860) Indian civil servant.
PR M.GAUCI, after George, tql, lith, BM.

BAYLY, Thomas Haynes (1797-1839) miscellaneous writer.
D F.R.SAY, 1831, hl seated, chalk, NPG 2647.
PR H.P.RIVIÈRE, after C.Jagger, hl, lith, BM. R.COOPER, after a miniature by S.Lover, hl, stipple and line, NPG. J.SANDS, after T.Sampson, hl, stipple, NPG.

BAYNING, Charles Townshend, 1st Baron (1728-1810) politician.
PR W.C.EDWARDS, after D.Gardner, hl, line, oval, BM.

BAYNTUN, Sir Henry William (1766-1840) admiral.
P SIR WILLIAM BEECHEY, tql in uniform, Louisiana State University, Baton Rouge, USA. UNKNOWN, c1835, hl seated with orders, NMM, Greenwich.

BAZLEY, Sir Thomas (1797-1885) manufacturer and politician.
D 'APE', CARLO PELLEGRINI, 1875, wl profile, w/c, for *Vanity Fair*, 21 August 1875, NPG 2566.
G S.BELLIN, after J.R.Herbert of 1847, 'The Anti-Corn Law League', mixed engr, pub 1850, BM, NPG. EASTHAM, 'The Treaty of Commerce, 1862', woodcut, for *Illust London News*, 1862, NPG.
PR Two woodcuts, after photographs by KILBURN and J. and C.WATKINS, for *Illust London News*, 1851 and 1863, NPG.

BEACH, Thomas (1738-1806) portrait painter.
P Self-portrait, 1802, hs, NPG 3143.

BEADON, Richard (1737-1824) bishop of Bath and Wells.
P L.F.ABBOTT, hl seated, Bishop's Palace, Wells.
SC LUCIUS GAHAGAN, 1823, plaster statuette, wl seated, NPG 4901.
PR S.FACIUS, after L.Abbott, hl seated, stipple, BM, NPG.

BEARD, John (1716?-1791) actor and singer.
G J.FINLAYSON, after J.Zoffany, wl in character with Mr Shuter and Mr Dunstall, in a scene from *Love in a Village*, mezz, pub 1768, BM, NPG.
PR UNKNOWN, hl seated, mezz, pub 1787, BM, NPG. J.MCARDELL, after T.Hudson, hl, mezz, BM, NPG. J.FABER jun, after J.M.Williams, tql, mezz, BM, NPG. Theatrical prints, BM, NPG.

BEARD, William (1772-1868) collector of bones.
PR UNKNOWN, hl with specimens, lith, for John Rutter's *Delineations of Somersetshire*, NPG.

BEATSON, Alexander (1759-1833) governor of St Helena.
D THOMAS HICKEY, 1799, hs, charcoal and chalk, Stratfield Saye, Hants.

BEATTIE, James (1735-1803) Scottish poet.
P SIR JOSHUA REYNOLDS, RA 1774, tql 'The Triumph of Truth', The University of Aberdeen.
SC JAMES TASSIE, 1789, paste medallion, SNPG 132.
PR W.RIDLEY, hs, profile, stipple, oval, for *European Mag*, 1801, BM, NPG.

BEATTIE, James Hay (1768-1790) professor of moral philo-

sophy and logic.
PR J.HEATH, hl, stipple, oval, for vol II of Dr Beattie's *Minstrel*, 1799, BM, NPG.

BEATTIE, William (1793-1875) physician and author.
PR J.ROGERS, after H.Room, hl seated, stipple, BM, NPG.

BEATTY, Sir William (c1770-1842) surgeon.
P A.W.DEVIS, c1806, hl, NMM, Greenwich. A.W.DEVIS, c1805–07, wl profile, kneeling beside the dying Nelson, NMM.

BEAUCLERK, Lord Amelius (1771-1846) admiral.
P JOHN JACKSON, begun 1831, finished by A.Fusell, 1863, wl in uniform with Bath star, NMM, Greenwich. ANDREW MORTON, tql with Bath ribbon and star, NMM.
PR S.WATTS, after C.J.Robertson, tql seated, in uniform, line, BM, NPG. W.H.SIMMONS, after W.Watson, hl, with orders, stipple, NPG.

BEAUCLERK, Lord Aubrey (1711-1741) post-captain, killed at Carthagena.
PR G.VERTUE, hl, line, oval, 1746, BM, NPG.

BEAUCLERK, Lady Diana, née Spencer (1734-1808) artist.
P SIR JOSHUA REYNOLDS, 1764–65, tql seated with portfolio and crayon, Kenwood House (The Iveagh Bequest), London.
G THOMAS HUDSON, The family of the 3rd Duke of Marlborough with Blenheim Palace in the background, oil, c1754, Blenheim Palace, Oxon.

BEAUCLERK, Topham (1739-1780) friend of Dr Johnson.
D G.P.HARDING, hs, w/c, BM.
G RICHARD BROMPTON, with HRH Duke of York and friends, oil, 1764, Fonmon Castle, S.Glamorgan, Wales.
PR S.BELLIN, after G.P.Harding, hl, line, BM, NPG.

BEAUFORT, Sir Francis (1774-1857) rear-admiral and hydrographer.
P STEPHEN PEARCE, 1850, hl seated, study for NPG 1208, NPG 918. S.PEARCE, 1855–56, related portrait, tql, NMM, Greenwich.
D WILLIAM BROCKEDON, 1838, hs, chalk, NPG 2515(90).
G S.PEARCE, 'The Arctic Council, 1851', oil, NPG 1208.

BEAUFORT, Henry Somerset, 7th Duke of (1792-1853) sportsman, aide-de-camp to the Duke of Wellington.
P WILLIAM GUSH, c1837, Badminton House, Avon. SIR EDWIN LANDSEER, wl on horseback at the Eglington Tournament, Badminton. HENRY ALKEN, 1845, wl, NPG 2806. N.SCHIAVONI, 1858, hl with his second wife, in a gondola at Venice, Badminton. F.X.WINTERHALTER, wl in Garter robes, Badminton.
D RICHARD COSWAY, c1812, wl in uniform with dog, pencil and w/c, Badminton. COUNT ALFRED D'ORSAY, 1838, hl, pencil and chalk, NPG 4026(5). JOHN DOYLE, 1841, equestrian, BM. J.R.SWINTON, c1854, hs, chalk, Badminton.
G SIR GEORGE HAYTER, 'The Trial of Queen Caroline, 1820', oil, NPG 999.

BEAUFOY, Henry (d1795) politician.
PR W.WARD, after T.Gainsborough, wl in landscape, mezz, pub 1797, BM, NPG.

BEAUFOY, Mark (1764-1827) astronomer and physicist.
PR HENRY BRETT, hs, silhouette, stipple, pub 1834, NPG.

BEAUMONT, Sir George Howland, Bart (1753-1827) connoisseur.
P JOHN HOPPNER, probably RA 1809, hl, NG 6333.
D GEORGE DANCE, 1807, hl profile, pencil, NPG 1137. J.WRIGHT, after Hoppner, hl, w/c, NPG 3157. B.R.HAYDON, c1815, two pencil sketches, TATE 2445 (ii).

G J.G.MURRAY, after J.Stephanoff, 'The Trial of Queen Caroline, 1820', stipple, pub 1823, BM. W.J.WARD, after J.Jackson, seated, with Lord Mulgrave, Hon Augustus Phipps and General Edmund Phipps, mezz, BM, NPG.
PR UNKNOWN, after J.Reynolds, hl, mezz, oval, BM, NPG.

BEAUMONT, John Thomas Barber (1774-1841) founder of insurance offices, painter.
PR J.THOMSON, after J.T.Barber Beaumont, hs, stipple, for *European Mag*, 1822, BM, NPG. J.H.LYNCH, after a bust by E.H.Baily, lith, BM, NPG.

BEAUMONT, Thomas Wentworth (1792-1848) politician.
P SIR THOMAS LAWRENCE, c1809, hl, a leaving portrait, Eton College, Berks.

BEAUVALE, Frederick James Lamb, Baron, see 3rd Viscount Melbourne.

BECHE, Sir Henry Thomas de la, see DE la Beche.

BECHER, Eliza, Lady Wrixon-, see Lady WRIXON Becher.

BECKFORD, Peter (1740-1811) sportsman and master of foxhounds.
P POMPEO BATONI, 1766, wl with dog, Royal Museum of Fine Arts, Copenhagen.

BECKFORD, William (1709-1770) lord mayor of London.
P Attrib SIR JOSHUA REYNOLDS, wl in mayor's robes, Upton House (NT), Warwicks. Attrib TILLY KETTLE, c1760–70, hl, Palace of Westminster, London.
G R.HOUSTON, tql seated with Alderman James Townsend and Alderman John Sawbridge, mezz, pub 1769, BM, NPG.
SC J.F.MOORE, 1767, marble statue, Ironmongers' Hall, London. NATHANIEL SMITH, 1770, terracotta sketch model, V & A. J.F.MOORE, 1772, statue on monument, Guildhall, London.
PR J.DIXON, wl in robes with Bill of Rights and Magna Carta, mezz, pub 1769, BM, NPG.

BECKFORD, William (1759-1844) author of *Vathek*, builder of Fonthill Abbey.
P GEORGE ROMNEY, c1781, wl, Upton Park (NT), Warwicks. JOHN HOPPNER, 1790s, tql seated, Salford City Art Gallery. WILLES MADDOX, 1844, on his deathbed, Brodick Castle (NT), Strathclyde region, Scotland.
PR J.DOYLE, equestrian, lith, *Equestrian Sketches*, pl 42, BM, NPG. F.BROMLEY, after J.Reynolds, hl, mezz, BM, NPG. A. DE St AUBIN, after P.Sauvage, profile head in circular medallion, line BM.
C UNKNOWN, wl, etch, pub 1826, NPG.

BECKFORD, William (d1799) historian.
PR UNKNOWN, after Miers, silhouette profile, stipple, for *Monthly Mirror*, 1799, BM, NPG.

BECKWITH, Sir George (1753-1823) general, governor of Barbadoes.
PR S.W.REYNOLDS, after J.Eckstein, wl in uniform, mezz, BM, NPG

BECKWITH, John Christmas (1750-1809) organist of Norwich Cathedral.
PR C.TURNER, after J.Clover, tql seated, mezz, pub 1812, BM.

BEDDOES, Thomas (1760-1808) physician.
M SAMPSON TOWGOOD ROCHE, 1794, hs, oval, NPG 5070.
D JAMES SHARPLES, hs, pastel, Bristol City Art Gallery. By or after EDWARD BIRD, pencil, Wellcome Institute, London, eng C.Warren, hs, line, pub 1810, NPG.

BEDFORD, Francis Russell, 5th Duke of (1765-1802) Whig politician and agriculturalist.

P JOHN HOPPNER, RA 1796, wl in robes, Woburn Abbey, Beds. JOHN HOPPNER, RA 1797, wl, Royal Coll; version, hs, Petworth (NT), W.Sussex.
D WILLIAM LANE, hs, pencil, NPG 1830.
M WILLIAM GRIMALDI, after Hoppner, hl, w/c, NPG L152(34).
G SIR JOSHUA REYNOLDS, 'St George and the Dragon', oil, 1776, Osterley Park (NT), Middx.
SL W.KIMPTON, c1800, hs profile, engr, NPG.
SC JOSEPH NOLLEKENS: 1802, bust, Woburn Abbey; 1803, Holkham Hall, Norfolk; 1808, Royal Coll. RICHARD WESTMACOTT, 1809, bronze statue, Russell Square, London.
C J.SAYERS, 'The Bedford level', engr, pub 1795, BM. J.GILLRAY, 'The Generae of Patriotism – or – the Bloomsbury Farmer, planting Bedfordshire Wheat', aquatint, pub 1796, BM. I.CRUIKSHANK, 'The Modern Leviathan', engr, pub 1796, BM.

BEDFORD, Georgiana Gordon, Duchess of (1781-1853) wife of the 6th Duke of Bedford.
P JOHN HOPPNER, 1800, wl, Woburn Abbey, Beds.
D SIR GEORGE HAYTER, pencil studies for a miniature, NPG 883 (4–5).
M WILLIAM GRIMALDI, after Hoppner?, 1805, tql, Woburn Abbey. HENRY BONE, after Sir G.Hayter, 1829, Woburn Abbey.
G W.SMITH, The Duke of Gordon with his family, oil, c1784, Goodwood, W.Sussex.
PR MACKENZIE, after R.W.Satchwell, hl, stipple, oval, for *Ladies' Monthly Museum*, 1804, BM, NPG. MACKENZIE, after W.M.Craig, hl, stipple, oval, for *Ladies' Monthly Museum*, 1807, BM, NPG. J.HOPWOOD, after a miniature, hl, stipple, oval, for *La Belle Assemblée*, 1807, BM, NPG. F.C.LEWIS, after T.Lawrence, hl, stipple, oval, BM. C.HEATH, after E.Landseer, tql, semi-profile, line, for *The Keepsake*, BM, NPG. J.H.ROBINSON, after G.Hayter, hl, line, BM, NPG.

BEDFORD, John Russell, 4th Duke of (1710-1771) statesman.
P GEORGE KNAPTON, 1747, hl with Garter star, The Society of Dilettanti, Brooks's Club, London. SIR JOSHUA REYNOLDS, c1759–62, tql in Garter robes, Woburn Abbey, Beds. THOMAS GAINSBOROUGH, 1764, hs, Woburn Abbey. THOMAS GAINSBOROUGH, c1768, wl, Trinity College, Dublin. THOMAS GAINSBOROUGH, c1770, hl, NPG 755.

BEDFORD, John Russell, 6th Duke of (1766-1839) lord-lieutenant of Ireland.
P SIR WILLIAM BEECHEY, 1790, Woburn Abbey, Beds. SIR HENRY RAEBURN, RA 1820, tql seated, Longleat House, Wilts. SIR THOMAS LAWRENCE, 1822, hs, Woburn Abbey. SIR GEORGE HAYTER, 1826, Woburn Abbey.
D J.D.INGRES, 1815, pencil, City Art Museum, St Louis, USA. SIR GEORGE HAYTER, hl, study for a miniature, pencil, pen and ink, wash, NPG 883(3).
M W.GRIMALDI, 1808, w/c, Woburn Abbey.
G SIR JOSHUA REYNOLDS, 'St George and the Dragon', oil, 1776, Osterley Park (NT), Middx. GEORGE GARRARD, 'Woburn Sheep-shearing', oil, 1804, Woburn Abbey. SIR G.HAYTER, 'The Trial of Queen Caroline, 1820', oil, NPG 999. SIR G.HAYTER, 'The House of Commons, 1833', oil, NPG 54. SIR G.HAYTER, 'The Coronation of Queen Victoria', oil, 1838, Royal Coll.
SC JOSEPH NOLLEKENS, 1808, two marble busts, Woburn Abbey; copy, 1811, Royal Coll. JOHN FRANCIS, 1832, marble bust, Woburn Abbey. UNKNOWN, recumbent tomb figure, Bedford Chapel, Chenies Parish Church, Bucks.
PR GEORGE GARRARD, wl, seated in park at Woburn, etch, pub 1806, BM, NPG. R.J.LANE, after E.Landseer, tql seated, lith, 1838, BM, NPG.

BEDFORD, Paul (1792?-1871) actor.
D ALFRED BRYAN, tql, w/c, NPG 2449.
PR R.J.LANE, hl, lith, pub 1839, NPG. C.BAUGNIET, tql, lith, pub 1847, BM. Several theatrical prints, BM, NPG.
PH F.R.WINDOW, wl seated, carte, NPG.

BEECHAM, John (1787-1856) methodist.
PR T.A.DEAN, after M.Claxton, hl, stipple and line, NPG.

BEECHEY, Frederick William (1796-1856) rear-admiral and geographer.
P GEORGE BEECHEY, begun c1812, RA 1828, hl, NMM, Greenwich. STEPHEN PEARCE, 1850, hs study for NPG 1208, NPG 911.
G STEPHEN PEARCE, 'The Arctic Council planning a search for Sir John Franklin', oil, 1851, NPG 1208.

BEECHEY, Sir William (1753-1839) portrait-painter.
P Self-portrait, 1799, hl, Detroit Institute of Arts, USA. By himself c1805, finished by JOHN WOOD c1836, hl, NPG 614. Self-portrait, c1814, hl, Royal Academy, London. Attrib RICHARD ROTHWELL, 1835, hl seated, Boston Museum of Fine Arts, Mass, USA.
D GEORGE DANCE, 1795, hl profile, chalk, Royal Academy. WILLIAM EVANS, after Sir William Beechey, 1799, hs, pencil, NPG 3158.
M Attrib JOSEPH SAUNDERS, c1800, V & A.
G HENRY SINGLETON, 'Royal Academicians, 1793', oil, Royal Academy.
SC E.H.BAILY, 1826, marble bust, NPG 5169.
PR E.SCRIVEN, after W.J.Newton, hs, stipple, for *Library of the Fine Arts*, vol III, 1832, BM. MISS TURNER, after Beechey (wrongly ascribed to M.A.Shee), hs, lith, 1830, BM, NPG. W.SKELTON, probably after T.Phillips, tql seated, with crayon and book, lith, 1837, BM, NPG. W.WARD, after W.Beechey, hl, mezz, BM.

BELCHER, Sir Edward (1799-1877) admiral.
P STEPHEN PEARCE, c1859, hl, in uniform, with orders, NPG 1217.
PR UNKNOWN, after a photograph by Beard, hl, for *Illust London News*, 1852, NPG. UNKNOWN, hs, woodcut, for *Illust London News*, 1877, NPG.
PH CAMILLE SILVY, wl, carte, NPG. Silvy Photographs 1860–61, vol II.

BELCHER, James (1781-1811) prize-fighter.
P UNKNOWN, hl, NPG 5214.

BELCHER, Thomas (1783-1854) pugilist.
PR C.TURNER, after G.Sharples, hl, mezz, pub 1811, BM. C.TURNER, after D.Guest, wl in the ring, mezz, BM.
C THOMAS ROWLANDSON, 1805–10, after Guest?, hl with another boxer, w/c, Brodick Castle (NT), Strathclyde region, Scotland.

BELCHIER, John (1706-1785) surgeon.
P Attrib OZIAS HUMPHRY, hl, Royal College of Surgeons, London.
SC Attrib L.F.ROUBILIAC, terracotta bust, Royal College of Surgeons, London.

BELFRAGE, Henry (1744-1835) Scottish presbyterian minister.
PR ROFFE, after J.R.Wildman, hl, stipple, for *Evangelical Mag*, BM, NPG.

BELL, Andrew (1726-1809) engraver.
P GEORGE WATSON, hl, SNPG 307.
C J.KAY, wl conversing with Smellie, printer, etch, 1787, BM, NPG.

BELL, Andrew (1753-1832) founder of Madras system of education.
SC WILLIAM BEHNES, wl marble relief figure, Westminster Abbey, London.

PR C.TURNER, after W.Owen, tql seated, mezz, pub 1813, BM, NPG.

BELL, Archibald (1755-1854) miscellaneous writer.
PR J.H.ROBINSON, after Allen, hl seated, line, BM, NPG.

BELL, Beaupré (1704-1745) antiquary.
D H.R.MORLAND, 1738, hs, chalk, Trinity College, Cambridge.

BELL, Benjamin (1749-1806) surgeon, of Edinburgh.
SC After JAMES TASSIE, 1792, plaster medallion, SNPG 423.
PR W. and J.WALKER, after H.Raeburn, tql seated, line, pub 1791, BM, NPG.
C J.KAY, wl, etch, 1791, BM, NPG.

BELL, Sir Charles (1774-1842) neurologist.
P JOHN STEVENS, tql, NPG 446a. UNKNOWN, SNPG 1294.
SC HENRY WEEKES, 1856, marble bust, Royal College of Surgeons, London. UNKNOWN, memorial tablet, Hallow Church, Worcester.
PR J.THOMSON, after Ballantyne, hl, stipple, for Pettigrew's *Medical Portrait Gallery*, 1839, BM, NPG. UNKNOWN, at table with skull and mace, lith, for *Lancet Gallery of Medical Portraits*, NPG.

BELL, George Joseph (1770-1843) jurist.
P SIR HENRY RAEBURN, 1816, tql seated, Faculty of Advocates, Parliament House, Edinburgh. JAMES TANNOCK, hl, SNPG 562.
C B.W.CROMBIE, wl, pencil study for *Modern Athenians*, pl 12, SNPG 2306. J.KAY, hs, etch, 1811, NPG.

BELL, Henry (1767-1830) marine engineer.
P JAMES TANNOCK, hl, SNPG 911.

BELL, Henry Nugent (1792-1822) legal antiquary.
PR E.SCRIVEN, after W.S.Lethbridge, hl, stipple, for his *Huntingdon Peerage*, 1821, BM, NPG.

BELL, John (1745-1831) publisher.
P GEORGE CLINT, V & A.
D WILLIAM DOUGLAS, pencil and w/c, SNPG 2265.
PR G.ARNALD, hl, polyautography, BM.
C RICHARD DIGHTON, wl 'A Real TB', coloured etch, pub 1821, BM, NPG, V & A.

BELL, John (1763-1820) surgeon.
P UNKNOWN, tql seated, NPG 1983.

BELL, John (1764-1836) barrister-at-law.
PR S.COUSINS, after T.Stewardson, hl seated, mezz, pub 1832, BM, NPG.

BELL, Sir John (1782-1876) general.
P JOHN LUCAS, RA 1857, tql seated in uniform, Royal Court House, Guernsey, engr H.Cousins, mezz, NPG.
PH CAMILLE SILVY, wl seated, carte, NPG Silvy Photographs 1860–61 vol II.

BELL, Maria, Lady, née Hamilton (d1825) artist.
PR G.CLINT, after a self-portrait, hl with crayon and portfolio, mezz, BM. E.SCRIVEN, after W.S.Lethbridge, hl, stipple, pub 1821, NPG.

BELL, Patrick (1799-1869) inventor of reaping machine.
PR UNKNOWN, hs, woodcut, for *Illust London News*, 1868, NPG.

BELL, Thomas (1792-1880) dental surgeon and zoologist.
P H.W.PICKERSGILL, RA 1856, Linnean Society, London.
SC PETER SLATER, RA 1862, marble bust, Linnean Society.
PR T.H.MAGUIRE, tql seated, lith, for *Ipswich Museum Portraits*, 1851, BM.
PH ERNEST EDWARDS, wl seated, for *Men of Eminence* ed L.Reeve, 1864, vol III, NPG.

BELLAMY, Daniel (1718-1788) minister of Kew and Petersham.
PR J.K.BALDREY, after Folkestone, hl, stipple, for his *Sermons*, 1789,

BM, NPG.

BELLAMY, George Anne (1731?-1788) actress.
P F.LINDO, wl, Garrick Club, London.
PR Several theatrical prints, BM, NPG.

BELLAMY, Thomas (1745-1800) writer and editor.
PR I.PURDEN, after S.Drummond, hl, stipple, oval, pub 1800, BM, NPG.

BELLAMY, Thomas Ludford (1770-1843) singer and actor.
PR S.FREEMAN, after Allingham, hs, stipple, oval, for *Monthly Mirror*, 1808, BM, NPG.

BELSHAM, Thomas (1750-1829) unitarian divine.
P HENRY HOWARD, RA 1809, tql seated, Dr Williams's Library, London.

BELZONI, Giovanni Battista (1778-1823) actor, engineer and traveller.
P WILLIAM BROCKEDON, hl profile in Egyptian dress, NPG 829.
D W.BROCKEDON, 1823, hs profile, chalk, NPG 2515(1).
G UNKNOWN, 'Five Remarkable Characters', etch, BM.
SC T.J.WELLS, 1818, medal, BM.
PR A. VAN ASSEN, after J.Parry, wl in costume in which he exhibited as a strong man, etch, pub 1804, BM, NPG. M.GAUCI, tql in oriental dress, with hookah, lith, pub 1820, BM, NPG. J.THOMSON, hl, stipple, for *European Mag*, 1822, BM, NPG.

BENAZECH, Charles (1767?-1794) painter.
P Self-portrait, *c*1790, hl, Uffizi Gallery, Florence.

BENGER, Elizabeth Ogilby (1778-1827) writer.
PR UNKNOWN, after T.C.Wageman, tql seated, stipple, for *La Belle Assemblée*, 1823, BM, NPG. T.WOOLNOTH, after T.C.Wageman, hl, stipple, for *Ladies' Monthly Museum*, 1825, BM, NPG.

BENNET, Agnes Maria, née Evans (d1808) writer.
PR K.MACKENZIE, after T.Braine, hl, stipple, oval, for *The Ladies' Monthly Museum*, 1804, BM, NPG.

BENNET, William (1746-1820) bishop of Cloyne.
P Attrib GILBERT STUART, 1787-93, hs, Emmanuel College, Cambridge.
SC UNKNOWN, monument, Cloyne Cathedral, Cork, Eire.

BENNETT, James (1774-1862) congregational minister.
PR T.BLOOD, after J.Renton, hs, stipple, for *Evangelical Mag*, 1818, BM, NPG. C.BAUGNIET, tql seated, lith, pub 1845, BM. UNKNOWN, tql, stipple and line, NPG.

BENNETT, William Mineard (1778-1858) miniature painter and singer.
P Self-portrait, 1815, hs, Exeter City Art Gallery.
PR S.FREEMAN, after W.M.Bennett, hs, stipple, oval, for *Monthly Mirror*, 1808, BM, NPG.

BENSLEY, Robert (1738?-1817) actor.
P SAMUEL DE WILDE, wl as Harold in *The Battle of Hastings*, Garrick Club, London. S. DE WILDE, wl as Oakly in *The Jealous Wife*, Garrick Club.
D J.ROBERTS, pencil, Garrick Club. ROBERT DIGHTON, wl as Prospero in *The Tempest*, Garrick Club.
G J.H.MORTIMER, in a scene from *King John*, oil, exhib 1768, Garrick Club.
PR W.DANIELL, after G.Dance of 1795, hl seated, profile, etch, pub 1814, BM, NPG. Various theatrical prints, BM, NPG.
C J.SAYERS, 'A Scene in the Fair Circassian', etch, NPG.

BENSON, Christopher (1789-1868) divine, master of the Temple.
P UNKNOWN, tql, Inner Temple, London.
PR UNKNOWN, hl profile, etch, NPG.

BENSON, Joseph (1749-1821) methodist minister.
PR J.HOLLOWAY jun, hs, line, pub 1804, BM, NPG. T.BLOOD, after J.Jackson, tql seated, stipple, BM, NPG.

BENTHAM, James (1708-1794) divine.
PR FACIUS, after T.Kerrich, hl, semi-profile, stipple, BM, NPG.

BENTHAM, Jeremy (1748-1832) social philosopher.
P THOMAS FRYE, c1761, wl, NPG 196. H.W.PICKERSGILL, 1829, wl seated, NPG 413. ANDREW GEDDES, hs, Queen's College, Oxford. UNKNOWN, hs, University College, London.
D J.WATTS, wl, crayon, Queen's College, Oxford.
SL JOHN FIELD, c1830, hs profile, NPG 3068.
SC DAVID D'ANGERS, bust, and bronze medallion, Musée des Beaux Arts, Angers.
PR J.THOMSON, after W.Derby, hl, stipple, for *European Mag*, 1823, BM. W.H.WORTHINGTON, hs, line, pub 1823, BM, NPG.

BENTHAM, Sir Samuel (1757-1831) naval architect.
P Unknown Russian artist, c1784, hl, NMM, Greenwich.
M HENRY EDRIDGE, hs, NPG 3069.
G J.F.SKILL, J.GILBERT, W. and E.WALKER, 'Men of Science Living in 1807-08', pencil and wash, NPG 1075.

BENTINCK, Sir Henry John William (1796-1878) general.
PR D.J.POUND, after a photograph by Watkins, tql, stipple and line, NPG.

BENTINCK, John Albert (1737-1775) captain.
P MASON CHAMBERLIN, 1775, wl seated with his son William, NMM, Greenwich.

BENTINCK, Lord William Cavendish (1774-1839) governor-general of India.
P THOMAS PHILLIPS, wl, Government House, Madras.
D J.A.D.INGRES, 1816, tql with his wife, pencil, Musée Bonnat, Bayonne. JAMES ATKINSON, set of sketches of head, pen and ink, NPG 848.
SC SIR RICHARD WESTMACOTT, 1835, statue, Calcutta. BERTEL THORVALDSEN, plaster bust, Thorvaldsen Museum, Copenhagen.
PR H.R.COOK, after T.Lawrence, hl, stipple, for *Military Panorama*, 1813, BM, NPG. G.PHILLIPS, after T.Phillips, wl, mezz, pub 1838, NPG.

BENTINCK, William Henry Cavendish, see 3rd Duke of Portland.

BENTLEY, Nathaniel (1735?-1809) 'Dirty Dick', beau.
PR I.MILLS, hl profile, etch, BM, NPG. Several popular prints, NPG.

BENTLEY, Richard (1708-1782) miscellaneous writer and artist.
PR J.HEATH, after J.G.Eccardt, hl in fancy dress, line, oval, for Walpole's *Works*, 1798, BM, NPG.

BENTLEY, Richard (1794-1871) publisher.
PR C.BAUGNIET, tql seated, lith, 1844, BM, NPG. J.BROWN, after a photograph by Lock and Whitfield, hl, stipple and line, NPG.

BENTLEY, Thomas (1731-1780) potter, partner of Josiah Wedgwood.
P UNKNOWN, hl, Walker Art Gallery, Liverpool. UNKNOWN, Wedgwood Museum, Barlaston, Staffs.
SC JOACHIM SMITH, 1773, Wedgwood medallion, Manchester City Art Galleries; similar medallion, modern cast, NPG 1949. Attrib HACKWOOD, c1778, two Wedgwood medallions, Wedgwood Museum. UNKNOWN, c1780, Wedgwood medallion, Wedgwood Museum.

BENWELL, Mary (fl 1761-1800) portrait painter.
M Self-portrait, 1779, hs, Uffizi Gallery, Florence.
PR H.KINGSBURY, hs, mezz, oval, pub 1779, BM.

BERDMORE, Samuel (1740-1802) headmaster of Charterhouse school.
PR W.NUTTER, after S.Shelley, hl seated, stipple, oval, pub 1788, BM, NPG.

BERESFORD, John (1738-1805) Irish statesman.
P G.C.STUART, NGI 1133.
G FRANCIS WHEATLEY, 'The Irish House of Commons, 1780', oil, Leeds City Art Galleries, Lotherton Hall, W.Yorks.
PR C.H.HODGES, after G.C.Stuart, hl seated, mezz, pub 1790, BM, NPG.

BERESFORD, Lord John George de la Poer (1773-1862) archbishop of Armagh.
P STEPHEN CATTERSON SMITH, wl in robes of chancellor of the University, Trinity College, Dublin.
D JOHN DOYLE, equestrian, chalk, BM.
PR C.TURNER, after T.Lawrence, tql seated, mezz, pub 1841, BM. UNKNOWN, hs, woodcut, for *Illust London News*, 1862, NPG. JOHN KIRKWOOD, tql seated, etch, NPG.
PH WALKER, tql seated, NPG Album of Photographs 1949.

BERESFORD, Sir John Poo, Bart (1766-1844) admiral.
G SIR GEORGE HAYTER, 'The House of Commons, 1833', oil, NPG 54.
PR T.HODGETTS, after W.Beechey, hl, mezz, pub 1828, BM, NPG.

BERESFORD, William Carr Beresford, Viscount (1768-1854) general.
P E.BERESFORD, after Sir William Beechey of c1814, hs with orders, NPG 1180. SIR THOMAS LAWRENCE, c1818, wl in uniform of Marshal of Portugal, Wellington Museum, Apsley House, London. RICHARD ROTHWELL, c1831, hl, NPG 300. REUBEN SAYERS, 1849, hl seated, formerly United Service Club, London (c/o The Crown Commissioners).
D D.A. DE SEQUEIRA, c1810, wl, chalk, Museu Nacional de Arte Antiga, Lisbon. THOMAS HEAPHY, 1813-14, wl in uniform, with orders, w/c, NGI 2551; hs, w/c study, NPG 1914(4).
G F.BROMLEY, after J.P.Knight, 'Peninsular Heroes', mixed, pub 1847, BM, NPG.
PR C.TURNER, after W.Beechey, hl in uniform, mezz, pub 1814, BM, NPG. J.COCHRAN, after E.Kendrick, hl, stipple, pub 1830, BM.
C JOHN DOYLE, 'A Political Riddle', pencil and chalk, 1829, BM.

BERKELEY, Francis Henry Fitzhardinge (1794-1870) politician and reformer.
PR H.B.HALL, after J.W.Childe, tql, stipple, pub 1839, BM, NPG.

BERKELEY, George Cranfield Berkeley, 17th Baron (1753-1818) admiral.
P FRANCIS COTES, 1769, hl as midshipman, Berkeley Castle, Glos. THOMAS GAINSBOROUGH, 1784-86, wl, Berkeley Castle.
M Attrib MISS PAYE, hs, oval, Berkeley Castle.
G OZIAS HUMPHRY, wl with members of his family, oil, 1780, Berkeley Castle.

BERKELEY, George Monck (1763-1793) writer.
PR W.SKELTON, after W.Peters, hs, line, oval, for his *Poems*, 1797, BM, NPG.

BERKELEY, Maurice Frederick Fitzhardinge, see Baron Fitzhardinge.

BERKENHOUT, John (1730?-1791) physician and naturalist.
PR T.HOLLOWAY, hl semi-profile, line, oval, for *European Mag*, 1788, BM, NPG.

BERNAL, Ralph (d1854) politician and collector.
G SIR GEORGE HAYTER, 'The House of Commons, 1833', oil, NPG

54.
PR J.THOMSON, after A.Wivell, hl, stipple, pl 7 set of portraits of persons connected with trial of Queen Caroline, pub 1822, BM, NPG.

BERNARD, Sir Francis (c1712-1779) governor of Massachusetts.
P JOSEPH BLACKBURN, 1760, tql, Wadsworth Atheneum, Hartford, Conn, USA. Attrib JOHN SINGLETON COPLEY or GILBERT STUART, hs, oval, Christ Church, Oxford.

BERNARD, John (1756-1828) actor, writer and manager.
P SAMUEL DE WILDE, wl as Jack Meggot in *The Suspicious Husband*, Garrick Club, London. P.MARSHALL, hs, Garrick Club.
PR W.RIDLEY, after Barry, hl, stipple, oval, for Parson's *Minor Theatre*, 1794, BM.

BERNARD, Sir Thomas (1750-1818) philanthropist.
P After JOHN OPIE, hl, Royal Institution, London.
PR S.W.REYNOLDS, after J.Opie, tql seated, mezz, pub 1805, BM.

BERRIDGE, John (1716-1793) evangelical divine.
PR UNKNOWN, hl profile, line, oval, for *Gospel Mag*, 1774, BM, NPG. J.OGBORNE, hl profile, in pulpit, stipple, pub 1788, BM, NPG.

BERRY, Sir Edward, Bart (1768-1831) admiral.
P JOHN SINGLETON COPLEY, 1815, tql in uniform with medals, NMM, Greenwich.
G W.BROMLEY, J.LANDSEER and LENEY, after R.Smirke, 'Naval Victories', 'Victors of the Nile', line, pub 1803, BM, NPG.
PR W.RIDLEY, after W.Grimaldi, hs, stipple, oval, pub 1799, BM, NPG. D.ORME, hl, stipple, oval, for *Naval Chronicle*, 1799, BM, NPG. G.KEATING, after H.Singleton, hl, mezz, pub 1799, BM.

BERRY, Mary (1763-1852) writer.
SC ANNE SEYMOUR DAMER, 1793, bronze bust, Chillington Hall, Staffs.
PR H.ADLARD, after J.Zoffany, wl with her sister and a dog, as children, stipple and line, NPG. H.ROBINSON, after J.R.Swinton, hs, aged 86, stipple, pub 1850, BM, NPG. H.ADLARD, after a miniature by Miss Foldson, (Mrs Mee), hs, stipple, oval, NPG.

BERTIE, Sir Albemarle (1755-1824) admiral.
G BARTOLOZZI, LANDSEER, RYDER and STOW, after R.Smirke, 'Naval Victories', 'Commemoration of the victory of June 1st 1794', line, pub 1803, BM, NPG.

BERTIE, Sir Thomas (1758-1825) admiral.
PR PAGE, after Lea, hs profile, stipple, pub 1811, NPG.

BERTIE, Willoughby, see 4th Earl of Abingdon.

BERWICK, William Noel-Hill, 3rd Baron (1773-1842) ambassador.
P UNKNOWN, c1800, Attingham Park (NT), Salop.

BESSBOROUGH, John William Ponsonby, 4th Earl of (1781-1847) politician.
P STEPHEN CATTERSON SMITH, hl with robes, and Garter star, NGI 248.
G SIR GEORGE HAYTER, 'The House of Commons, 1833', oil, NPG 54.
C SIR EDWIN LANDSEER, c1835, hl profile, pen and wash, NPG 4915. JOHN DOYLE, several drgs, BM.

BESSBOROUGH, William Ponsonby, 2nd Earl of (1704-1793) collector.
P GEORGE KNAPTON, 1743, hl in Turkish dress, Society of Dilettanti, Brooks's Club, London. By or after G.KNAPTON, hl in Turkish dress, Hardwick Hall (NT), Derbys.
G JOHN SINGLETON COPLEY, 'The Collapse of the Earl of Chatham in the House of Lords, 7 July 1778', oil, TATE 100, on loan to NPG.

SC JOSEPH NOLLEKENS, 1793, bust, Derby Cathedral.
PR R.DUNKARTON, after J.S.Copley, tql with antique vase, mezz, pub 1794, BM, NPG.

BEST, Samuel (1738-1825) (alias Poor Help), pretended prophet.
PR FARN, after Lewis, hs, stipple, for *Wonderful Museum*, 1804, BM, NPG.

BEST, William Draper, see 1st Baron Wynford.

BETAGH, Thomas (1739-1811) jesuit.
D HENRY BROCAS, pencil, NGI 2643.
SC PETER TURNERELLI, monument, St Michael and St John's Church, Dublin.

BETHAM, William (1749-1839) antiquary.
PR MISS TURNER, after M.Betham, hs, aged 81, lith, BM, NPG.

BETHAM, Sir William (1779-1853) Ulster king of arms.
SC J.E.JONES, RA 1846?, bust, Dublin Castle.
PR W.DRUMMOND, after D.Maclise, hl, lith, *Athenaeum Portraits*, No 20, pub 1836, BM, NPG.

BETHELL, Christopher (1773-1859) bishop of Bangor.
PR T.LUPTON, after J.W.Gordon, tql seated, mezz, BM, NPG.

BETTESWORTH, George Edmund Byron (1780-1808) naval captain.
SC The Coade firm, 1812, statue, St Michael's Church, St Michael Caerhays, Cornwall.

BETTY, William Henry West (1791-1874) actor.
P JAMES NORTHCOTE, RA 1805?, hl, Petworth (NT), W.Sussex. JOHN OPIE, wl as Young Norval in *Douglas*, Garrick Club, London; version, NPG 1392. JAMES NORTHCOTE, wl, Royal Shakespeare memorial Theatre Museum, Stratford-upon-Avon.
D SAMUEL DE WILDE, 1805, wl as Orestes, pencil, chalk and w/c, BM. G.H.HARLOW, 1810, chalk, NPG 1333. HENRY SINGLETON, pencil, BM.
PR Numerous theatrical prints, BM, NPG.

BEVAN, Edward (1770-1860) physician and apiarian.
PR UNKNOWN, hs, semi-profile, lith, for Neville Wood's *Naturalist*, NPG.

BEVERLEY, Henry Roxby (1796-1863) comedian.
PR Several theatrical prints, BM, NPG.

BEVERLEY, John (1743-1827) esquire bedell of Cambridge University.
C RICHARD DIGHTON, wl, coloured etch, NPG.

BEWICK, Thomas (1753-1828) wood engraver.
P JAMES RAMSAY, 1823, hl, NPG 319. WILLIAM NICHOLSON, tql, Laing Museum and Art Gallery, Newcastle upon Tyne. JAMES RAMSAY, Laing Museum and Art Gallery.
D Attrib R.E.BEWICK, pen and ink sketch, BM. MISS E.D.CRAWHALL, w/c, Laing Museum and Art Gallery.
SC E.H.BAILY, marble bust, Newcastle Literary and Philosophical Society.
PR T.A.KIDD, after Miss Kirkley, hs, line, pub 1798, BM, NPG. J.SUMMERFIELD, after D.B.Murphy, hs, stipple, pub 1816, BM. T.RANSON, after W.Nicholson, tql seated with pencil, line, pub 1816, BM, NPG. F.BACON, after J.Ramsay, wl, line, BM, NPG.

BEWICK, William (1795-1866) portrait and historical painter.
P Self-portrait, hl at easel, Dean and Chapter of Durham.
SC JOHN GIBSON, 1853, after model of 1827, marble bust, NG 2240.

BEXLEY, Nicholas Vansittart, 1st Baron (1766-1851) chancellor of the exchequer.
P WILLIAM OWEN, 1815, tql seated in robes of the chancellor of the

exchequer, Christ Church, Oxford.
D GEORGIANA M.ZORNLIN, 1848, hs, pencil, NPG 641.
P.STEPHANOFF, study for 'Coronation of George IV', w/c, V & A.
PR T.A.DEAN, after Sir Thomas Lawrence, tql seated in peer's robes, stipple, for Jerdan's *Nat Portrait Gallery*, 1831, BM, NPG. C.TURNER, after J.Rand, nearly wl seated, mezz, pub 1836, BM, NPG.
C JOHN DOYLE, wl, entitled 'A small tea party of superannuated politicians', pen over pencil, BM.

BICHENO, James Ebenezer (1785-1851) statesman.
P E.U.EDDIS, Linnean Society, London.

BICKERSTETH, Edward (1786-1850) evangelical divine.
PR S.W.REYNOLDS, after A.Mosses, tql seated, mezz, pub 1826, BM, NPG. H.MEYER, after A.Robertson, hl, stipple, pub 1827, BM, NPG. T.A.DEAN, after H.Room, hl, stipple, NPG.

BICKERSTETH, Henry, see Baron Langdale.

BICKERTON, Sir Richard Hussey (1759-1832) admiral.
SC SIR FRANCIS CHANTREY, medallion on marble monument, Bath Abbey.
PR W.RIDLEY, after T.Maynard, hl, stipple, oval, pub 1803, NPG.

BIDDULPH, Thomas Tregenna (1763-1838) minister of St James's, Bristol.
SC E.H.BAILY, bust, St James' Church, Bristol.
PR W.RIDLEY, hs, stipple, oval, for *Evangelical Mag*, 1805, BM, NPG.

BIDLAKE, John (1755-1814) divine and poet.
PR UNKNOWN, hs profile, etch, NPG.

BIFFIN, Sarah (1784-1850) miniature painter.
PR R.W.SIEVIER, after S.Biffin, tql seated, stipple, pub 1821, BM. H.GRÉVEDON, 1823, hl, lith, BM, NPG.

BIGG, William Redmore (1755-1828) painter.
PR W.BARNARD, after W.Fisk, hl, mezz, pub 1831, BM, NPG.

BIGLAND, John (1750-1832) schoolmaster and author.
PR H.MEYER, after T.Uwins, hs, stipple, oval, pub 1806, NPG. W.WARD, after J.R.Smith, hl seated, mezz, pub 1811, BM, NPG.

BIGLAND, Ralph (1711-1784) herald, Garter king of arms.
PR C.TOWNLEY, after R.Brompton, hl as Somerset herald, mezz, BM, NPG.

BILLING, Archibald (1791-1881) physician.
PR C.BAUGNIET, tql seated, lith, BM, 1846, NPG.

BILLINGTON, Elizabeth, née Weichsel (1768-1818) singer.
P J.J.MASQUERIER, hl, Garrick Club, London. GEORGE ROMNEY, wl seated as St Cecilia, Boston Museum of Fine Arts, USA.
D FRANCESCO BARTOLOZZI, hs, chalk, Royal Coll. W.WELLINGS, in *Artaxerxes*, w/c, BM.
M Possibly FREDERICK BUCK, V & A.
PR F.BARTOLOZZI, after R.Cosway, hl as the Peruvian in opera *The Peruvian*, stipple, oval, pub 1786, BM. T.BURKE, after S. de Koster, hs, semi-profile, stipple, pub 1802, BM, NPG. J.WARD, after J.Reynolds, wl as St Cecilia, with choir of angels, mezz, pub 1803, BM. Various theatrical prints, BM, NPG.
C J.GILLRAY, several etchs, NPG.

BINDLEY, Charles (1795-1859) sporting writer.
PR H.ADLARD, after J.W.Childe, tql, stipple, pub 1846, BM, NPG.

BINDLEY, James (1737-1818) commissioner of stamps, book collector.
PR J.PARRY, wl, etch, pub 1813, BM, NPG. W.HOLL, after W.Behnes, hl seated, stipple, BM, pub 1819, NPG. W.SAY, hl, mezz, for Dibdin's *Typographical Antiquities*, 1819, BM.

BINGHAM, Sir George Ridout (1777-1833) major-general.

PR W.J.WARD, after H.W.Pickersgill, wl in uniform, mezz, pub 1835, BM.

BINGHAM, Margaret, Lady, see Countess of Lucan.

BINGLEY, William (1774-1823) author.
PR W.WARD, hl seated, mezz, BM.

BINNEY, Thomas (1798-1874) nonconformist divine.
P UNKNOWN, hl, Dr Williams's Library, London; tql version, Memorial Hall Trust, London.
D 'MD', GEORGES MONTBARD, 1872, hl, w/c, for *Vanity Fair*, NPG 2182.
G B.E.HAYDON, 'The Anti-Slavery Society Convention, 1840', oil, NPG 599.
PR W.HOLL, after J.R.Wildman, hl, stipple, pub 1830, NPG. C.BAUGNIET, tql, lith, pub 1846, BM, NPG. F.CROLL, hs, line, for Hogg's *Instructor*, BM, NPG. J.COCHRAN, after W.Gush, tql seated, stipple and line, BM.
PH Several photographs and engravings after photographs, NPG.

BINNS, John (1772-1860) journalist and politician.
PR MATT HAUGHTON, after Moses Haughton, hs, stipple, oval, pub 1797, NPG.

BIRCH, John (1745?-1815) surgeon.
PR J.LEWIS, after T.Phillips, tql, line and stipple, NPG.

BIRCH, Samuel (1757-1841) alderman of London, dramatist.
P UNKNOWN, Corporation of London.
PR W.RIDLEY, after S.Drummond, hs, stipple, oval, for *European Mag*, 1805, BM, NPG.

BIRCH, Thomas (1705-1766) historian.
P UNKNOWN, 1735, hs, oval, BM. UNKNOWN, c1735, hl seated, NPG 522. JAMES WILLS, 1737, hl, Royal Society, London.

BIRD, Edward (1772-1819) painter.
D SIR FRANCIS CHANTREY, 1816, hs profile, pencil, NPG 3648.
SC SIR FRANCIS CHANTREY, 1816, plaster bust, NPG 986.
PR H.JACKSON, after B.Murphy, hs, lith, BM.

BIRD, Edward Joseph (1799-1881) admiral.
G STEPHEN PEARCE, 'The Arctic Council planning a search for Sir John Franklin', oil, 1851, NPG 1208.

BIRD, John (1709-1776) astronomical instrument maker.
PR V.GREEN, after C.Lewis, hl seated, with diagrams, mezz, pub 1776, BM, NPG.

BIRKBECK, George (1776-1841) promoter of mechanics' institutes.
P WILLIAM BEWICK, The Royal Technical College, Glasgow.
PR H.DAWE, after S.Lane, tql, mezz, BM, NPG. G.ADCOCK, hl, stipple, BM. T.WOOLNOTH, after Wageman, hs, stipple, NPG.

BIRNIE, Sir Richard (1760?-1832) police magistrate.
PR W.SAY, after J.Green, hl seated, mezz, pub 1819, BM, NPG. 'H.B.', 1829, wl, coloured lith, NPG.

BISHOP, George (1785-1861) astronomer.
SC H.G.MAY, 1866, marble bust, Royal Astronomical Society, London.

BISHOP, Sir Henry Rowley (1786-1855) composer of operas and glees.
P Attrib G.H.HARLOW, c1810, hl, NPG 617. ISAAC POCOCK, 1813, hs, NPG 275.
PR S.W.REYNOLDS, after T.Foster, tql seated with music, mezz, pub 1822, BM, NPG.

BISHOP, Samuel (1731-1795) poet, headmaster of Merchant Taylors' school.
PR C.TOWNLEY, after G.Dance, hl profile, stipple, oval, for his *Works*, 1796, BM, NPG. H.D.THIELCKE, after Clarkson, hl, stipple, pub 1814, BM, NPG.

BISSET, William (1758-1834) bishop of Raphoe.
P SIR THOMAS LAWRENCE, c1827, hl seated, Christ Church, Oxford.

BLAAUW, William Henry (1793-1870) antiquary.
P SIR WILLIAM BEECHEY, 1811, hl, a leaving portrait, Eton College, Berks.

BLACK, Adam (1784-1874) publisher.
D UNKNOWN, chalk, SNPG 1691.
PR W.STEWART, hl, lith, BM. UNKNOWN, hl, line and stipple, NPG.
C B.W.CROMBIE, wl, coloured etch, 1848, NPG.

BLACK, John (1783-1855) journalist, editor of the 'Morning Chronicle'.
P W.H.WORTHINGTON, hl, SNPG 321, engr W.H.Worthington, hl seated with newspaper, line, pub 1835, NPG.

BLACK, Joseph (1728-1799) chemist and physician.
P DAVID MARTIN, c1770, hl, Edinburgh University. DAVID MARTIN, 1787, tql with chemist's equipment, SNPG L259.
D UNKNOWN, hs, oval, chalk, SNPG 283.
SC JAMES TASSIE, 1788, paste medallion, NPG 3238.
PR J.ROGERS, after H.Raeburn, tql seated, stipple, for Chambers's Dict of Eminent Scotsmen, BM, NPG. ROBERTSON, after Thornton, hl in cloak, line, oval, BM. J.BEUGO, after J.Brown, hs profile, stipple, oval, BM.
C J.KAY, several etchs, BM, NPG.

BLACK, William (1749-1829) physician and author.
PR R.STANIER, hs profile, stipple, oval, for European Mag, 1790, BM, NPG.

BLACKALL, John (1771-1860) physician.
P R.R.REINAGLE, hl, Royal College of Physicians, London.
PR S.COUSINS, after R.Reinagle, hl, mezz, pub 1844, BM, NPG.

BLACKBURNE, Francis (1705-1787) archdeacon of Cleveland.
P GEORGE CUITT, hs, St Catherine's College, Cambridge. UNKNOWN, hl, St Catherine's College.
PR SCHIAVONETTI, hl, stipple, oval, NPG.

BLACKBURNE, Francis (1782-1867) lord chancellor of Ireland.
P By or after STEPHEN CATTERSON SMITH, King's Inns, Dublin.
PR C.H.JEENS, hs in judicial robes, line, for his Life, 1874, BM. J.KIRKWOOD, after C.Grey, hl seated, stipple, NPG.

BLACKET, Joseph (1786-1810) poet.
PR H.R.COOK, after J.J.Masquerier, hl, stipple, for his Remains, 1811, BM, NPG.

BLACKLOCK, Thomas (1721-1791) poet.
P WILLIAM BONNAR, hs profile, SNPG 319, engr W. and F.Holl, stipple, NPG.

BLACKNER, John (1770-1816) historian of Nottingham.
PR UNKNOWN, after R.Bonington, hl, mezz, BM, NPG.

BLACKSTONE, Sir William (1723-1780) jurist.
P THOMAS GAINSBOROUGH, 1774, hl, TATE 2637. Attrib SIR JOSHUA REYNOLDS, tql seated, NPG 388. TILLY KETTLE, tql, Bodleian Library, Oxford.
SC JOHN BACON, 1784, marble statue, All Souls College, Oxford.

BLACKWELL, Thomas (1701-1757) classical scholar.
PR J.RECORD, after J.Richardson of 1735, hs, etch, pub 1783, BM, NPG.

BLACKWOOD, Sir Henry, Bart (1770-1832) vice-admiral.
P JOHN HOPPNER, 1806, hl in uniform, NMM, Greenwich, engr C.Turner, mezz, pub 1833, BM.

BLACKWOOD, William (1776-1834) publisher.

PR UNKNOWN, probably after Sir William Allan, hl seated, line, SNPG.

BLAGDEN, Sir Charles (1748-1820) physician, secretary of the Royal Society.
PR MRS D.TURNER, after T.Phillips, hs, semi-profile, etch, BM, NPG.

BLAIR, Hugh (1718-1800) Scottish divine.
P DAVID MARTIN, c1775, hl, Edinburgh University.
SC JAMES TASSIE, 1791, paste medallion, SNPG 134.
PR J.CALDWALL, after D.Martin, hl seated, line, oval, for his Discourses, 1783, BM, NPG. F.BARTOLOZZI, after H.Raeburn, tql seated, stipple, pub 1802, BM, NPG.
C J.KAY, hl preaching, line, oval, 1798, BM, NPG.

BLAIR, Sir James Hunter (1741-1787) lord-provost of Edinburgh.
C J.KAY, wl, etch, 1785, NPG. J.KAY, wl with Thomas, 7th Earl of Haddington and Sir William Forbes of Pitsligo, etch, 1785, BM, NPG.

BLAIR, Robert (1741-1811) president of the College of Justice in Scotland.
P SIR HENRY RAEBURN, Society of Writers to the Signet, Edinburgh.
SC JAMES TASSIE, 1792, paste medallion, SNPG 1265. SIR FRANCIS CHANTREY, marble statue, Faculty of Advocates, Parliament House, Edinburgh.
PR J.HEATH, after H.Raeburn, tql with mace, line, pub 1813, BM.
C J.KAY, wl, etch, 1793, NPG. J.KAY, tql profile, etch, oval, 1799, BM, NPG.

BLAIR, William (1766-1822) surgeon.
P HENRY MEYER, hl profile, St Giles-in-the-Fields, London.

BLAKE, John Bradby (1745-1773) naturalist.
SC JOACHIM SMITH, Wedgwood medallion, City Museum and Art Gallery, Stoke-on-Trent.

BLAKE, William (1757-1827) poet and painter.
P THOMAS PHILLIPS, 1807, hl seated, NPG 212.
D JOHN FLAXMAN, 1804, hs, pencil, Fitzwilliam Museum, Cambridge. J.FLAXMAN, c1804, hs profile, pencil, Yale Center for British Art, New Haven, USA. Self-portrait, before 1810, head, pencil sketch (the 'Rosetti MS') BL Add Ms 49460, fol 67. JOHN LINNELL, 1820–25, 6 pencil drgs: hl at Hampstead; hl seated with John Varley; hl seated; 3 hs profile sketches, Fitzwilliam Museum, Cambridge. GEORGE RICHMOND, c1825, wl, pencil, Fitzwilliam Museum. Attrib CATHERINE BLAKE, c1828, hs as a young man, probably from memory, pencil, Fitzwilliam Museum. FREDERICK TATHAM, c1830, hs, in youth and age, sepia wash and pencil, Yale Center for British Art, New Haven, USA. GEORGE RICHMOND, c1857–59, two drgs from memory, head, Fitzwilliam Museum. JOHN LINNELL, 1861, after a miniature of 1821, hs, w/c, NPG 2146.
M JOHN LINNELL, 1821, hs profile, Fitzwilliam Museum.
SC JAMES S.DEVILLE, 1823, plaster cast of life mask, NPG 1809.
PR THOMAS STOTHARD, c1780–81, with Stothard and Ogleby, camping by the Medway, etch, BM.

BLAKE, William (1773-1821) dissenting minister.
PR MOSES HAUGHTON, after F.Webb, hs profile, stipple, NPG.

BLAKELY, Johnston (1781-1814) commander in United States navy.
PR T.GIMBREDE, hl, stipple, for Analectic Mag and Naval Chronicle, NPG.

BLAKENEY, Sir Edward (1778-1868) field-marshal.
P STEPHEN CATTERSON SMITH, wl in uniform, formerly United

Service Club, London (c/o The Crown Commissioners).

PR G.SANDERS, after S.Catterson Smith, tql, mezz, NPG. R.J.LANE, after J.Nogues, 1840, hl, lith, NPG.

BLAKEWAY, John Brickdale (1765-1826) topographer.

PR C.HULLMANDEL, after P.Corbet, hl, lith, NPG.

BLANCHARD, William (1769-1835) actor.

P SAMUEL DE WILDE, hl as the Marquis de Grand Chateau in *The Cabinet*, Garrick Club, London.

G G.H.HARLOW, 'Court for the Trial of Queen Catherine', oil, 1817, Royal Shakespeare Memorial Theatre Museum, Stratford-on-Avon. GEORGE CLINT, in a scene from *Love, Law and Physic*, oil, RA 1830, Garrick Club.

PR H.COOK, hs, line, for *European Mag*, 1817, BM, NPG. Several theatrical prints, BM, NPG.

BLAND, Maria Theresa, née Romanzini (1769-1838) singer.

D SAMUEL DE WILDE, three w/c drgs, in character, Garrick Club, London.

PR J.CONDÉ, hl, stipple, oval, for *Thespian Mag*, 1792, BM, NPG. Various theatrical prints, BM, NPG.

BLANDY, Mary (1719-1752) murderess.

PR T.RYLEY, after F.Wilson, hl, mezz, oval, BM, NPG. B.COLE, tql, line, BM, NPG. Several popular prints, BM.

BLANE, Sir Gilbert (1749-1834) physician.

P SIR MARTIN ARCHER SHEE, hs, Royal College of Physicians, London.

BLESSINGTON, Charles John Gardiner, 1st Earl of (1782-1829) man of fashion.

P JAMES HOLMES, c1812, hs, NPG 1523.

G SIR GEORGE HAYTER, 'The Trial of Queen Caroline, 1820', oil, NPG 999.

BLESSINGTON, Marguerite Power, Countess of (1789-1849) writer and beauty.

P SIR THOMAS LAWRENCE, RA 1822, hl, Wallace Coll, London; copy Hughenden Manor (NT), Bucks.

D P.E.STRÖHLING, 1812, hl profile, chalk, BM. After A.E.CHALON, c1836, hs, w/c, NPG 1309. CHARLES MARTIN, 1844, wl, pencil, NPG 1645a. GEORGE CATTERMOLE, hs, pencil, BM.

PR R.J.LANE, after E.Landseer, hl, lith, 1833, BM. W.GILLER, after E.T.Parris, tql, mezz, pub 1835, BM, NPG. R.J.LANE, after Count d'Orsay 1841, tql, lith, NPG. J.COCHRAN, after Le Comte, tql, stipple, BM, NPG. D.MACLISE, wl, lith, for *Fraser's Mag*, BM.

BLIGH, Sir Richard Rodney (1737-1821) admiral.

PR RIDLEY, after J.Opie, hs, stipple, oval, pub 1805, NPG.

BLIGH, William (1754-1817) admiral, commander of *The Bounty*.

D GEORGE DANCE, 1794, hl seated, pencil, NPG 1138. JOHN SMART, hl, pencil and w/c, 4317.

G BROMLEY, after Benezach, 'The hospitable behaviour of the Governor of Timor to Lieutenant Bligh', line, pub 1802, NPG. G.NOBLE and J.PARKER, after J.Smart, 'Naval Victories', 'Commemoration of 11th Oct 1797', line, pub 1803, BM, NPG.

PR J.CONDÉ, after J.Russell, hl in uniform, coloured stipple, oval, BM, NPG.

BLIGHT, William (c1780-1862) rear-admiral.

P UNKNOWN, c1857, tql seated, NMM, Greenwich.

BLISS, Philip (1787-1857) antiquary.

P WILLIAM RIVIERE, 1850, tql seated, Oriel College, Oxford. JOHN ? BRIDGES, tql seated, Oriel College.

BLIZARD, Sir William (1743-1835) surgeon.

P JOHN OPIE, RA 1804, tql seated, Royal College of Surgeons, London.

D SIR FRANCIS CHANTREY, c1815, hs profile, pencil, NPG 316a(5). W.H.CLIFT, c1823, hs profile, pencil, album of portrait studies, BM.

SC SIR FRANCIS CHANTREY, 1815, marble bust, Royal College of Surgeons. C.A.RIVERS, 1834, wax bust, Royal College of Surgeons.

PR E.EDWARDS, hs, profile, etch, 1796, NPG.

C R.MARTIN, after J.K.Meadows, wl, lith, c1830, NPG.

BLOMFIELD, Charles James (1786-1857) bishop of London.

P SAMUEL LANE, RA 1826, tql seated, Bishop's House, Chester; version, Fulham Palace, London.

G C.R.LESLIE, 'Queen Victoria Receiving the Sacrament after her Coronation, 1838', oil, Royal Coll. SIR GEORGE HAYTER, 'The Christening of the Prince of Wales, 1842', oil, Royal Coll. GEORGE RICHMOND, wl with Henry Edward Manning and Sir John Gurney, ink, pencil and wash, 1840–45, NPG 4166.

SC GEORGE RICHMOND, 1859–67, recumbent figure?, St Paul's Cathedral, London.

PR C.S.TAYLOR, after C.Penny, hl, stipple, pub 1826, BM, NPG. J.S.TEMPLETON, hl, lith, BM, pub 1840, NPG. J.THOMSON, after G.Richmond, hs, stipple, pub 1847, BM, NPG.

C JOHN DOYLE, 'Dives and Lazarus', pen and pencil, 1840, BM and 'A Scene from Henry IV', pen and pencil, 1842, BM.

BLOMFIELD, Ezekiel (1778-1818) nonconformist divine.

PR UNKNOWN, hl, etch, NPG.

BLOOMFIELD, Benjamin Bloomfield, 1st Baron (1768-1846) lieutenant-general.

D FRANCIS PHILIP STEPHANOFF or JAMES STEPHANOFF, an illustration of the Coronation of King George IV, 19th July 1821, V & A.

PR C.TURNER, after T.C.Thompson, wl in court dress, mezz, pub 1819, BM. C.TURNER, after T.Lawrence, hl in uniform, mezz, pub 1829, BM. E.MCINNES, after J.Lilley, wl in uniform of Royal Horse Artillery, with busby, mezz, pub 1844, BM.

BLOOMFIELD, Robert (1766-1823) poet.

D HENRY EDRIDGE, c1805, hs, w/c, NPG 2926.

M HENRY BONE, after Richard Cosway, c1800, hs, NPG 1644.

PR BROWN, after S.Polack, hl, line, oval, pub 1800, BM, NPG. W.RIDLEY, after S.Drummond, hs, stipple, oval, for *Monthly Mirror*, 1800, BM, NPG. J.YOUNG, after J.Rising, hl seated, mezz, pub 1805, BM, NPG. YOUNG, after a miniature by P.Violet, hl, mezz, pub 1805, BM, NPG.

BLORE, Edward (1787-1879) architect and antiquary.

P Attrib WILLIAM HILTON, hl, University Press, Cambridge.

D GEORGE KOBERWEIN, 1868, hs, chalk, NPG 3163.

SC JOHN TERNOUTH, 1845, marble bust, University Press, Cambridge.

PR UNKNOWN, hs, woodcut, for *Illust London News*, 1879, NPG.

BLUNDELL, Henry (1724-1810) collector.

SC GEORGE BULLOCK, bust, Liverpool Corporation. JOHN GIBSON, 1813, statue, on monument, Sefton Church, Lancs.

BLUNDELL, James (1790-1877) physician.

PR J.COCHRAN, after H.Room, hl, line and stipple, pub 1847, NPG.

BLUNT, Henry (1794-1843) divine.

PR J.BROWN, after R.Fadanza, hl, stipple and line, NPG.

BLUNT, John James (1794-1855) divine.

PR J.A.VINTER, tql seated, lith, NPG.

BOADEN, James (1762-1839) dramatist and biographer.

PR E.BELL, after J.Opie, hl, mezz, pub 1801, BM.

BOBBIN, Tim, see John Collier.

BODKIN, Sir William Henry (1791-1874) legal writer.

P JOHN PRESCOTT KNIGHT, RA 1864, tql, Guildhall, Westminster.
PR UNKNOWN, hs, woodcuts, for *Illust London News*, 1859 and 1874, NPG.

BOGUE, David (1750-1825) divine.
PR UNKNOWN, hs, stipple, oval, for *Evangelical Mag*, 1794, NPG. FREEMAN, after Orme, hs, stipple, for *New Evangelical Mag*, NPG. THOMSON, hl, stipple, pub 1826, NPG.

BOILEAU, Sir John Peter, Bart (1794-1869) archaeologist.
PR T.H.MAGUIRE, tql seated, lith, one of set of *Ipswich Museum Portraits*, 1851, BM, NPG.

BOLLAND, Sir William (1772-1840) judge and bibliophile.
P JAMES LONSDALE, c1830, hl, NPG 730.
SC R.W.SIEVIER, 1830, marble bust, Trinity College, Cambridge.
PR R.J.LANE, hs, lith, 1840, NPG. T.BRIDGFORD, tql seated in judge's robes, lith, 1840, NPG.

BOLTON, Harry Paulet, 6th Duke of (1719-1794) admiral.
P FRANCIS COTES, tql, Metropolitan Museum of Art, New York, USA.

BOLTON, Lavinia, née Fenton, Duchess of (1708-1760) actress.
P WILLIAM HOGARTH, c1740, hl, Tate 1161.
G WILLIAM HOGARTH, A Scene from *The Beggar's Opera*, oil, 1729, Yale Center for British Art, New Haven, USA; version, Tate 2437.
PR J.FABER jun, after J.Ellys, hl, mezz, oval, BM, NPG. J.TINNEY, after J.Ellys, tql with shepherdess's staff, mezz, BM, NPG.

BOLTON, Thomas Orde-Powlett, 1st Baron (1746-1807) chief secretary of Ireland.
P After ROMNEY, King's College, Cambridge.
PR J.JONES, after G.Romney, tql seated, mezz, pub 1786, BM, NPG.

BOND, John Linnell (1766-1837) architect.
P HENRY SINGLETON, RIBA, London.

BONE, Henry (1755-1834) enamel painter.
P JOHN OPIE, 1799, hl, NPG 869. H.P.BONE, 1805, hl, Musée d'Ixelles, Brussels. G.H.HARLOW, c1818, hs, Woburn Abbey, Beds.
D JOHN JACKSON, c1814, hs, w/c, NPG 3155. SIR FRANCIS CHANTREY, c1816, hs profile, pencil, NPG 316a (13b).
SC SIR FRANCIS CHANTREY, 1820, marble bust, Royal Academy, London.

BONE, Robert Trewick (1790-1840) history painter.
P JOHN PARTRIDGE, 1836, hl, study for a group portrait of 'The Sketching Society', NPG 4233.
G JOHN PARTRIDGE, 'A Meeting of the Sketching Society', pen, ink and wash, BM.

BONOMI, Joseph (1739-1808) architect.
P J.F.RIGAUD, 1794, Royal Academy, London.
D GEORGE DANCE, 1793, hs profile, Royal Academy.
PR A.WIVELL, hl with crayon and compasses, etch, BM.

BONOMI, Joseph (1796-1878) sculptor and draughtsman.
P MATILDA SHARPE, 1868, hs, NPG 1477.
PR UNKNOWN, hs, for *Illust London News*, 1878, NPG.

BOOKER, Luke (1762-1835) divine and poet.
PR W.SAY, after W.J.Pringle, tql, mezz, pub 1828, BM, NPG.

BOONE, James Shergold (1799-1859) author.
PR E.COCKING, after a photograph by R.Hogg, tql, lith, pub 1852, NPG.

BOOTH, Abraham (1734-1806) dissenting minister.
PR J.COLLYER, after J.Robinson, hl, stipple, pub 1806, NPG.

BOOTH, Junius Brutus (1796-1852) actor.

P JOHN NEAGLE, 1827, hl as Brutus, Museum of the City of New York, Theatre and Music Coll, USA. THOMAS LE CLEAR, hl as Brutus in *The Fall of Tarquin*, oval, Garrick Club, London. Three portraits in Harvard University, USA: THOMAS SULLY; JOSEPH AMES, as Richard III; UNKNOWN, as Iago.
PR Several theatrical prints, NPG.

BOOTH, Sarah (1793-1867) actress.
P UNKNOWN, as Juliet, Royal Shakespeare Memorial Theatre Museum, Stratford upon Avon.
PR H.MEYER, after H.W.Pickersgill, tql seated, mezz, pub 1813, BM, NPG. Several theatrical prints, BM, NPG.

BOOTHBY, Sir Brooke, 7th Bart (1744-1824) poet.
P JOSEPH WRIGHT of Derby, 1781, wl reclining in landscape, TATE 4132. SIR JOSHUA REYNOLDS, 1784, hl, Detroit Institute of Arts, USA.
M ANDREW PLIMER, hs, oval, Fitzwilliam Museum, Cambridge. ANDREW PLIMER, V & A. Attrib R.COSWAY, hs, Fonmon Castle, Barry, S.Glamorgan.

BOOTHROYD, Benjamin (1768-1836) independent minister and Hebrew scholar.
PR UNKNOWN, hl seated, stipple, NPG.

BOOTT, Francis (1792-1863) physician.
P E.U.EDDIS, 1840, hl, Royal College of Physicians, London.

BORINGDON, John Parker, 2nd Baron, see 1st Earl of Morley.

BORUWLASKI, Joseph (1739-1837) dwarf.
D JOHN DOWNMAN, 1812, hl, BM.
PR W.HINKS, wl holding up a bird to a child seated on a lady's lap, stipple, oval, for his *Memoirs*, 1788, BM, NPG.
C J.KAY, wl with Neil Fergusson returning to their carriage from the Parliament House, Edinburgh, etch, 1802, NPG. SIR EDWIN LANDSEER, 1830-35, wl, pen and ink wash, NPG 3097 (8).

BOSANQUET, Sir John Bernard (1773-1847) judge.
PR W.J.WARD, after H.W.Pickersgill, tql seated, mezz, BM, NPG.

BOSCAWEN, Edward (1711-1761) admiral.
P After SIR JOSHUA REYNOLDS of c1755, hl, NPG 44. ALLAN RAMSAY, c1758, wl, Badminton, Avon.
PR J.FABER, jun, 1751, after A.Ramsay, tql, mezz, BM. J.McARDELL, after J.Reynolds, wl in uniform, mezz, 1757, BM.

BOSCAWEN, Edward (1787-1841), see 1st Earl of Falmouth.

BOSTOCK, John (1773-1846) physician and writer.
PR W.DRUMMOND, after J.Partridge, hs, lith, No 19 of set of *Athenaeum Portraits*, 1836, BM.

BOSWELL, Alexander (1706-1782), see Lord Auchinleck.

BOSWELL, Claud Irvine, see Lord Balmuto.

BOSWELL, James (1740-1795) diarist and biographer of Dr Johnson.
P GEORGE WILLISON, 1765, tql seated, SNPG 804. SIR JOSHUA REYNOLDS, 1785, hs, NPG 4452; studio version, NPG 1675.
D GEORGE LANGTON, c1790, wl profile, pen and wash, Gunby Hall (NT), Lincs. GEORGE DANCE, 1793, hl profile, pencil, NPG 1139. H.W.BUNBURY, hl seated with Dr Johnson, chalk, V & A.
G DAVID ALLAN, Boswell speaking in the General Assembly of the Kirk of Scotland, 1783, etch, SNPG. H.W.BUNBURY, with Johnson, pencil illustrations for episodes in Boswell's *Journal of a Tour to the Hebrides*, V & A. D.G.THOMPSON, after J.E.Doyle, 'A Literary Party at Sir Joshua Reynolds's', stipple and line, pub 1851, NPG.
PR J.MILLER, after S.Wale, in the dress of an armed Corsican Chief as he appear'd at Shakespeare's Jubilee, at Stratford upon Avon,

1769, line, for *London Mag*, 1769, BM, NPG.
C T.ROWLANDSON, after S.Collings, 'Picturesque Beauties of Boswell', etch, pub 1786, V & A. SIR THOMAS LAWRENCE, *c*1790–95, two sketches, hs profile, pencil, NPG 2755, and Yale University, New Haven, USA.

BOSWORTH, Joseph (1789-1876) Anglo-Saxon scholar.
PR UNKNOWN, hs, lith, NPG.

BOUCHER, Jonathan (1738-1804) divine.
D DANIEL GARDNER, hs, pastel, Yale University Art Gallery, New Haven, USA.
SC L.A.GOBLET, bust, Epsom Parish Church, Surrey.
PR P.CONDÉ, after W.J.Thomson, hs, stipple, pub 1815, NPG.

BOULTON, Matthew (1728-1809) engineer, worked with James Watt.
P C.F. VON BREDA, tql seated, Institution of Civil Engineers, London. L.F.ABBOTT, hs, City Museum and Art Gallery, Birmingham. UNKNOWN, hs, NPG 1532.
M After SIR WILLIAM BEECHEY, hs, NPG 1595.
SC S.BROWN, 1807, paste medallion, NPG 1451. JOHN FLAXMAN, marble bust on monument, St Mary's Church, Handsworth, Birmingham. BENEDETTO PISTRUCCI, wax medallion, BM.
PR W.SHARP, after W.Beechey, tql seated, line, pub 1801, BM, NPG.

BOURCHIER, Sir Thomas (1791-1849) captain in Royal Navy.
P SAMUEL LAWRENCE, 1846, hs, NPG 720.

BOURGEOIS, Sir Peter Francis (1756-1811) painter, founder of the Dulwich Gallery.
P JAMES NORTHCOTE, RA 1794, hl, Dulwich College Picture Gallery, London. Self-portrait, *c*1800, hs, oval, Dulwich College Picture Gallery. SIR WILLIAM BEECHEY, *c*1810, hl, NPG 231.
D GEORGE DANCE, 1793, hs profile, pencil and chalk, Royal Academy, London. PAUL SANDBY, *c*1795, wl seated with Mt Desenfans, w/c, Dulwich College Picture Gallery.
G HENRY SINGLETON, 'Royal Academicians, 1793', oil, Royal Academy.
SC CHRISTOPHER PROSPERI, marble bust, Mausoleum attached to Dulwich Gallery.
PR W.RIDLEY, after T.Collopy, hl, stipple, oval, for *Monthly Mirror*, 1804, BM, NPG. UNKNOWN, possibly a self-portrait, *c*1805, hs, mezz, NPG.

BOURKE, Sir Richard (1777-1855) colonial governor.
SC E.H.BAILY, 1841, statue, Sydney, New South Wales.

BOURN, Thomas (1771-1832) schoolteacher and writer.
PR J.FASSELL, hs, lith, NPG.

BOURNE, Hugh (1772-1852) founder of the primitive methodists.
P UNKNOWN, hl, Methodist Publishing House, London.

BOUVERIE, William Pleydell-, see 3rd Earl of Radnor.

BOWATER, Sir Edward (1787-1861) general.
P WILLIAM SALTER, tql study for 'Waterloo Banquet', NPG 3700.
G W.SALTER, 'Waterloo Banquet at Apsley House', oil, 1836, Wellington Museum, Apsley House, London.
PH CAMILLE SILVY, wl seated, carte, NPG Silvy Photographs, 1860, vol I.

BOWDEN, John William (1798-1844) ecclesiastical writer.
P JOHN HOPPNER, *c*1803, wl seated with his sister, The Detroit Institute of Arts, USA.

BOWDICH, Thomas Edward (1791-1824) African traveller and author.
PR J.THOMSON, after W.Derby, hs, stipple, for *European Mag*, 1824, BM, NPG.

BOWDLER, Henrietta Maria (1754-1830) religious writer.
PR I.W.SLATER, after J.Slater, hl, lith, pub 1830, BM, NPG.

BOWDLER, Jane (1743-1784) writer.
PR R.M.MEADOWS, after T.Lawrence, hl, stipple, oval, for her *Poems and Essays*, 1798, BM, NPG.

BOWDLER, John (1746-1823) author.
PR M.GAUCI, hs, lith, BM, NPG.

BOWDLER, John (1783-1815) barrister and author.
PR E.SCRIVEN, after A.W.Devis, hl, stipple, for his *Select Pieces in Verse and Prose*, 1816, BM, NPG.

BOWEN, James (1751-1835) admiral.
P UNKNOWN, hl, NMM, Greenwich.
PR I.W.SLATER, after J.Slater, hl seated, lith, BM.

BOWERBANK, James Scott (1797-1877) geologist.
PR T.H.MAGUIRE, tql seated, lith, one of set of *Ipswich Museum Portraits*, 1851, BM.
PH ERNEST EDWARDS, wl seated, for *Men of Eminence*, ed L.Reeve, 1864, vol II, NPG.

BOWLE, John (1725-1788) writer on Spanish literature.
PR UNKNOWN, hl seated, stipple, for Hoare's *Wiltshire*, 1838, BM, NPG.

BOWLES, William Lisle (1762-1850) poet, canon of Salisbury and antiquary.
D DANIEL MACLISE, pencil sketch, V & A.
PR J.THOMSON, after Mullar, hl, stipple, for *New Monthly Mag*, 1820, BM, NPG. D.MACLISE, wl seated, lith, BM, NPG.

BOWRING, Sir John (1792-1872) linguist and traveller.
P JOHN KING, 1826, hl seated, NPG 1113.
D WILLIAM BROCKEDON, 1831, hs, chalk, NPG 2515(56). CHARLES MARTIN, 1844, wl, pencil, BM. UNKNOWN, 1854, hl seated, profile, pencil, NPG 2550. R.LEHMANN, 1867, BM.
G F.BROMLEY, after B.R.Haydon, 'The Reform Banquet, 1832', etch, pub 1835, NPG. B.R.HAYDON, 'The Anti-Slavery Society Convention, 1840', oil, NPG 599. S.BELLIN, after J.R.Herbert of 1847, 'The Anti-Corn Law League', mixed, pub 1850, NPG.
SC P.D.D'ANGERS, 1832, bronze medallion, NPG 1082.
PR W.WARD, after H.W.Pickersgill, tql seated, mezz, pub 1832, BM, NPG. W.HOLL, after B.E.Duppa, hl, stipple, for J.Saunders's *Political Reformers*, 1840, BM, NPG. J.STEPHENSON, after C.A. du Val, hl, mixed, pub 1844, BM.
C JOHN DOYLE, 'We, the People of England', chalk, 1837, BM.
PH ELLIOTT and FRY, hs, carte, NPG Cunnington Coll. UNKNOWN, wl seated, carte, NPG Twist Album 1892.

BOWYER, Sir George, Bart (1740-1800) admiral.
P Attrib THOMAS HUDSON, Abingdon Guildhall, Oxon.
G BARTOLOZZI, LANDSEER, RYDER and STOW, 'Naval Victories', 'Commemoration of the victory of June 1st 1794', line, pub 1803, BM, NPG.
PR G.H.EVERY, after J.Reynolds, tql in uniform, mezz, BM, NPG.

BOYCE, William (1711-1779) composer.
P THOMAS HUDSON, *c*1750, wl, Examination Schools, Oxford.
D JOHN RUSSELL, 1776, hs, pastel, NPG 4212.
PR J.K.SHERWIN, tql seated, line, pub 1775, BM, pub 1788 NPG.

BOYD, Henry (d1832) translator of Dante.
G Attrib THOMAS ROBINSON, 'A political group at the Bishop's Palace at Dromore', oil, *c*1801–08, Castleward (NT), Co Down, N.Ireland.

BOYD, Hugh (1746-1794) essayist.
PR J.BROWN, after R.Home, hs, stipple, oval, pub 1795, NPG. W.EVANS, after R.Home, hl, stipple, pub 1799, NPG. C.WATSON, hl, stipple, oval, for Almon's *Letters of Junius*, 1806,

BM, NPG.

BOYD, Sir Robert (1710-1794) general, governor of Gibraltar.
SC After WILLIAM TASSIE, plaster medallion, SNPG 374.
PR UNKNOWN, hs in uniform, line, oval, pub 1783, BM, NPG. J.HALL, after A.Poggi, hl profile, line, oval, pub 1785, BM, NPG. C.WATSON, after J.Smart, hs, stipple, oval, pub 1785, BM, NPG.

BOYD, William (1704-1746), see 4th Earl of Kilmarnock.

BOYDELL, John (1719-1804) engraver, print publisher and alderman of London.
P JOHN GRAHAM, RA 1792, tql, Stationers' Hall, London. SIR WILLIAM BEECHEY, c1801, wl in lord mayor's robes, Guildhall Art Gallery, London; version, NPG 934.
G Attrib studio of REYNOLDS, hl with his wife, oil, c1775, Sir Thomas Adams Grammar School, Newport, Salop. FRANCIS WHEATLEY, 'Interior of the Shakespeare Gallery', drg, V & A.
SC THOMAS BANKS, bust, V & A.
PR V.GREEN, after Josh Boydell, tql seated with print of St George and the Dragon, mezz, pub 1772, BM, NPG. J.CONDÉ, after A.Pope, hl in lord mayor's robes, stipple, oval, for *European Mag*, 1792, BM, NPG. H.MEYER, after G.Stuart, tql seated in alderman's gown, stipple, for *Contemporary Portraits*, 1814, BM, NPG.

BOYDELL, Josiah (1752-1817) painter and engraver.
P GILBERT STUART, mid 1780s, thought to be the sitter, hl with portfolio, Holburne of Menstrie Museum, Bath.
G FRANCIS WHEATLEY, 'Interior of the Shakespeare Gallery', drg, V & A.

BOYLE, David Boyle, Lord (1772-1853) president of session.
P SIR JOHN WATSON-GORDON, probably RA 1850, wl seated, Faculty of Advocates, Parliament Hall, Edinburgh; study, SNPG 949.
SC SIR JOHN STEELL, plaster statue, SNPG 227; marble statue, Faculty of Advocates, Parliament Hall.
PR R.M.HODGETTS, after a miniature by Sir W.J.Newton, hl, mezz, NPG.

BOYLE, John (1706/7-1762), see 5th Earl of CORK and Orrery.

BRADBURN, Samuel (1751-1816) methodist minister.
PR UNKNOWN, hs, line, oval, for *Arminian Mag*, 1785, BM.

BRADFORD, Sir Thomas (1777-1853) general.
PR W.J.EDWARDS, after G.Sanders, tql, stipple and line, NPG.

BRADLEY, Thomas (1751-1813) physician.
G N.BRANWHITE, after S.Medley, 'Institutors of the Medical Society of London', stipple, pub 1801, BM.

BRADY, Sir Maziere (1796-1871) lord chancellor of Ireland.
P SIR T.A.JONES, wl in chancellor's state robes, NGI 132.

BRAHAM, John (1774?-1856) singer.
P UNKNOWN, c1800, hs, Garrick Club, London.
D SAMUEL DE WILDE, 1819, hl, w/c, NPG. RICHARD DIGHTON, wl profile, w/c, NPG 1637. W.M.THACKERAY, pencil sketch, V & A.
M Attrib W.C.ROSS, hl, NPG 1870.
PR A.CARDON, after J.G.Wood, hl, stipple, oval, pub 1806, BM, NPG. Several theatrical prints, BM, NPG.

BRAITHWAITE, John (1797-1870) engineer.
PR F.C.LEWIS, after J.Boaden, hl, lith, for *Mechanic's Mag*, NPG.

BRAMAH, Joseph (1748-1814) inventor.
G J.F.SKILL, J.GILBERT, W. and E.WALKER, 'Men of Science Living in 1807-08', pencil and wash, NPG 1075.

BRAMSTON, James Yorke (1763-1836) catholic bishop.

PR H.ROBINSON, after W.Derby, hl, stipple, pub 1828, NPG. W.HOLL, hs, stipple, oval, pub 1836, NPG.

BRAND, John (1743/4-1806) antiquary.
PR T.CORAM, wl seated, etch, NPG. UNKNOWN, hs profile, silhouette, line, NPG.

BRAND, John (d1808) rector of St George's, Southwark.
PR UNKNOWN, hs profile, line, BM.

BRANDE, William Thomas (1788-1866) chemist.
P H.W.PICKERSGILL, RA 1830, hl seated, Royal Institution, London. HENRY WEIGALL, RA 1859, wl, Apothecaries' Hall, London.
G SHAPPEN, after daguerreotypes by Mayall, 'Celebrated English Chemists', lith, pub 1850, BM.
SC TROYE, c1820, plaster relief, oval, NPG 4819.
PR T.BRIDGFORD, hs, lith, BM. M.GAUCI, after L.Wyon, hs, lith, BM. C.W.SHARPE, after L.Wyon, tql seated, stipple and line, BM, NPG.

BRANDER, Gustavus (1720-1787) merchant and antiquary.
P NATHANIEL DANCE, hl, BM (Natural History).

BRANDRETH, Jeremiah (d1817) the 'Nottingham Captain', rebel.
D W.G.SPENCER, hs profile, ink on ivory, BM.
PR UNKNOWN, wl in irons, coloured etch, BM, NPG. NEELE, after W.Pegg, his severed head held by hands of the executioner, stipple, BM.

BRANDRETH, Joseph (1746-1815) physician at Liverpool.
PR W.WARD, hl, mezz, BM. E.SCRIVEN, after J.Allen, hl, line and stipple, NPG.

BRAXFIELD, Robert Macqueen, Lord (1722-1799) lord justice clerk of Scotland.
P SIR HENRY RAEBURN, hl, Faculty of Advocates, Parliament House, Edinburgh. SIR HENRY RAEBURN, SNPG 1615.
PR W. and D.LIZARS, after H.Raeburn, hl, for Lockhart's *Peter's Letters to his Kinsfolk*, 1819, line, BM, NPG.
C J.KAY, tql, etch, oval, 1793, BM. J.KAY, hs, etch, pub 1842, NPG.

BRAY, Anna Eliza, née Kempe (1790-1883) novelist.
D WILLIAM BROCKEDON, 1834, hl, chalk, NPG 2515(71)
PR F.C.LEWIS, after a miniature by W.Patten, hl, stipple, BM, NPG.

BRAY, Edward Atkyns (1778-1857) miscellaneous writer.
PR R.J.LANE, hs, lith, NPG.

BRAY, William (1736-1832) historian, antiquary, editor of *Evelyn's Diary*.
SL JOHN MIERS, V & A.
PR J.LINNELL, tql seated, mezz, pub 1833, BM, NPG.

BRAYBROOKE, John Griffin, Lord, see 4th Baron HOWARD de Walden.

BRAYBROOKE, Richard Aldworth Griffin-Neville, 2nd Baron (1750-1825) politician.
G Attrib PHILIP WICKSTEAD, 'Conversation Piece', oil, c1773-74, DoE (Audley End, Essex); version, Springhill (NT), Co Londonderry, N.Ireland.
PR C.TURNER, after J.Hoppner, hl in peer's robes, mezz, BM.

BRAYBROOKE, Richard Griffin Neville, 3rd Baron (1783-1858) editor of Pepys' Diary.
P JOHN HOPPNER, hl, a leaving portrait, Eton College, Berks. JOHN JACKSON, 1822, hs, DoE (Audley End, Essex).
PR M.GAUCI, after E.U.Eddis, hs, lith, BM.

BREADALBANE, John Campbell, 2nd Marquess of - (1796-1862) politician.
P SIR GEORGE HAYTER, 1834, hl, study for NPG 54, NPG 2510.

G SIR GEORGE HAYTER, 'The House of Commons, 1833', oil, NPG 54. SIR GEORGE HARVEY, with the Earl of Dalhousie and Lords Cockburn and Rutherfurd, oil, SNPG 1497.

SC BERTEL THORVALDSEN, bust, Thorvaldsen Museum, Copenhagen.

BRENT, Charlotte (d1802) singer.
PR UNKNOWN, with John Beard in Bickerstaffe's *Thomas and Sally*, line, BM.

BRENTON, Edward Pelham (1774-1839) author of the *Naval History*.
PR UNKNOWN, after Franklin, hl seated, line and stipple, for his *Naval History*, 1837, BM, NPG.

BRERETON, Owen Salusbury (1715-1798) recorder of Liverpool and antiquary.
G JAMES BARRY, 'The Society for the Encouragement of Arts', oil, Royal Society of Arts, London.
PR UNKNOWN, hs profile, silhouette, BM. W.EVANS, after a miniature, hl, stipple, oval, BM, NPG.

BRETLAND, Joseph (1742-1819) dissenting minister.
PR THOMSON, hl seated, stipple, pub 1820, NPG.

BRETT, Sir Peircy (1709-1781) admiral.
PR J.S.MÜLLER, hl, line, oval, for Smollett's *Hist of England*, 1757, BM, NPG.

BREWER, Jehoiada (1752?-1818) dissenting minister.
P HENRY WYATT, National Museum of Wales 363, Cardiff.
PR UNKNOWN, hl, stipple, for *Christian's Mag*, 1791, NPG. RIDLEY, hs, stipple, oval, for *Evangelical Mag*, 1799, NPG.

BREWSTER, Abraham (1796-1874) Irish lawyer.
P FRANK REYNOLDS, King's Inns, Dublin.

BREWSTER, Sir David (1781-1868) inventor of the kaleidoscope.
P JAMES WILSON, 1852, hl, Glasgow University. SIR JOHN WATSON-GORDON, 1864, tql seated, NPG 691. NORMAN MACBETH, c1869, Royal Society, Edinburgh. WIGHTON, tql, University of Edinburgh.
D WILLIAM BEWICK, 1824, hs, chalk, SNPG 1044. RUDOLPH LEHMANN, 1857, hs, crayon, BM.
G D.MACLISE, 'The Fraserians', lith, for *Fraser's Mag*, 1835, BM; 2 pencil studies, V & A. C.G.LEWIS, after T.J.Barker, 'The Intellect and Valour of Great Britain', engr, pub 1863, BM, pub 1864, NPG.
SC WILLIAM BRODIE, 1871, statue, University of Edinburgh.
PR W.HOLL, after H.Raeburn, hl, stipple, for Jerdan's *Nat Portrait Gallery*, 1832, BM, NPG. D.MACLISE, wl, lith, for *Fraser's Mag*, 1832, NPG; pencil study, V & A.
PH D.O.HILL, three photographs, SNPG. Several photographs, NPG.

BREWSTER, John (1753-1842) author.
PR W.B., after J.C., hs, stipple, pub 1827, BM. J.BURNET, after J.Ramsay, hl seated, line, BM.

BREWSTER, Patrick (1788-1859) Scottish divine.
SC J.G.MOSSMAN, 1863, statue, Paisley Cemetery, Scotland.

BRIDGES, Charles (1794-1869) evangelical divine.
PR J.H.LYNCH, after S.Laurence, hs profile, lith, NPG.

BRIDGES, Thomas (fl 1760-75) dramatist and parodist.
PR C.J.SMITH, wl with Laurence Sterne, as mountebanks, line, for Dibdin's *Bibliographical Tour in England and Scotland*, 1838, BM.

BRIDGETOWER, George Augustus Polgreen (1779-1840?) violinist.
D HENRY EDRIDGE, hl with violin, oval, pencil and w/c, BM.

BRIDGEWATER, Francis Egerton, 3rd Duke of (1736-1803) promoter of the Bridgewater canal.

M RICHARD CROSSE, hs, Tatton Park (NT), Cheshire.
SC PETER ROUW, after W.M.Craig, 1803, wax medal, NPG 4276.
PR UNKNOWN, wl, canal in background, line, for Whitworth's *Advantages of Inland Navigation*, 1766, BM, NPG. E.SCRIVEN, after W.M.Craig, hl, profile, stipple, for Jerdan's *Nat Portrait Gallery*, 1833, BM, NPG.

BRIDGEWATER, Francis Henry Egerton, 8th Earl of (1756-1829) founder of the *Bridgewater Treatises*.
PR COUPÉ, after F.Gérard, hl, stipple, oval, BM, NPG. COUPÉ, after a medallion by Donadio, line, NPG.

BRIDPORT, Alexander Hood, 1st Viscount (1727-1814) admiral.
P SIR JOSHUA REYNOLDS, 1764, tql, NMM, Greenwich. L.F.ABBOTT, 1795, tql, in undress uniform with Bath star, NMM; hl sketch, NMM. L.F.ABBOTT, hs with Bath star, NPG 138.
D Attrib MATHER BROWN, chalk, SNPG 2256.
G K.A.HICKEL, 'The House of Commons, 1793', oil, NPG 745.

BRIGGS, Henry Perronet (1791?-1844) artist.
P Self-portrait, hs, Uffizi Gallery, Florence.
D CARL CHRISTIAN VOGEL, 1834, hs, Staatliche Kunstsammlungen, Dresden.

BRIGGS, John (1788-1861) catholic divine.
PR JOHN M'ELHERAN, 1851, hl seated, coloured lith, NPG.

BRIGHT, Richard (1789-1858) physician.
P F.R.SAY, 1860, tql seated, replica, Royal College of Physicians, London.
SC WILLIAM BEHNES, marble bust, Royal College of Physicians.
PH UNKNOWN, Royal College of Physicians.

BRINDLEY, James (1716-1772) civil engineer.
P FRANCIS PARSONS, hl, Institution of Civil Engineers, London, engr, R.Dunkarton, mezz, BM, NPG.

BRINKLEY, John (1763-1835) bishop and astronomer.
P UNKNOWN, Caius College, Cambridge. MARTIN CREGAN, exhib 1827, Royal Irish Academy.
SC JOHN HOGAN, relief seated figure on marble monument, Trinity College, Dublin.

BRISBANE, Sir Charles (1769?-1829) rear-admiral.
PR H.R.COOK, after J.Northcote, hl, stipple, oval, pub 1808, NPG.

BRISBANE, Sir Thomas Makdougall (1773-1860) soldier and astronomer.
P SIR JOHN WATSON-GORDON, 1848, Royal Society, Edinburgh; tql pencil study, SNPG 1075.

BRISTOL, Augustus John Hervey, 3rd Earl of (1724-1779) admiral.
P SIR JOSHUA REYNOLDS, c1762, tql with cannon, The Town Hall, Bury St Edmunds, Suffolk; hs version, Wilton House, Wilts, copy, NPG 1835. THOMAS GAINSBOROUGH, c1768, wl, Ickworth (NT), Suffolk. UNKNOWN, wl, battle in background, Ickworth.
M RICHARD COSWAY, hs, Ickworth.
G UNKNOWN, 'The Earl of Bristol taking leave on his appointment to the command of a ship', oil, c1750, Ickworth.

BRISTOL, Elizabeth Chudleigh, 3rd Countess of (1720-1788) bigamous wife of 2nd Duke of Kingston.
M UNKNOWN, hs, oval, V & A.
SC After JAMES TASSIE, plaster medallion, SNPG 1906.
PR F.BARTOLOZZI, hs in character of Iphigenia, at the ambassador's ball, 1749, stipple, oval, BM. UNKNOWN, wl in same character, stipple, BM, NPG. UNKNOWN, wl taken at the bar of the House of Lords, 1776, line, BM, for *Lady's Mag*, NPG. R.BROOKSHAW, after R.Pyle, tql, mezz, BM. Popular prints, BM, NPG.

BRISTOL, Frederick Augustus Hervey, 4th Earl of (1730-1803) bishop of Derry.

P MADAME VIGÉE LE BRUN, 1790, tql seated, Vesuvius in background, Ickworth (NT), Suffolk. ANGELICA KAUFFMANN, wl seated, Ickworth. JOHAN ZOFFANY, tql, Ickworth.

D H.D.HAMILTON, wl seated, Janiculum Hill in background, pastel, Ickworth.

M S.SHELLEY, hs, Ickworth. GERVASE SPENCER, hs, Ickworth.

G WILLIAM HOARE, 'The Bishop of Derry presenting Lord Hervey to Lord Chatham', oil, 1771, Ickworth.

SC CHRISTOPHER HEWETSON, marble bust, NPG 3895.

C JAMES SAYERS, 'A Whisper Cross the Channel', etch, pub 1785, NPG.

BRISTOL, George William Hervey, 2nd Earl of (1721-1775) politician.

P JOHAN ZOFFANY, 1769, wl in peer's robes, Ickworth (NT), Suffolk. By or after RAPHAEL MENGS, hs, Ickworth.

C GEORGE TOWNSHEND, wl, drg, NPG 4855(7).

BRITTON, John (1771-1857) antiquary.

P JOHN WOOD, 1845, tql seated, NPG 667.

D WILLIAM BROCKEDON, 1831, hs, chalk, NPG 2515 (44).

PR J.THOMSON, after T.Uwins, tql seated, stipple, for *European Mag*, 1820, BM, NPG. J.THOMSON, after J.Wood, hl seated, stipple, pub 1828, BM, NPG. S.WILLIAMS, after a bust by W.Scoular, hs in medallion, line, pub 1841, NPG. J.H. LE KEUX, after a photograph by Claudet, hl, mezz, BM.

BROADBENT, Thomas Biggin (1793-1817) dissenting minister.

PR J.THOMSON, after J.Partridge, hl, stipple, for his *Folly of Vice*, 1817, BM, NPG.

BROADWOOD, John (1732-1812) pianoforte maker.

PR W.SAY, after J.Harrison, tql seated, mezz, pub 1812, BM, NPG.

BROCK, Sir Isaac (1769-1812) major-general.

P J.W.L.FORSTER, hl, Parliament Buildings, Toronto, Canada.

BROCKEDON, William (1787-1854) painter, author and inventor.

P Self-portrait, 1822, hs, Uffizi Gallery, Florence.

D CLARKSON STANFIELD, hs, pencil and chalk, NPG 4653.

PR C.TURNER, tql with sketch-book and crayon, mezz, pub 1835, BM.

BROCKLESBY, Richard (1722-1797) physician.

D GEORGE DANCE, 1795, hs profile, BM. JOHN SINGLETON COPLEY, head, chalk, Metropolitan Museum of Art, New York, USA.

G JOHN SINGLETON COPLEY, 'The Collapse of the Earl of Chatham in the House of Lords, 7 July 1778', oil, TATE 100, on loan to NPG.

PR W.RIDLEY, after J.S.Copley, tql seated, stipple, for *European Mag*, 1798, BM, NPG.

BRODERIP, William John (1789-1859) lawyer and naturalist.

PR UNKNOWN, hs, woodcut, for *Illust London News*, 1856, NPG.

BRODIE, Sir Benjamin Collins, Bart (1783-1862) surgeon.

P A.THOMPSON, after G.F.Watts, hl, Royal Society, London.

D SIR FRANCIS CHANTREY, hs and hs profile, pencil, NPG 316a (6).

SC WILLIAM BEHNES, 1835, plaster bust, University Museum, Oxford. WILLIAM WYON, 1841, bronze medal, Royal College of Surgeons, London. HENRY WEEKES, 1863, marble bust, Royal College of Surgeons.

PR C.TURNER, after J.J.Halls, tql seated, mezz, pub 1821, BM. J.BRAIN, after H.Room, hl, stipple and line, NPG. D.J.POUND, after a photograph by Maull and Polyblank, tql seated, stipple and line, presented with the *Illust News of the World*, NPG.

BRODIE, William (d1788) Scottish gambler and criminal.

C J.KAY, wl with George Smith, entitled 'The First Interview in

1786', etch, BM. J.KAY, 1788, wl, etch, NPG. J.HALDANE, wl seated in cell, etch, NPG.

BROKE, Sir Philip Bowes Vere (1776-1841) rear-admiral.

P After SAMUEL LANE of c1814, wl in uniform, NMM, Greenwich.

PR H.R.COOK, after G.Engleheart, hl, stipple, pub 1814, BM. T.BLOOD, hs, stipple, oval, for *Naval Chronicle*, 1815, BM, NPG.

BROMFIELD, William (1712-1792) surgeon to Queen Charlotte.

P NATHANIEL DANCE, tql with plans, Royal College of Surgeons, London.

D FRANCIS COTES, hs, pastel, Royal Academy, London.

PR W.HUMPHREY, hs, mezz, pub 1774, BM. UNKNOWN, hs, mezz, pub 1774, BM. J.R.SMITH, after B. vr. Gucht, tql seated, mezz, pub 1777, BM. D.ORME, after R.Cosway, hl, line, pub 1792, BM, NPG.

BROMLEY, Henry, see Anthony WILSON.

BRONTË, Patrick (1777-1861) curate of Haworth, Yorkshire, writer.

PH UNKNOWN, tql seated, York Minster Library, York. UNKNOWN, hl semi-profile, Brontë Society, Brontë Parsonage Museum, Haworth.

BROOK, Benjamin (1776-1848) nonconformist divine.

PR FREEMAN, hs, stipple, pub 1820, NPG.

BROOKE, Frances, née Moore (1724-1789) writer.

PR M.BOVI, after C.Read, tql seated, stipple, oval, pub 1790, BM.

BROOKE, Henry (1703?-1783) dramatist and novelist.

PR R.CLAMP, after H.Brooke, hs, stipple, for Harding's *Biographical Mirrour*, 1793, BM, NPG.

BROOKE, John Charles (1748-1794) herald.

PR E.BELL, after T.Maynard, hl in tabard and chain, mezz, pub 1794, BM, NPG. UNKNOWN, after the Earl of Leicester, 1794, hl, etch, NPG.

BROOKES, Joshua (1754-1821) chaplain of the collegiate church, Manchester.

PR E.SCRIVEN, after J.Minasi, hl, stipple, pub 1822, BM, NPG.

BROOKES, Joshua (1761-1833) anatomist.

P THOMAS PHILLIPS, 1815, tql seated, NPG 5002.

PR W.WARD, after B.E.Duppa, hl, mezz, pub 1833, NPG.

BROTHERS, Richard (1757-1824) enthusiast.

PR J.CHAPMAN, hs profile, stipple, oval, pub 1795, BM. W.SHARP, hl, line, pub 1795, BM, NPG. BARLOW, after S.Collings, hl profile, etch, oval, BM. G.MURRAY, after I.Cruikshank, hs, line, oval, BM, NPG.

BROTHERTON, Joseph (1783-1857) parliamentary reformer.

G SIR GEORGE HAYTER, 'The House of Commons, 1833', oil, NPG 54.

SC MATTHEW NOBLE, 1856, marble bust, Gawsworth Hall, Cheshire. MATTHEW NOBLE, 1858, lead statue, Gawsworth Hall.

PR MACLURE etc, hl profile, lith, BM, NPG.

BROUGHAM AND VAUX, Henry Peter Brougham, 1st Baron (1778-1868) lord chancellor.

P JAMES LONSDALE, 1821, hl profile, replica, NPG 361; related drg, hs, chalk, NPG 5038. SIR THOMAS LAWRENCE, 1825, hl, NPG 3136. ANDREW MORTON, 1836, wl, SNPG 882. SPIRIDIONI GAMBARDELLA, c1845, tql, Wellington Museum, Apsley House, London. SIR DANIEL MACNEE, 1863, wl, Faculty of Advocates, Parliament Hall, Edinburgh. J.MAYALL, c1864, wl seated with Pierre-Antoine Berryer, Middle Temple, London.

D S.F.DIEZ, 1841, hl, Staatliche Museen Zu Berlin. DANIEL MACDONALD, 1847, two sketches, during the hearing of the

Tracy Peerage Case, BM. C.H.LEAR, 1857, hl seated and wl sketches, pen and ink, NPG 1457(a, b).

G SIR GEORGE HAYTER, 'The Trial of Queen Caroline, 1820', oil, NPG 999.

SC WILLIAM BEHNES, 1830, marble bust, Lincoln's Inn, London. Attrib JOHN FRANCIS, 1831, circular marble relief, of Grey, Brougham and Lord John Russell, Yale Center for British Art, New Haven, USA. J.P.DANTAN, 1833, caricature plaster statuette, Musée Carnavalet, Paris. MATTHEW NOBLE, 1864, marble statue, Brown's Institute, Liverpool. J.A.ACTON, 1867, marble bust, NPG 2004; related plaster bust, NPG 1588.

PR S.W.REYNOLDS, after T.Phillips, hl, mezz, pub 1820, BM. DANIEL MACLISE, wl seated in robes, 'The Editor of the Times', lith, for *Fraser's Mag*, 1831, BM, NPG.

C HEATH, CRUIKSHANK, LEECH, DOYLE, etc, various cartoons and satires, BM.

PH Several photographs, NPG.

BROUGHAM AND VAUX, William Brougham, 2nd Baron (1795-1886) master in Chancery.

G SIR GEORGE HAYTER, 'The House of Commons, 1833', NPG 54.

BROUGHTON, John (1705-1789) pugilist.

PR F.ROSS, after W.Hogarth, wl, lith, pub 1842, BM, NPG. J.YOUNG, after J.H.Mortimer, wl engaged in prize-fight with George Stevenson, mezz, BM. J.FABER, after J.Ellys, hl, mezz, oval, BM, NPG.

C GEORGE TOWNSHEND, wl, 'The Townshend Album', NPG 4855 (29).

BROUGHTON, Thomas (1712-1777) divine.

PR R.DUNKARTON, after N.Dance, hl, mezz, BM, NPG.

BROUGHTON, William Grant (1788-1853) bishop of Australia.

SC J.G.LOUGH, 1855, recumbent figure on monument, Canterbury Cathedral.

BROUGHTON de Gyfford, John Cam Hobhouse, Baron (1786-1869) statesman and friend of Byron.

P HENRY GRAVES, 1866, tql, The Society of Dilettanti, Brooks's Club, London.

D DANIEL MACLISE, sketch, V & A. G.CRUIKSHANK, pencil, BM.

G SIR GEORGE HAYTER, 'The House of Commons, 1833', oil, NPG 54.

PR H.MEYER, after A.Buck, hs profile, stipple, pub 1819, NPG. C.TURNER, after J.Lonsdale, hl seated, mezz, pub 1826, BM, NPG. J.HOPWOOD, after A.Wivell, hl, stipple, for Finden's *Byron*, BM, NPG.

C RICHARD DIGHTON, wl, coloured etch, pub 1819, NPG. Two JOHN DOYLE political sketches, drgs, BM.

BROWN, Sir George (1790-1865) general.

G M.ALOPHE, 'Les Défenseurs du Droit et de la Liberté de l'Europe', lith, pub 1854, BM.

PR D.J.POUND, tql, stipple and line, NPG. C.HOLL, after a photograph by Fenton, tql seated, stipple and line, NPG. UNKNOWN, tql, mezz, NPG.

BROWN, James Baldwin (1785-1843) miscellaneous writer.

PR C.PENNY, hl, stipple, NPG.

BROWN, John (1722-1787) biblical commentator.

PR UNKNOWN, hl profile, stipple and line, pub 1832, BM, NPG. A.WILSON, hl, stipple, NPG.

BROWN, John (1735-1788) physician.

D JOHN BROWN, c1780, hs, pencil, SNPG L71.

M JOHN BOGLE, 1788, believed to be the sitter, NGS 1793.

PR W.BLAKE, after J.Donaldson, hs, stipple, oval, pub 1795, BM, NPG. J.HEATH, after J.Donaldson, hl, line, oval, BM. J.CALDWALL,

after J.Donaldson, hl, line, oval, BM, pub 1799, NPG.

C JOHN KAY, 1786, wl, etch, NPG.

BROWN, John (1754-1832) minister of the Burgher Church in Whitburn.

M JOHN PAIRMAN, hs, SNPG L150, engr Blood, stipple, oval, pub 1813, NPG.

BROWN, John (1784-1858) Scottish divine.

PR S.FREEMAN, hs, stipple, for *Evangelical Mag*, 1821, BM. J.PAIRMAN, hl, line, NPG. W.H.EGLETON, after H.Anelay, hs, stipple, NPG. A.HAEHNISCH, after W.Trautschold, hs, lith, NPG. L.STOCKS, tql seated, line, NPG.

BROWN, Lancelot (1715-1783) 'Capability Brown', landscape gardener.

P NATHANIEL DANCE, c1769, hl, NPG L107; copy, NPG 1490.

BROWN, Robert (1773-1858) botanist.

P H.W.PICKERSGILL, hl seated, Linnean Society, London. STEPHEN PEARCE, 1854, Kew Gardens, London.

D WILLIAM BROCKEDON, 1849, hs, chalk, NPG 2515(100).

G J.F.SKILL, J.GILBERT, W. and E.WALKER, 'Men of Science Living in 1807–08', pencil and wash, NPG 1075.

SC PETER SLATER, RA 1860, bust, Linnean Society.

PR T.H.MAGUIRE, tql seated, lith, one of set of *Ipswich Museum Portraits*, 1851, BM, NPG.

BROWN, Thomas (1778-1820) metaphysician.

P GEORGE WATSON, tql seated, Edinburgh University.

BROWN, Ulysses Maximilian von (1705-1757) Count, Baron de Camus and Mountany, Austrian general.

P UNKNOWN, Museum of Military History, Prague.

BROWN, William (1777-1857) admiral.

P RAFAEL DEL VILLAR, 1931, after the miniature of c1820, hl in uniform, NMM, Greenwich.

M UNKNOWN, c1820, National Gallery, Buenos Aires.

BROWN, Sir William, Bart (1784-1864) founder of the Liverpool library and museum.

P SIR JOHN WATSON-GORDON, 1857, wl, Walker Art Gallery, Liverpool.

SC PATRICK MACDOWELL, 1858, statue, St George's Hall, Liverpool.

PR C.BAUGNIET, tql seated, lith, 1858, BM.

BROWNE, Isaac Hawkins (1705-1760) wit and poet.

P JOSEPH HIGHMORE, 1732 and 1744, hl and tql, both Trinity College, Cambridge.

SC JOHN FLAXMAN, 1805, relief medallion on monument, Trinity College Chapel, Cambridge.

PR S.F.RAVENET, after J.Highmore, hs, line, oval, for his *Poems*, 1768, BM, NPG.

BROWNE, Isaac Hawkins (1745-1818) essayist.

SC SIR FRANCIS CHANTREY, wl relief figure?, St Giles's Church, Badger, Salop.

PR J.FITTLER, tql seated, line, BM, NPG.

BROWNE, Moses (1704-1787) poet.

PR J.S.MÜLLER, after P.Brookes, hs, line, oval, for his *Sunday Thoughts*, 1752, BM. UNKNOWN, hl, line, oval, for *Gospel Mag*, 1778, BM. C.BLACKBERD, hs, stipple, oval, pub 1785, NPG.

BROWNRIGG, Elizabeth (d1767) murderess.

PR N.DANCE, wl seated in her cell in Newgate, etch, pub 1767, BM. UNKNOWN, tql in cell, line, BM. Several popular prints, NPG.

BROWNRIGG, Sir Robert, Bart (1759-1833) general, governor of Ceylon.

P SIR THOMAS LAWRENCE, c1810, hl, National Army Museum, London.

PR W.WARD, after J.Jackson, hl with star, mezz, BM, NPG.

BROWNRIGG, William (1711-1800) chemist.

P UNKNOWN, c1790–95, possibly the sitter, hs, Whitehaven Hospital, Cumbria.

BRUCE, James (1730-1794) explorer.

P POMPEO BATONI, 1762, hs, SNPG 141. UNKNOWN, hl seated, profile, NPG 100.

D UNKNOWN, after David Martin, wash, SNPG 1667.

M JOHN SMART, 1776, hs, NPG 5008. UNKNOWN, SNPG 1460.

G JOHAN ZOFFANY, 'The Tribuna of the Uffizi', oil, 1772–78, Royal Coll.

PR R.STAINIER, hs, stipple, oval, for *European Mag*, 1790, BM, NPG. J.HEATH, after D.Martin, hl, stipple, for his *Travels*, BM, NPG.

C E.TOPHAM, wl, 'The Abyssinian Traveller', etch, pub 1775, NPG. J.KAY, wl with Peter Williamson, entitled 'Travells eldest son in conversation with a Cherokee Chief', etch, pub 1791, BM.

BRUCE, Sir James Knight-, see KNIGHT-Bruce.

BRUCE, John (1745-1826) historian.

P SIR HENRY RAEBURN, tql seated, SNPG 1016.

BRUCE, Thomas (1766-1841), see 7th Earl of Elgin.

BRUCE, William (1757-1841) principal of Belfast Academy.

PR T.HODGETTS, after T.C.Thompson, tql seated, mezz, BM. G.ADCOCK, after a miniature by Hawksett, hl, stipple, NPG.

BRUDENELL, James Thomas, see 7th Earl of Cardigan.

BRÜHL, John Maurice, Count of (1736-1809) diplomatist and astronomer.

P JAMES NORTHCOTE, tql, Petworth (NT), W.Sussex.

BRUMMELL, George Bryan (1778-1840) known as 'Beau' Brummel.

P SIR JOSHUA REYNOLDS, 1781–82, as a child, with his brother William, Kenwood, The Iveagh Bequest (GLC), London.

PR J.COOK, after a miniature,.hs, line, oval, for his *Life* by W.Jesse, pub 1844, BM, NPG. R.H.COOKE, wl, etch, NPG.

BRUNEL, Sir Marc Isambard (1769-1849) civil engineer.

P JAMES NORTHCOTE, 1813, tql seated, NPG 978. SAMUEL DRUMMOND, tql seated, NPG 89. E.V.RIPPINGILLE, c1820, hs, Bristol City Art Gallery.

D WILLIAM BROCKEDON, c1834, hs, chalk, NPG 2515(28). CARL CHRISTIAN VOGEL, 1834, hs, Staatliche Kunstsammlungen, Dresden.

SC UNKNOWN, plaster bust, Science Museum, London.

PR A.BRY, after A.Farcy, hl, lith, NPG.

BRUNTON, Alexander (1772-1854) professor of Hebrew and Oriental languages.

P SIR JOHN WATSON-GORDON, 1846, wl, Edinburgh University.

C B.W.CROMBIE, wl, coloured etch, 1839, reprinted in *Modern Athenians*, 1882, NPG.

BRUNTON, Elizabeth, see Yates.

BRUNTON, Louisa, see Craven.

BRUNTON, Mary, née Balfour (1778-1818) novelist.

PR J.THOMSON, after G.Clint, hl, stipple, BM, pub 1820, NPG. UNKNOWN, hl seated, stipple, BM.

BRYAN, Margaret (fl 1790-1815) schoolmistress and scientist.

PR W.NUTTER, after S.Shelley, tql seated, with two girls, stipple, for her *System of Astronomy*, 1797, BM, NPG. J.HEATH, after T.Kearsley, hl, stipple, for her *Lectures on Natural Philosophy*, 1806, BM, NPG.

BRYAN, Michael (1757-1821) picture dealer.

PR W.HAINES, after A.Pope, hl, stipple, pub 1813, BM, NPG.

BRYANT, Jacob (1715-1804) classical scholar.

PR H.R.COOK, after J.Bearblock, tql seated, profile, stipple, oval, for his *Analysis of Ancient Mythology*, 1807, BM; related wl etch, pub 1801, NPG.

BRYDGES, Sir Harford Jones (1764-1847) diplomatist.

P SIR THOMAS LAWRENCE, 1829, hl, Kentchurch Court, Hereford and Worcester.

BRYDGES, Sir Samuel Egerton, Bart (1762-1837) bibliographer and genealogist.

D BENJAMIN BURNELL, 1817, hs, chalk, NPG 2393. FRANCIS DANBY, wl, V & A.

PR G.B.NOCCHI, after P.Carloni, hl seated, line, 1820, BM, NPG. FRANCIS DANBY, hl, etch, 1834, NPG. DANIEL MACLISE, wl, lith, for *Fraser's Mag*, 1834, NPG.

BRYDONE, Patrick (1736-1818) traveller and author.

PR W.WARD, after A.Geddes, wl reclining on sofa, with crutches, mezz, BM.

BUCCLEUCH, Henry Scott, 3rd Duke of (1746-1812) president of the Royal Society of Edinburgh.

P Buccleuch Estates, Selkirk, Scotland: SIR JOSHUA REYNOLDS, 1768, tql; THOMAS GAINSBOROUGH, 1770, tql with dog; M.F.QUADAL, 1780, wl equestrian; attrib CATHERINE READ, tql.

D JOHN DOWNMAN, 1783, hl with Thistle star, w/c, Buccleuch Estates. H.D.HAMILTON, hs, oval, Beaulieu Abbey, Hants.

G R.B.PAUL, 1892, after Sir J.Reynolds of 1758, tql with Hon Campbell Scott and Lady Frances Scott, oil, Buccleuch Estates. H.P.DANLOUX, 1798, wl with his family, oil, Buccleuch Estates.

PR H.MEYER, after T.Heaphy, tql as an old man with star, stipple, BM.

BUCHAN, David Steuart Erskine, 11th Earl of (1742-1829) antiquary.

P After SIR JOSHUA REYNOLDS of c1764, hl in Vandyck dress, Edinburgh University. ALEXANDER RUNCIMAN, c1785, hl with bust, Perth Museum and Art Gallery. SIR HENRY RAEBURN, hl, NGI 523.

D JOHN BROWN, 1780–81, head, pencil, SNPG L72.

SC After JAMES TASSIE, 1783, plaster medallion, SNPG 471.

PR J.FINLAYSON, after J.Reynolds, hl in Vandyck dress, mezz, pub 1765, BM, NPG. C.TURNER, after G.Watson, hl, mezz, pub 1807, BM.

C J.KAY, wl profile, in Highland uniform, with Duke of Montrose, etch, 1784, BM.

BUCHAN, William (1729-1805) author of the popular *Domestic Medicine*.

D UNKNOWN, hl profile, pen and wash, Royal College of Surgeons, London.

SC JOHN FLAXMAN, jun, 1783, Wedgwood medallion, BM. UNKNOWN, medallion, Westminster Abbey, London.

PR J.MILLS, after A.Mills, hl, line, for the *Wonderful Museum*, 1803, NPG. W.RIDLEY, after Wales, hl, stipple, oval, for *European Mag*, 1805, BM, NPG.

BUCHANAN, Claudius (1766-1815) chaplain to the East India Co.

PR F.C.LEWIS, after J.Slater, hl, stipple, pub 1815, BM, NPG. R.PAGE, hl seated, stipple, BM.

BUCK, Adam (1759-1833) portrait-painter.

M Self-portrait, 1804, hs, V & A.

BUCK, Charles (1771-1815) independent minister.

PR W.RIDLEY, after Robinson, hs, stipple, oval, for *Evangelical Mag*, 1803, BM, NPG.

BUCK, Zachariah (1798-1879) composer.

PR R.J.LANE, after S.Gambardella, hl, lith, NPG.

BUCKINGHAM, George Nugent-Temple-Grenville, 1st Marquess of (1753-1816) statesman.
P UNKNOWN, after 1786, wl profile, NPG 5168. JOHN JACKSON, wl in Garter robes, Christ Church, Oxford. After THOMAS GAINSBOROUGH, 1787, Hughenden (NT), Bucks.
G SIR JOSHUA REYNOLDS, 1780–82, wl with his family, NGI 733. J.K.SHERWIN, 'Installation Dinner of the Order of St Patrick, 1783', line, pub 1803, BM.
SC EDWARD SMYTH, 1783, stone statue, St Patrick's Cathedral, Dublin. J.C.LOCHÉE, after a portrait by Vincent Waldré, 1788, Wedgwood medallion, Wedgwood Museum, Barlaston, Staffs.
PR J.K.SHERWIN, after Gainsborough, tql in Garter robes, line, pub 1788, BM, NPG.
C Three JAMES SAYERS etchs, NPG. R.DIGHTON, 'A View of a Temple near Buckingham', coloured etch, pub 1811, V & A.

BUCKINGHAM, James Silk (1786-1855) writer and traveller.
P CLARA LANE, c1850, hs profile, NPG 2368.
M EDWIN DALTON SMITH, 1837, tql, NPG 5003.
SC E.D.SMITH, bust, Cutlers' Hall, Sheffield.
PR R.HAVELL, jun, after W.H.Brooke, on horseback, in oriental dress, coloured aquatint, for his *Travels in Assyria*, 1829, BM. G.T.DOO, hl, for his *Autobiography*, 1855, BM, NPG.

BUCKINGHAM and CHANDOS, Richard Grenville, 1st Duke of (1776-1839) statesman and print collector.
P SIR WILLIAM BEECHEY, 1802, wl, Stowe School, Bucks.
G SIR JOSHUA REYNOLDS, 1780–82, with his father and the family, NGI 733. SIR GEORGE HAYTER, 'The Trial of Queen Caroline, 1820', oil, NPG 999.
PR R.COOPER, after a miniature by G.L.Saunders, hl in fancy dress, stipple, oval, BM, NPG.

BUCKINGHAM and CHANDOS, Richard Grenville, 2nd Duke of (1797-1861) writer.
P JOHN JACKSON, wl, Stowe School, Bucks.
G SIR GEORGE HAYTER, 'The House of Commons, 1833', oil, NPG 54.
PR R.COOPER, tql in uniform, stipple, BM.
C Several JOHN DOYLE drgs, BM.

BUCKINGHAMSHIRE, John Hobart, 2nd Earl of (1723-1793) lord-lieutenant of Ireland.
P FRANCIS COTES, 1766, hs, Melbourne Hall, Derbys. THOMAS GAINSBOROUGH, c1784, wl in robes, Blickling Hall (NT), Norfolk; tql version, North Carolina Museum of Art, Raleigh, USA.
PR GUERCISSIMOFF, hs profile, line, oval, 1766, BM, NPG. UNKNOWN, wl, line, BM.

BUCKINGHAMSHIRE, Robert Hobart, 4th Earl of (1760-1816) statesman.
P SIR THOMAS LAWRENCE, c1795, on loan to DoE (Marlborough House, London). SIR THOMAS LAWRENCE, tql, National Gallery of Victoria, Melbourne, Australia. JOHN HOPPNER, tql seated, NPG 3892.
PR W.W.BARNEY, after W.Beechey, tql seated, mezz, pub 1806, BM, NPG.

BUCKLAND, William (1784-1856) geologist.
P SAMUEL HOWELL, RA 1829, Corpus Christi College, Oxford. THOMAS PHILLIPS, 1832, hl in academic robes, with skull, The Deanery, Westminster Abbey, London. THOMAS PHILLIPS, hs, NPG 1275. A.HOOKER, 1894, after T.C.Thompson, RA 1845, hl seated, University Museum, Oxford.
D WILLIAM BROCKEDON, 1838, hs, chalk, NPG 2515 (87).
SL AUGUSTIN EDOUART, 1828, Woodwardian Museum, Cambridge.

SC Several busts by HENRY WEEKES: 1856, marble, Westminster Abbey, London; RA 1858, marble, University Museum, Oxford, related bronze, NPG 255; 1860, Geological Museum, London.
PR T.H.MAGUIRE, after a daguerreotype by Claudet, hl, lith, for *Ipswich Museum Portraits*, 1852, NPG. C.HULLMANDEL, after G.Rowe, hl with geological specimens, lith, NPG.

BUCKLER, Benjamin (1718-1780) antiquary.
P THOMAS GAINSBOROUGH, tql seated, All Souls College, Oxford.

BUCKLER, John (1770-1851) topographical artist.
PR J.OUTRIM, after W.J.Newton, 1847, hl, line, pub 1850, NPG.

BUDD, Henry (1774-1853) theologian.
PR R.WOODMAN, hl, stipple and line, pub 1855, NPG.

BUDD, Richard (1746-1821) physician.
PR W.DANIELL, after G.Dance of 1798, hl seated, profile, soft-ground etch, pub 1812, BM, NPG.

BULL, William (1738-1814) congregationalist minister.
PR R.M.MEADOWS, after J.Robinson, hl, stipple, pub 1801, NPG.

BULLEN, Sir Charles (1769-1853) naval officer.
P UNKNOWN, 1843–46, hl with orders, NMM, Greenwich. A.GRANT, 1849, hl with orders, NMM.

BULLER, Sir Francis, Bart (1746-1800) judge.
P MATHER BROWN, tql seated, NPG 458.
D MATHER BROWN, chalk, SNPG 357.

BULMER, William (1757-1830) printer.
PR J.RAMSAY, hl, lith, pub 1827, NPG; related engr, P.Audinet, hl, line, for *Gent Mag*, 1830, BM.

BUNBURY, Henry William (1750-1811) artist and caricaturist.
D SIR THOMAS LAWRENCE, 1789, hl, pastel, NPG 4696.
PR T.BLACKMORE, after J.Reynolds, hl as a boy, mezz, BM. T.RYDER, after T.Lawrence, tql seated, stipple, oval, pub 1789, BM, NPG.
C THOMAS PATCH, 1769, hl, pen and ink, Yale Center for British Art, New Haven, USA.

BUNN, Alfred (1796?-1860) theatrical manager.
PR R.J.LANE, hl, lith, BM, NPG.

BUNN, Margaret Agnes, née Somerville (1799-1883) actress.
PR Several theatrical prints, BM, NPG.

BUNTING, Edward (1773-1843) musician.
PR W.BROCAS, jun, wl, etch, pub 1811, BM, NPG. H.GRIFFITHS, wl seated, etch, pub 1847, NPG.

BUNTING, Jabez (1779-1858) Wesleyan methodist.
SC WILLIAM BEHNES, 1852, bronze cast of relief, NPG 4880.
PR S.W.REYNOLDS, jun, after J.Bostock, tql seated, mezz, pub 1855, BM, NPG. T.THOMSON, after J.Jackson, hl, stipple, for *Methodist Mag*, BM, NPG. J.COCHRAN, after W.Gush, tql seated, stipple and line, NPG.

BURCH, Edward (fl 1771) painter.
D GEORGE DANCE, hs profile, Royal Academy, London.
G JOHAN ZOFFANY, 'Royal Academicians, 1772', oil, Royal Coll.

BURCHELL, William John (1782?-1863) explorer and naturalist.
D JOHN SELL COTMAN, 1818, pencil, V & A.
PR MRS D.TURNER, after J.S.Cotman, hl, etch, BM, NPG. T.H.MAGUIRE, 1854, hl, lith, NPG.

BURCKHARDT, John Lewis (1784-1817) traveller in the East.
PR ANGELICA CLARKE, after Slater, hs profile, etch, pub 1819, NPG.

BURDER, George (1752-1832) secretary of the Missionary Society.
PR H.MEYER, after H.W.Pickersgill, hl seated, mezz, pub 1812, BM, NPG. W.HOLL, after J.R.Wildman, hl, stipple, pub 1824, NPG.

BURDER, Henry Forster (1783-1864) dissenting minister.
P G.B.MORRIS, hl, Dr Williams's Library, London.
PR T.BLOOD, after J.Jackson, hs, stipple, for *Evangelical Mag*, 1817, BM, NPG. C.BAUGNIET, tql, aged 62, lith, BM, NPG. J.COCHRAN, after E.B.Morris, tql seated, stipple, BM, NPG.

BURDER, Samuel (1773-1837) dissenting minister.
PR P.ROBERTS, after A.Buck, hs, stipple, oval, pub 1799, NPG. I.TAYLOR, hs, stipple, pub 1802, NPG. RIDLEY and BLOOD, hl, stipple, oval, for *Evangelical Mag*, 1808, BM, NPG. FREEMAN, hs, stipple, for *New Evangelical Mag*, NPG.

BURDETT, Sir Francis, Bart (1770-1844) parliamentary reformer.
P SIR THOMAS LAWRENCE, 1793, finished after his death, wl, NPG 3820. THOMAS PHILLIPS, 1834, hl, NPG 34. SIR EDWIN LANDSEER, c1840, wl profile, NPG 3140. SIR MARTIN ARCHER SHEE, 1843, hl, NPG 432.
M ADAM BUCK, 1810, tql seated, w/c, NPG 1229. SIR W.C.ROSS, RA 1844, wl seated, NPG 2056.
SL J.BRUCE, c1832, wl, NPG.
G SIR GEORGE HAYTER, 'The Trial of Queen Caroline, 1820', oil, NPG 999. SIR GEORGE HAYTER, 'The House of Commons, 1833', oil, NPG 54.
SC SAMUEL PERCY, RA 1803, wax relief, V & A. SIR FRANCIS CHANTREY, plaster model of RA 1811, Ashmolean Museum, Oxford. JOHN TERNOUTH, 1827, marble bust, Palace of Westminster, London. G.G.ADAMS, c1854, marble bust, Westminster School, London.
PR A.CARDON, after R.Cosway, hs in fancy dress, stipple, oval, pub 1804, BM, NPG. W.WARD, after J.R.Smith, wl with Magna Carta, mezz, pub 1811, BM, NPG. W.SHARP, after J.Northcote, hl, line, pub 1811, BM, NPG.
C R.DIGHTON, wl, coloured etch, pub 1820, NPG. JOHN DOYLE, several political satires, drgs, BM.

BURDON, William (1764-1818) miscellaneous writer.
PR C.PICART, after R.W.Satchwell, hs, stipple, pub 1819, NPG. UNKNOWN, hs, etch, pub 1826, NPG.

BURGES, Sir James Bland, see Lamb.

BURGESS, Richard (1796-1881) divine.
PR UNKNOWN, hs, lith, NPG.

BURGESS, Thomas (1756-1837) bishop of Salisbury.
P WILLIAM OWEN, RA 1819, tql seated, Corpus Christi College, Oxford, engr in garter robes, by S.W.Reynolds, mezz, 1825, NPG.
G SIR GEORGE HAYTER, 'The Trial of Queen Caroline, 1820', oil, NPG 999.
SC UNKNOWN, wax bust, Corpus Christi College.
PR THOMSON, hs profile, stipple, pub 1825, NPG. UNKNOWN, wl seated, profile, aquatint, for his *Life*, 1840, BM.

BURGESS, Thomas (1791-1854) catholic prelate.
PR H.ADLARD, hs, stipple and line, pub 1854, NPG.

BURGH, Walter Hussey (1742-1783) chief baron of the exchequer in Ireland.
P G.F.JOSEPH, 1820, wl in robes of chief baron, Trinity College, Dublin.
D H.D.HAMILTON, hl, pastel, oval, NGI 2925.
G FRANCIS WHEATLEY, 'The Irish House of Commons, 1780', oil, Leeds City Art Galleries, Lotherton Hall, W.Yorks.
PR UNKNOWN, wl, line, NPG.

BURGH, William (1741-1808) politician and controversialist.
PR J.R.SMITH, hl, mezz, pub 1809, BM, NPG.

BURGON, Thomas (1787-1858) assistant in department of coins, British Museum.
PR H.CORBOULD, hs profile, lith, 1839, BM, NPG.

BURGOYNE, John (1722-1792) dramatist and soldier.
P After ALLAN RAMSAY of 1756, tql, NPG 4158. SIR JOSHUA REYNOLDS, 1766, tql, Frick Collection, New York, USA.
PR Several popular prints, NPG.
C J.SAYERS, wl, etch, pub 1782, NPG.

BURGOYNE, Sir John Fox, Bart (1782-1871) military engineer.
P H.W.PHILLIPS, 1858, wl, Royal Engineers, Chatham, Kent.
D THOMAS HEAPHY, hs, pencil and w/c, NPG 4321. THOMAS HEAPHY, hs, w/c, NPG 1914(5).
SC SIR J.E.BOEHM, 1874, bronze statue, Waterloo Place, London.
PR D.J.POUND, after a photograph by Mayall, tql, stipple and line, for *Illust News of the World*, 1859, BM, NPG. W.J.EDWARDS, after Victor Plumier, tql seated, stipple, for Nolan's *History of the War against Russia*, BM. J.S.TEMPLETON, after G.F.Mulvany, hl, lith, NPG.

BURKE, Edmund (1729-1797) statesman.
P SIR JOSHUA REYNOLDS, 1766-68, tql seated, with Lord Rockingham, sketch, Fitzwilliam Museum, Cambridge. Studio of REYNOLDS, 1771, hs, NPG 655. JAMES BARRY, 1771, hl, NGI 128; miniature copy, NPG 854. SIR JOSHUA REYNOLDS, RA 1774?, hl, SNPG 2362, on loan to NGI. JOHN OPIE, 1792, hl, Knole (NT), Kent. JOHN HOPPNER, 1795, wl in gown, Trinity College, Dublin. THOMAS HICKEY, wl with Charles James Fox, NGI 258.
G JAMES BARRY, 'The Society for the Encouragement of the Arts', oil, Royal Society of Arts, London.
SC JOHN HICKEY, bust, BM. UNKNOWN, bust, Trinity College, Dublin. T.R.POOLE, 1791, wax medallion, NPG 1607. After WILLIAM TASSIE, plaster medallion, SNPG 406. After J.C.LOCHÉE, a plaster medallion after a Wedgwood medallion, SNPG 1878.
PR J.WATSON, after J.Reynolds of 1767-69, hl, mezz, pub 1770, BM, NPG. J.JONES, after G.Romney, hl, mezz, pub 1790, BM, NPG.
C JOHN NIXON, 'The Wrangling Friends or Opposition in Disorder, 1791', Palace of Westminster, London. Various caricatures by Gillray, Sayers and others, BM, NPG.

BURKE, William (1792-1829) murderer.
SL AUGUSTIN EDOUART, SNPG 841.
G UNKNOWN, with his associates, 'Life and Transactions of the Murderer Blake and his Associates', 1829, a broadside, BM.
PR UNKNOWN, wl, etch, BM.

BURN, Edward (1762-1837) writer.
PR A.CARDON, after Hancock, hl, stipple, pub 1837, NPG.

BURN, Richard (1709-1785) chancellor of Carlisle, writer of law.
PR T.TROTTER, hl profile, seated, line, oval, for his *Law Dictionary*, 1791, BM, NPG.

BURNET, John (1784-1868) painter and engraver.
P WILLIAM SIMSON, 1841, hl seated, NPG 935.
D S.P.DENNING, hl, w/c, SNPG 2.
PR UNKNOWN, possibly after a self-portrait, woodcut, for *Art Journal*, 1850, NPG. UNKNOWN, after a photograph by J.Watkins, hs, woodcut, for *Illust London News*, 1868, NPG.
PH JOHN WATKINS, hs, carte, NPG Album of Artists vol II.

BURNETT, James (1714-1799), see Lord Monboddo.

BURNEY, Charles (1726-1814) musician and historian of music.

P SIR JOSHUA REYNOLDS, 1781, hl, NPG 3884.
D GEORGE DANCE, 1794, hl seated, profile, pencil, NPG 1140.
SC JOSEPH NOLLEKENS, 1801, marble bust, BM. SEBASTIAN GAHAGAN, 1819, tablet, Westminster Abbey, London.
G D.G.THOMPSON, after J.E.Doyle, 'A Literary Party at Sir Joshua Reynolds's', stipple and line, pub 1851, NPG. JAMES BARRY, 'The Triumph of Thames', oil, Royal Society of Arts, London.

BURNEY, Charles (1757-1817) classical scholar.
D GEORGE DANCE, 1794, hs seated, profile, pencil, BM. HENRY EDRIDGE, hl seated, pencil, BM.
SC L.A.GOBLET, 1818, relief bust, on monument, St Paul's Church, Deptford. JOSEPH NOLLEKENS, bust, BM. L.A.GOBLET, 1818, relief bust on monument, Westminster Abbey, London.
PR W.SHARP, after T.Lawrence?, hl, line, BM, NPG. MRS D.TURNER, after T.Phillips, hs, semi-profile, etch, BM, NPG.

BURNEY, Charles Rousseau (1747-1819) musician.
P THOMAS GAINSBOROUGH, hl with music, Metropolitan Museum of Art, New York, USA.
D E.F.BURNEY, hl, w/c, NPG 1860.

BURNEY, Frances, see D'ARBLAY.

BURNHAM, Richard (1711-1752) clergyman.
PR ROTHWELL, after Peat, hl, line and stipple, NPG. J.DEAN, after W.Smith, tql, mezz, NPG.

BURNHAM, Richard (1749?-1810) baptist minister.
PR R.WOODMAN, hl, stipple, pub 1811, NPG. H.KINGSBURY, hl, stipple, BM.

BURNS, Sir George, 1st Bart (1795-1890) founder of the Cunard Line.
SL AUGUSTIN EDOUART, SNPG 786.

BURNS, James (1789-1871) shipowner.
PR E.BURTON, after D.Macnee, tql seated, mezz, BM.

BURNS, John (1774-1850) surgeon.
PR J.FAED, after J.Gilbert, tql, mezz, pub 1851, BM. L.GHÉMAR, after Stewart Watson, tql seated, with dog, lith, oval, BM.

BURNS, Robert (1759-1796) poet.
P PETER TAYLOR, 1786, hl, SNPG 1085. ALEXANDER NASMYTH, 1787, hs, oval, SNPG 1063; version, NPG 46. ALEXANDER NASMYTH, c1827-28, wl in landscape, SNPG 1062.
D ARCHIBALD SKIRVING, after Nasmyth?, hs, chalk, SNPG 745.
M ALEXANDER REID, 1796, hs profile, SNPG 341.
SL By or after JOHN MIERS, 1787, hs, SNPG 113.
G STEWART WATSON, The installation of Burns as Poet Laureate of the Lodge Canongate, Kilwinning, oil, SNPG 946.
SC JOHN FLAXMAN, marble statue, SNPG L139.

BURNS, Robert (1789-1869) theologian.
PR J.SWAN, hl, line, NPG.

BURRELL, Sir William (1732-1796) antiquary.
PR R.LAURIE, after R.Cosway, hs, mezz, oval, BM.

BURROUGH, Sir James (1750-1839) judge.
PR T.LUPTON, after T.Phillips, tql seated in judicial robes, mezz, BM, NPG.

BURROW, Sir James (1701-1782) editor of law reports.
P ARTHUR DEVIS, wl seated in landscape, Uppark (NT), W.Sussex. J.B.VANLOO, tql seated, Royal Society, London. UNKNOWN, tql, Law Courts, London.
PR J.BASIRE, after A.Devis, wl in official dress, line, 1780, BM, NPG.

BURROWES, Peter (1753-1841) Irish politician.
PR UNKNOWN, wl seated, lith, pub 1849, NPG. J.WATTS, hs, line, NPG. R.J.LANE, wl sleeping in chair, lith, NPG.

BURROWS, George Man (1771-1846) physician.

P J.G.MIDDLETON, tql seated, Apothecaries Hall, London.

BURTON, Edward (1794-1836) regius professor of divinity at Oxford.
P PHILIP CORBET, tql seated, Christ Church, Oxford. PHILIP CORBET, 1838, hs, Christ Church.
SC UNKNOWN, marble medallion in profile, Christ Church Cathedral.

BURY, Lady Charlotte Susan Maria (1775-1861) novelist.
P JOHN OPIE, c1784, wl seated with dog, Inveraray Castle, Strathclyde region, Scotland. JOHANN WILHELM TISCHBEIN, wl seated with faun, SNPG 2275. JOHN HOPPNER, wl as Aurora, Inveraray Castle.
D ALEXANDER BLAIKLEY, 1841, hl, oval, chalk, SNPG 645.
PR UNKNOWN, hs, lith, 1795, NPG. T.WRIGHT, after T.Lawrence, hl, stipple, for La Belle Assemblée, 1830, BM, NPG. J.POSSELWHITE, after G.Hayter, hl with dove, stipple, for her Three Sanctuaries of Tuscany, 1833, BM, NPG.

BUSBY, Thomas (1755-1838) composer.
P JAMES LONSDALE, Magdalene College, Cambridge.
PR R.WHITE, head, profile, soft-ground etch, BM.

BUSHE, Charles Kendal (1767-1843) chief justice of the king's bench, Ireland.
P MARTIN CREGAN, c1828, tql in robes, NGI 865. MARTIN CREGAN, NGI 1375.
SC PETER TURNERELLI, 1816, plaster bust, NGI 8188.
PR J.HEATH, after J.Comerford, hs, stipple, for Sir J.Barrington's Historic Memoirs, 1809, BM, NPG.

BUTCHELL, Martin van (1735-1812?) eccentric.
PR UNKNOWN, wl equestrian, stipple, pub 1803, NPG. J.MILLS, after A.Mills, wl equestrian, line, for the Wonderful Museum, NPG.

BUTE, John Stuart, 3rd Earl of (1713-1792) prime-minister.
P SIR JOSHUA REYNOLDS, 1773, wl, NPG 3938. Attrib ALLAN RAMSAY, called 3rd Earl, SNPG 308.
D ALLAN RAMSAY, wl, chalk, study for a portrait, NGS.
M LUKE SULLIVAN, 1767, on ivory, V & A.
PR J.HALL, after Allan Ramsay, wl standing in peer's robes, line, for Smollett's Hist of England, 1757, BM.

BUTLER, Alban (1711-1773) hagiographer.
PR UNKNOWN, hl, stipple, oval, pub 1781, NPG.

BUTLER, Charles (1750-1832) roman catholic lawyer and legal author.
SC UNKNOWN, 1832, bust, Lincoln's Inn, London.
PR R.W.SIEVIER, after J.Barry, hl, line and stipple, oval, pub 1817, BM, NPG. MRS DAWSON TURNER, hl seated, lith, 1829, NPG.

BUTLER, Lady Eleanor Charlotte (1745?-1829) one of the 'Ladies of Llangollen'.
PR R.J.LANE, after Lady Leighton, hl seated at a table with Miss Ponsonby, lith, BM; related lith, NPG. J.H.LYNCH, wl in walking dress with Miss Ponsonby, lith, NPG.

BUTLER, George (1774-1853) headmaster of Harrow and dean of Peterborough.
PR R.J.LANE, after F.W.Wilkin, hs, lith, BM, NPG.

BUTLER, John (1717-1802) bishop of Hereford.
D WILLIAM PETHER, hs, pastel, Bishop's Palace, Hereford.
PR UNKNOWN, hs, line, oval, pub 1783, NPG. P.J.SIMON, after T.H.Hull, hs, stipple, oval, BM, NPG.

BUTLER, Samuel (1774-1839) bishop of Lichfield.
P UNKNOWN, tql seated, Bishop's Palace, Lichfield.
SC E.H.BAILY, 1843, seated statue, Moser Building, Shrewsbury.
PR S.COUSINS, after T.Phillips, tql seated, mezz, pub 1838, BM, NPG. W.WARD, after T.Kirkby, tql seated, mezz, BM, NPG.

BUTLER, Simon (1757-1797) Irish politician.
C J.KAY, 1793, wl with Hamilton Rowan, etch, NPG.

BUTT, George (1741-1795) poet.
PR T.NUGENT, after M.Kean, hl, stipple, for his *Poems*, 1793, BM, NPG.

BUTTERWORTH, John (1727-1803) baptist minister.
PR W.RIDLEY, hs, aged 75, stipple, oval, for *Evangelical Mag*, 1804, BM, NPG.

BUXTON, Jedidiah (1707-1772) illiterate calculating genius.
PR J.SPILSBURY, after B.Killingbeck, hl, mezz, pub 1773, BM, NPG. M.HARTLEY, hl profile, aged 57, etch, BM. R.HOLME, wl seated, aged 60, etch, BM. TOPHAM, wl aged 63, etch, BM, NPG. J.CORNER, tql seated, line, oval, for *Literary Mag*, NPG.

BUXTON, Sir Thomas Fowell, Bart (1786-1845) philanthropist.
D B.R.HAYDON, hs, chalk, NPG 3782.
G SIR GEORGE HAYTER, 'The House of Commons, 1833', oil, NPG 54. B.R.HAYDON, 'The Anti-Slavery Society Convention, 1840', oil, NPG 599.
SC FREDERICK THRUPP, 1846, statue, Westminster Abbey, London. JOHN BELL, 1848, bust, Freetown Cathedral, Sierra Leone.
PR W.HOLL, after H.P.Briggs, hl, stipple and line, pub 1835, NPG. J.BRAIN, after G.Hayter, hl profile, line, for Saunders's *Political Reformers*, 1840, BM, NPG. H.J.ROBINSON, after G.Richmond, tql, stipple, 1848, NPG. J.THOMSON, after A.Wivell, hs, stipple, pl 4 of set of portraits of persons connected with the trial of Queen Caroline, BM, NPG.

BYNG, John (1704-1757) admiral.
P THOMAS HUDSON, 1749, tql, NMM, Greenwich. By or after HUDSON, hl, NMM.

BYNG, Sir John (1772-1860), see 1st Earl of Strafford.

BYRES, James (1734-1817) architect and antiquary.
P Attrib ANTON MARON, 1767, hs, Accademia di San Luca, Rome.
G Attrib PHILIP WICKSTEAD, wl with a group of Englishmen, discussing bronze group, 'The Lion and the Horse', oil, c1773, DoE (Audley End, Essex); version, Springhill (NT), Co Londonderry, N.Ireland.

SC By or after JAMES TASSIE, three medallions, SNPG 368, 1879, 2189.
PR J.BOGLE, hl profile, mezz, pub 1782, NPG.

BYRNE, Charles (1761-1783) Irish giant.
C Several JOHN KAY etch, BM, NPG. THOMAS ROWLANDSON, wl, w/c, Royal College of Surgeons, London.

BYRNE, William (1743-1805) landscape engraver.
D HENRY EDRIDGE, tql seated, pencil and ink, BM.
PR E.EDWARDS, 1804, hs, etch, BM, NPG.

BYRON, Anne Isabella, née Milbanke, Lady (1792-1860) wife of the poet Byron.
G B.R.HAYDON, 'The Anti-Slavery Society Convention, 1840', oil, NPG 599.

BYRON, George Gordon, 6th Baron (1788-1824) poet.
P GEORGE SANDERS, 1807-10, wl landing from a dinghy, Royal Coll. RICHARD WESTALL, 1813, tql seated, NPG 4243; versions, Hughenden Manor (NT), Bucks, NPG 1047. THOMAS PHILLIPS, 1813-14, tql in Arnaout costume, DoE (British Embassy, Athens); replica, NPG 142. THOMAS PHILLIPS, 1813, hl in cloak, Newstead Abbey, Nottingham. WILLIAM EDWARD WEST, 1822, hl, SNPG 1561.
D GILCHRIST, c1807, wl in nobleman's academic robes, w/c, (probably a later concoction based on Harlow's drg of 1814-15), Newstead Abbey. COUNT A.D'ORSAY, 1823, wl, pencil, V & A.
M JAMES HOLMES, replica of miniature of 1818, hl, aquatint, NPG 4167.
SC LAURENCE GAHAGAN, 1814, bronze bust, DoE (British Embassy, Berne). BERTEL THORVALDSEN, 1817, clay bust, Thorvaldsen Museum, Copenhagen; marble copy, Royal Coll. LORENZO BARTOLINI, 1822, marble bust, NPG 1367. BERTEL THORVALDSEN, 1829-34, statue, Trinity College, Cambridge.
PR H.MEYER, after G.H.Harlow, hs profile, stipple, for *Contemporary Portraits*, 1816, BM, NPG. S.FREEMAN, after Mrs Leigh Hunt, wl seated, silhouette, stipple, for *Lord Byron and some of his Contemporaries*, 1828, BM, NPG. ADAM FRIEDEL, 1823, hs with helmet, lith, NPG.

BYRON, John (1723-1786) navigator.
P SIR JOSHUA REYNOLDS, 1759, hl, NMM, Greenwich.
PR UNKNOWN, hs, line, oval, entitled 'The Nautical Lover', for *Town and Country Mag*, 1773, BM, NPG.

C

CABBELL, Benjamin Bond (1781-1874) patron of art.
B.P.GIBBON, after W.Mulready, head profile, etch, for J.Pye's *Patronage of British Art*, 1845, BM.

CADELL, Thomas (1742-1802) bookseller and publisher.
H.MEYER, after W.Beechey, hl seated, stipple, BM, NPG. J.G.WALKER, after T.Stothard, hs, line, pub 1824, NPG.

CADOGAN, Henry (1780-1813) colonel.
SIR FRANCIS CHANTREY, wl relief figure on monument, St Paul's Cathedral, London.

CADOGAN, William (1711-1797) physician.
R.E.PINE, 1769, hl, Royal College of Physicians, London.

CALCRAFT, John (1765-1831) politician.
J.POSSELWHITE, after A.Wivell, hl, pl 19 of set of portraits of persons connected with trial of Queen Caroline, stipple, pub 1825, BM, NPG. C.TURNER, after J.Lonsdale, tql, mezz, pub 1826, BM, NPG.

CALDER, Sir Robert (1745-1818) admiral.
L.F.ABBOTT, c1790, hl, National Gallery of Art, Washington DC, USA. L.F.ABBOTT, c1798, hl in uniform, NMM, Greenwich. WORTHINGTON and PARKER, after R.Smirke, 'Naval Victories', 'Commemoration of the 14th February 1797', line, pub 1803, BM, NPG. H.R.COOK, hs, stipple, oval, pub 1807, NPG.

CALDWELL, Sir Benjamin (1737?-1820) admiral.
R.HORNE, 1784, hl in uniform, NMM, Greenwich. Attrib SAMUEL MEDLEY, hl, NMM. BARTOLOZZI, LANDSEER, RYDER and STOW, after R.Smirke, 'Naval Victories', 'Commemoration of the victory of June 1st 1794', line, pub 1803, BM, NPG. RIDLEY, hs, stipple, oval, pub 1804, NPG.

CALDWELL, Sir James Lillyman (1770-1863) general.
UNKNOWN, hl, oval, Royal Engineers, Kitchener Barracks, Chatham, Kent.

CALL, Sir John (1732-1801) military engineer.
UNKNOWN, hs, oval, Royal Engineers, Chatham, Kent.

CALLANDER, James (1745-1832), see Campbell.

CALLCOTT, Sir Augustus Wall (1779-1844) landscape painter.
JOHN LINNELL, 1831, hl, Yale Center for British Art, New Haven, USA. SIR EDWIN LANDSEER, 1833, head, NPG 3336. PERCY WILLIAMS, c1825, hs, pencil, BM. CARL VOGEL, 1827, hs, pencil, Staatliche Kunstsammlungen, Dresden. SIR FRANCIS CHANTREY, c1830, hs profile, pencil, NPG 316a (8).

CALLCOTT, John Wall (1766-1821) composer.
F.C.LEWIS, after A.W.Callcott, hl, stipple, for his *Collection of Glees*, 1824, BM, NPG. H.MEYER, hl seated, stipple, BM.

CALLCOTT, Maria, Lady, née Dundas (1785-1842) writer.
SIR THOMAS LAWRENCE, 1819, head, NPG 954. SIR AUGUSTUS CALLCOTT (her husband), c1830, tql seated in Vandyck dress, DoE (British Embassy, Santiago). C.L.EASTLAKE, 1818, head, chalk, BM. CHARLES PHILIPS, head, chalk, BM.

PR MRS D.TURNER, after C.L.Eastlake, hl in turban, etch, BM, NPG.

CALVERT, Frederick (1731-1771), see 6th Baron Baltimore.

CALVERT, Sir Harry (1763-1826) general.
P THOMAS PHILLIPS, 1825, hl, Claydon House (NT), Bucks.

CAMBRIDGE, Duke of (1774-1850), see ADOLPHUS Frederick.

CAMBRIDGE, Richard Owen (1717-1802) poet.
PR C.BESTLAND, after O.Humphry, hl, stipple, for his *Works*, 1803, BM, NPG. E.FINDEN, after O.Humphry, hl profile, stipple, pub 1835, BM.

CAMDEN, Charles Pratt, 1st Earl and 1st Baron (1714-1794) lord chancellor.
P BENJAMIN WILSON, 1759, tql, Harvard University Law School, Cambridge, USA. THOMAS HUDSON, 1764, wl, Exeter Guildhall. SIR JOSHUA REYNOLDS, 1764, nearly wl, Guildhall Art Gallery, London. NATHANIEL DANCE, tql, NPG 336. After REYNOLDS, hl seated, NPG 459.
D J.S.COPLEY, head, Metropolitan Museum of Art, New York, USA. N.DANCE, hs, chalk, study for NPG 336, BM.
SC WILLIAM BEHNES, 1846, bust, Eton College, Berks. Two Wedgwood medallions, one from a medal by THOMAS PINGO, 1766, the other in robes of lord chancellor, Wedgwood Museum, Barlaston, Staffs.
PR J.OGBORNE, after G.Dance, hl profile, stipple, pub 1794, BM, NPG.

CAMDEN, Sir John Jeffreys Pratt, 2nd Earl and 1st Marquess of (1759-1840) statesman.
P SIR THOMAS LAWRENCE, 1802, wl, NGI 299; version, Trinity College, Cambridge.
D SIR FRANCIS CHANTREY, 1830, hs sketch and hs profile, pencil, NPG 316a (9).
G K.A.HICKEL, 'The House of Commons, 1793', oil, NPG 745. SIR GEORGE HAYTER, 'The Trial of Queen Caroline, 1820', oil, NPG 999.
SC SIR FRANCIS CHANTREY, 1835, marble bust, NPG 5241. SIR F.CHANTREY, bust, Ashmolean Museum, Oxford.
PR W.WARD, after J.Hoppner, wl in Garter robes, mezz, pub 1807, BM, NPG.

CAMELFORD, Thomas Pitt, 1st Baron (1737-1793) politician.
SC UNKNOWN, c1779, Wedgwood medallion, Wedgwood Museum, Barlaston, Staffs.

CAMELFORD, Thomas Pitt, 2nd Baron (1775-1804) killed in a duel.
G UNKNOWN, 'Death of Lord Camelford', line, NPG.
PR UNKNOWN, wl, line, for Kirby's *Wonderful Museum*, 1805, BM, NPG. UNKNOWN, after S.Band, hs, line, NPG.
C JAMES GILLRAY, 'Caneing in Conduit Street', with Captain Vancouver, coloured etch, pub 1796, BM, NPG.

CAMERON, Alexander (1747-1828) Scottish catholic bishop.
PR W.NICHOLSON, hs with mitre and crozier, etch, BM, NPG.

CAMERON, Archibald (1707-1753) Jacobite.
PR UNKNOWN, tql, mezz, BM.

CAMERON, Charles Hay (1795-1880) Indian jurist.
PR W.DRUMMOND, hs profile, lith, *Athenaeum Portraits*, No 35, BM, pub 1836, NPG.
PH JULIA MARGARET CAMERON, wl as Merlin with Annie Cameron? as Vivien, NPG.

CAMERON, John (1771-1815) colonel.
PR C.TURNER, hl profile, pub 1815, BM.

CAMIDGE, John (1790-1859) organist.
P WILLIAM ETTY, *c*1820-25, hl, Fitzwilliam Museum, Cambridge.

CAMPBELL, Alexander (1764-1824) musician and poet.
C J.KAY, wl with his brother John, and James Duff, etch, BM.

CAMPBELL, Sir Archibald (1739-1791) governor of Jamaica and Madras.
P By or after GEORGE ROMNEY, *c*1792, tql in uniform with Bath star, National Gallery of Art, Washington DC, USA. TILLY KETTLE, tql, Government House, Madras.
SC Three plaster medallions, after JAMES TASSIE, SNPG 405, 442, 482.
PR D.ORME, after Smart of 1788, hs, stipple, oval, pub 1794, NPG.

CAMPBELL, Sir Archibald (1769-1843) general.
PR J.COCHRAN, after J.Wood, tql, stipple, for Jerdan's *Nat Portrait Gallery*, 1833, BM, NPG.

CAMPBELL, Lady Charlotte Susan Maria, see BURY.

CAMPBELL, Sir Colin (1776-1847) governor of Nova Scotia and of Ceylon.
P WILLIAM SALTER, tql study for 'Waterloo Banquet', NPG 3702.
D THOMAS HEAPHY, 1813, hs, pencil and w/c, NPG 4320. ROBERT DIGHTON, wl, w/c, SNPG 2178, etch Richard Dighton, as 'Young Colin', pub 1827, BM.
G W.SALTER, 'Waterloo Banquet at Apsley House', oil, 1836, Wellington Museum, Apsley House, London.

CAMPBELL, Colin (1792-1863), see Baron Clyde.

CAMPBELL, Lord Frederick (1729-1816) lord clerk register of Scotland.
P Attrib THOMAS GAINSBOROUGH, hs, Inveraray Castle, Strathclyde region, Scotland. UNKNOWN, tql seated, Inveraray Castle. SIR HENRY RAEBURN, *c*1810, wl, General Register House, Edinburgh. SIR THOMAS LAWRENCE, 1815, Society of Dilettanti, Brooks's Club, London.
SC After JOHN HENNING, plaster medallion, SNPG 409.
PR J.STOW, after H.Edridge, tql seated, line, pub 1817, BM, NPG. G.DUPONT, after Gainsborough, hl in robe, mezz, BM.

CAMPBELL, George (1719-1796) theologian.
PR C.WATSON, after J.Bogle, hs, stipple, oval, pub 1798, BM, NPG.

CAMPBELL, Sir Ilay, Bart (Lord Succoth) (1734-1823) Scottish judge.
P JOHN PARTRIDGE, tql, Faculty of Advocates, Parliament Hall, Edinburgh.
C J.KAY, 1805, wl, etch, NPG.

CAMPBELL, Sir James (1745-1832) soldier and writer.
PR UNKNOWN, tql seated, profile, stipple, for *Memoirs Written by Himself*, 1832, BM, NPG.

CAMPBELL, Sir James, Bart (1763-1819) general, governor of the Ionian Islands.
PR C.TURNER, after H.Thomson, hl in uniform, mezz, pub 1815, BM.

CAMPBELL, John (1705-1782), see 4th Earl of Loudoun.

CAMPBELL, John (1766-1840) philanthropist.
PR T.HODGETTS, after J.Renton, tql, mezz, pub 1819, BM, NPG. THOMSON, after J.Partridge, hl seated, stipple, pub 1821, NPG. H.MEYER, after W.T.Strutt, wl in landscape, stipple, BM, NPG.

CAMPBELL, Sir John (1780-1863) general in the Portugue service.
PR C.BAUGNIET, tql, lith, BM. C.BAUGNIET, tql with La Campbell, lith, BM.

CAMPBELL, John (1794-1867) miscellaneous writer.
PR T.WOOLNOTH, after W.Gush, hl, mezz, NPG.

CAMPBELL, John (1796-1862), see 2nd Marquess Breadalbane.

CAMPBELL, John Campbell, 1st Baron (1779-1861) lo chancellor.
P SIR FRANCIS GRANT, 1850, tql seated in chancellor's robes, N 460; study, SNPG 560. THOMAS WOOLNOTH, *c*1851, hl, NPG 37 G.F.WATTS, *c*1860, wl in chancellor's robes, with mace and se Palace of Westminster, London.
G SIR GEORGE HAYTER, 'The House of Commons, 1833', oil, N 54. SIR DAVID WILKIE, 'The First Council of Queen Victor 1837', oil, Royal Coll.
SC SIR JOHN STEELL, 1843, marble bust, SNPG 912.
C JOHN DOYLE, 3 drgs, BM.
PH Several photographs, NPG.

CAMPBELL, Sir Neil (1776-1827) general.
P EDWARD PINGRET, 1819, wl, National Army Museur Camberley, Surrey.

CAMPBELL, Thomas (1777-1844) poet.
P SIR THOMAS LAWRENCE, *c*1820, hl, NPG 198. HENRY ROO 1841, hl, SNPG 11. ALEXANDER CRAIG, tql, Glasgow City A Gallery.
D SIR THOMAS LAWRENCE, 1808-09, hs, chalk, pencil and w SNPG 1034. JOHN HENNING, 1813, hs, pencil, NPG 1429. DAN MACLISE, 1830, w/c, V & A. COUNT A.D'ORSAY, 1832, hl profi pencil and chalk, NPG 4026 (10). DANIEL MACLISE, 1833, w V & A. WILLIAM BROCKEDON, 1847, chalk, NPG 2515 (93).
SC E.H.BAILY, 1826, marble bust, Glasgow City Art Galler W.CALDER MARSHALL, RA 1849, marble statue, Westminst Abbey, London.
PR S.W.REYNOLDS, after J.Lonsdale, tql seated, mezz, oval, p 1826, BM, NPG. E.FINDEN, after T.Phillips, tql in fancy dre stipple, pub 1841, BM.

CAMPBELL, Willielma, see Viscountess Glenorchy.

CANN, Abraham (fl 1820) wrestling champion.
PR H.B., wl, lith, BM.

CANNING, Elizabeth (1730-1773) imposter.
D THOMAS WORLIDGE, hs profile, pencil, BM.
PR L.P.BOITARD, hl seated, line, pub 1754, BM, NPG. T.WORLIDG 1754, hl profile, etch, BM. J.MCARDELL, after W.Smith, hl, mez oval, BM. Several popular prints, BM, NPG.

CANNING, George (1770-1827) prime minister.
P THOMAS GAINSBOROUGH, *c*1787, hl in Vandyck dress, ov Harewood House, W.Yorks. JOHN HOPPNER, 1797, tql, Et College, Berks. SIR THOMAS LAWRENCE, 1809, tql, Chr Church, Oxford. SIR THOMAS LAWRENCE, RA 1825, v Harewood House. SIR THOMAS LAWRENCE, 1825, wl, NPG 18
D SIR FRANCIS CHANTREY, *c*1818, hs, pencil, NPG 316a (10).
G K.A.HICKEL, 'The House of Commons, 1793', oil, NPG 745.
SC JOSEPH NOLLEKENS, 1810, marble bust, Wellington Museu Apsley House, London. SIR FRANCIS CHANTREY, 1819, mar bust, Palace of Westminster, London. SIR FRANCIS CHANTRE 1821, marble bust, NPG 282. DAVID D'ANGERS, 1827, bron bust, Musée d'Angers, France. SIR FRANCIS CHANTREY, *c*182 statue, Westminster Abbey, London. SIR RICHAR WESTMACOTT, 1832, statue, Parliament Square, London.
C Political satires by DOYLE, CRUICKSHANK and others, BM.

CANNING, Richard (1708-1775) Suffolk antiquary.
THOMAS GAINSBOROUGH, c1757, hl, Christchurch Mansion, Ipswich.

CANNING, Stratford, see 1st Viscount STRATFORD de Redcliffe.

CANNON, Richard (1779-1865) historian.
C.BAUGNIET, 1850, wl seated, lith, BM, NPG.

CANTERBURY, Charles Manners Sutton, 1st Viscount (1780-1845) speaker of the House of Commons.
SIR THOMAS LAWRENCE, c1810–15, tql, Niedersächsische Landesgalerie, Hannover. H.W.PICKERSGILL, 1833, wl, NPG 1987.
COUNT ALFRED D'ORSAY, 1833, hl, pencil and chalk, NPG 4026 (11).
SIR GEORGE HAYTER, 'The House of Commons 1833', oil, NPG 54.
H.B.HALL, after A.E.Chalon, hl seated, stipple, for *Eminent Conservative Statesmen*, 1838, BM, NPG.
R.DIGHTON, 'Elegant Manners', coloured etch, pub 1821, V & A, NPG. J.DOYLE, 'Make way for the Speaker', pencil and chalk, 1830, BM.

CANTON, John (1718-1772) scientist.
UNKNOWN, hs, NPG 809.

CAPELL, Edward (1713-1781) Shakespearean commentator.
UNKNOWN, hl, possibly the sitter, St Catherine's College, Cambridge.
F.BARTOLOZZI, after L.F.Roubiliac, from plaster medallion, line, for his *Notes to Shakespeare*, 1779, BM, NPG.

CAPEL(L)-CONINGSBY, Catherine, see Countess of Essex.

CAPEL(L)-CONINGSBY, George, see 5th Earl of Essex.

CAPON, William (1757-1827) scene-painter and architectural draughtsman.
W.BOND, after W.Bone, hl seated with compasses, line, for *Gent Mag*, 1828, BM, NPG.

CAPPE, Newcome (1733-1800) unitarian.
Attrib WILLIAM STAVELEY, 1799, hl, Dr Williams's Library, London.

CAPPER, Joseph (1727-1804) eccentric.
G.SCOTT, hl seated, stipple, pub 1804, NPG. UNKNOWN, wl seated, aquatint, pub 1804, NPG.

CARADOC, Sir John Francis, see 1st Baron Howden.

CARD, Henry (1779-1844) writer.
W.RIDLEY, after Harding, hl, stipple, for *Monthly Mirror*, 1804, BM, NPG.

CARDIGAN, George Brudenell Montagu, 4th Earl of, see Duke of Montagu.

CARDIGAN, James Thomas Brudenell, 7th Earl of (1797-1868) general.
Attrib H.W.PHILLIPS, 1856, hl, Deene Park, Northants. A.F. DE PRADES, 1868, wl in Hussar's uniform, on horseback, Deene Park. A.F. DE PRADES, wl equestrian, National Army Museum, London. RICHARD BUCKNER, wl, Deene Park. R.BUCKNER, wl equestrian, leading the Charge of the Light Brigade, Deene Park.
SIR GEORGE HAYTER, 'The House of Commons, 1833', oil, NPG 54. J.E.FERNELEY, at the Whissendine Brook, oil, 1850, Deene Park. JAMES SANT, relating the story of the cavalry charge at Balaclava to the Prince Consort and the Royal Children at Windsor, oil, 1855, Deene Park. G.H.LAPORTE, leading the Charge of the Light Brigade, oil, 1868, Deene Park.
SC LAWRENCE MACDONALD, marble bust, Gawsworth Hall, Cheshire. UNKNOWN, bust, formerly United Service Club, London (c/o The Crown Commissioners). SIR J.E.BOEHM, recumbent figure on monument, St Peter's Church, Deene, Northants.

CARDON, Anthony (1772-1813) engraver.
PR A.FRESCHI, after A.W.Devis, hs, stipple, BM, NPG.

CARDONNEL (later Cardonnel-Lawson), Adam de, (d1820) surgeon and antiquary.
D JOHN BROWN, hs profile, pencil, SNPG L73.

CARDWELL, Edward (1787-1861) church historian.
PR W.HOLL, after G.Richmond, hs profile, stipple, NPG. UNKNOWN, lith, Brasenose College, Oxford.

CAREW, Sir Benjamin Hallowell (1760-1834) admiral.
P UNKNOWN, 1815–19, hl with Bath medal and other orders, NMM, Greenwich. JOHN HAYTER, hl, NPG 373. MARGARET THOMAS, hl with Bath star, NMM, Greenwich.
D SIR FRANCIS CHANTREY, 1815, hs profile, pencil, NPG 316a (64).
M SIR W.C.ROSS, c1833, Los Angeles County Museum, USA.

CAREW, John Edward (1782-1868) sculptor.
P GEORGE CLINT, tql with statuette, Petworth (NT), W.Sussex. J.SIMPSON, Petworth.

CAREY, George Saville (1743-1807) writer.
PR TERRY & CO, hl with mask and mirror, line, oval, pub 1776, BM, NPG. J.HALL, after W.Sherlock, hl, stipple, oval, BM, NPG.

CAREY, William (1761-1834) orientalist and missionary.
P ROBERT HOME, c1812, tql seated with Mritunjaya, his Brahmin pundit, Baptist Missionary Society, London, engr W.H.Worthington, line, pub 1813, BM, NPG.
PR UNKNOWN, hl, stipple, octagon, BM.

CAREY, William (1769-1846) bishop of Exeter.
P S.W.REYNOLDS, jun, RA 1823, tql seated, Christ Church, Oxford. UNKNOWN, hs, Christ Church.

CARGILL, Anne, née Brown (1748?-1784) actress.
PR Several theatrical prints, BM, NPG.

CARHAMPTON, Henry Lawes Luttrell, 2nd Earl of (1743-1821) soldier and politician.
D H.D.HAMILTON, hs, pastel, oval, NGI 6992.

CARLETON, Guy, see 1st Baron Dorchester.

CARLETON, Hugh Carleton, Viscount (1739-1826) Irish judge.
G FRANCIS WHEATLEY, 'The Irish House of Commons, 1780', oil, Leeds City Art Galleries, Lotherton Hall, W.Yorks.
PR W.DANIELL after G.Dance, hs, soft-ground etch, NPG.

CARLETON, William (1798-1869) Irish novelist.
P JOHN SLATTERY, hl, NGI 224.
D CHARLES GREY, wl, pen, NGI 2590, etch K.Kirkwood, pub 1841, NPG.
SC JOHN HOGAN, plaster sculpture, NGI 8196.
PR J.W.COOK, after W.Roe, tql seated, stipple, NPG.

CARLILE, James (1784-1854) divine.
G B.R.HAYDON, 'The Anti-Slavery Society Convention, 1840', oil, NPG 599.

CARLILE, Richard (1790-1843) freethinker and radical.
P UNKNOWN, hs, NPG 1435.
PR UNKNOWN, hs, on his liberation from Dorchester gaol, 1825, line, BM. UNKNOWN, hl, stipple, BM. UNKNOWN, hs, lith, BM, NPG.

CARLINI, Agostino (d1790) sculptor.
G JOHAN ZOFFANY, 'Royal Academicians, 1772', oil, Royal Coll. J.F.RIGAUD, tql with Francesco Bartolozzi and Giovanni Battista Cipriani, oil, 1777, NPG 3186.

CARLISLE, Sir Anthony (1768-1840) surgeon.
P SIR MARTIN ARCHER SHEE, tql with skull, Royal College of Surgeons, London.
PR MISS TURNER, after C.Ross, head, lith, BM, NPG.

CARLISLE, Frederick Howard, 5th Earl of (1748-1825) statesman.
P SIR JOSHUA REYNOLDS, 1757–58, wl as a boy in Vandyck dress, with dog, Castle Howard, N.Yorks. J.B.GREUZE, 1768, hl, Buccleuch Estates, Selkirk, Scotland. SIR JOSHUA REYNOLDS, 1769, wl in Thistle robes, Castle Howard. SIR JOSHUA REYNOLDS, 1769–70, hl with George Selwyn and dog, Castle Howard. GEORGE ROMNEY, 1781, hl, King's College, Cambridge. JOHN JACKSON, with his son Henry in the Long Gallery at Castle Howard, Castle Howard. JOHN HOPPNER, hl in Garter robes, Castle Howard.
D RICHARD COSWAY, wl seated, pencil, Castle Howard. H.D.HAMILTON, 1772, hs, crayon, oval, Castle Howard.
G FRANCIS WHEATLEY, 1781, wl equestrian with his family in Phoenix Park, Castle Howard.
SC JOSEPH NOLLEKENS, marble bust, Castle Howard.

CARLISLE, George Howard, 6th Earl of (1773-1848) statesman.
P JOHN JACKSON, c1808, with his eldest son, George, Castle Howard, N.Yorks. J.JACKSON, c1815–20, Castle Howard. SIR THOMAS LAWRENCE, after 1825, (finished by Tomlinson), in parliamentary robes, Castle Howard.
D HENRY EDRIDGE, pencil, Castle Howard.
PR T.TROTTER, after J.Reynolds, hl as a boy, line, BM, NPG.

CARLISLE, Nicholas (1771-1847) antiquary.
M SAMUEL BIRCH, 1798, Society of Antiquaries, London.

CARLYLE, Alexander (1722-1805) Scottish divine.
P ARCHIBALD SKIRVING, hs, SNPG 155.
D JOHN BROWN, hs, pencil, SNPG 1975. ARCHIBALD SKIRVING, hs profile, chalk, SNPG L154.
SC JOHN HENNING, 1805, porcelain medallion, SNPG 245.
PR W.ROFFE, after D.Martin of 1770, hs, stipple, NPG.
C J.KAY, wl profile, 'The preserver of the Church from Fanaticism', etch, 1789, BM, NPG. J.KAY, as 'The modern Hercules destroying the Hydra of Fanaticism', etch, oval, 1789, BM, NPG.

CARLYLE, Thomas (1795-1881) historian and essayist.
P JOHN LINNELL, 1844, tql seated, SNPG 893. R.S.TAIT, 1855, Carlyle's House (NT), London. R.S.TAIT, 1857–58, wl with his wife at 5 Cheyne Row, Carlyle's House, London. G.F.WATTS, c1868, hs profile, V & A; version, c1868–77, NPG 1002. J.M.WHISTLER, 1873, wl seated, Glasgow City Art Gallery. ROBERT HERDMAN, 1876, hl, SNPG 803. ALPHONSE LEGROS, 1877, tql seated, SNPG 940. J.E.MILLAIS, 1877, tql seated, NPG 968. WALTER GREAVES, c1879, SNPG 982.
D DANIEL MACLISE, 1832, wl, pencil, for engr pub *Fraser's Mag*, VII, 1833, V & A. SAMUEL LAURENCE, 1838, hs, Carlyle's House, London. WALTER GREAVES, 1870, partly based on a photograph, hs, pencil and wash, SNPG 1593 (one of many versions). HELEN ALLINGHAM, 1879, wl seated, w/c, SNPG 845. HELEN ALLINGHAM, 1881, two drgs after his death on Feb 5, Carlyle's House.
G FORD MADOX BROWN, 'Work', oil, c1860, Manchester City Art Gallery.
SC THOMAS WOOLNER, 1855, plaster medallion, NPG 1241. THOMAS WOOLNER, 1866, marble bust, University Library,

Edinburgh. SIR J.E.BOEHM, 1875, terracotta bust, NPG 658. SIR J.E.BOEHM, 1881, marble statue, SNPG 1218; related bronze statue, Chelsea Embankment, London. SIR ALFRED GILBERT, 1881, plaster death mask, NPG 1361.
PR UNKNOWN, after a w/c by Helen Allingham of 1875, wl seated in his garden, reading, woodcut, BM, NPG.
PH Several photographs, NPG, Carlyle's House, London, Carlyle birthplace, (NT), Ecclefechan, Scotland.

CARMICHAEL, John (1701-1767), see 3rd Earl of Hyndford

CARNABY, William (1772-1839) musical composer.
PR A.CARDON, after J.T.Barber, hl, stipple, oval, BM.

CARNAC, Sir James Rivett, 1st Bart (1785-1846) governor of Bombay.
P H.W.PICKERSGILL, hl, Oriental Club, London.
D SIR FRANCIS CHANTREY, 1839, hs and hs profile, pencil, NPG 316a (11, 12).
SC PATRICK MACDOWELL, marble bust, NPG 5128.

CARNAC, John (1716-1800) soldier.
M OZIAS HUMPHRY, 1786, hs semi-profile, oval, NPG L152 (22).

CARNEGIE, William, see 7th Earl of Northesk.

CAROLINE Amelia Elizabeth of Brunswick (1768-182 wife of George IV.
P GAINSBOROUGH DUPONT, 1795, wl in her wedding dress, with coronet, Royal Coll. SIR THOMAS LAWRENCE, 1798, wl landscape, V & A. SIR THOMAS LAWRENCE, 1800–01, wl with harp, with Princess Charlotte, Royal Coll. SIR THOMAS LAWRENCE, 1804, tql seated, NPG 244, JAMES LONSDALE, 182 tql seated, The Guildhall, London. SIR GEORGE HAYTER, c182 tql seated, profile study for NPG 999, NPG 4949.
D RICHARD COSWAY, 1798, wl with Princess Charlotte, pencil an w/c, Royal Coll. SIR GEORGE HAYTER, pencil studies for NP 999, NPG 1695 (a, b); others at BM.
M PHILIP JEAN, 1795, hs, Royal Coll.
G HENRY SINGLETON, 'The Marriage of George, Prince of Wale 1795', oil, Royal Coll. WILLIAM HAMILTON,, 'The Marriage George, Prince of Wales, 1795', oil, Royal Coll. SIR GEORGE HAYTER, 'The Trial of Queen Caroline, 1820', oil, NPG 999.
C Numerous caricatures by ISAAC CRUIKSHANK, GEORGE CRUIKSHANK, GILLRAY, WILLIAMS and others, BM.

CAROLINE Elizabeth, Princess (1713-1757) daughter George II.
P PHILIP MERCIER, 1728, wl in robe, with coronet, Shire Hall Hertford. JACOPO AMICONI, tql seated, Ickworth (NT), Suffolk.
G MARTIN MAINGAUD, hl with Princesses Anne and Amelia, o 1721, Royal Coll. WILLIAM HOGARTH, 'The Family of George II', oil, c1731–32, Royal Coll. PHILIP MERCIER, 'The Music Party', oil, 1733, NPG 1556; variant, Royal Coll. Attr P.MERCIER, Frederick Prince of Wales, with Duke Cumberland and his sisters, Chatsworth, Derbys.
PR B.LENS, wl seated on sofa, as a child, with flowers, mezz, ov BM. J.SIMON, after Maingo, aged 7, tql seated with garland flowers, mezz, BM, NPG. J.FABER, jun, after H.Hysing, tql wi mantle, mezz, BM, NPG.
SC JOHN SIGISMUND TANNER, medal, BM.

CARPENTER, Lant (1780-1840) unitarian.
SC HENRY WOOD, 1840, medallion on tablet, Lewins Mead Chapel Bristol.
PR R.WOODMAN, after N.C.Branwhite, tql seated, stipple, pu 1837, NPG.

CARPENTER, Margaret Sarah, née Geddes (1793-187 portrait-painter.
P WILLIAM CARPENTER, tql seated at easel, Town Hall, Salisbur

D Self-portrait, 1817, hs, w/c, BM.
R W.CARPENTER, jun, hl, lith, BM, NPG.
H HENRY WEBSTER, 1862, wl seated, carte, NPG.

CARPENTER, William Hookham (1792-1866) keeper of prints, British Museum.
D MARGARET CARPENTER, 1817, hs, w/c and pencil, BM.
SC J.H.FOLEY, bust, BM.
R W.CARPENTER, jun, hs, etch, BM.
H CALDESI, BLANFORD & CO, wl, carte, NPG Distinguished Persons Album vol I.

CARPUE, Joseph Constantine (1764-1846) surgeon.
C WILLIAM BEHNES, 1847, bust, St George's Hospital, London.
R C.TURNER, tql seated, mezz, pub 1822, BM, NPG. UNKNOWN, hs, woodcut, for *Illust London News*, 1846, NPG.

CARR, John (1723-1807) architect.
P SIR WILLIAM BEECHEY, *c*1786?, hl, Mansion House, York. SIR WILLIAM BEECHEY, *c*1791, tql seated, NPG 4062.
D Attrib JOHN RUSSELL, *c*1790, hs, pastel, York City Art Gallery.
SC JOSEPH NOLLEKENS, 1800, marble bust, York City Art Gallery.
R W.DANIELL, after G.Dance, hl seated profile, soft-ground etch, pub 1814, BM, NPG.

CARR, Sir John (1772-1832) traveller.
D WILLIAM BROCKEDON, 1832, hs, pencil, NPG 2515 (42).
R R.M.MEADOWS, after Emma Smith, hs, stipple, BM, NPG. FREEMAN, after R.Westall, hs profile, stipple, pub 1809, NPG.

CARR, Robert James (1774-1841) bishop of Worcester.
R S.W.REYNOLDS, after G.Hayter, tql, mezz, pub 1828, BM, NPG.

CARR, William Holwell, see HOLWELL-Carr.

CARRINGTON, Sir Codrington Edmund (1769-1849) chief justice of Ceylon.
P SIR THOMAS LAWRENCE, *c*1801, V & A.
R W.DRUMMOND, hs, lith, *Athenaeum Portraits*, No 12, pub 1836, BM.

CARRINGTON, Noel Thomas (1777-1830) poet.
D UNKNOWN, *c*1807, hl seated, pencil, NPG 1797b.

CARRINGTON, Robert Smith, 1st Baron (1752-1838) politician.
G SIR GEORGE HAYTER, 'The Trial of Queen Caroline 1820', oil, NPG 999.
R M.GAUCI, after J.Reynolds, tql leaning on stump, lith, BM. M.GAUCI, tql in peer's robes, lith, BM.

CARRUTHERS, Robert (1799-1878) miscellaneous writer.
R UNKNOWN, hs, woodcut, for *Illust London News*, 1878, NPG.

CARTER, Elizabeth (1717-1806) writer.
P Attrib JOSEPH HIGHMORE, *c*1738, tql, The Town Hall, Deal, Kent. CATHERINE READ, *c*1765, hs, Dr Johnson's House, London.
D SIR THOMAS LAWRENCE, hl profile, chalk, NPG 28.
G RICHARD SAMUEL, 'The Nine Living Muses of Great Britain', oil, exhib 1779, NPG 4905.
R J.R.SMITH, after T.Kitchingman, hs, mezz, oval, pub 1781, BM. MACKENZIE, after Joachim Smith, hs, stipple, oval, for her *Memoirs*, 1807, BM, NPG.

CARTER, Francis (1741-1783) traveller and antiquary.
R J.BASIRE, after S.Howitt, hs profile, line, oval, for his *Journey from Gibraltar to Malaga*, 1777, BM, NPG.

CARTER, George (1737-1794) painter.
R W.SHARP, hs, line, oval, BM.

CARTER, John (1748-1817) draughtsman and architect.
D SYLVESTER HARDING, hl seated, pencil, BM.

CARTWRIGHT, Edmund (1743-1823) inventor.
G J.F.SKILL, J.GILBERT, W. and E.WALKER, 'Men of Science Living in 1807-08', pencil and wash, NPG 1075.
SC HENRY FEHR, seated marble statue, posthumous, City of Bradford Museum and Art Gallery.
PR T.O.BARLOW, after R.Fulton, hl, mezz, oval, one of set of *Portraits of Inventors*, 1862, BM, NPG. J.THOMSON, hs, stipple, NPG.

CARTWRIGHT, John (1740-1824) political reformer.
SC G.CLARKE, *c*1831, bronze statue, Cartwright Gardens, London.
PR G.S.FACIUS, after J.Hoppner, hl, aged 49, stipple, BM, NPG. UNKNOWN, hs profile, stipple, pub 1820, NPG, for Smeeton's *The Unique*, 1823, BM. H.MEYER, tql seated, aged 80, stipple, pub 1821, NPG, pub 1831, BM.

CARTWRIGHT, Samuel (1788-1864) dentist.
P UNKNOWN, British Medical Association, London.
SC BENEDETTO PISTRUCCI, marble bust, NPG 4983.

CARY, Henry Francis (1772-1844) translator of Dante.
PR H.ROBINSON, after F.Cary, hl semi-profile, seated, stipple, for his *Life*, 1847, BM, NPG.

CARYSFORT, John Joshua Proby, 1st Earl of and 2nd Baron (1751-1828) politician and writer.
D JOHN DOWNMAN, 1779, hl, chalk and w/c, Fitzwilliam Museum, Cambridge.
PR C.TOMKINS, after J.Reynolds, tql with his sister, mezz, BM, NPG.

CASSAN, Stephen Hyde (1789-1841) ecclesiastical biographer.
PR DAY and HAGHE, hl, lith, NPG.

CASTLEREAGH, Robert Stewart, Viscount (1769-1822), see 2nd Marquess of Londonderry.

CATALANI, Angelica (1780-1849) singer.
P JAMES LONSDALE, tql, Garrick Club, London.
SC L.ALEXANDER GOBLET, 1820, marble bust, NPG 5039.
PR Several theatrical prints, BM, NPG.

CATHCART, Charles Cathcart, 9th Baron (1721-1776) soldier.
P SIR JOSHUA REYNOLDS, 1753-54, tql, on loan to the Manchester City Art Gallery, engr J.McArdell and R.Houston, mezz, pub 1770, BM.

CATHCART, David, see Lord Alloway.

CATHCART, Sir George (1794-1854) general.
PR UNKNOWN, after a daguerreotype by Claudet, hl, woodcut, for *Illust London News*, 1852, NPG.

CATHCART, William Schaw Cathcart, 10th Baron and 1st Earl of (1755-1843) general and diplomatist.
D LUKE CLENNELL, pencil and w/c, SNPG 835.
SL UNKNOWN, hs, NPG.
PR H.MEYER, after J.Hoppner, hl in uniform, mezz, pub 1807, BM, NPG.

CATLEY, Anne (1745-1789) actress.
D JAMES ROBERTS, three drgs in character, BM.
PR Several theatrical prints, BM, NPG.

CATTON, Charles (1728-1798) painter.
P Self-portrait?, or possibly by Charles Catton, jun, hl, Castle Museum, Norwich.
D GEORGE DANCE, hs profile, Royal Academy, London.
G JOHAN ZOFFANY, 'Royal Academicians, 1772', oil, Royal Coll. HENRY SINGLETON, 'Royal Academicians, 1793', oil, Royal Academy.

CAULFIELD, James (1728-1799), see 1st Earl of Charlemont.

CAULFIELD, James (1764-1826) printseller and author.

G UNKNOWN, after P.Sandby, 'Sketches taken at Print Sales', line, pub 1798, BM.

PR R.COOPER, after H.Walton, hl, stipple, for his *Chalcographiana*, 1814, BM, NPG.

CAVALLO, Tiberius (1749-1809) scientist and inventor.

P UNKNOWN, wl, NPG 1412.

PR T.TROTTER, hs, stipple, oval, for *European Mag*, 1787, BM, NPG. W.DANIELL, after G.Dance, hl profile, soft-ground etch, pub 1809, BM, NPG. Two engr silhouettes, BM, NPG.

CAVAN, Richard Ford William Lambart, 7th Earl of (1763-1836) general.

SC UNKNOWN, bust, Royal Military Academy, Sandhurst, Camberley, Surrey.

CAVENDISH, Elizabeth (1759-1824), see Duchess of Devonshire.

CAVENDISH, Georgiana, see Duchess of Devonshire.

CAVENDISH, Henry (1731-1810) physicist.

P? UNKNOWN, Peterhouse, Cambridge.

D WILLIAM ALEXANDER, wl profile, pencil and ink wash, BM.

G G.F.SKILL, J.GILBERT, W. and E.WALKER, 'Men of Science Living in 1807–08', pencil and wash, NPG 1075.

CAVENDISH, Sir Henry, Bart (1732-1804) parliamentary reporter.

G FRANCIS WHEATLEY, 'The Irish House of Commons, 1780', oil, Leeds City Art Galleries, Lotherton Hall, W.Yorks.

CAVENDISH, Lord John (1732-1796) politician.

P GEORGE TOMLINSON, after Reynolds of 1767, hs, Hardwick Hall (NT), Derbys.

PR J.GROZER, after J.Reynolds, hl, mezz, pub 1786, BM.

C J.SAYERS, wl, etch, pub 1782, NPG.

CAVENDISH, William (1720-1764), see 4th Duke of Devonshire.

CAVENDISH, William (1748-1811), see 5th Duke of Devonshire.

CAVENDISH, William George Spencer, see 6th Duke of Devonshire.

CAYLEY, Cornelius (1729-1780?) methodist preacher and writer.

PR I.TAYLOR, after J.J.Schwanfelder, tql, line, for his *Autobiography*, 1778, BM, NPG.

CAYLEY, Sir George, Bart (1773-1857) pioneer of aviation.

P H.P.BRIGGS, 1840, hl seated, NPG 3977.

G SIR GEORGE HAYTER, 'The House of Commons, 1833', oil, NPG 54.

SC UNKNOWN, bronze bust, Royal Aeronautical Society.

PR J.J.PENSTONE, after a photograph by Beard, hs, stipple, pub 1843, NPG.

PH E.ANES, hs, oval, NPG.

CECIL, James (1748-1823), see 7th Earl and 1st Marquess of Salisbury.

CECIL, Richard (1748-1810) evangelical divine.

PR J.COLLYER, after J.Russell, hl, stipple, pub 1811, BM, NPG.

CENNICK, John (1718-1755) divine.

PR R.PURCELL, after Jenkins, hl aged 35, mezz, oval, BM, NPG. P.DAWE, after A.L.Brandt, hl, mezz, pub 1785, BM, NPG.

CERVETTO, Giacomo (1747?-1837) violoncellist.

C JOHN NIXON, 1789, 'A Bravura at the Hanover Square Concert', pen and wash, NPG 5179.

CHAFFERS, Richard (1731-1762) pottery manufacturer.

P THOMAS CHUBBARD, hl, Merseyside County Museums.

CHAFY, William (1779-1843) benefactor of Sidney Sussex College, Cambridge.

P UNKNOWN, Sidney Sussex College, Cambridge.

CHALMERS, Alexander (1759-1834) editor and biographer.

PR G.P.HARDING, after W.Behnes, hl, lith, pub 1837, BM, NPG. R.J.LANE, hl, lith, BM, NPG.

CHALMERS, George (1742-1825) Scottish antiquary.

P ANDREW GEDDES, SNPG 2037. JAMES TANNOCK, 1824, hl, SNPG 94.

D HENRY EDRIDGE, 1809, hs, w/c, NPG 2196.

SC JAMES TASSIE, 1796, paste medallion, SNPG 136.

CHALMERS, James (1782-1853) post-office reformer.

P UNKNOWN, Dundee City Art Gallery.

CHALMERS, Thomas (1780-1847) preacher and social reformer.

P SIR DANIEL MACNEE, 1843, hl, SNPG 853. WILLIAM BONNAR, SNPG 687. THOMAS DUNCAN, hl, SNPG 1394. SIR JOHN WATSON-GORDON, posthumous, SNPG 1094. D.O.HILL, with his grandson, SNPG.

D KENNETH MACLEAY, 1847, hs, w/c, SNPG 591.

SL AUGUSTIN EDOUART, four silhouettes, 1830, 1831, and two undated, SNPG 2150, 2282, 836 and 1211.

SC SIR JOHN STEELL, 1883, marble bust, SNPG 564. SIR JOHN STEELL statue, George Street, Edinburgh.

PH D.O.HILL and ROBERT ADAMSON, hl, NPG P6(5, 6). Album Vol I.

CHALON, Alfred Edward (1780-1860) portrait painter.

D Self-portrait, 1847, hs, BM.

G JOHN PARTRIDGE, 'A Meeting of the Sketching Society', pen, ink and wash, BM. C.R.LESLIE, with Clarkson Stanfield and J.J.Chalon, in fancy dress, painted on Twelfth Night, pencil and wash, BM.

CHALON, John James (1778-1854) landscape and genre painter.

P JOHN PARTRIDGE, 1836, tql seated, NPG 4230.

G JOHN PARTRIDGE, 'A Meeting of the Sketching Society', pen and wash, BM. C.R.LESLIE, with Clarkson Stanfield and A.E.Chalon, in fancy dress, painted on Twelfth Night, pencil and wash, BM.

CHAMBERLAINE, Frances, see Mrs Frances Sheridan.

CHAMBERLIN, Mason (d1787) portrait painter.

G JOHAN ZOFFANY, 'Royal Academicians, 1772', oil, Royal Coll.

SC JOHN BACON, sen, marble relief, NPG 2653.

CHAMBERS, Sir Robert (1737-1803) Indian judge.

P ROBERT HOME, tql in robes, University College, Oxford. Attrib TILLY KETTLE, wl seated, Yale Center for British Art, New Haven, USA.

PR UNKNOWN, after Sir Joshua Reynolds, hl, mezz, BM.

CHAMBERS, Sir William (1726-1796) architect.

P SIR JOSHUA REYNOLDS, hl seated, NPG 27. SIR JOSHUA REYNOLDS, RA 1780, tql with plans, Royal Academy, London.

D FRANCIS COTES, 1764, hs, chalk, SNPG 629. GEORGE DANCE 1793, hs profile, Royal Academy. After REYNOLDS, hs, wash NPG 3159. P.E.FALCONET, head, pencil, BM.

M JEREMIAH MEYER, hs, NPG 4044.

G JOHAN ZOFFANY, 'Royal Academicians, 1772', oil, Royal Coll. J.F.RIGAUD, hl with Sir Joshua Reynolds and Joseph Wilton 1782, oil, NPG 987. HENRY SINGLETON, 'Royal Academicians 1793', oil, Royal Academy.

CHAMBERS, William Frederick (1786-1855) physician to William IV and Queen Victoria.

PR H.DROEHMER, after J.Hollins, tql, mezz, pub 1850, BM, NPG.

CHAMBRÉ, Sir Alan (1739-1823) judge.
PR H.MEYER, after Allan, tql, mezz, NPG.

CHAMIER, Anthony (1725-1780) under-secretary of state.
P SIR JOSHUA REYNOLDS, exhib 1762, tql seated, Pennsylvania Museum, Philadelphia, USA, engr W.Ward, mezz, BM, NPG.

CHAMIER, Frederic (1796-1870) historical writer and novelist.
R S.FREEMAN, after L.Schmitz, hl seated, stipple, for *New Monthly Mag*, 1838, BM, NPG.

CHAMPION, Anthony (1725-1801) barrister and poet.
R C.TURNER, after B.Wilson of 1766, tql, mezz, pub 1807, BM, NPG.

CHAMPION, Joseph (b1709) writing-master.
PR UNKNOWN, hl, mezz, oval, BM, NPG. J.HULETT, after H.Gravelot, hl, line, NPG.

CHANTREY, Sir Francis Legatt (1781-1841) sculptor.
P Self-portrait, c1810, hl, TATE 1591. THOMAS PHILLIPS, RA 1818, hl, NPG 86. JOHN JACKSON, RA 1830, tql with bust, TATE 3672. SIR MARTIN ARCHER SHEE, c1832, hl, Royal Scottish Academy, Edinburgh. Self-portrait, hs, Graves Art Gallery, Sheffield.
D SIR HENRY RAEBURN, 1818, pencil, SNPG 602. E.U.EDDIS, 1838, hs, chalk, NPG 1731. Self-portrait, hl, chalk, NPG 654.
M ANDREW ROBERTSON, hl with a bust of George IV, Royal Coll.
G GEORGE JONES, 'Opening of London Bridge, 1831', oil, Sir John Soane's Museum, London.
SC F.W.SMITH, 1824, plaster bust, TATE 2441. F.W.SMITH, RA 1826, marble bust, Royal Academy, London. JAMES HEFFERNAN, 1842, bronze plaque, SNPG 1222.

CHAPMAN, William (1749-1832) civil engineer.
G W.WALKER and G.ZOBEL, after J.F.Skill, J.Gilbert, W. and E.Walker, 'Men of Science Living in 1807-08', engr, NPG 1075a.

CHAPONE, Hester, née Mulso (1727-1801) essayist.
PR R.PAGE, after Miss Highmore's group, of Samuel Richardson reading *Sir Charles Grandison to his friends*, hl, stipple, pub 1812, NPG.

CHARKE, Charlotte (1713-1760?) actress.
PR F.GARDEN, aged 4, dressed as a gentleman, walking in a ditch, line, pub 1755, BM. UNKNOWN, wl as Scrub, etch, NPG. UNKNOWN, popular woodcut, for *The Table Book*, NPG. UNKNOWN, tql, mezz, NPG. UNKNOWN, wl, line, NPG.

CHARLEMONT, James Caulfield, 1st Earl of (1728-1799) Irish statesman.
P WILLIAM HOGARTH, c1764, hs, Smith College, Northampton, Mass, USA. RICHARD LIVESAY, c1783, wl seated, NGI 4051; version NPG 176. WILLIAM CUMING, tql profile seated, NGI 187.
SC WILLIAM MOSSOP, wax relief, NGI 8164. WILLIAM MOSSOP, bronze medallion, National Museum of Ireland.
PR T.NUGENT, after N.Hone, hl profile with ribbon and star, stipple, oval, pub 1790, BM, NPG. W.DANIELL, after G.Dance, hl profile, soft-ground etch, pub 1814, BM, NPG.
C SIR JOSHUA REYNOLDS, wl with Sir Thomas Kennedy, Mr Ward and Mr Phelps, oil, c1751, NGI 737.

CHARLES, David (1762-1834) author of sermons.
PR T.BLOOD, hs, stipple, oval, for *Evangelical Mag*, 1818, BM, NPG.

CHARLES Edward Stuart, Prince (1720-1788) grandson of James II, 'Bonnie Prince Charlie'.
P Attrib B.GENNARI, wl pointing to a coronet, aged 6, Stonyhurst College, Lancs. Studio of ANTONIO DAVID, c1729, hl as a child, oval, NPG 434. ANTONIO DAVID, 1732, hl, oval, SNPG 887. LOUIS GABRIEL BLANCHET, 1739, tql, Royal Coll. Attrib HUGH

DOUGLAS HAMILTON, c1780-88, hs, oval, NPG 376; versions, SNPG 622, Towneley Hall, Lancs, Dundee Art Gallery and Lennoxlove, Lothian. UNKNOWN, hl in Scots costume, SNPG 1510.
D After MAURICE QUENTIN DE LA TOUR, 1748, hs, pastel, NPG 2161. CHARLES ELPHINSTONE DALRYMPLE, ink, SNPG 1690. GILES HUSSEY, red chalk, BM. UNKNOWN, w/c and ink, SNPG 929.
M UNKNOWN, hs aged 5, copper, SNPG 2060. GILES HUSSEY, c1735, hs profile, Blair Castle, Tayside region, Scotland.
SC THOMAS PINGO, 1745, bronze medal, NPG 1052.
PR G.WILL, c1745, after Wassdail, wl holding sword, SNPG. N.J.B. DE POILLY, 1746, after D.Dupra, wl standing, holding truncheon, ships in background, line, BM, SNPG. SIR ROBERT STRANGE, hl with riband and star, line, oval, BM.

CHARLES, Thomas (1755-1814) of Bala, Welsh preacher.
P UNKNOWN, hs, British and Foreign Bible Society, London.

CHARLESWORTH, Edward Parker (1783-1853) pioneer in mental health.
SC THOMAS MILNES, 1853, statue, Union Road, Lincoln.

CHARLETON, Rice (1710-1789) physician.
P THOMAS GAINSBOROUGH, 1764, wl, Holburne of Menstrie Museum, Bath.
D WILLIAM HOARE, 1755, hs profile, chalk, Witt Collection, Courtauld Institute Galleries, London.

CHARLOTTE Augusta of Wales, Princess (1796-1817) daughter of George IV.
P SIR THOMAS LAWRENCE, 1802, hl seated with birdcage, Royal Coll. JAMES LONSDALE, 1816, Guildhall, London. GEORGE SANDERS, 1816, hl with coronet, Belgian Royal Coll. SIR THOMAS LAWRENCE, 1817, hl, Belgian Royal Coll; copy, Royal Coll. GEORGE DAWE, 1817, wl walking on terrace, Belgian Royal Coll. GEORGE DAWE, c1817, tql seated, profile, with star of St Catherine of Russia, NPG 51.
D SIR THOMAS LAWRENCE, c1797, as a baby, City Art Gallery, Birmingham. RICHARD COSWAY, 1798, wl with her mother, pencil and wash, Royal Coll. GEORGE SANDERS, hs, pencil, SNPG 730. THOMAS HEAPHY, 1815, wl, w/c, NPG 1914 (19). SIR GEORGE HAYTER, 1816, pencil and sepia, BM. GEORGE DAWE, 1817, 'Princess Charlotte and Prince Leopold in their Box at Covent Garden', pencil, Royal Coll. Attrib R.WESTALL, the marriage ceremony at Carlton House, 1816, Royal Coll. RICHARD WOODMAN, hl, w/c, NPG 206. ANNE MEE, tql seated, w/c, Royal Coll.
M R.COSWAY, 1796, with crouching British lion, Royal Coll. CHARLOTTE JONES, 1807, with Maltese lapdog, Royal Coll. GEORGE SANDERS, 1812, tql, Bowood, Wilts, and Royal Coll. CHARLOTTE JONES, 1814, Palais Royale, Brussels. SIMON JACQUES ROCHARD, hs, Royal Coll.
SC SAMUEL PERCY, 1814, wax relief, NPG 3086. PETER TURNERELLI, 1816, marble bust, NPG 4470. PETER TURNERELLI, terracotta bust, Dynastic Museum, Brussels.
C Various engravings by CRUIKSHANK, GILLRAY, etc, BM.

CHARLOTTE Augusta Matilda, Princess Royal, afterwards Queen of Würtemberg (1766-1828) eldest daughter of George III.
P FRANCIS COTES, 1767, with her mother, Royal Coll. JOHAN ZOFFANY, c1770, wl with Prince William, Royal Coll. BENJAMIN WEST, 1776, tql seated sewing with her mother, Royal Coll. THOMAS GAINSBOROUGH, c1782, hs, oval, Royal Coll. SIR WILLIAM BEECHEY, c1797-1800, tql seated with ribbon of an order, Royal Coll.

D FRANCIS COTES, 1767, with her mother, pastel, oval, Royal Coll. P.W.TOMKINS, hs, chalk, BM.

M OZIAS HUMPHRY, 1769, wl seated, oval, Royal Coll. J.G.P.FISCHER, 1827, tql seated as Dowager Queen, Royal Coll. GEORGE ENGELHEART, after R.Cosway?, hs, oval, Wallace Coll, London. EDWARD MILES, hs, oval, Royal Coll.

G JOHAN ZOFFANY, 'George III, Queen Charlotte and their six Eldest Children', in Vandyck dress, oil, 1770, Royal Coll. J.ZOFFANY, in a family group, oil, RA 1773, Royal Coll. THOMAS GAINSBOROUGH, with her sisters Augusta and Elizabeth, oil, 1784, Royal Coll.

CHARLOTTE, Sophia of Mecklenburg-Strelitz (1744-1818) Queen of George III.

P ALLAN RAMSAY, c1762, wl in robes of state, Royal Coll; studio version, NPG 224. ALLAN RAMSAY, c1764, wl seated with her two eldest sons, Royal Coll. JOHAN ZOFFANY, c1765, with her two eldest sons, Royal Coll. FRANCIS COTES, 1767, wl seated with Princess Royal as a baby, Royal Coll. JOHAN ZOFFANY, 1771, tql seated, Royal Coll. JOHAN ZOFFANY, c1771-72, hs in robes of state, oval, Royal Coll. BENJAMIN WEST, 1776, tql seated, sewing with the Princess Royal, Royal Coll. SIR JOSHUA REYNOLDS, c1779-80, wl in robes of state, Royal Academy, London. THOMAS GAINSBOROUGH, RA 1781, wl with a fan and a small dog, Royal Coll. BENJAMIN WEST, 1782, wl with dog, her children in background, and 1789, with George III, both Royal Coll. SIR THOMAS LAWRENCE, 1789, wl seated, NG 4257. SIR WILLIAM BEECHEY, 1796, wl with dogs, Royal Coll. P.E.STROEHLING, 1807, wl seated with crown, orb and sceptre, Royal Coll.

D FRANCIS COTES, 1767, with the Princess Royal as a baby, pastel, Royal Coll. JOHN DOWNMAN, c1783, hl, Royal Coll. ISAAC CRUIKSHANK, hs, wash, NPG 2788.

M OZIAS HUMPHRY, 1766, tql seated, Royal Coll. RICHARD COSWAY, c1795?, hs, oval, Royal Coll. HENRY BONE, 1801, hs, oval, NPG L152 (28). JEREMIAH MEYER, two hs, oval, Royal Coll.

G SIR JOSHUA REYNOLDS, 'The Marriage of George III, 1761', oil, Royal Coll. JOHAN ZOFFANY, 'George III, Queen Charlotte and their Six Eldest Children', in Vandyck dress, 1770, Royal Coll. JOHAN ZOFFANY, a family group, oil, RA 1773, Royal Coll.

SC PETER TURNERELLI, 1818, marble bust, Leeds City Art Galleries, Temple Newsam House.

CHARNOCK, John (1756-1807) author.

PR E.SHIRT, after M.Singleton, hs, stipple, pub 1810, NPG.

CHATHAM, John Pitt, 2nd Earl of (1756-1835) general.

P Studio of JOHN HOPPNER, hl, Royal Marines' Mess, Chatham.

G SIR GEORGE HAYTER, 'The Trial of Queen Caroline, 1820', oil, NPG 999.

CHATHAM, William Pitt, 1st Earl of (1708-1778) prime-minister.

P Studio of WILLIAM HOARE, c1754, tql seated, NPG 1050. W.HOARE, c1766, wl in peer's robes, The Guildhall, Bath. After RICHARD BROMPTON of 1772, hl, NPG 259. JOHN SINGLETON COPLEY, sketch for 'The Death of Chatham', NPG L139. W.HOARE, hl seated, DoE (War Office).

M JEAN ROUQUET, V & A.

G JOHN SINGLETON COPLEY, 'The Collapse of the Earl of Chatham in the House of Lords, 7 July 1778', Tate Gallery 100, on loan to NPG.

SC WILLIAM BEHNES, 1847, bust, Eton College, Berks. JOSEPH WILTON, 1759, marble bust, SNPG 1493. J.WILTON, 1766, statue, Crawford School, Cork. J.WILTON, 1766, bust, Fitzwilliam Museum, Cambridge. PATIENCE WRIGHT, 1775?, wax effigy, Westminster Abbey, London. JOHN FLAXMAN, jun, 1778,

Wedgwood medallion, Wedgwood Museum, Barlaston, Staffs. J.WILTON, 1780, marble bust, Belvoir Castle, Leics. JOHN BACON, sen, 1782, statue, Guildhall, London. J.BACON, jun, 1784, statue, Westminster Abbey, London. JOSEPH NOLLEKENS 1811, bust, Belvoir Castle.

CHATTERLEY, William Simmonds (1787-1822) actor.

PR J.THOMSON, after Chater, wl as Justice Woodcock in Bickerstaffe's *Love in a Village*, stipple, for *Theatrical Inquisitor* 1817, BM, NPG.

CHATTERTON, Thomas (1752-1770) poet.

P HENRY WALLIS, 1856, wl, the death scene, TATE 1685.

PR Several posthumous popular prints, BM, NPG.

CHAUNCEY, Charles (1706-1777) physician and antiquary.

SC After JAMES TASSIE, plaster medallion, SNPG 488.

PR C.WATSON, after F.Cotes, hl, stipple, BM.

CHEDWORTH, John Howe, 4th Baron (1754-1804) scholar.

P GEORGE KNAPTON, 1741, hl with globe and goblet, The Society of Dilettanti, Brooks's Club, London.

PR UNKNOWN, hs, outline, lith, BM.

CHEESMAN, Thomas (1760-1835) engraver.

P FRANCESCO BARTOLOZZI, 1777, hs profile, NPG 780.

D HENRY EDRIDGE, tql, pencil, BM.

CHELMSFORD, Frederick Thesiger, 1st Baron (1794-1878) lord chancellor.

P E.U.EDDIS, c1859, in robes of chancellor, with mace, Abingdon Guildhall, Oxfordshire.

D FREDERICK SARGENT, c1870-80, hl, pencil, NPG 1834(g).

G HENRY GALES, 'The Derby Cabinet of 1867', w/c, 1868, NPG 4893.

PR W.WALKER, after E.U.Eddis, tql, mezz, pub 1847, BM. W.HOLL, after George Richmond, stipple, for the 'Grillion's Club' series BM. D.J.POUND, after a photograph by Mayall, nearly wl seated by table, line, for *Illustrated News of the World*, NPG.

PH UNKNOWN, hs in wig and robes, carte, NPG 'Twist' album.

CHELSUM, James (1740?-1801) author.

SC Two plaster medallions, after JAMES TASSIE, 1788, SNPG 375 and SNPG 469.

CHENEVIX, Richard (1774-1830) chemist and mineralogist.

PR J.HOPWOOD, after Pescorsky, hs, stipple, NPG.

CHERRY, Andrew (1762-1812) actor.

P SAMUEL DE WILDE, hl as Item in *The Deserted Daughter*, Garrick Club, London.

D SYLVESTER HARDING, hl, w/c, Garrick Club.

PR Several theatrical prints, BM, NPG.

CHESNEY, Francis Rawdon (1789-1872) general and explorer.

P UNKNOWN, over a photograph, tql, NPG 2659.

PR UNKNOWN, wl, etch, NPG.

CHESTERFIELD, Philip Stanhope, 5th Earl of (1755-1815) privy councillor.

PR J.SCOTT, after T.Gainsborough, wl seated on a bank, with a dog mezz, BM, NPG. J.R.SMITH, after W.Beechey, hl, mezz, pub 1798, NPG.

CHEVALIER, Thomas (1767-1824) surgeon.

PR J.LINNELL, hl, etch, and line, BM, NPG.

CHEVALLIER, Temple (1794-1873) astronomer.

P C.W.COPE, RA 1870, wl, University College, Durham.

CHEYNE, John (1777-1836) medical writer.

PR J.COCHRAN, after W.Deey, hl seated, stipple, for Pettigrew's

Medical Portrait Gallery, 1839, BM, NPG.

CHICHESTER, Thomas Pelham, 1st Earl of (1728-1805) politician.
P GILBERT STUART, 1785, hs, oval, Saltram House (NT), Devon.

CHICHESTER, Thomas Pelham, 2nd Earl of (1756-1826) statesman.
R S.W.REYNOLDS, after J.Hoppner, hl, mezz, pub 1802, BM, NPG.

CHIFNEY, or CHIFFNEY, Samuel (1753?-1807) jockey.
P GEORGE STUBBS, 1791, riding 'Baronet', Royal Coll; versions, Belvoir Castle, Leics and Huntington Library and Art Gallery, San Marino, USA.

CHIFNEY, or CHIFFNEY, Samuel (1786-1854) jockey.
P H.B.CHALON, 1808, riding 'Sir David', Royal Coll. BEN MARSHALL, 1812, riding 'Sorcery', Belvoir Castle, Leics. BEN MARSHALL, 1818, Fonmon Castle, S.Glamorgan.
R C.TURNER, wl preparing to be weighed after a race, mezz, pub 1807, BM. R.WOODMAN, after B.Marshall, hl in racing dress, stipple, for *Sporting Mag*, 1828, BM, NPG.
C JOHN DOYLE, 'Two personages of Great Weight on the Turf', pencil, 1829, BM.

CHILDREN, George (1742-1818) electrician.
P A.J.OLIVER, 1806, hl, NPG 5150, engr M.Gauci, lith, BM, NPG.

CHILDREN, John George (1777-1852) scientist.
P Attrib STEPHEN PEARCE, hl, Royal Society, London. UNKNOWN, hl, NPG 5151.
R W.DRUMMOND, after E.U.Eddis, hl, lith, one of set of *Athenaeum Portraits*, 1835, BM. MISS TURNER, after B.R.Faulkner, hs, lith, BM.

CHINNERY, George (1774-1852) painter.
P Several self-portraits: c1825, hs, Metropolitan Museum of Art, New York, USA; c1835-40, hl, The Peabody Museum, Salem, Mass, USA; c1840, wl seated at easel, NPG 779; hl at easel, SNPG 1251.
D Self-portrait, 1824, tql, pen and ink, BM. Self-portrait, 1832, hl seated, pencil, NPG 4096. G.T.DURRAN, 1844, hs sketch, The Peabody Museum, Salem.
M Self-portrait, c1810-15, hs, oil, Royal Academy, London.
C SIR CHARLES D'OYLY, 'Tom Raw Sits for His Portrait', coloured engr, for *Tom Raw the Griffin* 1828, BM.

CHOLMONDELEY, George James Cholmondeley, 1st Marquess of (1749-1827) chamberlain to the Prince of Wales.
P SIR JOSHUA REYNOLDS, RA 1780, wl in peer's robes, Houghton Hall.
G JOHN SINGLETON COPLEY, 'The Collapse of the Earl of Chatham in the House of Lords, 7 July 1778', oil, TATE 100, on loan to NPG. WILLIAM LANE, 'Whig Statesmen and their Friends, c1810', chalk, NPG 2076.
R W.BRETT, after J.Simpson, hs, with Garter star, mezz, NPG.

CHRISTIAN, Sir Hugh Cloberry (1747-1798) rear-admiral.
R H.R.COOK, after J.Northcote, hs, stipple, oval, pub 1809, NPG.

CHRISTIE, James (1730-1803) auctioneer.
P THOMAS GAINSBOROUGH, RA 1778, tql, J.Paul Getty Museum, Malibu, California, USA.
C R.DIGHTON, hl, etch, pub 1794, NPG. UNKNOWN, wl at auctioneer's desk, etch, NPG.

CHRISTIE, James (1773-1831) auctioneer and antiquary.
D E.TURNER, two pencil drgs, one dated 1821, V & A.
R R.GRAVES, after a bust by W.Behnes, line, BM, NPG.

CHRISTIE, Samuel Hunter (1784-1865) mathematician.
H ERNEST EDWARDS, wl seated, for *Men of Eminence*, ed L.Reeve, 1865, vol III.

CHRISTISON, Sir Robert (1797-1882) toxicologist.
P SIR JOHN WATSON-GORDON, RA 1864, Royal College of Physicians, Edinburgh.
SC WILLIAM BRODIE, RA 1870, marble bust, Edinburgh University.
PR C.COOK, after a photograph by Moffat, hl, stipple and line, NPG. F.SCHENCK, after W.Stewart, hs, lith, NPG.

CHUDLEIGH, Elizabeth, see 3rd Countess of Bristol.

CHURCHILL, Charles (1731-1764) satirist.
P J.S.C.SCHAAK, hl, NPG 162.
PR COOK, after C.Catton, hl seated, line, oval, for Bell's ed of his *Poems*, 1784, BM, NPG. A.SMITH, after O'Neal, hl seated, line, BM, NPG.
C W.HOGARTH, 'The Bruiser', line, pub 1763, NPG.

CIBBER, Charlotte, see Charke.

CIBBER, Susannah Maria, née Arne (1714-1766) actress and singer.
P THOMAS HUDSON, c1739, hl, Garrick Club, London. THOMAS HUDSON, c1749?, hl, NPG 4526.
G PETER VAN BLEECK, wl as Cordelia in *King Lear*, oil, 1755, Yale Center for British Art, New Haven, USA. JOHAN ZOFFANY, in *The Farmer's Return*, oil, (type of c1762), Yale Center for British Art. JOHAN ZOFFANY, in *Venice Preserved*, oil, (type of c1763), Garrick Club.
SC UNKNOWN, c1729, ivory medallion, NPG 1984.

CIBBER, Theophilus (1703-1758) actor.
D WILLIAM ROBINS, 1715, hl, pencil, Royal Coll. THOMAS WORLIDGE, 1735, wl, pencil, Royal Coll.
PR R.CLAMP, tql in character of a *Fine Gentleman*, stipple, BM, NPG.

CIPRIANI, Giovanni Battista (1727-1785) painter and engraver.
P NATHANIEL DANCE, hs, Royal Academy, London.
D FRANCESCO BARTOLOZZI, Cipriani painting, Royal Coll.
G JOHAN ZOFFANY, 'Royal Academicians, 1772', oil, Royal Coll. J.F.RIGAUD, with Francesco Bartolozzi and Agostino Carlini, oil, 1777, NPG 3186.
PR M.BOVI, after F.Bartolozzi, hs profile, stipple, oval, pub 1785, BM, NPG. R.EARLOM, after J.F.Rigaud, hl with palette, stipple, oval, pub 1789, BM, NPG.

CLAIRMONT, Clara Mary Jane (1798-1879) mistress of Lord Byron.
P AMELIA CURRAN, Newstead Abbey, Nottingham.

CLANWILLIAM, Richard Charles Francis Meade, 3rd Earl of (1795-1879) diplomat.
P Attrib LAWRENCE, hs as a young man, Pen-y-Ian, Meifod, Powys. G.F.WATTS, Uppark (NT), W.Sussex.
G SIR GEORGE HAYTER, 'The Trial of Queen Caroline, 1820', oil, NPG 999.

CLAPPERTON, Hugh (1788-1827) African explorer.
P G.MANTON, hs, SNPG 1114, engr T.Lupton, mezz, for his *Journal of a Recent Expedition*, 1829, BM, NPG.
D UNKNOWN, hs, w/c, SNPG 5.

CLARE, John (1793-1864) poet.
P WILLIAM HILTON, 1820, hl seated, NPG 1469, engr E.Scriven, stipple, for his *Village Minstrel*, 1821, BM, NPG. THOMAS GRIMSHAWE, 1844, hl, Northampton Public Library.
D GEORGE MAINE, 1848, Clare seated in the portico of All Saints' Church, Northampton, w/c, Northampton Public Library. UNKNOWN, hs, as an old man, w/c, Peterborough Museum and Art Gallery. Several drgs, Northampton Public Library and Peterborough Museum and Art Gallery.
SC HENRY BEHNES, 1828, bronze bust, Northampton Public Library. UNKNOWN, death mask, Northampton Public Library.

PH W.W.LAW AND SON, 1862, hl seated, Northampton Public Library.

CLARE, John Fitzgibbon, 1st Earl of (1749-1802) lord chancellor of Ireland.

P H.D.HAMILTON, wl in chancellor's robes, NGI 292. GILBERT STUART, wl in chancellor's robes, Trinity College, Dublin.

PR F.BARTOLOZZI, after R.Cosway, hl, stipple, oval, pub 1790, BM, NPG. C.TURNER, after J.Hoppner, hl, mezz, pub 1802, BM, NPG. J.HEATH after J.Comerford, hs in chancellor's robes, stipple, for Sir J.Barrington's *Historic Memoirs*, 1809, BM, NPG. W.DANIELL, after G.Dance, hl profile, soft-ground etch, NPG.

CLARENDON, Thomas Villiers, 1st Earl of (1709-1786) diplomat.

P Attrib ENOCH SEEMAN, jun, c1740, hl wearing Polish dress, Earl of Clarendon Coll (on loan to the British Embassy, Warsaw).

PR C.BESTLAND, after T.Hudson, aged 47, stipple, for the *Works of R.O.Cambridge*, pub 1803, BM.

CLARENDON, Thomas Villiers, 2nd Earl of (1753-1824) politician.

P ROBERT TREWICK BONE, 1824, hl, Hatfield House, Herts.

CLARINA, Eyre Massey, 1st Baron (1719-1804) general.

SC After JAMES TASSIE, plaster medallion, SNPG 495.

PR J.J. VR. BERGHE, after R.Bull, hs, stipple, oval, pub 1800, BM.

CLARK, Sir James (1788-1870) court physician.

P JOHN ANDREWS, 1853, tql seated, Royal College of Physicians, London.

D HOPE JAMES STEWART, 1849, wl, pencil and w/c, SNPG 1168.

G SIR GEORGE HAYTER, 'The Christening of HRH Prince of Wales 1842', oil, Royal Coll.

PR UNKNOWN, hs, woodcut, for *British Medical Journal*, 1870, NPG.

PH UNKNOWN, hs profile, daguerreotype, Royal College of Surgeons.

CLARK, Richard (1739-1831) chamberlain of the city of London.

P SIR THOMAS LAWRENCE, RA 1827, tql seated in robes, Guildhall, London. LADY BELL, tql seated in gown, Bridewell Royal Hospital, Surrey.

PR RIDLEY and HOLL, after M.Brown, hs, stipple, oval, for *European Mag*, 1806, BM, NPG. W.DANIELL, after G.Dance of 1798, hs profile, soft-ground etch, NPG.

CLARK, William (1788-1869) anatomist.

SC TIMOTHY BUTLER, two marble busts, c1856(?) and 1866-67, Trinity College, and Department of Zoology, Cambridge.

CLARKE, Adam (1762?-1832) theologian.

P UNKNOWN, hl, Methodist Publishing House, London.

G ROBINSON, after Mosses, wl seated, with two priests of Buddha, line, pub 1844, NPG.

PR J.THOMSON, after J.Jenkinson, hl, stipple, for Jerdan's *Nat Portrait Gallery*, 1833, BM, NPG. W.WARD, after J.Jackson, hl, mezz, BM, NPG.

CLARKE, Sir Alured (1745?-1832) field-marshal.

P SIR WILLIAM BEECHEY, RA 1813, wl in Bath robes, Eton College, Berks.

PR J.BROMLEY, after W.Beechey, tql with cannon, mezz, pub 1833, BM.

CLARKE, Charles Cowden (1787-1877) author and lecturer.

D UNKNOWN, tql, w/c on marble, NPG 4506.

CLARKE, Sir Charles Mansfield, Bart (1782-1857) obstetrician.

P SAMUEL LANE, 1832?, tql seated, Royal College of Physicians, London.

D SIR FRANCIS CHANTREY, 1833, hs and hs profile, pencil, NPG 316a (15, 16).

SC SIR FRANCIS CHANTREY, c1840, plaster bust, Ashmolean Museum, Oxford.

CLARKE, Edward Daniel (1769-1822) mineralogist.

P JOHN OPIE, hs, NPG 813. Attrib OPIE, hl, Jesus College, Cambridge.

D THOMAS UWINS, wl seated, w/c, BM. JOHN JACKSON, c1816-17, hs, w/c, BM.

SC SIR FRANCIS CHANTREY, RA 1824, marble bust, Fitzwilliam Museum, Cambridge. After unknown artist, plaster medallion, SNPG 376.

PR H.MEYER, after J.Jackson, hl in robes, stipple, for *Contemporary Portraits*, 1814, BM. E.SCRIVEN, after J.Opie, hl in robes, stipple, pub 1825, BM, NPG.

CLARKE, James Stanier (1765?-1834) author.

D JOHN RUSSELL, called J.S.Clarke, pastel, V & A.

CLARKE, John (1761-1815) physician.

PR C.TURNER, after W.Wood, hs, stipple, pub 1813, BM.

CLARKE, Mary Anne, née Thompson (1776-1852) mistress of the Duke of York.

M ADAM BUCK, 1803, tql seated, NPG 2793.

SC LAWRENCE GAHAGAN, 1811, marble bust, NPG 4436.

PR BATE, wl reclining, stipple, pub 1809, BM, NPG. W.HOPWOOD after T.Rowlandson, standing in witness box, with letter, stipple and line, for *Trial of Duke of York*, 1809, BM. C.WILLIAMS, wl etch, pub 1809, BM. FREEMAN, after A.Buck, hs profile, stipple pub 1810, BM. Several popular prints, NPG.

CLARKSON, Thomas (1760-1846) philanthropist.

P C.F. VON BREDA, 1789, hl seated, NPG 235. SAMUEL LANE, RA 1834, tql seated, Wisbech Corporation, Cambs. HENRY ROOM RA 1839, tql, St John's College, Cambridge.

D A.E.CHALON, w/c, Wilberforce House, Hull.

G B.R.HAYDON, 'The Anti-Slavery Society Convention, 1840' oil, NPG 599.

SC WILLIAM BEHNES, marble bust, Corporation of London. After CATHERINE ANDRAS, plaster medallion, SNPG 496.

PR T.S.ENGLEHEART, after W.Hazlitt, hl, line, pub 1833, BM C.TURNER, after A.E.Chalon, wl seated, mezz, BM, NPG.

CLATER, Francis (1756-1823) farrier and druggist.

PR HOPWOOD, after Clater, hs, stipple, oval, pub 1810, NPG.

CLAY, Sir William, Bart (1791-1869) politician.

G SIR GEORGE HAYTER, 'The House of Commons, 1833', oil, NPG 54.

PR R.J.LANE, after E.U.Eddis?, 1853, tql, lith, NPG.

CLAYTON, John (1754-1843) congregationalist.

PR RIDLEY & CO, hs, stipple, oval, for *Evangelical Mag*, 1808, BM NPG. C.TURNER, after W.McCall, hl, mezz, pub 1831, BM, NPG

CLAYTON, John (1780-1865) minister of Poultry chapel London.

PR J.THOMSON, after S.Drummond, hl, stipple, for *European Mag* 1820, BM, NPG. C.TURNER, after W.McCall, hl, mezz, pub 1831 BM, NPG. C.BAUGNIET, 1845, tql, lith, NPG.

CLEAVER, Euseby (1746-1819) archbishop of Dublin.

P GEORGE ROMNEY, 1796, tql, Christ Church, Oxford. THOMAS PHILLIPS, RA 1800, hl, Petworth (NT), W.Sussex.

CLEAVER, William (1742-1815) bishop of St Asaph.

P JOHN HOPPNER, tql seated, Brasenose College, Oxford, eng J.Ward, mezz, BM, NPG.

C R.DIGHTON, wl, coloured etch, pub 1808, NPG.

CLEGG, Samuel (1781-1861) civil engineer.

P 'UNKNOWN, hl, Science Museum, London.

CLEGHORN, George (1716-1789) physician.
P UNKNOWN, hs, Trinity College, Dublin.
PR C.SHERWIN, hl, stipple, oval, for Lettsom's *Memoirs*, 1786, BM, NPG.

CLEMENT, William Innell (d1852) part proprietor of the 'Observer'.
P? Two portraits, The Observer Newspaper, London.

CLENNELL, Luke (1781-1840) wood engraver and painter.
D Self-portrait, pencil, Laing Museum and Art Gallery, Newcastle-upon-Tyne.

CLÉRISSEAU, Charles Louis (1721-1820) architectural draughtsman.
C P.L.GHEZZI, 1751, hs, pen and ink, Gabinetto Nazionale delle Stampe, Rome. P.L.GHEZZI, wl, pen and ink, BM.

CLERK, Sir George (1787-1867) statesman.
P WILLIAM DYCE, RA 1834, tql, Penicuik House, Lothian region, Scotland. SIR JOHN WATSON-GORDON, RA 1857, tql seated, Penicuik House.

CLERK, John (1728-1812) naval writer.
P SIR HENRY RAEBURN, hl, The Currier Gallery of Art, Manchester, New Hampshire, USA. JAMES SAXON, tql seated, SNPG L30.

CLERK, John (1757-1832), see Lord Eldin.

CLERKE, Charles (1741-1779) circumnavigator.
P SIR NATHANIEL DANCE, 1776, hl with a Maori warrior, Government House, Wellington, New Zealand.

CLERKE, Thomas Henry Shadwell (1792-1849) military journalist.
PR W.DRUMMOND, after E.U.Eddis, tql seated, lith, *Athenaeum Portraits*, No 11, pub 1835, BM, NPG.

CLEVELAND, William Harry Vane, 1st Duke of (1766-1842) politician and patron of the turf.
P A.W.DEVIS, c1810, wl in peer's robes, Harris Museum and Art Gallery, Preston.
D JOHN DOWNMAN, 1813, hl, pencil and w/c, Smith College Museum of Art, Northampton, USA. SIR FRANCIS CHANTREY, hs and hs profile, pencil, NPG 316a (17).
SC SIR RICHARD WESTMACOTT, 1842, recumbent figure on monument, Staindrop, Durham.
PR W.T.FRY, hl, stipple, pub 1821, BM, NPG.

CLEVELEY, Robert (1747-1809) marine painter.
PR S.FREEMAN, after W.Beechey, hl, stipple, for *Monthly Mirror*, 1810, BM, NPG.

CLIFFORD, Sir Augustus William James, Bart (1788-1877) usher of the black rod.
G SIR GEORGE HAYTER, 'The Christening of HRH Prince of Wales, 1842', oil, Royal Coll.
PR W.GILLER, after F.R.Say, tql with rod, mezz, pub 1844, BM, NPG. LACRETELLE, hl, etch, NPG. UNKNOWN, hs, woodcut, for *Illust London News*, 1877, NPG.

CLIFFORD, Hugh Charles, 7th Baron Clifford of Chudleigh (1790-1858) political writer.
P JAMES RAMSAY, 1829, hl, Ugbrooke Park, Devon.
D JAMES GREEN, 1819, with his wife and son Charles, chalk, 1819, Ugbrooke Park.

CLIFT, William (1775-1849) naturalist.
P HENRY SCHMIDT, 1833, hl, Royal Society, London.
D SIR FRANCIS CHANTREY, 1831, head, pencil, BM. W.H.CLIFT, three pencil sketches, BM.

SC UNKNOWN, plaster bust, Royal College of Surgeons, London.
PR BOSLEY, after a daguerreotype, hl seated, line, pub 1849, BM.

CLINE, Henry (1750-1827) surgeon.
D SIR FRANCIS CHANTREY, hs profile, NPG 316a (18).
SC SIR FRANCIS CHANTREY, 1825, marble bust, Royal College of Surgeons, London.

CLINT, George (1770-1854) portrait-painter and engraver.
P Self-portrait, hs, NPG 2064.
D EDWARD BELL, hs, pen and ink, BM.
G GEORGE CLINT, The Last Scene in *A New Way to Pay Old Debts*, oil, 1820, Garrick Club, London.
PR J.H.ROBINSON, after W.Mulready, hs profile, etch, for Pye's *Patronage of British Art*, 1845, BM. T.LUPTON, after a self-portrait, hl, mezz, pub 1854, NPG.

CLINTON, Sir Henry (1738?-1795) general.
P UNKNOWN, c1760, tql, National Army Museum, London.
M JOHN SMART, c1777, National Army Museum. SARA ADDINGTON, 1793, V & A.

CLINTON, Sir Henry (1771-1829) general.
PR UNKNOWN, wl in uniform, aquatint, pub 1817, BM. S.W.REYNOLDS, sen, after S.W.Reynolds, jun, hl with Bath star, mezz, pub 1827, NPG.

CLINTON, Henry Fiennes (1720-1794), see 2nd Duke of Newcastle-under-Lyme.

CLINTON, Henry Pelham Fiennes Pelham (1785-1851), see 4th Duke of Newcastle-under-Lyme.

CLIVE, Catherine, or Kitty, née Raftor (1711-1785) actress.
P JEREMIAH DAVISON, 1735, tql seated, Longleat, Wilts. WILLEM VERELST, 1740, tql seated, with music at harpsichord, Garrick Club, London. Attrib JONATHAN RICHARDSON, hl, NGI 642. UNKNOWN, wl as Mrs Riot, The Fine Lady in *Lethe*, Garrick Club.
PR Several theatrical prints, BM, NPG.

CLIVE, Edward (1754-1839), see 1st Earl of Powis.

CLIVE, Robert Clive, 1st Baron (1725-1774) governor of Bengal.
P NATHANIEL DANCE, c1772–74, wl, Powis Castle (NT), Powys; tql version, NPG 39. UNKNOWN, tql with Bath star, National Army Museum, London.
SC PETER SCHEEMAKERS, 1764, marble statue, India Office Library and Records, London. JOHN VAN NOOST and 'C.G.', 1766, silver medal, NPG 1688.
PR J.MCARDELL, after T.Gainsborough, hs, mezz, NPG.

CLOBERY, Robert Glyn (1719-1800) physician.
PR J.PAGE, hl, line, NPG.

CLONMELL, John Scott, 1st Earl of (1739-1798) Irish judge.
PR P.CONDÉ, after R.Cosway, hs in robes, oval, stipple, BM. UNKNOWN, hs, stipple, NPG.

CLONMORE, Ralph Howard, 1st Baron (d1786) Irish politician.
P POMPEO BATONI, 1752, hl, J.B.Speed Art Museum, Louisville, Kentucky, USA.

CLOSE, Sir Barry (1756-1813) major-general.
P SIR MARTIN ARCHER SHEE, tql, City Art Gallery, Manchester. MOORE, after an unknown artist, tql, Oriental Club, London.
D THOMAS HICKEY, 1801, hs, chalk, Stratfield Saye, Hants.

CLOSE, Francis (1797-1882) dean of Carlisle.
PR J.R.JACKSON, after H.W.Phillips, tql, mezz, pub 1850, BM. DAY & SON, hl, lith, NPG. D.J.POUND, after a photograph by Mayall,

tql, stipple, presented with *Illust News of the World*, BM, NPG.

CLOUTT, Thomas (1781?-1846) independent divine.
PR R.WOODMAN, hs, stipple, pub 1822, NPG.

CLOWES, Butler (*d*1782) mezzotint engraver and printseller.
PR UNKNOWN, hs, stipple, oval, pub 1802, BM, NPG. B.CLOWES, hl in cap, mezz, oval, BM.

CLOWES, John (1743-1831) Swedenborgian.
P JOSEPH ALLEN, 1818, Chetham's Library, Manchester.
SC JOHN FLAXMAN, relief plaster model for memorial, University College, London.

CLOWES, William (1780-1851) methodist.
P UNKNOWN, Methodist Publishing House, London.

CLUTTERBUCK, Henry (1767-1856) medical writer.
PR J.COCHRAN, after H.Room, hl, stipple, BM, NPG. C.MEASOM, hl profile, line and etch, NPG.

CLUTTERBUCK, Robert (1772-1831) topographer.
PR UNKNOWN, 1818, hs profile, lith, BM. W.BOND, after W.Hunt, head, semi-profile, stipple, BM, NPG. R.J.LANE, hs, lith, NPG. J.E.CLUTTERBUCK, after G.F.Joseph, hl, mezz, oval, NPG.

CLYDE, Colin Campbell, Baron (1792-1863) field-marshal.
P J.W.PIENEMAN, 1821, head, Wellington Museum, Apsley House, London. H.W.PHILLIPS, *c*1856, tql, Glasgow City Art Gallery. T.J.BARKER, 1860, hl, SNPG 284.
D SIR FRANCIS GRANT, *c*1860, wl study, pen, ink and w/c, NPG 619. T.BLAKE WIRGMAN, with the 1st Lord Sandhurst, pencil, SNPG 1976.
G J.W.PIENEMAN, 'The Battle of Waterloo', oil, 1824, Rijksmuseum, Amsterdam. T.J.BARKER, after sketches by E.Lundgren, 'Relief of Lucknow', oil, 1857, City Art Gallery, Glasgow.
SC G.G.ADAMS, 1855 and 1861, plaster busts, NPG 1201, SNPG 597. MATTHEW NOBLE, 1866, marble relief (meeting of Clyde, Havelock and Outram at Lucknow), Outram memorial, Westminster Abbey, London. J.H.FOLEY, *c*1868, bronze statue, George's Square, Glasgow. CARLO MAROCHETTI, statue on memorial, Waterloo Place, London.
PH ROGER FENTON, 1855, tql, NPG P20. F.BEATO, 1857-58, wl seated, with Sir W.R.Mansfield, National Army Museum, London. UNKNOWN, tql seated, Royal Coll. HERBERT WATKINS, wl, caricature, carte, NPG.

COATES, Robert (1772-1848) actor.
D SAMUEL DE WILDE, wl as Romeo, w/c, Garrick Club, London.
PR Several theatrical prints, BM, NPG.

COBB, James (1756-1818) playwright.
D GEORGE DANCE, hl profile, pencil, NPG 3900.
PR CHAPMAN, after S.Drummond, hs, stipple, oval, for *European Mag*, 1796, BM, NPG. W.RIDLEY, after Birch, hs, stipple, oval, for *Monthly Mirror*, 1803, BM, NPG. T.BLOOD, hl, stipple, pub 1809, BM.

COBBETT, William (1763-1835) essayist.
P UNKNOWN, hl seated, NPG 1549.
D UNKNOWN, hl seated, w/c, NPG 2877.
G SIR GEORGE HAYTER, 'The House of Commons, 1833', oil, NPG 54.
SC J.P.DANTAN, 1834, plaster statue, caricature, with Daniel O'Connell, Musée Carnavalet, Paris.
PR F.BARTOLOZZI, after J.R.Smith, hl, stipple, pub 1801, BM, NPG. W.WARD, after J.R.Smith, wl seated, mezz, pub 1812, BM. After A.BUCK, *c*1817, hl profile, etch, NPG. G.V.PALMER, after a miniature by G.M.Brighty, hs, line, pub 1817, NPG. E.SMITH, from a drg made on board the *Importer*, 1817, BM. D.MACLISE, wl seated, for *Fraser's Mag*, 1835, BM. N.MAURIN, after G.Cooke,

wl, lith, NPG.
C JOHN DOYLE, 2 drgs, BM.

COBBIN, Ingram (1777-1851) congregational minister.
PR R.WOODMAN, hl, stipple, pub 1822, NPG. W.FINDEN, after E.B.Morris, hl, stipple, NPG.

COBBOLD, Elizabeth (1767-1824) poet.
PR W.H.WORTHINGTON, after Gardiner, hl, line, for her *Poems* 1825, BM, NPG.

COBHAM, Thomas (1786-1842) actor.
PR Several theatrical prints, NPG.

COCHRANE, Sir Alexander Forrester Inglis (1758-1832) admiral.
P ROBERT FIELD, 1809, hs with Bath ribbon and star, SNPG 1578. SIR WILLIAM BEECHEY, 1815-19, tql with Bath ribbon and star NMM, Greenwich.

COCHRANE, Archibald, see 9th Earl of Dundonald.

COCHRANE, John Dundas (1780-1825) traveller.
PR H.MEYER, after Harding, hl in uniform, stipple, BM, NPG.

COCHRANE, Thomas (1775-1860), see 10th Earl of Dundonald.

COCHRANE, Sir Thomas John (1789-1872) admiral of the fleet.
P RICHARD BUCKNER, tql in uniform, NMM, Greenwich. SIR W.C.ROSS, 1854, The Admiralty, Portsmouth.

COCKBURN, Sir George (1772-1853) admiral.
P J.J.HALLS, 1817, wl in uniform, NMM, Greenwich. SIR WILLIAM BEECHEY, 1820, wl with Bath ribbon and star, NMM T.W.MACKAY, 1851, wl, formerly United Service Club (c/o The Crown Commissioners). JOHN LUCAS, tql with telescope DoE (Ministry of Defence, London).
PR C.TURNER, hl in uniform, mezz, for Brenton's *Naval History* 1825, BM, NPG.

COCKBURN, Henry Thomas Cockburn, Lord (1779-1854) Scottish judge.
P SIR JOHN WATSON-GORDON, wl, SNPG 709. JOHN SYME, exhib 1831, tql, Faculty of Advocates, Parliament Hall, Edinburgh. SIR HENRY RAEBURN, hl, Faculty of Advocates, Parliament Hall.
SL AUGUSTIN EDOUART, 1831, SNPG 2281. UNKNOWN, SNPG 1175.
G SIR GEORGE HARVEY, with the Marquess of Breadalbane, the Earl of Dalhousie and Lord Rutherfurd, oil, SNPG 1497.
SC A.H.RITCHIE, 1848, marble bust, NPG 4700. WILLIAM BRODIE 1855, marble bust, SNPG 1392. SIR JOHN STEELL, marble bust Faculty of Advocates, Parliament Hall. WILLIAM BRODIE, 1862 marble statue, Faculty of Advocates, Parliament Hall.
C B.W.CROMBIE, pencil study for *Modern Athenians*, pl 14, SNPG 2306.

COCKBURN, Sir James, Bart (1771-1852) major-general.
P F.R.SAY, RA 1849, tql with Guelphic order star and ribbon, formerly United Services Club (c/o The Crown Commissioners) A.J.DUBOIS DRAHONET, wl with KCH insignia, Royal Coll.

COCKBURN, Sir William (1768-1835) general.
P THOMAS BARKER, 1816, wl, Victoria Art Gallery, Bath.
M JOHN SMART, 1791, hs, Powis Castle (NT), Powys.

COCKERELL, Charles Robert (1788-1863) architect.
P SIR WILLIAM BOXALL, hl, RIBA, London.
D CARL CHRISTIAN VOGEL, 1817, hs, Staatliche Kunstsammlungen, Dresden. Attrib A.E.CHALON, hl seated, w/c NPG 5096.

COCKERELL, Samuel Pepys (1754-1827) architect.
D GEORGE DANCE, hs profile, pencil, BM.

PR T.HODGETTS, after W.Beechey, hl, mezz, pub 1824, BM.

COCKERILL, William (1759-1832) inventor.
M UNKNOWN, hs, V & A.

COCKINGS, George (d1802) writer, registrar of the Society of Arts.
PR W.EVANS, hs, stipple, oval, BM, NPG.

CODRINGTON, Sir Edward (1770-1851) admiral.
P H.PATTERSON, RA 1840, Town Hall, Devonport. H.P.BRIGGS, 1843, hl seated, profile, NPG 721.
D SIR FRANCIS CHANTREY, 1819, V & A. JOHN DOYLE, 2 drgs, BM.
G SIR GEORGE HAYTER, 'The House of Commons, 1833', oil, NPG 54.
SC SIR FRANCIS CHANTREY, plaster bust, Ashmolean Museum, Oxford.
PR C.TURNER, after T.Lawrence, hl in uniform, mezz, pub 1830, BM. B.HOLL, after G.Hayter, hl, stipple, BM, NPG. Various popular prints, BM, NPG.

COETLOGON, Charles Edward de, see DE Coetlogon.

COFFIN, Sir Isaac, Bart (1759-1839) admiral.
SC WILLIAM BEHNES, 1826, bust, Boston Athenaeum, USA.
PR W.RIDLEY, after a miniature, hs in uniform, stipple, oval, for *Naval Chronicle*, 1804, BM, NPG.

COGAN, Eliezer (1762-1855) dissenting minister and schoolmaster.
PR S.COUSINS, after T.Phillips, tql seated, mezz, BM. UNKNOWN, hl, lith, oval, BM, NPG.

COGAN, Thomas (1736-1818) philosopher.
PR J.BASIRE, after F.Gérard, hs profile, line, oval, pub 1814, BM, NPG. UNKNOWN, hs, silhouette profile, stipple, BM, NPG.

COKE, Daniel Parker (1745-1825) politician.
G JOSEPH WRIGHT of Derby, tql with Rev d'Ewes Coke, and his wife Hannah, oil, c1780-82, Derby Museum and Art Gallery.
PR T.GAUGAIN, after T.Barber, hl seated, stipple, pub 1809, NPG.

COKE, Jeremiah, see Brandreth.

COKE, Thomas (1747-1814) methodist bishop.
D HENRY EDRIDGE, 1799, hl seated, pencil, NPG 1434a.

COKE, Thomas William, see 1st Earl of Leicester.

COLBORNE, Sir John (1778-1863), see 1st Baron Seaton.

COLBY, Thomas Frederick (1784-1852) director of the Ordnance Survey.
D WILLIAM BROCKEDON, 1837, hs, chalk, NPG 2515 (82).

COLCHESTER, Charles Abbott, 1st Baron (1757-1829) speaker of the House of Commons.
P Attrib JOHN HOPPNER, 1801, hl, NPG 1416. JAMES NORTHCOTE, 1802, tql in speaker's robes, with mace, Christ Church, Oxford. SIR THOMAS LAWRENCE, 1824, hs in peer's robes, Palace of Westminster, London.
D S.J.B., wl, w/c, Palace of Westminster.
PR H.MEYER, after S.Drummond, hl in peer's robes, stipple, for *European Mag*, 1817, BM, V & A.
C JAMES GILLRAY, head, pencil, BM.

COLE, Sir Christopher (1770-1837) captain in the navy.
PR G.H.PHILLIPS, after W.Owen, tql, mezz, BM.

COLE, Sir Galbraith Lowry (1772-1842) general.
P WILLIAM DYCE, hl, NPG 946.
SC TERENCE FARRELL, statue, Enniskillen, N.Ireland. UNKNOWN, bust, Royal Military Academy, Camberley, Surrey.
PR C.PICART, after T.Lawrence, hl, stipple, for *Contemporary Portraits*, 1816, BM, NPG.

COLE, William (1714-1782) antiquary.
D REV THOMAS KERRICH, hs, chalk, BM.
PR UNKNOWN, hs, line, pub 1805, BM, NPG.

COLEBROOKE, Henry Thomas (1765-1837) sanskrit scholar.
D SIR FRANCIS CHANTREY, hs, pencil, NPG 316a (19).
SC SIR FRANCIS CHANTREY, 1820, marble bust, India Office Library and Records, London.

COLERAINE, George Hanger, 4th Baron (1751?-1824) eccentric.
PR S.SPRINGSGUTH, after R.R.Reinagle, wl on horseback, stipple, pub 1816, NPG.
C JAMES GILRAY, wl, 'Georgey in the Coal-Hole', coloured etch, pub 1800, NPG.

COLERIDGE, Sir John Taylor (1790-1876) judge.
P H.W.PICKERSGILL, 1835, hl seated, in robes, Exeter College, Oxford.
PR S.COUSINS, after M.Carpenter, tql seated in robes, mezz, BM, NPG.

COLERIDGE, Samuel Taylor (1772-1834) poet and philosopher.
P PETER VANDYCK, 1795, hs, NPG 192. JAMES NORTHCOTE, 1804, hl, Jesus College, Cambridge. WASHINGTON ALLSTON, 1814, hl seated, NPG 184. WASHINGTON ALLSTON, 1806, hl seated, unfinished, Fogg Art Museum, Cambridge, USA. COOPER, c1830, hl, Highgate Literary and Scientific Institute, London. MOSES HAUGHTON, 1832, hs, Christ's Hospital, Horsham, Sussex.
D ROBERT HANCOCK, 1796, hs, pencil and wash, NPG 452. DANIEL MACLISE, 1833, wl, for *Fraser's Mag*, V & A.
SC HAMO THORNYCROFT, RA 1884, marble bust, Westminster Abbey, London.
PR W.WAGSTAFF, after A.Wivell, hl seated, stipple, one of Finden's set of illustrations to Moore's *Life of Byron*, 1833, BM, NPG. L.HAGHE, after T.Phillips, tql seated, lith, pub 1835, BM, NPG.

COLERIDGE, William Hart (1789-1849) bishop of Barbadoes.
P THOMAS PHILLIPS, RA 1825, tql, Christ Church, Oxford.

COLLARD, Frederick William (1772-1860) pianoforte manufacturer.
PR C.TURNER, after J.Lonsdale, hl seated, mezz, pub 1829, BM, NPG.

COLLARD, William Frederick (1776-1866) pianoforte manufacturer.
PR T.LUPTON, after J.Lonsdale, tql, mezz, NPG.

COLLEDGE, Thomas Richardson (1796-1879) physician.
P GEORGE CHINNERY, with his wife, Hongkong and Shanghai Banking Corporation, Hongkong.

COLLES, Abraham (1773-1843) surgeon.
P MARTIN CREGAN, hl, Steeven's Hospital, Dublin.
SC THOMAS KIRK, exhib 1837, Royal College of Surgeons, Dublin.

COLLIER, John ('Tim Bobbin') (1708-1786) writer and artist.
PR J.SANDERS, hl, line, oval, for his *Works*, 1773, BM, NPG. UNKNOWN, hl, stipple, NPG.

COLLIER, John Payne (1789-1883) Shakespearean critic and forger.
PR UNKNOWN, hs, woodcut, BM.

COLLING, Charles (1751-1836) stock-breeder.
PR G.COOK, after J.M.Wright, hl, line, for *Farmer's Mag*, 1844, BM, NPG.

COLLINGS, Samuel (fl 1780-1790?) painter and caricaturist.
P Self-portrait, hl, Yale Center for British Art, New Haven, USA.

COLLINGWOOD, Cuthbert Collingwood, Baron (1748-1810) admiral.
P C.LONSDELL, c1810, wl, Mansion House, Newcastle-upon-Tyne. HENRY HOWARD, c1827, after Giuseppe Politi of 1807, wl in uniform, with medals, NMM, Greenwich. FRANK HOWARD, tql, copy, NPG 1496.
D VISCOUNT NELSON, 1784, hs, silhouette, NMM.
M UNKNOWN, c1790-95, hs, NMM.
SC SIR R.WESTMACOTT, 1813, recumbent figure on monument, St Paul's Cathedral, London. J.C.F.ROSSI, 1819, marble bust on monument, St Nicholas's Cathedral, Newcastle. Attrib J.G.LOUGH, probably RA 1845, marble bust, NPG 1296. J.G.LOUGH, stone statue, Galley Hill, Tynemouth.
PR GAUGAIN and SCRIVEN, wl, stipple, pub 1806, BM. W.SAY, tql, mezz, pub 1806, BM. H.R.COOK, after R.Bowyer, hs, stipple, oval, NPG.

COLLINS, David (1756-1810) colonial governor.
PR A.CARDON, after a miniature by I.T.Barber, hs, stipple, oval, pub 1804, NPG.

COLLINS, John (1743-1808) actor and poet.
D 'J.C.B.', wl, ink, BM.
PR UNKNOWN, hl, stipple, oval, BM.

COLLINS, Richard (1755-1831) miniature painter.
G PAUL SANDBY, 'Sketches taken at Print Sales', drg, Royal Coll.

COLLINS, Thomas (1775-1806) actor.
P SAMUEL DE WILDE, RA 1805, wl as Timothy Quaint in a scene from *The Soldier's Daughter*, Garrick Club, London. S. DE WILDE, wl, as Slender in *The Merry Wives of Windsor*, National Theatre, London.

COLLINS, William (1721-1759) poet.
SC JOHN FLAXMAN, 1795, wl seated, medallion on monument, Chichester Cathedral, E.Sussex.
PR UNKNOWN, hl aged 14, stipple, oval, for *European Mag*, 1811, BM, NPG.

COLLINS, William (1788-1847) painter.
P JOHN LINNELL, hl, NGI 844.
D C.A.COLLINS (his son), hs, chalk, NPG 1643.
PR UNKNOWN, after John Landseer, 1844, wl, woodcut, for *Illust London News*, 10 May 1845, NPG.

COLLYER, William Bengo (1782-1854) congregational minister and author.
P UNKNOWN, hs, Dr Williams's Library, London.
PR C.PICART, after J.H.Stevenson, hl seated, stipple, pub 1806, BM, NPG. J.YOUNG, after C.C.Coventry, wl, mezz, pub 1812, BM. FITTLER, hl, line, pub 1816, NPG. FREEMAN, after Wivell, hl, stipple, pub 1818, NPG. C.PENNY, tql, stipple and line, pub 1820, NPG.

COLMAN, George (1732-1794) playwright.
P Studio of REYNOLDS, 1767, hl seated, NPG 1364. THOMAS GAINSBOROUGH, hl seated, NPG 59. After ZOFFANY, hl, Garrick Club, London.
D JOHN JACKSON, 1810, after Reynolds, hl seated, BM.
PR E.SMITH, after J.Zoffany, hl, line, for *Effigies Poeticae*, BM, NPG.

COLMAN, George (1762-1836) dramatic poet.
PR W.RIDLEY, hl, stipple, oval, for *Monthly Mirror*, 1797, BM. RIDLEY and BLOOD, after S.Drummond, hs, stipple, for *European Mag*, 1808, BM, NPG. H.MEYER, after F.Stephanoff, wl, (in dress of lieutenant of the yeomen of the guard), coloured stipple, for Sir G.Nayler's work on coronation of George IV, 1826, BM, NPG.

W.GREATBACH, tql, line, for *Bentley's Miscellany*, 1837, BM, NPG.
T.LUPTON, after J.Jackson, hl, mezz, oval, BM, NPG.

COLNAGHI, Dominic Paul (1790-1879) printseller.
PR After C.BROCKY, hs, stipple, BM, NPG.

COLNAGHI, Paul (1751-1833) printseller.
PR E.MORTON, after J.R.Smith, hl, lith, BM, NPG. R.EASTON, after Danlan, hs aged 82, stipple, oval, BM, NPG.

COLONSAY AND ORONSAY, Duncan McNeill, Baron (1793-1874) judge.
P THOMAS DUNCAN, tql, SNPG 249. JOHN PHILIP, 1866, wl, Faculty of Advocates, Parliament House, Edinburgh.
D LESLIE WARD, 1873, wl, w/c, for *Vanity Fair*, NPG 2627.
SC SIR JOHN STEELL, 1856, marble bust, Faculty of Advocates, Edinburgh; related plaster bust, SNPG 171.

COLPOYS, Sir John (1742?-1821) admiral.
P W.SAVAGE, after Mather Brown, hl with Bath ribbon and star, NMM, Greenwich.
PR R.EARLOM, after Pellegrini, hl in uniform, mezz, pub 1777, BM, NPG. RIDLEY, after Mather Brown, hs, stipple, oval, pub 1804, NPG. J.YOUNG, hl, mezz, pub 1812, BM.

COLQUHOUN, Archibald Campbell (d1820) lord advocate of Scotland.
C J.KAY, 1813, wl, with Lord Meadowbank, etch, NPG.

COLQUHOUN, Janet, Lady, née Sinclair (1781-1846) religious writer.
PR H.T.RYALL, after C.Smith, tql, stipple, BM, NPG. UNKNOWN, tql seated, stipple and line, NPG.

COLQUHOUN, John (1748-1827) theological writer.
C J.KAY, 1793, hs, etch, oval, BM, NPG.

COLQUHOUN, Patrick (1745-1820) police magistrate and statistical writer.
P UNKNOWN, The Chamber of Commerce, Glasgow.
PR R.DUNKARTON, after S.Medley, tql seated, mezz, pub 1802, BM. H.MEYER, after S.Drummond, hl, stipple, for *European Mag*, 1818, BM, NPG.

COLVILLE, Sir Charles (1770-1843) general.
D ALEXANDER BLAIKLEY, 1849, chalk, SNPG 630.
PR G.T.PAYNE, after H.Raeburn, hl, mezz, pub 1844, BM.

COMBE, Andrew (1797-1847) physiologist and phrenologist.
P G.H.GARRAWAY, after Sir Daniel Macnee of 1836, hl, Edinburgh University.
SC JOHN HUTCHISON, 1889, marble bust, SNPG 555.

COMBE, Charles (1743-1817) physician and numismatist.
G N.BRANWHITE, after S.Medley, 'Institutors of the Medical Society of London', stipple, pub 1801, BM.

COMBE, George (1788-1858) phrenologist and social reformer.
P G.H.GARRAWAY, after Sir J.Watson-Gordon, tql, Edinburgh University.
SC LAWRENCE MACDONALD, marble bust, SNPG 556. SHAKSPERE WOOD, 1849, plaster medallion, SNPG 167.
PR HÄHNISCH, hl, lith, 1855, BM. C.H.JEENS, after D.Macnee, hs, for his *Life*, by C.Gibbon, 1878, BM.
C B.W.CROMBIE, 1849, wl, coloured etch, for *Modern Athenians*, NPG.
PH D.O.HILL and ROBERT ADAMSON, tql, NPG P6 (87).

COMBE, Taylor (1774-1826) numismatist.
P UNKNOWN, hs, Royal Society, London.
G ARCHER, 'The Temporary Elgin Room', 1819, BM.

COMBE, Thomas (1797-1872) printer.

P SIR J.E.MILLAIS, c1849, tql seated, Ashmolean Museum, Oxford.
D W.HOLMAN HUNT, 1860, hs, chalk, Ashmolean Museum.
SC THOMAS WOOLNER, RA 1864, marble bust, Ashmolean Museum.

COMBE, William (1741-1823) author of *Doctor Syntax*.
D GEORGE DANCE, 1793, hs profile, pencil, NPG 2029.
SL UNKNOWN, c1800, BM.

COMBERMERE, Sir Stapleton Cotton (1773-1865) field-marshal.
P MARY M.PEARSON, 1823, hl, NPG 351. JOHN HAYTER, c1829, wl in uniform, with horse, National Army Museum, London. J.P.KNIGHT, c1845, hl, Plas Newydd (NT), Gwynedd. SIR WILLIAM ROSS, c1850, wl, formerly United Service Club, London (c/o The Crown Commissioners).
D THOMAS HEAPHY, 1799, hs, chalk, Stratfield Saye, Hants. THOMAS HEAPHY, 1817, wl, w/c, NPG 4177.
SC BARON CARLO MAROCHETTI, 1864, equestrian statue, Grosvenor Road, Chester.
PR C.TURNER, after T.Heaphy, wl equestrian, mezz, pub 1823, BM.
PH MAULL and POLYBLANK, c1860, hl, NPG.

COMERFORD, John (1762?-1832?) miniature painter.
D WILLIAM BEWICK, hs, chalk, BM.

COMPTON, Sir Herbert Abingdon Draper (1770-1846) judge.
P R.R.REINAGLE, RA 1832, wl seated, Oriental Club, London.

COMPTON, Spencer Joshua Alwyne, see 2nd Marquess of Northampton.

CONDER, John (1714-1781) congregational minister.
P SAMUEL WEBSTER, 1775, hs, Dr Williams's Library, London.

CONDER, Josiah (1789-1855) bookseller.
G B.R.HAYDON, 'The Anti-Slavery Society Convention, 1840', oil, NPG 599.

CONGREVE, Sir William, Bart (1772-1828) military inventor.
P JAMES LONSDALE, hl, NPG 982 f. PHILIP REINAGLE, c1782, with his father, at Woolwich, NGI 1213.
G J.F.SKILL, J.GILBERT, W. and E.WALKER, 'Men of Science Living in 1807-08', pencil and wash, NPG 1075.

CONINGSBY, George Capel-, see 5th Earl of Essex.

CONNOR, Charles (d1826) actor.
PR UNKNOWN, wl as Dr O'Toole, playing violin, etch, BM, NPG. UNKNOWN, wl as Earl of Montrose, coloured etch, NPG.

CONOLLY, John (1794-1866) physician to the Hanwell Asylum.
SC G.M.BENZONI, 1866, marble bust, Royal College of Physicians, London.
PR W.WALKER, after J.W.Gordon, tql seated, mezz, BM. T.M.BAYNES, after T.Kirkby, tql seated, lith, Wellcome Institute, London. UNKNOWN, hs, woodcut, for *Illust London News*, March 31, 1866, NPG.

CONOLLY, Thomas (1738-1803) Irish politician.
G FRANCIS WHEATLEY, 'The Irish House of Commons, 1780', oil, Leeds City Art Galleries, Lotherton Hall, W.Yorks.
PR J.COLLYER, after R.Bull, hs, stipple, oval, pub 1800, NPG.

CONQUEST, John Tricker (1789-1866) man-midwife.
PR M.GAUCI, after T.Snellgrove, hl, lith, BM.

CONROY, Sir John, Bart (1786-1854) comptroller of household to Duchess of Kent.
M ALFRED TIDEY, 1836, hl, NPG 2175.
PR W.J.WARD, after W.Fowler, hl, mezz, pub 1839, BM, NPG.

H.T.RYALL, after H.W.Pickersgill, tql, mixed, pub 1840, BM.

CONST, Francis (1751-1839) chairman of the Westminster sessions, writer.
PR C.TURNER, after B.Marshall, wl equestrian, mezz, pub 1806, BM, V & A. C.TURNER, after J.Jackson, hl, mezz, oval, pub 1824, BM.

CONSTABLE, Archibald (1774-1827) publisher, founder of the *Edinburgh Review*.
P ANDREW GEDDES, wl seated, SNPG 609.
PR G.T.PAYNE, after H.Raeburn, tql, mezz, BM.
C After J.KAY, wl, etch, 1823, NPG.

CONSTABLE, John (1776-1837) painter.
P DANIEL GARDNER, 1796, hl profile, V & A. R.R.REINAGLE, c1799, hl seated, NPG 1786. C.R.LESLIE, c1830, hl, Royal Academy, London.
D JOHN HARDEN, 1806, tql seated at easel, BM. Self-portrait, hl, pencil and w/c, NPG 901. DANIEL MACLISE, hl seated, profile, pencil, NPG 1458.
G Two drgs by JOHN HARDEN: Constable drawing a group of friends at Brathay Hall, and Constable with his friends at Brathay Hall, BM.
SC UNKNOWN, bronze cast of death mask by Samuel Joseph, NPG 4063.
PR R.J.LANE, after C.R.Leslie, hs, lith, for Leslie's, *Memoirs of the Life of John Constable Esq RA*, composed chiefly of his letters, 1843, BM, NPG.

CONWAY, Francis Charles Seymour, see 3rd Marquess of Hertford.

CONWAY, Lord Francis Seymour, see 1st Marquess of Hertford.

CONWAY, Henry Seymour (1721-1795) field-marshal.
P THOMAS GAINSBOROUGH, RA 1780, wl, Inveraray Castle, Strathclyde region, Scotland.
M RICHARD COSWAY, V & A.
SC ISAAC GOSSETT, 1760, wax medallion, NPG 1757.
PR W.ANGUS, after T.Stothard, hs, line, circular frame, for *European Mag*, 1782, BM, NPG. HEATH, hs, line and stipple, oval, NPG. W.GREATBATCH, after J.G.Eckardt, hs, stipple and line, oval, NPG. C.TOMKINS, after J.Reynolds, hl, mezz, oval, BM, NPG.

CONWAY, William Augustus (1789-1828) actor.
P G.H.HARLOW, hs, oval, Royal Shakespeare Theatre Museum, Stratford-on-Avon.
D SAMUEL DE WILDE, 1810, wl as Richmond in *Richard III*, Garrick Club, London.
G G.H.HARLOW, 'Court for the Trial of Queen Catherine', oil, RA 1817, Royal Shakespeare Theatre Museum.
PR W.SAY, after G.H.Harlow, hl, mezz, pub 1815, BM, NPG.

CONYBEARE, John Josias (1779-1824) geologist.
D THOMAS UWINS, wl, w/c and pencil, BM.

CONYBEARE, William Daniel (1787-1857) geologist.
PR UNKNOWN, hs, for *Illust London News*, 1857, NPG.

COOK, James (1728-1779) circumnavigator.
P NATHANIEL DANCE, 1776, tql seated with chart, NMM, Greenwich. JOHN WEBBER, 1782, tql, Trinity House, Hull; related hl, NPG 26.
G JOHAN ZOFFANY, 'The Death of Captain James Cook at Hawaii, 14 February 1779', oil, c1795, NMM.
SC JOHN FLAXMAN, jun, 1784, Wedgwood medallion, Castle Museum and Art Gallery, Nottingham. LUCIEN LE VIEUX, 1790, marble bust, NPG 984. THOMAS WOOLNER, c1879, statue, Sydney, Australia.

PR J.BASIRE, after W.Hodges, hs, line, oval, for his *Voyages*, 1777, BM, NPG. A.BIRRELL, after D.Dodd, wl in West Indian landscape, line, pub 1785, BM, NPG.

COOK, William (d1824) author.
PR UNKNOWN, after A.Pope, hs, stipple, oval, for *Monthly Mirror*, 1807, BM.

COOKE, Benjamin (1734-1793) musician.
PR W.SKELTON, hs profile, oval, NPG.

COOKE, Edward (1755-1820) under-secretary of state.
PR W.WARD, after W.Cuming, tql seated, mezz, pub 1799, BM. J.BURNET, after G.Sanders, hl, line, pub 1821, BM, NPG.

COOKE, Sir George (1768-1837) lieutenant-general.
P J.W.PIENEMAN, hs, Wellington Museum, Apsley House, London.

COOKE, George Frederick (1756-1811) actor.
P Several paintings at the Garrick Club, London: JAMES GREEN, RA 1801, tql as Iago; C.R.LESLIE, wl as Richard III; THOMAS PHILLIPS, hl as Shylock in *The Merchant of Venice*; HENRY SINGLETON, hs as Kitely in *Every Man in his Humour*; GILBERT STUART, hs profile; THOMAS SULLY, hs; UNKNOWN, hs. THOMAS SULLY, wl as Richard III, Pennsylvania Academy of Fine Arts, Philadelphia, USA.
D UNKNOWN, hs, pencil, oval, Garrick Club.
M OZIAS HUMPHRY, hs, Royal Coll.
PR Various theatrical prints, BM, NPG.

COOKE, Henry (1788-1868) Irish presbyterian leader.
P UNKNOWN, Ulster Museum, Belfast.
PR C.TURNER, after J.Syme, hl when young, mezz, BM. McFARLANE and ERSKINE, after a photograph, tql seated, lith, pub 1873, BM. W.HOLL, after a photograph, hl seated, stipple and line, NPG.

COOKE, John (1765-1805) naval officer.
P L.F.ABBOTT, hl, NMM, Greenwich. UNKNOWN, tql, NMM.

COOKE, Thomas (1722-1783) eccentric divine.
PR UNKNOWN, after Walker, tql profile, line, BM.

COOKE, Thomas Potter (1786-1864) actor.
P UNKNOWN, after a photograph by Mayall of c1853, wl, NMM, Greenwich. GEORGE CLINT, wl as Zenocles in *Ali Pacha*, Garrick Club, London.
PR S.W.REYNOLDS, sen, after S.W.Reynolds, jun, hl, mezz, pub 1825, BM, NPG. C.BAUGNIET, tql, lith, BM, NPG. Several theatrical prints, BM, NPG.

COOKE, Thomas Simpson (1782-1848) actor, singer and composer.
PR T.LUPTON, after G.Clint, hl, mezz, pub 1839, BM, NPG. Several theatrical prints, NPG.

COOKE, William (1711-1797) divine.
PR S.HARDING, tql seated, stipple, pub 1798, BM, NPG.

COOKWORTHY, William (1705-1780) porcelain-maker.
P JOHN OPIE, hs, City Art Gallery, Plymouth.
D Attrib JOHN OPIE, wl, pencil, City Art Gallery, Plymouth.

COOPER, Abraham (1787-1868) painter.
D C.H.LEAR, c1845, hs, pencil, NPG 1456 (2). C.W.COPE, 1862 and 1864, sketching, NPG 3182 (1, 19). JOHN JACKSON, pencil and w/c, Newport Museum and Art Gallery, South Wales.
PR J.H.ROBINSON, after W.Mulready, hs profile, etch, for Pye's *Patronage of British Art*, 1845, BM, NPG. C.E.WAGSTAFF, after A.D.Cooper, hl seated with easel, stipple, BM, NPG. J.THOMSON, after J.Jackson, hl, stipple, BM, NPG.
PH ELLIOTT and FRY, hs, carte, NPG Album of Artists vol III.

COOPER, Sir Astley Paston, Bart (1768-1841) surgeon.
P SIR THOMAS LAWRENCE, RA 1828, tql, Royal College of Surgeons, London.
D SIR FRANCIS CHANTREY, c1825, hs and hs profile, pencil, NPG 316a (20, 21).
SC JOSEPH TOWNE, 1841, bust, Guy's Hospital, London. E.H.BAILY, c1842, statue, St Paul's Cathedral, London. HENRY WEEKES, c1844, bust, Royal College of Surgeons.
PR H.MEYER, after F.Simonau, hl, stipple, 1819, NPG. J.S.AGAR, after A.Wivell, hl seated, stipple, pub 1825, BM, NPG. ROBINSON, after Penny, hs, stipple, pub 1829, NPG.

COOPER, Sir Grey (d1801) politician.
C J.SAYERS, 'The Comet', etch and mezz, pub 1789, NPG.

COOPER, John (1790-1870) actor.
PR Several theatrical prints, BM, NPG.

COOPER, Richard (d1764) engraver.
P JEREMIAH DAVISON, hs, SNPG 728.
PR R.COOPER, after W.Robinson, hl, line, oval, BM, NPG. UNKNOWN, after G.Schroider, hl, mezz, oval, BM.

COOPER, Richard (c1740-c1814) painter and engraver.
D JOHN HOPPNER, chalk, SNPG 1869.

COOPER, Samuel (1781-1848) surgical writer.
P ANDREW MORTON, RA 1838, tql seated, Royal College of Surgeons, London.
SC TIMOTHY BUTLER, 1851, marble bust, Royal College of Surgeons.

COOTE, Sir Eyre (1726-1783) general, commander-in-chief in Bengal.
P THOMAS HICKEY, wl, Government House, Madras. Attrib H.R.MORLAND, hl, NPG 124. J.T.SETON, wl, India Office Library and Records, London. UNKNOWN, tql, Oriental Club, London.
SC After JOSEPH NOLLEKENS, Wedgwood medallion, BM.

COOTE, Sir Eyre (1762-1823) general.
P SIR MARTIN ARCHER SHEE, wl, National Army Museum, London.
PR A.CARDON, after W.Lodder, hs in uniform, stipple, oval, pub 1805, BM, NPG.

COPE, Richard (1776-1856) independent minister.
PR UNKNOWN, hl, stipple, oval, for *Evangelical Mag*, 1815, BM, NPG. R.WOODMAN, hl, stipple, pub 1826, NPG.

COPELAND, Thomas (1781-1855) surgeon.
PR W.DRUMMOND, after T.Stewardson, hl, lith, No 26 of *Athenaeum Portraits*, 1836, BM. W. and F.HOLL, hl seated, stipple, for Pettigrew's *Medical Portrait Gallery*, 1840, BM, NPG.

COPELAND, William Taylor (1797-1868) porcelain manufacturer of Stoke-on-Trent.
P W.M.TWEEDIE, RA 1866, wl, Bridewell Royal Hospital, Surrey.

COPLAND, James (1791-1870) physician.
P HENRY ROOM, hl, Royal College of Physicians, London.

COPLESTON, Edward (1776-1849) bishop of Llandaff.
P THOMAS PHILLIPS, RA 1820, tql seated, Oriel College, Oxford. Attrib SIR MARTIN ARCHER SHEE, tql seated, Corpus Christi College, Oxford.
D JOHN DOWNMAN, 1810, hs, pencil and w/c, Ashmolean Museum, Oxford.
SC WILLIAM BEHNES, 1843, marble bust, Oriel College.

COPLEY, John Singleton (1737-1815) painter.
P Self-portrait, c1780-84, hs, Smithsonian Institution,

Washington DC, USA. GILBERT STUART, *c*1784, hs, NPG 2143.

D Self-portrait, 1769, hs, pastel, Henry Francis du Pont Winterthur Museum, Delaware, USA.

G Self-portrait, wl with his family, RA 1777, National Gallery of Art, Washington DC. HENRY SINGLETON, 'Royal Academicians, 1793', oil, Royal Academy, London.

PR W.DANIELL, after G.Dance, hl profile, soft-ground etch, BM, NPG.

COPLEY, John Singleton (1772-1863), see 1st Baron Lyndhurst.

CORBET, William (1779-1842) Irish rebel.

G UNKNOWN, 'The United Irish Patriots of 1798', coloured lith, NPG.

PR UNKNOWN, hl, mezz, NPG.

CORBOULD, Henry (1787-1844) painter.

SC CHARLES S.KELSEY, medallion on monument, The Assumption and St Nicholas Church, Etchingham, Sussex.

CORBOULD, Richard (1757-1831) painter.

D HENRY EDRIDGE, tql, pencil and ink, BM.

CORDINER, James (1775-1836) traveller.

PR W.BOND, after A.Birnie, hs, stipple, pub 1819, NPG.

COREHOUSE, George Cranstoun, Lord (d1850) Scottish judge.

D B.W.CROMBIE, hs profile, pencil, SNPG 100.

C J.KAY, 1810, hs profile, etch, reprinted in *Kay's Portraits*, vol II, NPG.

CORK and ORRERY, John Boyle, 5th Earl of (1706/7-1762) politician and man of letters.

P Attrib ISAAC SEEMAN, hl, NPG 4621.

PR J.FABER, jun, 1741, tql, mezz, Ashmolean Museum, Oxford.

CORK and ORRERY, Mary Monckton, Countess of (1746-1840) 'blue stocking'.

P SIR JOSHUA REYNOLDS, 1777-78, wl, with dog, TATE 4694.

CORNBURY, Henry Hyde, Viscount and Baron Hyde (1710-1753) statesman.

P GEORGE KNAPTON, 1741, hl with goblet, Society of Dilettanti, Brooks's Club, London.

CORNEWALL, Folliott Herbert Walker (1754-1831) bishop of Worcester.

P UNKNOWN, hl, The Deanery, Canterbury. UNKNOWN, *c*1830, hs in robes, Powis Castle (NT), Powys.

D SIR GEORGE HAYTER, hl sketch, NPG 1695n.

G SIR GEORGE HAYTER, 'The Trial of Queen Caroline, 1820', oil, NPG 999.

CORNWALL, Barry, see Bryan Waller PROCTOR.

CORNWALL, Charles Wolfran (1735-1789) politician, speaker of the House of Commons.

P THOMAS GAINSBOROUGH, *c*1785-86, wl in speaker's robes, National Gallery of Victoria, Melbourne.

C J.SAYERS, several etchings, NPG.

CORNWALLIS, Charles Cornwallis, 1st Marquess (1738-1805) general and diplomat.

P UNKNOWN, 1742, wl seated as a child with his brother Henry and a dog, DoE (Audley End, Essex). THOMAS GAINSBOROUGH, 1783, hl, NPG 281. ROBERT HOME, 1792, wl, Government House, Madras. A.W.DEVIS, RA 1796, wl, East India Company, London. SIR WILLIAM BEECHEY, RA 1799, wl in Garter robes, Audley End. JOHN SINGLETON COPLEY, tql with Garter ribbon and star, The Guildhall, London. HENRY WALTON, hs, on copper, Moyses Hall Museum, Bury St Edmunds.

D JOHN SMART, 1792, hs, pencil and wash, NPG 4316.

G MATHER BROWN, receiving the sons of Tipoo Sahib as hostages, Oriental Club, London.

SC JOHN BACON, sen, 1793, statue, India Office Library and Records, London. J.C.ROSSI, statue on monument, St Paul's Cathedral, London.

C JAMES GILLRAY, 'The Bengal Levée', 1792, etch, India Office Library and Records.

CORNWALLIS, Charles Cornwallis, 2nd Marquess (1774-1823) sportsman.

P GEORGE ROMNEY, 1795, hl, a leaving portrait, Eton College, Berks.

G SIR GEORGE HAYTER, 'The Trial of Queen Caroline, 1820', oil, NPG 999.

PR C.TURNER, hl in uniform, mezz, BM.

CORNWALLIS, Frederick (1713-1783) archbishop of Canterbury.

P UNKNOWN, 1750, hl, DoE (Audley End, Essex). NATHANIEL DANCE, 1768, tql, Lambeth Palace, London.

PR UNKNOWN, hs, line, circular frame, BM, NPG.

CORNWALLIS, James Cornwallis, 4th Earl of (1742-1824) bishop of Lichfield and Coventry.

P Attrib GEORGE ROMNEY, tql, The Deanery, Canterbury.

PR W.WARD, after H.W.Pickersgill, tql, mezz, BM, NPG. J.GOLDAR, hs, line, circular frame, BM, for *The New Christian's Magazine*, 1783, NPG.

CORNWALLIS, Sir William (1744-1819) admiral.

P W.N.SKINNER, after D.Gardner, wl, NMM, Greenwich.

PR F.HAWARD, after D.Gardner, hl, stipple, oval, pub 1784, BM. C.WARREN, after T.Uwins, hs, line, octagonal frame, pub 1805, BM. ROBERTS, after J.Barry, hs in uniform, stipple, oval, BM, NPG.

CORRIE, Daniel (1777-1837) bishop of Madras.

SC HENRY WEEKES, 1842, statue in group, Madras Cathedral.

PR UNKNOWN, hs profile, line, pub 1816, NPG. UNKNOWN, hl, stipple, NPG. UNKNOWN, hs, lith, NPG.

CORRIE, George Elwes (1793-1885) divine.

P UNKNOWN, hs, St Catherine's College, Cambridge.

CORRY, Isaac (1755-1813) Irish politician.

G FRANCIS WHEATLEY, 'The Irish House of Commons, 1780', oil, Leeds City Art Galleries, Lotherton Hall, W.Yorks.

CORT, Henry (1740-1800) ironmaster, inventor of the 'pudding' process.

SC UNKNOWN, medallion, Science Museum, London.

PR UNKNOWN, hl profile, lith, BM.

COSBY, Philips (1727?-1808) admiral.

PR RIDLEY, after Robinson, hs, stipple, oval, pub 1805, NPG.

COSTARD, George (1710-1782) astronomical writer.

PR J.BASIRE, after J.C.Barnes, hl seated, with compasses, line, oval, for *Gent Mag*, BM, NPG.

COSWAY, Maria Cecilia Louisa (1759-1838) miniature painter.

P Self-portrait, hs, Leeds City Art Galleries, Temple Newsam House, W.Yorks. RICHARD COSWAY, *c*1789, wl, Cincinnati Art Museum, USA.

D RICHARD COSWAY, tql sketch, Yale University Library, New Haven, USA.

PR R.COSWAY, wl with her husband in garden, etch, 1784, BM, NPG. F.BARTOLOZZI, after R.Cosway, wl seated, stipple, pub 1785, BM. V.GREEN, after M.Cosway, tql seated, mezz, pub 1787, BM, NPG. W.BIRCH, after R.Cosway and W.Hodges, wl seated, stipple, pub 1789, BM, NPG. R.THEW, after R.Cosway, wl with Mr Cosway in fancy dress, entitled 'Abelard and Eloisa', stipple, pub 1789, BM. L.SCHIAVONETTI, after R.Cosway, hl, stipple, pub 1791, BM, NPG.

COSWAY, Richard (1740-1821) miniature painter.
P Self-portrait, c1770, tql in Vandyck dress, Attingham Park (NT), Salop.
D GEORGE DANCE, 1793, hs profile, pencil and chalk, Royal Academy, London.
M Self-portrait, hl profile, NPG 304. Self-portrait, hl profile, NPG 1678.
G JOHAN ZOFFANY, 'Royal Academicians, 1772', oil, Royal Coll. HENRY SINGLETON, 'Royal Academicians, 1793', oil, Royal Academy.
SC RICHARD WESTMACOTT, medallion on monument, St Mary's Church, Marylebone. UNKNOWN, bronze medallion, V & A.
PR R.COSWAY, wl seated with his wife, in garden, etch, 1784, BM, NPG. M.BOVA, after R.Cosway, wl seated, stipple, pub 1786, BM, NPG. J.CLARKE, after R.Cosway, hl profile in fancy dress, stipple, pub 1788, BM, NPG. R.THEW, after R.Cosway, wl in fancy dress, entitled 'Abelard and Eloisa', stipple, pub 1789, BM.

COTES, Francis (1726?-1770) portrait painter.
D Attrib PAUL SANDBY, 1755, called Cotes, wl seated, pencil and chalk, Castle Museum and Art Gallery, Nottingham.
PR D.P.PARISET, after P.Falconet, hs profile, stipple, BM, NPG.

COTES, Samuel (1734-1818) miniature-painter.
D PAUL SANDBY, wl seated, w/c Royal Coll.

COTMAN, John Sell (1782-1842) landscape painter.
P ALFRED CLINT, c1833, tql seated, Thetford Town Hall.
D CORNELIUS VARLEY, c1810, hs profile, Graves Art Gallery, Sheffield. J.P.DAVIS, 1818, tql seated, pencil, V & A. H.B.LOVE, 1830, hl seated, pencil, NPG 1372. H.B.LOVE, 1830, hl seated, pencil and w/c, BM. J.J.COTMAN, 1841, hs, chalk, NPG 3013.

COTTENHAM, Sir Charles Christopher Pepys, 1st Earl of (1781-1851) lord chancellor.
P CHARLES ROBERT LESLIE, RA 1840, wl, NPG 5149.
D S.F.DIEZ, tql seated, Staatliche Kupferstichkabinett, Berlin.
G SIR GEORGE HAYTER, 'The House of Commons, 1833', oil, NPG 54.
SC BARON C.MAROCHETTI, 1852, bust, Palace of Westminster, London.
PR MACLURE, MACDONALD and MACGREGOR, tql in robes, NPG. R.STOTHARD, tql seated in robes, with purse, lith, BM.
C JOHN DOYLE, 'The flitch of Bacon', pen and pencil, BM.

COTTER, Patrick (1761?-1806) Irish giant.
G UNKNOWN, 'Five Remarkable Characters', one of a set, etch, BM. UNKNOWN, '30 Extraordinary Characters, etc', line, BM.
PR T.ROWLANDSON, wl surrounded by crowd, 'The surprizing Irish Giant of St James's Street', etch, pub 1785, BM. UNKNOWN, wl, etch, pub 1804, BM. A. VAN ASSEN, after J.Parry, wl profile, etch, for Kirby's *Wonderful Museum*, 1804, BM, NPG.
C J.KAY, 1803, wl, etch, NPG.

COTTESLOE, Thomas Francis Fremantle, 1st Baron (1798-1890) statesman.
G SIR GEORGE HAYTER, 'The House of Commons, 1833', oil, NPG 54.
PR W.HOLL, after G.Richmond, hs, stipple, for 'Grillion's Club', series, BM, NPG.
C SIR LESLIE WARD, 'Spy', 1876, wl, w/c, for *Vanity Fair*, NPG 3190.

COTTLE, Amos Simon (1766-1800) translator and poet.
P WILLIAM PALMER, 1787, hs, NPG 2470.

COTTON, Sir Charles, Bart (1753-1812) admiral.
G BARTOLOZZI, LANDSEER, RYDER and STOW, after R.Smirke, 'Naval Victories', 'Commemoration of the victory of June 1st 1794', line, pub 1803, BM, NPG.
PR H.MEYER, after J.Ramsay, hl, mezz, pub 1812, BM, NPG. PAGE, after a miniature, hs, stipple, oval, pub 1812, NPG.

COTTON, Joseph (1745-1825) deputy-master of the Trinity House.
PR W.WARD, after T.Stewardson, tql seated, mezz, pub 1808, BM. C.TURNER, after T.Lawrence, tql with document, mezz, pub 1818, BM, NPG.

COTTON, Nathaniel (1705-1788) physician and poet.
PR W.H.WORTHINGTON, after J.Thurston, hl profile, line, for *Effigies Poeticae*, 1820, BM.

COTTON, Richard Lynch (1794-1880) provost of Worcester College, Oxford.
P SIR WILLIAM BOXALL, tql seated, Worcester College, Oxford.

COTTON, Sir Stapleton, see Viscount Combermere.

COTTON, Sir Sydney John (1792-1874) lieutenant-general.
PR UNKNOWN, hs, woodcut, for *Illust London News*, 1858, NPG.

COTTON, William (1786-1866) philanthropist and governor of the Bank of England.
SC UNKNOWN(?), perhaps the bust by Matthew Noble, RA 1856, Bank of England, London.
PR UNKNOWN, hs, woodcut, for *Illust London News*, 1844-45, NPG.

COTTON, Sir Willoughby (1783-1860) general.
D JAMES ATKINSON, c1838, hs profile, w/c, NPG 824. COUNT A.D'ORSAY, 1842, hl profile, pencil and chalk, NPG 4026 (15).

COULSON, Walter (1794?-1860) journalist and lawyer.
PR R.J.LANE, after Fanny Corbaux, 1841, hl, lith, pub 1848, NPG.

COURTENAY, John (1741-1816) whig politician.
C J.SAYERS, 'The Biographers', etch, pub 1786, NPG. J.SAYERS, 'The Managers in Distress', etch, pub 1788, NPG. J.GILLRAY, 'Juge du Tribunal Correctionnel', etch, pub 1798, NPG. J.SAYERS, hs, entitled, 'Camille Desmoulins anglice Joe Miller', etch, BM, NPG. J.SAYERS, 'The Impeachment', etch, NPG.

COURTENAY, Thomas Peregrine (1782-1841) politician.
PR W.DRUMMOND, after E.U.Eddis, hs, lith, *Athenaeum Portraits* No 30, 1836, BM, NPG.

COURTENAY, Sir William (1799-1838), see John Nichols TOM.

COUTTS, Thomas (1735-1822) banker.
SC SIR FRANCIS CHANTREY, plaster seated statue, Ashmolean Museum, Oxford.
PR R.W.SIEVIER, after W.Beechey, hl, stipple, pub 1822, BM, NPG.
C GEORGE CRUIKSHANK, 'Management – or – Butts and Hogsheads', coloured engr, pub 1812, BM.

COVENTRY, Andrew (1764-1832) agriculturist.
SC JAMES TASSIE, 1794, paste medallion, SNPG 431.

COVENTRY, Maria Gunning, Countess of (1733-1760) famous beauty.
P FRANCIS COTES, 1751, hl, NGI 417. GAVIN HAMILTON, hs, Inveraray Castle, Strathclyde region, Scotland. GAVIN HAMILTON, tql as Venus, with a child, Woburn Abbey, Beds. JOSEPH HIGHMORE, tql, Waddesdon Manor (NT), Bucks.
D J.E.LIOTARD, c1749, wl in Turkish dress, Rijksmuseum, Amsterdam. FRANCIS COTES, 1751, hl, pastel, Inveraray Castle. H.D.HAMILTON, tql, pastel, oval, Courtauld Institute Galleries, London. CATHERINE READ, hs, pastel, oval, Inveraray Castle.
M PENELOPE COTES, 1757, hs, oval, Wallace Collection, London.

G R.HOUSTON, 'The Three Gunning Sisters', mezz, oval, the portrait of Maria is after Liotard, pub 1756, BM.

COWLEY, Hannah, née Parkhouse (1743–1809) dramatist.
PR J.HEATH, after R.Cosway, sitting writing, inspired by the muse of comedy, line, pub 1783, BM, NPG. J.FITTLER, after R.Cosway, tql seated, line and stipple, pub 1785, BM. T.HOLLOWAY, hl, line, for *European Mag*, 1789, BM, NPG. G.MURRAY, after R.Cosway, hl, line, oval, for *Biographical Mag*, BM.

COWLEY, Henry Wellesley, 1st Baron (1773–1847) diplomatist.
P JOHN HOPPNER, wl, Stratfield Saye, Hants.
D JOHN DOWNMAN, 1783, hs, w/c, Badminton, Avon.
M UNKNOWN, hs, Stratfield Saye, Hants.

COWPER, Henry (1758–1840) lawyer.
P JOHN JACKSON, RA 1829, hl, Palace of Westminster, London.
D SIR FRANCIS CHANTREY, 1823–27, hs and hs profile, pencil, NPG 316a (23).
G SIR GEORGE HAYTER, 'The Trial of Queen Caroline, 1820', oil, NPG 999.
SC SIR FRANCIS CHANTREY, 1828, marble bust, V & A.

COWPER, William (1731–1800) poet.
P L.F.ABBOTT, 1792, tql seated, NPG 2783. WILLIAM BLAKE, c1800, head, Manchester City Art Gallery. JOHN JACKSON, hl, Northampton Museum and Art Gallery.
D GEORGE ROMNEY, 1792, hs, pastel, NPG 1423. SIR THOMAS LAWRENCE, 1793, hs, pencil, Cowper Museum, Olney, Bucks. SIR THOMAS LAWRENCE, 1793, head, profile, pencil, Yale University Library, New Haven, USA. W.HARVEY, after L.F.Abbott, hl seated, pencil, NPG 806.

COX, David (1783–1859) landscape painter.
P WILLIAM RADCLYFFE, 1830, hl seated, NPG 1403. SIR JOHN WATSON-GORDON, 1855, tql seated, City Museum and Art Gallery, Birmingham. SIR WILLIAM BOXALL, 1856, hs, NPG 1986.
D UNKNOWN, 1855, hs, pencil, NPG 1074.
SC PETER HOLLINS, 1860, bust, City Museum and Art Gallery, Birmingham. G.MORGAN, bronze medallion, NPG, for the Art Union.
PH JOHN WATKINS, head, carte, NPG Album of Artists vol. I.

COX, Francis Augustus (1783–1853) baptist preacher.
G B.R.HAYDON, 'The Anti-Slavery Society Convention, 1840', oil, NPG 599.
PR C.PENNY, hs, stipple, pub 1820, NPG. C.BAUGNIET, tql, lith, BM, NPG. H.COOK, after Cockin, hl seated, stipple, NPG.

COXE, Peter (d1844) poet.
PR E.SCRIVEN, after A.Robertson, hl seated, stipple, for his *Social Day*, 1822, BM, NPG.

COXE, William (1747–1828) historian.
P SIR WILLIAM BEECHEY, 1805, hs profile, King's College, Cambridge.
D UNKNOWN, hs, w/c, NPG 3911.
PR W.PETHER, after C.Grignion of c1784–86, tql seated, mezz, BM, NPG.

CRABBE, George (1754–1832) poet.
P H.W.PICKERSGILL, c1818–19, hl seated, NPG 1495.
D SIR FRANCIS CHANTREY, 1821, head, pencil, NPG 316a(24).
M ROLINDA SHARPLES, Bristol City Art Gallery.
SC THOMAS THURLOW, 1847, bust on monument, St Peter and St Paul Church, Aldeburgh, Suffolk.
PR W.HOLL, after T.Phillips, tql seated, stipple, for his *Works*, 1847, BM, NPG. R.COOPER, hs, stipple, BM, NPG.

CRACHERODE, Clayton Mordaunt (1730–1799) book and print collector.
PR W.H.WORTHINGTON, after H.Edridge, tql seated, line, for Dibdin's *Bibliographical Decameron*, 1817, BM, NPG.

CRADOCK, Sir John Francis, see 1st Baron Howden.

CRADOCK, Joseph (1742–1826) author.
PR P.AUDINET, after a silhouette by Miers and Field, hs profile, line, pub 1827, BM, NPG. R.DYER, after a miniature by Hone of 1764, hs, stipple, pub 1828, NPG.

CRAIG, James (1740–1795) architect.
P DAVID ALLAN, wl, SNPG 729.

CRAIG, Sir James Gibson (1765–1850) politician.
D B.W.CROMBIE, 3 drgs, SNPG 2306.
SC THOMAS CAMPBELL, plaster bust, SNPG 351.

CRAIG, Sir James Henry (1748–1812) general.
D Attrib GERRITT SCHIPPER, 1807, hs profile, pastel, oval, McCord Museum, McGill University, Montreal, Canada.

CRAIG, Robert (1730–1823) advocate and political writer.
P ANDREAS VAN DER MIJN, 1765, SNPG 326.
C J.KAY, 1815, wl seated, etch, NPG.

CRAIG, William Craig, Lord (1745–1813) Scottish judge.
P SIR HENRY RAEBURN, tql seated, Faculty of Advocates, Parliament Hall, Edinburgh.
D ARCHIBALD SKIRVING, pastel, SNPG L279.
PR G.DAWE, after A.Skirving, tql, mezz, BM.
C J.KAY, 1799, hl seated in robes, etch, oval, BM, NPG.

CRAIG, Sir William Gibson (1797–1878) lord clerk register.
P SIR JOHN WATSON-GORDON, wl, SNPG 711.

CRAIG, William Marshall (fl 1788–1828) painter.
D Self-portrait, w/c, Castle Art Gallery, Nottingham.

CRAMER, Franz (1772–1848) violinist.
D Attrib JAMES STEPHANOFF, wl, one of a series illustrating the Coronation of George IV, V & A.
PR B.P.GIBBON, after W.Watts, tql with sheet of music, line, pub 1826, BM, NPG. I.W.SLATER, after J.Slater, hs, lith, pub 1832, BM. C.MOITTE, after Minasi, hs, lith, BM.

CRAMER, Johann Baptist (1771–1858) pianist and composer.
M G.L.SAUNDERS, 1827, hl seated, NPG 5190.
G G.H.HARLOW, 'Court for the Trial of Queen Catherine', oil, 1817, Royal Shakespeare Memorial Theatre Museum, Stratford on Avon.
PR E.SCRIVEN, after J.Pocock, hl, stipple, pub 1819, BM. J.THOMSON, after D.Barber, hl, stipple, pub 1826, BM. W.SHARP, hl, lith, pub 1830, BM. B.HOLL, after A.Wivell, hl, stipple, pub 1831, BM, NPG.

CRAMER, John Antony (1793–1848) historian.
D WILLIAM BROCKEDON, 1834, hs, chalk, NPG 2515(72).

CRAMER, Wilhelm (1745?–1799) violinist.
PR T.HARDY, hl, stipple, pub 1794, BM, NPG. T.BRAGG, after G.Place, hs, line, oval, pub 1803, BM.

CRAMPTON, Sir Philip, Bart (1777–1858) surgeon.
P S.CATTERSON SMITH, hl, NGI 309.
D CHARLES GREY, wl seated, pen, NGI 2594.
M CHARLES ROBERTSON, NGI 252b.
SC J.R.KIRK, c1859, marble bust, Royal College of Surgeons, Dublin. J.R.KIRK, 1862, bust on monument, Dublin.
PR A.D'ORSAY, hl, profile, lith, BM.

CRANCH, John (1751–1821) painter.
PR J.T.SMITH, hl, line and stipple, pub 1795, NPG.

CRANSTOUN, George, see Lord Corehouse.

CRANSTOUN, Helen d'Arcy (1765-1838) song-writer.
D WILLIAM NICHOLSON, hs, w/c and pencil, NGS.

CRANSTOUN, William Henry (1707-1752) lover of Mary Blandy.
PR B.COLE, hl, line, BM, NPG.

CRANWORTH, Robert Monsey Rolfe, Baron (1790-1868) lord chancellor.
P GEORGE RICHMOND, 1860, tql, NPG 285.
G SIR JOHN GILBERT, 'The Coalition Ministry, 1854', pencil and wash, NPG 1125.
PR G.C.LEIGHTON, after A.Blaikley, wl, woodcut, for *Illust London News*, 1857, NPG. W.HOLL, after G.Richmond, hs stipple, for 'Grillion's Club' series BM, NPG. UNKNOWN, after a photograph by Mayall, hs, woodcut, for Cassell's *Illust Family Paper*, 1858, NPG.
PH UNKNOWN, hl seated, carte, NPG 'Twist Album' 1892.

CRAVEN, Elizabeth, Countess of, see Margravine of ANSPACH.

CRAVEN, Keppel Richard (1779-1851) traveller.
D COUNT A.D'ORSAY, 1832, hl profile, pencil and chalk, NPG 4026 (18).
PR R.PAGE, hl, stipple, pub 1821, BM, NPG.

CRAVEN, Louisa, née Brunton, Countess of (1785?-1860) actress.
PR Several theatrical prints, BM, NPG.

CRAWFORD, Mrs Ann, see Mrs Spranger BARRY.

CRAWFORD, John Lindsay, 20th Earl of (1702-1749) military commander.
PR T.WORLIDGE, hl in armour and fur mantle, etch, oval, for his *Life*, by Rolt, 1753, BM, NPG.

CRAWFORD, William Sharman (1781-1861) politician.
PR T.LUPTON, after J.P.Knight, hl, mezz, pub 1844, NPG.

CRAWFURD, John (1783-1868) orientalist.
P UNKNOWN, *c*1858, tql, National Museum, Singapore.

CREECH, William (1745-1815) publisher and lord provost of Edinburgh.
P SIR HENRY RAEBURN, SNPG 1041.

CREGAN, Martin (1788-1870) painter.
P Self-portrait, 1820, head, Royal Hibernian Academy, Dublin.
D SIR GEORGE HAYTER, hs, w/c, NGI 2145.

CREWDSON, Isaac (1780-1844) author.
G B.R.HAYDON, 'The Anti-Slavery Society Convention, 1840', oil, NPG 599.
PR F.C.LEWIS, after B.R.Faulkner of 1840, tql, mezz, pub 1843, NPG.

CREWE, Frances Anne, née Greville, Lady (*d*1818) leader of fashion and friend of Fox, Burke and Sheridan.
PR J.MCARDELL, after J.Reynolds, wl as Hebe, with her brother as Cupid, mezz, pub 1762, BM, NPG. J.MARCHI, after J.Reynolds, seated by monument, with Mrs Bouverie, mezz, pub 1770, BM, NPG. T.WATSON, after J.Reynolds, wl seated at St Geneviève, mezz, pub 1773, BM. T.WATSON, after D.Gardner, tql, stipple, oval, pub 1780, BM, NPG.

CREWE, John Crewe, 1st Baron (1742-1829) politician.
G WILLIAM LANE, 'Whig Statesmen and their Friends, *c*1810', chalk, NPG 2076.
PR W.SAY, after T.Lawrence, hl, mezz, BM, NPG. J.G.WOOD, hl profile, etch, BM.

CRIBB, Thomas (1781-1848) pugilist.
PR J.EMERY, wl, etch, pub 1811, NPG. C.WARREN, after S. de Wilde, hl, line, pub 1812,'BM, NPG. P.ROBERTS, after J.Sharples, hl, stipple, for Egan's *Boxiana*, 1824, BM.
C THOMAS ROWLANDSON, the fight between Cribb and Molineux, w/c, Brodick Castle (NT), Strathclyde region, Scotland.

CRISTALL, Joshua (1767-1847) painter.
P Self-portrait, hs, Royal Society of Painters in Watercolours, London.
D C.H.LEAR, 1846, hs, pencil, NPG 1456(3). JOHN VARLEY, hs, profile, pencil, Victoria Art Gallery, Bath. DANIEL MACLISE, sketch, V & A. JOHN VARLEY, chalk, V & A.
G JOHN PARTRIDGE, 'A Meeting of the Sketching Society', pen, ink and wash, BM.

CROCKFORD, William (1775-1844) proprietor of 'Crockford's' gambling club.
D THOMAS ROWLANDSON, hs, pen and ink, BM.
PR T.JONES, wl profile, etch, pub 1828, BM, NPG. R.S., wl profile, lith, BM, NPG.

CROFT, George (1747-1809) divine.
PR F.EGINGTON, after G.Heape, hl seated, stipple, BM, NPG.

CROFT, Sir Herbert, 5th Bart (1751-1816) author.
P LEMUEL ABBOTT, tql with busts of Johnson and Lowth, Croft Castle (NT), Herefordshire.

CROFT, Sir Richard, 6th Bart (1762-1818) accoucheur.
P J.J.HALLS, *c*1810, Croft Castle (NT), Herefordshire.
PR W.HOLL, after G.Hayter, hl profile, stipple, BM.

CROKER, John Wilson (1780-1857) politician and essayist.
P WILLIAM OWEN, RA 1812, hl, NPG 355. SIR THOMAS LAWRENCE, RA 1825, hl, NGI 300.
D UNKNOWN, *c*1810, hl, NPG.
PR T.BLOOD, after S.Drummond, hl, stipple, for *European Mag*, 1812, BM, NPG. D.MACLISE, wl seated, lith, for *Fraser's Mag*, 1831, BM, NPG. KIRKWOOD, tql seated, etch, NPG.

CROKER, Marianne (*d*1854) artist.
PR UNKNOWN, wl seated on bank, with sketchbook and pencil, lith, BM.

CROKER, Thomas Crofton (1798-1854) Irish antiquary.
P UNKNOWN, wl seated, NPG 4555.
D DANIEL MACLISE, 1827, V & A.
PR D.MACLISE, wl, lith, for *Fraser's Mag*, 1831, BM, NPG; w/c, study, Castle Museum, Norwich, pencil study, V & A.

CROLY, George (1780-1860) author and divine.
D WILLIAM BROCKEDON, 1832, hs, chalk, NPG 2515(31).
SC WILLIAM BEHNES, bust, St Stephen's Church, Walbrook.
PR UNKNOWN, after a daguerreotype by R.Beard, hs, for *Illust London News*, 1854, NPG. W.STEVENSON, after J.Kirkwood, hl, line, pub 1840, NPG. C.BAUGNIET, tql seated, lith, BM.

CROME, John (1768-1821) landscape painter.
P JOHN OPIE, *c*1798–1803, hs, Castle Museum, Norwich. MICHAEL SHARP, *c*1818, hl with palette, Castle Museum. J.T.WOODHOUSE, Castle Museum.
D J.S.COTMAN, 1809, hs, sketch, BM. D.B.MURPHY, 1821, hs, w/c, NPG 2061; related drg, Castle Museum.
SC PELLEGRINO MAZOTTI, *c*1820, plaster bust, NPG 1900.

CROME, John Bernay (1794-1842) landscape painter.
D H.B.LOVE, pastel and w/c, Castle Museum, Norwich.
PR UNKNOWN, hl seated, mixed engr, BM, NPG.

CROMEK, Robert Hartley (1771-1812) engraver.
D THOMAS STOTHARD, head, pencil, BM.

CROMPTON, Samuel (1753-1827) inventor.
G J.F.SKILL, J.GILBERT, W. and E.WALKER, 'Men of Science Living in 1807–08', pencil and wash, NPG 1075.
SC WILLIAM CALDER MARSHALL, c1862, statue, Nelson Square, Bolton, Lancs.
PR S.W.REYNOLDS, after C.Allingham, hl seated, mezz, pub 1828, BM, NPG.

CROSBIE, Andrew (1733-1785) Scottish advocate.
P UNKNOWN, tql, Faculty of Advocates, Parliament Hall, Edinburgh.

CROSBY, Brass (1725-1793) lord mayor of London.
P JOHN SINGLETON COPLEY, wl, Chicago Art Institute, USA.
PR W.DICKINSON, after R.E.Pine, hs, mezz, pub 1771, BM, NPG.

CROSSE, John Green (1790-1850) surgeon.
PR UNKNOWN, after Frederick Sandys, hs, lith, NPG 2083a.

CROSSE, Richard (1742-1810) miniature-painter.
P Self-portrait, 1760s, tql seated at easel, Royal Albert Memorial Museum, Exeter.
M Self-portrait, hs, oval, V & A, engr R.Thew, stipple, pub 1792, BM, NPG.

CROTCH, William (1775-1847) musician.
P SIR WILLIAM BEECHEY, RA 1786, wl, Royal Academy of Music, London.
D JOHN CONSTABLE, 1806, head, sketch, Norfolk and Norwich Record Office. THOMAS UWINS, c1814, wl, w/c and pencil, BM. JOHN LINNELL, c1839, two hs, w/c, NPG 1812 and 1813. W.DE LA MOTTE, wl playing the violin, sketch, Norfolk and Norwich Record Office.
SC J.FAZI, 1853, plaster bust, Christ Church, Oxford.
PR J.SANDERS, wl seated, aged 3, playing the organ, etch, pub 1778, BM. Three anonymous engravings, one after a silhouette by MRS HARRINGTON of 1778, BM.

CROUCH, Anna Maria, née Phillips (1763-1805) singer and actress.
P GEORGE ROMNEY, 1787, tql, Kenwood House, London. SAMUEL DE WILDE, wl as Polly in *The Beggar's Opera*, Garrick Club, London.
D REV THOMAS, wl, pencil, Garrick Club.
PR Various theatrical prints, BM, NPG.

CROWE, Eyre Evans (1799-1868) historian.
D DANIEL MACLISE, pencil and w/c, V & A.

CROWE, William (1745-1829) poet and divine.
P UNKNOWN, hs, New College, Oxford.
C R.DIGHTON, wl profile, coloured etch, pub 1808, BM, NPG.

CROWTHER, Jonathan (1760-1824) methodist preacher.
PR W.HOLL, after J.Jackson, hs, stipple, oval, for *Methodist Mag*, 1813, BM.

CROWTHER, Jonathan (1794-1856) Wesleyan minister.
PR T.A.DEAN, after J.Hill, hl, stipple and line, NPG.

CROZIER, Francis Rawdon Moira (1796?-1848) navy captain and adventurer.
M UNKNOWN, Royal Geographical Society, London.

CRUDEN, Alexander (1701-1770) author of the *Concordance to the Bible*.
PR T.TROTTER, after T.Frye, hs, line, oval, for his *Concordance*, 1785, BM, NPG.

CRUDEN, William (1725-1785) Scottish divine.
PR T.TROTTER, after D.Allen, hl, line, for his *Sermons*, 1786, BM.

CRUIKSHANK, George (1792-1878) caricaturist and illustrator.

P UNKNOWN, 1836, hl, in Vandyck dress, NPG 1385.
D Several self-portraits, BM. UNKNOWN, hs, w/c, NPG 3150. Three self-portrait sketches, in pencil, pen and ink, NPG 4259.
SC WILLIAM BEHNES, RA 1855, marble bust, Kensal Green Cemetery, London; related plaster bust, NPG 1300. JOHN ADAMS, bust, St Paul's Cathedral, London.
PR D.MACLISE, wl seated on barrel, sketching, lith, for *Fraser's Mag*, 1833, BM, NPG; pencil study, NPG 5170. F.W.PAILTHORPE, hs, etch, pub 1883, BM, NPG. C.BAUGNIET, tql seated, lith, BM. C.E.WAGSTAFF, after F.Stone, hs, stipple, BM, NPG.
PH Several photographs: cartes by LONDON STEREOSCOPIC CO., ELLIOTT & FRY and MAYALL, C. & R. LAVIS, cabinet; unknown, wl with his wife, NPG.

CRUIKSHANK, William Cumberland (1745-1800) anatomist.
P GILBERT STUART, hl, Royal College of Surgeons, London.
G THOMAS ROWLANDSON, 'The Dissecting Room', drg, Royal College of Surgeons.
SC After JAMES TASSIE, 1795, plaster medallion, SNPG 377.
PR J.CORNER, hs profile, line, oval, for *European Mag*, 1787, BM. T.DICKINSON, after J.Roberts, hl, stipple, oval, pub 1801, BM.

CRUSIUS, Lewis (1701-1775) biographer.
P UNKNOWN, 1765, hs, Charterhouse Museum, Goldalming, Surrey.

CUBBON, Sir Mark (1784-1861) commissioner of Mysore.
D CAPTAIN MARTIN, c1856-61, hs, w/c and pencil, NPG 4250.
SC UNKNOWN, equestrian statue, Bangalore, India.
PR F.C.LEWIS, sen, after a portrait by his son of 1845, wl, mezz, NPG.

CUBITT, Lewis (b1799) architect.
P SIR WILLIAM BOXALL, 1845, tql seated, NPG 4099.

CUBITT, Thomas (1788-1855) builder.
P H.W.PICKERSGILL, RA 1849, (cut down from wl), London Master-Builders Collection. UNKNOWN, tql seated, NPG 4613.
SC PATRICK MACDOWELL, 1856, marble bust, Denbies, Dorking.
PR G.R.WARD, after H.W.Pickersgill, wl, mezz and line, NPG.

CUBITT, Sir William (1785-1861) civil engineer.
P SIR WILLIAM BOXALL, tql seated, Institute of Civil Engineers, London.
G H.W.PHILIPS, 'The Royal Commissioners for the Great Exhibition of 1851', oil, V & A.
PR T.H.MAGUIRE, tql seated, lith, one of set of *Ipswich Museum Portraits*, 1851, BM, NPG.

CUBITT, William (1791-1863) lord mayor of London.
PR UNKNOWN, after a photograph by Mayall, wl, woodcut, for *Illust London News*, 1860, NPG. T.L.ATKINSON, after Sir F.Grant, tql seated, mezz, NPG.

CUFF, James Dodsley (1780-1853) numismatist.
PR UNKNOWN, 1837, hs profile, lith, NPG.

CUITT, George (1743-1818) painter.
PR G.CUITT, jun, hl, after death, etch, BM.

CUITT, George (1779-1854) etcher.
PR UNKNOWN, hs, etch, BM.

CULBERTSON, Robert (1765-1823) Scottish divine.
C J.KAY, 1811, hs, etch, NPG.

CULLEN, Robert Cullen, Lord (d1810) Scottish judge.
C J.KAY, 1799, hs, etch, oval, NPG.

CULLEN, William (1710-1790) physician.
P DAVID MARTIN, 1776, tql, SNPG L260. WILLIAM COCHRANE, hl, SNPG 1479. J.RUSSELL, tql, Wellcome Institute, London.
D DAVID ALLAN, 1774, hs profile, pencil and w/c, SNPG 98.

SC JAMES TASSIE, 1786, paste medallion, SNPG 268.

C J.KAY, wl profile, etch, BM, NPG.

CULLUM, Sir John, 6th Bart (1733-1785) antiquary and divine of Hardwick, Suffolk.

P ANGELICA KAUFFMAN, *c*1778-80, hl seated, Moyses Hall Museum, Bury St Edmunds, Suffolk, engr J.Basire, line, for Cullum's *Hist of Hawsted and Hardwick*, 1813, BM, NPG.

CULLUM, Sir Thomas Gery, 7th Bart (1741-1831) Bath king-at-arms.

P Attrib GEORGE KEITH RALPH, *c*1800, hl seated, Moyses Hall Museum, Bury St Edmunds, Suffolk.

D MRS DAWSON TURNER, 1822, pen and ink, V & A.

CUMBERLAND, Ernest Augustus, Duke of, and King of Hanover (1771-1851) 5th son of George III.

P JOHAN ZOFFANY, 1772, wl as a baby, Royal Coll. THOMAS GAINSBOROUGH, 1782, hs in Windsor uniform, oval, Royal Coll. SIR WILLIAM BEECHEY, RA 1802, wl in uniform with Garter ribbon and star, Royal Coll. WILLIAM OWEN, RA 1814, wl in Hussar uniform with Garter ribbon and star, on loan to DoE (War Office). GEORGE DAWE, *c*1828, hl, NPG 3309.

D HENRY EDRIDGE, 1802, wl with Garter star, Royal Coll.

M J.G.P.FISCHER, *c*1823, hl, Royal Coll.

G SIR BENJAMIN WEST, wl with Princess Augusta, Princess Elizabeth, Prince Augustus, Prince Adolphus and Princess Mary, oil, 1776, Royal Coll. SIR B.WEST, 'Queen Charlotte with her children', oil, 1779, Royal Coll. SIR B.WEST, 'Queen Charlotte with her children', oil, 1782, Royal Coll. SIR DAVID WILKIE, 'The First Council of Queen Victoria', oil, 1837, Royal Coll.

SC J.C.LOCHÉE, 1787, Wedgwood medallion, Royal Coll. PETER TURNERELLI, 1809, marble bust, Trinity College, Dublin. JOSEPH NOLLEKENS, 1814, marble bust, Royal Coll. WILLIAM BEHNES, 1828, marble bust, Royal Coll. J.P.DANTAN, 1834, caricature plaster statue with the Duke of Gloucester, NPG L167.

C JOHN DOYLE, numerous drgs, BM.

CUMBERLAND, George (1754?-1847) writer on art.

M UNKNOWN, hs, enamel, NPG 5162.

PR T.WOOLNOTH, after N.Branwhite, hl seated, stipple, BM, NPG.

CUMBERLAND and STRATHEARN, Henry Frederick, Duke of (1745-1790) fourth son of Frederick, Prince of Wales.

P SIR JOSHUA REYNOLDS, RA 1773, hs in Garter robes, Royal Coll. THOMAS GAINSBOROUGH, RA 1777, wl in robes of state, with Garter collar, Royal Coll. THOMAS GAINSBOROUGH, 1783, hs in robes, unfinished, Royal Coll.

D GEORGE KNAPTON, *c*1748, hs in white frock, pastel, Royal Coll. J.E.LIOTARD, hs seated at card table, with card house, pastel, Royal Coll.

G BARTHELEMY DU PAN, 'The Children of Frederick, Prince of Wales', oil, 1746, Royal Coll. GEORGE KNAPTON, 'The Children of Frederick, Prince of Wales', Prince Henry Frederick, with Princess Elizabeth and Prince William Henry, pastel, 1848, Royal Coll. GEORGE KNAPTON, 'The Family of Frederick, Prince of Wales', oil, 1751, Royal Coll. THOMAS GAINSBOROUGH, with the Duchess of Cumberland and Lady Elizabeth Luttrell, oil, *c*1785-88, Royal Coll. JOHN SINGLETON COPLEY, 'The Collapse of the Earl of Chatham in the House of Lords, 7 July 1778', oil, TATE 100, on loan to NPG.

CUMBERLAND, Richard (1732-1811) playwright.

P GEORGE ROMNEY, *c*1768, wl seated, NPG 19. GEORGE ROMNEY, hs, oval, Pollock House, Glasgow. Manner of ROMNEY, hs, TATE T63. J.CLOVER, hl seated, Tunbridge Wells Council, engr E.Scriven, stipple, for *Contemporary Portraits*, 1814, BM, NPG.

PR V.GREEN, after G.Romney, tql seated, mezz, pub 1771, BM. UNKNOWN, hs, stipple, oval, for *Register of the Times*, 1795, BM.

W.RIDLEY, after W.Lane, hl, stipple, for *European Mag*, 1809, BM, NPG.

CUMBERLAND, William Augustus, Duke of (1721-1765) third son of George II, general.

P Type attrib KELBERG, *c*1725, as a child, Plas Newydd, Gwynedd. CHARLES JERVAS, *c*1728, wl as a child, wearing robes of state and collar of the Bath, NPG 802. Studio (?) of CHARLES JERVAS, *c*1728, with Caroline of Ansbach, wl in robes of the Bath, Royal Coll. Several equestrian portraits attrib DAVID MORIER, *c*1745-50, sitter in uniform, wearing orders, Royal Coll. Studio of DAVID MORIER, *c*1748-9, wl in uniform, dog lying in foreground, NPG 537. Studio of SIR JOSHUA REYNOLDS, *c*1758-60, hl in uniform, NPG 625. SAWREY, GILPIN and WILLIAM MARLOW, the Duke of Cumberland visiting his stud, Royal Coll.

M Attrib C.F.ZINCKE, hs, NPG L152(23).

SC English school, *c*1760, lead, V & A. JOSEPH NOLLEKENS, 1814, marble bust, Royal Coll. Numerous medals and medallions commemorating battles, SNPG.

C GEORGE TOWNSHEND, three drgs, NPG 4855 (37-39).

CUMING, Hugh (1791-1865) naturalist.

PH ERNEST EDWARDS, wl seated, for ed L.Reeve, *Men of Eminence*, 1864, vol II, NPG.

CUMING, William (1769-1852) portrait-painter.

P Self-portrait, NGI 1725. E.D.LEAHY, Royal Hibernian Academy, Dublin.

CUMMING, Alexander (1733-1814) mathematician.

P SAMUEL DRUMMOND, hs, Clockmakers' Company, London.

CUMMING, James (d1827) official in the India Office.

PR J.THOMSON, hl, stipple, pub 1827, NPG.

CUMMING, Thomas (d1774) the 'fighting Quaker'.

PR J.S.MÜLLER, hs, line, oval, for Smollett's *Hist of England*, 1757, BM, NPG.

CUNNINGHAM, Sir Alexander, see DICK.

CUNNINGHAM, Allan (1784-1842) writer.

P HENRY ROOM, *c*1840, hl profile, NPG 1823. H.W.PICKERSGILL, SNPG 1490.

D WILLIAM BROCKEDON, 1832, hs, chalk, NPG 2515 (39). J.J.PENSTONE, hs, wash, SNPG 659.

SC HENRY WEEKES, 1842, marble bust, SNPG 1494. SIR FRANCIS CHANTREY, plaster bust, SNPG 276.

PR D.MACLISE, wl seated, lith; for *Fraser's Mag*, 1832, BM, NPG, pencil study, V & A. F.W.WILKIN, hs, lith, BM. J.JENKINS, after J.Moore, hl, stipple, for Jerdan's *Nat Portrait Gallery*, 1832, BM, NPG.

CUNNINGHAM, Allan (1791-1839) botanist.

P J.E.H.ROBINSON, Linnean Society, London.

PR A.PICKEN, hl, lith, BM.

CUNNINGHAM, Sir Charles (1755-1834) rear-admiral.

P HENRY WYATT, *c*1833-34, hl with order of a Knight Commander of Hanover, NMM, Greenwich.

CUNNINGHAM, James (1749-1791), see 14th Earl of Glencairn.

CUNNINGHAM, John (1729-1773) actor and poet.

PR P.AUDINET, hs, line, oval, for *Biographical Mag*, 1794, BM, NPG. W.H.WORTHINGTON, after T.Bewick, hl profile, line for *Effigies Poeticae*, 1821, BM, NPG.

CUNNINGTON, William (1754-1810) antiquary, of Heytesbury.

P SAMUEL WOODFORDE, hl seated, Stourhead (NT), Wilts.

PR J.BASIRE, after S.Woodforde, tql seated, with view of

Stonehenge, line, for Hoare's *Wiltshire*, 1810, BM, NPG.

CURETON, Charles Robert (1789-1848) brigadier-general.
P UNKNOWN, *c*1844, hl, Royal United Services Institution, London.

CURRAN, John Philpot (1750-1817) Irish judge.
P H.D.HAMILTON, *c*1790, hs, NGI 592. SIR THOMAS LAWRENCE, RA 1800, hl, NGI 520. UNKNOWN, 1807, hl, NPG 379. Two portraits by unknown artists, NGI 545 and 820.
SC SIR FRANCIS CHANTREY, *c*1812, bust, Ashmolean Museum, Oxford. UNKNOWN, 1817, plaster death mask, NGI 8132.
PR J.HEATH, after J.Comerford, hs, stipple, for Sir J.Barrington's *Historic Memoirs*, 1809, BM, NPG. S.FREEMAN, hl in judicial robes, stipple, for *Contemporary Portraits*, 1815, BM. T.WAGEMAN, after J.Saxon, hl, aged 60, stipple, pub 1818, BM.

CURRIE, James (1756-1805) physician.
PR R.H.CROMEK, after H.Hone, hl, line, pub 1807, BM, NPG. W.T.FRY, after T.Hargreaves, hl, stipple, for *Contemporary Portraits*, 1816, BM, NPG. UNKNOWN, hl, stipple, NPG.

CURTIS, John (1791-1862) entomologist.
PR T.H.MAGUIRE, tql seated, lith, one of set of *Ipswich Museum Portraits*, 1851, BM, NPG.

CURTIS, Sir Roger (1746-1816) admiral.
P MATHER BROWN, 1794, hl in uniform, NMM, Greenwich. UNKNOWN, *c*1800, hl in uniform, NMM.
G BARTOLOZZI, LANDSEER, RYDER and STOW, after R.Smirke, 'Naval Victories', 'Commemoration of the victory of June 1st 1794', line, pub 1803, BM, NPG.
PR W.RIDLEY, after Rivers, hl in uniform, stipple, oval, for *Naval*

Chronicle, 1801, BM, NPG. J.CALDWALL, after W.Hamilton, 1783, hl, semi-profile, in uniform, line, BM, NPG.

CURTIS, William (1746-1799) botanist and entomologist.
P Attrib JOSEPH WRIGHT of Derby, hl, Royal Horticultural Society, London.
PR UNKNOWN, hl, stipple, oval, pub 1800, BM. W.EVANS, hs, stipple, oval, for Thornton's *Sexual System of Linnaeus*, 1802, BM, NPG.

CURTIS, Sir William, Bart (1752-1829) Lord Mayor of London.
P SIR THOMAS LAWRENCE, RA 1824, hl seated in mayoral robe and chain of office, Royal Coll.
D SIR FRANCIS CHANTREY, 1827, hs and hs profile, pencil, NPG 316a (25, 26).
SC SIR FRANCIS CHANTREY, *c*1828, bust, Ashmolean Museum, Oxford.
PR W.BROMLEY, after S.Drummond, hs, line, oval, for *European Mag*, 1799, BM, NPG. W.SHARP, after T.Lawrence, wl seated, line, pub 1814, BM, NPG. T.L.BUSBY, wl in Highland dress, entitled 'A True Character', coloured line, pub 1822, BM.
C R.DIGHTON, 1820, wl, coloured etch, pub 1824, NPG, V & A. G.CRUIKSHANK, wl in Highland dress, coloured etch, pub 1822, NPG.

CUST, Sir John, 3rd Bart (1718-1770) speaker of the House of Commons.
P SIR JOSHUA REYNOLDS, *c*1767, wl in speaker's robes, with mace, Belton House, Lincs.
G ENOCH SEEMAN, *c*1743, with his family at tea, Belton House.

D

DALBIAC, Sir James Charles (1776-1847) lieutenant-general.

P F.R.SAY, posthumous, based on portrait attrib Andrew Morton 1837, hl with orders, Floors Castle, Borders region, Scotland.

D MISS SHARPLES, 1832, hs with his daughter, NPG.

G MISS ROLINDA SHARPLES, 'The Trial of Colonel Brereton – after the Bristol Riots, 1831', Bristol City Art Gallery.

PR UNKNOWN, hs, woodcut, for *Illust London News*, 1847–48, NPG.

DALBY, Isaac (1744-1824) professor of mathematics at Sandhurst.

P J.J.HALLS, RA 1817, Staff College, Camberley, Surrey.

PR J.THOMSON, after W.Derby, hl, stipple, pub 1827, BM, NPG.

DALE, David (1739-1806) originator of cotton mills in Scotland.

P UNKNOWN, The Glasgow Art Collections.

SC JAMES TASSIE, 1791, paste medallion, SNPG 2219.

PR H.THOMSON, after a medallion by J.Henning, profile bust, stipple, pub 1822, BM, NPG.

DALE, Thomas (1729-1816) physician.

PR UNKNOWN, silhouette profile bust, stipple, BM, NPG.

DALE, Thomas (1797-1870) dean of Rochester.

PR H.COUSINS, after J.Lonsdale, tql, mezz, pub 1836, NPG. W.O.GELLER, after J.Lucas, tql, mezz, c1842, NPG. UNKNOWN, after a photograph by J.Watkins, hl, woodcut, for *Illust London News*, 31 Dec, 1859, NPG. D.J.POUND, after a photograph by Mayall, tql, line and stipple, for *Illust News of the World*, BM, NPG.

DALLAS, Alexander Robert Charles (1791-1869) divine.

PR R.J.LANE, (after Louisa Brock?), 1852, tql, lith, NPG.

DALLAS, Sir Robert (1756-1824) judge.

G SIR GEORGE HAYTER, 'The Trial of Queen Caroline, 1820', oil, NPG 999.

PR W.HOLL, after a bust by R.W.Sievier, stipple, pub 1824, BM, NPG.

DALLAS, Sir Thomas (d1839) lieutenant-general.

D THOMAS HICKEY, 1801, hs, chalk, Stratfield Saye, Hants.

PR J.S.AGAR, after a miniature by C.Jagger, hs in uniform, stipple, pub 1827, NPG.

DALRYMPLE, Alexander (1737-1808) hydrographer to the Admiralty.

PR UNKNOWN, after J.Brown, hl, line, oval in dedication of Arrowsmith's *Map of the World*, 1794, BM. W.DANIELL, after G.Dance, hl profile, soft-ground etch, pub 1809, BM, NPG.

DALRYMPLE, Sir David, see Lord Hailes.

DALRYMPLE, Sir Hew Whitefoord, Bart (1750-1830) general.

M ANTHONY STEWART, hl, NGS 1987.

PR UNKNOWN, hs, near profile, stipple, pub 1808, NPG. C.TURNER, after J.Jackson, hl, mezz, pub 1831, BM, NPG.

DALRYMPLE, Sir John, 4th Bart of Cranstoun (1726-1810) judge and author.

D JOHN BROWN, c1780, hs, pencil, SNPG L74.

DALRYMPLE, Sir John Hamilton Macgill, see 8th Earl of Stair.

DALTON, John (1766-1844) chemist, founder of modern atomic theory.

P After JOSEPH ALLEN of 1816, tql seated, Salford City Art Gallery. JAMES LONSDALE, 1825, Manchester University B.R.FAULKNER, c1840–41, tql seated, Royal Society, London

D SIR FRANCIS CHANTREY, 1834, several sketches, head and wl, pencil NPG 316a (27–30). CHARLES JORDAN, c1840, w/c, Manchester Medical Society. UNKNOWN, hs, w/c, SNPG 145.

SC SIR FRANCIS CHANTREY, RA 1837, marble seated statue, Royal Institution, Manchester. HOLME CARDWELL, c1840, marble bust, Christie Library, Manchester. WILLIAM THEED jun, 1854, statue, Piccadilly, Manchester. SIR FRANCIS CHANTREY, plaster bust Ashmolean Museum, Oxford.

DALTON, Richard (1715?-1791) draughtsman, engraver and librarian.

G JOHAN ZOFFANY, with his wife and their niece Mary de Heulle oil, c1765–68, TATE T1895.

DALY, Denis (1747-1791) Irish politician.

P UNKNOWN, NGI 1165.

D H.D.HAMILTON, hs, pastel, oval, NGI 6993.

G FRANCIS WHEATLEY, 'The Irish House of Commons, 1780', oil Leeds City Art Galleries, Lotherton Hall, W.Yorks.

DALY, Richard (d1813) theatrical manager.

PR UNKNOWN, hs profile, line, oval, for *Town & Country Mag* 1787, BM, NPG.

DALYELL, Sir John Graham, 6th Bart (1775-1851) antiquary and naturalist.

P SIR JOHN WATSON-GORDON, tql seated, The Binns (NT) Lothian region, Scotland. UNKNOWN, tql seated, The Binns.

DALZEL, Andrew (1742-1806) classical scholar.

P SIR HENRY RAEBURN, tql seated, SNPG 199.

C J.KAY, wl, etch, reprinted in *Kay's Portraits*, 1842, vol. I, NPG.

DAMER, Anne Seymour, née Conway (1749-1828) sculptress.

P Studio of SIR J.REYNOLDS, 1772, hs, NPG 594.

D H.CARR, 1788, w/c, SNPG 2125.

SC ANNE SEYMOUR DAMER, marble bust, BM. GIUSEPPE CERACCHI c1777, marble statue, as the Muse of Sculpture, BM.

PR J.R.SMITH, after J.Reynolds, tql, mezz, pub 1774, BM L.SCHIAVONETTI, after R.Cosway, hl, stipple, pub 1791, BM NPG. T.RYDER, after A.Kauffman, tql seated, stipple, pub 1792 BM, NPG. J.HOPWOOD, after G.C., hs, stipple, pub 1812, BM, NPG

DAMPIER, Thomas (1748-1812) bishop of Ely, book collector.

PR UNKNOWN, after J.Masquerier, head, etch, BM. H.MEYER, after J.Northcote, tql seated, mezz, BM, NPG.

DANBY, Francis (1793-1861) painter.

P H.T.MUNNS, NGI 770.

SC CHRISTOPHER MOORE, 1827, plaster bust, NGI 8059.

DANBY, William (1752-1833) miscellaneous writer.

PR E.SCRIVEN, after J.Jackson, hl seated, stipple, pub 1822, NPG, V & A.

DANCE, George (1700-1768) architect, designed the Mansion House.

P SIR NATHANIEL DANCE, 1767, hl with plans, Guildhall Art Gallery, London. FRANCIS HAYMAN, wl, Fitzwilliam Museum, Cambridge.

DANCE, George (1741-1825) architect and portrait draughtsman.

P JOHN JACKSON, tql seated, Leicester Museum and Art Gallery.

D Self-portrait, 1795, hs, profile, pencil, Ashmolean Museum, Oxford. Self-portrait, 1814, hl seated, pencil and chalk, NPG 2812.

G HENRY SINGLETON, 'Royal Academicians, 1793', oil, Royal Academy, London.

SC J.C.F.ROSSI, 1827, marble bust, Royal Academy, London.

DANCE, James (1722-1774), see Love.

DANCE, Sir Nathaniel (1748-1827) commander under the East India Company.

D UNKNOWN, hl, chalk, India Office Library and Records, London.

PR C.KNIGHT, after G.Dance, hs, coloured stipple, oval, pub 1804, BM, NPG. J.FITTLER, after G.Dance, hl, line, oval, for *Naval Chronicle*, 1804, BM, NPG. J.R.SMITH, wl with charts and plans, mezz, pub 1805, BM. C.TURNER, after R.Westall, hl in uniform, mezz, BM.

DANCE, William (1755-1840) musician.

D GEORGE DANCE, 1800, hl profile, pencil, NPG 3058. GEORGE DANCE, hs profile, pencil, Royal Society of Musicians, London.

PR UNKNOWN, after W.P.Sherlock, hs, lith, NPG.

DANCE-HOLLAND, Sir Nathaniel, 1st Bart (1735-1811) painter.

P Self-portrait, c1780, hs, NPG 3626.

DANCER, Mrs Anne, see Mrs Spranger BARRY.

DANCER, Daniel (1716-1794) miser.

D Attrib ROBERT COOPER, hl, pencil and chalk, NPG 4369. UNKNOWN, wl, NPG.

PR J.CHAPMAN, hl with bag of money, stipple, oval, pub 1801, BM, NPG.

DANICAN, François André, see Philidor.

DANIEL, George (1789-1864) writer and book-collector.

PR R.GRAVES, after T.Wageman, tql seated, line, 1835, BM.

C GEORGE CRUIKSHANK, 'Sir Lionel Flamstead and his Friends', etch, V & A.

DANIEL, William Barker (1753?-1833) author of *Rural Sports.*

PR P.W.TOMKINS, after G.Engleheart, hl profile, stipple, for his *Rural Sports,* 1811, BM, NPG.

DANIELL, John Frederic (1790-1845) physicist.

P UNKNOWN, King's College, London.

DANIELL, Thomas (1749-1840) landscape-painter.

P SIR DAVID WILKIE, 1838, hs, TATE 231.

D GEORGE DANCE, hs profile, Royal Academy, London.

DANIELL, William (1769-1837) landscape-painter.

D GEORGE DANCE, 1794, hs profile, chalk, BM.

D'ARBLAY, Frances, née Burney (1752-1840) diarist and novelist.

P E.F.BURNEY, (her cousin), c1782-5, tql seated in Vandyck dress, Parham Park, W.Sussex. E.F.BURNEY, c1784-85, hl seated, NPG 2634.

DARBY, George (d1790) admiral.

P GEORGE ROMNEY, 1783-86, wl in uniform, NMM, Greenwich.

PR C.KNIGHT, after C.Sherriff, hs in uniform, stipple, oval, pub 1781, BM.

D'ARCY, Robert (1718-1778), see 4th Earl of Holderness.

DARGAN, William (1799-1867) Irish railway projector.

P STEPHEN CATTERSON SMITH, 1862, hs, NGI 141.

SC J.E.JONES, 1854, marble bust, NGI 8204. J.E.JONES, plaster sculpture, NGI 8111. WILLIAM WOODHOUSE, medal, National Museum of Ireland. SIR THOMAS FARRELL, bronze statue, in front of the NGI.

PR W.J.EDWARDS, after G.F.Mulvany, hs, stipple and line, NPG.

DARLEY, George (1795-1846) poet and mathematician.

D RICHARD EVANS, 1837, hs, Staatliche Kunstsammlungen, Dresden.

DARLINGTON, William Harry Vane, 3rd Earl of, see 1st Duke of Cleveland.

DARLY, Matthew (fl 1770) printseller and caricaturist.

PR Self-portrait?, tql, etch and line, pub 1771, BM, NPG. UNKNOWN, wl with mule, etch, pub 1772. NPG. UNKNOWN, hs profile, medallion, line, pub 1775. NPG.

DARTMOUTH, George Legge, 3rd Earl of (1755-1810) statesman.

G JOHAN ZOFFANY, 'The Tribuna of the Uffizi', oil, 1772–78, Royal Coll.

PR J.SPILSBURY, after J.Reynolds, hl as a boy, mezz, BM. W.EVANS, after W.Lane, tql seated with Garter, stipple, pub 1808, BM, NPG. W.DANIELL, after G.Dance, hs, soft-ground etch, pub 1809, BM, NPG. C.HEATH jun, after T.Phillips, tql seated with wand of lord chamberlain, and bust of George III, line, BM, NPG.

DARTMOUTH, William Legge, 2nd Earl of (1731-1801) secretary of state.

P SIR JOSHUA REYNOLDS, c1757–59, wl in peer's robes, Thomas Coram Foundation for Children, London.

PR W.EVANS, after T.Gainsborough, hl, stipple, oval, BM, NPG. UNKNOWN, hl, line, oval, for *London Mag,* 1780, BM, NPG. C.WARREN, hs, line, oval, the *The Senator,* 1792, BM, NPG.

DARWIN Erasmus (1731-1802) physician.

P JOSEPH WRIGHT of Derby, 1770, hs, NPG 88. JOSEPH WRIGHT of Derby, 1792–93, hl with pen, Wolverhampton Art Gallery. JAMES RAWLINSON, (perhaps based on Wright of 1792–93?), hl, Derby Corporation. JAMES RAWLINSON, hl, Royal College of Surgeons, Down House, Kent.

D JAMES SHARPLES, hs, pastel, Bristol City Art Gallery.

SL Attrib FRANCIS TOROND, c1785, wl seated with his son, playing chess, Royal College of Surgeons, Down House.

PR B.PYM, after S.J.Arnold, tql seated, mezz, pub 1801, BM.

DASHWOOD, Francis (1708-1781), see 15th Baron LE Despencer.

DAUBENY, Charles (1745-1827) archdeacon of Salisbury.

PR J.S.AGAR, after C.Jagger, tql, stipple, pub 1828, BM.

DAUBENY, Charles Giles Bridle (1795-1867) chemist and botanist.

P Attrib THOMAS PHILLIPS, hs, Library of the Botanic Garden, Oxford. UNKNOWN, hl, Magdalen College, Oxford.

PR UNKNOWN, after M.Haughton, hs, lith, *Athenaeum Portraits,* No 27, pub 1836, BM.

DAVENPORT, Mary Ann, née Harvey (1765?-1843) actress.

P SAMUEL DE WILDE, before 1805, hl as Dame Ashfield in *Speed the Plough,* Garrick Club, London. BENJAMIN BURNELL, probably RA 1818, hs as Lady Denny in *Henry VIII,* Garrick Club.

D S. DE WILDE, 1802, hs as Dame Ashfield in *Speed the Plough,* V & A.

S. DE WILDE, 1809, wl as Fiametta in *The Tale of Mystery*, w/c, Garrick Club.
PR Several theatrical prints, BM, NPG.

DAVIDSON, John (d 1797) Scottish antiquary.
C J.KAY, 'Conversion – Demonstration', etch, BM, NPG.

DAVIDSON, John (1797-1836) physician and traveller.
SC CHARLES PUY, 1858, posthumous bust, Royal Geographical Society, London.
PR M.GAUCI, after E.U.Eddis, hs, lith, BM.

DAVIDSON, Thomas (1747-1827) theologian.
C J.KAY, 1790, hl, etch, oval, NPG.

DAVIES, or Davis, John Scarlett (fl 1841) painter.
D Self-portrait, 1829, hl seated, sepia, BM.

DAVIES, Sneyd (1709-1769) poet and canon of Lichfield.
PR H.MEYER, hs, stipple, oval, for Nichols's *Illustrations of Literature*, 1817, BM, NPG.

DAVIES, Thomas (1712?-1785) bookseller, actor and author.
PR L.SCHIAVONETTI, after T.Hickey, hl, stipple, pub 1794, BM, NPG.

DAVIS, Sir John Francis, Bart (1795-1890) diplomatist, governor of Hong Kong.
PR W.DRUMMOND, hl, lith, No 38 of *Athenaeum Portraits*, 1836, BM.

DAVIS, John Philip (called 'Pope' Davis) (1784-1862) painter.
D Self-portrait, 1818, probably rightly named, pencil and wash, V & A.

DAVIS, John Scarlett, see Davies.

DAVIS, William (1771-1807) mathematician and bookseller.
PR J.S.DICKSON, after W.Allen, hs, stipple, oval, BM, NPG.

DAVISON, Alexander (1750-1829) government contractor.
PR W.BARNARD, after L.Abbott, hl, mezz, pub 1804, BM, NPG.

DAVISON, Maria Rebecca, née Duncan (1783-1858) actress.
P HENRY SINGLETON, RA 1805, wl as Juliana in *The Honey Moon*, Garrick Club, London. MICHAEL SHARP, as Juliana, in *The Honey Moon*, V & A.
PR Various theatrical prints, BM. C.TURNER, after G.H.Harlow, hl seated, mezz, pub 1809, BM, NPG.

DAVY, Sir Humphry, Bart (1778-1829) chemist.
P HENRY HOWARD, 1803, tql, NPG 4591. SIR THOMAS LAWRENCE, RA 1821, tql, Royal Society, London. THOMAS PHILLIPS, hl seated, NPG 2546.
D Attrib JOHN JACKSON, tql seated, w/c, NPG 1794. JAMES SHARPLES, hs, pastel, Bristol City Art Gallery.
SC SAMUEL JOSEPH, bust, Royal Institution, London. A.B.JOY, plaster medallion, NPG 1273. ANNE SEYMOUR DAMER, bust, Royal Institution.
PR W.H.WORTHINGTON, after J.Lonsdale, tql seated, as president of the Royal Society, line, BM, NPG.
C J.GILLRAY, 'Scientific Researches', etch, pub 1802, NPG.

DAVY, Martin (1763-1839) physician and master of Caius College, Cambridge.
P JOHN OPIE, c1803, Caius College, Cambridge. UNKNOWN, Caius College, Cambridge.
SC UNKNOWN, memorial brass effigy, Ante Chapel, Caius College, Cambridge.

DAVYS, George (1780-1864) bishop of Peterborough, tutor to Queen Victoria.
P UNKNOWN, Christ's College, Cambridge.

DAWE, George (1781-1829) portrait painter.

D CARL CHRISTIAN VOGEL, 1828, hs, Staatliche Kunstsammlungen, Dresden. Self-portrait, chalk, Castle Museum and Art Gallery, Nottingham.
G A.E.CHALON, 'Study at the British Institution, 1806', pen, ink and w/c, BM.
PR UNKNOWN, tql seated with crayon, stipple, BM.

DAWES, Richard (1793-1867) dean of Hereford.
SC MATTHEW NOBLE, 1869, recumbent effigy, Hereford Cathedral.
PH UNKNOWN, Downing College, Cambridge.

DAWKINS, James (1722-1757) archaeologist and Jacobite.
G J.HALL, 1773, after G.Hamilton 1758, with Robert Wood, first discovering sight of Palmyra, line, pub 1775, NPG.
PR J.McARDELL, after J.Stuart, hl, mezz, oval, BM.

DAWSON, John (1734-1820) surgeon and mathematician.
PR W.W.BURNEY, after J.Allen, hl, mezz, pub 1809, NPG.

DAWSON, Nancy (1730?-1767) dancer.
P UNKNOWN, wl, Garrick Club, London.
PR C.SPOONER, tql, mezz, BM, NPG. M.JACKSON?, wl dancing a hornpipe, mezz, BM.

DAY, Alexander (1773-1841) painter and art dealer.
D UNKNOWN, head, pencil, NPG 3113.

DAY, Thomas (1748-1789) author of *Sandford and Merton*.
P JOSEPH WRIGHT of Derby, tql, NPG 2490. JOSEPH WRIGHT, wl, Yale Center for British Art, New Haven, USA.
PR J.CONDÉ, hs, stipple, oval, for *European Mag*, 1794, BM, NPG.

DAYES, Edward (1763-1804) water-colour painter.
P Self-portrait, hs, NPG 2091.

DEALTRY, Thomas (1796-1861) third bishop of Madras.
SC E.B.STEPHENS, 1851, bust, Calcutta Cathedral.

DEAN, John (d 1747) shipwrecked mariner.
P WILLIAM VERELST, 1743, tql, NPG 949.

DEANE, Sir Thomas (1792-1871) builder and architect in Cork.
P JAMES BUTLER BRENAN, exhib 1852, Royal Hibernian Academy, Dublin.

DEASE, William (1752?-1798) surgeon.
SC JOHN SMYTH, posthumous, bust, Royal College of Surgeons, Dublin. SIR THOMAS FARRELL, posthumous statue, Royal College of Surgeons, Dublin.

DE COETLOGON, Charles Edward (1746?-1820) vicar of Goldstone, Surrey.
PR UNKNOWN, hs profile, line, oval, for *Gospel Mag*, 1744, BM, NPG. J.WATSON, after G.James, wl seated with Martin Madan, mezz, pub 1774, BM. W.GRAINGER, after T.Peat, tql seated, stipple, pub 1791, BM. UNKNOWN, hs, line, oval, for Edward Young's *Night Thoughts*, NPG.

DE DUNSTANVILLE, Francis Basset, Baron (1757-1835) political writer and patron of fine arts.
P SIR JOSHUA REYNOLDS, c1775, hs, Eton College, Berks. THOMAS GAINSBOROUGH, c1786, tql, Corcoran Gallery of Art, Washington DC, USA. Attrib GAINSBOROUGH DUPONT, hs oval, Norton Simon Foundation, Los Angeles, USA. L.F.ABBOTT, c1780-90, King's College, Cambridge.
SC SIR RICHARD WESTMACOTT, medallion bust on monument, S Illogan Church, Illogan, Cornwall.

DE FERRARS, George Townshend, Baron, see 2nd Marquess Townshend.

DE FLAHAULT, Margaret Mercer Elphinstone, see Viscountess Keith.

DE GREY, Thomas Philip Weddell Robinson de Grey, 2nd Earl (1781-1859) statesman.

P H.W.PICKERSGILL, 1826, wl in peer's robes, formerly United Service Club, London (c/o The Crown Commissioners). SIR FRANCIS GRANT, 1849, wl in uniform, York City Art Gallery. JOHN WOOD, after William Robinson, tql in peer's robes, RIBA, London.

G S.W.REYNOLDS, after J.Reynolds, wl with his brothers, Frederick John Robinson and Philip Robinson, with dogs in landscape, mezz, BM. SIR GEORGE HAYTER, 'The Trial of Queen Caroline, 1820', oil, NPG 999.

SC MATTHEW NOBLE, recumbent effigy, De Grey Mausoleum, St John Baptist Church, Flitton, Beds.

DE GREY, William (1719-1781), see 1st Baron Walsingham.

DE LA BECHE, Sir Henry Thomas (1796-1855) geologist.

D WILLIAM BROCKEDON, 1842, hs, chalk, NPG 2515 (94).

M H.P.BONE, RA 1847, hl, Geological Museum, London.

SC E.G.PAPWORTH, bust, Geological Museum, London.

R T.H.MAGUIRE, tql seated, lith, for *Ipswich Museum Portraits*, 1851, BM, NPG. UNKNOWN, after a photograph by Claudet, for *Illust London News*, 1851, NPG.

DE LANCEY, Oliver (1749-1822) general.

P HENRY BENBRIDGE, hl, Pennsylvania Museum, Philadelphia, USA.

DELANE, Solomon (1727-1784?) landscape-painter.

D GEORGE DANCE, 1795, hs profile, Castle Museum and Art Gallery, Nottingham.

DELANY, Mary, née Granville (1700-1788) memoir and letter writer.

P JOHN OPIE, hl, Royal Coll; version NPG 1030. UNKNOWN, hl at Windsor, Royal Coll. French school, called MRS DELANEY, tql seated, Manchester City Art Gallery.

D Attrib JOHN HOPPNER, hl, pencil, V & A.

DELATRE or Delattre, Jean Marie (1745-1840) engraver.

D EDWARD BELL, head as an old man, w/c, BM.

DE LA WARR, George John Sackville West, 5th Earl (1791-1869) politician.

G SIR GEORGE HAYTER, 'The Trial of Queen Caroline, 1820', oil, NPG 999.

R W.H.MOTE, after E.D.Smith, tql in peer's robes, line and stipple, NPG. UNKNOWN, wl in fancy dress?, lith, NPG.

DE LA WARR, John West, 2nd Earl (1729-1777) general.

R S.W.REYNOLDS, after J.Reynolds, hl in uniform, mezz, pub 1823, BM, NPG.

DE LOLME, John Louis (1740?-1807) writer on the English constitution.

R HEATH, after Stoddart, hs, line, oval, pub 1784, NPG.

DE LOUTHERBOURG, Philip James (1740-1812) painter.

P Self-portrait, tql, NPG 2493. THOMAS GAINSBOROUGH, RA 1778, hl, Dulwich College Picture Gallery, London.

G HENRY SINGLETON, 'Royal Academicians, 1793', oil, Royal Academy, London.

R UNKNOWN, after S.Singleton, hl, stipple, pub 1798, BM, NPG. H.MEYER, hs, stipple, for *Contemporary Portraits*, 1813, BM, NPG. PAGE, hl, stipple, oval, pub 1814, BM, NPG.

DELPINI, Carlo Antonio (d 1828) clown and stage-manager.

R J.NIXON, hl with glass, etch, BM. Two theatrical prints, BM.

C J.SAYERS, wl in female dress, entitled 'Delpini a la Rossi; Grace was in all her steps', etch, pub 1785, BM, NPG.

DE LUC, Jean André (1727-1817) geologist and meteorologist.

PR C.PENNY, hs profile, stipple, BM, NPG. SCHROEDER, after W. de Stetten, hs profile, mezz, BM.

DEMAINBRAY, Stephen Charles Triboudet (1710-1782) electrician and astronomer.

SL UNKNOWN, hs profile, Radcliffe Observatory, Oxford.

DEMPSTER, George (1732-1818) agriculturalist and politician.

P J.T.NAIRN, hs, SNPG 138. GEORGE WILLISON, hl, Dundee City Art Gallery.

SC JAMES TASSIE, paste medallion, SNPG 257.

DENHAM, Dixon (1786-1828) soldier and traveller.

P THOMAS PHILLIPS, 1826, hs, NPG 2441.

DENHAM, Sir James Steuart, Bart (1744-1839) general.

P UNKNOWN, wl with horse, Arniston House, Lothian region, Scotland. SIR HENRY RAEBURN, tql with orders, NGI 430.

D RICHARD DIGHTON, 1836-37, wl profile, w/c, NPG 2756.

DENIS, Sir Peter (d 1778) vice-admiral.

P SIR NATHANIEL DANCE, 1767-70, probably rightly named, hl, NMM, Greenwich.

DENISON, William Joseph (1770-1849) politician and millionaire.

PR W.GILLER, after F.R.Say, wl seated, mezz, BM, NPG.

DENMAN, Thomas (1733-1815) physician.

P UNKNOWN, hl, Royal College of Physicians, London.

PR W.SKELTON, after L.Abbott, hl, line, pub 1792, BM, NPG.

DENMAN, Thomas Denman, 1st Baron (1779-1854) lord chief justice.

P J.J.HALLS, hs, NPG 372. SIR MARTIN ARCHER SHEE, wl in robes, NPG 463. THOMAS BARBER, tql seated, Castle Art Gallery, Nottingham.

D SIR GEORGE HAYTER, pen and wash, study for NPG 999, NPG 1695f. JOHN DOYLE, c1851, equestrian, pen and pencil, BM.

G SIR GEORGE HAYTER, 'The Trial of Queen Caroline, 1820', oil, NPG 999. SIR DAVID WILKIE, 'The First Council of Queen Victoria, 1837', oil, Royal Coll.

SC J.E.JONES, RA 1845, marble bust, Lincoln's Inn, London.

PR W.WALKER, after E.U.Eddis, tql seated, mezz, pub 1852, BM, NPG.

D'ÉON DE BEAUMONT, Charles Geneviève Louis Auguste André Timothée (1728-1810) chevalier.

D GEORGE DANCE, 1793, hs profile, chalk and w/c, BM.

PR T.BURKE, after J.G.Huquier, hs, mezz, pub 1771, BM. T.CHAMBARS, after R.Cosway, hl in female dress, stipple, pub 1787, BM. F.HAWARD, after A.Kauffmann (after Latour), hl in female dress, stipple, oval, pub 1788, BM, NPG. J.CONDÉ, head, profile, as Minerva, in oval medallion, entitled 'Proprio Marte Tuta', stipple, pub 1791, BM, NPG. Several popular prints, BM, NPG.

DE QUINCEY, Thomas (1785-1859) author of *Confessions of an Opium Eater*.

P SIR JOHN WATSON-GORDON, c1845, tql seated, NPG 189. JAMES ARCHER, tql seated, City Art Gallery, Manchester.

D JAMES ARCHER, 1855, tql seated, chalk, Dove Cottage, Grasmere, Cumbria.

SC SIR JOHN ROBERT STEELL, 1875, marble bust, SNPG 581; related plaster bust, NPG 822. JOHN CASSIDY, bust, Moss Side Public Library, Glasgow. SHAKSPERE WOOD, plaster medallion, SNPG 220.

PR F.CROLL, after a daguerreotype, by Howie jnr, hs, stipple, for *Portrait Gallery of Hogg's Instructor*, BM, NPG. F.SCHENCK of 1845, after 'W H D', hs, lith, SNPG.

PH Two photographs, Dove Cottage.

DERBY, Edward George Stanley, 14th Earl of (1799-1869) prime-minister.
P G.H.HARLOW, hl, a leaving portrait, Eton College, Berks. FREDERICK RICHARD SAY, 1844, tql, NPG 1806. SIR FRANCIS GRANT, 1858, wl in his robes as chancellor of Oxford University, Examination Schools, Oxford.
G SIR GEORGE HAYTER, 'The House of Commons, 1833', oil, NPG 54. H.W.PHILLIPS, 'The Royal Commissioners for the Exhibition, 1851', V & A. HENRY GALES, 'The Derby Cabinet of 1867', w/c, NPG 4893.
SC WILLIAM THEED, c1868, statue, St George's Hall, Liverpool. H.P.MACCARTHY, 1871, bust, Merchant Taylors' Company, London. MATTHEW NOBLE, 1871, bust, Guildhall Museum, London. F.GLEICHEN, 1892, marble bust, Houses of Parliament.
PH UNKNOWN, hl, oval, carte, NPG Twist Album, 1892.

DERBY, Edward Smith Stanley, 13th Earl of (1775-1851) politician and president of the Zoological Society.
P SIR THOMAS LAWRENCE, hl, a leaving portrait, Eton College, Berks.
M UNKNOWN, Trinity College, Cambridge.
G J.BARENGER, probably rightly named, on horseback with staghounds, oil, 1819, Yale Center for British Art, New Haven, USA.
PR F.C.LEWIS, after W.Derby, tql seated, mezz, pub 1844, BM, NPG.

DERBY, Elizabeth Farren, Countess of (1759?-1829) actress.
P JOHAN ZOFFANY, c1780, wl as Hermione in *The Winter's Tale*, National Gallery of Victoria, Melbourne, Australia. SIR THOMAS LAWRENCE, RA 1790, wl, Metropolitan Museum of Art, New York, USA. Attrib RICHARD COSWAY, hl, oval, Garrick Club, London.
D JOHN DOWNMAN, 1787, hs, chalk, NPG 2652. E.F.BURNEY, playing a guitar, ink, BM. OZIAS HUMPHRY, hs, pastel, oval, NGI 315. JOHN NIXON, hs profile, wash, BM.
M Attrib HORACE HONE, hs, oval, Garrick Club. UNKNOWN, hs, oval, Royal Coll.
SC ANNE SEYMOUR DAMER, c1789, marble bust, NPG 4469.
PR Several theatrical prints, BM, NPG.
C R.DIGHTON, in box at theatre, with her husband, entitled 'Darby and Joan', coloured etch, pub 1795, BM. J.SAYERS, 'A Moving Scene in the Fair Circassian', etch, NPG.

DERMODY, Thomas (1775-1802) Irish poet.
P CHARLES ALLINGHAM, 1802, hl, NGI 138.

DERRICK, Samuel (1724-1769) poet.
PR W.HIBBERT, after Vespris, hl, etch, oval, BM, NPG.

DE SAUMAREZ, James Saumarez, Baron (1757-1836) admiral.
P EDWIN WILLIAMS, after Thomas Phillips, hl wearing the ribbon and star of the Bath, NMM, Greenwich. Attrib SAMUEL LANE, hl wearing orders, NMM.
M PHILIP JEAN, 1801, hl, NPG 2549.
SC SIR JAMES STEELL, 1840, statue, NMM.
PR C.TURNER, after Carbonier, hs in uniform, mezz, for Brenton's *Naval History*, 1823, BM, NPG.

DESBARRES, Joseph Frederick Walsh or **Wallet (1722-1824)** military engineer.
P UNKNOWN, hl semi-profile, Public Archives of Canada, Ottawa, Canada.

DESENFANS, Noel Joseph (1745-1807) picture dealer.
P UNKNOWN, wl with bust of Fénelon, Dulwich College Picture Gallery, London. JAMES NORTHCOTE, hs, Dulwich College Picture Gallery.
D PAUL SANDBY, c1795, wl seated with Sir P.F.Bourgeois, w/c, Dulwich College Picture Gallery.
SC C.PROSPERI, bust, Dulwich College Picture Gallery.

DESPARD, Edward Marcus (1751-1803) executed for treason.
PR BARLOW, hs, etch, oval, pub 1803, BM. UNKNOWN, wl on the gallows, line, for the *Wonderful Museum*, 1804, BM, NPG.

DE TABLEY, Sir John Fleming Leicester, 1st Baron (1762-1827) art patron.
PR H.MEYER, tql in robes, stipple, BM, NPG. S.W.REYNOLDS, after J.Reynolds and J.Northcote, wl in uniform, with horse, mezz, BM, NPG.

DEVIS, Arthur (1711?-1787) portrait-painter.
P Self-portrait, hl with palette, Harris Museum and Art Gallery, Preston.
M Three miniatures, Harris Museum and Art Gallery.

DEVIS, Arthur William (1763-1822) painter.
P Self-portrait, hl, Harris Museum and Art Gallery, Preston.
D Self-portrait, c1808, hs profile, pencil, Ashmolean Museum, Oxford; related w/c, hs profile, Harris Museum and Art Gallery, and related stipple engraving by T.Cheesman, hs profile in Elizabethan ruff, NPG.
PR J.H.ROBINSON, after W.Mulready, hs profile, etch, for Pye's *Patronage of British Art*, 1845, BM.

DEVISME, Louis (1720-1776) diplomatist.
P RAPHAEL MENGS, tql, Christ Church, Oxford.

DEVONSHIRE, Elizabeth Hervey, Duchess of (1759-1824) famous beauty.
P ANGELICA KAUFFMANN, 1786, tql, Ickworth (NT), Suffolk, SIR JOSHUA REYNOLDS, 1787, hl, Chatsworth, Derbys. SIR THOMAS LAWRENCE, RA 1805, wl, NGI 788. J.W.CHANDLER, tql seated, NPG 2355.
D JOHN DOWNMAN, 1785, wl with Georgiana, Duchess of Devonshire, Ickworth. SIR THOMAS LAWRENCE, hl, Royal Coll.

DEVONSHIRE, Georgiana Spencer, Duchess of (1757-1806) beauty and leader of Whig society.
P SIR JOSHUA REYNOLDS, 1759, hs with her mother, sketch, Chatsworth, Derbys. SIR JOSHUA REYNOLDS, 1760-62, wl with her mother and a dog, Althorp, Northants. THOMAS GAINSBOROUGH, 1763, hl, oval, Althorp. R.E.PINE, 1773, hl with miniature harp, Althorp. ANGELICA KAUFFMANN, 1771-74, wl with Countess of Bessborough and 2nd Earl Spencer, Althorp. SIR JOSHUA REYNOLDS, RA 1776, wl, Huntington Library and Art Gallery, San Marino, USA. SIR JOSHUA REYNOLDS, c1780, 1784 and RA 1786, three portraits, two with her daughter, Chatsworth. THOMAS GAINSBOROUGH, c1783, wl, National Gallery of Art, Washington DC, USA.
D CATHERINE READ, hs as a child, pastel, Althorp. JOHN DOWNMAN, 1785, wl with Lady Elizabeth Foster, Ickworth (NT), Suffolk. JOHN DOWNMAN, 1787, wl, w/c, Chatsworth. CATHERINE READ, with Viscount Althorp and her sisters, pastel, Althorp. LADY DIANA BEAUCLERK, tql seated, Royal Coll.
M RICHARD COSWAY, hs, oval, Royal Coll.
C THOMAS ROWLANDSON, 1790, wl with Lady Duncannon, ink and w/c, Yale Center for British Art, New Haven, USA.

DEVONSHIRE, William Cavendish, 4th Duke of (1720-1764) lord lieutenant of Ireland.
P WILLIAM HOGARTH, 1741, hl, oval, Yale Center for British Art, New Haven, USA. Attrib THOMAS HUDSON, tql, Chatsworth, Derbys. Attrib GEORGE KNAPTON, hl with dog, Hardwick Hall (NT), Derbys. By or after SIR JOSHUA REYNOLDS, tql, J.B.Speed

Art Museum, Louisville, USA.

DEVONSHIRE, William Cavendish, 5th Duke of (1748-1811) Lord High Treasurer of Ireland.

P POMPEO BATONI, 1768, tql, Chatsworth, Derbys. SIR JOSHUA REYNOLDS, RA 1776, hs, Althorp, Northants. A.VAN MARON. tql, (the head altered), Chatsworth.

G WILLIAM LANE, 'Whig Statesmen and their Friends, c1810', chalk, NPG 2076.

R W.T.HULLAND, after J.Reynolds, tql in fancy dress, mezz, BM, NPG.

DEVONSHIRE, William George Spencer Cavendish, 6th Duke of (1790-1858) lord chamberlain.

P HENRY HOWARD, RA 1799, hl with cricket bat, Althorp, Northants. SIR M.A.SHEE, RA 1806, Hardwick Hall (NT), Derbys. GEORGE SANDERS, 1812–13, tql in fancy dress, Chatsworth, Derbys. SIR GEORGE HAYTER, 1816, tql in peer's robes, Chatsworth. SIR THOMAS LAWRENCE, c1824, hs with Garter star, Royal Coll. SIR EDWIN LANDSEER, RA 1832, tql, Chatsworth. SIR FRANCIS GRANT, RA 1850, wl with Garter star, Chatsworth.

G SIR GEORGE HAYTER, 'The Trial of Queen Caroline, 1820', oil, NPG 999. SIR GEORGE HAYTER, 'Coronation of Queen Victoria', oil, 1838, Royal Coll.

C JOSEPH NOLLEKENS, 1812, marble bust, Royal Coll. THOMAS CAMPBELL, 1823, bust, Chatsworth. SIR GEORGE HAYTER, 1858, marble bust, Chatsworth.

C RICHARD DIGHTON, wl, coloured etch, pub 1820, NPG. SIR EDWIN LANDSEER, c1835, tql seated at the opera, pen and wash, NPG 4916.

DE WILDE, Samuel (1748-1832) portrait-painter.

R UNKNOWN, hs, stipple, BM.

DE WINT, Peter (1784-1849) painter.

D Self-portrait, hs, pencil, The Usher Art Gallery, Lincoln.

M WILLIAM HILTON, called de Wint, oval, The Usher Art Gallery, Lincoln.

D'EYNCOURT, Charles Tennyson (1784-1861) politician.

G SIR GEORGE HAYTER, 'The House of Commons, 1833', oil, NPG 54.

R C.PICART, after A.Wivell, hs, stipple, for a set of portraits of persons present at the trial of Queen Caroline, pub 1822, BM, NPG. F.C.LEWIS, after J.Harrison, hs, aquatint and stipple, pub 1829, BM, NPG. E.MORTON, after J.Pelham, tql seated, lith, pub 1838, NPG.

DIBDIN, Charles (1745-1814) song-writer and dramatist.

P THOMAS PHILLIPS, 1799, hl, NPG 103. UNKNOWN, c1800, hl, Royal College of Music, London. S.J.ARNOLD, hs, Garrick Club, London.

R Several theatrical prints, BM, NPG. B.SMITH, after A.W.Devis, hl seated, stipple, octagon, for *Professional Life of Mr Dibdin*, 1803, BM.

DIBDIN, Charles Isaac Mungo (1768-1833) dramatist.

R J.THOMSON, after R.W.Satchwell, hl, stipple, for *European Mag*, 1819, BM.

DIBDIN, Thomas Frognall (1776-1847) bibliographer.

P UNKNOWN, hl, St John's College, Oxford.

D WILLIAM BEHNES, hl, chalk, BM. E.TURNER, pencil, V & A.

R H.MEYER, after H.Edridge, hl, stipple, pub 1816, BM, NPG. T.HODGETTS, after T.Phillips, hl seated, mezz, pub 1821, BM, NPG. J.POSSELWHITE, after G.Richmond, tql seated, stipple, pub 1835, BM. MRS D.TURNER, after Mrs F.Palgrave, hs profile, etch, BM, NPG.

DIBDIN, Thomas John (1771-1841) actor and dramatist.

P WILLIAM OWEN, hl, Museum of Fine Arts, Boston, USA.

PR R.DIGHTON, hl seated, entitled 'Sans Souci Junr', coloured etch, oval, 1799, BM. W.RIDLEY, after C.Allingham, hl, stipple, oval, for *Monthly Mirror*, 1802, BM, NPG. H.MEYER, after S.Drummond, hl seated, stipple, for *European Mag*, 1817, BM, NPG. D.MACLISE, wl seated, lith, BM, NPG.

DICK, Sir Alexander (1703-1785) physician and antiquary.

D JOHN BROWN, hs profile, pencil, SNPG L 83.

DICK, 'Dirty Dick', see Nathaniel Bentley.

DICK, Sir Robert Henry (1785?-1846) major-general.

P WILLIAM SALTER, tql study for 'Waterloo Banquet', NPG 3708.

G W.SALTER, 'Waterloo Banquet at Apsley House', oil, 1836, Wellington Museum, Apsley House, London.

DICK, Thomas (1774-1857) populariser of astronomy and science.

D UNKNOWN, tql, w/c, SNPG 2137.

PR H.COOK, hl seated, stipple, NPG. F.CROLL, hl, line, NPG.

DICKINSON, William (1756-1822) topographer and legal writer.

PR W.HOLL, after W.P.Sherlock, hl, stipple, for his *History of Southwell*, 1801, BM, NPG.

DICKONS, Maria, née Poole (1770?-1833) singer.

D WILLIAM BRADLEY, wl as Rosina in *The Barber of Seville*, pencil and w/c, Garrick Club, London. A.E.CHALON, pen and w/c sketch, NPG 1962 (c).

PR M.A.BOURLIER, hl with music, stipple, for *La Belle Assemblée*, BM, NPG.

DICKSON, Sir Alexander (1777-1840) major-general.

P WILLIAM SALTER, tql study for 'Waterloo Banquet', NPG 3709.

G W.SALTER, 'Waterloo Banquet at Apsley House', oil, 1836, Wellington Museum, Apsley House, London.

PR UNKNOWN, hs, aquatint, c1815, NPG.

DICKSON, David (1754-1820) presbyterian minister at Edinburgh.

PR W.RIDLEY, hs, stipple, oval, for *Evangelical Mag*, 1805, BM, NPG.

C J.KAY, hl, etch, oval, 1797, BM, NPG.

DICKSON, David (1780-1842) minister of St Cuthbert's church, Edinburgh.

PR W.HOLL, after J.R.Wildman, hl, stipple, for *Evangelical Mag*, 1829, BM, NPG.

C J.KAY, hl preaching, etch, 1812, NPG.

DICKSON, James (1737?-1822) botanist.

P H.P.BRIGGS, 1820, hl, Royal Horticultural Society, London.

DICKSON, William (1745-1804) Irish bishop.

PR W.DANIELL, after G.Dance, 1794, hl profile, soft-ground etch, pub 1808, BM, NPG. J.HEATH, hs, stipple, for Sir J.Barrington's *Historic Memoirs*, 1810, BM, NPG.

DIGBY, Robert (1732-1815) admiral.

PR J.CHAPMAN, hs, stipple, oval, pub 1802, NPG.

DIGGES, West (1720-1786) actor.

PR UNKNOWN, wl as Sir John Brute in Vanburgh's *The Provok'd Wife*, pub 1778, BM.

DIGHTON, Richard (fl 1795-1880) portrait draughtsman.

D Called a self-portrait, (identity doubtful), w/c, NPG 1836a.

DIGHTON, Robert (1752?-1814) portrait-painter and caricaturist.

D Self-portrait, hl, pen and wash, NPG 2815.

DIGNUM, Charles (1765?-1827) singer.

D SAMUEL DE WILDE, 1801, wl as Tom Tug in *The Waterman*, w/c,

Garrick Club, London.

M After SIR A.W.CALCOTT, hl, Garrick Club, London.

PR W.RIDLEY, after S.Drummond, hs, stipple, oval, for *European Mag*, 1799, BM, NPG. K.MACKENZIE, after R.Dighton, hs, stipple, oval, BM.

DILKE, Charles Wentworth (1789-1864) antiquary and critic.

P UNKNOWN, hs, Keats House, London.

DILLON, Sir John Talbot (1740?-1805) traveller and baron of the Holy Roman Empire.

PR W.BOND, 1798, hs, stipple, oval, NPG.

DILLON, Robert Crawford (1795-1847) divine.

PR R.SMITH, after E.Dixon, tql seated, stipple, NPG. UNKNOWN, after T.Bridgeford, tql seated, mezz, NPG.

DILLWYN, Lewis Weston (1778-1855) naturalist.

G SIR GEORGE HAYTER, 'The House of Commons, 1833', oil, NPG 54.

PR UNKNOWN, after E.U.Eddis, hl, lith, BM.

DIMSDALE, Thomas (1712-1800) physician, baron of the Russian Empire.

P UNKNOWN, hs, County Hall, Hertford.

D HENRY BONE, 1800, hs, pencil, NPG Bone's Drawings.

PR W.RIDLEY, hl, stipple, oval, for *European Mag*, 1802, BM, NPG. UNKNOWN, after C.L.Christeneke, hl seated, line, Russian Museum, Leningrad, USSR.

DINELEY-GOODERE, Sir John (1729?-1809) the eccentric Poor Knight of Windsor.

P UNKNOWN, wl profile, etch, pub 1799, BM, similar engr, NPG. UNKNOWN, wl profile, line, for *Wonderful Museum*, 1803, BM, NPG. J.MILLS, wl seated, line, pub 1803, NPG. W.HOPKINS, hs, etch, 1809, BM, NPG.

DISNEY, John (1746-1816) unitarian clergyman.

SC PATRICK MACDOWELL, plaster bust, Dr Williams's Library, London.

PR C.PICART, after Guy Head, hs, stipple, BM, NPG.

DISNEY, John (1779-1857) collector of classical antiquities.

SC UNKNOWN, marble bust, Fitzwilliam Museum, Cambridge.

D'ISRAELI, Isaac (1766-1848) writer.

P UNKNOWN, hl as a boy, Hughenden Manor (NT), Bucks.

D JOHN DOWNMAN, 1804, hl, pencil, NPG 4079. JOHN DOWNMAN, 1805, hl, w/c, Hughenden. DANIEL MACLISE, 1828, hl, Hughenden. COUNT ALFRED D'ORSAY, 1839, hl profile, pencil, NPG 3772. After DANIEL MACLISE, wl seated, pen and ink, NPG 3092. SIR WILLIAM ROSS, hs, pencil and chalk, BM.

DOBREE, Peter Paul (1782-1825) Greek scholar.

SC E.H.BAILY, RA 1828, marble bust, Trinity College, Cambridge.

DOBSON, John (1787-1865) architect.

P JOHN DIXON, Laing Art Gallery and Museum, Newcastle on Tyne.

D THOMAS HEATHFIELD CARRICK, pencil, Laing Art Gallery and Museum.

DODD, James William (1740?-1796) actor.

D Four portraits in the Garrick Club, London: SAMUEL DE WILDE, as Abel Drugger in *The Alchymist*, w/c; UNKNOWN, hs profile, gouache; ROBERT DIGHTON, wl as Lord Foppington in *The Trip to Scarborough*, w/c; ROBERT DIGHTON, wl as Sparkish in *The Country Girl*. JAMES ROBERTS, as Tensel in Addison's *Drummer*, BM.

PR R.LAURIE, after R.Dighton, hl, mezz, oval, pub 1779, BM, NPG. Several theatrical prints, BM, NPG.

DODD, Philip Stanhope (1775-1852) divine.

PR J.T.LINNELL, after Corton, tql, lith, NPG.

DODD, Thomas (1771-1850) auctioneer and printseller.

G UNKNOWN, 'Portraits from Sketches made at Rare Print Sales', etch, BM.

PR W.HOLL, after A.Wivell, hs, stipple, pub 1828, BM, NPG.

DODD, William (1729-1777) parson and forger.

P JOHN RUSSELL, 1769, tql, NPG 251.

PR T.L.ATKINSON, after T.Gainsborough, hl, mezz, oval, BM. UNKNOWN, hl, mezz, oval, pub 1777, BM, NPG. UNKNOWN, wl on the morning of his execution, line, pub 1777, BM, NPG.

DODDRIDGE, Philip (1702-1751) dissenting minister.

P UNKNOWN, hl, Dr Williams's Library, London.

PR G.VERTUE, after A.Soldi, hs, line, pub 1751, NPG. W.H.WORTHINGTON, after an unknown artist of 1750, hs, line pub 1829, BM, NPG.

DODSLEY, Robert (1703-1764) poet, dramatist and bookseller.

P Attrib WILLIAM ALCOCK, 1760, hl, oil on tin, NPG 1436. SIR JOSHUA REYNOLDS, *c*1760, hl, Dulwich College Picture Gallery, London.

DODSON, Sir John (1780-1858) judge of the prerogative court.

PR W.WALKER, tql seated, mezz, pub 1849, BM, NPG.

DODSWORTH, William (1798-1861) Roman Catholic writer.

PR W.WALKER, after E.Walker, hl, stipple, pub 1835, BM, NPG. C.BAUGNIET, tql, lith, 1845, BM, NPG.

DODWELL, Edward (1767-1832) traveller and archaeologist.

D COUNT A.D'ORSAY, 1828, hs profile, pencil, DoE (British Embassy, Athens).

DOHERTY, John (1783-1850) chief-justice of Ireland.

P MARTIN CREGAN, 1826, NGI 830.

PR UNKNOWN, tql seated, stipple, NPG.

DOLBEN, Sir William, Bart (1727?-1814) abolitionist.

P After JOHN OPIE of *c*1800, hl, Examination Schools, Oxford. MATHER BROWN, RA 1802, hs, Christ Church, Oxford.

SC JAMES TASSIE, 1779, Wedgwood medallion, Wedgwood Museum, Barlaston, Staffs.

DOLLOND, John (1706-1761) optician.

P BENJAMIN WILSON, exhib 1781, hl, Herstmonceux Observatory, E.Sussex; copy by W.F.Witherington, Royal Society, London.

DOLLOND, Peter (1730-1820) optician.

G J.F.SKILL, J.GILBERT, W. and E.WALKER, 'Men of Science Living in 1807-08', pencil and wash, NPG 1075.

PR J.THOMSON, after J.Hoppner, hl, stipple, for *European Mag*, 1820, BM, NPG.

DOMETT, Sir William (1754-1828) admiral.

G BARTOLOZZI, LANDSEER, RYDER and STOW, after R.Smirke, 'Naval Victories', 'Commemoration of the victory of June 1st 1794', line, pub 1803, BM, NPG.

PR RIDLEY & HOLL, after Bowyer, hs, stipple, oval, pub 1806, NPG.

DON, Sir George (1754-1832) general.

PR S.W.REYNOLDS, after C.G.Dillon, wl in uniform, in landscape, coloured mezz, pub 1808, BM.

DONALD, Adam (1703-1780) prophet.

D JOHN HARRIS, wl, w/c, BM.

PR UNKNOWN, after J.W., wl, aged 69, line, for *The Bee*, related to the above drg, BM, NPG.

DONALDSON, James (1751-1830) founder of Donaldson's Hospital.
L AUGUSTIN EDOUART, SNPG 1176.

DONALDSON, John (d1865) professor of music.
P WILLIAM SMELLIE WATSON, exhib 1849, tql, Edinburgh University.

DONALDSON, Thomas Leverton (1795-1885) architect.
P CHARLES MARTIN, hl profile, RIBA, London.
R F.B.BARWELL, head, lith, for *The Architect*, 1869, NPG. M.JACKSON, hs, woodcut, BM.

DONKIN, Bryan (1768-1855) civil engineer.
G J.F.SKILL, J.GILBERT, W. and E.WALKER, 'Men of Science Living in 1807-08', pencil and wash, NPG 1075.

DONKIN, Sir Rufane Shaw (1773-1841) general, founded Port Elizabeth.
P HENRY MAYER, tql seated in uniform, City Hall, Port Elizabeth, South Africa, engr W.Holl, stipple, for Jerdan's *Nat Portrait Gallery*, 1831, BM, NPG.
G SIR GEORGE HAYTER, 'The House of Commons, 1833', oil, NPG 54.

DONOUGHMORE, John Hely-Hutchinson, 2nd Earl of (1757-1832) general.
P THOMAS PHILLIPS, c1809, tql with Bath ribbon and star, Royal Coll.
R GOSS, hl, mezz, pub 1802, BM. H.MACKENZIE, after T.Phillips, hl seated, stipple, for *Contemporary Portraits*, 1809, BM, NPG. W.NICHOLLS, hl, stipple for *Military Panorama*, 1814, BM, NPG. J.HEATH, after Knight, hs, stipple, for Sir J.Barrington's *Historic Memoirs*, 1815, BM, NPG.

DONOUGHMORE, John Hely-Hutchinson, 3rd Earl of (1787-1851) soldier.
G A.J.BLANCHARD, after A.Neveu, 'Wilson, Hutchinson and Bruce', line, BM.

DONOUGHMORE, Richard Hely-Hutchinson, 1st Earl of (1756-1825) advocate of Catholic emancipation.
G SIR GEORGE HAYTER, 'The Trial of Queen Caroline, 1820', oil, NPG 999.
R W.LENEY, hl, stipple, oval, pub 1797, BM, NPG. H.BROCAS, after B.Stoker, hs, stipple, oval, NPG.

DORCHESTER, Guy Carleton, 1st Baron (1724-1808) governor of Quebec.
R UNKNOWN, hs, line, oval, NPG.

DORSET, Charles Sackville, 2nd Duke of (1711-1769) privy councillor and friend of Frederick, Prince of Wales.
P GEORGE KNAPTON, 1741, hl in Roman dress, Society of Dilettanti, Brooks's Club, London. F.RICHTER, wl as Roman Emperor, Knole (NT), Kent.
D ROSALBA CARRIERA, two hl pastels, Knole.
SC JOHANN LORENZ NATTER, silver and copper medal, BM.
R UNKNOWN, after O.Humphry, hs, stipple, oval, pub 1799, BM, NPG.

DORSET, John Frederick Sackville, 3rd Duke of (1745-1799) diplomatist.
P SIR JOSHUA REYNOLDS, 1769, wl in robes, coronet and Garter star on table, Knole (NT), Kent. THOMAS GAINSBOROUGH, 1782, hl, Knole. Attrib SIR J.REYNOLDS, hs with Garter star, oval, Knole.
M OZIAS HUMPHRY, 1778, Knole. OZIAS HUMPHRY, V & A.

DOUCE, Francis (1757-1834) antiquary.
D STEPHEN CATTERSON SMITH, hl seated, pencil, BM. E.TURNER, after a medallion by C.Prosperi, head, profile, pencil, V & A.

DOUGHTY, William (d1782) painter and mezzotint engraver.
P Self-portrait, c1776, hs, NPG 2513.
PR Self-portrait, c1780, hl in Vandyck dress, mezz, BM.

DOUGLAS, Alexander Hamilton (1767-1852), see 10th Duke of Hamilton.

DOUGLAS, formerly Stewart, Archibald James Edward Douglas, 1st Baron (1748-1827) claimant in the celebrated 'Douglas' lawsuit.
P GEORGE WILLISON, 1769, hl, SNPG L209. SIR THOMAS LAWRENCE, c1790, hl, Buccleuch Estates, Selkirk, Scotland.

DOUGLAS, Catherine, see Duchess of Queensberry.

DOUGLAS, David (1798-1834) botanist and traveller.
D SIR DANIEL MACNEE, 1828, hs, crayon, Royal Botanic Gardens, Kew.
PR UNKNOWN, hs, lith, for Curtis's *Botanical Magazine*, BM.

DOUGLAS, Frederick Sylvester North (1791-1819) author.
PR J.D.INGRES, hl, lith, 1815, BM, NPG. F.C.LEWIS, after J.Slater, hs, stipple, one of 'Grillion's Club' series, BM, NPG.

DOUGLAS, Sir Howard, 3rd Bart (1776-1861) general.
D SIR FRANCIS CHANTREY, hs and hs profile, pencil, NPG 316a (33).
PR W.HOLL, after a photograph by Williams, hs, stipple and line, oval, pub 1863, NPG.

DOUGLAS, James (c1702-1768), see 14th Earl of Morton.

DOUGLAS, James (1753-1819) divine, antiquary.
P Attrib THOMAS PHILLIPS, hl, Ashmolean Museum, Oxford.

DOUGLAS, John (1721-1807) bishop of Salisbury.
P SIR WILLIAM BEECHEY, RA 1789, tql seated with Garter badge, Lambeth Palace, London. R.MULLER, RA 1797, tql in robes of chancellor of the order of the Garter, Balliol College, Oxford.
PR G.BARTOLOZZI, after R.Muller, hl with Garter badge, stipple, for *Contemporary Portraits*, 1810, BM.

DOUGLAS, Neil (1750-1823) poet and preacher.
PR B.W., hs, profile, etch, 1817, NPG.

DOUGLAS, Sir Neil (1779-1853) soldier.
P SIR JOHN WATSON-GORDON, wl, SNPG 1866.
C B.W.CROMBIE, wl, coloured etch, 1847, reprinted in *Modern Athenians*, 1882, NPG.

DOUGLAS, Philip (1758-1822) master of Corpus Christi College, Cambridge.
P KIRKBY, Corpus Christi College, Cambridge.

DOUGLAS, Sylvester, see Baron Glenbervie.

DOUGLAS, William (1724-1810), see 4th Duke of Queensberry.

DOUGLASS, John (1743-1812) Roman Catholic prelate.
PR UNKNOWN, hs, stipple, oval, pub 1812, NPG.

DOVER, George James Welbore Agar-Ellis, 1st Baron (1797-1833) one of the founders of the National Gallery.
P SIR THOMAS LAWRENCE, c1825, tql seated, Yale Center for British Art, New Haven, USA.
G SIR GEORGE HAYTER, 'The Trial of Queen Caroline, 1820', oil, NPG 999. P.C.WONDER, 'Patrons and Lovers of Art, 1826', NPG 794.
SC BERTEL THORVALDSEN, 1818, plaster bust, Thorvaldsen Museum, Copenhagen.
PR W.WARD, after J.Jackson, hl, mezz, pub 1823, BM, NPG. E.SCRIVEN, after T.Phillips, hl, stipple, for Jerdan's *Nat Portrait Gallery*, 1830, BM, NPG. J.BURNET, after G.Sanders, tql in fancy dress and robe, line, BM, NPG.

DOVER, Joseph Yorke, Baron (1724-1792) diplomatist.
M J.ALEFOUNDER, hs on ivory, Antony House (NT), Cornwall.
PR UNKNOWN, hs, line, pub 1780, BM, NPG.

DOW, Alexander (d1779) translator and dramatist.
P SIR JOSHUA REYNOLDS, 1771-72, hs, Petworth (NT), W.Sussex.

DOWDESWELL, William (1761-1828) general, print collector.
PR R.GRAVES, hs, line, pub 1826, BM, NPG.

DOWNES, William Downes, 1st Baron (1752-1826) chief justice of the King's bench to Ireland.
P G.F.JOSEPH, 1821, wl in robes, Trinity College, Dublin.
PE S.W.REYNOLDS, after M.Cregan, wl in robes, mezz, pub 1827, BM.

DOWNMAN, Hugh (1740-1809) physician and poet.
D JOHN DOWNMAN, 1778, hl, chalk, Fitzwilliam Museum, Cambridge. JOHN DOWNMAN, 1796, hl profile, pencil and w/c, BM.

DOWNMAN, John (1750-1824) portrait-painter.
D Self-portrait, 1813, BM.
G UNKNOWN, after P.Sandby, 'Sketches taken at Print Sales', line, pub 1798, BM.

DOWNSHIRE, Arthur Hill, 2nd Marquess of (1753-1801) peer.
G ARTHUR DEVIS, '1st Marquess of Downshire and family', oil, c1760, NPG L160.

DOWNSHIRE, Wills Hill, 1st Marquess of (1718-1793) statesman.
P POMPEO BATONI, 1766, wl, on loan to the Ulster Museum, Belfast. JOHN RISING, after George Romney, hl in peer's robes, Hatfield House, Herts.
D JOHN DOWNMAN, 1786, tql, w/c, oval, Hatfield.
G ARTHUR DEVIS, '1st Marquess of Downshire and family', oil, c1760, NPG L160.

DOWTON, William (1764-1851) actor.
P Two hs sketches as Falstaff, by R.W.Buss, Garrick Club, London.
D SAMUEL DE WILDE, two portraits both 1812, as Dr Cantwell in *The Hypocrite*, chalk and w/c, and as Sir Oliver Cypress in *Grieving's a Folly*, w/c, BM and Garrick Club.
G SAMUEL DE WILDE, two pictures, in scenes from *The Soldier's Daughter*, RA 1805, and *The Mayor of Garratt*, RA 1810, Garrick Club.
PR Several theatrical prints, BM, NPG.

DOYLE, Sir Charles William (1770-1842) general.
P MARGARET CARPENTER, hl in uniform, Boston Museum of Fine Arts, USA.
PR J.GODBY, after Walton, hl, stipple, pub 1813, NPG. UNKNOWN, hl in uniform, stipple, for Clarke's *Life of Wellington*, 1814, BM.

DOYLE, James Warren (1786-1834) catholic bishop of Kildare and Leighlin.
SC JOHN HOGAN, 1840, statue, Carlow Cathedral, Eire. UNKNOWN, plaster bust, NGI 8101, death mask, NGI 8131.
PR R.COOPER, after J.C.Smith, hs, stipple, pub 1824, NPG. W.HOLL, after P.Turnerelli, after a marble bust, stipple, pub 1834, BM, NPG. J.HAVERTY, hl, lith, NPG.

DOYLE, Sir John, Bart (1750?-1834) general.
PR A.CARDON, hs, stipple, oval, for *Military Chronicle*, 1812, NPG. W.SAY, after J.Ramsay, tql with Egyptian servants and horse, mezz, pub 1817, BM, NPG. UNKNOWN, hs in uniform, stipple, oval, BM.

DOYLE, John (1797-1868) 'HB', caricaturist.

D H.E.DOYLE, (his son), head, profile, chalk, NPG 2130.
SC CHRISTOPHER MOORE, plaster bust, NGI.

D'OYLY, Sir John, 1st Bart (1774-1824) resident of Kandy
D Indian artist, c1800, wl at the Court of Newaub Moobaruck u Dowlah, w/c, V & A.

DRAGONETTI, Domenico (1755?-1846) musician.
SC J.P.DANTAN, 1834, plaster caricature statue, Musée Carnavelet, Paris.
PR F.HILLEMACHER, hl profile, etch, oval, BM. T.FAIRLAND, after C.Doane, hs, lith, pub 1846, NPG. M.GAUCI, hl, as an old man, lith, BM.

DRAKE, Nathan (1766-1836) physician and essayist.
PR P.W.TOMKINS, after H.Thomson, hl seated, stipple, BM, NPG.

DRAKE, William (1723-1801) antiquary and philologist.
PR W.BROMLEY, after N.Drake, tql seated, line, BM, NPG.

DRAPER, Sir William (1721-1787) lieutenant-general.
P THOMAS GAINSBOROUGH, late 1760s, tql in uniform, De Young Memorial Museum, San Francisco, USA.
PR UNKNOWN, probably after a drawing by Gainsborough, hs profile, stipple, oval, pub 1782, NPG. Similar engraving by W.Ridley, for *Letters of Junius*, 1805, BM.

DREW, Samuel (1765-1833) metaphysician.
PR HICKS, after Griffiths, hl seated, stipple, pub 1819, NPG. W.T.FRY, after J.Moore, hl seated, stipple, pub 1834, NPG. Similar engraving by R.Hicks, for Jerdan's *Nat Portrait Gallery*, 1835, BM.

DROGHEDA, Charles Moore, 6th Earl and 1st Marquess of (1730-1822) major-general.
PR R.B.PARKES, after Sir J.Reynolds, hl in uniform, mezz, BM, NPG.

DRUMMOND, Henry (1786-1860) politician.
PR W.WALKER, hl, stipple, pub 1849, BM. W.HOLL, after G.Richmond, hs, stipple, one of 'Grillion's Club' series, BM.
C JOHN DOYLE, 'Extremes Meet', pencil, 1848, BM.

DRUMMOND, James (1713-1746) see 6th Earl and 3rd titular Duke of Perth.

DRUMMOND, John (1714-1747) see 7th Earl and 4th titular Duke of Perth.

DRUMMOND, Robert Hay (1711-1776) archbishop of York.
P SIR JOSHUA REYNOLDS, 1764-65, tql seated in robes of chancellor of the order of the Garter, City Art Museum, St Louis, Missouri, USA; version, SNPG 903. THOMAS HUDSON, tql seated, Bishopthorpe Palace, York; version, Christ Church, Oxford.

DRUMMOND, Samuel (1765-1844) portrait and history painter.
D G.H.WHITE, 1842, hs profile, ink and pencil, NPG 4216. J.T.SMITH, hs, pencil, BM.
PR W.BARNARD, after S.Drummond, wl seated, with his wife, mezz, pub 1805, BM.

DRUMMOND, Thomas (1797-1840) under-secretary for Ireland and engineer.
P H.W.PICKERSGILL, 1834, wl, Edinburgh University. H.W.PICKERSGILL, tql, NGI 409.
SC JOHN HOGAN, 1840-43, bronze statue, City Hall, Dublin.
PR J.C., hl profile, lith, BM.

DRUMMOND, Sir William (1770?-1828) scholar and diplomatist.
PR After A. DE MEYER, hs, coloured stipple, NPG.

DRURY, Henry Joseph Thomas (1778-1841) scholar.
PR T.HODGETTS, after M.Carpenter, hl, mezz, BM, NPG.

DRYANDER, Jonas (1748-1810) botanist.
W.DANIELL, after G.Dance, hs profile, soft-ground etch, pub 1811, BM, NPG.

DUANE, Matthew (1707-1785) lawyer and numismatist.
J.MITAN, after G.Hussey, hs profile, line, oval, pub 1798, BM, NPG.

DUBOIS, Edward (1774-1850) wit and author.
E.DUMÉE, after A. van Assen, hl, stipple, oval, for *Thespian Mag*, 1794, BM. 'UNKNOWN', hl seated (similar pose), stipple, BM. RIDLEY, after Allingham, hl seated, stipple, pub 1839, NPG.

DUCAREL, Andrew Coltee (1713-1785) antiquary.
F.PERRY, after A.Soldi, hl, etch, oval, for his *Norman Coins*, 1757, BM, NPG. P.AUDINET, after F.Towne, hs, line, for Nichols's *Illustrations of Literary History*, 1818, BM, NPG.

DUCK Stephen (1705-1756) poet.
Attrib BERNARD LENS, c1740, hs, NPG 4493.
G.BICKHAM jun, after J.Thornhill, tql seated, line, for his *Poems*, 1736, BM, NPG. UNKNOWN, wl in farmyard, line, BM, NPG.

DUCKWORTH, Sir John Thomas, 1st Bart (1748-1817) admiral.
SIR WILLIAM BEECHEY, replica of c1809–10, tql with medals, NMM, Greenwich.
H.R.COOK, after R.Bowyer, hs, stipple, oval, for *The Naval Chronicle*, 1807, BM, NPG.

DUCROW, Andrew (1793-1842) equestrian performer.
J.W.GEAR, head, Theatre Collection, Harvard College Library, Cambridge, Mass, USA.
Several theatrical prints, NPG. Numerous theatrical prints, Harvard Theatre Collection.

DUDLEY, Sir Henry Bate, 1st Bart (1745-1824) journalist and canon of Ely.
THOMAS GAINSBOROUGH, RA 1780, wl in landscape with dog, Marlborough House, London. THOMAS GAINSBOROUGH, c1780, hs, oval, TATE 1044.

DUDLEY, John William Ward, 1st Earl of (1781-1833) secretary of state.
F.C.LEWIS, after J.Slater, hs, one of 'Grillion's Club' series, stipple, BM, NPG. E.BERENS, aged 19, hs, lith, BM, NPG.

DUFF, James (1729-1809), see 2nd Earl of Fife.

DUFF, James (1776-1857), see 4th Earl of Fife.

DUIGENAN, Patrick (1735-1816) Irish politician.
J.HEATH, after J.Comerford, hs, stipple, for Sir J.Barrington's *Historic Memoirs*, 1810, BM, NPG.

DUNBAR, George (1774-1851) classical scholar.
SIR JOHN WATSON-GORDON, hl, Edinburgh University.

DUNCAN, Adam Duncan, 1st Viscount (1731-1804) admiral.
SIR JOSHUA REYNOLDS, exhib 1760, tql, NGS 1215. JOHN HOPPNER, RA 1798, wl, Forfar Town Hall, Scotland; hl version, NPG 1839. DANIEL ORME, c1797, wl, NMM, Greenwich. SIR HENRY RAEBURN, c1797, wl, Trinity House, Leith. JOHN SINGLETON COPLEY, 1793–95, hl, oval, NMM. J.S.COPLEY, 1798, tql, NMM. H.P.DANLOUX, wl with telescope, NPG 1084. H.P.DANLOUX, wl with cannon, SNPG 1065.
JOHN SMART, 1798, hs, pencil and wash, NPG 4315.
SAMUEL DRUMMOND, Duncan receiving the surrender of the Dutch admiral, aboard the Venerable at the Battle of Camperdown, 1797, oil, NMM.
JOHN DE VAERE, 1798, Wedgwood medallion, NPG L152(8). SIR RICHARD WESTMACOTT, 1804, statue, St Paul's Cathedral, London. Several medallions, SNPG.

DUNCAN, Andrew (1744-1828) physician and professor at Edinburgh University.
P DAVID MARTIN, hl, SNPG 165. SIR JOHN WATSON-GORDON, hl, SNPG L258.
D JOHN BROWN, c1780, head, pencil, SNPG L77.
SC PETER SLATER, after Benjamin Cheverton, porcelain bust, SNPG 238.
C J.KAY, wl profile, etch, 1785, BM, NPG. J.KAY, wl profile with umbrella, etch, 1797, BM.

DUNCAN, Henry (1774-1846) propounder of Savings Bank.
PH D.O.HILL and ROBERT ADAMSON, wl seated, calotype, P 6 (88).

DUNCAN, John Shute (1769-1844) writer and keeper of the Ashmolean Museum, Oxford.
P THOMAS KIRKBY, c1825–26, hs, Ashmolean Museum, Oxford. KILBERT, hl, Winchester College, Hants. W.SMITH, hs, New College, Oxford.
SC J.S.DEVILLE, RA 1825, plaster bust, Oriel College, Oxford.

DUNCAN, Jonathan (1756-1811) governor of Bombay.
PR W.WARD, after J.J.Masquerier of 1792, hs, mezz, NPG.

DUNCAN, Philip Bury (1772-1863) keeper of the Ashmolean Museum, Oxford.
P THOMAS KIRKBY, RA 1825, hs, New College, Oxford. W.SMITH junr, hl, New College, Oxford.

DUNCANNON, John William Ponsonby, Viscount, see 4th Earl of Bessborough.

DUNCOMBE, John (1729-1786) miscellaneous writer.
P JOSEPH HIGHMORE, 1766, hl, Corpus Christi College, Cambridge.

DUNCOMBE, Thomas Slingsby (1796-1861) radical politician.
D JAMES CHILDE, 1836, tql, pencil and wash, NPG 1651a. COUNT A. D'ORSAY, 1839, hs, pencil and chalk, NPG 4026(20).
G F.BROMLEY, after B.R.Haydon, 'The Reform Banquet, 1832', etch, pub 1835, NPG, and J.C.BROMLEY, mezz, pub 1837, BM.
PR S.W.REYNOLDS sen, after S.W.Reynolds jun, tql, mezz, pub 1831, BM. D.J.POUND, after a photograph by Mayall, tql seated, stipple and line, NPG.

DUNDAS, Charles, see Baron Amesbury.

DUNDAS, Sir David (1735-1820) general.
P SIR HENRY RAEBURN, 1809, hl, Arniston House, Lothian region, Scotland. SAMUEL DRUMMOND, hl, SNPG 1281.
D SIR FRANCIS CHANTREY, hs profile, pencil, NPG 316a (38).
PR H.R.COOK, after W.Owen, hl with order of Bath, stipple, for *Royal Military Panorama*, BM, NPG.
C R.DIGHTON, wl in uniform, coloured etch, pub 1810, BM, NPG.

DUNDAS, Francis (d1824) general.
P SIR HENRY RAEBURN, hl, Arniston House, Lothian region, Scotland. SIR HENRY RAEBURN, hl, with his wife, Arniston House.
D JOHN DOWNMAN, 1793, hl, chalk, and w/c, oval, Arniston House. DANIEL GARDNER, wl, pastel and gouache, Arniston House.
C J.KAY, 'Military Promenade', etch, BM.

DUNDAS, Henry (1742-1811), see 1st Viscount Melville.

DUNDAS, Sir James Whitley Deans (1785-1862) admiral.
G SIR GEORGE HAYTER, 'The House of Commons, 1833', oil, NPG 54.
PR W.H.GIBBS, after F.Piercy, hs, stipple, pub 1855, NPG. D.J.POUND, tql, stipple and line, NPG.

DUNDAS, Robert (1713-1787), see Lord Arniston.

DUNDAS, Robert (1771-1851), see 2nd Viscount Melville.

DUNDAS, Thomas Dundas, 1st Baron (1741-1820) vice admiral of Orkney and Shetland.
P SIR THOMAS LAWRENCE, 1817, hl, The Society of Dilettanti, Brooks's Club, London.
D SIR FRANCIS CHANTREY, hs, pencil, NPG 316a (39).
SC SIR FRANCIS CHANTREY, bust, Ashmolean Museum, Oxford.

DUNDAS, William (1762-1845) secretary of state.
P JOHN HOPPNER, hl, Arniston House, Lothian region, Scotland; version, SNPG 289.
D JOHN DOWNMAN, wl, w/c, Arniston House.

DUNDAS of Arniston, Robert (1758-1819) judge.
P J.J.MASQUERIER, hl, Arniston House, Lothian region, Scotland.
  SIR HENRY RAEBURN, hl seated, Arniston House.
D SIR FRANCIS CHANTREY, hs profile, pencil, NPG 316a (40).
G K.A.HICKEL, 'The House of Commons, 1793', oil, NPG 745.
SC SIR FRANCIS CHANTREY, RA 1817?, marble bust, Arniston House. SIR FRANCIS CHANTREY, 1824, marble statue, Faculty of Advocates, Parliament Hall, Edinburgh. After JOHN HENNING, plaster medallion, SNPG 408.
C J.KAY, wl with Lord Melville, etch, 1790, BM, NPG. J.KAY, tql profile, etch, 1799, BM, NPG.

DUNDONALD, Archibald Cochrane, 9th Earl of (1747/8-1831) chemist.
G J.F.SKILL, J.GILBERT, W. and E.WALKER, 'Men of Science Living in 1807-08', pencil and wash, NPG 1075.

DUNDONALD, Thomas Cochrane, 10th Earl of (1775-1860) admiral and politician.
P JAMES RAMSAY, RA 1811, wl with telescope, DoE (Admiralty). UNKNOWN, posthumous, after a photograph, tql with orders, NMM, Greenwich.
PR C.TURNER, after G.F.Stroehling, wl, mezz, pub 1809, BM. R.COOPER, after W.Walton, tql, stipple, pub 1819, BM, NPG. BOUVIER, after J.Ramsay, tql, lith, pub 1827, BM. H.MEYER, after same portrait, wl, mezz, NPG.

DUNDRENNAN, Thomas Maitland, Lord (1792-1851) Scottish judge.
C B.W.CROMBIE, wl, coloured etch, for *Modern Athenians*, 1847, NPG.

DUNFERMLINE, James Abercromby, 1st Baron (1776-1858) politician.
P SIR JOHN WATSON-GORDON, tql, SNPG 990. JOHN JACKSON, hl, Hardwick Hall (NT), Derbys.
G SIR GEORGE HAYTER, 'The House of Commons, 1833', oil, NPG 54. SIR DAVID WILKIE, 'The First Council of Queen Victoria, 1837', oil, Royal Coll.
SC WILLIAM BRODIE, 1858, marble bust, SNPG 330.
PR UNKNOWN, after J.Hayter, hs in speaker's robes, stipple, pub 1838, BM, NPG. H.COOK, after J.Stewart, tql seated in speaker's robes, line, BM, NPG. T.LUPTON, after Colvin Smith, hl, mezz, BM, NPG.

DUNGANNON, Arthur Hill-Trevor, 3rd Viscount (1798-1862) politician.
P STEPHEN CATTERSON SMITH, c1856, wl, V & A, engr J.J.Chant, mezz, pub 1858, NPG, V & A.
PR W.SAY, after J.Burnet, tql as a boy with his brother and a dog, mezz, BM.

DUNK, George Montagu, see 2nd Earl of Halifax.

DUNLOP, Frances Anna, née Wallace (1730-1815) friend of Robert Burns.
D 'A.C.', w/c, SNPG 1208.

DUNLOP, John (1755-1820) song-writer and provost of Glasgow.
P SIR HENRY RAEBURN, hs, Glasgow City Art Gallery.

DUNLOP, William (1792-1848) pioneer in Canada and writer.
D DANIEL MACLISE, 1833, wl seated, pencil and w/c, NPG 3029, finished study for No 35 of 'Gallery of Illustrious Literary Characters', for *Fraser's Mag*, 1833, BM, NPG.

DUNMORE, John Murray, 4th Earl of (1732-1809) governor of New York and Virginia.
P SIR JOSHUA REYNOLDS, 1765, wl in Scottish dress, SNPG L163.
PR J.SCOTT, after J.Reynolds, wl, mezz, NPG.

DUNN, Robert (1799-1877) writer on medical psychology.
PR G.B.BLACK, tql seated, lith, BM.

DUNN, Samuel (1798-1882) expelled Wesleyan minister.
P Attrib HENRY ANELAY, tql, Methodist Publishing House, London, engr W.H.Egleton, stipple, NPG.
PR UNKNOWN, hl, woodcut, for *Illust London News*, 1849, BM.

DUNNING, John (1731-1783), see 1st Baron Ashburton.

DUNSINANE, Sir William Nairne, Lord (1731?-1811) Scottish judge.
P SIR HENRY RAEBURN, tql in robes, Faculty of Advocates, Parliament Hall, Edinburgh.
C J.KAY, hl seated in robes, etch, oval, 1799, BM, NPG.

DUNSTAN, Jeffrey (1759?-1797) 'mayor' of Garratt.
PR UNKNOWN, wl, coloured etch, pub 1779, BM, similar etch, by T.Wilkes, for *Wonderful Mag*, 1794, BM, NPG.

DUNSTANVILLE, Francis Basset, Baron de, see De Dunstanville.

DUNTHORNE, John (1770-1844) landscape-painter.
D JOHN CONSTABLE, 1813, probably rightly named, wl, pencil sketch, V & A.

DUNTHORNE, John (1798-1832) painter.
P Self-portrait, hs, oval, Ipswich Museum and Art Gallery (Christchurch Mansion).

DUPONT, Gainsborough (1754?-1797) portrait painter and mezzotint engraver.
P THOMAS GAINSBOROUGH, c1770-75, hs, TATE 6242. THOMAS GAINSBOROUGH, hs, semi-profile, oval, Mansfield College, Oxford.
D THOMAS GAINSBOROUGH, 1775, head, w/c and chalk, V & A.

DUPPA, Richard (1770-1831) artist and author.
PR C.TURNER, after H.Edridge, tql, mezz, pub 1819, BM, NPG.

DUPUIS, Thomas Sanders (1733-1796) musician.
PR C.TURNER, after J.Russell, hl in robes, mezz, pub 1797, BM, NPG. UNKNOWN, hl, mezz, NPG.

DURHAM, John George Lambton, 1st Earl of (1792-1840) governor-general of Canada.
P THOMAS PHILLIPS, after his portrait of 1819, hl, NPG 2547. After SIR THOMAS LAWRENCE of 1829, hl, Reform Club, London.
SL UNKNOWN, wl, woodcut, NPG.
G SIR GEORGE HAYTER, 'The Trial of Queen Caroline, 1820', oil, NPG 999. S.W.REYNOLDS, 'The Reform Bill Receiving the King's Assent, 1832', oil, Palace of Westminster, London. J.KNIGHT, 'William IV holding a Council', lith, c1832, BM.
PR C.E.WAGSTAFF, G.DALZIEL, tql in masonic dress, mixed engraving, pub 1841, BM. R.J.LANE, after A.d'Orsay, hl profile, lith, NPG.
C JOHN DOYLE, several political satires, drgs, BM.

DURHAM, Sir Philip Charles Henderson Calderwood

(1763-1845) admiral.
P SIR FRANCIS GRANT, c1833, tql with orders, SNPG 1605. JOHN WOOD, 1844, wl with orders, NMM, Greenwich.

DUTENS, Louis (1730-1812) diplomatist and author.
C Attrib JOHN FLAXMAN, 1787, Wedgwood medallion, Wedgwood Museum, Barlaston, Staffs. After JAMES TASSIE, plaster medallion, SNPG 513.
R E.FISHER, hs, mezz, pub 1777, BM.

DWYER, Michael (1771-1826) Irish rebel.
G UNKNOWN, 'The United Irish Patriots of 1798', coloured lith, NPG.

DYCE, Alexander (1798-1869) scholar and editor of Shakespeare.
R C.H.JEENS, tql seated, line, BM, NPG.

DYER, George (1755-1841) author.

P HENRY MEYER, hl seated with dog, Fitzwilliam Museum, Cambridge.
PR E.CRISTALL, after J.Cristall, hl, stipple and aquatint, oval, BM, NPG.

DYER, John (1700-1758) poet.
PR DALZIEL, hs, woodcut, BM.

DYER, Joseph Chessborough (1780-1871) inventor.
D WILLIAM BROCKEDON, 1831, hs, chalk, NPG 2515(55).
PR E.SCRIVEN, after J.Allen, hl seated, line, BM.

DYER, Samuel (1725-1772) writer and translator.
PR G.MARCHI, after J.Reynolds, hl profile, seated, mezz, pub 1773, BM.

DYKES, Thomas (1761-1847) divine.
SC W.D.KEYWORTH, 1840, bust, St John's Church, Hull.
PR R.J.LANE, 1847, hl, lith, NPG.

E

EARLE, Henry (1789-1838) surgeon.
SC WILLIAM BEHNES, 1838, bust, St Bartholomew's Hospital, London.

EARLE, William Benson (1740-1793) philanthropist.
PR W.EVANS, after W.Hoare, hs profile, stipple, oval, BM, NPG.

EARLOM, Richard (1743-1822) engraver.
PR T.LUPTON, after G.Stuart, hl, mezz, pub 1819, BM, NPG.

EARNSHAW, Thomas (1749-1829) watchmaker and inventor.
P SIR MARTIN ARCHER SHEE, hl, NMM, Greenwich.

EAST, Sir Edward Hyde (1764-1847) chief justice of Calcutta.
D SIR FRANCIS CHANTREY, hs and hs profile, pencil, NPG 316a (42).
SC SIR FRANCIS CHANTREY, c1829, marble seated statue, Calcutta.
PR G.B.BLACK, after G.Chinnery, hl in robes, lith, NPG.

EAST, Sir James Buller (1789-1878) barrister.
PR F.C.LEWIS, after J.Slater, hs, stipple, one of 'Grillion's Club', series, BM.

EASTHOPE, Sir John, 1st Bart (1784-1865) politician.
PR G.B.BLACK, after J.Holmes, hl seated, lith, octagon, BM.

EASTLAKE, Sir Charles Lock (1793-1865) President of the Royal Academy and Director of the National Gallery.
P JOHN PRESCOTT KNIGHT, c1857, tql seated, Royal Academy, London. D.HUNTINGTON, RA 1852, New York Historical Society, USA.
D Attrib JOHN HAYTER, 1814, hs, pencil and ink, BM. SIR GEORGE HAYTER, 1816, head, with S.Kirkup, pencil and wash, BM. JOHN PARTRIDGE, 1825, hs, pencil, NPG 3944 (22). WILLIAM BROCKEDON, 1828, hs, chalk, NPG 2515 (16). CARL CHRISTIAN VOGEL, 1834, hs, Kupferstichkabinett, Staatliche Kunstsammlungen, Dresden. THOMAS BRIDGFORD, c1844, tql, Royal Hibernian Academy, Dublin. C.B.BIRCH, c1858, head, sketch, pencil, NPG 2477. C.B.BIRCH, 1859, head, profile, pencil, NPG 2478.
G JOHN PARTRIDGE, 'The Fine Arts Commissioners, 1846', NPG 342, 3.
SC JOHN GIBSON, marble bust, NPG 953.
C C.W.COPE, c1862, head, profile, pen and ink, NPG 3182 (12).
PH CALDESI, BLANDFORD & CO., wl, carte, NPG.

EATON, Daniel Isaac (d1814) publisher.
PR W.SHARP, after L.Abbott, hl, line, pub 1794, NPG; pencil drg for Sharp's engraving, BM. UNKNOWN, hs, stipple and line, for his *Trial*, 1812, BM.

EBSWORTH, Joseph (1788-1868) musician and dramatist.
D J.W.EBSWORTH, 1848, w/c, SNPG 1118.

EDEN, George (1784-1849), see 1st Earl of Auckland.

EDEN, William (1744-1814), see 1st Baron Auckland.

EDGCUMBE, George (1721-1795), see 1st Earl of Mount-Edgcumbe.

EDGCUMBE, Richard (1764-1839), see 2nd Earl of Mount-Edgcumbe.

EDGCUMBE, Richard Edgcumbe, 2nd Baron (1716-

1761) friend of Horace Walpole.
P SIR JOSHUA REYNOLDS: c1748, tql, Mount Edgcumbe, Cornwall; exhib 1760, tql in peer's robes, Mount Edgcumbe.
G SIR JOSHUA REYNOLDS, 'The Committee of Taste', some times called 'The "Out of Town" party', oil, 1761, City Art Gallery, Bristol.

EDGEWORTH DE FIRMONT, Henry Essex (1745-180 confessor to Louis XVI.
PR A.CARDON, after A. de St Aubin, hl, stipple, oval, pub 1800, BM, NPG.

EDGEWORTH, Maria (1767-1849) writer.
PH UNKNOWN, hs, daguerreotype, NPG P 5.

EDGEWORTH, Richard Lovell (1744-1817) writer and inventor.
P H.D.HAMILTON, c1783, hl, NGI 1350.
M HORACE HONE, 1785, hs, oval, NPG 5069.
SC JOHN HENNING, 1803, paste medallion, SNPG 2135.

EDMONDSON, Joseph (d1786) herald and genealogist.
PR J.JONES, after T.Beach, hl in tabard and collar, mezz, pub 178 BM. F.BARTOLOZZI, after an unknown artist, hs, line, oval, for h *Heraldry*, 1780, BM.

EDMONSTONE, Neil Benjamin (1765-1841) India civilian.
PR M.GAUCI, after W.Bradley, hl, lith, BM, NPG.

EDWARD Augustus, Duke of Kent and Strathearn, se KENT.

EDWARD Augustus, Duke of York and Albany, se YORK and Albany.

EDWARDS, Bryan (1743-1800) West India merchant.
PR HOLLOWAY, after L.Abbot, hl, line, pub 1800, NPG.

EDWARDS, Edward (1738-1806) painter.
D GEORGE DANCE, 1793, hs, profile, pencil, BM. Self-portrait, h chalk and wash, BM.
PR A.CARDON, after E.Edwards, hs, stipple, for his *Anecdotes Painters*, 1808, BM, NPG. MRS D.TURNER, after O.Humphry head, etch, BM, NPG.

EDWARDS, John (1714-1785) dissenting minister at Leeds
PR J.WATSON, after J.Russell, hl, mezz, oval, pub 1772, BM, NPG

EDWARDS, William (1719-1789) bridge builder.
PR W.SKELTON, after T.Hill, hl seated with plan of Taaffe bridg line, oval, BM, NPG.

EDWARDS, William Camden (1777-1855) engraver.
PR MRS D.TURNER and W.C.EDWARDS, after J.P.Davis, head etch, and line, BM, NPG.

EDWIN, Elizabeth Rebecca, née Richards (1771?-1854 actress.
P SAMUEL DE WILDE, hl as Eliza in *Riches*, Garrick Club, London
D S. DE WILDE, wl as Lady Traffic in *Riches*, Garrick Club. S. D WILDE, as Albina Mandeville in *The Will*, Garrick Club.
PR Several theatrical prints, BM, NPG.

EDWIN, John (1749-1790) actor.
P Attrib THOMAS GAINSBOROUGH, hs, Garrick Club, London

THOMAS BEACH, hs as Justice Woodcock in *Love in a Village*, Garrick Club. T.BEACH, as Peeping Tom, Garrick Club.
D JAMES ROBERTS, two hs pencil drgs, Garrick Club.
R Various theatrical prints, BM, NPG.

EDWIN, John (1768-1805) actor.
R UNKNOWN, small wl, aged 12, as Tom Thumb in Fielding's *Tom Thumb*, line, pub 1780, BM.

EFFINGHAM, Kenneth Alexander Howard, 1st Earl of (1767-1845) general.
G SIR GEORGE HAYTER, 'The Trial of Queen Caroline, 1820', oil, NPG 999.

EGAN, John (1750?-1810) chairman of Kilmainham.
R J.HEATH, after J.Comerford, hs, stipple, for Sir J.Barrington's *Historic Memoirs*, 1811, BM, NPG.

EGAN, Pierce (1772-1849) author of *Life in London*.
R C.TURNER, after G.Sharples, tql seated, mezz, pub 1823, BM, NPG.

EGERTON, Daniel (1772-1835) actor.
D SAMUEL DE WILDE, 1816, wl as Clytus, w/c and chalk, BM.

EGERTON, Francis (1736-1803), see 3rd Duke of Bridgewater.

EGERTON, Francis Henry (1756-1829), see 8th Earl of Bridgewater.

EGERTON, John (1721-1787) bishop of Durham.
P UNKNOWN, hl, Bishop Auckland Palace, Durham. UNKNOWN, hl profile, Durham Cathedral.
R F.BARTOLOZZI, after I.Gosset, hs profile, oval medallion, stipple, BM, NPG.

EGERTON, Sarah, née Fisher (1782-1847) actress.
D SAMUEL DE WILDE, 1816, wl as Meg Merrilees in *Guy Mannering*, w/c and chalk, BM.
R Several theatrical prints, BM, NPG.

EGINTON, Francis (1737-1805) painter on glass.
P JAMES MILLAR, 1796, hl, City Art Gallery, Birmingham.

EGLINTON, Archibald Montgomerie, 11th Earl of (1726-1796) lieutenant-general.
P SIR JOSHUA REYNOLDS, *c*1783-84, hs sketch, Royal Coll.
R S.W.REYNOLDS, after C.F. von Breda, tql in robes, mezz, pub 1797, BM. J.SCOTT, after J.Reynolds, hs, mezz, BM.

EGLINTON, Hugh Montgomerie, 12th Earl of (1739-1819) captain in the army during the American war.
P JOHN SINGLETON COPLEY, wl in Highland dress, SNPG 1516; version, *c*1780, County Art Museum, Los Angeles, USA.
C JOHN KAY, hl in highland uniform, etch, BM.

EGMONT, Sir John Perceval, 2nd Earl of (1711-1770) statesman.
P SIR JOSHUA REYNOLDS, *c*1756, tql with his 2nd wife Catherine, Bradford City Art Gallery. THOMAS HUDSON, tql in peer's robes, NPG 2481.
SC UNKNOWN, marble bust, Castle Ashby, Northants.
R J.FABER, jun, after C.F.Zincke, hl, mezz, for *Hist of House of Yvery*, 1742, BM. J.FABER, jun, after F.Hayman, wl, mezz, BM, NPG. 'ADAM STANUP', wl, line, a broadside entitled 'Vain Glory: A Pretty Independent Print', NPG.

EGREMONT, Sir Charles Wyndham, 2nd Earl of (1710-1763) statesman.
P WILLIAM HOARE, nearly wl, Petworth (NT), W.Sussex. Attrib WILLIAM HOARE, nearly wl, NPG 4589. UNKNOWN, wl as a child, dressed as a classical huntsman, in landscape, Petworth. RICHARD WILSON, tql in robes, Dulwich College Picture Gallery, London.

EGREMONT, Sir George O'Brien Wyndham, 3rd Earl of (1751-1837) patron of fine art.
P THOMAS PHILLIPS, 1798, tql in uniform, Petworth (NT), W.Sussex. THOMAS PHILLIPS, 1799, hl, Petworth. J.LUCAS, 1834, hl, Petworth. Several other portraits by THOMAS PHILLIPS at Petworth: wl seated at desk with a dog, tql with dog and book, tql with his daughter. THOMAS PHILLIPS, tql with letter, NPG 3323. GEORGE CLINT, tql at desk with young child, Petworth. GEORGE CLINT, wl in uniform, Brighton Art Gallery.
D SIR FRANCIS CHANTREY, pencil, NPG 316a (43).
G SIR GEORGE HAYTER, 'The Trial of Queen Caroline, 1820', oil, NPG 999. P.C.WONDER, 'Patrons and Lovers of Art, 1826', wl, NPG 795.
SC J.E.CAREW, marble bust, Petworth. UNKNOWN, marble bust, Petworth.

ELCHO, David Wemyss, Lord (1721-1787) Jacobite.
PR A.LALAUZE, after A.Ramsay, tql, etch, BM.

ELDER, Thomas (1737-1799) lord provost of Edinburgh.
P SIR HENRY RAEBURN, 1797, tql, Edinburgh University.
SC JAMES TASSIE, 1795, paste medallion, SNPG 1271.
C J.KAY, wl profile, 1790, etch, BM, NPG. J.KAY, wl with his son-in-law, Dr G.H.Baird, 1793, etch, BM.

ELDIN, John Clerk, Lord (1757-1832) judge.
P SIR HENRY RAEBURN, *c*1815, tql, SNPG 1491. ANDREW GEDDES, tql seated, SNPG 625. COLVIN SMITH, hl, Faculty of Advocates, Parliament Hall, Edinburgh.
D WILLIAM BEWICK, 1824, chalk, SNPG 1052.
SC SAMUEL JOSEPH, plaster bust, SNPG 346.
C J.KAY, hs, etch, 1810, reprinted in *Kay's Portraits*, 1842, vol II, NPG.

ELDON, John Scott, 1st Earl of (1751-1838) lord chancellor.
P WILLIAM OWEN, RA 1812, tql University College, Oxford. H.W.PICKERSGILL, 1832, wl seated with dog, Merchant Taylors' Company, London. H.P.BRIGGS, RA 1835, hl, Middle Temple, London. SIR THOMAS LAWRENCE, hl, Royal Coll; version, NPG 464. WILLIAM OWEN, wl, Convocation House, Oxford.
D SIR GEORGE HAYTER, study for NPG 999, NPG 1695 (k, l, s).
G SIR G.HAYTER, 'The Trial of Queen Caroline, 1820', oil, NPG 999.
SC FREDERICK TATHAM, 1831, marble bust, NPG 181. M.L.WATSON and G.NELSON, *c*1843-47, marble group, University College Library, Oxford. WILLIAM BEHNES, bust, Inner Temple, London.
PR S.W.REYNOLDS and E.SCRIVEN, after F.Stephanoff, wl in robes, holding purse and coronet, with page, for Sir G.Nayler's work on coronation of George IV, mezz, pub 1824, BM.
C Several JOHN DOYLE political sketches, drgs, BM.

ELGIN, Thomas Bruce, 7th Earl of (1766-1841) diplomatist and collector of the 'Elgin Marbles'.
D G.P.HARDING, after Anthony Graff, wl, wash over pencil, BM.

ELIAS, John (1774-1841) Welsh methodist preacher.
P WILLIAM ROOS, 1839, hs, National Museum of Wales 96, Cardiff.
PR S.FREEMAN, after an unknown artist, hs, stipple, for *Evangelical Mag*, 1820, BM, NPG.

ELIOT, Edward Granville, see 3rd Earl of St Germans.

ELIOTT, George Augustus, see 1st Baron Heathfield.

ELIZABETH, Princess of England and Landgravine of Hesse-Homburg (1770-1840) daughter of George III, artist.
P THOMAS GAINSBOROUGH, 1782, hs, oval, Royal Coll. SIR WILLIAM BEECHEY, RA 1797, hl with crayon, Royal Coll. P.E.STROEHLING, 1807, wl in ermine-lined robe, with canvas,

Royal Coll.

D HENRY EDRIDGE, 1802–04, wl seated with pencil and sketchbook, Royal Coll.

M ANDREW ROBERTSON, c1807, hs, Royal Coll.

G SIR BENJAMIN WEST, 'The children of George III and Queen Charlotte', oil, 1776, Royal Coll. SIR BENJAMIN WEST, 'Queen Charlotte with her children', oil, 1779, Royal Coll. THOMAS GAINSBOROUGH, with Charlotte, Princess Royal and Augusta, 'The Three Eldest Princesses', oil, 1784, Royal Coll.

PR W.WARD, after H.Ramberg, tql seated, profile, stipple, oval, pub 1788, BM, NPG.

ELLENBOROUGH, Anne, Lady, née Towry (1769-1843) wife of 1st Baron Ellenborough.

P SIR THOMAS LAWRENCE, RA 1813, hs, Metropolitan Museum of Art, New York, USA.

D SIR GEORGE HAYTER, study for a miniature, NPG 883 (9).

ELLENBOROUGH, Edward Law, 1st Baron (1750-1818) lord chief-justice of England.

P SAMUEL DRUMMOND, hs, NPG 1123. After LAWRENCE of c1806, tql in robes, Lincoln's Inn, London.

SC B.F.HARDENBERG, 1820, marble bust, Royal Coll.

C THOMAS ROWLANDSON, c1815, 'We three Logger Heads be', Laing Art Gallery, Newcastle.

ELLENBOROUGH, Edward Law, 1st Earl of (1790-1871) governor general of India.

P F.R.SAY, c1845, tql, NPG 1805.

D SIR GEORGE HAYTER, head, pen and pencil, BM.

G SIR GEORGE HAYTER, 'The Trial of Queen Caroline, 1820', oil, NPG 999. Attrib ISAAC CRUICKSHANK, 'Members of the House of Lords, c1835', pen and wash, NPG 2789.

PR UNKNOWN, hs, woodcut, oval, for Illust London News, 1872, NPG.

C Several JOHN DOYLE political sketches, drgs, BM.

ELLERTON, Edward (1770-1851) founder of scholarships.

P UNKNOWN, hs, Magdalen College, Oxford.

ELLEY, Sir John (d1839) lieutenant-general.

P WILLIAM SALTER, tql study for 'Waterloo Banquet', NPG 3713. J.W.PIENEMAN, hs, Wellington Museum, Apsley House, London.

G W.SALTER, 'Waterloo Banquet at Apsley House', oil, 1836, Wellington Museum.

SC R.TRENTANOVA, c1815, bust, St George's Chapel, Windsor.

ELLICE, Edward (1781-1863) secretary at War.

G SIR GEORGE HAYTER, 'The House of Commons, 1833', oil, NPG 54. JOHN PHILLIP, 'The House of Commons, 1860', oil, Palace of Westminster, London.

PR UNKNOWN, hs profile, woodcut, for Illust London News, 1863, NPG. UNKNOWN, hl seated, lith, pub 1878, BM.

ELLICOTT, John (1706?-1772) clockmaker.

PR R.DUNKARTON, after N.Dance, tql seated, aged 67, mezz, BM.

ELLIOT, Sir George (1784-1863) admiral.

P SIR GEORGE HAYTER, 1834, hs, NPG 2511.

G SIR G.HAYTER, 'The House of Commons, 1833', oil, NPG 54.

ELLIOT, Sir Gilbert (1751-1814), see 1st Earl of Minto.

ELLIOT, Gilbert (1782-1859), see 2nd Earl of Minto.

ELLIOT, Jane (1727-1805) poet.

D UNKNOWN, wash, SNPG 1672.

ELLIOTSON, John (1791-1868) physician.

P JAMES RAMSAY, hl, Royal College of Physicians, London.

PR C.BAUGNIET, hl, lith, BM. R.MARTIN, after J.K.Meadows, wl, lith, NPG.

ELLIOTT, Ebenezer (1781-1849) 'the corn-law rhymer'.

SC N.N.BURNARD, 1854, statue, Weston Park, Sheffield.

PR UNKNOWN, hl, woodcut, for Howitt's Journal, 1847, NPG UNKNOWN, hs, woodcut, for Illust London News, 1849, NPG.

ELLIOTT, Grace, née Dalrymple (1758?-1823) mistress c the Prince of Wales.

P THOMAS GAINSBOROUGH, RA 1778, wl, Metropolitan Museum of Art, New York, USA. T.GAINSBOROUGH, RA 1782, hs, oval Frick Collection, New York, USA.

PR J.BROWN, after R.Cosway, head, stipple, oval, for her Memoir 1859, BM, NPG.

ELLIOTT, Henry Venn (1792-1865) divine.

PR C.BAUGNIET, tql, lith, BM, NPG.

ELLIS, Charles Rose, see 1st Baron Seaford.

ELLIS, George James Welbore Agar-, see 1st Baron Dover

ELLIS, Sir Henry (1777-1869) principal librarian of the Britis Museum.

PR H.CORBOULD, hl profile, lith, No 53 of Athenaeum Portraits, BM NPG.

ELLIS, Sir Henry Walton (1783-1815) colonel.

PR UNKNOWN, hs, stipple, NPG.

ELLIS, John (1789-1862) railway promoter.

P JOHN LUCAS, 1858, wl, Museum of British Transport, York UNKNOWN, tql, Leicester Museum and Art Gallery.

G B.R.HAYDON, 'The Anti-Slavery Society Convention, 1840' oil, NPG 599.

ELLIS, Sarah, née Stickney (d1872) writer.

PR P.GREATBACH, after W.Gush, tql seated, stipple and line, NPG W.HOLL, after P.A.Gaugain, hs, stipple and line, NPG. DALZIE hs, woodcut, oval, BM.

ELLIS, Thomas Flower (1796-1861) law reporter.

SC WILLIAM BEHNES, 1842?, plaster bust, Trinity College Cambridge.

ELLIS, Welbore (1713-1802), see 1st Baron Mendip.

ELLIS, William (1794-1872) missionary.

PR C.TAYLOR, after Derby, hl seated, stipple, pub 1826, NPG.

ELLIS, Wynne (1790-1875) picture collector.

SC SIR J.E.BOEHM, marble bust, TATE 2243. UNKNOWN, bust, TAT 2239.

PR UNKNOWN, hs, woodcut, for Illust London News, 1876, NPG.

ELLISTON, Robert William (1774-1831) actor.

P SAMUEL DE WILDE, hs as Duke Aranza in The Honey Moon Garrick Club, London. G.H.HARLOW, hs, NPG 2136; version Garrick Club. HENRY SINGLETON, hs as Octavian in Th Mountaineers, Garrick Club.

D G.H.HARLOW, 1814, hs, pencil and sanguine, Garrick Club.

PR W.RIDLEY, after S.Drummond, hl, stipple, for Monthly Mirror 1796, BM, NPG. A.CARDON, after W.M.Bennet, hl, stipple, pu 1810, BM, NPG. Several theatrical prints, BM, NPG.

ELLMAN, John (1753-1832) agriculturist.

PR E.SCRIVEN, after J.Lonsdale, hl, stipple, pub 1830, BM, NPG.

ELMES, James (1782-1862) architect and antiquary.

P JAMES LONSDALE, RA 1810?, RIBA, London.

ELPHINSTON, James (1721-1809) educationalist.

PR J.CALDWELL, after J.Graham, hl, line, oval, BM, NPG.

ELPHINSTONE, George Keith, see Viscount Keith.

ELPHINSTONE, Hester Maria, see Viscountess Keith.

ELPHINSTONE, Margaret Mercer, see Viscountess Keith

ELPHINSTONE, Mountstuart (1779-1859) Indian statesman.

P SIR THOMAS LAWRENCE, 1829, wl seated (finished by Simpson), Elphinstone College, Bombay. H.W.PICKERSGILL, wl seated, Oriental Club, London.

SC MATTHEW NOBLE, 1832, statue, St Paul's Cathedral, London. SIR FRANCIS CHANTREY, RA 1833, statue, Bombay; model, Ashmolean Museum, Oxford. SIR F.CHANTREY, bust, Ashmolean Museum. After WILLIAM WYON, 1833, plaster medal, SNPG 84.

ELPHINSTONE, William George Keith (1782-1842) aide-de-camp to George IV.

P WILLIAM SALTER, tql study for 'Waterloo Banquet', NPG 3714.

G W.SALTER, 'Waterloo Banquet at Apsley House', oil, 1836, Wellington Museum, Apsley House, London.

ELRINGTON, Thomas (1760-1835) bishop of Leighlin and Ferns.

P THOMAS FOSTER, 1820, hl seated in bishop's robes, Trinity College, Dublin.

SC Attrib THOMAS KIRK, marble bust, Trinity College, Dublin.

ELTON, Sir Charles Abraham (1778-1853) writer.

P THOMAS BARKER, as a boy, Clevedon Court (NT), Avon. EDWARD BIRD, hl, Clevedon Court.

M UNKNOWN, c1804, hs, oval, Clevedon Court.

ELWES, John (1714-1789) politician and miser.

PR W.AUSTIN, after an unknown artist, tql profile, etch, oval, pub 1790, BM. G.SCOTT, hl, stipple, pub 1805, NPG.

EMERSON, William (1701-1782) mathematician.

PR C.TURNER, after Sikes, hl, mezz, oval, pub 1812, BM, NPG.

EMERY, John (1777-1822) actor.

P SAMUEL DE WILDE, Garrick Club London: hs as John Lump in *The Review*; hl as Dan in *John Bull*; wl as Tyke in *The School of Reform*.

D Four drawings in the Garrick Club: C.LINSELL, 1815, as Sam in *Raising the Wind*; JOHN VARLEY, 1816, head, pencil; SAMUEL DE WILDE, as Farmer Ashfield in *Speed the Plough*; JOHN TURMEAU, head, w/c.

M SAMUEL RAVEN, hl seated, NPG 1661.

G GEORGE CLINT, in a scene from *Love, Law and Physic*, oil, RA 1830, Garrick Club.

PR Various theatrical prints, BM, NPG.

EMMET, Robert (1778-1803) Irish patriot.

P JAMES SLEATOR, Abbey Theatre, Dublin.

D UNKNOWN, tql, w/c, oval, NGI 2363.

M JOHN COMERFORD, hs, oval, NGI 7341.

G UNKNOWN, 'The United Irish Patriots of 1798', coloured lith, NPG.

SC JAMES PETRIE, plaster death mask, NGI 8130.

PR J.HEATH, after J.Petrie, head, stipple, for Sir J.Barrington's *Historic Memoirs*, 1812, BM, NPG. W.READ, wl, stipple and line, BM, NPG.

EMMET, Thomas Addis (1764-1827) Irish nationalist.

D UNKNOWN, hs, pastel, oval, NGI 211.

G UNKNOWN, 'The United Irish Patriots of 1798', coloured lith, NPG.

EMPSON, William (1791-1852) editor of the *Edinburgh Review*.

PR W.WALKER, after J.Linnell, tql seated, mezz, BM.

ENFIELD, William (1741-1797) dissenting minister and writer.

PR ANKER SMITH, after an unknown artist, hs, silhouette profile, line, oval, pub 1798, BM, NPG.

ENGLAND, Sir Richard (1793-1883) general.

PR C.HOLL, after a miniature, hl with orders, stipple, NPG.

ENGLEFIELD, Sir Henry Charles (1752-1822) antiquary.

P THOMAS PHILLIPS, 1815, hl seated, NPG 4659. SIR THOMAS LAWRENCE, 1812, hl seated, The Society of Dilettanti, Brooks's Club, London.

D GEORGE DANCE, 1794, hl seated, pencil, NPG 1142. SIR FRANCIS CHANTREY, 1817, head, profile, V & A.

SC UNKNOWN, 1817, medal, NPG 2000. SIR FRANCIS CHANTREY, bust, Ashmolean Museum, Oxford.

PR C.PICART, after H.Edridge, hl, stipple, for *Contemporary Portraits*, 1812, BM, NPG.

ENGLEHEART, George (1752-1839) miniature painter.

M Self-portrait, hs, oval, NPG 2753. Self-portrait, profile, V & A.

ENGLEHEART, John Cox Dillman (1783-1862) miniature painter.

M Self-portrait, c1810, hl, NPG 2754.

ENSOR, George (1769-1843) political writer.

PR H.MEYER, after J.Comerford, hl, stipple, BM, NPG.

ENTICK, John (1703?-1773) schoolmaster and author.

PR W.P.BENOIST, after Burgess, hl, line, oval, for his *Hist of the late War*, 1763, BM, NPG.

ENTWISLE, Joseph (1767-1841) methodist preacher.

PR W.RIDLEY, hs, stipple, oval, for *Arminian Mag*, BM, NPG.

ÉON, Chevalier d', see D'ÉON de Beaumont.

ERLE, Sir William (1793-1880) judge.

P SIR FRANCIS GRANT, RA 1851, tql seated, New College, Oxford.

D F.A.TILT, 1868, tql seated, w/c, NPG 464a.

SC THOMAS WOOLNER, exhib 1883, marble bust, Temple Library, London.

ERNEST Augustus, Duke of Cumberland and King of Hanover, see CUMBERLAND.

ERSKINE, David Steuart, see 11th Earl of Buchan.

ERSKINE, Henry (1746-1817) lord advocate.

P Attrib WILLIAM YELLOWLEES, after Sir Henry Raeburn, SNPG 2047.

D JOHN BOGLE, hl, pencil and w/c, SNPG 121.

SC JAMES TASSIE, 1791, paste medallion, SNPG 265. PETER TURNERELLI, 1814, marble bust, Faculty of Advocates, Parliament Hall, Edinburgh. MARY GRANT, marble relief monument, SNPG 1582.

C Several JOHN KAY etchings, BM, NPG.

ERSKINE, James (1722-1796) Scottish judge.

P DAVID ALLAN, 1765, hs, Royal Scottish Academy, Edinburgh.

ERSKINE, Sir James St Clair, see 2nd Earl of Rosslyn.

ERSKINE, John (1721-1803) theologian.

SC After WILLIAM TASSIE, plaster medallion, SNPG 432.

PR G.DAWE, after H.Raeburn, hl, mezz, pub 1804, BM.

C J.KAY, hl in pulpit, etch, oval, 1793, BM, NPG.

ERSKINE, Thomas Erskine, 1st Baron (1750-1823) lord chancellor.

P SIR JOSHUA REYNOLDS, RA 1786, tql, Royal Coll. SIR THOMAS LAWRENCE, RA 1802, hl, Lincoln's Inn, London. SIR W.C.ROSS, hl, with Thistle star, NPG 960.

G K.A.HICKEL, 'The House of Commons, 1793', oil, NPG 745. SIR GEORGE HAYTER, 'The Trial of Queen Caroline, 1820', oil, NPG 999.

SC JOSEPH NOLLEKENS, 1815, marble bust, Royal Coll. SIR RICHARD WESTMACOTT, 1830, marble statue, Lincoln's Inn, London.

PR J.WALKER, after L.Abbott, hl, mezz, pub 1783, BM.

ERSKINE, Thomas (1788-1864) judge.
G SIR DAVID WILKIE, 'The First Council of Queen Victoria, 1837', oil, Royal Coll.

ERSKINE, Thomas (1788-1870) advocate and theologian.
PR F.HOLL, after G.Richmond, hl, stipple, BM, NPG.

ERSKINE, Thomas Alexander, see 6th Earl of Kellie.

ERSKINE, Sir William (1769-1813) major-general.
P RICHARD COSWAY, c1810, hs, oval, Royal Coll.

ERSKINE, William (1769-1822), see Lord Kinneder.

ESDAILE, William (1758-1837) banker and print collector.
D GEORGE SHARPLES, c1826, tql seated, pastel, NPG 4660.

ESKGROVE, Sir Davie Rae, 1st Bart, Lord (1724?-1804) lord justice clerk.
P SIR HENRY RAEBURN. tql, Faculty of Advocates, Parliament Hall, Edinburgh.
M UNKNOWN, SNPG 1198.
C J.KAY, hl seated, profile, etch, oval, 1799, BM, NPG.

ESSEX, Catherine Stephens, Countess of (1794-1882) singer and actress.
P SAMUEL DE WILDE, 1813, as Mandane in *Artaxerxes*, Garrick Club, London. G.H.HARLOW, c1816, Petworth (NT), W.Sussex. G.H.HARLOW, c1819, hs as Diana Vernon in *Rob Roy MacGregor*, Garrick Club, London; w/c copy, Garrick Club, London. JOHN JACKSON, 1822, hl, NPG 702.
M MISS L.SHARPE, c1824, Garrick Club, London.
SL UNKNOWN, profile, Garrick Club, London.
G G.H.HARLOW, 'Court for the Trial of Queen Catherine' ('Henry VIII'), oil, 1817, Royal Shakespeare Memorial Theatre Museum, Stratford on Avon.
PR Various theatrical prints, BM, NPG.

ESSEX, George Capel-Coningsby, 5th Earl of (1757-1839) lord lieutenant of Hereford.
P SIR JOSHUA REYNOLDS, 1767-68, wl with his sister Elizabeth, Metropolitan Museum of Art, New York, USA. After GEORGE CLINT, hs in peer's robes, Althorp, Northants.
G SIR GEORGE HAYTER, 'The Trial of Queen Caroline, 1820', oil, NPG 999.
PR C.TURNER, after J.Hoppner, tql in peer's robes, mezz, pub 1812, BM, NPG. HARDING, after Danloux, hs, stipple, NPG.
C SIR EDWIN LANDSEER, c1825-35, wl, pen and ink, NPG 3097(6). JAMES GILLRAY, head, pencil, BM.

ESSEX, James (1722-1784) builder and architect.
SL FRANCIS TOROND, c1780, with his family, Worthing Museum.

ESTLIN, John Bishop (1785-1855) surgeon.
SC E.H.BAILEY, 1856, bust, Bristol City Art Gallery.

ETTY, William (1787-1849) painter.
P Self-portrait, hs profile, Manchester City Art Gallery; related version, Fogg Art Museum, Cambridge, Mass, USA. UNKNOWN, after a photograph by Hill and Adamson of 1844, hl, NPG 1368.
D Self-portrait, c1830, wl, pen and ink, Ashmolean Museum, Oxford. Self-portrait, c1840, head, York City Art Gallery. C.H.LEAR, c1845, three sketches, head, hl and wl, NPG 1456 (6-8). WILLIAM NICHOLSON, hl profile, Royal Scottish Academy, Edinburgh. HENRY BAINES, 1847, hs profile, King's Lynn Museum and Art Gallery, Norfolk.
SC MATTHEW NOBLE, 1850, marble bust, NPG 595.
PH D.O.HILL and ROBERT ADAMSON, hl, NPG P 6 (7). J.WATKINS, hs, NPG Album of Artists vol III.

EVANS, Christmas (1766-1838) Welsh preacher.

P WILLIAM ROOS, 1835, hs, National Museum of Wales 95, Cardiff.
PR FREEMAN, after Branwhite, hs, stipple, pub 1822, NPG.

EVANS, Daniel (1797-1846) Welsh poet, Daniel Du C Geredigion.
P? UNKNOWN, St David's University College, Lampeter.

EVANS, Sir George de Lacy (1787-1870) general.
M UNKNOWN, c1840, hs, NPG 2158.
SC UNKNOWN, marble bust, Brighton Pavilion.
PR M.O'CONNOR, wl, lith, BM, pub 1833, NPG. M.GAUCI, after A.E.Chalon, hs, lith, pub 1834, BM, NPG. J.H.LYNCH, after a photograph by R.Fenton c1855, hl in uniform, lith, BM, NPG G.ZOBEL, after R.Buckner, tql, mezz, pub 1856, NPG.
PH E.EDWARDS, wl seated, for ed L.Reeve, *Men of Eminence*, 1865 vol III, NPG. UNKNOWN, hs, NPG 'Twist' album, 1892.

EVANS, John (1767-1827) baptist minister.
PR H.MEYER, after J.Hazlitt, hl, mezz, pub 1812, BM R.WOODMAN, after J.Wiche, hl seated, stipple, NPG.

EVANS, Lewis (1755-1827) mathematician.
P UNKNOWN, hl, Royal Astronomical Society, London.

EVANS, Richard (1784-1871) portrait-painter and copyist.
D CARL CHRISTIAN VOGEL, 1837, hs, Staatliche Kunstsammlungen, Dresden.

EVANS, Robert (1773-1849) estate agent. Father of George Eliot.
M CAROLINE BRAY, 1841, after a miniature, hs, w/c, NPG 1232a

EVANS, Robert Harding (1778-1857) bookseller and auctioneer.
PR After W.BEHNES, tql seated, stipple, BM.

EVANS, Thomas Simpson (1777-1818) mathematician.
PR UNKNOWN, hs, silhouette profile, stipple, oval, BM.

EVANS, Sir William David (1767-1821) recorder o Bombay.
PR E.SCRIVEN, hs, stipple, oval, BM.

EVELEIGH, John (1748-1814) provost of Oriel College Oxford.
P JOHN HOPPNER, tql seated, Oriel College, Oxford.
C R.DIGHTON, wl, 'A View from Oriel College, Oxford' coloured etch, pub 1808, NPG.

EVEREST, Sir George (1790-1866) surveyor-general o India.
P LADY BURRARD, after a photograph, Royal Artillery Institution, Woolwich.
D Attrib WILLIAM TAYLER, 1843, hs profile, pencil, NPG 2553.
PH RUSSELL & SONS, tql in uniform, NPG. MAULL & FOX, wl seated NPG. ELLIOTT & FRY, hs, NPG.

EVERETT, James (1784-1872) miscellaneous writer.
PR H.ADLARD, after Parry, hl, stipple, for Holland and Everett' *Memoir of J.Montgomery*, 1854, BM, NPG. W.H.EGLETON, afte H.Anelay, hl, stipple, NPG.

EVERSLEY, Charles Shaw-Lefevre, Viscount (1794-1888) speaker of the House of Commons.
P SIR MARTIN ARCHER SHEE, wl in speaker's robes, Palace o Westminster, London.
D JOHN DOYLE, equestrian, pen and pencil, BM.
G SIR GEORGE HAYTER, 'The House of Commons, 1833', oil, NPG 54. JOHN PARTRIDGE, 'The Fine Arts Commissioners, 1846', oil NPG 342, 3.
PR W.HOLL, after G.Richmond, hs in speaker's wig, stipple, fo 'Grillion's Club' series, BM, NPG. UNKNOWN, after F.Sargent, hl etch, NPG. R.T., in old age, woodcut, for *Illust London News*

FROUDE, Robert (1771?-1859) divine.

D WILLIAM BROCKEDON, 1832, hs, chalk, NPG 2515 (35).

FRY, Caroline, see Wilson.

FRY, Elizabeth (1780-1845) prison reformer.

P After C.R.LESLIE, hl seated, NPG 898.
D GEORGE SCHARF senr, 1819, hl seated in Newgate, pencil, BM.
M SAMUEL DRUMMOND, hl seated, NPG 118.
PR R.DIGHTON, wl profile, seated in a prison, entitled 'In Prison and ye came unto me', coloured etch, pub 1820, BM. S.COUSINS, after G.Richmond, wl, mezz, pub 1850, BM.

FRYE, Thomas (1710-1762) portrait painter and engraver.

PR T.FRYE, hs with crayon, mezz, BM, NPG. T.FRYE, hs, semi-profile, mezz, BM, NPG.

FULLER, Andrew (1754-1815) baptist theologian.

PR N.BRANWHITE, hl, stipple, pub 1816, NPG.

FUSELI, Henry (Johann Heinrich Fuessli) (1741-1825) painter and author.

P JOHN WILLIAMSON, 1789, hl, Walker Art Gallery, Liverpool. SIR THOMAS LAWRENCE, c1825, tql seated, Musée Bonnat, Bayonne. JOHN OPIE, hl, NPG 744. Self-portrait, wl seated with J.J.Bodmer, Kunsthaus, Zurich.
D GEORGE DANCE, 1793, hs profile, Royal Academy, London. SIR THOMAS LAWRENCE, c1795, hs, black lead, BM. THOMAS COOLEY, 1810, hs study, pencil, NPG 4913 (2). GEORGE HAYTER, 1812, head, pen and ink, BM. Self-portrait, head, pencil, NPG 4538. Two self-portrait studies, head, V & A.
G HENRY SINGLETON, 'Royal Academicians, 1793', oil, Royal Academy, London.
PR J.H.LIPS, hs profile, stipple and line, oval, for Lavater's *Essay on Phisiognomy*, 1779, BM, NPG. W.EVANS, after M.Haughton, tql seated, stipple, pub 1808, BM, NPG. T.THOMSON, after E.H.Baily, from a bust, stipple, for *European Mag*, 1825, BM, NPG. F.C.LEWIS, after G.S.Newton, hs profile, with hat, stipple, BM, NPG.

FUST, Sir Herbert Jenner (1778-1852) vicar-general to the archbishop of Canterbury.

PR W.WALKER, after F.Y.Hurlstone, tql, mezz, 1835, NPG.

G

GADSBY, William (1773-1844) baptist minister.
PR J.H.LYNCH, after E.Benson, tql seated, lith, pub 1844, BM. W.BARNARD, after F.Turner, in pulpit, preaching, mezz, BM, NPG.

GAGE. Rokewode, John, see ROKEWODE.

GAGE, Thomas (1721-1787) general.
P DAVID MARTIN, wl, Firle Place, E.Sussex.
M JEREMIAH MEYER, hs, NPG 4070.
PR R.POLLARD, hs, line, oval, NPG.

GAHAN, William (1730-1804) Irish ecclesiastic and author.
PR MAGUIRE, hs, stipple, NPG.

GAINSBOROUGH, Thomas (1727-1788) portrait and land-scape painter.
P Self-portrait, 1754, hs with hat, Houghton Hall, Norfolk. Self-portrait, c1758–59, hl, NPG 4446. Attrib WILLIAM HOARE, mid 1760's, hs, Museum of Art, Santa Barbara, California, USA. JOHAN ZOFFANY, c1772, hs, NPG 3913. Self-portrait, after 1782, hs, Holkham Hall, Norfolk. Self-portrait, c1787, hs, oval, Royal Academy, London.
G Self-portrait, 1751–52, wl seated with his wife and daughter in landscape, Houghton Hall.

GAIRDNER, John (1790-1876) medical reformer.
P J.M.BARCLAY, 1867, hs, oval, Royal College of Surgeons, Edinburgh.

GAISFORD, Thomas (1779-1855) dean of Christ Church, Oxford.
P H.W.PICKERSGILL, hl seated, Christ Church, Oxford.
SC UNKNOWN, plaster bust, Christ Church, Oxford.

GALT, John (1779-1839) novelist.
P CHARLES GREY, 1835, hs, SNPG 1144.
D WILLIAM BROCKEDON, 1834, hs, pencil, NPG 2515 (37). COUNT A.D'ORSAY, pencil, SNPG 1823.
G D.MACLISE, 'The Fraserians', lith, for *Fraser's Mag*, 1835, BM.
PR T.WOOLNOTH, after E.Hastings, tql seated, stipple, for *Ladies' Monthly Museum*, 1824, BM, NPG. D.MACLISE, wl with bust of Byron, lith, for *Fraser's Mag*, 1830, BM, NPG. R.GRAVES, after J.Irvine, tql seated, line, for his *Autobiography*, 1833, BM, NPG.

GAMBIER, James Gambier, 1st Baron (1756-1833) admiral.
D JOSEPH SLATER, 1813, wl seated, pencil, NPG 1982.
G BARTOLOZZI, LANDSEER, RYDER & STOW, 'Naval Victories', 'Commemoration of the Victory of June 1st 1794', line, pub 1803, BM, NPG. J.G.MURRAY, after J.Stephanoff, 'Trial of Queen Caroline, 1820', stipple, pub 1823, BM.
PR G.CLINT, after W.Beechey, hl in uniform, mezz, pub 1808, BM, NPG.

GAMBOLD, John (1711-1771) Moravian minister.
PR J.SPILSBURY, after A.Brandt, hl, mezz, pub 1771, BM, NPG; related engraving by Bath, after a drawing by Hibbert, etch, NPG.

GANDON, James (1743-1823) architect.
P TILLY KETTLE and WILLIAM CUMING, tql with plans, NGI 1783.
M HORACE HONE, hs, NGI 2157. H.HONE, 1799, hs, oval, Fitzwilliam Museum, Cambridge.

G PAUL SANDBY, wl with his family, pencil and wash, c1780, Ya Center for British Art, New Haven, USA.
PR H.MEYER, after J.Comerford, hs, stipple, BM, NPG. H.MEYEI after H.Hone, hl seated, stipple, BM.

GARDELLE, Theodore (1721-1761) miniature-painter.
PR S.IRELAND, after W.Hogarth, hl profile, on his way to executio aquatint, pub 1788, BM, NPG.

GARDEN, Francis, see Lord Gardenstone.

GARDENSTONE, Francis Garden, Lord (1721-179 Scottish judge.
C J.KAY, wl equestrian, etch, NPG.

GARDINER, Arthur (1716?-1758) captain in the navy.
PR BENOIST, hs, line, oval, NPG.

GARDINER, Charles John (1782-1829), see 1st Earl Blessington.

GARDINER, Marguerite, see Countess of Blessington.

GARDINER, Sir Robert William (1781-1864) governor Gibraltar.
P WILLIAM SALTER, tql study for 'Waterloo Banquet', NPG 371 UNKNOWN, c1860, hl, The Convent, Gibraltar.
G W.SALTER, 'Waterloo Banquet at Apsley House', oil, 183 Wellington Museum, Apsley House, London.

GARDINER, William (1748-1806) diplomatist.
P SIR JOSHUA REYNOLDS, RA 1773, hs, Petworth (NT), W.Susse

GARDINER, William (1770-1853) musical composer.
P Attrib WILLIAM ARTAUD, hl, Leicester Museum and A Gallery.

GARDINER, William Nelson (1766-1814) engraver ai publisher.
PR UNKNOWN, hl profile, stipple, oval, BM, NPG.

GARDNER, Alan Gardner, 1st Baron (1742-1809) admir.
P ANTON HICKEL, 1794, hl in uniform, NMM, Greenwic THEOPHILUS CLARKE, c1799, hs, NPG 2103. After SIR WILLIA BEECHEY, hl in uniform, NMM.
G BARTOLOZZI, LANDSEER, RYDER & STOW, 'Naval Victorie 'Commemoration of the victory of June 1st 1794', line, p 1803, BM, NPG.
PR PIERSON, hs profile, stipple, oval, for *European Mag*, 1794, B NPG. W.DANIELL, after G.Dance, hl profile, soft-ground etc pub 1809, BM, NPG.

GARDNER, Alan Hyde Gardner, 2nd Baron (1770-181 admiral.
PR H.COOK, after T.Lawrence, hl with orders, stipple, for Jerdar *Nat Portrait Gallery*, 1832, BM, NPG. A.CARDON, after H.Edridg hs, stipple, BM, NPG.

GARDNER, Daniel (1750?-1805) portrait painter.
P Self-portrait, hs, NPG 1971. Self-portrait, called Gardner, hl wi a member of the Pennington family, Abbot Hall Art Galler Kendal.

GARDNER, Mrs, née Cheney (fl 1770) actress.
PR WALKER, after D.Dodd, with John Palmer, as Lady Plyant an Careless in Congreve's *The Double Dealer*, line, for *New Engli*

Theatre, 1777, BM.

GARNETT, John (1709-1782) bishop of Clogher.
P Two portraits, St John's College, Cambridge, and Sidney Sussex, Cambridge.
R J.McARDELL, after Gainsborough, hl, mezz, oval, BM.

GARNETT, John (1748-1813) dean of Exeter.
R C.TURNER, after J.J.Halls, tql seated, mezz, pub 1813, BM, NPG.

GARNETT, Thomas (1766-1802) physician and scientist.
P SIR DAVID WILKIE, The Royal Technical College, Glasgow.
R S.PHILLIPS, after T.Phillips, tql, stipple, BM. UNKNOWN, tql mezz, BM.
C JAMES GILLRAY, 'Scientific Researches!' etch, pub 1802, NPG.

GARNIER, Thomas (1776-1873) dean of Winchester.
SC R.C.LUCAS, 1850, wax medallion, oval, NPG 4844.
R UNKNOWN, hs, stipple and line, NPG.
H C.SILVY, wl seated, carte; UNKNOWN, head, carte, both in NPG Distinguished Men and Woman Album vol II.

GARRETT, Jeremiah Learnoult (fl 1809) dissenting minister.
R UNKNOWN, hs, stipple, oval, pub 1801, NPG.

GARRICK, David (1717-1779) actor.
P WILLIAM HOGARTH, c1745, wl as Richard III, Walker Art Gallery, Liverpool. THOMAS WORLIDGE, 1752, as Tancred, V & A. W.HOGARTH, 1757, tql with his wife Eva Maria, Royal Coll. FRANCIS HAYMAN, 1760, wl as Richard III, National Theatre, London. After SIR JOSHUA REYNOLDS (type of 1761–62), Garrick between Tragedy and Comedy, Garrick Club, London. POMPEO BATONI, 1764, hl, Ashmolean Museum, Oxford. ANGELICA KAUFFMANN, 1764, hl, Burghley House, Northants. SIR JOSHUA REYNOLDS, exhib 1768, hl as Kitely, Royal Coll. THOMAS GAINSBOROUGH, c1768, hl with book, Yale Center for British Art, New Haven, USA. THOMAS GAINSBOROUGH, exhib 1770, hl, NPG 5054. NATHANIEL DANCE, 1771, wl as Richard III, Stratford upon Avon Town Council. BENJAMIN VAN DER GUCHT, 1772, hl profile, as Steward of the Stratford Jubilee, Althorp, Northants. SIR JOSHUA REYNOLDS, RA 1776, hl, Knole (NT), Kent. FRANCIS HAYMAN, 1770, wl with Hannah Pritchard in a scene from *The Suspicious Husband*, Museum of London. P.J. DE LOUTHERBOURG, wl as Don Juan in *The Chances*, Garrick Club. R.E.PINE, hl seated, NPG 82. Several paintings by JOHAN ZOFFANY: 1762, wl seated in the garden of Hampton House, Petworth (NT), W.Sussex; c1765, as Sir John Brute in *The Provoked Wife*, Somerset Maugham Collection at the National Theatre; 1770, wl as Abel Drugger in *The Alchemist*, Castle Howard, N.Yorks; wl as Lord Chalkstone in *Lethe*, Birmingham City Art Gallery; as Jaffier in *Venice Preserved*, with Mrs Cibber as Belvidera, Garrick Club; as Macbeth, Mrs Pritchard as Lady Macbeth, Garrick Club; hl, NGI 539. After BENJAMIN WILSON, hl profile as Romeo, Garrick Club.
D J.E.LIOTARD, 1751, hl, pastel, Chatsworth, Derbys. NATHANIEL DANCE, 1771, hl, pencil, NPG 3639. E.F.BURNEY, wl seated, pen and wash, BM. JAMES ROBERTS, 5 portraits in character, BM.
M JAMES SCOULER, 1768, tql with his wife, oval, V & A. J.K.SHERWIN, hl, profile, pencil, NPG 1187.
G JOHAN ZOFFANY, wl with Mrs Cibber and 2 others in *The Farmer's Return*, oil, exhib 1752, Yale Center for British Art.
SC W.HACKWOOD, from a cast by Thomas Pingo of 1772, Wedgwood medallion, Wedgwood Museum, Barlaston, Staffs. HENRY WEBBER, c1797, statue on monument, Westminster Abbey, London. JOSEPH NOLLEKENS, marble bust, Althorp, L.F.ROUBILIAC, plaster bust, NPG 707a. UNKNOWN, marble bust, Royal Coll.
R Numerous theatrical prints, BM, NPG.

GARROW, Sir William (1760-1840) lawyer.
P GEORGE HARLOW, tql seated, Lincoln's Inn, London.
D GEORGE HAYTER, head, sketch, study for NPG 999, NPG 169 (s).
G SIR GEORGE HAYTER, 'The Trial of Queen Caroline, 1820', oil, NPG 999.
PR J.PURDEN, hl profile, stipple, pub 1801, BM, NPG. R.DUNKARTON, after A.W.Devis, hl, mezz, pub 1810, NPG. UNKNOWN, head, stipple, BM, NPG.

GARTHSHORE, William (1764-1806) lord of the admiralty.
PR S.FREEMAN, hl, stipple, oval, BM, NPG.

GARVEY, Edmund (d1813) painter.
D GEORGE DANCE, hs profile, Royal Academy, London.
G HENRY SINGLETON, 'Royal Academicians, 1793', oil, Royal Academy.

GASCOYNE, Bamber (c1729-1791) lord of the admiralty.
C J.SAYER, wl, etch, pub 1782, Hatfield House, Herts, NPG.

GASCOYNE, Sir Crisp (1700-1761) lord mayor of London.
P WILLIAM KEABLE, tql in official robes, Hatfield House, Herts.

GASKIN, George (1751-1829) divine.
PR S.W.REYNOLDS, after W.Owen, hl, mezz, BM, NPG.

GASTINEAU, Henry (c1791-1876) water-colour painter.
PH UNKNOWN, c1860s, tql, carte, NPG Album of Artists vol. I.

GATES, Horatio (1728-1806) major-general in United States Service.
D JOHN TRUMBULL, Metropolitan Museum of Art, New York, USA.
PR J.A.O'NEILL, after G.Stuart, hs, stipple, oval, NPG. UNKNOWN, hs profile, line, oval, for *Westminster Mag*, NPG. UNKNOWN, wl, line, NPG.

GATTIE, Henry (1774-1844) actor.
PR R.COOPER, after M.W.Sharpe, wl as Monsieur Morbleu in *Monsieur Tonson*, stipple, pub 1822, NPG.

GAUNTLETT, Henry (1762-1833) divine.
PR M.GAUCI, after A.Rippingille, hl, lith, for his *Sermons*, 1835, BM.

GAYTON, Clark (c1720-1787) admiral.
P J.S.COPLEY, 1779, tql in uniform, NMM, Greenwich.

GEARY, Sir Francis, Bart (1709/10-1796) admiral.
P UNKNOWN, c1780, hl with telescope, NMM, Greenwich. GEORGE ROMNEY, 1782-83, wl in uniform, NMM.

GEDDES, Alexander (1737-1802) biblical critic.
P SAMUEL MEDLEY, RA 1802, hl, Dr Williams's Library, London.

GEDDES, Andrew (1783-1844) painter.
P Self-portrait, 1812, hl, SNPG L42. Self-portrait, hl, SNPG 577. Self-portrait, 1816, hl, Royal Scottish Academy, Edinburgh.

GELL, John (c1740-1805) admiral.
P SIR JOSHUA REYNOLDS, 1786, tql in uniform, NMM, Greenwich.

GELL, Sir William (1777-1836) archaeologist.
D CORNELIUS VARLEY, 1816, hs, pencil, NPG 5086. THOMAS UWINS, 1830, hs, pencil, NPG 1491. COUNT D'ORSAY, 1828, hs profile, pencil, DoE (British Embassy, Athens).

GENDALL, John (1790-1865) painter.
P JOHN PRESCOTT KNIGHT, hl, Royal Albert Memorial Museum, Exeter.

GEORGE III (George William Frederick) (1738-1820) Reigned 1760-1820.
P RICHARD WILSON, c1751, wl seated, with the Duke of York, NPG 1165. SIR JOSHUA REYNOLDS, 1759, tql in cloak with Garter ribbon, coronet beside him, Royal Coll. ALLAN RAMSAY, c1761,

wl in coronation robes, Royal Coll. DAVID MORIER, c1760–65, 4 equestrian portraits, in uniform, with Garter ribbon and/or star, Royal Coll. NATHANIEL DANCE, 1769, wl in coronation robes, Drapers' Company, London. JOHAN ZOFFANY, 1771, tql with Garter ribbon and star, Royal Coll. SIR JOSHUA REYNOLDS, c1779, wl in coronation chair, with robes of state, sceptre and crown, Royal Academy, London. SIR BENJAMIN WEST, 1779, wl with Garter ribbon and star, with orb, sceptre and crown, sea-battle in background, Royal Coll. SIR WILLIAM BEECHEY, c1779–1800, wl wearing Garter star with his charger and a groom, Royal Coll. THOMAS GAINSBOROUGH, RA 1781, wl in uniform with Garter ribbon, star and the garter, Royal Coll. THOMAS GAINSBOROUGH, 1782, hs with Garter ribbon and star, oval, Royal Coll. SIR BENJAMIN WEST, 1789, in Garter robes with Queen Charlotte, oval, Royal Coll. SIR THOMAS LAWRENCE, RA 1792, wl in Garter robes, St Mary's Guildhall, Coventry. GAINSBOROUGH DUPONT, probably RA 1794, wl in robes of state with regalia, Royal Coll. G.DUPONT, c1795, wl in Garter robes, with crown and sceptre, Royal Coll. P.E.STROEHLING, 1807, wl in uniform with orders, with spaniel, Royal Coll.

D J.E.LIOTARD, c1754, hs with Garter ribbon, pastel, Royal Coll.
M JEREMIAH MEYER, hs, oval, Royal Coll. UNKNOWN, hs, profile, oval, NPG L152 (26).
G J.B.VANLOO, 'Augusta Princess of Wales, with Members of her Family and Household', oil, 1739?, Royal Coll. BARTHELEMY DU PAN, 'The Children of Frederick, Prince of Wales', oil, 1746, Royal Coll. SIR JOSHUA REYNOLDS, 'The Marriage of George III, 1761', oil sketch, Royal Coll. JOHAN ZOFFANY, 'George III, Queen Charlotte and their Six Eldest children', oil, 1770, Royal Coll. M.F.QUADAL, 'George III at a Review', oil, 1772, Royal Coll. PHILIPP JAKOB, or PHILIP JAMES DE LOUTHERBOURG, 'Warley Camp: The Mock Attack', oil, RA 1779, and 'Warley Camp: The Review', oil, RA 1780, Royal Coll. HENRY SINGLETON, 'The Marriage of George Prince of Wales', oil, 1795, Royal Coll. SIR W.BEECHEY, 'George III at a Review', oil, 1797–98, Royal Coll. Attrib JOHN WOOTTON, 'George III's procession to the Houses of Parliament', oil, Royal Coll. H.P.BRIGGS, 'Visit of George III and Queen Charlotte to Howe aboard his flagship, 26 June 1794', oil, 1828, NMM, Greenwich.
SC AGOSTINO CARLINI, 1769, plaster equestrian statue, Royal Academy. A.CARLINI, 1773, marble bust, Royal Academy. JOSEPH NOLLEKENS, 1773, marble bust, Royal Coll. JOHN BACON snr, 1775, marble bust, Royal Coll. JOHN BACON snr, 1789, statue on monument, Somerset House, London. PETER TURNERELLI, 1809, marble bust, NPG 3903. P.TURNERELLI, c1810, marble bust, V & A. SIR FRANCIS CHANTREY, c1812, marble statue, Guildhall, London. SIR FRANCIS CHANTREY, 1814, bust, Royal College of Surgeons, London. SIR RICHARD WESTMACOTT, 1822, statue, Monument Place, London Road, Liverpool.
PR S.W.REYNOLDS, tql seated as an old man, bearded, mezz, pub 1820, BM, NPG.

GEORGE IV (1762-1830) Regent 1811–1820. Reigned 1820–30.
P RICHARD BROMPTON, c1770, wl in Garter robes, Royal Coll. JOHAN ZOFFANY, c1770, wl in Vandyck dress and Garter ribbon, with Prince Frederick, Royal Coll. SIR BENJAMIN WEST, 1777, wl with state robe and Garter star, with his brother Prince Frederick, Royal Coll. THOMAS GAINSBOROUGH, 1782, hs with Garter star, oval, Royal Coll. THOMAS GAINSBOROUGH, RA 1782, wl with horse, Waddesdon Manor (NT), Bucks. SIR JOSHUA REYNOLDS, RA 1785, hs with Garter star, TATE 890. SIR JOSHUA REYNOLDS, RA 1787, wl in Garter robes, with negro

page, Arundel Castle, W.Sussex. C.J.ROBINEAU, 1787, wl with Garter star, in landscape, Royal Coll. MATHER BROWN, c1789–91, wl in uniform with Garter ribbon and star, Garter robes beside him, Royal Coll. GEORGE STUBBS, 1791, wl equestrian with dogs, Royal Coll. JOHN RUSSELL, RA 1792, wl in uniform of Royal Kentish Bowmen, with Garter ribbon and star, Royal Coll. JOHN HOPPNER, probably RA 1796, wl in Garter robes, Royal Coll. SIR WILLIAM BEECHEY, 1803, tql in uniform, with Garter star, Royal Coll. Several portraits by SIR THOMAS LAWRENCE: Studio of Lawrence, related to portrait RA 1815, wl in uniform, in landscape, NPG 2503; RA 1818, wl in Garter robes, NGI; 1821, wl in Coronation robes, with Imperial Crown, Royal Coll; 1822, wl seated with Garter star, garter and the Golden Fleece, Wallace Collection, London. SIR DAVID WILKIE, 1829, wl in Highland dress, with orders, Royal Coll. SIR THOMAS LAWRENCE, hs profile, unfinished, NPG 123.
D SIR FRANCIS CHANTREY, hs profile sketches, with sketches of robes, NPG 316a (53–57).
M H. de JANVRY, 1793, hs, NPG 1761. RICHARD COSWAY, hs, Royal Coll. PAUL FISCHER, hs, oval, NPG L152 (33).
SL UNKNOWN, wl profile with Duke of York, NPG 1691a.
G ALLAN RAMSAY, 'Queen Charlotte with her two eldest sons', oil, c1764, Royal Coll. JOHAN ZOFFANY, 'George III, Queen Charlotte and their six eldest children', oil, 1770, Royal Coll. C.J.ROBINEAU, 'The Fencing Match between the Chevalier de Saint George and the Chevalier D'Éon', oil, 1787, Royal Coll. WILLIAM HAMILTON, 'The Marriage of George, Prince of Wales, 1795', oil, Royal Coll. SIR WILLIAM BEECHEY, 'George III at a Review', oil 1797–98, Royal Coll. J.S.COPLEY, RA 1810, equestrian group, Museum of Fine Arts, Boston, USA. GEORGE JONES, 'The Banquet at the Coronation of George IV, 1821', oil, Royal Coll. SIR DAVID WILKIE, 'The Entrance of George IV at Holyrood House', oil, 1822–30, Royal Coll.
SC CHARLES LOCHÉE, 1787, Wedgwood medallion, Castle Museum, Nottingham. T.R.POOLE, 1804, wax medallion, Royal Coll. JOSEPH NOLLEKENS, 1815, after a model of c1807, marble bust, Belvoir Castle, Leics. UNKNOWN, c1821, bronze bust, Royal Coll. SIR FRANCIS CHANTREY, 1826, marble bust, Royal Coll. SIR FRANCIS CHANTREY, 1829, bronze equestrian statue, Trafalgar Square, London. SIR FRANCIS CHANTREY, 1830, marble bust, Royal Coll. T.R.POOLE, hs profile, wax relief, with Duke of York, NPG 3308.
C JOHN DOYLE, several satirical drgs, BM.

GERARD, Alexander (1728-1795) philosophical writer.
C J.KAY, 'The Sapient Septemviri', etch, 1786, reprinted in *Kay's Portraits*, 1842, vol I, NPG.

GERMAIN, George Sackville, see 1st Viscount Sackville.

GERRALD, Joseph (1763-1796) political reformer.
PR J.KAY, hs profile, etch, oval, 1794, NPG. S.W.REYNOLDS, after C.Smith, hl, mezz, pub 1795, BM.

GIBBES, Sir George Smith (1771-1851) physician.
P JOHN KEENAN, 1797, hl, Royal College of Physicians, London.

GIBBON, Edward (1737-1794) historian, author of *Decline and Fall of the Roman Empire*.
P HENRY WALTON, hs, NPG 1443.
D J. or T.WALPOLE, wl sketch, pencil, with two head sketches, BM. UNKNOWN, wl seated, chalk, NPG 4854.
SC UNKNOWN, Wedgwood medallion, probably after Sir Joshua Reynolds of 1779, V & A.
PR J.HALL, after J.Reynolds, hl, line, for his *Decline and Fall of the Roman Empire*, 1780, BM. C.CONSTANS, after C.Brandoin, wl seated in his garden at Lausanne, lith, BM, NPG. J.ROMNEY, after G.M.Brighty, wl profile, line, NPG.

C UNKNOWN, hs, 'The Luminous Historian', coloured etch, pub 1788, NPG. LADY DIANA BEAUCLERK, hs profile, pen and sepia, BM. UNKNOWN, wl profile, posthumous, w/c, NPG 3317.

GIBBONS, Thomas (1720-1785) dissenting minister.
R J.SPILSBURY, after S.Webster, hl, mezz, BM, NPG. J.BODEN, 1785, wl seated, coloured engr, Dr Williams's Library, London.

GIBBS, Joseph (1700?-1788) organist and composer.
P THOMAS GAINSBOROUGH, hs, NPG 2179.

GIBBS, Mrs Mary, née Logan (1770-1844?) actress.
P SAMUEL DE WILDE, hl as Blanch in *The Iron Chest*, Garrick Club, London. S. DE WILDE, wl as Selina in *The Tale of Mystery*, Garrick Club.
D S. DE WILDE, 1809, head as Blanch, w/c, Garrick Club.
R Several theatrical prints, BM, NPG.

GIBBS, Sir Vicary (1751-1820) judge.
R S.W.REYNOLDS and T.LUPTON, after W.Owen, tql seated in robes, mezz, pub 1815, BM, NPG.
C THOMAS ROWLANDSON, c1815, 'We Three Logger Heads be', Laing Art Gallery, Newcastle.

GIBSON, John (d 1852) artist.
L UNKNOWN, SNPG 1428.

GIBSON, John (1790-1866) sculptor.
P ANDREW GEDDES, 1830, tql seated, Walker Art Gallery, Liverpool. PENRY WILLIAMS, c1844, hl, Academy of St Luke, Rome. JOHN GRAHAM GILBERT, 1847, hl, NGS 198. SIR EDWIN LANDSEER, c1850, hl, Royal Academy, London. MARGARET CARPENTER, 1857, hl, NPG 232. SIR WILLIAM BOXALL, 1864, hl, Royal Academy.
D JOHN PARTRIDGE, 1825, hs, pencil, NPG 3944 (32). CARL VOGEL, 1843, Küpferstichkabinett, Staatliche Kunstsammlungen, Dresden. WILLIAM BROCKEDON, 1844, hs, chalk, NPG 2515 (96). RUDOLPH LEHMANN, 1853, hs, crayon, BM. FIELD TALFOURD, 1859, hs profile, BM. UNKNOWN, hs profile, pencil, NPG 1370.
C WILLIAM THEED, RA 1852, bust, Parish Church, Conway. J.ADAMS, 1866, marble bust, St. George's Hall, Liverpool. W.THEED, RA 1868, marble bust, Royal Academy; reduced replica, NPG 1795.
H F.JOUBERT, hs, carte, NPG Album of Photographs 1949. UNKNOWN, wl seated, carte, NPG Album of Artists vol 1.

GIBSON, Patrick (c1782-1829) artist and writer on art.
D Self-portrait, w/c, SNPG 118.

GIFFORD, Andrew (1700-1784) baptist minister and assistant librarian at the British Museum.
P JOHN RUSSELL, 1775, hl, BM.

GIFFORD, Robert Gifford, 1st Baron (1779-1826) judge.
D SIR GEORGE HAYTER, study for NPG 999, NPG 1695 (E. 1).
G SIR GEORGE HAYTER, 'The Trial of Queen Caroline, 1820', oil, NPG 999.
R T.WRIGHT, after A.Wivell, tql, stipple, pub 1821, BM, NPG. H.MEYER, after C.Penny, hl seated, stipple, pub 1829, BM, NPG. C.HULLMANDEL, after M.Gauci, tql seated, lith, NPG.

GIFFORD, William (1756-1826) editor of the *Quarterly Review*.
P JOHN HOPPNER, hl seated, (replica), NPG 1017.
R UNKNOWN, hl reading a book, line, for *Gent Mag*, 1827, BM, NPG.

GILBART, James William (1794-1863) writer on banking and manager of the London and Westminster bank.
R H.ADLARD, after G.B.Black, hs, stipple, NPG. D.J.POUND, after a photograph by Mayall, hs, stipple, NPG. G.ZOBEL, after a photograph by T.R.Williams, tql seated, mezz, NPG.

UNKNOWN, hs, lith, BM.

GILBERT, Mrs Ann, see Taylor.

GILBERT, Ashurst Turner (1786-1870) bishop of Chichester.
P THOMAS PHILLIPS, RA 1835, tql, Brasenose College, Oxford.
SL AUGUSTIN EDOUART, 1827, wl, NPG.
C UNKNOWN, 'The Chichester Extinguisher', woodcut, for *Punch*, 1868 NPG.

GILBERT, Davies (1767-1839) president of the Royal Society.
P THOMAS PHILLIPS, tql, The Royal Society, London.
D WILLIAM BROCKEDON, 1838, hs, pencil, NPG 2515 (88).
G J.F.SKILL, J.GILBERT, W. and E.WALKER, 'Men of Science Living in 1807-08', pencil and wash, NPG 1075.
SC RICHARD WESTMACOTT junr, RA 1833, marble bust, Pembroke College, Oxford.
PR S.COUSINS, after H.Howard, hl seated, mezz, BM, NPG.

GILBERT, John Graham-, see GRAHAM-Gilbert.

GILBERT, Joseph (1779-1852) congregational divine.
PR M.GAUCI, after T.Barber, hl, lith, pub 1833, BM. J.COCHRAN, after J.Gilbert, hl seated, stipple, NPG.

GILBERT, Sir Walter Raleigh (1785-1853) lieutenant-general.
PR UNKNOWN, tql in uniform with Bath star, woodcut, for *Illust London News*, 1846, NPG. T.LUPTON, after G.F.Atkinson, tql, mezz, pub 1852, NPG.

GILCHRIST, John Borthwick (1759-1841) orientalist.
SC C.F.VOIGT, bronze medal, NPG 4064.

GILCHRIST, Octavius Graham (1779-1823) antiquary.
PR FREEMAN, after J.Lonsdale, hl, stipple, pub 1810, NPG.

GILFILLAN, Robert (1798-1850) poet.
SL UNKNOWN, SNPG 772.

GILLESPIE, James (1726-1797) founder of hospital at Edinburgh.
C J.KAY, hl profile, with John Gillespie, etch, oval, 1797, NPG.

GILLESPIE, Sir Robert Rollo (1766-1814) general.
SC SIR FRANCIS CHANTREY, c1816, statue, St Paul's Cathedral, London.
PR H.R.COOK, after W.Haines, hl, stipple, for *Military Panorama*, 1814, BM, NPG.

GILLIES, Adam Gillies, Lord (1760-1842) Scottish judge.
PR T.LUPTON, after C.Smith, tql, mezz, NPG.
C J.KAY, two etchings, reprinted in *Kay's Portraits*, 1842, vol II, NPG.

GILLIES, John (1747-1836) historian and scholar.
P JOHN OPIE, hl, SNPG 1397.
PR J.CALDWELL, after J.Bogle, hs, line, oval, for his *Hist of Greece*, 1788, BM, NPG.

GILLILAND, Thomas (fl 1804) writer.
PR T.CHEESMAN, after S. de Wilde, hs, stipple, oval, for his *Dramatic Mirror*, 1807, BM, NPG.

GILLINGWATER, Edmund (1735?-1813) historian of Lowestoft.
PR MISS TURNER, after H.Walton, hl, lith, BM, NPG.

GILLOW, John (1753-1828) president of Ushaw College and catholic missionary at York.
PR C.TURNER, after J.Ramsay, hl in lay dress, mezz, pub 1814, BM, NPG.

GILLRAY, James (1756-1815) caricaturist.

D Self-portrait, hs, pencil, BM.
M Attrib himself, hs, oval, NPG 83.
PR UNKNOWN, hs, caricatures on wall behind, coloured etch, BM, NPG.

GILLY, William Stephen (1780-1855) divine.
P JOHN JACKSON, 1833, tql, University College, Durham.
SC J.G.LOUGH, 1858, statue, Durham.

GILPIN, Sawrey (1733-1807) painter of horses.
D GEORGE DANCE, 1798, hs profile, Royal Academy, London. WILLIAM SHERLOCK, hl, w/c, NPG 4328. GEORGE DANCE, hs profile, pencil, BM.
SC GEORGE GARRARD, 1803, plaster bust, Burghley, Northants.

GILPIN, William (1724-1804) writer, exponent of 'the picturesque'.
P HENRY WALTON, 1781, hs, NPG 4418.

GIPPS, Sir George (1791-1847) colonial governor.
P UNKNOWN, tql seated, Mitchell Library, Sydney, Australia.
SC HENRY WEEKES, c1849, marble bust, Canterbury Cathedral.

GIRTIN, Thomas (1775-1802) water-colour painter.
P JOHN OPIE, hl, NPG 882.
D GEORGE DANCE, hs profile, pencil, BM. HENRY EDRIDGE, seated, sketching, pencil, BM. Self-portrait, tql seated, pencil, BM.

GISBORNE, Thomas (1758-1846) prebendary of Durham.
P JOSEPH WRIGHT of Derby, 1786, wl with his wife, Yale Center for British Art, New Haven, USA. UNKNOWN, tql, University College, Durham.
SC C.R.SMITH, 1841, bust, Durham University.
PR H.MEYER, after J.Hoppner, hs, stipple, for *Contemporary Portraits*, 1814, BM, NPG.

GLADSTONE, Sir John (1764-1851) merchant and politician.
P THOMAS GLADSTONE, hl seated, NPG 5042.
PR S.W.REYNOLDS, after W.Bradley, wl, mezz, pub 1844, BM, NPG.

GLASS, Thomas (d1786) physician.
P JOHN OPIE, tql seated, Royal Devon and Exeter Hospital.

GLASSE, Samuel (1735-1812) rector of Wanstead.
PR W.BOND, after G.F.Joseph, hs, stipple, pub 1803, NPG. M.N.BATE, after D.B.Murphy, hs, stipple, oval, BM, NPG.

GLASSFORD, John (1715-1783) tobacco merchant.
G ARCHIBALD MCLAUCHLAN, with his family, oil, c1770, Glasgow City Art Gallery.

GLEIG, George (1753-1840) bishop of Brechin.
PR W.WALKER, after S.B.Cudlip, hl, mezz, BM. H.ADLARD, hs, stipple, NPG.

GLEIG, George Robert (1796-1888) writer.
PR W.DRUMMOND, after E.U.Eddis, hl, lith, *Athenaeum Portraits*, No 31, 1836, BM. D.MACLISE, wl, lith, NPG; related drg, V & A.

GLENBERVIE, Sylvester Douglas, Baron (1743-1823) statesman.
D JOHN HENNING, 1805, chalk, SNPG 2032.
SC JOHN HENNING, 1808, porcelain medallion, SNPG 1276.
PR E.HARDING, after T.Lawrence, tql seated, stipple, pub 1794, BM, NPG. C.S.TAYLOR, after A.Buck, hl, stipple, for *New European Mag*, 1823, BM, NPG. J.D.INGRES, tql seated, lith, BM, NPG.

GLENCAIRN, James Cunningham, 14th Earl of (1749-1791) soldier.
PR H.ROBINSON, after K.Macleay, hl, stipple, oval, NPG.

GLENELG, Charles Grant, Baron (1778-1866) statesman.
PR C.TURNER, after T.C.Thompson, tql, mezz, pub 1820, BM. F.C.LEWIS, after J.Slater, hs, stipple, one of 'Grillion's Club'

series, BM, NPG.
C JOHN DOYLE, 'Playing off a joke upon an old friend', 1839, chalk, BM. J.DOYLE, 'The Somnambulist', 1839, chalk, BM.

GLENLEE, Sir Thomas Miller, Lord (1717-1789) lor[d] president of the Court of Session.
SC JAMES TASSIE, paste medallion; SNPG 131.
PR D.BLACKMORE, after J.Reynolds, hs, line, oval, for *Edinburg[h] Mag*, 1793, NPG.

GLENLEE, Sir William Miller, Lord (1755-1846) Scottis[h] judge.
P SIR HENRY RAEBURN, hs, Faculty of Advocates, Parliamen[t] Hall, Edinburgh. SIR H.RAEBURN, wl, Huntington Library an[d] Art Gallery, San Marino, USA.
PR JOHN KAY, hs, etch, 1799, NPG.

GLENNY, George (1793-1874) horticultural writer.
P UNKNOWN, Royal Horticultural Society, London.

GLENORCHY, Willielma Campbell, née Maxwell[,] Viscountess (1741-1786) religious enthusiast.
P RAMSAY, 1750, hl, Dunrobin Castle, Highland Region[,] Scotland.
PR HOPWOOD, hs, stipple, oval, pub 1815, NPG.

GLOUCESTER, Maria (Walpole), Duchess of (1739-1807[)] wife of HRH William Henry, Duke of Gloucester.
P SIR JOSHUA REYNOLDS, c1762, hl with her daughter, Musé[e] Condé, Chantilly, France. SIR JOSHUA REYNOLDS, RA 1774, w[l] seated, Royal Coll. After SIR WILLIAM BEECHEY, hs in widow[s] dress, Althorp, Northants. THOMAS GAINSBOROUGH, h[s] Cincinnati Institute of Fine Arts, USA. By or after SIR JOSHU[A] REYNOLDS, tql, Euston Hall, Suffolk.
D RICHARD COSWAY, wl with Princess Sophia and Princess Mary[,] Royal Coll.
M OZIAS HUMPHRY, 1769, hs, Royal Coll. UNKNOWN, hs, ova[l] Euston Hall.
SC CHRISTOPHER HEWETSON, marble bust, Royal Coll.
PR J.MCARDELL, after J.Reynolds, hl with headdress, mezz, pu[b] 1762, BM, NPG. J.FINLAYSON, after J.Reynolds, tql in widow[s] dress, mezz, pub 1773, BM, NPG. S.W.REYNOLDS, afte[r] J.Reynolds, tql seated in white sprigged gown, mezz, pub 182[0] BM, NPG.

GLOUCESTER, William Frederick, 2nd Duke of (1776[-] 1834) field-marshal.
P SIR JOSHUA REYNOLDS, 1780, wl as a boy, Trinity Colleg[e] Cambridge. GEORGE ROMNEY, c1793, wl, Trinity Colleg[e] JOHN OPIE, wl, Trinity College. SIR WILLIAM BEECHE[Y] c1808-12, wl in uniform, with Garter star, in landscape, Roy[al] Coll. UNKNOWN, c1815-20, hl in uniform, with orders, Roy[al] Coll.
M JOSEPH PASTORINI, hs, Royal Coll. JOHN TROSSARELLI, h[s] Royal Coll.
G SIR GEORGE HAYTER, 'The Trial of Queen Caroline, 1820', oi[l] NPG 999. GEORGE JONES, 'The Banquet of the Coronation o[f] George IV, Royal Coll.
SC J.P.DANTAN, 1834?, wl with Ernest Augustus, Duke o[f] Cumberland and King of Hanover, plaster caricature statuett[e] NPG L167.

GLOUCESTER, William Henry, 1st Duke of (1743-1805[)] third son of Frederick Louis, Prince of Wales.
P SIR WILLIAM BEECHEY, hs in uniform with Garter star, Roya[l] Coll. UNKNOWN, hs, Royal Coll.
D J.E.LIOTARD, hs as a young man, pastel, Royal Coll. FRANCI[S] COTES, 1769, hs with Garter star, pastel, Royal Col[l] UNKNOWN, hs, pastel, Royal Coll.

UNKNOWN, *c*1775, hs, Royal Coll. RICHARD CROSSE, hs with Garter star, Royal Coll.

BARTHÉLÉMY DE PAN, 'The Children of Frederick, Prince of Wales, oil, 1746, Royal Coll. GEORGE KNAPTON, 1748, with Princess Elizabeth and Prince Henry Frederick, pastel, Royal Coll. GEORGE KNAPTON, 'The Family of Frederick, Prince of Wales', oil, 1751, Royal Coll.

CHRISTOPHER HEWETSON, 1772, marble bust, Royal Coll.

GLOVER, John (1767-1849) landscape painter.

UNKNOWN, hs, woodcut, for *Art Journal*, 1850, BM, NPG.

GLOVER, Julia, née Betterton (1779-1850) actress.

SAMUEL DRUMMOND, hs, pastel, Garrick Club, London. W.S.LETHBRIDGE, wl as Lady Allworth in *A New Way to Pay Old Debts*, w/c, Garrick Club.

Several theatrical prints, BM, NPG.

GLOVER, Richard (1712-1785) poet.

T.HOLLOWAY, after N.Hone, hs, line, oval, for *European Mag*, 1786, BM, NPG. B.GRANGER, hs, stipple, oval for an ed of the Poets, 1800, BM, NPG.

GLYN, Sir Richard Carr, 1st Bart (1755-1838) lord mayor of London.

W.SAY, after J.Hoppner, wl in robes with sword and mace, mezz, pub 1804, BM, NPG. H.COOK, after a bust by Baily, line, pub 1830, NPG. T.L.BUSBY, hs, line, pub 1835, BM.

GLYN, Robert (1719-1800), see CLOBERY.

GLYNN, John (1722-1779) politician and lawyer.

RICHARD HOUSTON, hl seated with John Wilkes and John Horne Tooke, oil, *c*1768, NPG 1944.
UNKNOWN, hs, line, oval, for *Universal Mag*, BM, NPG. UNKNOWN, wl, line for *Political Register*, NPG.

GODDARD, William Stanley (1757-1845) headmaster of Winchester.

JOHN LUCAS, *c*1830, hl, Winchester College, Hants. H.W.PICKERSGILL, *c*1835, tql seated, Winchester College.

GODERICH, Viscount Frederick John Robinson, see 1st Earl of Ripon.

GODWIN, Mrs Mary, née Wollstonecraft (1759-1797) miscellaneous writer.

JOHN OPIE, hl, NPG 1237. JOHN OPIE, *c*1790–91, hl, TATE 1167.

GODWIN, William (1756-1836) philosopher and novelist.

JAMES NORTHCOTE, 1802, hl profile, NPG 1236. H.W.PICKERSGILL, hl, NPG 411.

WILLIAM BROCKEDON, 1832, hs, pencil and chalk, NPG 2515 (29). SIR THOMAS LAWRENCE, hl, chalk, BM. DANIEL MACLISE, drg for *Gallery of Illustrious Literary Characters*, for *Fraser's Mag*, V & A.

ROBERTS, after T.Kearsley, hl, stipple, pub 1821, BM, NPG.

'A.C.', wl, lith, NPG.

GOLDSMID, Abraham (1756?-1810) financier.

F.BARTOLOZZI, after S.Medley, hl, stipple, pub 1802, BM.

GOLDSMID, Sir Isaac Lyon, Bart (1778-1859) financier and philanthropist.

UNKNOWN, tql seated, University College, London.

R.DIGHTON, 'Will you let me a loan?' coloured etch, pub 1824, NPG, V & A.

GOLDSMITH, Oliver (1728-1774) writer.

SIR JOSHUA REYNOLDS, RA 1770, hl profile, Woburn Abbey, Beds; replicas, Knole (NT), Kent. NPG 130.

UNKNOWN, hs profile, NPG 676.

JOSEPH NOLLEKENS, medallion on monument, Westminster Abbey, London.

PR J.BRETHERTON, after H.Bunbury, hs, semi-profile, etch, BM, NPG. P.AUDINET, after an unknown artist, hs, semi-profile, line, oval, for *Biographical Mag*, 1795, BM, similar to type engr by Cook, pub 1780, NPG.

C J.BRETHERTON, after H.Bunbury, wl, 'The Full Blown Macaroni', etch, pub 1772, NPG.

GOMM, Sir William Maynard, (1784-1875) field-marshal.

P WILLIAM SLATER, 1834–40, tql study for 'Waterloo Banquet', NPG 3717. JAMES BOWLES, 1873–74, tql, oil over photograph, NPG 1071.

D SIR LESLIE WARD, 'Spy', 1873, wl, w/c, drawn for *Vanity Fair*, NPG 2715.

G W.SALTER, 'Waterloo Banquet at Apsley House', oil, 1836, Wellington Museum, Apsley House, London.

SC SIR JOHN STEELL, 1843, marble bust, Keble College, Oxford.

GOOCH, Robert (1784-1830) physician.

P R.J.LANE, 1823, hl, Royal College of Physicians, London.

PR J.LINNELL, hl seated, line, pub 1831, BM, NPG.

GOOD, John Mason (1764-1827) physician and author.

PR C.PICART, after W.Russell, hs, stipple, for his *Life*, 1828, BM, NPG.

GOOD, Thomas Sword (1789-1872) painter.

P Self-portrait, Castle Art Gallery, Nottingham.

GOODALL, Charlotte, née Stanton (1765-1830) actress.

P SAMUEL DE WILDE, wl as Sir Henry Wildair in *The Constant Couple*, Garrick Club, London.

PR Several theatrical prints, BM, NPG.

GOODALL, Joseph (1760-1840) provost of Eton.

P JOHN JACKSON, tql, Eton College, Berks.

SC HENRY WEEKES, 1845, statue, Eton College.

PR H.E.DAWE, tql, mezz, BM, NPG.

GOODALL, Thomas (1767-1832?) admiral of Hayti.

PR RIDLEY & BLOOD, after S.Drummond, hs in uniform, stipple, BM, NPG.

GOODE, Francis (1797-1842) divine.

PR C.TURNER, after W.E.Frost, hl, mezz, pub 1843, BM, NPG.

GOODE, William (1762-1816) divine.

PR UNKNOWN, hs, stipple, oval, for *Evangelical Mag*, 1796, NPG.

GOODENOUGH, Samuel (1743-1827) bishop of Carlisle.

P JAMES NORTHCOTE, 1810, tql seated, Christ Church, Oxford.

GOODRICKE, John (1764-1786) astronomer.

D UNKNOWN, tql, pastel, Royal Astronomical Society, London.

GOODYEAR, Joseph (1797-1839) engraver.

P HENRY ROOM, Birmingham City Art Gallery.

GORDON, Lord Adam (c1726-1801) general.

P JOHN ALEXANDER, 1738, hl, Lennoxlove, Lothian region, Scotland. HENRI-PIERRE DANLOUX, 1799, hl, SNPG 192. Attrib J.T.SETON, hl, Crathes Castle (NT), Grampian region, Scotland.

PR F.BARTOLOZZI, after D.A. de Sequeire, hl, stipple, oval, BM, 1797, NPG.

C J.KAY, two etchings, NPG.

GORDON, Sir Alexander (1786-1815) lieutenant-colonel, aide-de-camp to Wellington.

SC JOHN HENNING, 1809, paste medallion, NPG 1801.

GORDON, Alexander Gordon, 4th Duke of (1743-1827) keeper of the Great Seal of Scotland.

P SIR JOSHUA REYNOLDS, 1761, hl, Eton College, Berks. JOHN MOIR, 1817, hl, SNPG 207. SIR HENRY RAEBURN, hl with Thistle star, Goodwood, W.Sussex. Attrib SIR HENRY RAEBURN, hl, Manchester City Art Gallery, POMPEO BATONI, wl with horse

and dogs, Goodwood.
M GEORGE PLACE, V & A. W.SMITH, 1782, on vellum, Goodwood.
G W.SMITH, wl with his family, Goodwood.
SC JAMES TASSIE, paste medallion, SNPG 1194.
PR S.W.REYNOLDS, after Colvin Smith, hl aged 82, mezz, pub 1825, BM.

GORDON, Elizabeth Gordon, née Brodie, Duchess of (1794-1864) wife of 5th Duke of Gordon.
P UNKNOWN, wl seated, Brodie Castle, Grampian region, Scotland.
PR M.GAUCI, hl, lith, BM. UNKNOWN, tql seated, mezz, BM.

GORDON, Lord George (1751-1793) agitator.
G J.HEATH, after F.Wheatley, 'The Riot in Broad Street, 7 June 1780', line, pub 1790, NPG.
SC JAMES TASSIE, 1781, glass intaglio, NPG 4603. JAMES TASSIE, 1781, plaster medallion, SNPG 465.
PR UNKNOWN, after R.Bran, wl, line, pub 1780, BM, NPG. (TROTTER), after J. de Fleur, hs profile, line, oval, BM, NPG.

GORDON, George (1761-1853), see 9th Marquess of Huntly.

GORDON, George Gordon, 5th Duke of (1770-1836) raised the Gordon Highlanders.
P SIR HENRY RAEBURN, wl in Highland dress, Goodwood, W.Sussex. GEORGE SANDERS, tql in full Highland costume, Goodwood. A.E.CHALON, wl equestrian, Goodwood. UNKNOWN, wl seated with gun and dog in landscape, Brodie Castle, Grampian region, Scotland.
M ANDREW ROBERTSON, Aberdeen Art Gallery.
G BEN MARSHALL, wl equestrian with hounds and grooms, oil, c1815, Yale Center for British Art, New Haven, USA.
PR H.MEYER, after J.Jackson, hl, mezz, pub 1812, BM, NPG. C.TURNER, after J.McKenzie, tql seated, mezz, pub 1830, BM, NPG.

GORDON, George Hamilton, see 4th Earl of Aberdeen.

GORDON, Georgiana, Lady (1781-1853), see Duchess of Bedford.

GORDON, Sir James Alexander (1782-1869) admiral of the fleet.
P ANDREW MORTON, 1837-43, hl with Bath star, NMM, Greenwich.
PR UNKNOWN, hs, stipple, oval, for *Naval Chronicle*, 1814, BM, NPG.

GORDON, Sir James Willoughby, 1st Bart (1773-1851) general.
PR J.HOPWOOD, after T.Rowlandson, tql seated, profile, line, for *Investigation of charges against the Duke of York*, 1809, BM.

GORDON, Jane (or Jean) Maxwell, Duchess of (c1749-1812) wife of the 4th Duke of Gordon.
P SIR JOSHUA REYNOLDS, RA 1775, hl, Goodwood, W.Sussex. GEORGE ROMNEY, called Duchess of Gordon, with her son, SNPG 2208.
D JOHN BROWN, 1786, hl, pencil, SNPG 1153. J.BROWN, head, with Lady Wallace, pencil, SNPG 927.
G W.SMITH, wl seated with her husband and children, Goodwood.
PR W.EVANS, after W.Lane, tql reclining, stipple, pub 1806, BM, NPG.

GORDON, Sir John Watson (1788-1864) artist.
P JOHN GRAHAM GILBERT, 1854, wl, SNPG 715. Self-portrait, hl, Royal Scottish Academy, Edinburgh.
D Self-portrait, head, pencil, chalk and wash, SNPG 1771.
SC PATRIC PARK, bust, Royal Scottish Academy.
PH J.G.TUNNY, hs, carte, NPG Album of Artists vol 1.

GORDON, Pryse Lockhart (fl 1834) writer.

PR H.MEYER, hs, stipple, pub 1830, NPG.

GORDON, Robert (1786-1853) professor of Divinity in t Free Church College.
SL AUGUSTIN EDOUART, 1830, SNPG 2152. A.EDOUART, with w background, SNPG 1213.

GORDON, Sir Robert (1791-1847) diplomatist.
PR KRIEHUBER, tql with Bath ribbon and star, lith, BM, NPG.

GORDON, Thomas (1788-1841) general in the Greek servic
PR F.HANFSTAENGL, after Kraxcisen, hl in Greek uniform, lith, B

GORDON-LENNOX, Charles, see 5th Duke RICHMOND and Lennox.

GORE, Mrs Catherine Grace Frances, née Moody (179 1861) novelist and dramatist.
PR I.W.SLATER, after J.Slater, head, lith, pub 1829, BM. Similar en by S.Freeman, stipple, BM, NPG. UNKNOWN, hl, stipple, p 1848, BM.

GORHAM, George Cornelius (1787-1857) divine a antiquary.
PR After A.H.FORRESTER, wl, lith, for *Bentley's Miscellany*, 18 BM, NPG.

GORT, Charles Vereker, 2nd Viscount (1768-184 politician.
D CHARLES GREY, wl, pencil, NGI 2598.
PR J.HEATH, after J.Comerford, hs, stipple, for Sir J.Barringto *Historic Memoirs*, 1809, BM, NPG.

GOSFORD, Archibald Acheson, 2nd Earl of (1776-184 governor of Canada.
G SIR GEORGE HAYTER, 'The Trial of Queen Caroline, 1820', c NPG 999.
PR R.J.LANE, after T.Phillips of 1826, hl in peer's robes, lith, 182 BM, NPG.

GOSSET, Isaac (1735?-1812) bibliographer.
PR S.SPRINGSGUTH, wl seated, line, for Kirby's *Wonderful Museu 1813, BM, NPG. UNKNOWN, hl seated in Lochee's auction roo entitled 'A Pretty Copy', etch, BM, NPG. R.COOPER, after a w model by W.Behnes, hs, stipple, BM, NPG. J.BEUGO, wl, etch, B

GOUGH, Sir Hugh Gough, 1st Viscount (1779-1869) fie marshal.
P GENERAL A.Y.SHORTT, after Edwin Long of c1850, East Inc and Sports Club, London. LOWES DICKINSON, c1851, wl uniform, Oriental Club, London. SIR FRANCIS GRANT, c185 wl, formerly United Services Club, London (c/o The Crow Commissioners). JAMES HARWOOD, c1851, wl, NGI 30 UNKNOWN, East India and Sports Club.
D SIR FRANCIS GRANT, after the portrait of c1853, tql, pen and in NPG 805.
SC G.G.ADAMS, 1850, plaster bust, NPG 1202. J.H.FOLE 1874-80, bronze equestrian statue, Phoenix Park, Dubl UNKNOWN, bust, India Office Library and Records, Londo
PR J.H.LYNCH, after E.Long, hs, lith, pub 1850, NPG. H.B.HA after J.R.Jackson, hl, stipple, BM, NPG.
PH UNKNOWN, tql, NPG Photographs – Portraits vol. 1.

GOUGH, Richard (1735-1809) antiquary.
PR UNKNOWN, silhouette, hs profile, woodcut, BM.

GOULBURN, Henry (1784-1856) chancellor of t exchequer.
G SIR GEORGE HAYTER, 'The House of Commons, 1833', oil, N 54.
PR F.HOLL, after H.W.Pickersgill, hl, stipple, NPG.
C Several JOHN DOYLE political sketches, drgs, BM.

GOULD, Sir Henry (1710-1794) judge.
P UNKNOWN, Harvard Law Library, Cambridge, Mass, USA.
R T.HARDY, tql seated in robes, mezz, pub 1794, BM, NPG.

GOW, Neil or Niel (1727-1807) violinist and composer.
P SIR HENRY RAEBURN, tql seated playing violin, SNPG 160. After
DAVID ALLAN, wl seated playing violin with another musician,
SNPG 2126.

GOWER, Sir Erasmus (1742-1814) admiral.
P RICHARD LIVESAY, National Museum of Wales 1112, Cardiff.
R W.RIDLEY, after R.Livesay, hl in uniform, stipple, oval, for
Naval Chronicle, 1800, BM, NPG.

GOWER, Foote (1726?-1780) antiquary.
R W.SKELTON, after J.Taylor, hl profile, line, circular frame, pub
1790, NPG.

GOWER, Richard Hall (1767-1833) naval architect.
R UNKNOWN, hl, lith, BM, NPG.

GRACE, Mary, née Hodgkiss (d1786?) painter.
R UNKNOWN, hs, stipple, pub 1785, BM, NPG.

GRACE, Sheffield (1788?-1850) historical writer.
R R.GRAVE, after F.Manskirsch, tql seated, line, for his *Memoirs of
the Family of Grace*, 1823, BM, NPG. F.DELEU, after A.Robertson,
hl in uniform, line, for same work, BM.

GRADWELL, Robert (1777-1833) Roman catholic prelate.
R J.HOLL, hs, stipple, oval, pub 1833, NPG.

**GRAFTON, Augustus Henry Fitzroy, 3rd Duke of (1735-
1811)** prime-minister.
P POMPEO BATONI, 1762, hl, NPG 4899. Several portraits at Euston
Hall, Suffolk: R.E.PINE, 1776, hl with robes and Garter George;
JOHN HOPPNER, c1805, hl with Garter star; NATHANIEL
DANCE, hl.
M Attrib JEREMIAH MEYER, hs, oval, Euston Hall.
G JOHN SINGLETON COPLEY, 'The Collapse of the Earl of Chatham
in the House of Lords, 7 July 1778', oil, TATE 100, on loan to NPG.
C Several engravings by J.Bretherton, Dighton and J.Sayers, BM,
NPG.

**GRAFTON, George Henry Fitzroy, 4th Duke of (1760-
1844)** politician.
P SIR THOMAS LAWRENCE, c1816, wl in robes, completed by John
Simpson after 1830, Trinity College, Cambridge. JOHN
HOPPNER, hl, Euston Hall, Suffolk. WILLIAM OWEN, tql in
robes, Euston Hall. GEORGE ROMNEY, tql, Euston Hall.
D JOHN DOWNMAN, 3 hl chalk drgs, two dated 1777, one dated
1779, oval, Fitzwilliam Museum, Cambridge.
G SIR GEORGE HAYTER, 'The Trial of Queen Caroline, 1820', oil,
NPG 999.
C JOSEPH NOLLEKENS, 1813, marble bust, Castle Howard,
N.Yorks.

GRAHAM, Catharine Macaulay, see Macaulay.

GRAHAM, Clementina Stirling (1782-1877) writer.
D UNKNOWN, w/c, SNPG 1252.

GRAHAM, James (1745-1794) quack doctor.
C THOMAS ROWLANDSON, 'Dr Graham's Earth Bathing
Establishment, c1790-95', pen, w/c, and pencil, Yale Center for
British Art, New Haven, USA. J.KAY, wl on a bridge in high
wind, etch, 1785, NPG. J.KAY, lecturing to a crowd of men, etch,
1785, BM, NPG.

GRAHAM, James (1755-1836), see 3rd Duke of Montrose.

GRAHAM, James (1791-1845) army pensioner.
D UNKNOWN, hl, w/c, NGI 2605.

GRAHAM, James (1799-1874), see 4th Duke of Montrose.

**GRAHAM, Sir James Robert George, 2nd Bart (1792-
1861)** first lord of the admiralty.
D S.F.DIEZ, 1842, tql seated, Staatliche Museen zu Berlin; related
engr, E.Desmaisons, lith, pub 1842, BM, NPG.
G SIR GEORGE HAYTER, 'The House of Commons, 1833', oil, NPG
54. JOHN PARTRIDGE, 'The Fine Arts Commissioners, 1846', NPG
342, 3. JOHN GILBERT, 'The Coalition Ministry, 1854', pencil and
wash, NPG 1125.
PR BROWN, after Doyle, tql, stipple, pub 1863, NPG.
C BENJAMIN WILLIAM CROMBIE, pencil, Crombie Sketchbook, fo
5, pencil, SNPG 2036. Several JOHN DOYLE, drgs, BM.

GRAHAM, John (1794-1865) bishop of Chester.
D UNKNOWN, pencil sketch, Christ's College, Cambridge.

GRAHAM, Maria, see Lady Callcott.

GRAHAM, Sir Robert (1744-1836) judge.
P JOHN SINGLETON COPLEY, 1804, tql as baron of the Exchequer,
National Gallery of Art, Washington DC, USA.

GRAHAM, Robert (1786-1845) botanist and physician.
P COLVIN SMITH, hl, Edinburgh University.
PR UNKNOWN, hs, lith, NPG.

GRAHAM, Robert Cunninghame (d1797) poet and
politician.
P DAVID MARTIN, SNPG 885.

GRAHAM, Thomas (1748-1843), see 1st Baron Lynedoch.

GRAHAM-GILBERT, John (1794-1866) artist.
P Self-portrait, hl, Royal Scottish Academy.
SL AUGUSTIN EDOUART, SNPG 789.
SC WILLIAM BRODIE, 1870, statue, City Art Gallery and Museum,
Glasgow.

GRAHAME, James (1765-1811) advocate, clergyman and
poet.
SC JOHN HENNING, c1810, porcelain medallion, SNPG 1541.
PR S.FREEMAN, hl, stipple, for Chambers's *Dict of Eminent Scotsmen*,
BM, NPG.

GRAINGER, Edward (1797-1824) anatomical teacher.
SC PETER HOLLINS, marble bust, Royal College of Surgeons,
London.

GRAINGER, Richard (1798-1861) architect.
P DAVID MOSSMAN, Laign Art Gallery, Newcastle-upon-Tyne.
PR G.H.PHILLIPS, after T.Carrick, tql, mezz, pub 1840, BM, NPG.

GRAINGER, Thomas (1794-1852) civil engineer.
P SIR JOHN WATSON-GORDON, Institute of Civil Engineers,
London.

GRANARD, George Forbes, 6th Earl of (1760-1837)
general.
PR J.HEATH, after Wright, hs, stipple, for Sir J.Barrington's *Historic
Memoirs*, 1815, BM.

GRANBY, John Manners, Marquess of (1721-1770)
commander-in-chief of the British Army.
P ALLAN RAMSAY, 1745, wl, DoE (Audley End, Essex). SIR
JOSHUA REYNOLDS, 1766, wl with horse, Ringling Museum of
Art, Sarasota, Florida, USA; version, Royal Coll.
D J.E.LIOTARD, 1740, hs, crayon, Belvoir Castle, Leics. After SIR
JOSHUA REYNOLDS of c1759, hs, chalk, NPG 1186.
G DAVID MORIER, wl equestrian, battle in background, oil, c1760,
Royal Coll. EDWARD PENNY, wl equestrian giving alms, oil,
exhib 1765, Ashmolean Museum, Oxford. M.F.QUADAL,
'George III at a Review', oil, 1772, Royal Coll.
SC JOSEPH CERACCHI, 1778, marble bust, Belvoir Castle. JOSEPH
NOLLEKENS, 1814, marble bust, Royal Coll.

GRANDISON, George Bussy Villiers, 7th Viscount, see 4th Earl of Jersey.

GRANDISON, George Child Villiers, 8th Viscount, see 5th Earl of Jersey.

GRANGER, James (1723-1776) biographer and print collector.
M JOHN CORNISH, 1765, hs on copper, NPG 2961.
PR D.P.PARISET, after P.Falconet, hs, stipple, circular frame, BM.

GRANT, Anne, née MacVicar (1755-1838) writer.
P JAMES TANNOCK, hl, SNPG 274.
D WILLIAM BEWICK, 1824, chalk, SNPG 1046.
SL AUGUSTIN EDOUART, 1831, SNPG 1177.

GRANT, Charles (1746-1823) statesman and philanthropist.
P MISS LANCASTER LUCAS, after Sir Henry Raeburn, wl seated, India Office Library and Records, London.
C 'ARGUS', 'The Storming of Monopoly Fort', coloured engr, c1813, India Office, London.

GRANT, Charles (1778-1866), see Baron Glenelg.

GRANT, Colquhoun (d1792) Jacobite.
C J.KAY, wl with Allan Macdougall and Alexander Watson, etch, BM.

GRANT, James (of Ballindalloch) (1720-1806) general.
P Attrib RAMSAY, hl, Dunrobin Castle, Highland region, Scotland.
C J.KAY, hl profile, etch, 1798, NPG.

GRANT, Sir James, 8th Bart (1738-1811) politician.
P WILLIAM STAVELEY, 1797, SNPG 1956.
G NATHANIEL DANCE, wl, a conversation piece, with 2nd Baron Grantham and John Mytton, oil, 1700–66, Yale Center for British Art, New Haven, USA.
C J.KAY, wl in uniform, etch, 1798, NPG.

GRANT, Sir Robert (1779-1838) governor of Bombay.
G SIR GEORGE HAYTER, 'The House of Commons, 1833', oil, NPG 54.
PR F.C.LEWIS, after J.Slater, hs, stipple, one of 'Grillion's Club' series, BM.

GRANT, Robert Edmond (1793-1874) comparative anatomist.
PR T.H.MAGUIRE, tql seated, lith, for *Ipswich Museum Portraits*, BM, NPG.

GRANT, William (1701?-1764), see Lord Prestongrange.

GRANT, Sir William (1752-1832) master of the rolls.
P SIR THOMAS LAWRENCE, RA 1802, hl in private dress, Graves Art Gallery, Sheffield. SIR T.LAWRENCE, RA 1820, wl in robes, NPG 671. G.H.HARLOW, tql seated in robes, Lincoln's Inn, London.
PR J.R.SMITH, after J.Barry, hs, stipple, oval, BM, pub 1793, NPG.

GRANTHAM, Thomas Robinson, 2nd Baron (1738-1786) politician.
P Attrib GEORGE ROMNEY, c1779–80, tql seated, Newby Hall, N.Yorks. GILBERT STUART, 1781, hs, Saltram House (NT), Devon.
G NATHANIEL DANCE, wl, in a conversation piece, with James Grant and John Mytton, oil, c1760–66, Yale Center for British Art, New Haven, USA.
PR H.ROBINSON, hl, stipple, pub 1829, NPG.

GRANTLEY, Fletcher Norton, 1st Baron (1716-1789) barrister.
P SIR WILLIAM BEECHEY, tql in speaker's gown, Palace of Westminster, London.

PR UNKNOWN, hs, stipple, NPG. UNKNOWN, hs, stipple and line, oval, 'Sir Bullface Doublefees', for *Town and Country Magazine*, NPG.
C JAMES SAYERS, wl, etch, pub 1782, NPG. J.SAYERS, 'Razor Levée', etch, pub 1783, NPG.

GRANTON, Charles Hope, Lord (1763-1851) president of the court of session.
P SIR JOHN WATSON-GORDON, wl, Faculty of Advocates, Parliament Hall, Edinburgh. SIR HENRY RAEBURN, Boston Museum of Fine Arts, USA. SIR HENRY RAEBURN, SNPG L21.
PR C.M.HOPE, tql seated, lith, BM.
C Three JOHN KAY etchings, reprinted in *Kay's Portraits*, 1842, NPG.

GRANVILLE, Lord Granville Leveson-Gower, 1st Earl (1773-1846) diplomatist.
G GEORGE ROMNEY, 'The Gower Children', oil, 1776–77, Abbot Hall Art Gallery, Kendal. SIR GEORGE HAYTER, 'The Trial of Queen Caroline, 1820', oil, NPG 999.
PR J.S.AGAR, after T.Phillips, hl, stipple, for *Contemporary Portraits*, 1813, BM, NPG.

GRATTAN, Henry (1746-1820) Irish statesman.
P FRANCIS WHEATLEY, 1782, hs, NPG 790. NICHOLAS KENNY, wl moving the Declaration of Irish Rights in 1782, Trinity College, Dublin. SIR MARTIN ARCHER SHEE, hs, NGI 1788. GILBERT STUART, hs, NGI 1163. T.A.JONES, after James Ramsay, tql NGI 123.
D ALEXANDER POPE, hl, w/c, BM. T.SCOTT, after A.Pope, wl, ink, NGI 2273.
G FRANCIS WHEATLEY, 'The Irish House of Commons, 1780', oil, Leeds City Art Galleries, Lotherton Hall, W.Yorks.
SC PETER TURNERELLI, 1812, plaster bust, NPG 1341. SIR FRANCIS CHANTREY, RA 1826, bronze statue, City Hall, Dublin. J.E.CAREW, 1844, statue, St Stephen's Hall, Westminster, London.

GRATTAN, Thomas Colley (1792-1864) novelist.
PR J.THOMSON, after F.R.Say, hl seated, stipple, for *New Monthly Mag*, 1831, BM, NPG. UNKNOWN, wl with dog and gun, lith, pub 1853, NPG.

GRAVES, Richard (1715-1804) poet and novelist.
PR S.W.REYNOLDS, after J.Northcote, tql seated, mezz, pub 1800, BM, NPG. J.BASIRE, after T.Gainsborough, hs, line, oval, for Nichols's *Literary Anecdotes*, 1812, BM.
C UNKNOWN, wl, line, NPG.

GRAVES, Richard (1763-1829) dean of Ardagh.
PR R.GRAVES, hl, line, for his *Works*, 1840, BM.

GRAVES, Robert (1798-1873) line-engraver.
PR J.R.JACKSON, after R.W.Buss, 1835, tql seated, mezz, BM. T.FAIRLAND, after J.Miller, tql seated, lith, BM, NPG.
PH JOHN and CHARLES WATKINS, tql, carte, NPG Album of Artists vol 2, MAULL & POLYBLANK, wl seated, carte, NPG Album of Artists vol 2.

GRAVES, Robert James (1796-1853) physician.
D CHARLES GREY, pencil, NGI 2589.
SC JOHN HOGAN, 1854, marble bust, Royal College of Physicians of Ireland.

GRAVES, Sir Thomas (1747?-1814) admiral.
P JAMES NORTHCOTE, 1802, tql with Bath star, NMM, Greenwich.

GRAVES, Thomas Graves, 1st Baron (1725?-1802) admiral.
G BARTOLOZZI, LANDSEER, RYDER and STOW, after R.Smirke, 'Naval Victories', 'Commemoration of the victory of June 1, 1794', line, pub 1803, BM, NPG.
PR F.BARTOLOZZI, after J.Northcote, tql with arm in sling, mezz, BM, NPG.

GRAY, Edward Whitaker (1748-1806) botanist.
P SIR AUGUSTUS CALLCOTT, hl profile, The Royal Society, London.

GRAY, Sir George, Bart (d1773) soldier and founder of The Society of Dilettanti.
P GEORGE KNAPTON, 1744, hl seated at writing desk, The Society of Dilettanti, Brooks's Club, London.

GRAY, Sir James, Bart (d1773) diplomatist and antiquary.
P GEORGE KNAPTON, 1741, tql, The Society of Dilettanti, Brooks's Club, London.

GRAY, Maria Emma, née Smith (1787-1876) conchologist.
R G.STODART, after J.Ayling, hs, stipple, oval, BM.

GRAY, Robert (1762-1834) bishop of Bristol.
P EVANS, tql, University College, Durham.
SC E.H.BAILY, medallion on marble monument, Bristol Cathedral.
R J.JENKINS, after J.W.Wright, tql seated, stipple, for Jerdan's *Nat Portrait Gallery*, 1831, BM, NPG.

GRAY, Thomas (1716-1771) poet and classical scholar.
P JOHN GILES ECCARDT, 1747-48, hl, NPG 989. UNKNOWN, c1771, hl profile, Minster Library, York. BENJAMIN WILSON, hl profile, posthumous, Pembroke College, Cambridge.
D WILLIAM MASON, hs profile, pencil, Pembroke College, Cambridge. JAMES BASIRE, after a sketch by the Rev William Mason of c1771, hs profile, pencil, NPG 425.
SL FRANCIS MAPLETOFT, c1760, hs profile, Pembroke College.
SC UNKNOWN, plaster bust, NPG 781. JOHN BACON sen, medallion on monument, Westminster Abbey, London.
R W.DOUGHTY, after W.Mason, hs profile, etch, oval, for his *Poems*, 1778, BM, NPG. J.CHAPMAN, after B.Wilson, hs, stipple, circle, for his *Poems*, 1799, BM.

GRAY, Thomas (1788-1848) railway pioneer.
P R.A.CLACK, 1848, tql seated, Royal Albert Memorial Museum, Exeter, Devon.

GREATHEAD, Henry (1757-1816) lifeboat inventor.
P UNKNOWN, hl, NMM, Greenwich.
R W.RIDLEY, hs, stipple, oval, for *European Mag*, 1804, BM, NPG.

GREAVES, James Pierrepont (1777-1842) mystic.
R UNKNOWN, hs, stipple, NPG.

GREEN, Amos (1735-1807) painter.
R W.T.FRY, after Hancock, hl, stipple, NPG.

GREEN, Charles (1785-1870) aeronaut.
P HILAIRE LEDRU, 1835, hl seated with balloon in background, NPG 2557.
G JOHN HOLLINS, 'A Consultation prior to the Aerial Voyage to Weilburg, 1836', oil, NPG 4710.
R G.T.PAYNE, after J.Hollins, tql seated, mezz, pub 1838, BM, NPG. G.P.HARDING, hl with balloon, lith, pub 1839, BM, NPG. After a daguerreotype by J.E.MAYALL, hl, in balloon, woodcut, for *Illust London News*, 1852, NPG. UNKNOWN, after a photograph by J.E.Mayall, hs, woodcut, for *Illust London News*, 1870, NPG.

GREEN, James (1771-1834) portrait-painter.
G A.E.CHALON, 'Study at the British Institution 1805', pen, ink and w/c, BM.

GREEN, Jane, née Hippisley (d1791) actress.
G W.HUMPHREY, after T.Parkinson, in a scene from Goldsmith's *She Stoops to Conquer*, mezz, BM.
R J.H.GREEN, hl, etch, pub 1803, BM. UNKNOWN, as Duenna in Sheridan's *The Duenna*, etch, BM.

GREEN, Joseph Henry (1791-1863) surgeon.
P THOMAS PHILLIPS, RA 1829, tql, Royal College of Surgeons, London.

SC HENRY WEEKES, marble busts, Royal Academy, London, Royal College of Surgeons, London.
PR G.H.LYNCH, after G.Teniswood, hs profile, lith, BM.

GREEN, Thomas (1769-1825) miscellaneous writer.
PR W.H.WORTHINGTON, after W.M.Bennett, hl, line, NPG.

GREEN, Valentine (1739-1813) mezzotint engraver.
P L.F.ABBOTT, hl, NPG 1260.
G UNKNOWN, after P.Sandby, 'Sketches taken at Print Sales', line, pub 1798, BM. A.E.CHALON, 'Study at the British Institution, 1805', pen, ink, and w/c, BM.

GREEN, Sir William, 1st Bart (1725-1811) general.
P After G.CARTER, 1785, wl, Royal Engineers Conservatory, HQ Mess, Chatham, Kent.

GREENE, Richard (1716-1793) surgeon and antiquary.
PR UNKNOWN, hl profile, etch, oval, BM, NPG.

GREENFIELD, William (1799-1831) philologist.
PR W.HOLL, after G.Hayter, hl seated, stipple, pub 1834, BM, NPG.

GREENOUGH, George Bellas (1778-1855) geographer and geologist.
PR M.GAUCI, after E.U.Eddis, hs, lith, BM, NPG.

GREENWOOD, John (1727-1792) mezzotint engraver and auctioneer.
PR W.PETHER, hs, mezz, oval, BM.

GREGG, John (1798-1878) Irish bishop.
PR UNKNOWN, hs, woodcut, for *Illust London News*, 1878, NPG.

GREGORY, James (1753-1821) physician and writer.
SC JAMES TASSIE, 1791, paste medallion, SNPG 128. SAMUEL JOSEPH, 1821, plaster bust, SNPG 287.
PR G.DAWE, after H.Raeburn, tql seated, mezz, pub 1805, BM.
C J.KAY, hs profile, etch, oval, 1795, BM, NPG. J.KAY, 'The Craft in Danger', etch, NPG.

GREGORY, John (1724-1773) professor of medicine at Edinburgh.
PR R.EARLOM, after G.Chalmers, tql seated, mezz, pub 1774, BM. J.BEUGO, after F.Cotes, hl, aged 40, stipple, oval, for his *A Father's Legacy to his Daughters*, 1788, BM.

GREGORY, Olinthus Gilbert (1774-1841) mathematician and author.
PR THOMSON, after Derby, hl, stipple, pub 1823, NPG. H.ROBINSON, after R.Evans, tql seated, stipple, for Jerdan's *Nat Portrait Gallery*, 1834, BM, NPG.

GREGSON, Matthew (1749-1824) antiquary.
PR M.GAUCI, after W.Bigg, hl, lith, for 2nd ed of his *Fragments of Lancashire*, NPG.

GREIG, Sir Samuel (1735-1788) admiral of the Russian navy.
PR J.WALKER, after Dm. Levitsky, hl in uniform, mezz, pub 1788, NPG.

GRENFELL, Pascoe (1761-1838) politician.
PR S.COUSINS, after M.A.Shee, tql seated, mezz, BM, NPG.

GRENVILLE, George (1712-1770) statesman.
P WILLIAM HOARE, 1764, tql seated in chancellor's robes, Christ Church, Oxford. SIR JOSHUA REYNOLDS, c1764-67, wl in chancellor's robes, John Bass Museum, Miami, Florida, USA; tql version, Petworth (NT), W.Sussex.

GRENVILLE, George Nugent (1788-1850), see Baron Nugent.

GRENVILLE, George Nugent-Temple (1753-1813), see 1st Marquess of Buckingham.

GRENVILLE, Richard (1776-1839), see 1st Duke of

BUCKINGHAM and Chandos.

GRENVILLE, Richard (1797-1861), see 2nd Duke of BUCKINGHAM and Chandos.

GRENVILLE, Richard Temple (1711-1779), see Earl Temple.

GRENVILLE, Thomas (1755-1846) book collector and diplomat.
P After JOHN HOPPNER, c1807, Hughenden Manor (NT), Bucks. THOMAS PHILLIPS, RA 1810?, hs, Althorp, Northants.
M CAMILLE MANZINI, 1841, hl, NPG 517.
SC J.B.COMELLI, marble bust, on loan to the Plymouth Museum.
PR C.TURNER, after J.Hoppner, hl seated, mezz, pub 1805, BM, NPG. LADY DELAMERE, hl profile, aged 80, lith, BM. J.POSSELWHITE, after G.Richmond, hs aged 90, stipple, BM.

GRENVILLE, William Wyndham Grenville, 1st Baron (1759-1834) foreign secretary.
P GEORGE ROMNEY, 1781, hl, a leaving portrait, Eton College, Berks. THOMAS PHILLIPS, RA 1810, tql in robes of the chancellor of the University of Oxford, Royal College of Surgeons, London. WILLIAM OWEN, RA 1812, wl in chancellor's robes, Christ Church, Oxford. JOHN HOPPNER, tql seated, North Carolina Museum of Art, Raleigh, USA. J.HOPPNER, hl, NPG 318.
G GEORGE JONES, 'Reception of the Prince Regent in Oxford, June 1814', oil, Magdalen College, Oxford. SIR GEORGE HAYTER, 'The Trial of Queen Caroline, 1820', oil, NPG 999.
SC JOSEPH NOLLEKENS, 1810, marble bust, Royal Coll.
PR T.A.DEAN, after J.Jackson, hl, stipple, for Jerdan's *Nat Portrait Gallery*, 1829, BM, NPG. M.GAUCI, after C.Proby, tql seated, lith, BM, NPG.
C J.SAYERS, 'Achitopel an old Jew Scribe, lately turned Greek, Greeks, Persians (stowed together) worshipping the rising Sun', etch, 1804, NPG. CHARLES WILLIAMS (Argus), 'The New Minister or – as it should be', coloured etch, pub 1806, V & A. WILLIAM HEATH (Paul Pry), 'A Pair of Broad Bottoms', coloured etch, pub 1810, V & A.

GRESSE, John Alexander (1741-1794) painter and royal drawing-master.
D UNKNOWN, c1770, head, chalk, NPG 4196.

GRETTON, William (1736-1813) master of Magdalene College, Cambridge.
P UNKNOWN, Magdalene College, Cambridge.
C DIGHTON, wl, 'A View from Magdalen College, Cambridge', coloured etch, pub 1809, NPG.

GREVILLE, Algernon Frederick (1798-1864) private secretary to Duke of Wellington.
D SIR THOMAS LAWRENCE, c1803, tql as a child, Goodwood, W.Sussex.

GREVILLE, Charles Cavendish Fulke (1794-1865) political diarist.
P UNKNOWN, hl, Goodwood, W.Sussex.
D COUNT ALFRED D'ORSAY, 1840, hs profile, chalk, NPG 3773.
G SIR DAVID WILKIE, 'The First Council of Queen Victoria', oil, 1837, Royal Coll.
PR T.C.WILSON, wl profile, lith, for Wildrake's *Cracks of the day*, 1841, BM, NPG. J.BROWN, after a photograph by J.E.Mayall, hs, stipple, pub 1864, NPG.

GREVILLE, Robert Kaye (1794-1866) botanist.
D WILLIAM BEWICK, chalk, SNPG 1045.
G B.R.HAYDON, 'The Anti-Slavery Society Convention, 1840', oil, NPG 599.
PR MISS TURNER, after D.Macnee, hl, lith, BM. UNKNOWN, after D.Macnee of 1830, hl, lith, NPG.

GREY, Sir Charles Grey, 1st Earl (1729-1807) general.
PR J.COLLYER, after T.Lawrence, tql, stipple, BM, NPG. W.RIDLEY after a miniature, hs in uniform, stipple, oval, for *European Ma* 1797, BM, NPG.

GREY, Charles Grey, 2nd Earl (1764-1845) prime-ministe.
P GEORGE ROMNEY, 1784, hl seated, Eton College, Berk THOMAS PHILLIPS, 1810, hs, Althorp, Northants. Attrib THOMA PHILLIPS, c1820, tql, NPG 4137.JOHN JACKSON, c1826, hl, V & A After SIR THOMAS LAWRENCE, c1828, hl, NPG 1190 B.R.HAYDON, c1836, wl seated by fireside, Laing Art Gallery Newcastle. J.RAMSAY, c1837, Literary and Philosophic Society, Newcastle-upon-Tyne.
D SIR FRANCIS CHANTREY, after 1830, hs profile, pencil, NPG 316 (59). B.R.HAYDON, 1834, hs, NPG 3784, a study for Haydon 'Reform Banquet', 3 studies are in the Laing Art Gallery Newcastle.
G SIR GEORGE HAYTER, 'The Trial of Queen Caroline, 1820', oi NPG 999. F.BROMLEY, after B.R.Haydon, 'The Reform Banquet, 1832', etch, pub 1835, NPG. J.KNIGHT, 'William I' Holding a Council', lith, c1832, BM. S.W.REYNOLDS, 'Th Reform Bill Receiving the King's Assent', oil, 1832, Palace c Westminster, London. This is based on a drawing by John Doyl also in the Palace of Westminster. SIR G.HAYTER, 'The House c Commons, 1833', oil, NPG 54. SIR DAVID WILKIE, 'The Fir Council of Queen Victoria', oil 1837, Royal Coll.
SC THOMAS CAMPBELL, 1827, marble bust, Palace of Westminste JOSEPH NOLLEKENS, 1803, bust, Woburn Abbey, Bed E.H.BAILY, 1838, statue, Grey Street, Newcastle-upon-Tyn CHRISTOPHER MOORE, 1853, bust, Eton College. UNKNOWN bronze bust, Wellington Museum, Apsley House, London.
C Several JOHN DOYLE political sketches, drgs, BM.

GREY, Sir George, 2nd Bart (1799-1882) home secretary
G SIR JOHN GILBERT, 'The Coalition Ministry, 1854', pencil an wash, NPG 1125. JOHN PHILLIPS, 'The House of Commons, 1860 oil, Palace of Westminster, London.
PR W.HOLL, after G.Richmond, hs, stipple, one of 'Grillion's Club series, BM.
C JOHN DOYLE, 'Rowing in the Same Boat', 1848, pencil, BM.
PH W. & D.DOWNEY, wl seated, carte, NPG 1860s MPs/Franci Album. JOHN and CHARLES WATKINS, hs, carte, NPG 1860 MPs/Francis Album.

GREY, Henry (1778-1859) presbyterian minister a Edinburgh.
SC PATRIC PARK, 1853, bust, New College, Edinburgh.
PR W.WALKER, after W.Douglas, tql, stipple, BM, NPG.
C J.KAY, hl profile, etch, oval, 1815, NPG.

GREY, Thomas Philip de (1781-1859), see 2nd Earl DE Grey

GREY, William de (1719-1781), see 1st Baron Walsingham

GRIFFIN, John (1719-1797), see 4th Baron HOWARD d Walden.

GRIFFITH, Elizabeth (1720?-1793) playwright and novelis
G RICHARD SAMUEL, 'The Nine Living Muses of Great Britain oil, exhib 1779, NPG 4905.
PR MACKENZIE, after J.Thomas, hs, stipple, oval, for *Lady's Month* *Museum*, 1801, BM, NPG. UNKNOWN, hl, line, oval, BM, NPG.

GRIFFITH, John (1714-1798) independent minister.
PR UNKNOWN, hl, line, oval, for *Gospel Mag*, 1778, BM, NPG.

GRIFFITH, Moses (1747-1819) draughtsman.
P Self-portrait, 1811, hl, National Library of Wales.
PR G.SCOTT, hs, stipple, oval, NPG.

GRIFFITHS, Ralph (1720-1803) proprietor of the *Monthly Review*.
c UNKNOWN, c1790, Wedgwood medallion, Wedgwood Museum, Barlaston, Staffs.
R W.RIDLEY, hs, profile, stipple, oval, for *European Mag*, 1803, BM, NPG.

GRIGNION or **GRIGNON, Charles (1717-1810)** line-engraver.
D THOMAS UWINS, tql seated, aged 92, pencil, BM.

GRIMALDI, Joseph (1778-1837) entertainer.
P JOHN CAWSE, hl, NPG 827. UNKNOWN, hs, Garrick Club, London.
D J.E.T.ROBINSON, 1819, hl seated, w/c, Garrick Club, London. SAMUEL DE WILDE, wl as Clown in *Mother Goose*, w/c, Garrick Club.
R T.BLOOD, after T.Wageman, hs, stipple, pub 1820, BM, NPG. Several theatrical prints, BM, NPG.

GRIMALDI, William (1751-1830) miniature painter.
D MARY GRIMALDI, after Louisa Edwards, wl seated, profile, pencil, NPG 3114.

GRIMSHAW, William (1708-1763) incumbent of Haworth, Yorkshire.
R J.THOMSON, hs, stipple, NPG.

GRONOW, Rees Howell (1794-1865) writer of reminiscences.
G SIR GEORGE HAYTER, 'The House of Commons, 1833', oil, NPG 54.
R J.C.ARMYTAGE, after a miniature, hs, stipple, oval, NPG.

GROSE, Francis (1731?-1791) antiquary and draughtsman.
P UNKNOWN, tql, SNPG 891.
D NATHANIEL DANCE, 1787, wl, chalk, SNPG 116.
R Several popular prints, BM, NPG.

GROSE, Sir Nash (1740-1814) judge.
C J.KAY, hl, etch, 1800, NPG.

GROSVENOR, John (1742-1823) surgeon at Oxford.
C R.DIGHTON, wl profile, entitled 'A view from St Aldgate's Oxford', coloured etch, pub 1808, BM.

GROSVENOR, Richard (1795-1869), Earl of, see 2nd Marquess of Westminster.

GROSVENOR, Richard Grosvenor, 1st Earl (1731-1802) horse-breeder and politician.
R H.R.COOK, after J.Reynolds, hl, stipple, BM, pub 1808, NPG. T.L.ATKINSON, after Gainsborough, hl, mezz, BM, NPG. W.DICKINSON, after B.West, wl in robes of mayor of Chester, mezz, BM.

GROSVENOR, Robert, 2nd Earl of, see 1st Marquess of Westminster.

GROSVENOR, Thomas (1764-1851) field-marshal.
P UNKNOWN, head, NPG 3982.
R J.YOUNG, after J.Hoppner, tql in uniform, with canon, etch, for Young's *Grosvenor Gallery*, 1821, BM. R.SEYMOUR, wl at entrance to Tattersall's, for Wildrake's *Cracks of the Day*, 1841, BM.

GROTE, George (1794-1871) historian.
P THOMAS STEWARDSON, 1824, hl seated, NPG 365. SIR J.E.MILLAIS, 1870, tql in robes as vice-chancellor, Senate House, University of London.
G SIR GEORGE HAYTER, 'The House of Commons, 1833', oil, NPG 54.
C WILLIAM BEHNES, 1852, marble bust, University College, London. MISS S.DURANT, 1862, marble medallion, University

College, London. CHARLES BACON, 1872, marble bust, Westminster Abbey, London.
PR UNKNOWN, hl, stipple, pub 1838, BM. H.ROBINSON, after S.P.Denning, hl, stipple, for Saunders's *Political Reformers*, 1840, BM, NPG. L.DICKINSON, hs, aged 50, lith, BM, NPG.
C JOHN DOYLE, wl in 'Don Giovanni in London', 1839, chalk, BM.
PH HERBERT WATKINS, 1857, hs, albumen, NPG Portraits and Autographs vol 1. MAULL & POLYBLANK, tql seated, carte, NPG Album of Photographs 1949. MAULL & CO, tql seated, carte, NPG. UNKNOWN, tql, NPG Photographs and Portraits vol 1.

GROTE, Harriet, née Lewin (1792-1878) biographer.
PR C.LEWIS, after C.Landseer, hl, lith, BM.

GROZER, Joseph (fl 1784-1798) mezzotint engraver.
G UNKNOWN, after P.Sandby, 'Sketches taken at Print Sales', line, pub 1798, BM.

GRUNDY, John (1782-1843) unitarian minister and writer.
PR S.W.REYNOLDS, after H.Wyatt, hl, mezz, pub 1825, BM, NPG.

GUEST, Sir Josiah John, Bart (1785-1852) ironmaster.
P UNKNOWN, tql, National Museum of Wales 269, Cardiff.
G SIR GEORGE HAYTER, 'The House of Commons, 1833', oil, NPG 54.
PR R.J.LANE, after J.Thompson, hl, lith, pub 1839, BM, NPG. W.WALKER, after R.Buckner, tql seated, mezz, pub 1852, BM, NPG.

GUILFORD, Francis North, 4th Earl of (1761-1817) soldier.
PR C.TURNER, after T.Lawrence, tql seated, mezz, pub 1820, BM, NPG.

GUILFORD, Frederick North, 2nd Earl of (1732-1792) prime-minister.
P NATHANIEL DANCE, tql seated in Chancellor's robes, with Garter ribbon, NPG 3627; versions, Bodleian Library, Oxford, Trinity College, Oxford. Studio of REYNOLDS, hl, Petworth (NT), W.Sussex.
D JOHN SINGLETON COPLEY, c1779, hs, crayon, Library of the Boston Athenaeum, Boston, USA. JOHN DOWNMAN, 1780, hl, profile, oval, w/c, V & A. JOHN SINGLETON COPLEY, hs, Metropolitan Museum of Art, New York, USA. N.DANCE, hl with Garter ribbon, pastel, NPG 276.
G J.S.COPLEY, 'The Collapse of the Earl of Chatham in the House of Lords, 7 July 1778', oil, TATE 100, on loan to NPG.
SC After MATTHEW GOSSET, c1782, Wedgwood medallion, Wedgwood Museum, Barlaston, Staffs. JOHN BACON, marble bust, Bodleian Library, Oxford. WILLIAM BEHNES, bust, Eton College, Berks. JOHN FLAXMAN, 1806, bust, Examination Schools, Oxford. After JAMES TASSIE, plaster medallion, SNPG 506.
PR J.JONES, after A.Ramsay of 1761, hl, stipple, pub 1787, BM, NPG. Several popular prints, BM, NPG.
C Numerous political satires, BM. Various etch, James Sayers, NPG.

GUILFORD, Frederick North, 5th Earl of (1766-1827) traveller, lover of Greece.
D T.HICKEY, 1799, hs, drg, Stratfield Saye, Hants.
PR J.D.INGRES, hl seated, lith, 1815, BM, NPG. W.T.FRY, after J.Jackson of 1817, tql, stipple, NPG.

GUINNESS, Sir Benjamin Lee, 1st Bart (1798-1868) brewer.
SC ISAAC PARKES, bronze medallion, National Museum of Ireland. J.H.FOLEY, bronze statue, Churchyard, St Patrick's Cathedral, Dublin.
PR UNKNOWN, hl, woodcut, for *Illust London News*, 1865, NPG.

GULLY, John (1783-1863) pugilist and sportsman.

P DRUMMOND, c1820, hs, NPG 4817.

G SIR GEORGE HAYTER, 'The House of Commons, 1833', oil, NPG 54.

PR R.SEYMOUR, wl profile, lith, for Wildrake's *Cracks of the Day*, 1841, BM. UNKNOWN, wl with antique group of wrestlers, mezz, BM. J.B.HUNT, after A.Cooper, hl, stipple, pub 1863, NPG.

GULSTON, Joseph (1745-1786) print collector.

PR V.GREEN, after F.Cotes, tql as a boy with his brother, both in Vandyck dress, mezz, pub 1771, BM. J.WATSON, after H.D.Hamilton, hl, semi-profile, mezz, 1776, BM, NPG.

GUNN, William (1750-1841) antiquarian writer.

PR R.J.LANE, after J.Flaxman, hs, lith, 1841, BM, NPG. MRS D.TURNER, after E.Turner, hs profile, etch, BM.

GUNNING, Elizabeth (1734-1790), see Duchess of HAMILTON and Argyll.

GUNNING, Elizabeth (1769-1823), see Mrs Plunkett.

GUNNING, Henry (1768-1854) senior esquire bedell of Cambridge University.

P UNKNOWN, Christ's College, Cambridge.

GUNNING, Maria (1733-1760), see Countess of Coventry.

GUNNING, Sir Robert, Bart (1731-1816) diplomatist.

P GEORGE ROMNEY, wl in Bath robes, Montreal Museum of Fine Arts, Canada.

GURNEY, Hudson (1775-1864) antiquary and poet.

PR J.COCHRAN, after A.Wivell, hl profile seated, stipple, for a set of portraits of persons present at trial of Queen Caroline, 1823, BM, NPG. MRS D.TURNER, after J.Opie, hs, etch, BM, NPG.

GURNEY, Sir John (1768-1845) judge.

G GEORGE RICHMOND, wl with Charles James Blomfield and Henry Edward Manning, ink, pencil and wash, c1840-45, NPG 4166.

PR W.HOLL, after G.H.Harlow, hl, stipple, pub 1821, BM, NPG. J.POSSELWHITE, after G.Richmond, wl seated, stipple, BM, NPG. UNKNOWN, hl, stipple, BM.

GURNEY, Joseph John (1788-1847) quaker philanthropist and writer.

PR After S.DEBENHAM, hs profile, lith, NPG. R.J.LANE, after G.Richmond, tql seated, lith, BM. C.E.WAGSTAFFE, after G.Richmond, tql seated, mezz, BM, NPG.

GURNEY, Samuel (1786-1856) 'The Banker's Banker', philanthropist.

G B.R.HAYDON, 'The Anti-Slavery Society Convention, 1840', oil, NPG 599.

PR UNKNOWN, tql seated, stipple and line, pub 1857, NPG. After J.R.Dicksee, hs, lith, NPG.

C R.DIGHTON, wl profile, entitled 'They'll be done. We are obliged to thee', coloured etch, pub 1820, BM, NPG.

GURNEY, Thomas (1705-1770) stenographer.

PR J.COLLYER, hs, line, oval, for his *Brachygraphy*, 9th ed, BM, NPG. UNKNOWN, hl, line, BM, NPG.

GURNEY, William Brodie (1777-1855) shorthand writer and philanthropist.

G SIR GEORGE HAYTER, 'The Trial of Queen Caroline, 1820', oil, NPG 999.

PR T.WRIGHT, after A.Wivell, hs profile, stipple, one of set of portraits of persons present at the trial of Queen Caroline, 1821, BM, NPG.

GURWOOD, John (1790-1845) editor of the 'Wellington Despatches'.

P JAMES HALL, tql, Wellington Museum, Apsley House, London. ANDREW MORTON, with the Duke of Wellington, Wallace Collection, London. WILLIAM SALTER, tql study for 'Waterloo Banquet', NPG 3719.

D A.D'ORSAY, 1845, hl profile, pencil, DoE (Paris Chancery).

G W.SALTER, 'Waterloo Banquet at Apsley House', oil, 1836, Wellington Museum.

SC SAMUEL JOSEPH, 1840, marble bust, Wellington Museum.

GUTCH, John (1746-1831) antiquary and divine.

PR T.WAGEMAN, hs, stipple, for his *Antiquities of Oxford University*, 1786, BM, NPG.

GUTCH, John Mathew (1776-1861) journalist.

PR UNKNOWN, hs seated, lith, BM.

GUTCH, Robert (1777-1851) divine.

PR UNKNOWN, hs, stipple, BM.

GUTHRIE, George James (1785-1856) surgeon.

D A.D'ORSAY, hl, profile, pencil, Royal College of Physicians Library, London.

M REGINALD EASTON, hl, NPG 932. HENRY ROOM, hs, Royal College of Surgeons, London.

SC EDWARD DAVIS, 1857, marble bust, Royal College of Surgeons.

GUTHRIE, William (1708-1770) political and historical writer.

PR I.TAYLOR, hs, line, oval, for his *History of Scotland*, 1767, BM, NPG.

GWILT, George (1775-1856) architect.

PR UNKNOWN, hs aged 72, lith, BM.

GWYNN, John (d1786) architect.

P UNKNOWN, hl seated, NPG 4680.

G JOHAN ZOFFANY, 'Royal Academicians, 1772', oil, Royal Coll.

PR UNKNOWN, hs, etch, BM.

GWYNN, Mary, née Horneck (1754/5-1840) Goldsmith's 'Jessamy Bride'.

P JOHN HOPPNER, hl, Taft Museum, Cincinnati, USA.

D DANIEL GARDNER, tql with her sister, gouache and pastel, unfinished, Leicester Museum and Art Gallery.

M DANIEL GARDNER, after Sir Joshua Reynolds (type of c1765-66), hl with her sister, as the 'Merry Wives of Windsor', oil, oval, Castle Museum, Nottingham. HENRY EDRIDGE, hl profile, NPG 3152.

PR R.DUNKARTON, after J.Reynolds, wl seated on ground in Persian dress, mezz, pub 1778, BM, NPG. J.YOUNG, after J.Hoppner, tql seated, mezz, pub 1791, BM.

GYE, Frederick (1781-1869) entertainment manager.

PR C.BAUGNIET, 1844, tql seated, lith, BM, NPG.

H

HACKMAN, James (1752-1779) murderer.
R R.LAURIE, after R.Dighton, hs, profile, mezz, oval, pub 1779, BM, NPG.

HADDINGTON, Thomas Hamilton, 9th Earl of (1780-1858) lord lieutenant of Ireland.
R J.BROWN, after R.McInnes, hl in peer's robes, stipple, BM, NPG.

HADLEY, John (1731-1764) physician and professor of chemistry at Cambridge.
R E.FISHER, after B.Wilson, hl seated, aged 28, mezz, BM.

HAGUE, Charles (1769-1821) professor of music at Cambridge.
P G.H.HARLOW, c1813, hl, Fitzwilliam Museum, Cambridge.
D THOMAS UWINS, wl, w/c, BM.
R A.CARDON, after Gilchrist, hs, stipple, oval, pub 1803, BM.

HAIGHTON, John (1755-1823) physician.
G N.BRANWHITE, after S.Medley, 'Institutors of the Medical Society of London', stipple, pub 1801, BM.

HAILES, Sir David Dalrymple, Lord (1726-1792) Scottish judge.
P After J.T.SETON, hl, Dunrobin Castle, Highland region, Scotland.
C J.KAY, 1793, hl, etch, oval, NPG.

HAILSTONE, John (1759-1847) geologist.
P UNKNOWN, hl, Sedgwick Museum, Cambridge. UNKNOWN, hs, Trinity College, Cambridge.

HALDANE, James Alexander (1768-1851) religious writer.
R G.ZOBAL, after C.Smith, hl aged 77, stipple, NPG.
C J.KAY, 1801, hl, etch, NPG.

HALDIMAND, Sir Frederick (1718-1791) governor and commander-in-chief of Canada.
P Studio of SIR JOSHUA REYNOLDS, c1778, hl, NPG 4874.

HALE, John (d1806) gneral, governor of Londonderry.
R T.LUPTON, after J.Reynolds, tql seated, temple of Janus in background, mezz, BM.

HALE, Warren Stormes (1791-1872) lord mayor of London.
P J.R.DICKSEE, RA 1859, Corporation of London. J.W.ALLEN, Corporation of London.
C CHARLES BACON, RA 1865, bust, City of London Schools.
R UNKNOWN, tql seated in mayor's robes, woodcut, for *Illust London News*, 1864, NPG.

HALE, William Hale (1795-1870) divine and antiquary.
R W.WALKER, after T.A.Woolnoth, hl, mezz, pub 1850, BM.

HALES, William (1747-1831) chronologist.
P UNKNOWN, tql, Trinity College, Dublin.

HALFORD, Sir Henry, 1st Bart (1766-1844) physician.
P SIR WILLIAM BEECHEY, 1811, tql seated, NPG 1068. SIR THOMAS LAWRENCE, after 1820, tql seated, Royal College of Physicians, London, engr C.Turner, mezz, pub 1830, BM.
C SIR FRANCIS CHANTREY, 1826, marble bust, Royal College of Physicians; model for the bust, Ashmolean Museum, Oxford.
R J.COCHRAN, after H.Room, hl seated, stipple, for Pettigrew's *Medical Portrait Gallery*, 1838, BM, NPG.

HALHED, Nathaniel Brassey (1751-1830) orientalist.
PR WHITE, after I.Cruikshank, hl seated, stipple, oval, pub 1795, BM, NPG.

HALIBURTON, Thomas Chandler (1796-1865) politician and writer.
P BEATHAM, tql seated, Nova Scotia Legislative Library, Canada.
PR M.GAUCI, after E.U.Eddis, hl, lith, pub 1839, BM, NPG. UNKNOWN, hs lith, BM. D.J.POUND, after a photograph by Mayall, tql seated, stipple and line, NPG.

HALIFAX, George Montagu Dunk, 2nd Earl of (1716-1771) president of the board of trade.
G Attrib DANIEL GARDNER, after H.D.Hamilton, c1765-67, with his two secretaries, gouache, NPG 3328.
PR S.WHEATLY, hs, mezz, oval, at head of his *Answer to the Dublin House of Commons*, 1762, BM.

HALKETT, Sir Colin (1774-1856) general.
P WILLIAM SALTER, tql study for 'Waterloo Banquet', NPG 3720. J.W.PIENEMAN, hs, Wellington Museum, Apsley House, London.
G W.SALTER, 'Waterloo Banquet at Apsley House', oil, 1836, Wellington Museum.

HALKETT, Hugh Halkett, Baron von (1783-1863) Hanoverian general and British colonel.
PR UNKNOWN, hs, woodcut, for *Illust London News*, 1863, NPG.

HALL, Basil (1788-1844) naval commander and fellow of the Royal Society.
D SIR FRANCIS CHANTREY, hs profile, pencil, NPG 316a (62).
SC SAMUEL JOSEPH, marble bust, Pollok House, Glasgow.
PR J.SWAINE, after Bonnor, hl, stipple and line, pub 1842, NPG. J.SWAINE, hl, line, BM.

HALL, Chambers (1786-1855) virtuoso.
D JOHN LINNELL, hs, crayon, oval, Ashmolean Museum, Oxford.
SC Attrib R.C.LUCAS, wax medallion, Ashmolean Museum.

HALL, Charles Henry (1763-1827) dean of Durham.
P G.S.NEWTON, hl, Christ Church, Oxford.

HALL, George (1753-1811) bishop of Dromore.
P WILLIAM CUMING, hl in episcopal robes, Trinity College, Dublin.

HALL, James (1755-1826) presbyterian divine at Edinburgh.
SC After JAMES TASSIE, plaster medallion, SNPG 522.
PR J.BLOOD, hl, stipple, oval, for *Evangelical Mag*, 1814, BM, NPG.

HALL, Sir James, 4th Bart (1761?-1832) geologist and chemist.
P SIR JOHN WATSON-GORDON, tql seated, Royal Society, Edinburgh.
SC PATRIC PARK, marble bust, Geological Museum, London.

HALL, John (1739-1797) engraver.
P GILBERT STUART, hl seated, NPG 693.
D Attrib WILLIAM LAWRANSON, hs pastel, NPG 3992.
SC After JAMES TASSIE, plaster medallion, SNPG 445.
PR MRS D.TURNER, after O.Humphry, hl with graver, etch, BM.

HALL, Robert (1764-1831) baptist divine.
SC THOMAS R.POOLE, 1814, wax medallion, NPG 5066.

PR RIDLEY, after Branwhite, hs, stipple, oval, pub 1810, NPG. R.J.LANE, after E.Eden, hs, lith, pub 1850, NPG. UNKNOWN, after J.Flowers, hl, mezz, BM. UNKNOWN, hs profile, stipple, for *New Evangelical Mag*, NPG.

HALL, Sir William Hutcheon (1797?-1878) admiral.
PR UNKNOWN, hs, woodcut, for *Illust London News*, 1854, NPG.

HALLAM, Henry (1777-1859) historian.
P SIR WILLIAM BEECHEY, 1795, hl, Eton College, Berks. THOMAS PHILLIPS, 1835, hl, Clevedon Court (NT), Avon.
D GEORGE RICHMOND, 1843, hs, chalk, NPG 5139. Attrib G.S.NEWTON, hs, profile, chalk, NPG 2810.
G JOHN PARTRIDGE, 'The Fine Arts Commissioners, 1846', NPG 342, 3.
SC R.C.LUCAS, 1851, wax medallion, NPG 3119. WILLIAM THEED, 1863, statue, St Paul's Cathedral, London; related bust, 1864, Royal Coll.

HALLEY, Robert (1796-1876) nonconformist divine and historian.
P UNKNOWN, after a photograph by Elliott and Fry, hs, Dr Williams's Library, London.
PR COOK, after J.R.Wildman, hl, stipple, pub 1832, NPG.

HALLIFAX, Samuel (1733-1790) bishop of Gloucester and St Asaph.
P By or after VAN DER MIJN, tql in doctoral robes, Trinity Hall, Cambridge.

HALLOWELL, Sir Benjamin, see CAREW.

HAMILTON, Alexander (1739-1802) professor of midwifery at Edinburgh.
P SIR HENRY RAEBURN, c1800, hl, Breamore, Hants.
C J.KAY, wl, etch, BM, NPG.

HAMILTON, Alexander Hamilton Douglas, 10th Duke of (1767-1852) diplomat.
P SIR JOSHUA REYNOLDS, 1782, hl, NGS 2183. THOMAS GAINSBOROUGH, 1786, hs, oval, Waddesdon Manor (NT), Bucks. SIR DANIEL MACNEE, tql with Garter star, Lennoxlove, Lothian region, Scotland. Attrib DAVID WILKIE, hs sketch, Lennoxlove. WILLIAM MADDOX, Brodick Castle (NT), Strathclyde region, Scotland.
D UNKNOWN, wl, pencil, SNPG 2062.
G SIR GEORGE HAYTER, 'The Trial of Queen Caroline, 1820', oil, NPG 999.
C J.GILLRAY, wl equestrian 'Equestrian Elegance – or – a Noble Scot, metamorphosed', etch, pub 1803, NPG. J.DOYLE, 1851, equestrian, chalk, BM.

HAMILTON, Lady Anne (1766-1846) lady-in-waiting to Queen Caroline.
P Attrib THOMAS GAINSBOROUGH, wl, Detroit Institute of Arts. JAMES LONSDALE, V & A. UNKNOWN, NGI 1149.
G SIR GEORGE HAYTER, 'The Trial of Queen Caroline, 1820', oil, NPG 999.
PR UNKNOWN, hl, stipple, for Adolphus's *Memoirs of Queen Caroline*, 1820, BM, NPG.

HAMILTON, Lord Archibald (1769-1827) politician.
P THOMAS GAINSBOROUGH, 1786, Waddesdon Manor (NT), Bucks.

HAMILTON, Sir Charles, 2nd Bart (1767-1849) admiral.
P SIR WILLIAM BEECHEY, c1800, hl, NMM, Greenwich.

HAMILTON, David (1768-1843) architect.
SL AUGUSTIN EDOUART, SNPG 788.

HAMILTON, Sir Edward, 1st Bart (1772-1851) admiral.
PR W.RIDLEY, after W.Thompson, hs, stipple, oval, for *The Naval Chronicle*, 1801, BM, NPG.

HAMILTON, Elizabeth (1757-1816) writer and educationalist.
P SIR HENRY RAEBURN, tql seated, SNPG 1486.
PR J.HOPWOOD, after G.Clint, hl, stipple, octagon, for *Ladies Monthly Mag*, 1815, BM, NPG. J.HOPWOOD, jun, hl, stipple, pub 1823, BM, pub 1825, NPG.

HAMILTON, Emma, Lady, née Lyon (1761?-1815) mistress of Lord Nelson.
P Numerous paintings by GEORGE ROMNEY: 1782, hl as Nature with a dog, Frick Collection, New York, USA; c1782, head, a Circe, TATE 5591; 1782–84, tql seated as Ariadne, NMM Greenwich; 1782–86, tql at prayer, Kenwood House (GLC) London; 1782–86, wl, 'The Spinstress', Kenwood; c1783, tql, Huntington Library and Art Gallery, San Marino, USA; c1785, hl, NPG 294; c1785, hs, NPG 4448; c1785–86, as Cassandra, TATE 1668; c1786, as a Bacchante, TATE 312; wl seated in landscape, Waddesdon Manor (NT), Bucks. GAVIN HAMILTON, 1786, tql as Hebe, Burghley House, Northants. ANGELICA KAUFFMANN 1796, wl seated, V & A. MADAME VIGÉE LE BRUN, hl as a Bacchante with tambourine, Lady Lever Art Gallery, Port Sunlight. JOHN RISING, after Sir Joshua Reynolds of c1784, as a Bacchante Waddesdon Manor.
D SIR THOMAS LAWRENCE, 1791, hl, profile, pencil, oval, BM RICHARD COSWAY, wl, pencil and w/c, NPG 2941. FREDERICK REHBERG, series of drgs, 'Lady Hamilton's Attitudes', BM.
SC JOSEPH NOLLEKENS, marble bust, Ashmolean Museum, Oxford
C JAMES GILLRAY, 'Dido in Despair', coloured etch, pub 1801, BM THOMAS ROWLANDSON, 'Lady Hxxxxxxxx Attitudes', etch, BM

HAMILTON, Gavin (1723-1798) artist.
D Self-portrait, 1767, hs, pencil, SNPG 198.
SC CHRISTOPHER HEWETSON, 1784, marble bust, University of Glasgow.
PR R.SCOTT, after A.Skirving, hs, stipple, for vol 16 of *The Bee* 1793, BM, NPG.

HAMILTON, Hugh (1729-1805) bishop of Ossory.
P WILLIAM CUMING, after Gilbert Stuart, hl in episcopal robes Trinity College, Dublin.
PR W.EVANS, after G.Stuart, hl, stipple, pub 1807, BM, NPG.

HAMILTON, Hugh Douglas (1739-1808) portrait-painter
P GEORGE CHINNERY, hl seated, Royal Hibernian Academy.
D Self-portrait, hs, pastel, Uffizi Gallery, Florence.

HAMILTON, James (1712-1789), see 8th Earl of Abercorn.

HAMILTON, James (1749-1835) physician.
P WILLIAM DYCE, wl, SNPG 1070.
SL AUGUSTIN EDOUART, wl profile, SNPG 799.
PR C.TURNER, after H.Raeburn, hl, mezz, pub 1813, BM, NPG.
C J.KAY, wl profile, etch, BM.

HAMILTON, James Hamilton, 5th Duke of (1703-1743) lord of the bedchamber to George II.
P WILLIAM AIKMAN, wl, SNPG L281. WILLIAM AIKMAN, wl Holyroodhouse, Edinburgh. JOHN ALEXANDER, tql with the artist, Lennoxlove, Lothian region, Scotland. Attrib JEREMIAH DAVISON, hl semi-profile, with Thistle star, Lennoxlove. WILLIAM HOARE, hl with Thistle star, Brodick Castle (NT) Strathclyde region, Scotland. JOHN VANDERBANK, 1732, wl in Thistle robes, Lennoxlove.
D ROSALBA DE CARRIERA, hs with Thistle star, pastel Lennoxlove.

HAMILTON, John (d 1755) captain in the navy.
G S.W.REYNOLDS, after J.Reynolds, 'The Eliot Family', mezz pub 1823, BM.

PR R.JOSEY, after Sir Joshua Reynolds, of c1746, tql in Russian dress, mezz, pub 1876, NPG.

HAMILTON, Sir John, 1st Bart (1755-1835) lieutenant-general.
PR F.DELEU, after D.Wilkie, hl in uniform, line, for Grace's *Memoirs of the Family of Grace*, 1823, BM.

HAMILTON, Richard Winter (1794-1848) independent minister at Leeds.
PR BLOOD, after J.R.Wildman, hl, stipple, pub 1826, NPG. C.TURNER, after C.Schwanfelder, hl seated, mezz, pub 1836, BM, NPG. C.BAUGNIET, tql, lith, BM, NPG.

HAMILTON, Robert (1721-1793) physician.
SL AUGUSTIN EDOUART, SNPG 798.

HAMILTON, Robert (1743-1829) mathematician.
PR W.HOLL, hl, stipple, for Chambers's *Dict of Eminent Scotsmen*, BM, NPG.

HAMILTON, Thomas (1780-1858), see 9th Earl of Haddington.

HAMILTON, Thomas (1784-1858) architect.
P WILLIAM NICHOLSON, hs, Royal Scottish Academy, Edinburgh.

HAMILTON, Thomas (1789-1842) writer.
P SIR JOHN WATSON GORDON, tql, SNPG L277.

HAMILTON, William (1704-1754) of Bangour, poet.
P Attrib GAVIN HAMILTON, hs profile, SNPG 310.
PR UNKNOWN, hl seated, line, NPG.

HAMILTON, Sir William (1730-1803) diplomat and archaeologist.
P DAVID ALLAN, 1770, wl seated, his wife playing the spinet, Blair Castle, Tayside region, Scotland. DAVID ALLAN, 1775, wl, NPG 589. Studio of REYNOLDS, 1777, wl seated, NPG 680. CHARLES GRIGNION jun, hs, oval, Lennoxlove, Lothian region, Scotland.
D THOMAS GAINSBOROUGH, hs profile, pencil, oval, Castle Howard, N.Yorks.
G SIR JOSHUA REYNOLDS, 'The Society of Dilettanti', oil, 1777–79, The Society of Dilettanti, Brooks's Club, London.
SC JAMES TASSIE, 1784, paste medallion, SNPG 133. JOACHIM SMITH, Wedgwood medallion, SNPG 210.
C Several engravings, NPG. J.GILLRAY, 'A Cognocenti contemplating ye Beauties of ye Antique', etch, BM.

HAMILTON, William (1751-1801) painter.
D GEORGE DANCE, 1793, hs profile, Royal Academy, London.
G HENRY SINGLETON, 'The Royal Academicians, 1793', oil, Royal Academy, London.

HAMILTON, Sir William, Bart (1788-1856) metaphysician.
P JOHN BALLANTYNE, hl, SNPG 717.
D HOPE JAMES STEWART, 1845, tql seated, w/c, SNPG L43.

HAMILTON, William Gerard (1729-1796) politician.
PR W.EVANS, after J.R.Smith, hl profile, stipple, for his *Parliamentary Logick*, 1808, BM, NPG.

HAMILTON, William Richard (1777-1859) antiquary and diplomatist.
P DOROFIELD HARDY, after T.Phillips, tql seated, The Society of Dilettanti, Brooks's Club, London.
PR R.J.LANE, after H.Phillips, tql seated, lith, BM, NPG. C.BAUGNIET, tql seated, lith, oval, BM, NPG.

HAMILTON and ARGYLL, Elizabeth Gunning, Duchess of (1733-1790) famous beauty.
P GAVIN HAMILTON, c1752–55, wl with dog, Holyroodhouse, Edinburgh. SIR JOSHUA REYNOLDS, 1758-60, wl, Lady Lever Art Gallery, Port Sunlight. F.H.DROUAIS, 1763, hl, Inveraray

Castle, Strathclyde region, Scotland. FRANCIS COTES, 1767, **wl**, Inveraray Castle.
D FRANCIS COTES, 1751, hl, pastel, NPG 4890. CATHERINE READ, hs, pastel, oval, Inveraray Castle.
G R.HOUSTON, 'The Three Gunning Sisters', (the portrait of Elizabeth is after Hamilton), mezz, oval, pub 1756, BM.
PR R.HOUSTON, after F.Cotes, hl, mezz, oval, BM, NPG.

HAMOND, Sir Andrew Snape, 1st Bart (1738-1828) comptroller of the navy.
SC SIR FRANCIS CHANTREY, c1821, bust, Ashmolean Museum, Oxford.
PR G.H.PHILLIPS, after T.Lawrence, hl, mezz, pub 1830, BM, NPG.

HAMOND, Sir Graham Eden, 2nd Bart (1779-1862) admiral.
G MATHER BROWN, 1794, from a life sketch, on the quarterdeck of the *Queen Charlotte*, NMM, Greenwich.

HAMPDEN, Renn Dickson (1793-1868) bishop of Hereford.
P After SIR DANIEL MACREE, tql seated, Oriel College, Oxford. Attrib H.W.PICKERSGILL, hl seated, Christ Church, Oxford. UNKNOWN, tql seated, Bishop's Palace, Hereford.
D D.W., hs, chalk, Oriel College, Oxford.

HAMPDEN, Robert Hampden-Trevor, 1st Viscount (1706-1783) diplomatist.
P J.S.COPLEY, tql in robes, Glynde Place, E.Sussex.
PR S.HARDING, after W.Gardiner, hl, stipple, oval, pub 1802, NPG. UNKNOWN, hs, from a medal, line BM, NPG.

HAMPER, William (1776-1831) antiquary.
SC G.CLARKE, 1822, bust, Birmingham Reference Library.

HAMPSON, John (1760-1817?) writer.
PR UNKNOWN, hs semi-profile, line, oval, for *Arminian Mag*, 1785, BM.

HAMPTON, Sir John Somerset Pakington, 1st Baron (1799-1880) statesman.
D ALFRED THOMPSON, 1870, wl, w/c, for *Vanity Fair*, 12 February 1870, NPG 2628.
G JOHN PHILLIP, 'The House of Commons, 1860', oil, Houses of Parliament, London. HENRY GALES, 'The Derby Cabinet of 1867', w/c, NPG 4893.
SC BARON CHARLES MAROCHETTI, c1860, marble bust, Haslar Hospital, Portsmouth.
PR E.BURTON, after J.W.Gordon, tql seated, mezz, BM.
C JOHN DOYLE, 'A Game of Knock-em Downs', 1851, pen and pencil, BM. FAUSTIN, wl, coloured lith, BM.
PH HERBERT WATKINS, hs, NPG Portraits and Autographs 1856–57. UNKNOWN, hs, NPG Twist Album 1892.

HANBURY, William (1725-1778) clergyman.
P EDWARD PENNY, 1763, wl, Church Langton School, Leics, engr R.Earlom, tql, mezz, BM.
SC UNKNOWN, portrait bust, in relief, St Peter's Church, Church Langton, Leics.

HANCOCK, Robert (1730-1817) engraver.
PR R.HANCOCK, after J.Wright, hl, mezz, BM.

HANCOCK, Thomas (1786-1865) founder of the india rubber trade in England.
PR DALZIEL, hs, woodcut, circle, BM.
PH UNKNOWN, Science Museum, London.

HANCOCK, Walter (1799-1852) engineer.
PR W.ROFFE, after C.Hancock, hl, stipple, for *The Mechanic's Magazine*, 1836, BM, NPG.

HANDASYDE, Charles (fl 1760-1780) miniature painter.
PR Four self-portraits, hl with book, etch, oval, BM; hs in hat, mezz,

oval, BM; head, with long hair, mezz, oval, BM; hs, mezz, BM. C.SHARP, head, mezz, oval, BM.

HANGER, George, see 4th Baron Coleraine.

HANNAH, John (1792-1867) methodist minister.
PR ARMITAGE & IBBETSON, hs, lith, oval, BM. J.THOMSON, after Paradise, hs, stipple, NPG.

HANOVER, Ernest Augustus, King of, see Duke of CUMBERLAND.

HANSARD, Luke (1752-1828) printer.
P SAMUEL LANE, hl, Palace of Westminster, London.

HANSON, 'Sir' Levett (1754-1814) writer.
P Three portraits by unknown artists, hs as a boy, hl, and tql, Bury St Edmunds Athenaeum, Suffolk.

HANWAY, Jonas (1712-1786) merchant and philanthropist.
P EDWARD EDWARDS, 1779, wl seated, Marine Society, London. JAMES NORTHCOTE, c1785, hl, NPG 4301.
SC JOSEPH DICKSON, after a wax by Patience Wright, 1774–75, marble bust, Marine Society, London. UNKNOWN, after T.Orde, 1780–81, Wedgwood medallion, Wedgwood Museum, Barlaston, Staffs. J.F.MOORE, relief medallion on marble monument, Westminster Abbey, London.
PR T.HOLLOWAY, hs profile, line, oval, for *European Mag*, 1786, BM, NPG. J.BRETHERTON, after T.Orde, tql seated, writing, profile, etch, oval, BM, NPG.

HARBORD, Edward, see 3rd Baron Suffield.

HARCOURT, Edward Venables (1757-1847) archbishop of York.
P JOHN HOPPNER, RA 1803, tql seated, Christ Church, Oxford. WILLIAM OWEN, 1807, tql seated, Bishopsthorpe Palace, York. THOMAS PHILLIPS, 1819, tql seated, All Souls College, Oxford. SIR THOMAS LAWRENCE, RA 1823, wl in robes, Sudbury Hall (NT), Derbys.
G SIR GEORGE HAYTER, 'The Trial of Queen Caroline, 1820', oil, NPG 999.
SC MATTHEW NOBLE, 1855, recumbent effigy, York Minster. M.NOBLE, 1858, recumbent effigy on tomb chest, St Michael's Church, Stanton Harcourt, Oxon.
PR H.MEYER, after J.Jackson, tql seated, mezz, pub 1815, BM, NPG. G.BROWN, after G.Richmond, hs aged 89, stipple, BM.

HARCOURT, Simon Harcourt, 1st Earl (1714-1777) lord lieutenant of Ireland.
P BENJAMIN WILSON, 1750, hl with a plan of Nuneham, DoE (British Embassy, Bonn). ROBERT HUNTER, hl, Ulster Museum, R.Hunter, NGI 1002.
PR D.PARISET, after P.Falconet, hs profile, aged 54, stipple, circular frame, BM. UNKNOWN, hs profile, line, oval, BM.

HARCOURT, William Harcourt, 3rd Earl (1743-1830) field-marshal.
G SIR GEORGE HAYTER, 'The Trial of Queen Caroline, 1820', oil, NPG 999. C.A.TOMKINS, after J.Reynolds, 'Harcourt Family', mezz, BM, NPG.
SC R.W.SIEVIER, 1828, marble bust, Royal Coll. R.W.SIEVIER, 1832, statues, St George's Chapel, Windsor Castle, and St Michael's Church, Stanton Harcourt, Oxon.
PR S.W.REYNOLDS, after H.Edridge of 1818, tql seated in robes, mezz, BM, NPG.

HARCOURT, William Vernon (1789-1871) general secretary to first meeting of British Association.
SC SIR FRANCIS CHANTREY, c1833, marble bust, Yorkshire Museum, York. SIR F.CHANTREY, bust, Ashmolean Museum, Oxford.

PH JOHN and CHARLES WATKINS, hs profile, carte, NPG Distinguished Persons vol III.

HARDING, Edward (1755-1840) librarian to Queen Charlotte.
PR S.W.REYNOLDS, after M.A.Shee, hl seated, mezz, BM.

HARDING, George Perfect (1781-1853) portrait painter copyist and antiquary.
M Self-portrait, 1804, hl, NPG 4615.
PR J.BROWN, after J.P.Harding, hs, stipple, BM.

HARDING, James Duffield (1798-1863) water-colourist and lithographer.
P H.P.BRIGGS, c1840, hl, NPG 1781, J.P.KNIGHT, hl, Castle Museum, Nottingham.
D LAURENCE THEWENETI, 1825, wl seated, pencil and w/c, NPG 3125.
PH CUNDALL and DOWNES, tql, carte, NPG Album of Artists vol I.

HARDING, Silvester (1745-1809) artist and publisher.
G UNKNOWN, after P.Sandby, 'Sketches taken at Print Sales', line, pub 1798, BM.
PR E.HARDING, jun, after S.Harding, hl with crayon and canvas, stipple and etch, oval, BM. UNKNOWN, head, lith, BM.

HARDINGE, George (1743-1816) author, politician and judge.
P NATHANIEL DANCE, RA 1769, tql seated, Lambeth Palace, London.

HARDINGE, George Nicholas (1781-1808) captain in the navy.
PR H.R.COOK, after W.S.Lethbridge, hl, stipple, oval, for *European Mag*, 1810, BM, NPG.

HARDINGE, of Lahore, Henry Hardinge, 1st Viscount (1785-1856) governor-general of India.
P WILLIAM SALTER, c1834–40, tql study for 'Waterloo Banquet', NPG 3721. JOHN LUCAS, 1844, tql, Victoria Memorial Hall, Calcutta. SIR FRANCIS GRANT, after his portrait of 1849, tql with Bath star, in Indian landscape, NPG 437; study for the 1849 portrait, NPG 508.
G SIR GEORGE HAYTER, 'The House of Commons, 1833', oil, NPG 54. W.SALTER, 'Waterloo Banquet at Apsley House', oil, 1836, Wellington Museum, Apsley House, London.
SC G.G.ADAMS, 1845, plaster medallion, NPG 1207a. J.H.FOLEY c1853, bronze equestrian statue, Government House, Calcutta. J.H.FOLEY, RA 1860, marble bust, Royal Coll.

HARDWICK, Thomas (1752-1829) architect.
PR W.DANIELL, after G.Dance, hs profile, soft-ground etch, pub 1814, BM, NPG.

HARDWICKE, Charles Philip Yorke, 4th Earl of (1799-1873) admiral.
G SIR G.HAYTER, 'The House of Commons, 1833', oil NPG 54.
PR UNKNOWN, wl, woodcut, for *Illust London News*, 1843–44, NPG.

HARDWICKE, Philip Yorke, 2nd Earl of (1720-1790) writer and statesman.
PR M.BOVI, after G.Romney, tql in robes, stipple, pub 1796, NPG. F.BARTOLOZZI, after W.Gardiner, hl in robes, stipple, for Adolphus's *British Cabinet*, 1799, BM, NPG. W.RIDLEY, after G.Romney, hl in robes, stipple, oval, for *European Mag*, 1803 BM, NPG.

HARDWICKE, Philip Yorke, 3rd Earl of (1757-1834) lord lieutenant of Ireland.
P WILLIAM CUMING, 1802, Mansion House, Dublin. SIR HENRY RAEBURN, tql seated with Garter star, Baltimore Museum of Art, USA.

M JAMES TANNOCK, tql, V & A.
SC RICHARD WESTMACOTT junr, 1844, recumbent figure with Garter robes, on monument, St Andrew Church, Wimpole, Cambridgeshire.
PR W.GILLER, after T.Lawrence, tql in Garter robes, mezz, pub 1836, BM, NPG. W.WARD, tql, mezz, BM, NPG.

HARDY, Sir Charles (1716?-1780) admiral.
P GEORGE ROMNEY, 1780, tql in uniform, NMM, Greenwich. JOHN WOLLASTON, tql, Brooklyn Museum, New York, USA.
PR R.DAWE, after T.Hudson, tql in uniform, mezz, pub 1779, BM, NPG. R.STEWART, hs profile, mezz, oval, pub 1779, BM.

HARDY, Francis (1751-1812) Irish politician.
PR J.HEATH, after J.R.Maguire, head, stipple, for Sir J.Barrington's *Historic Memoirs*, 1811, BM, NPG.

HARDY, John Stockdale (1793-1849) antiquary and lawyer.
PR J.BROWN, after J.T.Mitchell, hs, aged 28, stipple, for his *Literary Remains*, 1852, BM, NPG.

HARDY, Thomas (1752-1832) radical politician.
P MISS McCREERY, National Liberal Club, London.
SC UNKNOWN, medal, NPG.
PR UNKNOWN, after A.Jameson, hs, line, oval, pub 1794, BM, NPG. UNKNOWN, hs, stipple, oval, pub 1794, NPG. UNKNOWN, tql seated in dock, line, NPG.

HARDY, Sir Thomas Masterman, 1st Bart (1769-1839) admiral.
P UNKNOWN, c1801, hl, NMM, Greenwich. A.W.DEVIS, 1805-07, wl, from a life sketch, for the 'Death of Nelson' painting, NMM. RICHARD EVANS, 1833-44, tql with Bath ribbon and star, NMM. L.F.ABBOTT, small wl with telescope, DoE.
G I.HILL, after C.A.Pugin, Nelson's funeral procession from Greenwich to Whitehall, engr, NMM, Greenwich.
SC WILLIAM BEHNES, 1836, marble bust, Royal Coll. W.BEHNES, 1843, bust, Greenwich Palace Chapel.

HARE, Augustus William (1792-1834) writer.
PR J.S.AGAR, after a marble bust by J.Gibson, stipple, pub 1836, BM, NPG.

HARE, James (1749-1804) politician and friend of C.J.Fox.
P After REYNOLDS, hl, oval, Hardwick Hall (NT), Derbys.
SC JOSEPH NOLLEKENS, 1804, bust, Woburn Abbey, Beds.
PR S.W.REYNOLDS, after J.Reynolds, hl, mezz, BM.

HARE, Julius Charles (1795-1855) archdeacon of Lewes, writer.
SC THOMAS WOOLNER, 1861, marble bust, Trinity College, Cambridge.
PR H.ROBINSON, after G.Richmond, hs, stipple, pub 1852, NPG. W.TAYLOR, after S.Laurence, hs, lith, NPG.

HARE, William (fl 1829) murderer, turned king's evidence against William Burke.
G UNKNOWN, with William Burke, Helen McDougall and one of their victims James Wilson, four rough cuts in a broadside entitled *Life and Transactions of the Murderer Burke and his Associates*, 1829, BM.
PR UNKNOWN, wl, etch, BM.

HAREWOOD, Henry Lascelles, 2nd Earl of (1767-1841) politician.
P SIR THOMAS LAWRENCE, RA 1823, wl, Harewood House, W.Yorks. Two portraits by E.U.EDDIS, one wl and one hl, Harewood House. Attrib JOHN JACKSON, tql, Harewood House.
D SIR GEORGE HAYTER, study for NPG 999, NPG 1695 (p). UNKNOWN, c1820, hl, chalk, Harewood House.
G SIR GEORGE HAYTER, 'The Trial of Queen Caroline, 1820', oil, NPG 999.

PR S.W.REYNOLDS, after J.Jackson, tql, mezz, pub 1820, BM, NPG. M.GAUCI, wl riding with a hunt and Harewood House in distance, lith, BM.

HARFORD, John Scandrett (1785-1866) biographer.
P UNKNOWN, St David's University College, Lampeter.

HARGOOD, Sir William (1762-1839) admiral.
P F.R.SAY, c1835, tql in uniform with orders, NMM, Greenwich.
PR J.THOMSON, tql seated, in uniform with orders, stipple, NPG.

HARGRAVE, Francis (1741?-1821) recorder of Liverpool.
P SIR JOSHUA REYNOLDS, RA 1787, hl, Lincoln's Inn, London.

HARGREAVES, Thomas (1774-1846) miniature-painter.
M Self-portrait, hs, oval, Walker Art Gallery, Liverpool.

HARINGTON, Henry (1727-1816) physician and musical composer.
PR C.TURNER, after T.Beach, tql seated, mezz, pub 1799, BM, NPG. UNKNOWN, after J.Slater, hs, lith, BM.

HARLAND, Sir Robert, Bart (1715?-1796?) admiral.
P Attrib D.HEINS, c1747-48, hl, NMM, Greenwich.
PR R.EARLOM, after H.Dance, tql in uniform, mezz, pub 1788, BM.

HARLEY, George (c1762-1811) actor and author.
P SAMUEL DE WILDE, wl as Caled in *The Siege of Damascus*, Garrick Club, London.
D SAMUEL DE WILDE, 1794, as Kent in *King Lear*, w/c, V & A.
PR Several theatrical prints, BM, NPG.

HARLEY, John Pritt (1786-1858) actor.
P GEORGE CLINT, hs, Garrick Club, London.
D SAMUEL DE WILDE, 1816, as Wellborn in *A New Way to Pay Old Debts*, w/c and chalk, Garrick Club. UNKNOWN, wl as Somno in *The Sleepwalker*, w/c, Garrick Club.
G GEORGE CLINT, the last scene in *A New Way to Pay Old Debts*, oil, 1820, Garrick Club.
PR Several theatrical prints, BM, NPG.

HARLEY, Thomas (1730-1804) lord mayor of London.
PR J.HALL, after H.Edridge, tql seated, hands in muff, stipple, BM, NPG.

HARLOW, George Henry (1787-1819) portrait-painter.
P Self-portrait, 1818, hl, Uffizi Gallery, Florence.
D Self-portrait, 1813, hs, chalk, Huntington Library and Art Gallery, San Marino, USA. JOHN JACKSON, after a self-portrait, hs, pencil, NPG 782.
G G.H.HARLOW, 'Court for the Trial of Queen Catherine', oil, c1817, Royal Shakespeare Memorial Theatre Museum, Stratford-on-Avon.

HARLOWE, Sarah (1765-1852) actress.
D S.HARDING, hl in *Heigho for a Husband*, w/c, Garrick Club, London. W.WELLINGS, 1795, wl as Adeline in *The Battle of Hexham*, w/c, Garrick Club. S. DE WILDE, 1805, wl as Beatrice in Ravenscroft's *The Anatomist*, Royal Coll.
G SAMUEL DE WILDE, wl as Mrs Sneak in a scene from *The Mayor of Garratt*, oil, RA 1810, Garrick Club. GEORGE CLINT, wl as Miss Pickle in a scene from *The Spoiled Child*, oil, RA 1823, Garrick Club.

HARMER, James (1777-1853) solicitor and alderman of London.
P UNKNOWN, c1850, wl, Gravesend Town Hall, Kent.
PR T.WRIGHT, after A.Wivell, hs, stipple, pub 1820, BM, pub 1822, NPG.

HARMER, Thomas (1714-1788) independent minister of Wattisfield, Suffolk.
PR T.WRIGHT, after an unknown artist, hl, stipple, for *Essex, Suffolk & Norfolk Characters*, 1820, BM, NPG.

HARNESS, William (1790-1869) divine and author.
P GEORGE LANCE, V & A.
PR B.HOLL, after T.C.Wageman, hl, stipple, pub 1828, BM. J.R.JACKSON, after H.W.Phillips, tql seated, mezz, BM.

HARPER, Thomas (1787-1853) trumpet player.
PR L.HAGHE, hl profile with trumpet, lith, BM.

HARRINGTON, Charles Stanhope, 3rd Earl of (1753-1829) general.
P SIR JOSHUA REYNOLDS, c1782, Yale Center for British Art, New Haven, USA.
PR S.RAWLE, hs profile wearing uniform, line, for European Mag, 1804, BM, NPG.
C J.GILLRAY, wl equestrian, coloured etch, pub 1803, NPG.

HARRINGTON, Charles Stanhope, 4th Earl of (1780-1851) lord of the bedchamber.
PR F.BARTOLOZZI, after Sir Joshua Reynolds, with his mother and brother, stipple, pub 1789, BM. R.DIGHTON, wl on horseback, entitled 'A Noble Aiddecamp', etch, BM, NPG.

HARRINGTON, Leicester Fitzgerald Charles Stanhope, 5th Earl of (1784-1862) soldier.
P JOHN POWELL, after Reynolds, NGI 1660.
PR F.BARTOLOZZI, after Sir Joshua Reynolds, tql as a child, playing a drum, stipple, pub 1789, BM, NPG.

HARRINGTON, Maria Foote, Countess of (1797?-1867) actress.
PR R.COOPER, after R.E.Drummond, hs, stipple, pub 1817, NPG. C.PICART, after G.Clint, hl as Maria Darlington in A Roland for an Oliver, stipple, pub 1822, BM, NPG. T.LUPTON, after G.Clint, similar, but wl, mezz, pub 1824, BM.

HARRIOT, John (1745-1817) projector of the London Thames police.
PR PAGE, hl profile, stipple, for Essex, Suffolk and Norfolk Characters, 1820, BM. H.COOK, after Hervé, hs, line, oval, NPG. H.R.COOK, after H.Hervé, hs profile, stipple, oval, BM, NPG.

HARRIS, George Harris, 1st Baron (1746-1829) commander in India.
D THOMAS HICKEY, 1800, hs, charcoal and chalk, Stratfield Saye, Hants.
SC GEORGE RENNIE, 1835, statue, St Michael and All Angels Church, Throwley, Kent. WILLIAM THEED, jun, bust, Royal Military Academy, Sandhurst, Camberley, Surrey.
PR J.CHAPMAN, hs, stipple, oval, pub 1799, NPG. W.EVANS, after A.W.Devis, hs, stipple, oval, for European Mag, 1800, BM, NPG.

HARRIS, James (1709-1780) philosopher and critic.
P UNKNOWN, tql seated, profile, NPG 186.
G JAMES BARRY, 'The Society for the Encouragement of Arts', oil, 1777-1782, Royal Society of Arts, London.
PR C.BESTLAND, after J.Highmore, tql aged 31, stipple, NPG. C.BESTLAND, after I.Gosset, hl profile, aged 67, from a wax model, stipple, oval, BM, NPG. F.BARTOLOZZI, hs profile, aged 67, line, oval, BM. W.EVANS, hs profile, stipple, for Works of R.O.Cambridge, 1803, BM, NPG.

HARRIS, James (1746-1820), see 1st Earl of Malmesbury.

HARRIS, Joseph (1773-1825) Welsh writer.
PR W.T.FRY, hl seated, stipple, NPG.

HARRIS, Moses (fl 1766-1785) entomologist and artist.
PR M.HARRIS, hl profile, aged 49, etch, oval, 1780, BM. UNKNOWN, wl seated with tray of butterflies, entitled 'The Aurelian Macaroni', etch, BM.

HARRIS, William (1776?-1830) independent minister at Cambridge.

PR FREEMAN, hs, stipple, pub 1820, NPG. UNKNOWN, hs, stipple, for Evangelical Mag, 1823, BM. T.WOOLNOTH, after Uwins, hl, stipple, pub 1826, NPG.

HARRIS, William George Harris, 2nd Baron (1782-1845) lieutenant-general.
P WILLIAM SLATER, tql study for 'Waterloo Banquet', NPG 3722.
D THOMAS HICKEY, 1799, hs, charcoal and chalk, Stratfield Saye, Hants.
G W.SALTER, 'Waterloo Banquet at Apsley House', oil, 1836, Wellington Museum, Apsley House, London.

HARRISON, Sir George (d1841) legal writer.
PR C.TURNER, after T.Barber, tql seated, mezz, pub 1816, BM, NPG.

HARRISON, Robert (1715-1802) mathematician and linguist.
P WILLIAM BELL, c1791, hl, NPG 4898.

HARRISON, Samuel (1760-1812) singer.
PR W.DANIELL, after G.Dance, hs profile, soft-ground etch, pub 1814, BM, NPG.

HARRISON, Thomas (1744-1829) architect.
P HENRY WYATT, 1820, hl, Chester Town Hall.
D J.DOWNMAN, 1815, hl seated, pencil, Grosvenor Museum, Chester. J.DOWNMAN, 1815, similar to above but with Lord Hill's column at Shrewsbury in background, w/c, Grosvenor Museum, Chester.
PR A.R.BURT, wl, coloured, stipple, pub 1824, NPG.

HARROWBY, Dudley Ryder, 1st Earl of and 2nd Baron (1762-1847) statesman.
G K.A.HICKEL, 'The House of Commons, 1793', oil, NPG 745. SIR GEORGE HAYTER, 'The Trial of Queen Caroline, 1820', oil, NPG 999.
PR J.S.AGAR, after T.Phillips, hl, stipple, for Contemporary Portraits, 1813, BM, NPG. H.B.HALL, after Madame Meunier, hl seated, stipple, for Eminent Conservative Statesmen, 1837, BM, NPG.
C RICHARD DIGHTON, wl, coloured etch, pub 1818, NPG. JOHN DOYLE, wl, 'The Swearing of the Horatii', pen and pencil, 1832, BM. J.DOYLE, 'Coroner's Inquest', pen and chalk, BM.

HARROWBY, Dudley Ryder, 2nd Earl of (1798-1882) statesman.
PR F.C.LEWIS, after J.Slater, hs, stipple, for 'Grillion's Club' series, BM. H.ROBINSON, tql seated, stipple and line, NPG. H.C.BALDING, after a photograph by H.Barraud, hl, stipple and line, NPG.
G SIR GEORGE HAYTER, 'The House of Commons, 1833', oil, NPG 54.
PH UNKNOWN, tql seated, carte, NPG 'Twist Album', 1892.

HART, Sir Anthony (1754?-1831) lord chancellor of Ireland.
PR UNKNOWN, after T.Cahill, seated with chancellor's purse, line, for Irish Law Recorder, BM.

HART, Emma (1761?-1815), see Lady Hamilton.

HARTLEY, David (1705-1757) philosopher.
PR W.BLAKE, after J.Shackleton, hs, line, oval, for his Observations on Man, 1791, BM, NPG.

HARTLEY, David (1732-1813) statesman and inventor.
D LEWIS VASLET, 1789, hs, pastel, oval, Merton College, Oxford.
PR J.WALKER, after G.Romney, tql seated, mezz, BM.

HARTLEY, Elizabeth, née White (1751-1824) actress.
P ANGELICA KAUFFMANN, wl, Garrick Club, London. SIR JOSHUA REYNOLDS, RA 1773, hl as a nymph with a young Bacchus, TATE 1924.
D JAMES ROBERTS, five drgs in character, BM.
PR R.HOUSTON, after H.D.Hamilton, hl profile, mezz, oval, pub

1774, BM, NPG. Numerous theatrical prints, BM, NPG.

HARTLEY, James (1747-1800) lieutenant-colonel.
P GEORGE ROMNEY, 1783–89, wl, North Carolina Museum of Art, Raleigh, USA.

HARVEY, Daniel Whittle (1786-1863) politician, founder of the *Sunday Times.*
G SIR GEORGE HAYTER, 'The House of Commons, 1833', oil, NPG 54.
PR G.SHADE, after E.H.Latilla, hl, mezz, pub 1836, NPG. UNKNOWN, wl holding *Pension List*, lith, BM.

HARVEY, Sir Eliab (1758-1830) admiral.
P UNKNOWN, c1805–12, tql in uniform with Trafalgar medal, NMM, Greenwich.

HARVEY, Sir Henry (1737-1810) admiral.
G BARTOLOZZI, LANDSEER, RYDER and STOW, after R.Smirke, 'Naval Victories', 'Commemoration of the victory of June 1st 1794', line, pub 1803, BM, NPG.

HARVEY, John (1740-1794) captain in the navy.
G BARTOLOZZI, LANDSEER, RYDER and STOW, after R.Smirke, 'Naval Victories', 'Commemoration of the victory of June 1st 1794', line, pub 1803, BM, NPG.
SC JOHN BACON, jun, 1804, medallion on monument, Westminster Abbey, London.

HARVEY, William (1796-1866) designer and wood engraver.
PR UNKNOWN, hs profile, woodcut, for *Illust London News*, 1866, NPG.

HARWOOD, Sir Busick (1745?-1814) professor of anatomy at Cambridge.
P UNKNOWN, Christ's College, Cambridge.
D THOMAS UWINS, wl, w/c, BM.
PR W.N.GARDINER, after S.Harding, wl seated, stipple, pub 1790, BM, NPG. J.JONES, after S.Harding, tql, mezz, pub 1791, BM.

HASLAM, John (1764-1844) medical writer.
R H.DAWE, after G.Dawe, hl seated, mezz, pub 1812, BM.

HASTED, Edward (1732-1812) historian of Kent.
D UNKNOWN, c1790, hs, pastel, oval, Maidstone Museum, Kent.

HASTINGS, Sir Charles (1794-1866) founder of the British Medical Association.
PR S.W.REYNOLDS, jun, after B.R.Faulkner, tql, mezz, pub 1839, BM, NPG.

HASTINGS, Francis Rawdon Hastings, 1st Marquess of and 2nd Earl of Moira (1754-1826) soldier and statesman.
P SIR JOSHUA REYNOLDS, RA 1790, wl, Royal Coll. JOHN HOPPNER, 1794, wl, Royal Coll. J.HOPPNER, 1795, tql, Lady Lever Art Gallery, Port Sunlight. GEORGE CHINNERY, wl, Government of West Bengal, Raj Bhavan, Calcutta, India. THOMAS GAINSBOROUGH, wl, Museum de Arte de São Paolo, Brazil. SIR HENRY RAEBURN, wl with his wife, National Army Museum, Camberley, Surrey. SIR MARTIN ARCHER SHEE, wl, Royal Military Academy, Sandhurst, Camberley. SIR M.A.SHEE, hs, NGI 194. UNKNOWN, hs, NPG 2696.
D JOHN ATKINSON, 1820, hl, pen and ink, NPG 837.
M J.S.HARVIE, 1804, hs, w/c, SNPG L39. THOMAS MITCHELL, hs, oval, NPG L152 (31).
SC JOSEPH NOLLEKENS, 1802, marble bust, Holkham Hall, Norfolk. J.NOLLEKENS, 1810, marble bust, Royal Coll. UNKNOWN, wax, NGI 8160.

HASTINGS, Hans Francis, see 11th Earl of Huntingdon.

HASTINGS, Selina, see Countess of Huntingdon.

HASTINGS, Warren (1732-1818) governor-general of India.
P SIR JOSHUA REYNOLDS, 1766–68, tql seated, NPG 4445. TILLY KETTLE, 1772, wl seated, Victoria Memorial Hall, Calcutta. J.T.SETON, 1784, wl seated, Victoria Memorial Hall. Attrib A.W.DEVIS, 1784–85, wl seated, Government House, Calcutta. GEORGE STUBBS, 1791, wl equestrian on Wedgwood plaque, oval, Victoria Memorial Hall. GEORGE ROMNEY, c1795, wl, India Office, London. L.F.ABBOTT, c1796, hs, NPG 1845. J.J.MASQUERIER, 1806, tql, seated, Oriental Club, London. SIR THOMAS LAWRENCE, RA 1811, hl seated, NPG 390. TILLY KETTLE, hl, NPG 81.
D SIR THOMAS LAWRENCE, 1786, tql, pastel, NPG 3823.
M RICHARD COSWAY, 1787, hs, NPG L152 (24). OZIAS HUMPHRY, hs, unfinished V & A.
G JOHAN ZOFFANY, 1783–87, wl with his wife and an Indian servant, in landscape, Victoria Memorial Hall. UNKNOWN, a conference between Warren Hastings and the Nawab of Murshidabad, oil, Victoria Memorial Hall.
SC THOMAS BANKS, 1794, bronze bust, NPG 209. PETER ROUW, 1806, wax medallion, NPG 5065. JOHN FLAXMAN, 1823, marble statue, India Office, London. JOHN BACON, jun, bust, Westminster Abbey, London.

HATCHER, Henry (1777-1846) historian of Salisbury.
PR G.F.STORM, after W.Gray, hs, stipple, for J.Britton's *Autobiography*, BM, NPG.

HATCHETT, Charles (1765?-1847) chemist.
D SIR FRANCIS CHANTREY, 1820, hs, pencil, NPG 316a (65).
SC SIR FRANCIS CHANTREY, busts, Linnean Society, London, Ashmolean Museum, Oxford.
PR W.DRUMMOND, after T.Phillips, hs, lith, *Athenaeum Portraits*, No 15, pub 1836, BM, NPG.

HATFIELD, John (1758?-1803) forger.
PR J.CHAPMAN, hs profile, stipple, pub 1803, NPG. UNKNOWN, hs profile, aged 46, line, for Kirby's *Wonderful Museum*, 1803, BM, NPG. UNKNOWN, hs profile, stipple, octagon, pub 1810, BM.

HATHERTON, Edward John Littleton, 1st Baron (1791-1863) politician.
P SIR GEORGE HAYTER, 1834, hl profile, holding quill, (study for NPG 54) NPG 4658.
G SIR GEORGE HAYTER, 'The House of Commons, 1833', oil, NPG 54.
PR F.C.LEWIS, after J.Slater, stipple, for *Grillion Club* series, BM, NPG.

HATSELL, John (1743-1820) clerk of the House of Commons.
G K.A.HICKEL, 'The House of Commons, 1793', oil, NPG 745.
PR C.PICART, after J.Northcote, wl seated, stipple, pub 1806, BM, NPG.
C J.SAYERS, wl 'Cicero in Catilinam' etch, pub 1785, NPG.

HAVARD, William (1710?-1778) actor.
PR E.FISHER, after T.Worlidge, hl, mezz, BM.

HAVELOCK, Sir Henry, 1st Bart (1795-1857) general.
D MRS M.MANNIN, 1851, hs, w/c, Yorkshire County Record Office, Northallerton, N.Yorks. FREDERICK GOODALL, c1857, hl, pencil and wash, NPG 4835.
G T.J.BARKER, after sketches by E.Lundgren, 'The Relief of Lucknow, 1857', oil, Corporation of Glasgow, engr C.G.Lewis, 1860, NPG.
SC WILLIAM BEHNES, 1858, bust, Guildhall Museum, London. G.G.ADAMS, 1858, plaster bust, NPG 1204. W.BEHNES, c1861, bronze statue, Trafalgar Square, London. MATTHEW NOBLE, 1866, marble relief (meeting Clyde and Outram at Lucknow), Outram Memorial, Westminster Abbey, London.

PH UNKNOWN, daguerreotype, on loan to Yorkshire County Record Office.

HAWARD, Francis (1759-1797) engraver.
D OZIAS HUMPHREY, hl, chalk, NPG 1233.

HAWEIS, Thomas (1734-1820) divine.
P UNKNOWN, Christ's College, Cambridge.
PR W.RIDLEY, after H.Edridge, hl, stipple, pub 1796, BM, NPG. W.RIDLEY, hs, stipple, oval, for *Evangelical Mag*, 1796, NPG.

HAWES, Sir Benjamin (1797-1862) under-secretary for war.
G JOHN PARTRIDGE, 'The Fine Arts Commissioners, 1846', NPG 342, 3.

HAWES, William (1736-1808) medical writer, founder of Royal Humane Society.
PR W.RIDLEY, after a miniature, hs, stipple, oval, for *European Mag*, 1802, BM, NPG. UNKNOWN, silhouette, hs profile, stipple, BM.

HAWKE, Edward Hawke, 1st Baron (1705-1781) admiral.
P FRANCIS COTES, 1768–70, tql with Bath ribbon and star, NMM, Greenwich.
G UNKNOWN, George II receiving Sir E.Hawke, with Pitt and Anson, Shugborough (NT), Staffs.
PR C.SPOONER, hl with Bath ribbon and star, mezz, pub 1762, BM. J.MCARDELL, after G.Knapton, hl with Bath ribbon and star, mezz, oval, BM, NPG.

HAWKER, Peter (1786-1853) sporting writer and soldier.
PR M.GAUCI, after A.E.Chalon, hs, lith, for his *Instructions to Young Sportsmen*, 1830, BM. H.ROBINSON, after a bust by W.Behnes, stipple, NPG. UNKNOWN, after a daguerreotype by Claudet, hs, woodcut, for *Illust London News*, 1851, NPG.

HAWKER, Robert (1753-1827) calvinistic divine.
PR W.BLAKE, after J.Ponsford, tql seated, line, BM, NPG. M.R.COOPER, after J.S.Wetherall, hl, stipple, BM, NPG. A.SMITH, after Williams, hl, seated, line, BM, NPG.

HAWKESBURY, Lord Charles, see 1st Earl of Liverpool.

HAWKESBURY, Lord Robert, see 2nd Earl of Liverpool.

HAWKESWORTH, John (1715?-1773) author.
PR J.WATSON, after J.Reynolds, hl seated, mezz, pub 1773, BM.

HAWKINS, Sir Caesar, Bart (1711-1786) surgeon.
P WILLIAM HOGARTH, *c*1740, hl, Royal College of Surgeons, London.

HAWKINS, Caesar Henry (1798-1884) surgeon.
SC GEORGE HALSE, marble bust, Royal College of Surgeons, London.

HAWKINS, Edward (1780-1867) keeper of antiquities at the British Museum.
PR M.GAUCI, after E.U.Eddis, hs, lith, pub 1833, BM, NPG. H.CORBOULD, hs profile, lith, BM.

HAWKINS, Edward (1789-1882) provost of Oriel College, Oxford.
P SIR FRANCIS GRANT, tql seated, Oriel College, Oxford.

HAWKINS, Sir John (1719-1789) writer.
P JAMES ROBERTS, 1786, hl seated, Faculty of Music, Oxford.
SL UNKNOWN, *c*1781, hs, profile, NPG 5020.

HAWTREY, Edward Craven (1789-1862) provost of Eton.
P HÉLÈNE FEILLET, 1853, tql seated, Eton College, Berks.
PR C.BAUGNIET, hl, lith, BM.

HAY, Alexander Leith (1758-1838), see Leith.

HAY, Andrew (1762-1814) major-general.
P SIR HENRY RAEBURN, tql, North Carolina Museum of Art, Raleigh, USA.

PR W.SAY, hl in uniform, mezz, BM.

HAY, Sir Andrew Leith (1785-1862) soldier and author.
G SIR GEORGE HAYTER, 'The House of Commons, 1833', oil, NPG 54.

HAY, Charles (1740?-1811), see Lord Newton.

HAY, Sir George (1715-1778) lawyer and politician.
P SIR JOSHUA REYNOLDS, 1764, hl with spectacles and paper, Harvard University Law School, Cambridge, Mass, USA.

HAY, George (1729-1811) Roman catholic bishop of Daulis.
PR G.A.PERIAM, after G.Watson, tql seated, line, NPG.

HAY, George (1787-1876), see 8th Marquess of Tweeddale.

HAY, Thomas (1710-1787), see 9th Earl of Kinnoull.

HAYDON, Benjamin Robert (1786-1846) historical painter.
P GEORGINA M.ZORNLIN, 1828, hl, NPG 510. Self-portrait, hs profile, NPG 268. G.H.HARLOW, tql in Vandyck dress, City Museum and Art Gallery, Birmingham. WILLIAM NICHOLSON, hl, Plymouth City Museum and Art Gallery.
D SIR DAVID WILKIE, 1815, wl reclining, pencil, NPG 1505. J.P.DAVIS, 1816, hs, V & A. JOHN KEATS, 1816, hs, pen and ink, NPG 3250. G.H.HARLOW, chalk, Courtauld Institute Galleries, London.
SC Two plaster casts of life mask, NPG 2172, NPG 2802.

HAYES, Sir John Macnamara, 1st Bart (1750?-1809) physician.
G N.BRANWHITE, after S.Medley, 'Institutors of the Medical Society of London', stipple, pub 1801, BM.

HAYES, Philip (1738-1797) professor of music at Oxford.
P JOHN COOPER, 1758, hl, Examination Schools, Oxford.
D JAMES ROBERTS, hl, pastel, St John's College, Oxford.

HAYES, William (1706-1777) professor of music at Oxford.
P JOHN CORNISH, hl, Examination Schools, Oxford, engr T.Park, mezz, pub 1787, BM, NPG.

HAYGARTH, John (1740-1827) medical writer.
D JAMES SHARPLES, pastel, Bristol City Art Gallery.
PR W.COOK, after J.H.Bell, tql seated, line, oval, BM, NPG.

HAYLEY, Thomas Alfonso (1780-1800) sculptor.
P GEORGE ROMNEY, 1789-92, as Robin Goodfellow, TATE 5850.
G G.ROMNEY, 'The Four Friends', oil, 1796, Abbot Hall Art Gallery, Kendal.
PR W.BLAKE, after J.Flaxman, hs profile, from a medallion, stipple for his father's *Essay on Sculpture*, 1800, BM, NPG.

HAYLEY, William (1745-1820) poet and biographer.
P HENRY HOWARD, hs, NPG 662. GEORGE ROMNEY, hs, Dulwich College Picture Gallery, London.
M Attrib JAMES NIXON, hs?, V & A.
G GEORGE ROMNEY, 'The Four Friends', oil, 1796, Abbot Hall Art Gallery, Kendal. G.ROMNEY, with Charles Greville, Romney and Emma Hart, pencil, pen, ink and wash, *c*1784, BM.
PR H.R.COOK, after W.Haines, hs, stipple, for *The Cabinet*, 1807, BM, NPG. R.COOPER, after G.Engleheart, hl seated, stipple and line, for his *Memoirs*, 1823, BM, NPG.

HAYMAN, Francis (1708-1776) painter.
P Self-portrait, *c*1740-45, wl (with Grosvenor Bedford?), NPG 217. SIR JOSHUA REYNOLDS, 1756, hs, Royal Academy, London. Two self-portraits, wl and tql, seated at an easel in both, Royal Albert Memorial Museum, Exeter.
G JOHAN ZOFFANY, 'Royal Academicians, 1772', oil, Royal Coll. FRANCIS HAYMAN, with 'Lord Chesterfield and His Friends', oil, Yale Center for British Art, New Haven, USA.
PR D.P.PARISET, after P.Falconet, 1769, hs, stipple, oval, BM, NPG.

HAYTER, Charles (1761-1835) miniature painter.
D GEORGE HAYTER (his son), 1811, hl, pencil and wash, NPG 2617.
G SIR GEORGE HAYTER, 'The Trial of Queen Caroline, 1820', oil, NPG 999. JOHN HAYTER, 'A Controversy on Colour', oil, RA 1823, Shipley Art Gallery, Gateshead.
PR G.HAYTER, head, etch, 1819, BM, NPG.

HAYTER, Sir George (1792-1871) portrait and historical painter.
P Self-portrait, 1820, hs with artist's brushes, NPG 3104. Self-portrait, 1828, hl with palette, Uffizi Gallery, Florence.
D Several self-portraits drgs: c1816, head, w/c and pencil, BM; 1821, seven comic sketches, NPG 3082 and a; c1826, wl seated at easel with man in Turkish costume, pen and ink, Bolton Art Gallery; 1843, hs, Küpferstichkabinett, Staatliche Kunstsammlungen, Dresden.
G SIR GEORGE HAYTER, 'The Trial of Queen Caroline, 1820', oil, NPG 999. JOHN HAYTER, 'A Controversy on Colour', with Sir E.Landseer, C.Hayter and another, oil, RA 1823, Shipley Art Gallery, Gateshead. SIR G.HAYTER, 'The House of Commons, 1833', oil, NPG 54.

HAYTER, Thomas (1702-1762) bishop of Norwich and London.
P UNKNOWN, hs, Fulham Palace, London.

HAYTER, Sir William Goodenough, 1st Bart (1792-1878) liberal whip.
PR UNKNOWN, hs, woodcut, for *Illust London News*, 1850, NPG. UNKNOWN, after a photograph by John Watkins, tql, woodcut, for *Illust London News*, 1861, NPG.

HAZELDINE, William (1763-1840) ironfounder.
D SIR FRANCIS CHANTREY, 1831, hs and hs profile, pencil, NPG 316a (66, 67).
SC SIR FRANCIS CHANTREY, bust on monument, St Chad's Church, Shrewsbury.

HAZLITT, William (1778-1830) essayist.
P JOHN HAZLITT, hs, Maidstone Museum and Art Gallery.
D WILLIAM BEWICK, 1822, hs profile, chalk, Maidstone Museum and Art Gallery. W.BEWICK, hs profile, chalk, (replica), NPG 2697.
SC UNKNOWN, plaster face mask, Bodleian Library, Oxford. HORNE, death mask, Maidstone Museum and Art Gallery.

HEAD, Sir Francis Bond, 1st Bart (1793-1875) governor of Upper Canada, writer.
PR C.TURNER, after N.Cook, hl, mezz, pub 1837, BM. UNKNOWN, hs, woodcut, for *Illust London News*, 1875, NPG.

HEARD, Sir Isaac (1730-1822) Garter king-of-arms.
PR C.TURNER, after A.W.Devis, hl aged 87, mezz, BM, NPG.

HEARNE, Samuel (1745-1792) explorer of north-western America.
PR UNKNOWN, hl with chart of Hudson's Bay, stipple, oval, for *European Mag*, 1796, BM, NPG.

HEARNE, Thomas (1744-1817) water-colour painter.
D HENRY EDRIDGE, 1801, seated sketching, pencil and ink, BM. H.EDRIDGE, tql seated, pencil and ink, BM. HENRY MONRO, hl seated, chalk, NPG 1653.
M JOHN SMART, c1783, hs, National Museum, Stockholm.
PR W.DANIELL, after G.Dance, 1795, hl profile, soft-ground etch, pub 1809, BM, NPG.

HEATH, Benjamin (1704-1766) book-collector and critic.
P R.E.PINE, wl, Exeter Guildhall.
PR W.DICKINSON, hl, mezz, oval, pub 1773, BM, NPG.

HEATH, Charles (1785-1848) engraver.

PR MRS D.TURNER, after H.Corbould, hl, etch, BM, NPG.

HEATH, James (1757-1834) engraver.
P W.J.LONSDALE, 1830, hl seated, NPG 771. GILBERT STUART, hs, Wadsworth Athenaeum, Hartford, Conn, USA.
D HENRY EDRIDGE, tql, pencil, BM.
PR J.R.SMITH, after L.Abbott, hl, mezz, pub 1796, BM, NPG. S.W.REYNOLDS, after T.Kearsley, hl, mezz, pub 1796, BM, NPG. MRS D.TURNER, after W.Behnes, hl seated, etch, BM. R.J.LANE, after T.George, tql seated, lith, BM, NPG.

HEATHFIELD, George Augustus Eliott, 1st Baron (1717-1790) general, defender of Gibraltar.
P JOHN SINGLETON COPLEY, 1787, hl profile, NPG 170. SIR JOSHUA REYNOLDS, RA 1788, tql with Bath ribbon and star and key of Gibraltar, NG 111. MATHER BROWN, wl, East Sussex County Council, Lewes, East Sussex.
D ANTONIO POGGI, chalk, SNPG 2048.
G J.S.COPLEY, 'The siege and relief of Gibraltar, 13 September 1782', oil, possibly a replica, TATE 787. GEORGE CARTER, wl with other officers at Gibraltar, 1782, NPG 1752.
SC J.C.ROSSI, c1825, marble statue on monument, St Paul's Cathedral, London.
PR C. DE MECHEL, after G.F.Koehler, hs profile, line, oval, pub 1784, BM. F.BARTOLOZZI, after A.Poggi, tql on rock of Gibraltar, stipple, pub 1788, BM. Several popular prints, BM, NPG.

HEBER, Reginald (1783-1826) bishop of Calcutta.
P THOMAS PHILLIPS, 1823, tql, All Souls College, Oxford.
D E.TURNER, pencil, V & A.
SC SIR FRANCIS CHANTREY, 1827–35, marble statue on monument, St Paul's Cathedral, London; clay model, V & A.
PR F.C.LEWIS, after J.Slater, head, stipple, one of 'Grillion's Club' series, BM, NPG.

HEBER, Richard (1773-1833) book collector.
D JOHN HARRIS, tql, pencil, NPG 4886.

HEBERDEN, William (1710-1801) physician.
P SIR WILLIAM BEECHEY, c1780, hs, St John's College, Cambridge.

HELY-HUTCHINSON, Christopher (1767-1826) Irish politician.
PR C.TURNER, after J.Corbett, tql, mezz, pub 1813, BM.

HELY-HUTCHINSON, John (1724-1794) secretary of state for Ireland.
P By or after SIR JOSHUA REYNOLDS, hl, Trinity College, Dublin, type engr J.Watson, mezz, pub 1778, BM.
G FRANCIS WHEATLEY, 'The Irish House of Commons, 1780', oil, Leeds City Art Galleries, Lotherton Hall, W.Yorks.

HELY-HUTCHINSON, John, Baron Hutchinson (1757-1832), see 2nd Earl of Donoughmore.

HELY-HUTCHINSON, John (1787-1851), see 3rd Earl of Donoughmore.

HELY-HUTCHINSON, Richard, see 1st Earl of Donoughmore.

HEMANS, Felicia Dorothea, née Browne (1793-1835) poet.
SC ANGUS FLETCHER, marble bust, NPG 5198; plaster cast NPG 1046.
PR E.SMITH, after E.Robertson, hl seated, line, for Chorley's *Memorials of Mrs Hemans*, 1836, BM. W.HOLL, after W.E.West, tql seated, stipple, for *The Christian Keepsake*, 1837, BM, NPG. UNKNOWN, after a medallion by E.W.Wyon, hs profile, oval, collas-type, for Chorley's *Authors of England*, 1837, BM, NPG.

HENDERLAND, Lord Alexander Murray (1736-1795) Scottish judge.
C JOHN KAY, wl, 'Conservation – Demonstration', etch, 1842, BM,

NPG.

HENDERSON, Andrew (1783-1835) Glasgow portrait-painter.
P Self-portrait, hl with palette, Glasgow Technical College.

HENDERSON, Ebenezer (1784-1858) missionary.
P J.R.WILDMAN, hl, Dunfermline Town Council.
PR H.ROOM, after J.Cochran, hl seated, stipple, NPG. W.T.FRY, after T.Wageman, hl, stipple, NPG.

HENDERSON, John (1747-1785) actor.
P THOMAS BEACH, 1773, hs profile, Garrick Club, London. THOMAS GAINSBOROUGH, *c*1777, hl, NPG 980. GEORGE ROMNEY, hl as Macbeth, Garrick Club. Attrib GEORGE ROMNEY, hl as Hamlet, with Richard Wilson as Polonius, Garrick Club. UNKNOWN, hs, oval, Garrick Club.
D ROBERT DUNKARTON, 1776, tql seated, chalk, NPG 1919. JAMES ROBERTS, wl as Falstaff, chalk, Garrick Club.
PR Various theatrical prints, BM, NPG.

HENDERSON, John (1757-1788) linguist and astrologer.
P WILLIAM PALMER, hl seated, Pembroke College, Oxford.
D WILLIAM BURGESS, 1771, hs, pencil, oval, BM.
PR AMES, hs as a boy, stipple and line, BM. J.CONDÉ, hs, stipple, oval, for *European Mag*, 1792, BM, NPG.

HENLEY, Joseph Warner (1793-1884) conservative politician.
P SIR FRANCIS GRANT, 1860, wl seated, County Hall, Oxford.
PR D.J.POUND, after a photograph by Mayall, tql seated, stipple and line, NPG. H.C.BALDING, after a photograph by H.Barraud, hl, stipple and line, NPG.
PH HILLS & SAUNDERS, wl seated, carte, NPG Francis Album.

HENLEY, Robert (1708?-1772), see 1st Earl of Northington.

HENLEY, Robert (1747-1786), see 2nd Earl of Northington.

HENNIKER, John Henniker-Major, 2nd Baron (1752-1821) antiquary.
PR H.HUDSON, after G.Romney, hl, mezz, BM, NPG.

HENNING, John (1771-1851) sculptor.
P ROBERT SCOTT LAUDER, SNPG 1375.
SC After a self-portrait, plaster medallion, SNPG 411.

HENRY Benedict Stuart, see Cardinal YORK.

HENRY Frederick, Duke of Cumberland and Strathearn (1745-1790), see Cumberland.

HENRY, Robert (1718-1790) Scottish historian.
P DAVID MARTIN, hl, SNPG L 37, engr J.Caldwall, line, for his *Hist of Great Britain*, 1771, BM.

HENRY, William (1774-1836) chemist.
G J.F.SKILL, J.GILBERT, W and E.WALKER, 'Men of Science Living in 1807-08', pencil and wash, NPG 1075.
PR H.COUSINS, after J.Lonsdale, tql seated, mezz, pub 1836, BM, NPG.

HENSEY, Florence (fl 1758) spy.
PR UNKNOWN, wl in his cell, for Caulfield's *Remarkable Persons*, 1820, BM.

HENSLOW, John Stevens (1796-1861) botanist.
P UNKNOWN, tql with botanical drawing, Ipswich Museum.
SC THOMAS WOOLNER, 1861, marble bust, Museum, Kew Gardens; version, Fitzwilliam Museum, Cambridge.
PR J.H.MAGUIRE, tql seated, lith, for *Ipswich Museum Portraits*, 1851, BM, NPG.

HENSMAN, John (1780-1864) divine.
PR W.O.GELLER, after S.West, tql, mezz, NPG.

HERBERT, Edward (1785-1848), see 2nd Earl of Powis.

HERBERT, George Augustus, see 11th Earl of Pembroke.

HERBERT, Henry (1734-1794), see 10th Earl of Pembroke.

HERBERT, Sir Thomas (1793-1861) rear-admiral.
PR J.H.LYNCH, hs, lith, BM, NPG.

HERBERT, William (1718-1795) bibliographer.
PR W.SAY, tql seated, mezz, for vol 1 of Dibdin's ed of Ames's *Typographical Antiquities*, 1810, BM, NPG. T.SMYTH, hs, line, NPG.

HERBERT, William (1778-1847) dean of Manchester.
P SIR WILLIAM BEECHEY, hl, a leaving portrait, Eton College, Berks.

HERON, Sir Richard, Bart (1726-1805) chief-secretary to lord-lieutenant of Ireland.
P Attrib SIR JOSHUA REYNOLDS, 1770, hs, Princeton University Art Museum, USA.
G FRANCIS WHEATLEY, 'The Irish House of Commons, 1780', oil, Leeds City Art Galleries, Lotherton Hall, W.Yorks.

HERON, Sir Robert, 2nd Bart (1765-1854) whig politician.
G SIR GEORGE HAYTER, 'The House of Commons, 1833', oil, NPG 54.
PR UNKNOWN, tql seated, mixed, BM, NPG.

HERRIES, John Charles (1778-1855) chancellor of the exchequer.
G SIR GEORGE HAYTER, 'The House of Commons, 1833', oil, NPG 54.
PR W.WALKER, after W.Boxall, tql seated, mezz, BM, NPG. S.FREEMAN, hl seated, NPG.

HERRING, Ann, née Harris (1795-1838) first wife of John Frederick Herring.
D EDWARD HEATON, 1825, tql seated, w/c, NPG 4903.

HERRING, John Frederick (1795-1865) animal painter.
D G.JACKSON, 1822, hl, w/c, NPG 4902.
PR J.B.HUNT, after W.Betham, hs, stipple, pub 1848, BM, NPG. UNKNOWN, hl, woodcut, for *Illust London News*, 1865, NPG.
PH UNKNOWN, wl, carte, NPG Album of Artists vol 1.

HERSCHEL, Caroline Lucretia (1750-1848) astronomer.
PR J.BROWN, hs, aged 92, stipple, NPG.

HERSCHEL, Sir John Frederick William, 1st Bart (1792-1871) astronomer.
P H.W.PICKERSGILL, *c*1835, hl, St John's College, Cambridge; related drawing, NPG 1386. C.A.JENSEN, hl, Royal Society, London.
SL UNKNOWN, hl, profile, NPG 4148.
SC E.H.BAILY, 1850, marble bust, St John's College, Cambridge, plaster cast, NPG 4056. After WILLIAM TASSIE, plaster medallion, SNPG 511.
PR F.CROLL, after a daguerreotype by Mayall, hs, stipple, for *Hogg's Instructor*, NPG.
PH JULIA MARGARET CAMERON, hs, NPG P 18/1.

HERSCHEL, Sir William (1738-1822) astronomer.
P L.F.ABBOTT, 1785, hl, NPG 98. JOHN RUSSELL, *c*1795, hl, NMM, Greenwich. WILLIAM ARTAUD, hs with Guelphic Order of Hanover, Royal Astronomical Society, London.
D CHARLES FORD, after L.F.Abbott, hl, w/c, Holburne of Menstrie Museum, Bath. JAMES SHARPLES, hs, pastel, Bristol City Art Gallery.
SC Attrib JOHN FLAXMAN, *c*1781, Wedgwood medallion, Wedgwood Museum, Barlaston, Staffs. J.C.LOCHÉE, *c*1785, Wedgwood medallion, Wedgwood Museum. J.C.LOCHÉE, plaster bust, NPG 4055.
PR J.GODBY, after F.Rehberg, hl, moon and stars in background,

stipple, pub 1814, BM, NPG.

HERSCHELL, Solomon, see Hirschel.

HERTFORD, Francis Charles Seymour-Conway, 3rd Marquess of (1777-1842) statesman.
D JOHN DOWNMAN, 1781, as a child, tinted drg, oval, Wallace Collection, London.
PR E.SCRIVEN and S.W.REYNOLDS, after P.Stephanoff, wl in robes, coloured mezz, for Sir G.Nayler's work on coronation of George IV, 1824, BM. W.HOLL, after T.Lawrence, hl, stipple for Jerdan's *Nat Portrait Gallery*, pub 1833, BM, NPG. M.GAUCI, wl in shooting dress with gun, lith, BM.
C RICHARD DIGHTON, wl entitled 'A view of Yarmouth', coloured etch, pub 1818, NPG, V & A.

HERTFORD, Francis Ingram Seymour, 2nd Marquess of (1743-1822) lord chamberlain.
P Attrib SIR JOSHUA REYNOLDS, tql, Ragley Hall, Warwicks.
D JOHN DOWNMAN, 1783, hl, w/c, oval, Ragley Hall.
SC SIR FRANCIS CHANTREY, bust and statue, semi-recumbent figure, Ashmolean Museum, Oxford.

HERTFORD, Francis Seymour-Conway, 1st Marquess of (1719-1794) diplomat.
P SIR JOSHUA REYNOLDS, RA 1785, hl with Garter star, Ragley Hall, Warwicks. JOHN ASTLEY, Ragley Hall. GEORGE MORLAND, wl equestrian in scene with cottage and village characters, Ragley Hall.
PR C.WARREN, after W.H.Brown, hs, line, oval, for *The Senator*, 1791, BM, NPG. J.DIXON, after an unknown artist, hl, mezz, oval, BM, NPG.

HERVEY, Augustus John, see 3rd Earl of Bristol.

HERVEY, Elizabeth, see Duchess of Devonshire.

HERVEY, Frederick Augustus, see 4th Earl of Bristol.

HERVEY, George William, see 2nd Earl of Bristol.

HERVEY, James (1714-1758) devotional writer.
PR J.DIXON, after J.M.Williams, hl, mezz, BM, NPG.

HERVEY, Lady Mary, née Lepell (1700-1768) celebrated beauty.
P UNKNOWN, tql with garland, Ickworth (NT), Suffolk. Attrib ALLAN RAMSAY, hl, Ickworth.
D UNKNOWN, probably based on the above tql portrait with garland, hl, pastel, Ickworth.
M Two miniatures by unknown artists, hl, Ickworth.
G UNKNOWN, 'The Earl of Bristol taking leave on his appointment to the command of a ship', oil, *c*1750, Ickworth.
PR H.WATELET, after C.N.Cochin, jun, hs, profile, etch, oval, 1752, BM. J.HEATH, after an unknown artist, hl, line, oval, for Lord Orford's *Works*, 1798, BM, NPG.

HESKETH, Harriet, Lady (1733-1807) friend of the poet Cowper.
PR H.ROBINSON, after F.Cotes of *c*1755, hl, stipple, NPG.

HESSE, Princess of (1723-1772), see MARY.

HESSE-HOMBURG, Landgravine of, see Princess ELIZABETH.

HESSEL, Phoebe (1713?-1821) apple-woman at Brighton, centenarian.
PR UNKNOWN, wl seated, soft-ground etch, BM.

HEUGH, Hugh (1782-1846) presbyterian divine.
PR FENNER, SEARS & CO, after J.R.Wildman, hl, stipple, for *Evangelical Mag*, 1830, BM, NPG. E.BURTON, after D.Macnee, hl, mezz, BM.

HEWETT, Sir George, 1st Bart (1750-1840) general.

PR S.W.REYNOLDS, sen and S.COUSINS, after S.W.Reynolds, tql in uniform, mezz, BM.

HEWITT, James (1709-1789), see 1st Viscount Lifford.

HEWLETT, James (1768-1836) flower-painter.
P Self-portrait, Victoria Art Gallery, Bath.
D J.VARLEY, chalk, V & A.

HEWLETT, John (1762-1844) biblical scholar.
PR UNKNOWN, after H.Ashby, hl, mezz, pub 1795, BM, NPG. J.P.QUILLEY, after W.Brough, tql, mezz, BM, NPG.

HEWSON, William (1739-1774) surgeon and anatomist.
G THOMAS ROWLANDSON, 'The Dissecting Room', drg, Royal College of Surgeons, London.
PR R.STEWART, hl, mezz, oval, pub 1780, BM.

HEY, John (1734-1815) divine.
P UNKNOWN, Sidney Sussex College, Cambridge.

HEY, William (1736-1819) surgeon.
P WILLIAM ALLEN, tql seated with Lady Harewood and a child, Leeds General Infirmary, W.Yorks.
SC SIR FRANCIS CHANTREY, *c*1820, statue, Leeds General Infirmary.
PR W.HOLL, hl, stipple, BM, pub 1816, NPG.

HEY, William (1772-1844) surgeon.
D JOHN RUSSELL, hs, pastel, Leeds City Art Gallery.

HEYTESBURY, William A'Court, Baron (1779-1860) viceroy in Ireland.
P E.U.EDDIS, 1844, wl seated, NGI 464.

HEYWOOD, Sir Benjamin, 1st Bart (1793-1865) banker.
P WILLIAM BRADLEY, exhib 1844, wl, City Art Gallery, Manchester.

HEYWOOD, Peter (1773-1831) navy captain.
P JOHN SIMPSON, 1822, hl, NMM, Greenwich.

HIBBERT, George (1757-1837) West Indian merchant and collector.
P SIR THOMAS LAWRENCE, 1811, wl, Port of London Authority.
PR J.WARD, after J.Hoppner, tql seated, mezz, BM.

HICKEY, William (1749-1830?) attorney in India and memoirist.
P WILLIAM THOMAS, 1819, wl with his Indian servant, NPG 3249.

HIEOVER, Harry, see Charles Bindley.

HIGHMORE, Anthony (1719-1799) draughtsman.
P JOSEPH HIGHMORE, (his father), tql, National Gallery of Victoria, Melbourne, Australia.

HILL, Arthur (1753-1801), see 2nd Marquess of Downshire.

HILL, Arthur Trevor, see 3rd Viscount Dungannon.

HILL, George (1716-1808) king's serjeant.
D UNKNOWN, wl, w/c, BM (Engr Ports Coll.).

HILL, George (1750-1819) principal of St Mary's College, St Andrews.
P UNKNOWN, University of St Andrews, Scotland.
PR T.HODGETTS, after J.Syme, hl, mezz, BM.

HILL, James (d1817?) actor and singer.
D SAMUEL DE WILDE, 1805, wl as Leander in *The Padlock*, chalk and w/c, BM.

HILL, John (c1716-1775) writer and naturalist.
D FRANCIS COTES, 1757, hs, ink and wash, BM.

HILL, Mary Amelia, see 1st Marchioness of Salisbury.

HILL, Matthew Davenport (1792-1872) reformer of criminal law.
PR UNKNOWN, hl, woodcut, for Cassell's *Illust Family Paper*, 1858,

NPG.

HILL, Sir Richard, 2nd Bart (1732-1808) writer of religious pamphlets.

D JOHN RUSSELL, head, chalk, NPG 1465.

PR R.WOODMAN, hl, line, pub 1839, NPG.

HILL, Rowland (1744-1833) evangelical preacher.

P UNKNOWN, hl, Dr Williams's Library, London.

D JOHN RUSSELL, head, chalk, NPG 1464.

SC UNKNOWN, plaster bust, NPG 1401.

PR SPRINGFORTH, after Lovelace, tql seated, line, pub 1792, NPG. T.BLOOD, after S.Drummond, hl, stipple, for *European Mag*, 1814, BM, NPG.

C J.KAY, tql, etch, 1798, NPG.

HILL, Sir Rowland (1795-1879) initiator of penny post.

P J.A.VINTER, after a photograph of c1879, hl, NPG 838.

SC SIR THOMAS BROCK, marble sculpture, Town Hall Square, Kidderminster, Worcs. EDWARD ONSLOW FORD, bronze statue, King Edward Street, London.

PR W.O.GELLER, after A.Wivell, jun, tql seated, mezz, pub 1848, BM, NPG. D.J.POUND, after a photograph by J. and C. Watkins, tql seated, line, NPG.

PH UNKNOWN, wl, NPG 'Twist' Album 1892.

HILL, Rowland Hill, 1st Viscount (1772-1842) general.

P J.PRESCOTT KNIGHT, RA 1842, small wl study for 'The Heroes of Waterloo', DoE (British Embassy, Luxembourg). GEORGE DAWE, wl, National Army Museum, London. J.W.PIENEMAN, hs, Wellington Museum, Apsley House, London. WILLIAM SALTER, tql study for 'Waterloo Banquet', NPG 3724. C.SMITH, wl, formerly United Services Club (c/o The Crown Commissioners), London.

D S.F.DIEZ, 1841, tql seated, National Gallery, Berlin. LUKE CLENNELL, hs, w/c over pencil, BM. THOMAS HEAPHY, hs and tql, w/c NPG 1914 (6, 7). GEORGE RICHMOND, hl, w/c, NPG 1055.

G SIR GEORGE HAYTER, 'The Trial of Queen Caroline, 1820', oil, NPG 999. W.SALTER, 'Waterloo Banquet at Apsley House', oil, 1836, Wellington Museum, Apsley House.

SC JOSEPH PANZETTA, statue, London Road, Shrewsbury.

HILL, Thomas (1760-1840) book-collector.

PR J.BROWN, after Linnell, hs, stipple, pub 1838, NPG. D.MACLISE, wl seated, lith, originally pub in *Fraser's Mag*, pl to Maginn's *Gallery of Illustrious Literary Characters*, 1873, BM, NPG. C.MOON, wl, lith, NPG.

HILL, Thomas Wright (1763-1851) schoolmaster and stenographer.

P MRS CHARLES PEARSON, and unknown artist, both City Art Gallery, Birmingham.

HILL, William Noel, see 3rd Baron Berwick.

HILL, Wills, see 1st Marquess of Downshire.

HILLS, Robert (1769-1844?) water colour painter and etcher.

D JOHN JACKSON, RA 1820, hl, w/c, BM. SIR RICHARD OWEN, 1835, hs profile, pencil, BM.

HILLSBOROUGH, Margaretta, Countess of (1729-1766) first wife of 1st Marquess of Downshire.

G ARTHUR DEVIS, '1st Marquess of Downshire and family', oil, c1760, NPG L 160.

HILLSBOROUGH, Wills Hill, 1st Earl and 2nd Viscount, see 1st Marquess of Downshire.

HILTON, William (1786-1839) history painter.

P Self-portrait, hl, Lincoln City Art Gallery.

D C.H.LEAR, c1845, hs, pencil, NPG 1456 (11).

HINCHCLIFFE, John (1731-1794) bishop of Peterborough.

P W.PETERS, wl in pulpit, Trinity College, Cambridge.

D JOHN SINGLETON COPLEY, hs, chalk, Metropolitan Museum of Art, New York, USA. JOHN GREENWOOD, head, pencil, BM.

PR W.GRAINGER, after W.H.Brown, hs, line, oval, for *The Senator*, 1791, NPG.

HINCKS, Edward (1792-1866) orientalist.

P UNKNOWN, c1830, tql seated, Trinity College, Dublin.

HINDERWELL, Thomas (1744-1825) historian of Scarborough.

PR J.POSSELWHITE, after J.Jackson, head, profile, stipple, BM, NPG.

HINDMARSH, Robert (1759-1835) founder of the Swendenborgian Society.

PR S.W.REYNOLDS, after J.Allen, wl seated, mezz, pub 1824, BM, NPG.

HINDS, Samuel (1793-1872) bishop of Norwich.

PR T.H.MAGUIRE, tql seated, lith, one of set of *Ipswich Museum Portraits*, 1851, BM, NPG.

HINTON, John Howard (1791-1873) baptist minister.

G B.R.HAYDON, 'The Anti-Slavery Society Convention, 1840' oil, NPG 599.

HIRSCHEL, Solomon (1761-1841) Chief Rabbi in London.

P F.B.BARLIN, hl, NPG 1343.

PR W.HOLL, after J.Slater, hl, stipple, pub 1808, BM, NPG W.RIDLEY, after S.Drummond, hs, stipple, for *European Mag* 1811, BM. NPG.

HOADLY, Benjamin (1706-1757) physician.

P WILLIAM HOGARTH, 1740, hl, NGI 398. W.HOGARTH, wl seated with bust of Newton, Fitzwilliam Museum, Cambridge FRANCIS HAYMAN, wl with his wife, Wellcome Institute London.

HOADLY, John (1711-1776) dramatist and chaplain to the Prince of Wales.

P FRANCIS HAYMAN, 1747, wl with Maurice Green, NPG 2106.

HOARE, Prince (1755-1834) painter and dramatist.

P Two self-portraits, 1779 and 1780, both hs profile, Uffizi Gallery Florence.

D WILLIAM BROCKEDON, 1831, hs, pencil and chalk, NPG 2515 (27) GEORGE DANCE, hs profile, pencil, BM. JOHN JACKSON, hs Victoria Art Gallery, Bath.

PR W.RIDLEY, after J.Northcote, hl, stipple, oval, for *Monthly Mirror*, 1796, BM, NPG. J.HOPWOOD, after J.Opie, hl, stipple, fo *The Cabinet*, 1807, BM, NPG. C.TURNER, after T.Lawrence, head from an unfinished picture, mezz, pub 1831, BM, NPG.

HOARE, Sir Richard (1709-1754) lord mayor of London.

P ALLAN RAMSAY, 1746, tql in gown and chain, Stourhead (NT) Wilts. JOHN WOOTTON, 1746, wl equestrian, as Lord Mayor Stourhead.

HOARE, Sir Richard Colt, 2nd Bart (1758-1838) historian

P SAMUEL WOODFORDE, RA 1802, wl with his son, Stourhead (NT), Wilts. Attrib SAMUEL WOODFORDE, tql, Stourhead.

D WILLIAM HOARE, hl as Mercury, pastel, Stourhead. HENRY EDRIDGE, tql, pencil and w/c, Stourhead.

SC R.C.LUCAS, 1841, statue on monument, Salisbury Cathedral R.C.LUCAS, wax bust, Stourhead.

HOARE, William (1707?-1792) portrait-painter.

P Self-portrait, hl, Victoria Art Gallery, Bath.

D Self-portrait, 1742, hs, pastel, Royal National Hospital fo Rheumatic Diseases, Bath; similar self-portrait, Roya Academy, London.

G JOHAN ZOFFANY, 'Royal Academicians, 1772', oil, Royal Coll

SC SIR FRANCIS CHANTREY, 1828, medallion on monument, Bath

Abbey, Avon.

HOBART, John (1723-1793), see 2nd Earl of Buckingham-shire.

HOBART, Robert (1760-1816), see 4th Earl of Buckingham-shire.

HOBDAY, William Armfield (1771-1831) portrait-painter.
P Self-portrait, City Art Gallery, Birmingham.
M Self-portrait, 1793, V & A.

HOBHOUSE, Sir Benjamin, 1st Bart (1757-1831) politician.
D SIR FRANCIS CHANTREY, hs and hs profile, sketch, pencil, NPG 316a (69).
SC SIR FRANCIS CHANTREY, 1818, bust, Victoria Art Gallery, Bath.
PR P.AUDINET, after T.Phillips, tql seated, line, pub 1825, BM, NPG. J.COCHRAN, after J.Jackson, hl, stipple, for Jerdan's *Nat Portrait Gallery*, 1832, BM, NPG.

HOBHOUSE, John Cam, see Baron BROUGHTON de Gyfford.

HODGES, Charles Howard (1764-1837) mezzotint engraver and portrait-painter.
P Self-portrait, hl, Rijksmuseum, Amsterdam.

HODGES, William (1744-1797) landscape-painter.
D GEORGE DANCE, 1793, hs profile, Royal Academy, London.
G H.SINGLETON, 'Royal Academicians, 1793', oil, Royal Academy.
PR THORNTHWAITE, after R.Westall, hl, line, oval, for *Literary Mag*, 1792, BM, NPG.

HODGSON, Francis (1781-1852) provost of Eton.
P UNKNOWN, Eton College, Berks.
PR W.WALKER, after F.Grant, hl, mezz, pub 1850, BM, NPG.

HODGSON, John (1779-1845) antiquary.
D THOMAS MOGFORD, after a miniature, 1829, pencil, V & A.
PR E.SCRIVEN, after H.Macreth, hl seated, stipple, for vol 2 of his *Hist of Northumberland*, 1832, BM, NPG.

HODGSON, Joseph (1788-1869) surgeon.
PR S.COUSINS, after J.Partridge, tql seated, mezz, BM.

HODGSON, Studholme (1708-1798) field-marshal.
PR W.BOND, after G.Romney, hl, stipple, pub 1796, BM, NPG.

HODSON, Frodsham (1770-1822) principal of Brasenose College.
P THOMAS PHILLIPS, tql seated, Brasenose College, Oxford.

HODSON, Septimus (1768-1833) rector of Thrapston.
PR W.SKELTON, after T.Lawrence, hl seated, line, pub 1790, BM, NPG. W.SKELTON, after W.Beechey, hl, line, BM, NPG.

HOFLAND, Barbara, née Wreake (1770-1844) writer.
PR UNKNOWN, hs, stipple, oval, NPG. UNKNOWN, tql in turban, stipple, for *La Belle Assemblée*, 1823, BM, NPG. E.FINDEN, hl, stipple, for her *Life* by T.Ramsay, pub 1849, BM, NPG.

HOGARTH, George (1783-1870) music critic.
PH UNKNOWN, Dickens' House, London.

HOGG, James (1770-1835) poet, 'the Ettrick Shepherd'.
P WILLIAM NICHOLSON, hl, SNPG L 15.
D WILLIAM BEWICK, 1824, hs, chalk, SNPG 1320. WILLIAM BROCKEDON, 1832, hs, pencil and chalk, NPG 2515 (41). S.P.DENNING, hs seated, w/c, NPG 426.
PR W. & D.LIZARS, after 'P.M.', hl seated, etch, for Lockhart's *Peter's Letters to his Kinsfolk*, 1819, BM, NPG. W.C.EDWARDS, after C.Fox, hs aged 60, line, for his *Altrive Tales*, 1832, BM, NPG. D.MACLISE, wl, lith, for *Fraser's Mag*, 1832, BM, NPG. W.ARCHIBALD, after J.W.Gordon, tql seated, line, BM.

HOGG, Sir James Weir, 1st Bart (1790-1876) East India director.
PR R.J.LANE, after E.U.Eddis, tql, lith, 1856, NPG.

HOGHTON, Daniel (1770-1811) major-general.
SC SIR FRANCIS CHANTREY, wl relief figure on monument, St Paul's Cathedral, London.

HOLBURNE, Francis (1704-1771) admiral.
P SIR JOSHUA REYNOLDS, 1756-57, tql with his son, NMM, Greenwich.

HOLCROFT, Thomas (1745-1809) dramatist and author.
P JOHN OPIE, hl, NPG 512. J.OPIE, hl, NPG 3130.
D GEORGE DANCE, hs, pencil, BM.
PR J.CONDÉ, hs, stipple, oval, for *European Mag*, 1792, BM, NPG. W.RIDLEY, after S.Drummond, hl, stipple, oval, for *Monthly Mirror*, 1799, BM, NPG.

HOLDERNESS, Robert d'Arcy, 4th Earl of (1718-1778) secretary of state.
P Attrib JACOB HUYSMANS, wl as a boy in fancy dress, DoE (British Embassy, The Hague). GEORGE KNAPTON, 1749, hl as a gondolier, Society of Dilettanti, Brooks's Club, London. GEORGE KNAPTON, 1752, tql seated, on loan to Temple Newsam, Leeds, W.Yorks.
PR R.COOPER, after J.Reynolds, hl, stipple, for W.Mason's *Works*, 1811, BM, NPG.

HOLE, Richard (1746-1803) poet and antiquary.
PR W.DANIELL, after G.Dance, hl profile, soft-ground etch, pub 1809, BM, NPG.

HOLL, William (1771-1838) engraver.
D UNKNOWN, hs, pencil, NPG 2912.

HOLLAND, Charles (1733-1769) actor.
P After H.B., hs, oval, Garrick Club, London.
M J.HUTCHINSON, 1760, hs, NPG L 152 (25).
SC UNKNOWN, monumental bust, St Nicholas Church, Chiswick, London.
PR J.R.SMITH, after H.B., hl, mezz, oval, pub 1771, BM. J.S.MÜLLER, hl, line, oval, BM, NPG.

HOLLAND, Elizabeth Vassall Fox, Lady (1770-1845) wife of 3rd Baron Holland.
C SIR EDWIN LANDSEER, c1835, hs, pen and wash, NPG 4914.

HOLLAND, Henry (1746?-1806) architect.
SC GEORGE GARRARD, 1818, bust, Woburn Abbey, Beds.
PR G.GARRARD, wl seated, Hans Place in background, etch, pub 1806, BM, NPG.

HOLLAND, Sir Henry, 1st Bart (1788-1873) physician.
P THOMAS BRIGSTOCKE, c1860, hl seated, NPG 1656.
SC WILLIAM THEED, 1873, marble bust, NPG 1067.
PR F.W.WILKIN, hs, lith, NPG.

HOLLAND, Henry Fox, 1st Baron (1705-1774) Whig statesman.
P After SIR JOSHUA REYNOLDS, c1762, tql seated, NPG 2075. J.G.ECCARDT, after J.B.Van Loo, hs, NPG 2078.
G WILLIAM HOGARTH, wl holding a plan in the group sometimes called 'The Holland House Group', c1738, oil, Ickworth (NT), Suffolk.
PR UNKNOWN, after J.E.Liotard of 1754, hl, stipple, pub 1798, BM, NPG. J.HAYNES, after W.Hogarth, hs, etch, pub 1782, BM, NPG. J.McARDELL, after A.Ramsay, hl, mezz, oval, BM.

HOLLAND, Henry Richard Vassall Fox, 3rd Baron (1773-1840) Whig statesman and patron of arts and letters.
P F.X.FABRE, 1795, tql, NPG 3660. F.X.FABRE, 1796, tql, a leaving portrait, Eton College, Berks. JOHN SIMPSON, after C.R.Leslie,

hs, NPG 382. SIR GEORGE HAYTER, wl study for NPG 999, NPG 5192.

D THOMAS LAWRENCE, chalk, Courtauld Institute Galleries, London.

G WILLIAM LANE, 'Whig Statesmen and their Friends, c1810', chalk, NPG 2076. SIR GEORGE HAYTER, 'The Trial of Queen Caroline, 1820', oil, NPG 999. SIR G.HAYTER, 'The House of Commons, 1833', oil NPG 54.

SC JOSEPH NOLLEKENS, 1804, marble bust, Woburn Abbey, Beds. J.FRANCIS, 1838, marble bust, Royal Coll. SIR RICHARD WESTMACOTT, bust, St Michael's Church, Millbrook, Beds.

PR S.W.REYNOLDS, after J.R.Smith, wl seated, with bust of C.J.Fox, mezz, pub 1806, BM. G.PARKER, after A.Wivell, hl, stipple, pub 1822, BM, NPG.

C Several JOHN DOYLE political sketches, drgs, BM. SIR EDWIN LANDSEER, c1835, hl, pen and wash, NPG 4914.

HOLLAND, John (1794-1872) poet and miscellaneous writer.

PR H.ADLARD, after R.Smith, hl, stipple, for vol 5 of his *Memoir of J.Montgomery*, 1854, BM.

HOLLAND, Sir Nathaniel Dance-, see DANCE-Holland.

HOLLINS, John (1798-1855) painter.

G JOHN HOLLINS, 'A Consultation prior to the Aerial Voyage to Weilburg, 1836', oil, NPG 4710.

HOLLINS, William (1754-1843) architect and sculptor.

SC PETER HOLLINS, bust, St Paul's Church, Birmingham.

HOLLIS, Aiskew Paffard (1764-1844) vice-admiral.

P H.W.PICKERSGILL, RA 1838, hl, NMM, Greenwich.

HOLLIS, Thomas (1720-1774) writer and antiquary.

P RICHARD WILSON, 1752, hs, Harvard University Library, Cambridge, Mass, USA.

D JOHN GREENWOOD, head, pen and pencil, BM.

PR G.B.CIPRIANI, head, line, for his *Memoirs*, 1780, BM, NPG. W.BROMLEY, hs profile, line, oval, for *European Mag*, 1788, BM, NPG.

HOLMAN, James (1786-1857) blind traveller.

P GEORGE CHINNERY, 1830, hl, Royal Society, London.

D WILLIAM BROCKEDON, 1834, hs, chalk, NPG 2515 (69).

PR J.R.JACKSON, after J.P.Knight, tql seated, mezz, pub 1849, BM. R.COOPER, after Fabrioni, hl seated, stipple, NPG. E.FINDEN, after T.Wageman, hl seated, stipple, NPG.

HOLMAN, Joseph George (1764-1817) actor.

P GAINSBOROUGH DUPONT, hl as Edgar as Mad Tom, in *King Lear*, Garrick Club, London. Several paintings by SAMUEL DE WILDE at the Garrick Club: wl as Chamont in Otway's *The Orphan*; wl as Douglas wearing tartan dress, in landscape; wl as Alexander in *The Rival Queens*; wl as Cyrus in *Cynthia and Cyrus*. UNKNOWN, tql as Hamlet, Garrick Club.

M DANIEL DODD, ink, V & A.

PR Various theatrical prints, BM, NPG.

C JAMES SAYERS, wl in a burlesque of F.Reynold's *Werter*, etch, pub 1786, NPG.

HOLMES, Sir Charles (1711-1761) rear-admiral.

P Attrib NATHANIEL DANCE, after 1758, hl, NMM, Greenwich.

SC JOSEPH WILTON, marble statue on monument, Westminster Abbey, London.

HOLMES, Robert (1765-1859) Irish lawyer.

D EDWARD HAYES, 1844, chalk, NGI 2144.

HOLMES, William (1779-1851) treasurer of the ordnance and tory 'whip'.

PR S.FREEMAN, after J.Moore, hl, stipple, for *Eminent Conservative Statesmen*, 1832, BM, NPG.

HOLROYD, Sir George Sowley (1758-1831) judge.

P Attrib THOMAS PHILLIPS, tql seated in robes, Gray's Inn, London.

PR S.W.REYNOLDS, tql seated in judicial robes, mezz, pub 1834, BM, NPG.

HOLROYD, John Baker, see 1st Earl of Sheffield.

HOLT, John (1743-1801) antiquary.

PR H.ROGERS, tql seated, etch, BM, NPG.

HOLT, Joseph (1756-1826) general of the Irish rebels in 1798.

PR R.J.HAMERTON, after an unknown artist, hl, lith, for his *Memoirs*, 1838, BM.

HOLWELL-CARR, William (1758-1830) connoisseur.

P JOHN JACKSON, hl, NG 124.

D LEWIS VASLET, 1790, hs, pastel, Exeter College, Oxford.

G P.C.WONDER, 'Patrons and Lovers of Art, 1826', study for a large group, NPG 792.

HOME, Sir Everard, 1st Bart (1756-1832) surgeon.

P THOMAS PHILLIPS, hl, The Royal Society, London.

D SIR FRANCIS CHANTREY, head, profile, pencil, NPG 316a (70). W.H.CLIFT, wl, and hl, pencil, BM.

SC SIR FRANCIS CHANTREY, 1816, marble bust, Royal College of Surgeons, London.

PR W.SHARP, after W.Beechey, tql seated with anatomical drawing, line, pub 1810, BM, NPG.

HOME, Francis (1719-1813) physician and professor at Edinburgh.

P Attrib DAVID ALLAN, hl seated, University of Edinburgh.

C J.KAY, wl, etch, 1787, BM.

HOME, James (1760-1844) professor of materia medica at Edinburgh.

P Attrib ANDREW GEDDES, wl seated, Edinburgh University.

HOME, John (1722-1808) Scottish minister, and dramatist.

P WILLIAM MILLER, 1762, hl, SNPG 1564. SIR HENRY RAEBURN, hl, NPG 320. UNKNOWN, SNPG 1378.

M UNKNOWN, SNPG 1209.

SC JAMES TASSIE, 1791, paste medallion, SNPG 1253.

PR W.RIDLEY, after S.Drummond, hl, stipple, oval, for *Monthly Mirror*, 1799, BM, NPG.

HOME, Robert (1752-1834) portrait-painter.

P Self-portrait, hl, NPG 3162.

HOMER, Henry (1753-1791) classical scholar.

PR J.JONES, after S.Harding, hl, stipple, pub 1791, BM, NPG. T.WALKER, after P.S.Lamborn, hl seated, etch, BM.

HONE, Horace (1756-1825) miniaturist.

M Self-portrait, 1795, hs, oval, NPG 1879. Self-portrait, hs, oval, NGI 2629.

HONE, John Camillus (d 1837) miniature painter.

P NATHANIEL HONE, RA 1769, hl with flute, 'The Piping Boy', NGI 440.

HONE, Nathaniel (1718-1784) portrait-painter and enamellist.

P Several self-portraits: c1765, hs, Royal Academy, London; c1775, hl seated in landscape NGI 886; hl with porte crayon and portfolio, NPG 177; City Art Gallery, Manchester.

D Self-portrait, 1764, drawing at a table, BM. Self-portrait, hl sketch, BM.

M Self-portrait, hs, enamel, NPG 1878.

G JOHAN ZOFFANY, 'Royal Academicians, 1772', oil, Royal Coll.

PR E.FISHER, after N.Hone, tql with crayons and canvas, mezz, BM, NPG.

HONE, William (1780-1842) bookseller and pamphleteer.

P GEORGE PATTEN, hl, NPG 1183.
R ROGERS, after G.Cruikshank, hs, stipple, BM.

HOOD, Alexander (1727-1814), see 1st Viscount Bridport.

HOOD, Alexander (1758-1798) captain in the navy.
P UNKNOWN, after a portrait of c1790, hl, NMM, Greenwich.

HOOD, Maria Elizabeth Frederica Stewart Mackenzie, Lady (1783-1862) wife of Admiral Sir Samuel Hood.
P SIR THOMAS LAWRENCE, RA 1808, wl, Castle Ashby, Northants.

HOOD, Sir Samuel, 1st Bart (1762-1814) vice-admiral.
P JOHN HOPPNER, RA 1807, wl with several orders, NMM, Greenwich. UNKNOWN, 1808-11, hl, NMM.
R C.TURNER, after J.Downman, hl in uniform, mezz, pub 1806, BM. RIDLEY & BLOOD, hs in uniform, stipple, oval, from a miniature, for *European Mag*, 1807, BM, NPG. E.BOCQUET, after W.Beechey, hl in uniform, stipple, for *Contemporary Portraits*, 1813, BM, NPG.

HOOD, Samuel Hood, 1st Viscount (1724-1816) admiral.
P JOHN WOLLASTON, 1746, tql, NMM, Greenwich. SIR JOSHUA REYNOLDS, 1783, tql, City Art Gallery, Manchester. JAMES NORTHCOTE, 1784, hl, NMM. L.F.ABBOTT, 1794-95, wl, NMM; tql version, NPG 628. THOMAS GAINSBOROUGH, tql Ironmongers' Hall, London. J.NORTHCOTE, tql, The Admiralty, Portsmouth.
G K.A.HICKEL, 'The House of Commons, 1793', oil, NPG 745.
C J.C.LOCHÉE, Wedgwood medallion, Wedgwood Museum, Barlaston, Staffs. JAMES TASSIE, paste medallion, SNPG 1195.

HOOD, Thomas (1799-1845) poet.
P UNKNOWN, c1835, hl seated, NPG 855.
C MATTHEW NOBLE, 1854, bust on monument, Kensal Green Cemetery, London.
R W.HOLL, after T.Lewis (formerly attrib G.R.Lewis), tql seated, stipple, for *Hood's Own*, BM, NPG. F.CROLL, hl, line, for Hogg's *Weekly Instructor*, BM, NPG.

HOOK, James (1746-1826) musician.
P L.F.ABBOTT, hs, NPG 2519.
R T.BLOOD, after S.Drummond, hs, stipple, for *European Mag*, 1813, BM, NPG.

HOOK, James (1772?-1828) dean of Worcester.
R S.W.REYNOLDS, jun, after R.Evans, tql seated, mezz, pub 1836, BM, NPG.

HOOK, Theodore Edward (1788-1841) novelist and wit.
P E.U.EDDIS, hs, NPG 37.
D WILLIAM BROCKEDON, hs, chalk, NPG 2515 (101). Self-portrait, c1831, wl sketch, Denham Album, Yale University Library, New Haven, USA.
R S.FREEMAN, after Bennett, hs, stipple, for *Monthly Mirror*, 1807, BM. D.MACLISE, wl, lith, for *Fraser's Mag*, 1834, NPG. R.J.LANE, after A. d'Orsay, hl profile, lith, pub 1839, BM, NPG. Two engravings in stipple and line by unknown artists, 1839 and 1841, BM, NPG.

HOOK, Walter Farquhar (1798-1875) dean of Chichester.
C W.D.KEYWORTH, recumbent effigy, St Peter Church, Leeds. F.W.POMEROY, bronze statue, City Square, Leeds.
R C.E.WAGSTAFF, after F.Rosenberg, hl, mezz, pub 1838, BM, NPG. W.HOLL?, after G.Richmond, hs, stipple, pub 1849, BM, NPG. D.J.POUND, after a photograph by Navey, tql seated, stipple and line, NPG.
H RUSSELL & SONS, two photographs, hs and hl, cartes, NPG Distinguished Persons Album vol III.

HOOKER, Sir William Jackson (1785-1865) director of Kew Gardens.

P SPIRIDIONE GAMBARDELLA, hl, Linnean Society, London.
D SIR DANIEL MACNEE, Royal Botanic Gardens, Kew.
SC THOMAS WOOLNER, RA 1860, marble bust, Royal Botanic Gardens; related plaster cast, NPG 1673. Wedgwood medallion, after a model by T.Woolner, 1866, NPG 1032; similar medallion on his monument at Kew Church.
PR H.COOK, after T.Phillips, hl seated, stipple, for Jerdan's *Nat Portrait Gallery*, 1834, BM, NPG. W.DRUMMOND, hs, lith, *Athenaeum Portraits*, No 51, pub 1837, BM. T.H.MAGUIRE, tql seated, lith, one of set of *Ipswich Museum Portraits*, 1851, BM, NPG. MRS D.TURNER, after J.S.Cotman, hs profile, etch, BM, NPG.
PH MAULL and POLYBLANK, wl, carte, NPG Album of Photographs 1949. E.EDWARDS, wl seated, for *Men of Eminence*, ed L.Reeve, pub 1863, NPG.

HOOLE, Elijah (1798-1872) orientalist.
PR DEAN, after Lovatt, hl, stipple, NPG.

HOOLE, John (1727-1803) author and translator.
D GEORGE DANCE, 1793, hl profile, seated, pencil, NPG 1143.
PR A.SMITH, hs, line, oval, for *European Mag*, 1792, BM, NPG. MRS D.TURNER, after O.Humphry, hl seated, etch, BM, NPG.

HOOPER, Robert (1773-1835) physician.
P Attrib PHILIP REINAGLE, c1813, tql seated, Royal College of Physicians, London.

HOPE, Sir Alexander (1769-1837) general.
P FRIEDRICH HEINRICH FUGER, 1801, tql Hopetoun House, Lothian region, Scotland. SIR THOMAS LAWRENCE, hl, Hopetoun House.

HOPE, Charles (1763-1851), see Lord Granton.

HOPE, Frederick William (1797-1862) entomologist and collector.
P L.C.DICKINSON, 1864, tql, University Museum, Oxford.
D UNKNOWN, hl, chalk, Bodleian Library, Oxford.
PR W.RADDON, tql seated, line, BM. J.DICKSON, hs, lith, NPG.

HOPE, Henry Philip (d1839) picture and diamond collector.
SL AUGUSTIN EDOUART, V & A.
PR T.LUPTON, after Bouton, hl, mezz, 1823, BM, NPG.

HOPE, James (1741-1816), see 3rd Earl of Hopetoun.

HOPE, James (1764-1846?) Irish Nationalist.
P W.C.NIXON, 1840, Ulster Museum, Belfast.
G UNKNOWN, 'The United Irish Patriots of 1798', coloured lith, NPG.

HOPE, John (1725-1786) professor of botany at Edinburgh.
C J.KAY, wl, conversing with a gardener, etch, 1786, NPG.

HOPE, John (1765-1823), see 4th Earl of Hopetoun.

HOPE, John (1794-1858) Scottish judge.
P COLVIN SMITH, hl, SNPG 712. After C.SMITH, tql seated, Faculty of Advocates, Parliament Hall, Edinburgh.
D Attrib B.W.CROMBIE, hs profile, w/c, SNPG 101.
PR B.W.CROMBIE, hs profile, lith, NPG.

HOPE, Thomas (1770?-1831) virtuoso, collector and writer.
P J.F.SABLET, 1792, wl playing cricket, Marylebone Cricket Club, London. SIR WILLIAM BEECHEY, wl, NPG 4574; related w/c by Adam Buck, 1805, Society of Dilettanti, Brooks's Club, London.
SC BERTEL THORVALDSEN, c1817, marble bust, Thorvaldsen Museum, Copenhagen.

HOPE, Thomas Charles (1766-1844) professor of chemistry at Edinburgh.
PR T.HODGETTS, after H.Raeburn, tql seated, mezz, BM.
C J.KAY, 'The Craft in Danger', etch, 1817, NPG.

HOPE, Sir William Johnstone (1766-1831) vice-admiral.

G BARTOLOZZI, LANDSEER, RYDER & STOW, after R.Smirke, 'Naval Victories', 'Commemoration of the victory of June 1st 1794', line, pub 1803, BM, NPG.

PR H.R.COOK, after a miniature. hl, stipple, oval, pub 1807, BM, NPG. C.TURNER, after G.Watson, hl, mezz, pub 1812, BM.

HOPETOUN, James Hope Johnstone, 3rd Earl of (1741-1816) soldier.

P NATHANIEL DANCE, 1763, wl, Hopetoun House, Lothian region, Scotland. DAVID MARTIN, 1785, hs, Hopetoun House.

C J.KAY, wl, etch, 1795, NPG.

HOPETOUN, John Hope, 4th Earl of (1765-1823) general.

P SIR HENRY RAEBURN, c1820, wl with horse, County Hall, Cupar, Fife, Scotland. Attrib SIR JOHN WATSON-GORDON, 1822, hl with Bath star, Hopetoun House Lothian region, Scotland. By or after JOHN HOPPNER, hl, Gordon Barracks, Aberdeen. SIR JOHN WATSON-GORDON, hl in uniform of the Archer's Company, oval, Hopetoun House.

G SIR DAVID WILKIE, 'The Entrance of George IV at Holyrood House', oil, 1822-29, Royal Coll.

SC THOMAS CAMPBELL, statue, Royal Bank of Scotland, Edinburgh.

PR J.VENDRAMINI, after W.M.Craig, hl, stipple, for *Contemporary Portraits*, 1811, BM, NPG.

HOPKINS, William (1793-1866) mathematician and geologist.

P UNKNOWN, Peterhouse, Cambridge.

PR UNKNOWN, hs, woodcut, NPG.

HOPPER, Thomas (1776-1856) architect.

PR MISS TURNER, after J.Ternouth, hl, lith, BM.

HOPPNER, John (1758-1810) portrait painter.

P Self-portrait, c1800, hl, Royal Academy, London. Self-portrait, hs, Parham, W.Sussex. Self-portrait, hs with fish, NGI 566.

D GEORGE DANCE, hs profile, crayon, Royal Academy.

G H.SINGLETON, 'Royal Academicians, 1793', oil, Royal Academy.

HOPPUS, John (1789-1875) professor at University College, London.

PR FENNER, SEARS & CO, after J.R.Wildman, hs, stipple, NPG.

HOPWOOD James (1752?-1819) engraver.

PR J.H.ROBINSON, after A.Cooper, head, etch, for Pye's *Patronage of British Art*, 1845, BM.

HORN, Charles Edward (1786-1849) singer, composer and actor.

P POCOCK, as Seraskier in *The Siege of Belgrade*, The Royal Society of Musicians, London.

D SAMUEL DE WILDE, 1811, as Meddle in *Up All Night*, w/c, Garrick Club, London.

PR J.McDOUGALL, tql seated with sheet of music, lith, BM.

HORNBY, Sir Phipps (1785-1867) admiral.

P SIR JOHN LAVERY, hl, Royal Academy, London.

HORNE, George (1730-1792) bishop of Norwich.

P UNKNOWN, hs, The Deanery, Canterbury. T.OLIVE, hs, Magdalen College, Oxford.

HORNE, Thomas Hartwell (1780-1862) biblical scholar and bibliographer.

PR H.ADLARD, after a photograph, tql seated, line, BM. J.COCHRAN, after a photograph, hl seated, stipple and line, NPG.

HORNE, Sir William (1774-1860) master in Chancery.

G SIR GEORGE HAYTER, 'The House of Commons, 1833', oil, NPG 54.

HORNE TOOKE, John, see Tooke.

HORNER, Francis (1778-1817) political economist.

P SIR HENRY RAEBURN, 1812, tql seated, NPG 485. SIR HENRY RAEBURN, hs, SNPG 253.

D JOHN HENNING, head, profile, chalk, NPG 2677.

SC J.HENNING, 1806, wax medallion, NPG 2678. SIR FRANCIS CHANTREY, 1818, marble bust, SNPG 1221. SIR FRANCIS CHANTREY, 1820, statue on monument, Westminster Abbey, London.

HORNER, Leonard (1785-1864) geologist and educationalist.

PR S.WILLIAMS, head, profile, woodcut, BM. UNKNOWN, hs, from 'Meeting of the British Association at Southampton', woodcut for *Illust London News*, 1846-47, NPG.

HORSFIELD, Thomas (1773-1859) naturalist.

PR T.ERXLEBEN, hs, lith, BM, NPG.

HORSLEY, Samuel (1733-1806) bishop of St Asaph, secretary of the Royal Society.

M W.S.LETHBRIDGE, hl, NPG 155.

PR H.MEYER, after J.Green, tql seated with badge of the Bath, mezz, pub 1813, BM, NPG. T.BLOOD, after O.Humphry, seated, stipple, for *European Mag*, 1813, BM, NPG. J.STOW, after S.Roch, hl, line, pub 1822, BM, NPG. S.W.REYNOLDS, hl with badge of the Bath, mezz, BM.

C R.DIGHTON, wl, coloured etch, pub 1809, BM, NPG.

HORSLEY, William (1774-1858) composer and organist.

P WILLIAM OWEN, hl, NPG 1655.

PR R.J.LANE, after J.C.Horsley, hs, lith, BM, NPG.

HORTON, Sir Robert John Wilmot, 3rd Bart (1784-1841) politician.

C JOHN DOYLE, 'The Battle of the Pamphleteers', pencil, 1829, BM.

HOSACK, John (d 1887) police magistrate.

G R.A.BROOKS, 'Benchers of the Middle Temple, 1880', oil, Middle Temple, London.

HOSTE, Sir George Charles (1786-1845) colonel, Royal Engineers.

P WILLIAM SALTER, tql study for 'Waterloo Banquet', NPG 372.

G W.SALTER, 'Waterloo Banquet at Apsley House', oil, 1836, Wellington Museum, Apsley House, London.

HOSTE, Sir William, 1st Bart (1780-1828) captain in the navy.

P Called HOSTE (probably rightly), attrib Samuel Lane, c1815, NMM, Greenwich.

SC THOMAS CAMPBELL, statue, St Paul's Cathedral, London.

PR W.GREATBACH, tql, line, for his *Memoirs*, 1833, BM, NPG.

HOTHAM, Beaumont Hotham, 2nd Baron (1737-1814) baron of the exchequer.

PR V.GREEN, after N.Dance, tql in robes, mezz, pub 1796, BM, NPG.

HOTHAM, Beaumont Hotham, 3rd Baron (1794-1870) general.

P WILLIAM SALTER, tql study for 'Waterloo Banquet', NPG 372.

G SIR GEORGE HAYTER, 'The House of Commons, 1833', oil, NPG 54. W.SALTER, 'Waterloo Banquet at Apsley House', oil, 1836, Wellington Museum, Apsley House, London.

HOTHAM, Sir William (1772-1848) admiral.

P After SIR GEORGE HAYTER, c1840, wl seated with Bath ribbon and star, in his library, NMM, Greenwich.

G G.NOBLE and J.PARKER after J.Smart, 'Naval Victories', 'Commemoration of 11th Oct 1797', line, pub 1803, BM, NPG.

HOUSMAN, Robert (1759-1838) divine.

PR S.W.REYNOLDS, after J.Lonsdale, hl, mezz, pub 1822, BM.

HOUSTON, Sir William, 1st Bart (1766-1842) general.

WILLIAM THEED, jun, bust, Royal Military Academy, Sandhurst, Camberley, Surrey.

HOWARD, Bernard Edward, see 12th Duke of Norfolk.

HOWARD, Charles (1720-1786), see 10th Duke of Norfolk.

HOWARD, Charles (1746-1815), see 11th Duke of Norfolk.

HOWARD, Edward (*d*1841) sailor and novelist.
S.FREEMAN, after S.S.Osgood, tql seated, stipple, for *New Monthly Mag*, 1838, BM.

HOWARD, Edward Charles (1774-1816) sugar refiner.
J.F.SKILL, J.GILBERT, W. and E.WALKER, 'Men of Science Living in 1807-08', pencil and wash, NPG 1075.

HOWARD, Frederick (1748-1825), see 5th Earl of Carlisle.

HOWARD, Sir George (1720?-1796) field-marshal.
J.WATSON, after J.Reynolds, hl in uniform, mezz, oval, BM, NPG.

HOWARD, George (1773-1848), see 6th Earl of Carlisle.

HOWARD, Gorges Edmond (1715-1786) writer.
UNKNOWN, hs aged 63, line, oval, BM, NPG. UNKNOWN, wl satirical sketch, inscribed 'Candid Appeal by G.E.Howard', line, BM.

HOWARD, Henry (1757-1842) writer.
C.TURNER, after J.A.Oliver, hl, mezz, pub 1839, BM.

HOWARD, Henry (1769-1847) painter.
GEORGE DANCE, hs profile, Royal Academy, London.
A.E.CHALON, 'Students at the British Institution, 1805', pen, ink and w/c, BM.
JOHN FLAXMAN, plaster bust, Sir John Soane's Museum, London.

HOWARD, Henry Charles, see 13th Duke of Norfolk.

HOWARD, John (1726?-1790) prison reformer.
There is no portrait definitely taken from life. MATHER BROWN, hl seated, NPG 97. DAVID MARTIN, hs, Dean Orphanage, Edinburgh.
THOMAS HOLLOWAY, hl profile, chalk, BM.
JOHN BACON, statue, St Paul's Cathedral.
T.PRATTENT, hs profile, line, oval, for *European Mag*, 1786, BM, NPG. UNKNOWN, after M.Davis, hs in circular medallion, line, pub 1787, BM. T.COOK, after M.Brown, hl seated, line, oval, pub 1790, BM, NPG.

HOWARD, Kenneth Alexander, see 1st Earl of Effingham.

HOWARD, Ralph, see 1st Baron Clonmore.

HOWARD DE WALDEN, John Griffin (Whitwell), 4th Baron (1719-1797) field marshal.
SIR BENJAMIN WEST, *c*1772, wl seated in uniform, DoE (Audley End, Essex). BIAGIO REBECCA, wl in Bath robes, Audley End.

HOWDEN, Sir John Francis Caradoc, 1st Baron (1762-1839) general.
M.STEWART, after Sir T.Lawrence, hs, Government House, Cape Town.
W.SAY, after T.Lawrence, tql in uniform, mezz, pub 1805, BM.

HOWE, James (1780-1836) animal painter.
THOMAS SWORD GOOD, SNPG 1828.
Self-portrait, pencil, SNPG 2171.

HOWE, John (1754-1804), see 4th Baron Chedworth.

HOWE, Richard Howe, 1st Earl (1725-1799) admiral.
HENRY SINGLETON, wl, NPG 75. MATHER BROWN, 1794, wl, NMM, Greenwich. JOHN SINGLETON COPLEY, 1794, hl, NMM. GAINSBOROUGH DUPONT, wl, Trinity House, London.
JOHN FLAXMAN, wax relief, NPG 3313. JOHN FLAXMAN, statue on monument, St Paul's Cathedral, London. JOHN DE VAERE,

Wedgwood medallion, BM.

HOWE, Sir William Howe, 5th Viscount (1729-1814) general.
PR 'CORBUTT', tql, mezz, pub 1777, BM, NPG.

HOWICK, Charles Grey, Viscount, see 2nd Earl Grey.

HOWITT, Mary, née Botham (1799-1888) writer.
M MARGARET GILLIES, wl with her husband William, Castle Art Gallery, Nottingham.
PR J.B.HUNT, after T.J.Hughes, hs, stipple, pub 1852, BM, NPG. ALFRED HARRAL, after Margaret Gillies, tql, woodcut, NPG.

HOWITT, William (1792-1879) author.
P After THOMAS HEAPHY, hl, Castle Art Gallery, Nottingham.
M MARGARET GILLIES, wl with his wife Mary, Castle Art Gallery, Nottingham.
PR UNKNOWN, hs, woodcut, for *Illust London News*, 1879, NPG.

HOWLEY, William (1766-1848) archbishop of Canterbury.
P WILLIAM OWEN, 1813, tql, NPG 1552. SIR THOMAS LAWRENCE, 1816, tql, Winchester College. W.OWEN, RA 1818, hl, Fulham Palace, London. M.A.SHEE, tql seated, Lambeth Palace, London.
D S.F.DIEZ, 1841, pencil and ink, SNPG 1784.
G SIR GEORGE HAYTER, 'The House of Commons, 1833', oil, NPG 54.
SC SIR FRANCIS CHANTREY, 1821, marble bust, Canterbury Cathedral. RICHARD WESTMACOTT jun, 1848, recumbent effigy, Canterbury Cathedral.
C JOHN DOYLE, two sketches, one wl seated, pen and pencil, one in 'a scene from Henry IV', pen and pencil, BM.

HUDDART, Joseph (1741-1816) hydrographer and manufacturer.
P After JOHN HOPPNER, hl, Royal Institution of South Wales, Swansea.
G J.F.SKILL, J.GILBERT, W. and E.WALKER, 'Men of Science Living in 1807-08', pencil and wash, NPG 1075.
PR J.STOW, after J.Hoppner, tql seated with compasses, line, pub 1801, BM, NPG.

HUDDESFORD, George (1749-1809) artist and satirist.
P SIR JOSHUA REYNOLDS, 1777-79, tql with J.C.W.Bamfylde, TATE 754.
G Attrib JOHN MILLER, small wl as Sancho Panza in a landscape scene from *Don Quixote*, Trinity College, Oxford.

HUDSON, Thomas (1701-1779) portrait-painter.
D JONATHAN RICHARDSON, head, chalk, BM.

HUGFORD, Ignazio Enrico (1703-1778) painter and art critic at Florence.
P Self-portrait, hl, Uffizi Gallery, Florence.
D GIOVANNI FRATELLINI, head, chalk, BM.

HUGHES, Sir Edward (1720?-1794) admiral.
P SIR JOSHUA REYNOLDS, 1786-87, wl with Bath ribbon and star, NMM, Greenwich; variant hs version, Museum of Fine Arts, Budapest. Attrib WILLIAM BEECHEY, tql with cannon, National Art Gallery, Wellington, New Zealand. Attrib GILBERT STUART, tql with Bath ribbon and star, John Herron Art Museum, Indianapolis, Indiana, USA.
D A Madras artist, *c*1783, gouache, India Office Library and Records, London.

HUGHES, Edward Hughes Ball (*d*1863) gamester, known as 'Golden Ball'.
D COUNT ALFRED D'ORSAY, hl, pencil and chalk, NPG 4026 (36). G.CRUIKSHANK, drumming on his money bags, pencil, BM.
C RICHARD DIGHTON, wl, 'The Golden Ball', coloured etch, pub 1819, NPG.

HUGHES, Thomas Smart (1786-1847) writer.
D G.R.LEWIS, 1822, pencil, V & A.

HUISH, Robert (1777-1850) biographer.
PR R.PAGE, after R.Drummond, hl seated, stipple, pub 1820, BM, NPG. BRAIN, after D.Wilkie, hs, stipple, pub 1842, NPG.

HULL, Thomas (1728-1808) actor and playwright.
P J.GRAHAM, tql seated, Garrick Club, London. SAMUEL DE WILDE, wl as Jarvis in *The Gamester*, Garrick Club. UNKNOWN, hl seated, with bust of Shenstone, NPG 4625.
D GEORGE DANCE, 1799, hl, profile, pencil, NPG 3899.
G MATHER BROWN, in a scene from *The Gamester*, oil, RA 1787, Garrick Club.
PR Several theatrical prints, BM, NPG.

HULLMANDEL, Charles Joseph (1789-1850) lithographic printer.
PR G.B.BLACK, hl, lith, BM.

HULME, Nathaniel (1732-1807) physician.
G N.BRANWHITE, after S.Medley, 'Institutors of the Medical Society of London', stipple, pub 1801, BM.
PR UNKNOWN, hs, silhouette profile, stipple, BM.

HULSE, Sir Samuel, 3rd Bart (1747-1837) field-marshal.
P THOMAS HUDSON, wl with his brother Edward as children, Breamore House, Hants. SAMUEL LANE, hl, Breamore House, engr R.J.Lane, lith, BM, NPG.

HUME, Sir Abraham, 2nd Bart (1749-1838) connoisseur.
P SIR JOSHUA REYNOLDS, c1783, replica, hl, TATE 305.
G P.C.WONDER, 'Patrons and Lovers of Art, 1826', study for a large group, NPG 793.
PR J.JENKINS, after H.Edridge, tql seated, when old, stipple, for Jerdan's *Nat Portrait Gallery*, 1830, BM, NPG.
C THOMAS PATCH, 1769, wl, pen, Uffizi Gallery, Florence.

HUME, David (1711-1776) philosopher.
P ALLAN RAMSAY, 1766, hl, SNPG 1057.
D CHARLES NICOLAS COCHIN, 1754, hs, pencil and estampe, Fogg Art Museum, Harvard University, Cambridge, Mass, USA. LOUIS CARROGIS or DE CARMONTELLE, wl seated, pencil, chalk and w/c, SNPG 2238. LADY ABERCROMBY, hl, w/c, (posthumous), Edinburgh University.
SC JAMES TASSIE, paste medallion, SNPG 1196. J.TASSIE, glass paste medallion, NPG 4897.

HUME, David (1757-1838) judge.
P SIR HENRY RAEBURN, c1822, tql seated, Faculty of Advocates, Parliament Hall, Edinburgh.
SC SIR FRANCIS CHANTREY, 1832, marble bust, Faculty of Advocates.

HUME, Hugh (1708-1794), see 3rd Earl of Marchmont.

HUME, Joseph (1777-1855) radical politician.
P JOHN WHITEHEAD WALTON, 1854, wl, NPG 713. JOHN LUCAS, 1854, wl, University College, London. CHARLES LUCY, 1868, V & A. SIR JOHN GRAHAM GILBERT, tql, SNPG 698.
D C.B.LEIGHTON, 1849-50, hl, chalk, NPG 1098.
G F.BROMLEY, after B.R.Haydon, 'The Reform Banquet', etch, pub 1835, NPG. SIR GEORGE HAYTER, 'The House of Commons, 1833', oil, NPG 54.
SC JOSEPH BONOMI, c1822, bust, New York Historical Society, USA. A.H.RITCHIE, c1830, marble bust, Palace of Westminster, London.
C JOHN DOYLE, 1837, 'Political Sketches, no 490', lith, BM. J.DOYLE, 'The Financial Bobadil', pencil, 1849, BM. J.DOYLE, 1851, wl, equestrian, chalk, BM.

HUMPHREY, William (1740?-1810?) engraver.

PR C.H.HODGES, after C.Imhoff, hs profile, mezz, oval, pub 180 BM, NPG.

HUMPHRY, Ozias (1742-1810) portrait-painter.
P GILBERT STUART, hs, oval, Wadsworth Athenaeum, Hartfor Conn, USA.
D Self-portrait, c1770, head, chalk, BM. HENRY EDRIDGE, 1802, I pencil sketch, BM. GEORGE DANCE, hs profile, Royal Academ London.
G HENRY SINGLETON, 'Royal Academicians, 1793', oil, Roy Academy.
PR D.P.PARISET, after P.Falconet of 1768, hs profile, stipple, ov BM, NPG. V.GREEN, after G.Romney, hl, mezz, pub 1772, B NPG.

HUNT, Henry (1773-1835) radical politician and demagog
D ADAM BUCK, hl, w/c, NPG 956. A.BUCK, wl seated, w/c, N 957.
G H.ROBINSON, 'Political Reformers', stipple, pub 1820, BM.
PR J.KENNERLEY, after T.Clater, wl, St Paul's in the backgroun stipple, pub 1819, BM. UNKNOWN, hl, stipple, pub 1819, B

HUNT, James Henry Leigh (1784-1859) poet and essayi
P UNKNOWN, Christ's Hospital, Horsham, Sussex. SAMU LAWRENCE, 1837, tql seated, NPG 2508. B.R.HAYDON, hl, h 293.
D T.C.WAGEMAN, 1815, tql, pencil, NPG 4505. DANIEL MACLI wl seated, pencil, V & A.
M MARGARET GILLIES, tql, NPG 1267.
SC JOSEPH DURHAM, 1869, bust, Chelsea Town Hall, London.
PR S.FREEMAN, after J.Jackson, hl seated, stipple, BM, NI H.MEYER, after J.Hayter, hl, stipple, for his *Byron and Contemporaries*, 1828, BM, NPG. DANIEL MACLISE, wl lith, NI

HUNT, William Henry (1790-1864) painter.
P Self-portrait, hs, NPG 768.
D There are several self-portraits: hs, w/c, NPG 2636; wl, w/c, La Lever Art Gallery, Port Sunlight; head, w/c, BM; with I daughter and niece, w/c, V & A. J.G.P.FISCHER, hs, pencil, B
SC ALEXANDER MUNRO, bust, Royal Society of Painters in Wate Colours, London.
PH CUNDALL & DOWNES, tql seated, carte, NPG. W.JEFFREY, seated, carte, NPG.

HUNTER, Alexander (1729-1809) physician and writer.
PR J.R.SMITH, tql seated, mezz, pub 1805, BM.

HUNTER, Andrew (1743-1809) professor of divinity Edinburgh University.
SC After JAMES TASSIE, 1791, plaster medallion, SNPG 462.
PR DAWE & HODGETTS, after H.Raeburn, hl, mezz, pub 1810, B
C J.KAY, wl, etch, 1785, BM, NPG. J.KAY, wl, etch, 1789, NI J.KAY, 'The Five Alls', etch, BM.

HUNTER, Sir Claudius Stephen, 1st Bart (1775-1851) mayor of London.
P SIR WILLIAM BEECHEY, wl, Merchant Taylors' Hall, Londo
PR T.BLOOD, after S.Drummond, hl, stipple, for *European M* 1812, BM, NPG.

HUNTER, Henry (1741-1802) divine and author.
SC After JAMES TASSIE, 1795, plaster medallion, SNPG 382.
PR W.PLATT, after A.Buck, hs, stipple, for *Gospel Mag*, 1799, NI T.TROTTER, hs, line, oval, BM, NPG. HOLLOWAY, after Stevens hs, line, oval, BM.

HUNTER, John (1728-1793) surgeon and anatomist.
P SIR JOSHUA REYNOLDS, 1786, tql seated, Royal College Surgeons, London; copy by John Jackson, NPG 77. ROBE HOME, tql seated, Royal College of Surgeons. UNKNOWN, Royal College of Surgeons.

Attrib GEORGE DANCE, 1793, hl profile, pencil, Royal College of Surgeons.
Bronze and plaster casts of life mask, c1785, NPG 4288 and 1712. JOHN FLAXMAN, c1800–05, marble bust, Royal College of Surgeons. SIR FRANCIS CHANTREY, 1820, marble bust, Royal College of Surgeons. HENRY WEEKES, 1864, statue based on the Reynolds portrait, Royal College of Surgeons.

HUNTER, John (1738-1821) vice-admiral, Governor of New South Wales.
W.M.BENNETT, 1815, hl, Public Library of New South Wales, Sydney, Australia.
D.ORME, after R.Dighton, tql seated, stipple, for *Journal of Transactions at Port Jackson and Norfolk Island*, 1792, BM, NPG. RIDLEY, after an unknown artist, hs, stipple, oval, pub 1801, NPG.

HUNTER, John (1745-1837) classical scholar.
SIR JOHN WATSON-GORDON, University of St Andrews, Scotland.
JOHN BROWN, hs, pencil, SNPG 218.

HUNTER, Joseph (1783-1861) antiquary.
HENRY SMITH, 1852, tql seated, Society of Antiquaries, London. H.MEYER, after S.Catterson Smith, tql seated with scroll, stipple, NPG.

HUNTER, Samuel (1769-1839) editor of the 'Glasgow Herald'.
SIR DANIEL MACNEE, University of Glasgow.

HUNTER, William (1718-1783) anatomist.
After ALLAN RAMSAY, late 1750s, tql, Hunterian Museum, University of Glasgow; version, Royal College of Physicians, London. MASON CHAMBERLIN, 1763–69, tql, Royal Academy, London. Attrib JAMES BARRY, c1784, hl, Royal College of Physicians. R.E.PINE, tql seated, Royal College of Surgeons, London. SIR JOSHUA REYNOLDS, 1788–89, tql, (posthumous), Hunterian Museum.
CHARLES GRIGNION jun, head, Hunterian Museum.
Attrib RICHARD CROSSE, hs, oval, Royal College of Physicians. UNKNOWN, wl, wash, Royal College of Surgeons.
JOHAN ZOFFANY, 'Royal Academicians, 1772', oil, Royal Coll. JOHAN ZOFFANY, Hunter lecturing the Royal Academy, oil, c1775, Royal College of Physicians. JAMES BARRY, 'The Society for the Encouragement of Arts', oil, Royal Society of Arts, London.
THOMAS ROWLANDSON, Hunter's dissecting room, etch, Royal College of Surgeons.

HUNTINGDON, Hans Francis Hastings, 11th Earl of (1779-1828) sailor.
C.WARREN, after W.S.Lethbridge, hs, line, pub 1820, NPG.

HUNTINGDON, Selina Hastings, Countess of (1707-1791) friend and benefactor of Methodist movement.
UNKNOWN, c1728, hl, Walters Art Gallery, Baltimore, USA. Attrib JOSEPH HIGHMORE, tql, Worcester Art Gallery, Mass, USA. UNKNOWN, hl seated, as an old woman, NPG 4224.
J.CROSS, after F.Hurlstone, tql seated, stipple, pub 1824, BM, NPG. UNKNOWN, after J.Russell, wl beside cavern, holding crown of thorns, her foot on coronet, mezz, BM, NPG.

HUNTINGDON, or Huntington, William (1745-1813) coal-heaver and preacher.
DOMENICO PELLEGRINI, 1803, tql seated, NPG 141.
UNKNOWN, bust, V & A.
J.BORGNIS, tql seated, stipple, oval, pub 1791, BM, NPG. T.OVERTON, tql seated, stipple, pub 1814, BM, NPG.
THOMAS ROWLANDSON, hs, 'Pie-Us Ecstacy or Godliness (the Itinerant Preachers) Great Gain', coloured etch, pub 1825, NPG.

HUNTINGFORD, George Isaac (1748-1832) bishop of Hereford.
P SIR THOMAS LAWRENCE, RA 1805, tql seated, Winchester College, Hants.

HUNTLY, George Gordon, 9th Marquess of (1761-1853) lieutenant-colonel.
P JOHN PONSFORD, 1842, hl with Thistle star and tartan, Lennoxlove, Lothian region, Scotland.
G SIR GEORGE HAYTER, 'The Trial of Queen Caroline, 1820', oil NPG 999.
PR C.TURNER, after J.Hollins, wl in robes of order of the Thistle, mezz, pub 1837, BM.

HUQUIER, James Gabriel (1725-1805) portrait-painter and engraver.
D JEAN BAPTISTE PERRONEAU, 1747, hl, pastel, Louvre, Paris. JOHN GREENWOOD, hs, pencil, BM.

HURD, Richard (1720-1808) bishop of Worcester.
P THOMAS GAINSBOROUGH, RA 1781, hs, Royal Coll. T.GAINSBOROUGH, c1788, hs, Emmanuel College, Cambridge.
D WILLIAM HOARE, hs, Hartlebury Castle, Worcs.
SC ISAAC GOSSET, 1778, wax medallion, Hartlebury Castle.

HUSKISSON, William (1770-1830) statesman.
P SIR THOMAS LAWRENCE, 1829, hl, Harewood House, W.Yorks. RICHARD ROTHWELL, hl seated, NPG 21.
SC SAMUEL JOSEPH, 1831, marble bust, Petworth (NT), W.Sussex. JOHN EDWARD CAREW, 1832, statue, Chichester Cathedral. JOHN GIBSON, c1836, marble statue, Pimlico Gardens, London. J.GIBSON, 1847, statue, Custom House, Liverpool. WILLIAM SPENCE, relief bust, in profile, on marble roundel, Athenaeum Library, Liverpool.
PR W.J.WARD, after J.Graham, tql, mezz, pub 1831, BM, NPG.
C JOHN DOYLE, wl, pencil, BM.

HUSSEY, Giles (1710-1788) portrait-painter.
P Self-portrait, tql, Syon House, Middx.
PR UNKNOWN, after G.Hussey, head, profile, stipple, for Hutchins's *Hist of Dorset*, BM, NPG.

HUSSEY, Thomas (1741-1803) Roman catholic bishop of Waterford and Lismore.
P UNKNOWN, hl seated with architectural plans, St Patrick's College, Maynooth.
PR W.HINCKS, after T.Collopy, hl, stipple, pub 1783, BM, NPG. S.W.REYNOLDS, after C.F. de Breda, tql before an altar, mezz, pub 1796, BM.

HUTCHINSON, Christopher Hely- (1767-1826), see HELY-Hutchinson.

HUTCHINSON, John Hely- (1724-1794), see HELY-Hutchinson.

HUTCHINSON, John Hely-Hutchinson, Baron, see 2nd Earl of Donoughmore.

HUTCHINSON, Richard Hely-, see 1st Earl of Donoughmore.

HUTCHINSON, William (1732-1814) antiquary.
PR J.COLLYER, after J.Hay, tql seated with George Allan, line, for Nichols's *Literary Anecdotes*, vol ix, 1814, BM, NPG.

HUTT, John (1746-1794) captain in the navy.
G BARTOLOZZI, LANDSEER, RYDER & STOW, after R.Smirke, 'Naval Victories', 'Commemoration of the victory of June 1st 1794', line, pub 1803, BM, NPG.
SC JOHN BACON jun, 1804, medallion on monument, Westminster Abbey, London.

HUTTON, Catherine (1756-1846) writer.

PR J.W.COOK, hl in turban, aged 43, stipple, BM, NPG. W.READ, hl, stipple, for *La Belle Assemblée*, 1824, BM, NPG. T.WOOLNOTH, after T.Wageman, hl seated, stipple, pub 1825, NPG. T.W.COOK, after F.Lines, tql aged 83, stipple, BM, NPG.

HUTTON, Charles (1737-1823) mathematician.

PR C.TURNER, after H.Ashby, hl seated, aged 75, for his *Tracts on Mathematical and Philosophical Subjects*, 1812, BM, NPG. J.THOMSON, after S.Gahagan, from a bust, stipple, for *European Mag*, 1823, BM, NPG. UNKNOWN, after a medal by Wyon, stipple, pub 1823, BM.

HUTTON, James (1715-1795) secretary of the Moravian Society.

PR J.R.SMITH, after R.Cosway, tql seated, mezz, pub 1786, BM.

HUTTON, James (1726-1797) geologist.

D UNKNOWN, wash, SNPG 115.

SC JAMES TASSIE, 1792, paste medallion, SNPG. PATRIC PARK, bust, Geological Museum, London.

C J.KAY, hl with Dr J.Black, entitled 'Philosophers', etch, BM, NPG.

J.KAY, wl with hammer, etch, BM, NPG. J.KAY, 'Conversation-Demonstration', etch, BM, NPG.

HUTTON, William (1723-1815) topographer.

PR J.BASIRE, hs, line, oval, pub 1804, BM.

HYATT, John (1767-1826) minister of the London Tabernacle.

PR FREEMAN, after an unknown artist, hs, stipple, NPG.

HYDE, Catherine, see Duchess of Queensberry.

HYDE, Henry, Baron (1710-1753), see Viscount Cornbury

HYDE, Thomas Villiers, 1st Baron, see 1st Earl of Clarendon.

HYNDFORD, John Carmichael, 3rd Earl of (1701-1767 diplomat.

P JONATHAN RICHARDSON, 1726, wl, DoE (British Embassy Vienna). J.RICHARDSON, 1726, SNPG 1556. Attrib COSM ALEXANDER, hs with Thistle star, DoE (British Embassy Stockholm).

I

IBBETSON, Bella, née Thompson (1783?-1817) second wife of Julius Caesar Ibbetson.
P JULIUS CAESAR IBBETSON, 1803, tql, NPG L152 (6).
G JULIUS CAESAR IBBETSON, 'The Painter's Family at Masham', oil, 1809, Leeds City Art Gallery, Temple Newsam House, W.Yorks.

IBBETSON, Julius Caesar (1759-1817) painter.
P GEORGE CUITT, c1777, hs, Leeds City Art Gallery. Self-portrait, 1804, wl seated, NPG L152 (5).
D J.R.SMITH, 1805, hs, pastel, Leeds City Art Gallery, Temple Newsam House, W.Yorks.
R R.COOPER, after J.R.Smith, hl seated with crayon, line and stipple, for his *Accidence of Painting in Oil*, 1828, BM, NPG.

IMPEY, Sir Elijah (1732-1809) chief justice of Bengal.
P TILLY KETTLE, 1775, wl in robes, High Court of Calcutta, Calcutta, India. JOHAN ZOFFANY, 1783, wl, High Court of Calcutta. J.ZOFFANY, tql seated, NPG 335.
D SIR THOMAS LAWRENCE, 1786, hl seated, pastel, NPG 821.

INCHBALD, Elizabeth (1753-1821) actress and author.
P SAMUEL DE WILDE, wl as Lady Jane Grey, Garrick Club, London.
D GEORGE DANCE, 1794, hl profile, seated, NPG 1144. G.H.HARLOW, 1814, hl, pencil and sanguine, Garrick Club.
R S.FREEMAN, after T.Lawrence, hl, stipple, for *Monthly Mirror*, 1807, BM. Several theatrical prints, BM, NPG.

INCLEDON, Charles (1763-1826) singer.
P Attrib M.A.SHEE, c1815, hl, Royal College of Music, London.
D GEORGE DANCE, 1798, hl, pencil, NPG 1145. SAMUEL DE WILDE, wl as Captain Macheath in *The Beggar's Opera*, w/c, Garrick Club, London.
M After J.T.BARBER-BEAUMONT, hs singing 'The Storm', in *Ella Rosenberg*, oval, Garrick Club.
SL UNKNOWN, Garrick Club.
R Several theatrical and other prints, BM.

INGENHOUSZ, Jan (1730-1799) Dutch physician and physicist.
C UNKNOWN, Wedgwood medallion, Wedgwood Museum, Barlaston, Staffs.

INGHAM, Benjamin (1712-1772) Yorkshire evangelist.
R FREEMAN, hs, stipple, BM.

INGHAM, Charles Cromwell (1796-1863) portrait painter.
P Self-portrait, c1840-50, hs, National Academy of Design, New York, USA.

INGLEFIELD, John Nicholson (1748-1828) navy captain.
R B.SMITH, after G.Engleheart, hs, stipple, oval, pub 1815, BM.

INGLIS, Charles (c1731-1791) rear-admiral.
P SIR HENRY RAEBURN, c1790-91, tql, SNPG 1567.

INGLIS, Charles (1734-1816) first bishop of Nova Scotia.
P ROBERT FIELD, 1810, hl, NPG 1023.

INGLIS, John (1762-1834) Scottish divine.
P UNKNOWN, hl, SNPG 215.
SL AUGUSTIN EDOUART, 1830, wl, SNPG 2154. A.EDOUART, SNPG 832.

PR T.HODGETTS, after J.Syme, tql, mezz, NPG.

INGLIS, Sir Robert Harry, 2nd Bart (1786-1855) Tory politician.
P SIR GEORGE HAYTER, 1833-43, hs profile, study for NPG 54, NPG 4968. GEORGE RICHMOND, 1854, wl, Examination Schools, Oxford.
D Three drgs by GEORGE RICHMOND: 1836, hl, w/c, Ashmolean Museum, Oxford; c1837, tql, w/c, Castle Museum and Art Gallery, Nottingham; 1845, head, chalk, NPG 1062.
G SIR GEORGE HAYTER, 'The House of Commons, 1833', oil, NPG 54. JOHN PARTRIDGE, 'The Fine Arts Commissioners, 1846', NPG 342, 3.
PR F.C.LEWIS, after J.Slater, hs, stipple, one of 'Grillion's Club' series, BM, NPG. F.HOLL, after C.W.Cope, hs, stipple, NPG.
C Several JOHN DOYLE, drgs, BM.

INGRAM, James (1774-1850) Anglo-Saxon scholar.
P STEPHEN HEWSON, 1803, hs, oval, Trinity College, Oxford. T.C.THOMPSON, hl, Trinity College, Oxford.

INNES, Cosmo (1798-1874) antiquary.
SL AUGUSTIN EDOUART, SNPG 780.

INNES-KER, James, see 5th Duke of Roxburgh(e).

INSKIPP, James (1790-1868) painter.
PH UNKNOWN, tql, carte, NPG Album of Artists vol 1.

IRELAND, John (d1808) biographer of Hogarth.
P JOHN HAMILTON MORTIMER, called Ireland, wl with a boy, Yale Center for British Art, New Haven, USA.
D RICHARD WESTALL, tql seated, profile, w/c over pencil, BM.
G JOHN HAMILTON MORTIMER, probably represented in caricature group, oil, c1760-70, Yale Center for British Art.
PR W.SKELTON, after J.H.Mortimer, hl, line, for his *Hogarth Illustrated*, 1791, BM, NPG. I.MILLS, after J.R.Smith, hl seated, an old man, line, pub 1834, BM, NPG.

IRELAND, John (1761-1842) dean of Westminster.
D SIR FRANCIS CHANTREY, hs and hs profile, sketch, pencil, NPG 316a (72).
SC SIR FRANCIS CHANTREY, bust, Bodleian Library, Oxford. JOHN TERNOUTH, bust, Westminster Abbey, London.
PR S.W.REYNOLDS and W.BOND, after F.Stephanoff, wl in coronation robes, mezz, for Nayler's *Coronation of George IV*, 1824, BM.

IRELAND, Samuel (d1800) writer and engraver.
D H.D.HAMILTON, 1776, hl, chalk, NPG 4302.

IRELAND, William Henry (1777-1835) forger of Shakespeare manuscripts.
PR S.HARDING, hl profile, aged 21, stipple, BM, NPG. MACKENZIE, hs, stipple, oval, BM.

IRVING, Edward (1792-1834) Scottish minister.
P JOHN ALLAN, SNPG 868. SIR DAVID WILKIE, hs, City Art Gallery, Auckland, New Zealand. UNKNOWN, SNPG 820.
D JAMES ATKINSON, 1825, hl, pencil and ink, SNPG 360. JOSEPH SLATER, head, pencil, NPG 424. SIR DAVID WILKIE, hl, and head, pen and ink, BM. UNKNOWN, wl, w/c, NPG 2757.
SC HAMILTON W.MCCARTHY, 1867, marble bust, SNPG 1035. UNKNOWN, wax relief, hs, NPG 1689.

PR Various engravings and popular prints, BM, NPG.

IRWIN, Eyles (1751?-1817) poet.

PR J.WALKER, after G.Romney, hl, mezz, pub 1780, BM.

ISAACSON, Stephen (1798-1849) writer.

PR UNKNOWN, hl, lith, 1852, NPG.

IVES, John (1751-1776) Suffolk herald extraordinary.

PR P.AUDINET, after F.Perry, hs, line, for Nichols's *Literary Anecdotes*, 1818, BM, NPG. P.S.LAMBORN, after J.S., hl, etch, BM pub 1822, NPG.

IVIMEY, Joseph (1773-1834) author of history of English baptists.

PR PENNY, after J.Linnell, hl, mezz, pub 1820, NPG.

J

JACKSON, Cyril (1746-1819) dean of Christ Church.
P WILLIAM OWEN, 1810, tql seated, Christ Church, Oxford.
C SIR FRANCIS CHANTREY, RA 1824, statue, Christ Church, Oxford.
C R.DIGHTON, wl with James Webber, coloured etch, pub 1807, NPG.

JACKSON, Francis James (1770-1814) diplomatist.
D JAMES SHARPLES, 1810, pastel, Bristol City Art Gallery.

JACKSON, John (1769-1845) pugilist, 'Gentleman Jackson'.
G UNKNOWN, the fight between Jackson and Mendoza at Hornchurch 1795, oil, Brodick Castle (NT), Strathclyde region, Scotland.
C T.BUTLER, medallion on monument, Brompton Cemetery, London.
R C.TURNER, after B.Marshall, wl, mezz, pub 1810, BM, NPG. UNKNOWN, hs, stipple, pub 1823, NPG. I.R.CRUIKSHANK, aquatint and w/c, V & A.

JACKSON, John (1778-1831) portrait-painter.
P Several self-portraits, 1808, hs, Scarborough Art Gallery, N.Yorks; 1810, V & A; c1815, Ferens Art Gallery, Hull; c1820-25, Castle Howard, N.Yorks; c1826-31, hl with palette, NPG 443.
D Self-portrait, tql seated with palette, w/c, Yale Center for British Art, New Haven, USA.
M MRS MARY BREWER, 1830, hs, V & A.

JACKSON, Joseph (1733-1792) type-founder.
R UNKNOWN, hl, line, oval, for Nichols's *Literary Anecdotes*, vol II, BM.

JACKSON, Randle (1757-1837) barrister.
R J.THOMSON, after S.Drummond, hl, stipple, for *European Mag*, 1820, BM, NPG.

JACKSON, Samuel (1786-1861) president of Wesleyan conference.
R J.COCHRAN, after W.Gush, hs, stipple, NPG.

JACKSON, William (1730-1803) musical composer.
P THOMAS GAINSBOROUGH, (probably the sitter), tql with harp, Exeter City Museum and Art Gallery.
R UNKNOWN, after J.Downman, hl, mezz, oval, pub 1785, BM. J.WALKER, after an unknown artist, hs, aquatint, pub 1819, NPG.

JACKSON, William (1737?-1795) Irish revolutionist.
G UNKNOWN, 'The United Irish Patriots of 1798', coloured lith, NPG.

JACKSON, William (1751-1815) bishop of Oxford.
P WILLIAM OWEN, tql seated, Christ Church, Oxford, engr S.W.Reynolds, mezz, pub 1818, BM, NPG.

JACOB, Arthur (1790-1874) oculist.
P S.CATTERSON SMITH, exhib 1867, Royal College of Surgeons, Dublin.

JACOB, Edward (1710?-1788) surgeon and antiquary.
R C.HALL, hs, profile, line, oval, for his *Plantae Favershamienses*, 1777, BM.

JACOB, William (1762?-1851) statistical writer and traveller.
R M.GAUCI, after E.U.Eddis, wl seated, aged 86, lith, BM.

JACOBSEN, Theodore (d1772) architect.
P WILLIAM HOGARTH, 1742, hl with plans, Allen Memorial Art Museum, Oberlin College, Ohio, USA. THOMAS HUDSON, wl with architectural plan of the Foundling Hospital, Thomas Coram Foundation for Children, London.

JAMES, Charles (d1821) poet and military writer.
PR J.S.AGAR, after J.Russell, hs, aged 49, stipple, oval, NPG. M.BOVI, after J.Russell, hs, stipple, oval, BM, NPG.

JAMES, George Payne Rainsford (1799-1860) historian and novelist.
P STEPHEN PEARCE, 1846, tql seated, NPG 1259.
PR UNKNOWN, hs, stipple, pub 1839, NPG. J.C.ARMYTAGE, after F.Cruikshank, tql, stipple and line, pub 1847, NPG.

JAMES, John (1729-1785) schoolmaster.
D DANIEL GARDNER, hl, gouache and pastel, oval, Queen's College, Oxford.

JAMES, John Angell (1785-1859) independent minister.
G B.R.HAYDON, 'The Anti-Slavery Society Convention, 1840', oil, NPG 599.
PR W.DERBY, after R.Cooper, tql, stipple, pub 1820, NPG. J.COCHRAN, after H.Room, hl seated, stipple, NPG. D.J.POUND, after a photograph by J.Whitlock, tql seated, stipple, NPG.

JAMES John Haddy (1788-1869) surgeon.
P JAMES LEAKEY, Devon and Exeter Hospital, Exeter.

JAMES, John Thomas (1786-1828) bishop of Calcutta.
P B.R.FAULKNER, RA 1828, hl, Christ Church, Oxford.
PR E.FINDEN, after J.Slater, hs profile, stipple, one of 'Grillion's Club' series, BM, NPG.

JAMES, Thomas (1748-1804) head-master of Rugby School.
SC SIR FRANCIS CHANTREY, 1824, marble statue on monument, Rugby School Chapel, Warwicks.

JAMES, Sir William, 1st Bart (1721-1783) commodore of the Bombay marine.
P SIR JOSHUA REYNOLDS, 1784, hl, after a painting of 1780-82, NMM, Greenwich.

JAMES, William (1771-1837) railway engineer.
PR W.ROLFE, after Chalon, hl, stipple, for *Mechanic's Mag*, 1839, BM.

JAMESON, Anna Brownell (1794-1860) writer.
D CARL VOGEL, 1839, tql, Küpferstichkabinett, Staatliche Kunstsammlungen, Dresden. WILHELM HENSEL, hs, Hensel Album vol XIII, National Gallery, Berlin.
SC JOHN GIBSON, 1862, marble bust, NPG 689.
PR H.ADLARD, after D.B.Murphy of c1810, hs, stipple, for G.MacPherson's *Memoirs of the Life of Anna Jameson*, 1878, NPG. R.J.LANE, after H.P.Briggs of c1835, hl seated, lith, BM, NPG.
PH D.O.HILL, tql, SNPG.

JAMESON, Robert (1774-1854) mineralogist.
P GEORGE WATSON, hl, SNPG 2054.
PR LIZARS, after 'P.M.', hl, etch, for Lockhart's *Peter's Letters to his Kinsfolk*, 1819, BM, NPG. J.JENKINS, after K.Macleary, hl, stipple, for Jerdan's *Nat Portrait Gallery*, 1832, BM, NPG. F.SCHENCK, after W.Stewart, hs, lith, NPG.

JAMIESON, John (1759-1838) philologist.
P WILLIAM YELLOWLEES, hs, SNPG 10.
PR E.MITCHELL, hs, line, oval, for *Theological & Biblical Mag*, 1804, BM, NPG.
C J.KAY, hl, etch, oval, 1799, BM.

JARDINE, James (1776-1858) engineer.
D UNKNOWN, w/c, SNPG 1384.
SC PATRIC PARK, 1842, marble bust, SNPG 1203.

JAY, William (1769-1853) dissenting minister.
P UNKNOWN, hs, NPG 4892.
SC MISS S.E.COVELL, 1812, wax medallion, NPG 1793.
PR R.HANCOCK, after J.Hutchisson, hl, stipple, pub 1799, NPG. J.THOMSON, after W.Etty, tql seated, stipple, for *European Mag*, 1819, BM, NPG. W.HOLL, after R.Evans, hl, stipple, for Jerdan's *Nat Portrait Gallery*, 1836, BM, NPG.

JEACOCKE, Caleb (1706-1786) baker and orator.
P CHARLES CATTON snr, hl, posthumous, St Giles-in-the-Fields, London.

JEBB, John (1736-1786) theological and political writer.
PR C.KNIGHT, hl, stipple, oval, pub 1782, BM, NPG. J.YOUNG, after J.Hoppner, tql seated, pub 1786, BM. J.K.SHERWIN, after J.Flaxman, from a bust, line, oval, for his *Works*, 1787, BM, NPG.

JEBB, John (1775-1833) bishop of Limerick.
D GEORGE RICHMOND, 1832, hl, pencil, NGI 2252.
SC E.H.BAILY, statue, Limerick Cathedral.
PR T.LUPTON, after T.Lawrence, tql seated, aged 51, mezz, BM, NPG. G.ADCOCK, hs, stipple, pub 1834, NPG.

JEBB, Sir Joshua (1793-1863) surveyor-general of convict prisons.
SC PATRICK MACDOWELL, 1865, bust, Bethnal Green Museum, London.

JEBB, Sir Richard, 1st Bart (1729-1787) physician.
P Attrib JOHAN ZOFFANY, hl, Royal College of Physicians, London.

JEFFEREYS, James (1751-1784) historical painter.
P WILLIAM JEFFEREYS, hl with porte crayon, National Book League, on loan to the Maidstone Museum, a w/c copy by an unknown artist is also at the Maidstone Museum.
D Self-portrait, hs, pen and ink, NPG 4669. Self-portrait, hs, back view, pen and ink, Yale Center for British Art, New Haven, USA.

JEFFREY, Francis Jeffrey, Lord (1773-1850) Scottish judge, critic and editor of the *Edinburgh Review*.
P JOHN PAIRMAN, 1823, tql seated, SNPG 280. ANDREW GEDDES, 1826, tql, NPG 1628. COLVIN SMITH, hl, SNPG 569.
D JOHN HENNING, 1806, chalk, SNPG 2043. WILLIAM NICHOLSON, 1816, hl, w/c, Abbotsford House, Borders region, Scotland. WILLIAM BEWICK, hs, chalk, SNPG 667. JOHN LINNELL, hs, pencil, NPG 1815.
G SIR GEORGE HAYTER, 'The House of Commons, 1833', oil, NPG 54.
SC JOHN HENNING, 1801, wax medallion, SNPG 532. SAMUEL JOSEPH, 1822, plaster bust, SNPG 229. SIR JOHN STEELL, 1855, marble statue, Faculty of Advocates, Parliament Hall. PATRIC PARK, marble bust, NPG 133.
C B.W.CROMBIE, pencil and w/c study for *Modern Athenians*, SNPG 2306.

JEHNER, Isaac (1750-1806?) painter and engraver.
PR I.JEHNER, hl seated at easel, mezz, oval, pub 1818, BM.

JEKYLL, Joseph (1753-1837) wit and politician.
D GEORGE DANCE, 1796, hl profile, pencil, NPG 1146.

PR W.SAY, after T.Lawrence, hl, mezz, pub 1818, BM, NPG.
C J.SAYERS, with Lord Lansdowne, etch, 1798, NPG.

JELF, Richard William (1798-1871) principal of King's College, London.
PR T.H.MAGUIRE, tql seated, lith, pub 1850, BM.

JENKINS, Joseph (1743-1819) baptist minister.
PR J.FITTLER, after J.F.Burrell, hl seated, line, oval, pub 1805, BM.

JENKINS, Thomas (1722-1798) painter, art dealer and banker in Rome.
P ANGELICA KAUFFMANN, 1790, wl with his niece Anna Maria, NPG 5044. ANTON MARON, 1791, hs, Accademia di San Luca, Rome.
D RICHARD WILSON, c1753, tql, chalk, Pierpont Morgan Library, New York, USA.

JENKINSON, Charles (1727-1808), see 1st Earl of Liverpool.

JENKINSON, Robert Banks, see 2nd Earl of Liverpool.

JENKYNS, Richard (1782-1854) Balliol College, Oxford.
P H.P.BRIGGS, RA 1841, tql seated, Balliol College, Oxford.
D FRANK CRUICKSHANK, RA 1839, tql seated, w/c, Balliol College.

JENNER, Edward (1749-1823) discoverer of vaccination.
P After J.R.SMITH, 1800, tql, The Johns Hopkins University Library, Baltimore, USA. JAMES NORTHCOTE, 1802, tql, Plymouth Medical Society. SAMUEL MEDLEY, c1802, Medical Society of London. JAMES NORTHCOTE, 1803, tql, NPG 62. SIR THOMAS LAWRENCE, c1809, hl, Royal College of Physicians, London. WILLIAM HOBDAY, 1821, tql, Royal Society of Medicine, London. H.WYATT, 1828, tql, Wellcome Institute, London.
D J.R.SMITH, 1800, tql, pastel, Wellcome Institute, London. Attrib HENRY EDRIDGE, c1821, hl, pencil, Wellcome Institute.
SC R.W.SIEVIER, 1825, memorial statue, Gloucester Cathedral.

JENNER-FUST, Sir Herbert, see Fust.

JENNINGS, Henry Constantine (1731-1819) virtuoso.
G UNKNOWN, 'Portraits from Sketches made at rare print sales', etch, BM.
PR E.DORRALL, hl, etch, oval, pub 1815, BM, NPG. R.COOPER, hl stipple, for *Fifty Wonderful Portraits*, 1821, BM.

JENYNS, Soame (1704-1787) writer and politician.
G JAMES BARRY, 'The Society for the Encouragement of Arts', oil, Royal Society of Arts, London.
PR W.DICKINSON, after J.Reynolds, hl seated, mezz, 1776, BM, NPG.

JEPHSON, Robert (1736-1803) poet and dramatist.
PR J.SINGLETON, after Stoker, hs, stipple, oval, for his *Roman Portraits*, 1794, BM, NPG.

JERDAN, William (1782-1869) journalist.
D DANIEL MACLISE, 1830, wl seated, w/c, NPG 3028, a study for the print in *Fraser's Mag*, 1830, BM, NPG.
PR H.ROBINSON, after G.H.Harlow of 1815, hs, stipple, for *The Autobiography of William Jerdan*, 1852, NPG. T.WOOLNOTH, after J.Moore, hl, stipple, pub 1830, NPG. R.J.LANE, after A. d'Orsay of 1839, hl profile, lith, NPG.

JEREMIE, Sir John (1795-1841) colonial judge.
G B.R.HAYDON, 'The Anti-Slavery Society Convention, 1840' oil, NPG 599.
SC E.H.BAILY, 1846, bust, Sierra Leone Cathedral.

JERMYN, Henry (1767-1820) barrister, Suffolk antiquary.
PR J.GODBY, after Mrs Pulham, hl, stipple, BM.

JERNINGHAM, Edward (1727-1812) poet.
M Attrib ANDREW PLIMER, hs, V & A.
PR P.THOMSON, after M.A.Shee, hl, line, for *European Mag*, 1794

BM, NPG. W.RIDLEY, after S.Drummond, hl, stipple, oval, for *Monthly Mirror*, 1800, BM, NPG.

JERSEY, George Bussy Villiers, 4th Earl of (1735-1805) statesman.

P NATHANIEL DANCE, 1770, tql seated in landscape, Althorp, Northants.

G JOHN SINGLETON COPLEY, 'The Collapse of the Earl of Chatham in the House of Lords, 7 July, 1778', oil, TATE 100, on loan to NPG.

JERSEY, George Child Villiers, 5th Earl of (1773-1859) master of the horse to Queen Victoria.

G SIR G.HAYTER, 'The Trial of Queen Caroline, 1820', oil, NPG 999. SIR G.HAYTER, 'The House of Commons, 1833', oil, NPG 54.

R S.COUSINS, after T.Phillips, tql, mezz, pub 1836, BM, NPG. R.SEYMOUR, wl, lith, for Wildrake's *Cracks of the Day* [1841], BM. UNKNOWN, wl wearing the ancient uniform used at the Queen's Ball, 1842, lith, NPG.

JERVIS, John (1735-1823), see 1st Earl of St Vincent.

JERVIS, Thomas (1748-1833) unitarian minister.

C PATRICK MACDOWELL, plaster bust, Dr Williams's Library, London.

JESSE, Edward (1780-1868) natural historian.

D DANIEL MACDONALD, 1844, hl, chalk and wash, NPG 2453.

C UNKNOWN, marble bust, Brighton Art Gallery.

R B.LEIGHTON, hs aged 71, lith, BM.

JESSOP, William (1745-1814) civil engineer.

P EDWIN WILLIAMS, Institute of Civil Engineers, London.

D GEORGE DANCE, 1796, hl profile, seated, pencil, NPG 1147.

JOCELYN, Robert (1731-1797), see 1st Earl of Roden.

JOCELYN, Robert (1788-1870), see 3rd Earl of Roden.

JODRELL, Richard Paul (1745-1831) classical scholar and dramatist.

P THOMAS GAINSBOROUGH, hl, Frick Coll, New York, USA.

R C.HEATH, after M.Brown, hl, stipple, 1820, BM.

JODRELL, Sir Richard Paul, 2nd Bart (1781-1861) poet.

SL UNKNOWN, wl, NPG.

JOHNES, Thomas (1748-1816) translator of Froissart's *Chronicles*.

SC SIR FRANCIS CHANTREY, c1812, bust, Ashmolean Museum, Oxford.

R F.ENGLEHEART, hs, line, oval, pub 1810, BM, NPG. W.H.WORTHINGTON, after T.Stothard, hs, line, BM. W.N.GARDINER, tql seated, stipple, BM.

JOHNSON, Sir Henry, 1st Bart (1748-1835) general.

R R.DUNKARTON, after R.Woodburn, tql, mezz, BM, NPG. S.SANGSTER, after C.Jagger, hl, line, BM.

JOHNSON, James (1705-1774) bishop of Worcester.

SC JOSEPH NOLLEKENS, 1774, bust, Worcester Cathedral.

JOHNSON, James (1777-1845) physician to William IV.

P JOHN WOOD, c1833, tql seated, Royal College of Physicians, London.

R After T.BRIDGFORD, hs, lith, NPG.

JOHNSON, John (1777-1848) printer.

R W.HARVEY, hl aged 46, woodcut, for vol II of his *Typographia*, 1824, BM.

JOHNSON, Joseph (1738-1809) bookseller and publisher.

R W.SHARP, after M.Haughton, hl seated, line, BM, NPG.

JOHNSON, Samuel (1709-1784) lexicographer and man of letters.

P SIR JOSHUA REYNOLDS, 1756-57, tql seated, NPG 1597. SIR JOSHUA REYNOLDS, c1770, hl profile, Knole (NT), Kent; replica TATE 4506. SIR JOSHUA REYNOLDS, c1778, hl, TATE 887 on loan to NPG (L 142). JAMES BARRY, hs, NPG 1185. After JOHN OPIE, hl, NPG 1302. Attrib FRANCES REYNOLDS, sometimes attrib Theophila Palmer, hs, Trinity College, Oxford.

G JAMES BARRY, 'The Society for the Encouragement of the Arts', oil, Royal Society of Arts, London.

SC JOSEPH NOLLEKENS, c1777, marble bust, Westminster Abbey, London. JOHN FLAXMAN, 1784, Wedgwood medallion, Wedgwood Museum, Barlaston, Staffs. JOHN BACON sen, 1796, marble statue, St Paul's Cathedral, London.

PR T.TROTTER, after J.Harding, hs, etch, pub 1782, BM, NPG. J.HEATH, after J.Opie, hl, line, oval, for his *Dictionary*, 1786, BM, NPG. T.TROTTER, wl in his tavelling dress as described in Boswell's *Tour*, line, pub 1786, BM, NPG. J.HALL, after J.Reynolds, hl reading pamphlet, line, for his *Life*, 1787, BM, NPG. C.TOWNLEY, after J.Opie, hl, mezz, pub 1792, NPG.

C JAMES SAYERS, his ghost appearing to Mrs Piozzi, etch, pub 1788, NPG. THOMAS ROWLANDSON, hl with Boswell, chalk, V & A.

JOHNSON, Sir William, 1st Bart (1715-1774) superintendent of Indian affairs in North America.

PR C.SPOONER, after T.Adams, tql with cannon, mezz, pub 1756, BM. UNKNOWN, tql, line, BM, NPG.

JOHNSTON, Sir Alexander (1775-1849) judge and government reformer in Ceylon.

PR T.WOOLNOTH, after W.M.Craig, hl, stipple, pub 1821, BM, NPG. J.COCHRAN, after T.Phillips, tql in judicial robes, stipple, for Jerdan's *Nat Portrait Gallery*, BM, NPG.

JOHNSTON, David (1734-1824) founder of the Blind Asylum, Edinburgh.

PR G.DAWE, after H.Raeburn, hl, mezz, pub 1825, BM.

C J.KAY, hl, etch, 1814, reprinted in vol I *Kay's Portraits*, 1842, NPG.

JOHNSTON, Francis (1761-1829) architect.

P MARTIN CREGAN, Royal Hibernian Academy, Dublin.

SC THOMAS KIRK, marble bust, Royal Hibernian Academy.

PR H.MEYER, after T.C.Thomson, tql seated, stipple, 1823, BM, NPG.

JOHNSTON, George (1797-1855) naturalist.

PR UNKNOWN, tql, mezz, Royal Botanic Gardens, Kew.

JOHNSTON, Henry Erskine (1777-1830?) actor.

P SIR WILLIAM ALLAN, wl as Young Norval in *Douglas*, Garrick Club. London. HENRY SINGLETON, hs as Douglas, Garrick Club.

PR Various theatrical prints, BM, NPG.

JOHNSTON, James Henry (1787-1851) controller of the East India Company's steamers.

PR E.MORTON, hl, lith, NPG.

JOHNSTONE, George (1730-1787) commodore.

P After JOHN BOYLE of c1768-74, hl, NMM, Greenwich.

JOHNSTONE, James (1754-1783) physician.

PR J.ROSS, after J.Russell, hl seated, stipple, oval, BM.

JOHNSTONE, James Hope, see 3rd Earl of Hopetoun.

JOHNSTONE, John Henry (1749-1828) actor.

P SIR M.A.SHEE, RA 1803, as Sir Callaghan O'Brallaghan in *Love à la Mode*, Garrick Club, London.

D SAMUEL DE WILDE, wl as Major O'Flaherty in *The West Indian*, w/c, Garrick Club. S. DE WILDE, as Dennis Bulgruddery in *John Bull*, w/c, Garrick Club. WILLIAM WELLINGS, wl as O'Whack in *Notoriety*, w/c, Garrick Club.

SL UNKNOWN, Garrick Club.

PR Several theatrical prints, BM, NPG.

JOLLY, Alexander (1756-1838) bishop of Moray.
PR W.H.LIZARS, after J.Moir (1821), hl, stipple and line, pub 1839, NPG, pub 1840, BM.

JONES, David (1735-1810) Welsh revivalist.
PR UNKNOWN, hs, line, oval, for *Gospel Mag*, 1778, BM, NPG.

JONES, George (1786-1869) painter.
D C.H.LEAR, *c*1845, hs, pencil, NPG 1456(14).
SC HENRY WEEKES, 1870, bust, Royal Academy, London.
PH JOHN and CHARLES WATKINS, hs, carte, NPG Album of Artists vol 1.

JONES, Sir Harry David (1791-1866) lieutenant-general.
P E.U.EDDIS, tql, Royal Engineers, Gordon Barracks, Chatham, Kent.

JONES, John (1745?-1797) engraver.
G UNKNOWN, after P.Sandby, 'Sketches taken at Print Sales', line, pub 1798, BM.

JONES, John (1796-1857) Welsh preacher.
PR T.W.HUNT, after E.Williams, hl, stipple, pub 1848, BM.

JONES, John Gale (1769-1838) democratic politician.
PR UNKNOWN, hl, mezz, oval, pub 1798, BM, NPG.

JONES, John Paul (1747-1792) seaman adventurer.
D MOREAU LE JEUNE, hs, pastel, Louisiana State Museum, USA. UNKNOWN, hl, gouache, commemorates Louis XVI's award to Jones of the order of military merit, Pierpont Morgan Library, New York, USA.
SC AUGUSTIN DUPRÉ, 1779, bronze medal, Bibliothèque Nationale, Paris, and copper medal, SNPG 758. JEAN ANTOINE HOUDON, 1780, plaster bust, Boston Museum of Fine Arts, USA; copy SNPG 669. Attrib JEAN MARTIN RENAUD, wax medallion, SNPG L104.
PR UNKNOWN, wl on board the *Seraphis*, etch, oval, pub 1779, BM. J.CHAPMAN, hl, stipple, oval, pub 1796, NPG. C.GUTTENBERG, after C.J.Notté, tql on board ship in a battle, line, BM.

JONES, Sir John Thomas, 1st Bart (1783-1843) major-general.
P UNKNOWN, tql, Royal Engineers, Gordon Barracks, Chatham, Kent.
SC WILLIAM BEHNES, statue, St Paul's Cathedral, London.

JONES, Leslie Grove (1779-1839) political reformer.
PR PHILLIPS, after A.Wivell, head, stipple, for *Union Monthly Mag*, 1832, BM, NPG. M.GAUCI, after S.M.Smith, hl, lith, pub 1833, BM, NPG.

JONES, Sir Lewis Tobias (1797-1895) admiral.
PR UNKNOWN, hl, process block, for *Illust London News*, 1895, BM.

JONES, Owen (1741-1814) Welsh antiquary.
PR UNKNOWN, hs, lith, pub 1828, NPG.

JONES, Richard (1779-1851) actor and dramatist.
P BENJAMIN BURNELL, hs, Garrick Club, London. UNKNOWN, hs, Garrick Club.
D SAMUEL DE WILDE, 1813, as Young Contrast in *The Lord of the Manor*, w/c, Garrick Club. S. DE WILDE, as Jeremy Diddler, in *Raising the Wind*, Garrick Club.
G SAMUEL DE WILDE, in a scene from *The Lord of the Manor*, oil, RA

1814, Garrick Club. GEORGE CLINT, as Brush in a scene from *The Clandestine Marriage*, oil, RA 1819, Garrick Club.
PR S.FREEMAN, after C.Robertson, hl, stipple, for *Monthly Mirror*, 1809, BM, NPG. Two theatrical prints, NPG.

JONES, Richard (1790-1855) political economist.
PR M.GAUCI, after E.U.Eddis, hl, lith, BM.

JONES, Richard Roberts (1780-1843) eccentric and linguist.
PR MRS D.TURNER, hs, etch, for *Memoir*, by Roscoe, 1822, BM, NPG. A.R.BURT, wl, coloured etch, pub 1823, BM, NPG. W.CLEMENTS, hl, woodcut, BM, NPG.

JONES, Thomas (1742-1803) painter.
P GIUSEPPE MARCHI, 1768, National Museum of Wales 1113, Cardiff.
G FRANCESCO RENALDI, with his family, 1797, National Museum of Wales 955.

JONES, Thomas (1752-1845) evangelical divine.
P GEORGE CLINT, *c*1814, hl, NPG 4828.

JONES, Thomas (*c*1756-1807) fellow and tutor of Trinity College, Cambridge.
P DANIEL GARDNER, hl, Trinity College, Cambridge.
SC Attrib JOSEPH NOLLEKENS, 1807, marble bust, Trinity College Chapel.

JONES, Thomas (1756-1820) Calvinistic methodist.
PR J.BLOOD, hs, stipple, pub 1817, BM.

JONES, William (1726-1800) divine, vicar of Nayland.
PR R.M.MEADOWS, hl seated, stipple, BM, NPG. R.GRAVES, hl, line NPG.

JONES, Sir William (1746-1794) Indian judge and orientalist
P SIR JOSHUA REYNOLDS, 1767-69, hl, Althorp, Northants A.W.DEVIS, tql seated, Althorp.
SC JOHN FLAXMAN, RA 1797, relief marble monument, University College, Oxford. JOHN BACON, 1799, St Paul's Cathedral London.

JONES, William (1784-1842) independent minister at Bolton
PR R.WOODMAN, hl, stipple, pub 1826, NPG. BLOOD, afte J.R.Wildman, hl, stipple, pub 1830, NPG.

JONES-LOYD, Samuel, see Baron Overstone.

JORDAN, Dorothea, née Bland (1762-1816) actress, mistres of William IV.
P JOHN HOPPNER, RA 1786, wl as Thalia the Muse of Comedy Royal Coll. GEORGE ROMNEY, 1786-87, tql as Peggy in *The Country Girl*, Waddesdon Manor (NT), Bucks. SAMUEL D WILDE, wl as Peggy in *The Country Girl*, Garrick Club, London S. DE WILDE, wl as Phaedra in *Amphitryon*, Garrick Club. Attri GAINSBOROUGH DUPONT, hl as a gleaner, Garrick Club. JOH HOPPNER, hl as Viola in *Twelfth Night*, Kenwood House London.
D JOHN HOPPNER, RA 1785, hs sketch, DoE (Bushly House Middx).
SC SIR FRANCIS CHANTREY, statue with two children, Ashmolea Museum, Oxford.

JUPP, Richard Webb (1767-1852) clerk to the Carpenters Company.
P JOHN PRESCOTT KNIGHT, RA 1849, Carpenters' Hall, London

K

KATER, Henry (1777-1835) scientist.
D GEORGE RICHMOND, 1831, hl seated, wash, NPG 2165.
G J.F.SKILL, J.GILBERT, W. and E.WALKER, 'Men of Science Living in 1807-08', pencil and wash, NPG 1075.

KATTERFELTO, Gustavus (d 1799) conjurer and empiric.
R UNKNOWN, hl with cat, woodcut, for *European Mag*, 1783, BM.

KAUFFMANN, Angelica (1741-1807) painter.
P Self-portrait, *c*1754, hs, Tiroler Landesmuseum Ferdinandeum, Innsbruck, Austria. Self-portrait, 1763, tql in national dress, Uffizi Gallery, Florence. NATHANIEL DANCE, 1764, hl, Burghley, Northants. Self-portrait, *c*1765-70, hs, Tiroler Landesmuseum Ferdinandeum. SIR JOSHUA REYNOLDS, 1766-77, hl, Althorp, Northants. Self-portrait, *c*1780, tql, Bünder Kunsthaus Chur, Switzerland. Self-portrait, *c*1780-85, hs, The Hermitage, Leningrad. Self-portrait, 1782, as the character of Design, listening to the inspiration of Poetry, Kenwood House, London. Self-portrait, 1787, tql seated, Uffizi Gallery. Self-portrait, hl with porte crayon, NPG 430. Self-portrait, herself hesitating between the arts of music and painting, Nostell Priory (NT), W.Yorks.
D NATHANIEL DANCE, wl seated with Sir Joshua Reynolds, Harewood House, W.Yorks.
G JOHAN ZOFFANY, 'Royal Academicians, 1772', oil, Royal Coll. RICHARD SAMUEL, 'The Nine Living Muses of Great Britain', oil, exhib 1779, NPG 4905. HENRY SINGLETON, 'Royal Academicians, 1793', oil, Royal Academy, London.
C JOHANN PETER KAUFFMANN, bust, Protomoteca Capitolina, Rome.

KAY, John (fl 1733-1764) inventor of the fly-shuttle.
R T.O.BARLOW, hl, mezz, pub 1862, BM.

KAY, John (1742-1826) miniature-painter and caricaturist.
P Self-portrait, SNPG 892.
C Self-portrait, tql seated with a bust, and a cat, etch, 1786, BM, NPG. Self-portrait, wl, the artist under examination, etch, 1792, NPG.

KAYE, John (1783-1853) bishop of Lincoln.
P SIR THOMAS LAWRENCE, *c*1828, finished by Say, The Old Palace, Lincoln. UNKNOWN, Christ's College, Cambridge.
C JOHN TERNOUTH, 1834, marble bust, Brasenose College, Oxford. RICHARD WESTMACOTT jun, 1857, recumbent effigy, Lincoln Cathedral.

KEAN, Edmund (1787-1833) actor.
P Several portraits at the Garrick Club, London: GEORGE CLINT, hl as Richard III; HENRY MEYER, wl as the chief of the Huron Indians; UNKNOWN, three portraits, wl, probably as Richard III. GEORGE CLINT, as Sir Giles Overreach, V & A. Attrib DANIEL MACLISE, as Hamlet, NGI 1019.
D SAMUEL COUSINS, 1814, hs, pencil, NPG 1829. Several drawings at the Garrick Club; in character, by Gear, de Wilde etc. Attrib THOMAS WAGEMAN, tql, pencil, NPG 4623.
G GEORGE CLINT, in a scene from *A New Way to Pay Old Debts*, oil, 1820, Garrick Club.
SC S.JOSEPH, 1815, bust, Drury Lane Theatre, London. JOHN EDWARD CAREW, 1833, marble statue, as Hamlet, Drury Lane Theatre.

PR Theatrical prints, BM, NPG.

KEATE, George (1729-1797) writer.
PR J.K.SHERWIN, after J.Plott, hl seated, line, for his *Poems*, 1781, BM, NPG.

KEATE, John (1773-1852) head master of Eton.
SL AUGUSTE EDOUART, 1828, wl, NPG.
C R.DIGHTON, wl profile 'A View taken at Eton', etch, BM, NPG 1116.

KEATE, Robert (1777-1857) surgeon to Queen Victoria.
P JOHN PRESCOTT KNIGHT, RA 1850, tql, St George's Hospital, London.

KEATING, Sir Henry Sheehy (1775-1847) general.
P ANDREW MORTON, 1839, hl, NPG 1895.

KEATS, John (1795-1821) poet.
P JOSEPH SEVERN, 1821, wl, NPG 58. WILLIAM HILTON, after a miniature by J.Severn, hl, NPG 194.
D B.R.HAYDON, 1816, hs, pen and ink, NPG 3251. J.SEVERN, 1816, head, charcoal, V & A. C.A.BROWN, 1819, hs, profile, pencil, NPG 1963. J.SEVERN, 1821, head, Keats-Shelley Memorial House, Rome.
M J.SEVERN, RA 1819, hl, NPG 1605.
SL C.A.BROWN, 1819, hs, Keats House, London.
SC B.R.HAYDON, 1816, life mask, NPG 686 and Keats House. GIUSEPPE GIROMETTI, 1821, plaster medallion, Keats House. Death mask, NPG 4031.

KEATS, Sir Richard Goodwin (1757-1834) admiral.
P JOHN JACKSON, 1822, hl, NMM, Greenwich.
SC WILLIAM BEHNES, 1831, marble bust, Royal Coll. SIR FRANCIS CHANTREY, 1835, bust, Greenwich Palace Chapel.
PR RIDLEY & BLOOD, after H.Mathews, hl in uniform, stipple, for *European Mag*, 1808, BM.

KEBLE, John (1792-1866) poet and divine.
P GEORGE RICHMOND, 1876, hs, Keble College, Oxford.
D GEORGE RICHMOND, 1844, tql, w/c, Keble College, Oxford. GEORGE RICHMOND, 1863, hs, chalk, NPG 1043. G.RICHMOND, head, chalk, Walsall Museum and Art Gallery.
SC THOMAS WOOLNER, bust, 1872, Westminster Abbey. G.RICHMOND, 1874, marble bust, Keble College.
PH R.H.PRESTON, tql, carte, NPG. PRESTON & POOLE, wl with his wife, carte, NPG Album of Photographs 1949.

KEELEY, Robert (1793-1869) comedian.
P HENRY O'NEIL, RA 1863, tql, Garrick Club, London.
D THOMAS HARRINGTON WILSON, 1865, wl, w/c, Garrick Club. T.HARRINGTON WILSON, wl as Billy Black in *The £100 note*, w/c, Garrick Club.
PR Several theatrical prints, BM, NPG.
PH O.J.REJLANDER, two tql seated, carte, NPG Actor's Album.

KEENE, Edmund (1714-1781) bishop of Ely.
P UNKNOWN, tql seated, Bishop's House, Chester, engr by C.Turner, as after J.Zoffany, mezz pub 1812, BM.

KEIR, James (1735-1820) chemist.
PR W.H.WORTHINGTON, after Longastre, tql seated, line, BM.

KEITH, Alexander (1791-1880) Scottish minister and writer.

PR UNKNOWN, hs, lith, BM. UNKNOWN, hs, woodcut, for *Christian Herald*, April 1880, NPG.

KEITH, George Keith Elphinstone, Viscount (1746-1823) admiral.

P JOHN HOPPNER, 1799, tql with Bath ribbon and star, Royal Coll. WILLIAM OWEN, *c*1796-97, hl, NMM, Greenwich. GEORGE SAUNDERS, after 1815, tql, NMM.

SC After JOHN G.HANCOCK of 1801, plaster medal, SNPG 66.

PR P.AUDINET, after H.P.Danloux, hl, line, oval, pub 1801, BM. RIDLEY & HOLL, after M.Brown, hl with Bath star, stipple, for *European Mag*, 1806, BM, NPG.

KEITH, Hester Maria Elphinstone, née Thrale, Viscountess (1762-1857) 2nd wife of Viscount Keith.

PR J.MARCHI, after J.Zoffany, wl as a child, with dog, mezz, oval, BM.

KEITH, Margaret Mercer Elphinstone, Viscountess (1788-1867) confidante of Princess Charlotte.

P JOHN HOPPNER, wl, Bowood, Wilts. GEORGE SAUNDERS, tql in Eastern dress, Bowood.

D SIR GEORGE HAYTER, head, pencil and indian ink, BM.

KEITH, Sir Robert Murray (1730-1795) general and diplomatist.

P JOHN OPIE, hs in uniform, with Bath ribbon and star, DoE (British Embassy, Copenhagen).

PR J.JACOBÉ, after A.Graff, tql seated in kilt, mezz, 1788, BM, NPG. UNKNOWN, hs with Bath star, stipple, pub 1848, NPG.

KELLIE, Thomas Alexander Erskine, 6th Earl of (1732-1781) musical dilettante.

P ROBERT HOME, hl seated, SNPG L241, engr R.Blyth, line, pub 1782, NPG.

KELLY, Sir Fitzroy (1796-1880) lord chief baron.

P UNKNOWN, tql in robes, Lincoln's Inn, London. UNKNOWN, *c*1870, wl in legal robes, Inner Temple, London, on loan to the Royal Courts of Justice.

M ELIZABETH WALKER, hs, Lincoln's Inn.

PR SYDNEY MARKS, after A.Lucas, tql, mezz, BM. S.BULL, after S.Lane, hl, stipple and line, NPG. D.J.POUND, after a photograph by Mayall, tql seated, stipple and line, NPG. W.WALKER, tql in judicial robes, mezz, BM.

PH LONDON STEREOSCOPIC CO, hs, albumen, carte, NPG.

KELLY, Frances Maria (1790-1882) actress and singer.

D SAMUEL DE WILDE, 1809, as Floretta in *The Cabinet*, w/c, Garrick Club, London. W.FOSTER, 1811, hl, w/c, Garrick Club. J.SLATER, 1813, Huntington Library and Art Gallery, San Marino, USA. THOMAS UWINS, 1822, head, chalk, NPG 1791.

PR Several theatrical prints, BM, NPG.

KELLY, Hugh (1739-1777) barrister and author.

PR J.BOYDELL, after H.Hamilton, hl, mezz, oval, for his *Dramatic Works*, 1778, BM, NPG. UNKNOWN, hs, line, oval, NPG.

KELLY, Michael (1764?-1826) singer and composer.

P SAMUEL DE WILDE, wl as Cymon, Garrick Club, London. JAMES LONSDALE, hl, Garrick Club.

D THEODORE HOOK, hl, pen and ink, BM.

PR Several theatrical prints, BM, NPG. H.MEYER, after A.Wivell, hl, stipple, for his *Reminiscences*, 1825, BM, NPG. C.TURNER, after T.Lawrence, tql, mezz, pub 1825, BM, NPG.

KELLY, Patrick (1756-1842) mathematician and astronomer.

PR T.WOOLNOTH, after H.Ashby, hl, stipple, BM, NPG.

KELWAY, Joseph (*d*1782) organist and composer.

D JOHN RUSSELL, 1776?, hl, pastel, NPG 4213.

KEMBLE, Charles (1775-1854) actor.

P THOMAS SULLY, 1833, hs as Fazio, The Pennsylvania Academy of Fine Arts, Philadelphia, USA. H.P.BRIGGS, hl with two masks, Garrick Club, London. H.P.BRIGGS, hl, Dulwich College Picture Gallery, London. GEORGE CLINT, wl as Charles II in a scene from *The Merry Monarch*, Garrick Club. HENRY WYATT, hs, Royal Shakespeare Memorial Theatre Museum, Stratford-on-Avon. ANDREW MORTON, wl as Macbeth, Garrick Club. ABRAHAM WIVELL, hs as Romeo, Garrick Club.

D SAMUEL DE WILDE, hs, pencil, chalk and wash, BM. UNKNOWN, hs as Malcolm or Macbeth, w/c, oval, Garrick Club. UNKNOWN, hl, w/c, Garrick Club.

SL UNKNOWN, profile, Garrick Club.

G G.H.HARLOW, 'Court for the trial of Queen Catherine', oil, Royal Shakespeare Memorial Theatre Museum.

PR Several theatrical prints, BM, NPG.

KEMBLE, Elizabeth (1761-1836), see Mrs Whitlock.

KEMBLE, Mrs Elizabeth, née Satchell (1763?-1841) actress

P SAMUEL DE WILDE, wl as Imoinda in *Oroonoko*, Garrick Club London.

PR C.SHERWIN, after J.H.Ramberg, as Juliet, line, for Bell's *British Theatre*, 1785, BM. J.GOLDAR, tql seated, line, pub 1790, BM.

KEMBLE, Frances (1759-1822), see Mrs Twiss.

KEMBLE, John Philip (1757-1823) actor.

P UNKNOWN, 1794, as Vicentio in *Measure for Measure*, V & A. SIR THOMAS LAWRENCE, RA 1798, wl as Coriolanus, Guildhall Art Gallery, London. SIR THOMAS LAWRENCE, RA 1801, wl as Hamlet, TATE 142; pencil study NPG 2616. G.H.HARLOW, exhib 1815, as Hubert in *King John*, Royal Shakespeare Memorial Theatre Museum, Stratford-on-Avon. SIR W.BEECHEY, hl Dulwich College Picture Gallery, London. SAMUEL DE WILDE, wl as Penruddock in *The Wheel of Fortune*, Garrick Club. SIR THOMAS LAWRENCE, wl as Cato, Garrick Club. WILLIAM OWEN, in *The Stranger*, Graves Art Gallery, Sheffield. GILBERT STUART, hl, NPG 49.

D JOHN GIBSON, hs, profile, pencil, BM.

M HORACE HONE, 1809, hs, on copper, Garrick Club. RICHARD COSWAY, in classical dress, V & A.

G G.H.HARLOW, 'Court for the trial of Queen Catherine', oil, Royal Shakespeare Memorial Theatre Museum.

SC JOHN FLAXMAN, 1826, statue, Westminster Abbey, London. Two busts, one by John Flaxman, one by John Gibson, Sir John Soane's Museum, London.

PR Numerous theatrical prints, BM, NPG.

KEMBLE, Maria Theresa, née de Camp (1774-1838) actress wife of Charles Kemble.

P SAMUEL DE WILDE, wl as Patie in *The Gentle Shepherd* Garrick Club, London.

D A.E.CHALON, hs, pen and w/c, NPG 1962 (b). S. DE WILDE, wl as Mrs Ford in *The Merry Wives of Windsor*, w/c, Garrick Club. S. DE WILDE, hl, chalk, V & A.

SL UNKNOWN, in profile, Garrick Club.

PR Several theatrical prints, BM, NPG.

KEMBLE, Priscilla, née Hopkins (1756-1845) actress.

PR Several theatrical prints, BM, NPG. R.J.LANE, after T.Lawrence, hl, lith, NPG.

KEMBLE, Roger (1721-1802) actor and manager.

P THOMAS BEACH, hs, Victoria Art Gallery, Bath, engr W.Ridley stipple, oval, for *Monthly Mag*, 1808, BM, NPG.

M OZIAS HUMPHRY, hs, oval, Royal Shakespeare Memorial Theatre Museum, Stratford-on-Avon.

G G.H.HARLOW, 'Court for the Trial of Queen Catherine', oil, Royal Shakespeare Memorial Theatre Museum.

KEMBLE, Sarah, see Mrs Siddons.

KEMBLE, Stephen (1758-1822) actor and manager.
D SAMUEL DE WILDE, 1805, wl as Falstaff, w/c, Garrick Club, London.
G G.H.HARLOW, 'Court for the trial of Queen Catherine', oil, Royal Shakespeare Memorial Theatre Museum, Stratford-on-Avon.
PR J.R.SMITH, hl, stipple, BM, NPG. UNKNOWN, hl, stipple, BM.
C R.DIGHTON, wl as Hamlet, coloured etch, pub 1794, BM.

KEMP, George Meikle (1795-1844) architect and designer of the Scott monument.
P WILLIAM BONNAR, tql, SNPG 246.
SC ALEXANDER HANDYSIDE RITCHIE, plaster bust, SNPG 239.

KEMP, Thomas Read (1781?-1844) founder of Kemp Town, Brighton.
G SIR GEORGE HAYTER, 'The House of Commons, 1833', oil, NPG 54.
PR T.ILLMAN, after T.Lawrence, hl, stipple, pub 1812, BM.

KEMPE, Alfred John (1785?-1846) antiquary.
PR J.B.SWAINE, after W.Patten, tql seated, mezz, BM, NPG.

KEMPENFELT, Richard (1718-1782) admiral.
P TILLY KETTLE, RA 1782, wl, NMM, Greenwich. RALPH EARL, 1783, tql, NPG 1641.

KEMPT, Sir James (1764-1854) governor-general of Canada.
P WILLIAM SALTER, tql study for 'Waterloo Banquet', NPG 3728.
G W.SALTER, 'Waterloo Banquet at Apsley House', oil, 1836, Wellington Museum, Apsley House, London.
PR S.BELLIN, after R.McInnes, tql, mezz, pub 1841, NPG.

KENDRICK, James (1771-1847) botanist.
PR R.J.LANE, hs, lith, 1841, BM, NPG.

KENNEDY, Sir James Shaw (1788-1865) general.
P J.W.PIENEMAN, hs, Wellington Museum, Apsley House, London.

KENNEDY, Thomas Francis (1788-1879) politician.
P SIR GEORGE HAYTER, SNPG 1295.
G SIR GEORGE HAYTER, 'The House of Commons, 1833', NPG 54.
PR UNKNOWN, hl, stipple and line, NPG.

KENNEY, James (1780-1849) dramatist.
P G.S.NEWTON, hl, NGI 210.
D SAMUEL LAURENCE, c1840-49, head, chalk, NPG 4263. Attrib S. DE WILDE, hl, probably the sitter, w/c, Garrick Club, London.
PR J.HEATH, tql seated, stipple, pub 1809, BM, NPG.

KENNICOTT, Benjamin (1718-1783) biblical scholar.
P UNKNOWN, hl, Exeter College, Oxford.

KENRICK, John (1788-1877) classical scholar and historian.
PR T.LUPTON, after G.Patten, tql seated, mezz, 1847, BM, NPG.

KENRICK, William (1725?-1779) writer.
PR T.WORLIDGE, hl, etch and line, oval, BM, NPG.

KENT, James (1700-1776) organist and composer.
P G.M. hl, Winchester College, Hants.

KENT, Nathaniel (1737-1810) land valuer and agriculturist.
PR J.YOUNG, after J.Rising, tql seated, mezz, BM.

KENT AND STRATHEARN, Edward Augustus, Duke of (1767-1820) son of George III.
P Attrib FRANCIS COTES, wl as Cupid in landscape, Royal Coll. BENJAMIN WEST, 1778, wl with Prince William, Royal Coll. THOMAS GAINSBOROUGH, 1782, hs, oval, Royal Coll. THOMAS GAINSBOROUGH, c1786-88, wl, Yale Center for British Art, New Haven, USA. JOHN HOPPNER, 1796-99, tql in uniform with Garter star, Royal Coll. SIR WILLIAM BEECHEY, 1814, wl with Garter ribbon and star, Fishmongers' Hall, London. SIR W.BEECHEY, 1818, hl with Garter, ribbon and star, NPG 647. GEORGE DAWE, 1818, wl in orders, with cannon, Royal Coll. F.X.WINTERHALTER, wl, Royal Coll.
D JOHN DOWNMAN, hl, Royal Coll. HENRY EDRIDGE, wl, Royal Coll. H.D.HAMILTON, hs, Royal Coll.
G JOHAN ZOFFANY, 'George III, Queen Charlotte and their six eldest children', oil, 1770, Royal Coll. BENJAMIN WEST, Queen Charlotte with her children, 1779, oil, Royal Coll.
SC JOHN BACON, jun, 1813, marble bust, Royal Coll. PETER TURNERELLI, 1820, bust, Royal Coll.

KENT AND STRATHEARN, Victoria Mary Louisa, Duchess of (1786-1861) mother of Queen Victoria.
P GEORGE DAWE, c1818, Royal Coll. SIR WILLIAM BEECHEY, c1823, tql seated with Princess Victoria, Royal Coll. RICHARD ROTHWELL, RA 1832, hs with hat, Royal Coll. SIR GEORGE HAYTER, wl with dog in landscape, Royal Coll. F.X.WINTERHALTER, 1846, wl, Royal Coll; hs replica, NPG 2554.
M HENRY COLLEN, 1829, hs with hat, Royal Coll.
D A.E.CHALON, 1838, w/c, SNPG 1001. A.E.CHALON, wl, Royal Coll.
G SIR DAVID WILKIE, c1831, with Princess Victoria and members of her family, oil, Royal Coll.
SC EDWARD DAVIS, 1843, marble bust, Royal Coll. WILLIAM THEED, 1864, statue, Royal Coll.

KENTISH, John (1768-1853) unitarian divine.
P THOMAS PHILLIPS, 1840, hl, NPG 4971.

KENTON, Benjamin (1719-1800) vintner and philanthropist.
P UNKNOWN, Vintners' Hall, London.
PR W.RIDLEY, hl, stipple, oval, for European Mag, 1808, BM, NPG.

KENYON, John (1784-1856) poet and philanthropist.
PR R.J.LANE, after J.C.Moore, hl, lith, 1857, NPG.

KENYON, Lloyd Kenyon, 1st Baron (1732-1802) lord chief justice.
P GEORGE ROMNEY and M.A.SHEE, hl, Middle Temple, London; copy NPG 469.
PR J.FITTLER, after J.Opie, tql seated in robes of the master of the rolls, line, pub 1789, BM, NPG.
C J.GILLRAY, 'Ancient Music', etch, pub 1787, NPG.

KEPPEL, Augustus Keppel, 1st Viscount (1725-1786) admiral.
P Several portraits by SIR JOSHUA REYNOLDS: 1749, tql, NMM, Greenwich; 1753-54, wl, NMM; 1759, tql, Woburn Abbey, Beds; c1762-64, hl, NMM; 1780, tql, TATE 886; 1785, wl, Royal Coll. Studio of Reynolds, 1779, hl, NPG 179. GEORGE ROMNEY, hs, Goodwood, West Sussex.
SC JOSEPH CERACCHI, 1777, marble bust, Belvoir Castle, Leics.
C Two JAMES SAYERS etch, NPG.

KEPPEL, Frederick (1729-1777) bishop of Exeter.
P UNKNOWN, hl, The Bishop's Palace, Exeter.

KEPPEL, George (1724-1772), see 3rd Earl of Albemarle.

KEPPEL, George Thomas, see 6th Earl of Albemarle.

KEPPEL, William Anne, see 2nd Earl of Albemarle.

KEPPEL, William Charles (1772-1849), see 4th Earl of Albemarle.

KER, Charles Henry Bellenden (1785?-1871) legal reformer.
D G.R.LEWIS, hl, pencil, BM.

KER, James Innes-, see 5th Duke of Roxburgh(e).

KER, John (1740-1804), see 3rd Duke of Roxburgh(e).

KERR, William Henry (1710-1775), see 4th Marquess of Lothian.

KERRICH, Thomas (1748-1828) antiquary and artist.
P UNKNOWN, 1795, Magdalene College, Cambridge.
PR G.S.FACIUS, after H.P.Briggs, hl, stipple, pub 1815, BM, NPG.

KERRISON, Sir Edward (1774-1853) general.
P WILLIAM SALTER, tql study for 'Waterloo Banquet', NPG 3729.
G SIR GEORGE HAYTER, 'The House of Commons, 1833', oil, NPG 54. WILLIAM SALTER, 'Waterloo Banquet at Apsley House', oil, 1836, Wellington Museum, Apsley House, London.
PR W.C.EDWARDS, after M.A.Shee, hl in uniform, line, pub 1818, BM, NPG. T.H.MAGUIRE, tql seated, lith, one of set of *Ipswich Museum Portraits*, 1851, BM, NPG. JOSEPH BROWN, after a photograph by J.E.Mayall, hs, stipple, NPG.

KERSHAW, James (1730?-1797) methodist preacher.
SC After JAMES TASSIE, 1795, plaster medallion, SNPG 1905.

KETT, Henry (1761-1825) writer.
C R.DIGHTON, wl 'A View from Trinity College, Oxford', coloured etch, pub 1807, BM.

KETTLE, Tilly (1735-1786) portrait-painter.
D Indian artist after a presumed painting by Tilly Kettle, c1815, wl painting a portrait of Shuja-ud-daula-Nawab of Oudh and his ten sons, w/c, V & A.

KEY, Charles Aston (1793-1849) surgeon.
PR F.HOLL, after G.Richmond, hs, stipple, pub 1851, BM, NPG.

KEY, Sir John, 1st Bart (1794-1858) lord mayor of London.
PR C.TURNER, after M.Pearson, tql in lord mayor robes, mezz, pub 1832, BM. UNKNOWN, hs, woodcut, NPG.
C UNKNOWN, 'The Don-key turn'd Mayor or an Ass in the Chair', lith, NPG. UNKNOWN, 'The City Militia', lith, NPG.

KEY, Thomas Hewitt (1799-1875) Latin scholar.
PR UNKNOWN, hs, woodcut, for *Illust London News*, 1875, NPG.

KEYSE, Thomas (1722-1800) still-life painter and keeper of Bermondsey Spa.
PR J.CHAPMAN, after S.Drummond, hs, stipple, oval, pub 1797, NPG.

KEYWORTH, Thomas (1782-1852) congregational minister and hebraist.
PR R.WOODMAN, hs, stipple, BM.

KIDD, James (1761-1834) presbyterian divine.
PR J.THOMSON, after W.Derby, hl, stipple, pub 1826, NPG. R.GRAVES, hl, line, BM.

KIDD, John (1775-1851) physician.
D UNKNOWN, hs, chalk, Christ College, Oxford. UNKNOWN, hs, pencil and chalk, University Museum, Oxford.

KILMAINE, Charles Edward Saul Jennings (1751-1799) general in the French army.
PR BOURGEOIS, after Hilaire le Dru, wl, stipple, NPG. UNKNOWN, hs, stipple, pub 1807, NPG.

KILMARNOCK, William Boyd, 4th Earl of (1704-1746) Jacobite.
P Attrib ALLAN RAMSAY, hs, Dick Institute, Kilmarnock.
PR UNKNOWN, hl, with another of 6th Baron Balmerino, line, ovals, BM. N.PARR, hl, line, NPG. UNKNOWN, hs, stipple, NPG.

KILWARDEN, Arthur Wolfe, Viscount (1739-1803) chief justice of Ireland.
P H.D.HAMILTON, 1795, hs, NGI 578. G.F.JOSEPH, wl seated in robes, (posthumous), Trinity College, Dublin.

KINDERSLEY, Sir Richard Torin (1792-1879) vice-chancellor.

D GEORGE RICHMOND, hs, Lincoln's Inn, London.

KING, Frances Elizabeth, née Bernard (1757-1821) writer.
PR T.WOOLNOTH, tql seated in turban, stipple, for *Ladies' Monthly Museum*, 1824, BM, NPG. E.SCRIVEN, after E.Hastings, hl seated, stipple, pub 1833, NPG.

KING, James (1750-1784) explorer and captain in the navy.
PR F.BARTOLOZZI, after J.Webber, hl, stipple, oval, pub 1784, BM, NPG. J.HOGG, after S.Shelley, hs, line, medallion, BM.

KING, John Glen (1732-1787) numismatist.
PR G.SMITH, after P.Falconet, 1771, hs, stipple, BM, NPG.

KING, Philip Gidley (1758-1808) first governor of Norfolk island and governor of New South Wales.
M UNKNOWN, c1800, Mitchell Library, Sydney, Australia.
PR W.SKELTON, after J.Wright, hs, line, oval, for *Voyage of Governor Philip to Botany Bay*, 1789, BM.

KING, Philip Parker (1793-1856) rear-admiral.
SC THOMAS WOOLNER, 1825-29, plaster relief, Art Gallery of New South Wales, Sydney, Australia.

KING, Sir Richard, 1st Bart (1730-1806) admiral.
SC After WILLIAM TASSIE, 1804, plaster medallion, SNPG 470.

KING, Sir Richard, 2nd Bart (1774-1834) admiral.
PR W.RIDLEY, hs, stipple, oval, from a miniature, for *The Naval Chronicle*, 1803, BM. C.TURNER, after Saunders, hl, mezz, pub 1835, BM, NPG.

KING, Thomas (1730-1805) actor and dramatist.
P In the Garrick Club, London: SAMUEL DE WILDE, hs as Lord Ogleby in *The Clandestine Marriage*; BENJAMIN WILSON, wl with dog in landscape; Attrib B.WILSON, wl with bust of Shakespeare; JOHAN ZOFFANY, wl as Touchstone in *As you like it*.
G JAMES ROBERTS, as Sir Peter Teazle in a scene from *School for Scandal*, oil, RA 1779, Garrick Club. JOHAN ZOFFANY, as Lord Ogleby in a scene from *The Clandestine Marriage*, oil, Garrick Club.
PR W.DANIELL, after G.Dance, hl seated, soft-ground etch, pub 1809, BM, NPG. Numerous theatrical prints, BM, NPG.

KING, William (1701-1769) independent minister.
PR HOPWOOD, hs, stipple, NPG.

KING of Ockham, Peter King, 7th Baron (1775-1833) authority on currency.
P JOHN LINNELL, 1832, tql, NPG 4020.
G SIR GEORGE HAYTER, 'The Trial of Queen Caroline, 1820', oil, NPG 999.
SC RICHARD WESTMACOTT jun, bust, All Saints' Church, Ockham, Surrey.
PR M.GAUCI, after E.U.Eddis, hl, lith, BM, NPG.

KINGHORN, Joseph (1766-1832) baptist minister.
PR W.BOND, after A.Robertson of 1813, hl, stipple, pub 1833, NPG. J.M.JOHNSON, hl, lith, NPG.

KINGSBURY, William (1744-1818) dissenting minister.
PR UNKNOWN, hs, stipple, oval, for *Evangelical Mag*, 1795, NPG. H.DAWE, after M.Spilsbury, hl, mezz, BM.

KINGSDOWN, Thomas Pemberton (afterwards Pemberton-Leigh) Baron (1793-1867) politician.
PR W.WALKER, tql seated, mezz, pub 1846, BM, NPG. W.HOLL, after G.Richmond, hs, stipple, for 'Grillion's Club' series, BM, NPG.

KINGSMILL, Sir Robert Brice, 1st Bart (1730-1805) admiral.
P SIR JOSHUA REYNOLDS, c1764-66, TATE 5023.
G P.ROBERTS, 'British Admirals. Britannia Viewing the Conquerors of the Sea', stipple, pub 1800, BM.

PR W.RIDLEY, after L.Abbott, hl, stipple, oval, for *Naval Chronicle*, 1801, BM, NPG.

KINGSTON, Elizabeth Chudleigh, Duchess of, see Countess of Bristol.

KINNAIRD, Charles Kinnaird, 8th Baron (1780-1826) Scottish representative peer.

D WILLIAM BONE, after James Northcote of 1809, hs, pencil, NPG 'Bone's Drawings'.

KINNAIRD, Douglas James William (1788-1830) writer and friend of Byron.

G SIR GEORGE HAYTER, 'The Trial of Queen Caroline, 1820', oil, NPG 999.

KINNEDER, William Erskine, Lord (1769-1822) judge.

D WILLIAM NICHOLSON, w/c, SNPG 1100.

KINNOULL, Thomas Hay, 9th Earl of (1710-1787) statesman.

P DAVID MARTIN, SNPG 2276.

PR C.H.HODGES, after W.Hoare, tql, mezz, BM.

KIPPIS, Andrew (1725-1795) nonconformist divine and biographer.

P WILLIAM ARTAUD, hl, Dr Williams's Library, London, engr F.Bartolozzi, stipple, pub 1792, BM, NPG.

PR J.BAKER, after J.Hazlitt, hs, line, for *Universal Mag*, 1796, NPG.

C J.SAYERS, 'The Repeal of the Test Act', etch, pub 1790, NPG.

KIRBY, John Joshua (1716-1774) student of linear perspective.

P THOMAS GAINSBOROUGH, *c*1751, wl seated with his wife, NPG 1421. T.GAINSBOROUGH, mid 1750s, hs, V & A. T.GAINSBOROUGH, hl, Fitzwilliam Museum, Cambridge.

PR D.P.PARISET, after P.Falconet, hs, stipple, circle, BM.

KIRBY, William (1759-1850) entomologist.

P UNKNOWN, Caius College, Cambridge. UNKNOWN, Linnean Society, London.

D UNKNOWN, w/c, Linnean Society, London.

PR T.H.MAGUIRE, after F.H.Bischoff, tql seated, lith, one of set of *Ipswich Museum Portraits*, 1851, BM, NPG. T.LUPTON, after H.Howard, hl, mezz, BM, NPG. R.J.LANE, after W.B.Spence, tql aged 89, lith, NPG.

KIRKLAND, Thomas (1722-1798) medical writer.

PR J.R.SMITH, hl, mezz, pub 1797, BM.

KIRKUP, Seymour Stocker (1788-1880) artist.

D SIR GEORGE HAYTER, hs, pencil and wash, BM.

KIRWAN, Richard (1733-1812) chemist and scientist.

P UNKNOWN, tql seated, Royal Irish Academy, Dublin. H.D.HAMILTON, Royal Dublin Society.

D UNKNOWN, hs, National Library of Ireland, Dublin.

KIRWAN, Walter Blake (1754-1805) dean of Killala.

P SIR M.A.SHEE, NGI 1129.

PR W.WARD, after H.D.Hamilton, wl in pulpit, mezz, pub 1806, BM.

KITCHENER, William (1775?-1827) writer on science and music.

D WILLIAM BROCKEDON, *c*1826, hl, pencil and chalk, NPG 2515 (14).

PR C.TURNER, wl with stuffed tiger and telescope, mezz, pub 1827, BM, NPG. E.FINDEN, after W.H.Brooke, from a bust by J.Kendrick, stipple, pub 1829, NPG.

KNAPTON, Philip (1762-1833) musician.

P Attrib A.MAYER, York City Art Gallery.

KNATCHBULL, Sir Edward, 9th Bart (1781-1849)

statesman.

P THOMAS PHILLIPS, tql seated, Maidstone County Hall, Kent. J.S.COPLEY, wl with his brother, Maidstone County Hall; pencil and chalk study, 1800–02, University of Nebraska Art Galleries, Lincoln, USA.

G SIR GEORGE HAYTER, 'The House of Commons, 1833', oil, NPG 54.

KNIGHT, Charles (1791-1873) author and publisher.

P C.H.KERR, after W.C.Dobson, Corporation of London.

SC JOSEPH DURHAM, 1874, marble bust, NPG 393.

PR UNKNOWN, hs, woodcut, for *The Illust Review*, 1873, NPG. UNKNOWN, after a photograph by Edwards and Bult, tql seated, woodcut, for *The Family Friend*, No 69, 1875, NPG.

KNIGHT, Edward (1774-1826) actor.

D SAMUEL DE WILDE, 1810, as Robin Roughead in *Fortune's Frolic*, w/c, Garrick Club, London. W.FOSTER, wl as Jailor in *Plots*, w/c, Garrick Club. J.WICHE, 1814, hl, pencil and w/c, BM. W.FOSTER, hs as Jerry Blossom in *Hit or Miss*, pencil and w/c, Garrick Club.

G GEORGE CLINT, in a scene from *Lock and Key*, oil, RA 1821, Garrick Club.

PR H.DAWE, after J.Knight, hl seated at the theatre, mezz, pub 1825, BM. Theatrical prints, BM, NPG.

KNIGHT, Ellis Cornelia (1757-1837) writer.

P ANGELICA KAUFFMANN, 1793, tql seated, Manchester City Art Gallery.

KNIGHT, Gowin (1713-1772) librarian of the British Museum.

P BENJAMIN WILSON, hl seated, BM.

PR B.WILSON, tql seated, etch, 1751, BM, NPG.

KNIGHT, Henrietta, see Lady Luxborough.

KNIGHT, Henry Gally (1786-1846) writer on architecture.

G JOHN PARTRIDGE, 'The Fine Arts Commissioners, 1846', NPG 342, 3.

KNIGHT, Sir John (1748?-1831) admiral.

G G.NOBLE and J.PARKER, after J.Smart, 'Naval Victories', 'Commemoration of 11th Oct 1797', line, pub 1803, BM, NPG.

PR W.RIDLEY, after J.Smart, hs, stipple, oval, for *The Naval Chronicle*, 1804, BM, NPG.

KNIGHT, Richard Payne (1750-1824) collector.

P SIR THOMAS LAWRENCE, 1794, tql seated, Whitworth Art Gallery, Manchester. SIR THOMAS LAWRENCE, 1805, hl, The Society of Dilettanti, Brooks's Club, London.

SC JOHN BACON, *c*1811, marble bust, BM. JOHN BACON, 1814, marble and bronze bust, NPG 4887.

KNIGHT, Samuel (1759-1827) vicar of Halifax.

PR UNKNOWN, hs, stipple, pub 1837, BM, NPG.

KNIGHT, Thomas (1764?-1820) actor and dramatist.

P JOHAN ZOFFANY, *c*1795-96, wl as Roger in *The Ghost*, Garrick Club, London. SAMUEL DE WILDE, wl as Jacob Gawkey in *Chapter of Accidents*, Garrick Club.

D THOMAS WAGEMAN, hl, pencil, Garrick Club.

KNIGHT, Thomas Andrew (1759-1838) horticulturist.

D UNKNOWN, tql seated with plant, City Art Gallery, Hereford.

PR R.J.LANE, after S.Cole of 1834, hs, lith, NPG. S.COUSINS, after S.Cole, hl seated, mezz, pub 1836, BM.

KNIGHT-BRUCE, Sir James Lewis (1791-1866) vice-chancellor.

D UNKNOWN, hl, pencil, NPG 1576c.

SC J.EVANS, marble bust, Royal Courts of Justice, London.

PR W.WALKER, after T.Woolnoth, hl, mezz, pub 1850, BM.

UNKNOWN, hs, stipple, NPG.

KNIGHTON, Sir William, 1st Bart (1776–1836) keeper of the privy purse to George IV.

PR C.TURNER, after T.Lawrence, hl, mezz, pub 1823, BM, NPG.

KNOLLYS, Sir William Thomas (1797–1883) general.

PR UNKNOWN, hs, woodcut, for *Illust London News*, 1863, NPG. UNKNOWN, hs, woodcut, NPG.

KNOWLES, Sir Charles, 1st Bart (1704?–1777) admiral.

G G.BICKHAM, 'Six Admirals', c1765, line, BM.

PR RIDLEY, hs, stipple, oval, pub 1803, NPG. T.HUDSON, after J.Faber jun, tql, mezz, BM, NPG. UNKNOWN, tql, mezz, BM.

KNOWLES, Sir Charles Henry, 2nd Bart (1754–1831) admiral.

G WORTHINGTON and PARKER, after R.Smirke, 'Naval Victories', 'Commemoration of the 14th February 1797', line, pub 1803, BM, NPG.

KNOWLES, James (1759–1840) lexicographer.

PR J.SCOTT, after G.Lance, hl, mezz, BM, NPG.

KNOWLES, James Sheridan (1784–1862) dramatist and actor.

P WILHELM TRAUTSCHOLD, c1849, tql, NPG 2003.

PR R.J.LANE, after C.Harding, tql, lith, pub 1826, NPG. H.S.SADD, after S.S.Osgood, tql, mezz, pub 1840, BM. D.MACLISE, wl, lith, (from a drawing originally pub in *Fraser's Mag*) for Maginn's *Gallery of Illustrious Literary Characters*, 1873, BM. R.J.LANE, after A.d'Orsay, hl, profile, lith, NPG.

PH J.DOUGLAS, wl seated, carte, NPG Album of Photographs 1949.

KNOWLES, John (1781–1841) biographer of Fuseli.

PR W.DRUMMOND, after C.Landseer, hs, lith, *Athenaeum Portraits* No 25, BM, NPG.

KNOX, Alexander (1757–1831) theological writer.

PR H.ADLARD, after H.Weekes, from a bust by Chantrey, hs, stipple, pub 1834, NPG.

KNOX, Robert (1791–1862) anatomist and ethnologist.

SL AUGUSTIN EDOUART, wl, SNPG 831.

PR UNKNOWN, hl holding a skeleton of a hand, etch, BM.

KNOX, Vicesimus (1752–1821) miscellaneous writer.

PR J.THOMSON, after A.J.Oliver, hl, stipple, for *European Mag*, 1822, BM, NPG.

KNYVETT, Charles (1752–1822) musician.

G G.H.HARLOW, 'Court for the Trial of Queen Catherine', oil, c1817, Royal Shakespeare Memorial Theatre Museum, Stratford-on-Avon.

PR W.DANIELL, after G.Dance, hs, soft-ground etch, pub 1812, BM, NPG.

KNYVETT, Charles (1773–1852) organist.

PR W.DANIELL, after G.Dance, hs, soft-ground etch, pub 1803, BM. J.THOMSON, after A.Wivell, hl, stipple, BM, NPG.

KNYVETT, William (1779–1856) singer and composer.

G G.H.HARLOW, 'Court for the Trial of Queen Catherine', oil, c1817, Royal Shakespeare Memorial Theatre Museum, Stratford-on-Avon.

PR W.DANIELL, after G.Dance, hs, soft-ground etch, pub 1812, BM, NPG.

KÖNIG, Charles Dietrich Eberhard (1774–1851) mineralogist.

PR MISS TURNER, after E.U.Eddis, hs, lith, BM, NPG.

KRAUSE, William Henry (1796–1852) Irish divine.

PR W.H.COLLINGRIDGE, after a daguerreotype by Professor Glukman, hs, lith, NPG.

KYD, Stewart (d1811) politician and legal writer.

PR UNKNOWN, hs, profile, stipple, oval, pub 1794, NPG.

L

LABLACHE, Luigi (1794-1858) singer.
P FRANZ WINTERHALTER, hs, oval, Royal Coll.
D DANIEL MACLISE, sketch, V & A.
SC JEAN PIERRE DANTAN, 1831, bronze and plaster statue, as Figaro, Musée Carnavelet, Paris.
PR F.SALABERT, hl, lith, 1835, BM. H.ROBINSON, after T.Carrick, hl, stipple, oval, pub 1846, BM. Theatrical prints, BM, NPG.
C CHARLES F.TOMKINS, several drgs, BM.

LABOUCHERE, Henry (1798-1869), see 1st Baron Taunton.

LACKINGTON, James (1746-1815) bookseller.
PR J.GOLDAR, after E.Maybry, tql seated, for *New Wonderful Mag*, BM, pub 1790, NPG. E.SCOTT, after J.Keenan, hl, stipple, for his *Memoirs* 1792, BM.
C UNKNOWN, wl, his shop in background, etch, pub 1795, NPG.

LACROIX, Alphonse François (1799-1859) missionary.
PR J.COCHRAN, after H.Room, hl, stipple, NPG.

LACY, Michael Rophino (1795-1867) violinist, composer and actor.
PR A.CARDON, after J.Smart, hl as a boy, stipple, pub 1807, BM, NPG.

LADBROOKE, Robert (1768-1842) landscape-painter.
PR J.B.LADBROOKE, tql, lith, 1839, NPG.

LAIDLAW, William (1780-1845) friend and amanuensis of Sir Walter Scott.
D SIR WILLIAM ALLAN, head, chalk, SNPG 104.

LAING, Alexander Gordon (1793-1826) African traveller.
PR S.FREEMAN, hl, stipple, NPG.

LAING, David (1793-1878) Scottish antiquary.
P SIR WILLIAM FETTES DOUGLAS, 1862, tql, SNPG 2041. ROBERT HERDMAN, 1874, tql, SNPG L 45.
SC DAVID WATSON STEVENSON, c1880, plaster bust, SNPG 349.
PR F.HARRISON, hl, etch, BM.

LAING, Malcolm (1762-1818) historian.
D UNKNOWN, hs?, wash, SNPG 1675a.

LAING, William (1764-1832) bookseller.
SL AUGUSTIN EDOUART, 1830, wl, SNPG 2149.

LAKE, Gerard Lake, 1st Viscount (1744-1808) general.
P UNKNOWN, wl, Oriental Club, London.
SC JOSEPH NOLLEKENS, 1814, marble bust, Royal Coll. After J.Lake, bust, Oriental Club.
PR RIDLEY and BLOOD, after S.Drummond, hs, stipple, for *European Mag.* 1808, BM, NPG. R.COOPER, wl with his son and a fallen horse, stipple, BM.

LAMB, Lady Caroline (1785-1828) novelist.
P SIR THOMAS LAWRENCE, 1809, Bristol City Art Gallery. THOMAS PHILLIPS, 1813, hs as a page, Chatsworth House, Derbyshire. JOHN HOPPNER, hl, Althorp, Northants. MISS E.H.TROTTER, wl reclining, NPG 3312.
M MISS EMMA ELEONORA KENDRICK, tql, V & A.
PR F.BARTOLOZZI, after R.Cosway, tql as a child, stipple, oval, pub 1788, BM. H.MEYER, hl, from a miniature, stipple, for *New Monthly Mag*, 1819, BM, NPG.

LAMB, Charles (1775-1834) essayist.
P WILLIAM HAZLITT, 1804, hl, NPG 507. HENRY MEYER, 1826, tql, India Office, London; copy, NPG 1312. F.S.CARY, 1834, wl seated with his sister, NPG 1019.
D ROBERT HANCOCK, 1798, hl, pencil and chalk, NPG 449. G.F.JOSEPH, 1819, hs, w/c stipple, BM. DANIEL MACLISE, sketch for *Fraser's Mag*, V & A.
PR W.FINDEN, after T.Wageman, hs, stipple, pub 1836, NPG. D.MACLISE, wl seated, etch, NPG.
C B.PULHAM, wl profile, etch, BM.

LAMB, Frederick James, see 3rd Viscount Melbourne.

LAMB, George (1784-1834) under-secretary of state.
C R.DIGHTON, wl profile, etch, pub 1819, BM, V & A.

LAMB, Sir James Bland Burges (1752-1824) politician and writer.
D FRANCIS PHILIP STEPHANOFF or JAMES STEPHANOFF, an illustration of the Coronation of King George IV, 1821, V & A.
SC After W.WHITLEY, plaster medallion, SNPG 1877.
PR P.W.TOMKINS, hl, stipple, pub 1796, BM. W.RIDLEY, after Mosnier, hl, stipple, oval, for *Monthly Mirror*, 1801, BM, NPG.

LAMB, John (1789-1850) dean of Bristol.
P SIR WILLIAM BEECHEY, RA 1828, Corpus Christi College, Cambridge.

LAMB, Mary (1764-1847) sister and collaborator of Charles Lamb.
P F.S.CARY, 1834, wl with Charles Lamb, NPG 1019.

LAMB, Sir Matthew, 1st Bart (1705-1768) politician.
P After THOMAS HUDSON, tql seated, Melbourne Hall, Derbyshire.
D ROSALBA CARRIERA, hs, pastel, Melbourne Hall.

LAMB, William (1779-1848), see 2nd Viscount Melbourne.

LAMBART, Richard Ford William, see 7th Earl of Cavan.

LAMBERT, Aylmer Bourke (1761-1842) botanist.
D JOHN RUSSELL, Linnean Society, London. STEPHEN CATTERSON SMITH, wl chalk, BM.
SC A.C.LUCAS, 1834, miniature plaster bust, Linnean Society, London.
PR W.EVANS, after H.Edridge, tql, stipple, for *Contemporary Portraits*, 1810, BM, NPG. HOLL, 1805, after J.Russell, hs, stipple, oval, NPG.

LAMBERT, Daniel (1770-1809) the most corpulent man of whom authentic records exist.
P BENJAMIN MARSHALL, wl seated, Leicester Museum and Art Gallery. Several engravings after this type, BM, NPG.
G UNKNOWN, 'Five Remarkable Characters', etch, BM. UNKNOWN, '30 Extraordinary Characters, etc', line, BM.

LAMBERT, George (1710-1765) landscape painter.
PR J.FABER jun, after J.Vanderbank, hl, mezz, 1727, BM, NPG.

LAMBERT, James (1741-1823) Greek professor at Cambridge.
P DANIEL GARDNER, 1767, hl, Trinity College, Cambridge.

LAMBERT, Sir John (1772-1847) general.
P WILLIAM SALTER, tql study for 'Waterloo Banquet', NPG 3731.

G W.SALTER, 'Waterloo Banquet at Apsley House', oil, 1836, Wellington Museum, Apsley House, London.

LAMBTON, John George, see 1st Earl of Durham.

LAMBTON, William (1756-1823) lieutenant-colonel and geodesist.
P WILLIAM HAVELL, 1822, hl, Royal Asiatic Society, London.
D THOMAS HICKEY, 1800, hs, Stratfield Saye, Hants.

LAMPE, John Frederick (1703?-1751) musical composer.
PR J.MCARDELL, after S.Andrea, tql seated, mezz, BM.

LANCASTER, Joseph (1778-1838) educationalist.
P JOHN HAZLITT, hl, NPG 99.
PR DEQUEVAUVILLER, hs profile, stipple and line, NPG.

LANDMANN, George Thomas (1779-1854) military engineer and author.
P UNKNOWN, c1800, tql, Royal Engineers, Gordon Barracks, Chatham, Kent.

LANDOR, Walter Savage (1775-1864) writer.
P WILLIAM FISHER, hl seated, NPG 236. SIR WILLIAM BOXALL, hs as an old man, V & A.
D WILLIAM BEWICK, 1826, hs, pencil, BM. CHARLES BRANWHITE, 1847, hs, Trinity College, Oxford. N.BRANWHITE jun, indian ink, BM. ROBERT FAULKNER, hs, pastel, NPG 2658.
SC JOHN GIBSON, 1828, plaster bust, NPG 1950. After J.GIBSON, marble bust, NPG 2127.
PR J.BROWN, after N.Dance of 1804, head, stipple, for vol i of his *Life*, by Forster, 1869, BM, NPG. A.D'ORSAY, hl seated, lith, pub 1839, BM, NPG.
PH UNKNOWN, hs, albumen, NPG 'Portraits and Autographs' collected Herbert Fry 1856-57.

LANDSEER, Charles (1799-1879) painter.
D SOLOMON ALEXANDER, 184?, hs, pen and ink, BM. D.MACLISE, pencil, V & A. W.M.THACKERAY, sketch, V & A.
PR UNKNOWN, hs, woodcut, for *The Queen, The Lady's Newspaper*, 1879, NPG.
PH JOHN and CHARLES WATKINS, hs, albumen, carte, NPG Album of Artists vol III.

LANDSEER, John (1769-1852) engraver and archaeologist.
P SIR EDWIN LANDSEER, (his son), c1848, hl seated, NPG 1843.
D E.LANDSEER, hs, pencil, BM.

LANDSEER, Thomas (1795-1880) engraver.
D CHARLES LANDSEER, (his brother), hs, chalk, NPG 1120.
PR JESSICA LANDSEER, (his sister), hl profile, asleep, lith, 1858, BM. W.J.EDWARDS, after G.Landseer, hl, stipple, NPG. UNKNOWN, after a photograph by Watkins, hs, woodcut, for *Illust London News*, 1868, NPG.
PH JOHN and CHARLES WATKINS, wl, albumen, carte, NPG Album of Artists vol II.

LANGDALE, Henry Bickersteth, Baron (1783-1851) master of the rolls.
M HENRY COLLEN, 1829, hl seated, NPG 1773.
PR S.FREEMAN, after G.Richmond, hs, stipple, for *Bentley's Miscellany*, 1852, BM, NPG. R.J.STOTHARD, tql seated at bench, lith, NPG.

LANGFORD, Abraham (1711-1774) auctioneer and playwright.
D JOHN GREENWOOD, head, pencil, BM.
PR UNKNOWN, hl holding up hammer, mezz, BM, NPG.

LANGHORNE, John (1735-1779) poet.
PR C.PYE, after R.Corbould, hs in cap, line, oval, pub 1804, BM.

LANGRISHE, Sir Hercules, 1st Bart (1731-1811) Irish politician.

G FRANCIS WHEATLEY, 'The Irish House of Commons', oil, 1780, Leeds City Art Galleries, Lotherton Hall, W.Yorks.

LANGTON, Bennet (1737-1801) Greek scholar, friend of Dr Johnson.
P SIR JOSHUA REYNOLDS, 1761-62, tql seated, Gunby Hall (NT), Lincs. CARL VON BREDA, RA 1790?, hl, Gunby Hall. Attrib JOHAN ZOFFANY, hl with bust of Dr Johnson, The Samuel Johnson Birthplace Museum, Lichfield.
D GEORGE DANCE, 1798, hs, profile, pencil, BM.
SC UNKNOWN, plaster bust, Trinity College, Oxford.

LANSDOWNE, Sir Henry Petty-Fitzmaurice, 3rd Marquess of (1780-1863) statesman.
P GEORGE ROMNEY, c1784, wl, Bowood, Wilts. HENRY WALTON, c1805, hl, NPG 178. SIR THOMAS LAWRENCE, 1827, tql, Bowood. JOHN LINNELL, c1840, hl seated, Bowood. SIR FRANCIS GRANT, 1854, hl seated, Bowood.
D E.T.PARRIS, 1838, hs, chalk, NPG 1383.
G SIR G.HAYTER, 'The House of Commons, 1833', NPG 54. DAVID WILKIE, 'Queen Victoria Presiding at her First Council, 1837', oil, Royal Coll. SIR G.HAYTER, 'The Coronation of Queen Victoria, 1838', oil, Royal Coll. JOHN PARTRIDGE, 'The Fine Arts Commissioners, 1846', NPG 342, 3.
SC SIR J.E.BOEHM, c1872, marble bust, Westminster Abbey, London.

LANSDOWNE, William Petty, 1st Marquess of (1737-1805) statesman and patron of the arts.
P SIR JOSHUA REYNOLDS, c1786, tql seated in robes, Bowood, Wilts. After REYNOLDS, hl, NPG 43.
G JOHN SINGLETON COPLEY, 'The Collapse of the Earl of Chatham in the House of Lords, 7 July 1788', oil, TATE 100, on loan to NPG. G.F.STORM, after J.Reynolds, with Lord Ashburton and Lieutenant Colonel Barré, mezz, for Britton's *Essay on Junius*, 1848, BM, NPG.
C Several engravings by JAMES SAYERS, NPG. UNKNOWN, hs, etch, pub 1794, NPG.

LANZA, Gesualdo (1779-1859) teacher of music.
PR H.MINASI, after T.Cheeseman, hs, stipple, oval, for Lanza's *The Elements of Singing*, 1809, V & A.

LARDNER, Dionysius (1793-1859) scientific writer.
M FORTUNÉE DE LISLE, posthumous, tql, oil, NPG 1039.
PR D.MACLISE, wl profile, lith, for *Fraser's Mag*, 1832, BM, NPG; w/c study, V & A. UNKNOWN, after T.Bridgford, hs, lith, NPG.

LARKING, Lambert Blackwell (1797-1868) antiquary.
PR HERBERT SMITH, 1857, hs, lith, NPG.

LARPENT, Francis Seymour (1776-1845) civil servant.
P UNKNOWN, wl seated with his wife, NPG 3806.

LARPENT, Sir George Gerard de Hochepied, 1st Bart (1786-1855) politician.
PR UNKNOWN, hs, woodcut, for *Illust London News*, 1847-48, NPG

LASCELLES, Henry (1767-1841), see 2nd Earl of Harewood

LATHAM, John (1761-1843) physician.
P JOHN JACKSON, RA 1816, hl, Brasenose College, Oxford.
D GEORGE DANCE, 1798, hs profile, chalk, Royal College of Physicians.
M ALEXANDER POPE, c1806, hs, oval, Royal College of Physicians, London.
SC R.W.SIEVIER, 1824, bust, St Bartholomew's Hospital, London

LATROBE, Christian Ignatius (1758-1836) musical composer.
PR S.BELLIN, after T.Barber, tql, mezz, BM, NPG.

LAUDER, Sir Thomas Dick, 7th Bart (1784-1848) author

C SIR JOHN STEELL, plaster bust, SNPG 226.
C After B.W.CROMBIE, wl, woodcut, NPG.

LAUDERDALE, James Maitland, 8th Earl of (1759-1839) statesman and writer.
P THOMAS PHILLIPS, 1806-07, hl, SNPG 756.
D JOHN HENNING, 1806, pencil, SNPG 397. JOHN HENNING, hs, pencil, SNPG 119.
G SIR GEORGE HAYTER, 'The Trial of Queen Caroline, 1820', NPG 999.
C JOSEPH NOLLEKENS, 1803, marble bust, SNPG 1364. UNKNOWN, plaster bust, SNPG 348. JOHN HENNING, 1806, paste medallion, SNPG 212.
C J.SAYERS, hs, entitled 'Brissot', etch, pub 1794, BM, NPG.

LAURIE, Sir Peter (1779?-1861) lord mayor of London.
P THOMAS PHILLIPS, wl in robes, Bridewell Royal Hospital, Witley, Surrey.
R UNKNOWN, tql, woodcut, for *Illust London News*, 1842-43, NPG. C.HAMBURGER, after F.Cruikshank, hl, lith, BM. UNKNOWN, tql, stipple and line, for Cassell's *Old and New London*, NPG.

LAW, Charles Ewan (1792-1850) recorder of London.
P H.W.PICKERSGILL, St John's College, Cambridge.
D SIR GEORGE HAYTER, head, pencil, BM.

LAW, Edmund (1703-1787) bishop of Carlisle.
P After ROMNEY, Peterhouse, Cambridge.
R W.DICKINSON, after G.Romney, tql seated, mezz, BM.

LAW, Edward (1750-1818), see 1st Baron Ellenborough.

LAW, Edward (1790-1871), see 1st Earl of Ellenborough.

LAW, George Henry (1761-1845) bishop of Bath and Wells.
P Attrib SIR WILLIAM BEECHEY, c1828, tql seated, Bishop's Palace, Wells. Attrib PICKERSGILL, Bishop's Palace, Wells.
G SIR GEORGE HAYTER, 'The Trial of Queen Caroline, 1820', oil, NPG 999, study NPG 1695 (n).
R W.SAY, after H.Pickersgill, hl seated, mezz, pub 1820, BM, NPG.

LAWLESS, John (1773-1837) Irish agitator.
P RICHARD ROTHWELL, c1820, hs, Ulster Museum, Belfast.
L HARDING, hs, profile with top hat, NPG.
G UNKNOWN, one of four silhouette profiles of Irish Politicians, lith, BM.

LAWRENCE, Sir Soulden (1751-1814) judge.
R C.TURNER, after J.Hoppner, tql in robes, mezz, pub 1808, BM, NPG.

LAWRENCE, Thomas (1711-1783) physician.
C JOHN FLAXMAN, marble tablet on memorial, Canterbury Cathedral.

LAWRENCE, Sir Thomas (1769-1830) portrait painter, collector and President of the Royal Academy.
P Self-portrait, c1825, hl, Royal Academy, London; copy by R.E.Evans, NPG 260.
D Self-portrait, 1786, hs, Burghley, Northants. WILLIAM BROCKEDON, hs profile, NPG 2515 (21). GEORGE DANCE, hs profile, Royal Academy.
G HENRY SINGLETON, 'The Royal Academicians, 1793', oil, Royal Academy.
C LAURENCE, GAHAGAN, 1812, bronze sculpture, NGI 8068. R.W.SIEVIER, c1830, marble bust, Sir John Soane's Museum, London. E.H.BAILY, marble bust, NPG 239. Plaster cast of death mask and right hand, NPG 1634.
R R.J.LANE, after Sir T.Lawrence drawing of 1812, hs, lith, NPG. C.TURNER, hl, mezz, pub 1830, BM, NPG.

LAWRENCE, Sir William, 1st Bart (1783-1867) surgeon.
P H.W.PICKERSGILL, tql, St Bartholomew's Hospital, London.

G G.B.BLACK, after daguerreotypes by Mayall, 'English Physicians', lith, pub 1851, BM.
SC HENRY WEEKES, marble bust, Royal College of Surgeons, London.
PR C.TURNER, tql seated, mezz, pub 1839, BM. J.COCHRAN, after H.Wyatt, hl, stipple, NPG. UNKNOWN, hs, woodcut, for *Illust London News*, 1867, BM, NPG.

LAWRENSON, Thomas (fl 1760-1777) painter.
PR W.LAWRENSON, hl in cap, laughing, mezz, BM, NPG.

LAWSON, George (1749-1820) Presbyterian minister.
SC JAMES TASSIE, 1794, wax medallion, SNPG 1469.
PR J.HORSBURGH, after J.Pairman, hl, line, for his *Exposition of the Book of Proverbs*, 1821, BM.

LAWSON, John (1712-1759) writer on oratory.
SC PATRICK CUNNINGHAM, 1759, marble bust, Trinity College, Dublin.
PR A.MILLER, hs, mezz, oval, BM.

LEACH, Sir John (1760-1834) master of the rolls.
D G.R.LEWIS, hl, w/c stipple, BM.
PR T.WRIGHT, after A.Wivell, tql stipple, pub 1821, BM, NPG. H.DAWE, after C.Penny, wl seated, mezz, pub 1825, BM, NPG.

LEACH, Thomas (1746-1818) legal writer.
PR AUDINET, after Drummond, hs, line, oval, for *European Mag*, 1793, NPG.

LEAKE, John (1729-1792) male midwife.
PR F.BARTOLOZZI, after D.Gardner, hs, stipple, oval, for his *Medical Instructions*, 1781, BM, NPG.

LEAKE, Stephen Martin (1702-1773) Garter king of arms.
PR T.MILTON, after R.E.Pine, hl, line, for Noble's *College of Arms*, 1803, BM, NPG.

LEAKE, William Martin (1777-1860) classical topographer and numismatist.
SC WILLIAM BEHNES, marble bust, Fitzwilliam Museum, Cambridge.

LE BRUN, John (d 1865) independent missionary.
PR H.T.RYALL, after J.Andrews, hs, stipple, NPG.

LE DESPENCER, Francis Dashwood, 15th Baron (1708-1781) Chancellor of the Exchequer; founder of the Hell-fire Club.
P Attrib NATHANIEL DANCE, hl, NPG 1345. GEORGE KNAPTON, 1742, hl as a monk with chalice and statue, The Society of Dilettanti, Brooks's Club, London.
PR J.FABER, jun, after A.Carpentièr, hl, mezz, BM, NPG. PLATT, after W.Hogarth, as a monk worshipping a figure of Venus, line, BM, NPG.

LEDWICH, Edward (1738-1823) antiquary.
PR SHEA, after Cullen, hs aged 78, stipple, NPG.

LEE, Charles (1731-1782) American major-general.
PR G.R.HALL, hl, stipple, NPG. 'R.P.', hs, line, oval, for Murray's *History of the American War*, NPG. UNKNOWN, scene of his arrest, wl, line, oval, NPG.

LEE, Frederick Richard (1799-1879) painter.
PH Two photographs by JOHN and CHARLES WATKINS, both hs, albumen, carte, NPG Album of Artists vol I and vol III.

LEE, Sir George (1700-1758) lawyer and politician.
PR J.FABER, jun, after J.Wills, hl, mezz, oval, BM, NPG.

LEE, George Henry (1718-1772), see 3rd Earl of Lichfield.

LEE, James (1715-1795) nurseryman.
PR S.FREEMAN, hl with fuchsia, stipple, for his *Introduction to the Science of Botany*, 1810, BM, NPG.

LEE, John (1733-1793) attorney-general.
SC JOSEPH NOLLEKENS, 1795, bust on monument, Staindrop Church, Durham.
PR R.STEWART, hs, mezz, oval, pub 1778, BM. C.H.HODGES, after J.Reynolds, tql seated in robes, mezz, pub 1788, BM. NPG.
C J.SAYERS, wl, etch, pub 1784, NPG.

LEE, John (1779-1859) principal of Edinburgh University.
P Two portraits by SIR JOHN WATSON-GORDON, wl and tql, Edinburgh University.
SL AUGUSTIN EDOUART, wl, SNPG 781.
PR J.ARCHER, hs, lith, BM.
C B.W.CROMBIE, wl, coloured etch, 1847, reprinted *Modern Athenians*, 1882, NPG.

LEE, John (1783-1866) collector and scientist.
D R.INWARDS, chalk, Royal Astronomical Society, London.
PR T.H.MAGUIRE, tql seated, lith, for *Ipswich Museum Portraits*, 1852, BM, NPG. F.CROLL, hs, line, NPG. UNKNOWN, hl, lith, BM.

LEE, Rachel Fanny Antonina (1774?-1829) heroine of a criminal trial.
PR UNKNOWN, wl seated in nightclothes 'Ruminating on her extraordinary Dream', stipple, oval, BM.

LEE, Samuel (1783-1852) orientalist.
P Attrib R.EVANS, tql seated, Trinity College, Cambridge.
PR J.THOMPSON, after J.Gooch of 1821, hs, stipple, pub 1821, NPG. W.T.FRY, after R.Evans, tql seated, stipple, for Jerdan's *Nat Portrait Gallery*, 1833, BM, pub 1º46, NPG.

LEE, Sophia (1750-1824) writer.
PR W.RIDLEY, after T.Lawrence, hl in turban, stipple, oval, for *Monthly Mirror*, 1797, BM, NPG.

LEECHMAN, William (1706-1785) divine.
PR J.CALDWALL, after W.Millar, hl, line, pub 1789, BM, NPG.

LEEDS, Francis Osborne, 5th Duke of' (1751-1799) politician.
P Attrib GEORGE KNAPTON, after Reynolds, hl, NPG 801.
G SIR JOSHUA REYNOLDS, 'The Society of Dilettanti', oil, 1777–79, Brooks's Club, London.
PR R.M.MEADOWS, after T.Lawrence, wl in Garter robes, stipple, BM, NPG.

LEES, Sir Harcourt, 2nd Bart (1776-1852) political pamphleteer.
PR H.MEYER, after T.C.Thompson, tql seated, stipple, BM, NPG.

LEFEVRE, Charles Shaw, see 1st Viscount Eversley.

LEFEVRE, Sir John George Shaw, see Shaw.

LEFROY, Thomas Langlois (1776-1869) Irish judge.
P S.CATTERSON SMITH, King's Inns, Dublin.
G SIR GEORGE HAYTER, 'The House of Commons, 1833', oil, NPG 54.
SC CHRISTOPHER MOORE, 1839, marble bust, Trinity College, Dublin.
PR H.ROBINSON, after G.Hayter, hl, stipple and line, BM, NPG. UNKNOWN, tql seated in robes, mezz, BM, NPG.

LEGAT, Francis (1755-1809) engraver.
PR T.PRESCOTT, after Runciman, hs, stipple, NPG.

LEGGE, George (1755-1810), see 3rd Earl of Dartmouth.

LEGGE, Henry Bilson (1708-1764) chancellor of the exchequer.
P WILLIAM HOARE, tql in Chancellor's robes, DoE (Treasury Board Room, London). Attrib STEPHEN SLAUGHTER, with Sir Robert Walpole, Treasury Boardroom.

LEGGE, William (1731-1801), see 2nd Earl of Dartmouth.

LEICESTER, George Townshend, Earl of, see 2nd Marquess of Townshend.

LEICESTER, Sir John Fleming, see 1st Baron DE Tabley

LEICESTER, Thomas William Coke, 1st Earl of (1752 1842) agriculturalist.
P POMPEO BATONI, 1774, wl with dog, Holkham Hall, Norfolk THOMAS GAINSBOROUGH, 1778, wl with gun and dogs Holkham Hall. SIR THOMAS LAWRENCE, 1807, Shire Hall Norwich. R.R.REINAGLE, RA 1815, wl with dog, Shugborough (NT), Staffs; version, Holkham. SIR THOMAS LAWRENCE, c1818 hl, Walker Art Gallery, Liverpool. SIR GEORGE HAYTER, tql Holkham. JOHN OPIE, wl, Holkham.
D SIR FRANCIS CHANTREY, hs, pencil, NPG 316a (77, 78).
G THOMAS WEAVER, wl with a herd of sheep and several shepherds, Holkham.
SC GEORGE GARRARD, 1806, marble bust, Shugborough. SIR FRANCIS CHANTREY, 1829, marble bust, Holkham.

LEIFCHILD, John (1780-1862) independent minister.
PR R.WOODMAN, hl seated, stipple, for *Congregational Mag*, 1825 BM. T.BLOOD, after J.R.Wildman, hl, stipple, for *Evangelical Mag*, 1825, BM, NPG. J.LINNELL, tql, mezz, pub 1836, NPG W.DICKES, after C.Baugniet 1854, hl, stipple, NPG.

LEIGH, Chandos Leigh, 1st Baron (1791-1850) poet.
PR UNKNOWN, tql, stipple, BM.

LEIGH, Thomas Pemberton, see 1st Baron Kingsdown.

LEINSTER, James Fitzgerald, 1st Duke of (1722-1773 politician.
P Attrib ALLAN RAMSAY, hl, Goodwood, W.Sussex.
SC UNKNOWN, medal, BM.
PR J.McARDELL, after J.Reynolds, tql in peer's robes, mezz, BM NPG.

LEITH, Sir James (1763-1816) general and colonial governor
D BENJAMIN BURRELL, hs, pencil, chalk, w/c, SNPG 122.
PR C.PICART, after J.Wright, hl with orders, stipple, BM, NPG.

LEITH HAY, Alexander (1758-1838) general.
P J.W.CHANDLER, tql, Leith Hall (NT), Grampian region Scotland.
D ROBERT DIGHTON, wl, w/c, Leith Hall.

LELAND, Thomas (1722-1785) Irish historian.
P SIR JOSHUA REYNOLDS, c1776, hl, Staatsgalerie, Stuttgart W.Germany. Attrib THOMAS HICKEY, NGI 655.

LE MARCHANT, Sir Denis, 1st Bart (1795-1874 politician.
G JOHN PHILLIPS, 'The House of Commons, 1860', oil, Palace c Westminster, London.
PR UNKNOWN, after a photograph by Kilburn, tql, woodcut, fo *Illust London News*, 1851, NPG. UNKNOWN, hs, woodcut for *Illus London News*, 1874, NPG.

LE MARCHANT, John Gaspard (1766-1812) major general.
P UNKNOWN, tql, Staff College, Camberley, Surrey.
SC J.SMITH, medallion on monument, St Paul's Cathedral, London

LEMOINE, Henry (1756-1812) writer and itinerant bookseller.
PR UNKNOWN, wl, etch, for *Wonderful Mag*, 1806, BM, NPG.

LEMON, Robert (1779-1835) archivist.
PR M.GAUCI, tql seated, with bust of Milton, lith, BM, NPG.

LEMPRIÈRE, John (1765?-1824) classical scholar.
P UNKNOWN, hl, St John's College, Cambridge. UNKNOWN, h Pembroke College, Cambridge.

LENNOX, Charles (1701-1750), see 2nd Duke of RICHMOND and Lennox.

LENNOX, Charles (1735-1806), see 3rd Duke of RICHMOND and Lennox.

LENNOX, Charles (1764-1819), see 4th Duke of RICHMOND and Lennox.

LENNOX, Charles Gordon, see 5th Duke of RICHMOND and Lennox.

LENNOX, Charlotte, née Ramsay (1720-1804) writer.
G RICHARD SAMUEL, 'The Nine Living Muses of Great Britain', oil, exhib 1779, NPG 4905.
PR F.BARTOLOZZI, after J.Reynolds, hs, stipple, for Harding's *Shakespeare Illustrated*, 1793, BM, NPG.

LENNOX, George Henry (1737-1805) general.
P POMPEO BATONI, 1752–53, tql, with dog, Goodwood, W.Sussex.
G GEORGE STUBBS, wl equestrian, with his brother 3rd Duke of Richmond and General Jones, Goodwood.

LENNOX, Lord William Pitt (1799-1881) miscellaneous writer.
D F.P.STEPHANOFF, attending Lord Rowland Hill, at the Coronation of George IV, w/c, V & A, engr H.Meyer, stipple and aquatint, for Sir G.Nayler's work on the Coronation of George IV, 1824, BM.

LENS, Andrew Benjamin (fl 1765-1770) miniature painter.
M BENJAMIN LENS, 1723, tql as a child, V & A.

LENS, John (1756-1825) serjeant-at-law and commissioner of assize.
PR C.PENNY, hl, stipple, pub 1825, NPG, pub 1829 BM. F.C.LEWIS, after E.Coffin, hs, stipple, oval, BM, NPG.

LESLIE, Charles Robert (1794-1859) painter and writer.
P Self-portrait, 1814, hl profile, NPG 2618. JOHN PARTRIDGE, 1836, hl, NPG 4232.
D C.H.LEAR, 1846, hs, chalk, NPG 1456 (15). C.W.COPE, c1862, head, sketch, pencil, NPG 3182 (4, 5).
SC A.B.WYON, RA 1872, bronze medallion, NPG for the Art Union.
PH MAYALL, hs, albumen, carte, NPG Album of Artists vol 1.

LESLIE, Sir John (1766-1832) scientist and mathematician.
P J.CAW, after Sir D.Wilkie, hl, Edinburgh University.
D SIR FRANCIS CHANTREY, hs, pencil, NPG 316a (64). JOHN HENNING, head, chalk, SNPG 660.
SC JOHN RIND, after Samuel Joseph, marble bust, SNPG 291.
PR W.WASTLE, hl profile, etch, for Lockhart's *Peter's Letter to his Kinsfolk*, 1819, BM, NPG. H.COOK, after A.Chisholm, hl, stipple, for Jerdan's *Nat Portrait Gallery*, 1833, BM, NPG.

LETHIEULLIER, Smart (1701-1760) antiquary.
P GEORGE KNAPTON, hs, Breamore House, Hants.

LETTSOM, John Coakley (1744-1815) physician.
SC T.R.POOLE, wax medallion, Royal College of Physicians, London.
PR T.HOLLOWAY, hs, line, for *European Mag*, 1787, BM, NPG. W.SKELTON, hs, line, oval, for his *Memoirs* by Pettigrew, 1817, BM, NPG.

LEVER, Sir Ashton (1729-1788) collector.
SC JOHN FLAXMAN, Wedgwood medallion, Brooklyn Museum, New York.
PR W.ANGUS, hl, line, oval, for *European Mag*, 1784, BM. W.NUTTER, after S.Shelley, hl, stipple, oval, pub 1787, BM, NPG.

LEVERTON, Thomas (1743-1824) architect.

P UNKNOWN, hl, St Giles-in-the-Fields, London.

LEVESON-GOWER, George Granville, see 1st Duke of Sutherland.

LEVESON-GOWER, Granville (1721-1803), see 1st Marquess of Stafford.

LEVESON-GOWER, Lord Granville (1773-1846), see 1st Earl Granville.

LEVI, David (1740-1799) Jewish controversialist.
PR W.BROMLEY, after S.Drummond, hl, line and stipple, oval, for *European Mag*, 1799, BM, NPG.

LEWES, Charles Lee (1740-1803) actor.
P SAMUEL DE WILDE, wl as Bobadil in *Every Man in his Humour*, Garrick Club, London, w/c portrait by de Wilde, same subject, Garrick Club.
PR Various theatrical prints, BM, NPG.

LEWIS, Charles (1786-1836) bookbinder.
PR G.R.LEWIS, hl, stipple, BM, NPG.

LEWIS, Frederick Christian (1781-1856) engraver and landscape painter.
D J.F.LEWIS, hs, pencil, V & A, etch, C.G.Lewis, 1834, V&A.
G A.E.CHALON, 'Study at the British Institution 1806', pen and ink, BM.
PR C.G.LEWIS, after sketch by J.F.Lewis of 1834, hs, roulette, BM, NPG.

LEWIS, Griffith George (1784-1859), lieutenant-general.
P UNKNOWN, wl, Royal Engineers HQ Mess, Chatham, Kent.

LEWIS, Matthew Gregory (1775-1818) writer.
P H.W.PICKERSGILL, hl, NPG 421.
M G.L.SAUNDERS, hs, NPG 2171.
PR W.RIDLEY, after S.Drummond, hl, stipple, oval, for *Monthly Mirror*, 1796, BM, NPG. J.HOLLIS, after G.H.Harlow, hl, stipple, for *Life and Works of Lord Byron*, 1834, BM, NPG.

LEWIS, Sir Thomas Frankland, 1st Bart (1780-1855) politician.
P JOHN HOPPNER, hl, (a leaving portrait), Eton College, Berks.
PR T.WRIGHT, after A.Wivell, hs, stipple, pub 1822, BM, NPG. R.J.LANE, after J.Slater, hs, lith, one of 'Grillion's Club' series, BM, NPG. T.H.MAGUIRE, after F.Watts, tql seated, lith, BM, NPG.

LEWIS, William Thomas (1748?-1811) actor.
P SIR M.A.SHEE, RA 1792, wl as the Marquess in *The Midnight Hour*, NG 677. SIR M.A.SHEE, hs, Garrick Club, London. SAMUEL DEWILDE, wl as Pharnacles in *Cleonice*, Garrick Club. Attrib JOHN STEWART, hs, Garrick Club. GAINSBOROUGH DUPONT, hl in character, NPG 5148.
D GEORGE DANCE, 1798, hs profile, pencil, BM. S. DE WILDE, 1809, wl as Mercutio in *Romeo and Juliet*, w/c, Garrick Club.
G JOHAN ZOFFANY, as Tanjore in a scene from *Speculation*, oil, c1795–96, Garrick Club.
PR Theatrical prints, BM, NPG.

LEWSON, Jane (1700-1816) centenarian.
PR R.COOPER, wl, stipple, pub 1821, BM, NPG.

LEYDEN, John (1775-1811) physician poet.
D UNKNOWN, ink, SNPG 1686.

LIART, Matthew (1736-1782?) engraver.
PR P.AUDINET, after J.Liart, hl, holding crayon and portfolio, mezz, BM.

LICHFIELD, George Henry Lee, 3rd Earl of (1718-1772) chancellor of Oxford University.
P GEORGE HUDDESFORD, 1777, wl in chancellor's robes,

Examination Schools, Oxford. UNKNOWN, hs, Radcliffe Infirmary, Oxford.

G JOHN WOOTTON, 1744, 'Members of the Beaufort Hunt', TATE 4679.

LIDDELL, Sir Henry Thomas, see 2nd Baron and 1st Earl of Ravensworth.

LIFFORD, James Hewitt, 1st Viscount (1709-1789) lord chancellor of Ireland.

P SIR JOSHUA REYNOLDS, hs, National Collection of Fine Arts, Smithsonian Institution, Washington DC, USA. R.L.WEST, after Reynolds, hs, NGI 124.

PR R.DUNKARTON, after J.Reynolds, wl seated in chancellor's robes, with purse, mezz, pub 1790, BM.

LIGHT, William (1786-1839) surveyor-general of South Australia.

P GEORGE JONES, head, NPG 982 (c). Self-portrait, hs, unfinished, National Gallery of South Australia, Adelaide.

LIGONIER, Edward Ligonier, 1st Earl (d1782) lieutenant-general.

P THOMAS GAINSBOROUGH, RA 1771, wl with horse, Huntington Library and Art Gallery, San Marino, USA.

LIMERICK, Edmund Henry Percy, 1st Earl of (1758-1844) politician.

G SIR GEORGE HAYTER, 'The Trial of Queen Caroline, 1820', oil, NPG 999.

PR T.A.DEAN, after G.Dawe, tql seated in peer's robes, stipple, pub 1840, BM, NPG.

LINCOLN, Henry Fiennes Clinton, 9th Earl of, see 2nd Duke of Newcastle-under-Lyme.

LIND, James (1716-1794) physician.

PR J.WRIGHT, after Sir G.Chalmers of 1783, hl, stipple, oval, Wellcome Institute, London.

LIND, James (1736-1812) physician.

PR Two engraved silhouette profiles, BM.

LINDLEY, John (1799-1865) botanist.

P E.U.EDDIS, hs, Royal Horticultural Society, London.

D UNKNOWN, pencil, Royal Horticultural Society Gardens, Wisley, Ripley, Surrey.

PR MISS TURNER, after E.U.Eddis, hs, lith, BM. S.LINDLEY, after C.Fox, hl, etch, BM. T.H.MAGUIRE, hl, lith, for *Ipswich Museum Portraits*, BM, NPG.

LINDLEY, Robert (1776-1855) cellist.

P WILLIAM DAVISON, tql, NPG 1952.

D A.E.CHALON, hl with cello, pen and w/c, NPG 1962e.

LINDSAY, Lady Anne, see Barnard.

LINDSAY, James Bowman (1799-1862) electrician and philologist.

SC GEORGE WEBSTER, marble sculpture, Dundee City Art Gallery.

LINDSAY, John (1702-1749), see 20th Earl of Crawford.

LINDSAY, John (1737-1788) rear-admiral.

P ALLAN RAMSAY, hl, Glasgow Art Gallery and Museum.

SC After JAMES TASSIE of 1779, plaster medallion, SNPG 440.

LINDSEY, Theophilus (1723-1808) unitarian.

PR UNKNOWN, hs, stipple, oval, pub 1809, NPG. NEELE, hs, oval, engraved silhouette, NPG.

LINGARD, John (1771-1851) Roman Catholic historian.

M THOMAS SKAIFE, 1848, hl, NPG 4304.

PR C.FOX, after J.Ramsay, hl seated, line, pub 1823, BM, NPG. H.COUSINS, after J.Lonsdale, tql seated, mezz, pub 1836, BM, NPG. L.STOCKS, after S.Lover, hl, line, NPG.

LINLEY, Elizabeth, see Mrs Elizabeth Sheridan.

LINLEY, George (1798-1865) poet and musical composer.

P C.H.SCHWANFELDER, hs, Leeds City Art Gallery, Temple Newsam House.

LINLEY, Mary, see Mrs Tickell.

LINLEY, Ozias Thurston (1766-1831) organist.

D Attrib SIR THOMAS LAWRENCE, hl, chalk, Dulwich College Picture Gallery, London.

LINLEY, Thomas (1733-1795) musical composer.

P THOMAS GAINSBOROUGH, hl, Dulwich College Picture Gallery, London.

LINLEY, Thomas (1756-1778) violinist and composer.

P THOMAS GAINSBOROUGH, c1768, hs with his sister Elizabeth, Sterling and Francine Clark Art Institute, Williamstown, Mass, USA. THOMAS GAINSBOROUGH, c1773–74, hl, Dulwich College Picture Gallery, London.

LINLEY, William (1771-1835) writer and composer.

P SIR THOMAS LAWRENCE, RA 1789, hl as a boy, Dulwich College Picture Gallery, London.

LINNECAR, Richard (1722-1800) dramatist.

PR T.BARROW, after H.Singleton, tql, stipple, pub 1800, NPG.

LINNELL, John (1792-1882) portrait and landscape painter.

P Self-portrait, c1860, hl, NPG 1811.

D C.H.LEAR, c1845, hs, pencil, NPG 1456 (16).

G A.E.CHALON, 'Students at the British Association, 1807', w/c, BM.

PH MAULL & CO, tql, carte, NPG Album of Artists vol I. ELLIOTT & FRY, hs, carte, NPG Album of Artists vol III. UNKNOWN, hs, carte, NPG Photographs of Artists (Arundell Coll).

LINTON, William (1791-1876) painter.

PR C.K.CHILDS, hs, woodcut, for *Art Journal*, 1850, BM, NPG.

LINWOOD, Mary (1755-1845) artist in needlework and musical composer.

P JOHN HOPPNER, hl, V & A.

PR W.RIDLEY, after W.Beechey, tql seated, stipple, oval, for *Monthly Mirror*, 1800, BM, NPG. W.RIDLEY, after Rivers, tql seated, stipple, oval, for *Lady's Monthly Museum*, 1800, BM, NPG.

LIPSCOMB, Christopher (1781-1843) first bishop of Jamaica.

P By of after G.W.PEGLER, tql, New College, Oxford, engr C.Turner, mezz, pub 1829, BM, NPG.

LISLE, James George Semple, see SEMPLE.

LISTON, John (1776?-1846) actor.

P SAMUEL DE WILDE, 1812, as Pompey in *Measure for Measure*, V & A. S. DE WILDE, 1812, as Gaby Grim in *We Fly by Night*, Garrick Club, London. GEORGE CLINT, hs, Garrick Club.

D CHARLES BROCKY, hs, chalk, BM. Three drawings by DE WILDE, in character, w/c, Garrick Club.

SL UNKNOWN, wl, NPG 3098.

G S. DE WILDE, in a scene from *The Lord of the Manor*, oil, 1814, Garrick Club. GEORGE CLINT, in a scene from *Paul Pry*, oil, RA 1827, V & A. G.CLINT, in a scene from *Love, Law, and Physic*, oil, RA 1830, Garrick Club.

PR Numerous theatrical prints, BM, NPG.

LISTON, Sir Robert (1742-1836) diplomat.

P SIR DAVID WILKIE, 1811, hl, SNPG 1313.

LISTON, Robert (1794-1847) surgeon.

P S.J.STUMP, exhib 1848, hl, and W. or G.Clarkson Stanfield, hs, both Royal College of Surgeons, Edinburgh.

SC THOMAS CAMPBELL, 1851, marble bust, Royal College of

Surgeons, London.

M.GAUCI, after E.U.Eddis, hs, lith, pub 1836, BM. J.C.BROMLEY, after F.Grant, hs, mezz, pub 1839, BM. C.TURNER, tql, mezz, pub 1840, BM. A. D'ORSAY, hl, lith, BM. B.W.CROMBIE, hs profile, lith, SNPG.

LITCHFIELD, Harriett, née Hay (1777-1854) actress.
SAMUEL DRUMMOND, hl, Garrick Club, London.
W.RIDLEY, after C.Allingham, hl, stipple, oval, for *Monthly Mirror*, 1802, BM, NPG. W.SAY, after G.H.Harlow, hl seated, mezz, pub 1816, BM, NPG.

LITTLEDALE, Sir Joseph (1767-1842) judge.
THOMAS PHILLIPS, tql seated, Gray's Inn, London.

LITTLER, Sir John Hunter (1783-1856) lieutenant-general.
UNKNOWN, hs, woodcut, for *Illust London News*, 1845–46, NPG.

LITTLETON, Edward John, see 1st Baron Hatherton.

LIVERPOOL, Charles Jenkinson, 1st Earl of (1727-1808) statesman.
After GEORGE ROMNEY of 1786–87, tql, University College, Oxford.
JOHN FLAXMAN, Wedgwood medallion, Wedgwood Museum, Barlaston, Staffs.
UNKNOWN, hl, line, oval, for *European Mag*, 1785, BM, NPG.
J.MURPHY, after G.Romney, wl seated, mezz, pub 1788, BM, NPG.

LIVERPOOL, Robert Banks Jenkinson, 2nd Earl of (1770-1828) prime-minister.
SIR THOMAS LAWRENCE, c1820–23, tql with Garter star, Royal Coll. SIR T.LAWRENCE, RA 1827, wl, NPG 1804. SIR GEORGE HAYTER, Weston Park, Salop.
K.A.HICKEL, 'The House of Commons, 1793', oil, NPG 745. SIR GEORGE HAYTER, 'The Trial of Queen Caroline, 1820', oil, NPG 999.
JOSEPH NOLLEKENS, 1816, marble bust, Royal Coll. B.F.HARDENBERG, bust, Ickworth (NT), Suffolk.
H.MEYER, after J.Hoppner, hl, mezz, pub 1808, BM, NPG.
C.TURNER, hl, mezz, pub 1826, BM, NPG.

LIVESEY, Joseph (1794-1884) temperance advocate.
UNKNOWN, 'The Family of Joseph and Jane Livesey', line, 1838, BM.

LIZARS, William Home (1788-1859) artist.
Self-portrait, hl, chalk, SNPG 2175.

LLOYD, Bartholomew (1772-1837) provost of Trinity College, Dublin.
CAMPANILE, hl seated, Trinity College, Dublin.
THOMAS KIRK, c1830–37, marble bust, NGI 8043.
C.TURNER, after H.O'Neill, tql seated, mezz, pub 1838, BM.

LLOYD, Charles (1748-1828) quaker, and Birmingham banker.
PETER HOLLINS, c1831, bust, Birmingham General Hospital.
UNKNOWN, hs, profile, stipple, NPG.

LLOYD, Charles (1775-1839) poet.
JANE IRELAND, hs, w/c stipple, BM.

LLOYD, Charles (1784-1829) bishop of Oxford.
B.R.FAULKNER, hs, Christ Church, Oxford.
F.C.LEWIS, after B.R.Faulkner, hs, mezz, oval, BM, NPG.

LLOYD, Mary (d1819) see Mary Moser.

LÖBEL, Hirsch, see Hart LYON.

LOCH, James (1780-1855) economist.
SIR GEORGE HAYTER, 'The House of Commons, 1833', oil, NPG 54.

PR J.POSSELWHITE, after G.Richmond, hs, stipple, pub 1850, BM, NPG.

LOCKE, William (1732-1810) art connoisseur.
P SIR THOMAS LAWRENCE, RA 1790, hl, Boston Museum of Fine Arts, USA.
G JAMES BARRY, 'The Society for the Encouragement of Arts', oil, Royal Society of Arts, London.

LOCKE, William (1767-1847) artist.
PR C.TOWNLEY, after J.Hoppner, hl, mezz, pub 1784, BM.

LOCKER, Edward Hawke (1777-1849) commissoner of Greenwich Hospital.
P H.W.PHILLIPS, c1830, hl, oval, NMM, Greenwich.

LOCKER, William (1731-1800) captain in the navy.
P DOMINIC SERRES, 1769, hl, Yale Center for British Art, New Haven, USA. GILBERT STUART, c1785, hl, in uniform, oval, NMM, Greenwich. G.STUART, c1785, hl in green riding coat, NMM. L.F.ABBOTT, c1795, hl, NMM.

LOCKHART, John Gibson (1794-1854) biographer of Scott.
P SIR FRANCIS GRANT, hl, SNPG 1588.
D SIR JOHN WATSON-GORDON, pencil and chalk, SNPG 1821.
PR D.MACLISE, wl seated, lith, for *Fraser's Mag*, 1830, BM. G.T.DOO, after H.W.Pickersgill, hs, line, NPG. UNKNOWN, after R. Scott Lauder, hl, stipple, NPG.
PH DAVID OCTAVIUS HILL, hl, carbon print, NPG.

LOCKHART-Ross, Sir John, see Sir John Lockhart ROSS.

LOCOCK, Sir Charles, 1st Bart (1799-1875) obstetric physician.
PR C.BAUGNIET, tql seated, lith, BM. UNKNOWN, hs, woodcut, for *Illust London News*, 1875, BM.

LODER, John David (1791-1846) violinist.
PR J.BRANDARD, after F.Salabert, hl, lith, BM, NPG.

LODGE, Edmund (1756-1839) historian and biographer.
P L.F.ABBOTT, hs, NPG 1411.
D DANIEL MACLISE, 1828, hl, pencil, BM.
PR D.MACLISE, wl in tabard, etch, for *Fraser's Mag*, 1836, BM, NPG.

LOFFT, Capell (1751-1824) writer and whig politician.
PR W.RIDLEY, after Holloway, hl, stipple, oval, for *Monthly Mirror*, 1802, BM, NPG. UNKNOWN, wl, etch, BM, NPG.

LOGAN, John (1748-1788) divine and poet.
D JOHN BROWN, hs, pencil, SNPG 154.
PR Engravings after the above, by several artists, BM, NPG.

LOGAN, Sir William Edmund (1798-1875) Canadian geologist.
PH ERNEST EDWARDS, wl seated, albumen, for ed L.Reeve, *Men of Eminence*, vol III, 1865, NPG.

LOGIER, John Bernard (1780-1846) musician.
PR C.TURNER, after J.Lonsdale, tql seated, mezz, pub 1819, BM, NPG. H.MEYER, after J.R.Maguire, hs, stipple, BM, NPG.

LONDONDERRY, Charles William Stewart (Vane), 3rd Marquess of (1778-1854) general and diplomatist.
D Attrib ISAAC CRUIKSHANK, c1835, sketch, pencil and wash, NPG 2789.
SC RAFFAELE MONTI, c1858, bronze equestrian statue, Market Place, Durham.
PR J.HOPWOOD, after Sir Thomas Lawrence, hl, stipple, for *Military Panorama*, 1813, BM, NPG. J.JENKINS, after J.Bostock, hl seated, stipple, for *Eminent Conservative Statesmen*, 1837, BM, NPG.
C JOHN DOYLE, several satirical sketches, drgs, BM.

LONDONDERRY, Robert Stewart, 2nd Marquess of (Lord Castlereagh) (1769-1822) statesman.

P SIR THOMAS LAWRENCE, RA 1810, hl, NPG 891. SIR THOMAS LAWRENCE, replica of portrait RA 1814, tql with Garter star, Royal Coll.

D GEORGE DANCE, 1794, hl profile, pencil, NPG 1141. SIR FRANCIS CHANTREY, two hs pencil sketches, NPG 316a (13a, 14).

M WILLIAM BATE, 1822, enamel, NGI 2333.

G Attrib THOMAS ROBINSON, a political group at the Bishop's Palace at Dromore, oil, c1801–08, Castle Ward (NT), Co Down, N.Ireland. SIR GEORGE HAYTER, 'The Trial of Queen Caroline, 1820', oil, NPG 999.

SC SIR FRANCIS CHANTREY, 1822, bust, Royal Coll. SIR F.CHANTREY, marble bust, NPG 687. UNKNOWN, 1822, head, wax-relief, NPG 4384. J.E.THOMAS, 1844, marble statue, Westminster Abbey, London.

LONG, Amelia, see Lady Farnborough.

LONG, Lady Catherine, née Walpole (1797-1867) novelist and religious writer.

PR J.COCHRAN, after A.E.Chalon, hl, stipple, oval, for *The Court Magazine*, BM.

LONG, Charles (1761-1838), see 1st Baron Farnborough.

LONG, Edward (1734-1813) writer.

PR W.SHARP, after J.Opie, tql seated, line, pub 1796, BM.

LONG, John St John (1798-1834) philosopher.

PR J.FAHEY, hl profile, lith, pub 1831, NPG. UNKNOWN, tql, lith, BM, NPG.

LONG, Robert Ballard (1771-1825) lieutenant-general.

PR C.TURNER, after W.Fowler, hl, mezz, pub 1827, BM, NPG.

LONGLEY, Charles Thomas (1794-1868) archbishop of Canterbury.

P H.P.BRIGGS, RA 1838, tql, Christ Church, Oxford. SIR FRANCIS GRANT, c1849, wl, Bishop Mount, Ripon, N.Yorks. GEORGE RICHMOND, 1862, tql, Lambeth Palace, London.

D G.RICHMOND, c1862, head, chalk, study for Lambeth Palace portrait, NPG 1056.

SC EDWARD DAVIS, RA 1844, marble bust, Lambeth Palace.

PH MAYALL, wl, albumen, carte, NPG. UNKNOWN, tql seated, albumen, carte, NPG Twist Album, 1892.

LONGMAN, Thomas Norton (1771-1842) publisher.

SC CHRISTOPHER MOORE, c1845, bust, Parish Church St John, Hampstead.

LONSDALE, James (1777-1839) portrait-painter.

P Self-portrait, hl, Lancaster Museum and Art Gallery, engr C.Turner, hl, mezz, pub 1830, BM, NPG.

M Self-portrait, head, NPG 1854.

SC E.H.BAILY, 1844, marble bust, NPG 770.

LONSDALE, John (1788-1867) bishop of Lichfield.

SC G.F.WATTS, recumbent, alabaster effigy, Lichfield Cathedral.

PR D.J.POUND, after a photograph by Maull and Polyblank, tql seated, stipple and line, NPG.

PH ERNEST EDWARDS, wl seated, albumen, for ed L.Reeve, *Men of Eminence*, vol III, 1865, NPG.

LONSDALE, William Lowther, 1st Earl of (1757-1844) patron of Wordsworth.

D JOHN DOWNMAN, 1778, hl, chalk, Fitzwilliam Museum, Cambridge.

SC M.L.WATSON, 1845, statue, in front of Assize Court, Carlisle. E.B.STEPHENS, 1863, statue, Lowther Mausoleum, Westmorland.

PR H.MEYER, after T.Lawrence, tql seated with Garter star, mezz, BM, NPG. S.W.REYNOLDS, after J.Opie, hl in robes, mezz, BM, NPG. R.J.LANE, after J.Thompson, tql, lith, pub 1839, NPG. W.WARD, after J.Ward, tql, mezz, BM.

LONSDALE, William Lowther, 2nd Earl of (1787-187 statesman.

SC UNKNOWN, marble bust, Hughenden Manor (NT), Bucks.

PR R. and E.TAYLOR, hs, woodcut, for *Illust London News*, 187 NPG.

LORT, Michael (1725-1790) antiquary.

D JOHN DOWNMAN, 1777, hs, chalk, oval, Fitzwilliam Museum Cambridge. SILVESTER HARDING, hl, w/c, oval, BM.

PR F.GROSE, hs, 'The Antiquarian Mastiff', etch, BM, NP UNKNOWN, head, etch, BM.

LOTHIAN, William Henry Kerr, 4th Marquess of (171 **1775)** general.

P UNKNOWN, c1735, wl in peer's robes, on loan to Do (Marlborough House, London). DAVID MORIER, wl equestria SNPG 1426. Attrib MORIER, wl, equestrian, on loan to Do (British Embassy, Washington).

LOUDOUN, John Campbell, 4th Earl of (1705-178 general.

P ALLAN RAMSAY, hl, SNPG 2190.

PR J.FABER, jun, after A.Ramsay, wl in highland dress, line, p 1755, BM.

LOUDOUN, John Claudius (1783-1843) landscap gardener.

P JOHN LINNELL, hs, Linnean Society, London.

PR UNKNOWN, hl, stipple, pub 1845, NPG.

LOUGHBOROUGH, Alexander Wedderburn, Lord, 1st Earl of Rosslyn.

LOUIS, Sir Thomas, 1st Bart (1759-1807) rear-admiral.

G W.BROMLEY, J.LANDSEER and LENEY, 'Naval Victorie 'Victors of the Nile', line, pub 1803, BM, NPG.

PR RIDLEY and HOLL, after Freese, hs, stipple, oval, pub 1806, NF J.DANIELL, after R.Livesay, hl in uniform, mezz, pub 1807, B

LOUTHERBOURG, Philip de, see DE Loutherbourg.

LOVE, James (Dance) (1722-1774) comedian.

G J.R.SMITH, after F.Wheatley, a scene in *Twelfth Night*, Act I mezz, pub 1774, BM.

LOVE, Sir James Frederick (1789-1866) general.

P A.BACCARI, tql, formerly United Service Club, London, (o The Crown Commissioners).

LOVE, John (1757-1825) presbyterian divine.

PR W.RIDLEY, hs, stipple, oval, for *Evangelical Mag*, 1797, NPG.

LOVEGROVE, William (1778-1816) actor.

D SAMUEL DE WILDE, 1810, as Lord Ogleby in *The Clandest Marriage*, and wl in character, 1815, both w/c, Garrick Clu London.

PR Several theatrical prints, BM, NPG.

LOVEL and HOLLAND, Sir John Perceval, 1st Baron, 2nd Earl of Egmont.

LOVELL, Sir Lovell Benjamin Badcock (1786-18 major-general.

PR G.T.PAYNE, after T.W.Mackay, tql with battle in backgrour mezz, BM.

LOVER, Samuel (1797-1868) song-writer, novelist a painter.

P JAMES HARWOOD, 1856, wl seated, NGI 142. J.HARWOOD, N 986.

D Self-portrait, 1828, hs, chalk, NGI 2432.

M Self-portrait, hs, NGI 7340.

SC E.A.FOLEY, 1839, marble bust, NPG 627.

PR C.BAUGNIET, 1844, hl, lith, BM, NPG. UNKNOWN, after

photograph by Maull & Co, hl woodcut, for *Illust London News*, 1868, NPG.

LOW, David (1768-1855) bishop of Ross, Moray and Argyll.
R C.WARREN, after C.Lees, hl, stipple and line, BM, NPG.

LOWE, Sir Hudson (1769-1844) general.
P WYVILLE, hs, National Army Museum, London.
R J.M.FONTAINE, after J.N.Frémy, hl in uniform, line, BM.

LOWE, Thomas (d1783) actor and singer.
R J.McARDELL, after R.E.Pine, wl with Mrs Chambers, as Captain Macheath and Polly Peachum in *Beggar's Opera*, mezz, pub 1752, BM. UNKNOWN, wl singing song 'With early Horn salute the Morn', line, pub 1778, BM.

LOWRY, Wilson (1762-1824) engraver.
D Attrib MATILDA HEMING, hs, w/c, NPG 2875.
R J.THOMSON, hs, stipple, for *European Mag*, 1824, NPG. LINNELL and BLAKE, after J.Linnell, head, line, pub 1825, BM.

LOWTH, Robert (1710-1787) bishop of London.
P R.E.PINE, tql, New College, Oxford.

LOWTHER, William (1757-1844), see 1st Earl of Lonsdale.

LOWTHER, William (1787-1872), see 2nd Earl of Lonsdale.

LOYD, Samuel Jones, see 1st Baron Overstone.

LUARD, John (1790-1875) lieutenant-colonel.
R UNKNOWN, hs, woodcut, pub 1875, NPG.

LUCAN, Margaret Bingham, née Smith, Countess of (d1814) amateur painter.
P ANGELICA KAUFFMANN, wl in classical dress, Althorp, Northants.

LUCAS, Charles (1713-1771) Irish politician and physician.
D THOMAS HICKEY, hs, chalk, NGI 3437.
R J.McARDELL, after J.Reynolds, hl, mezz, BM, NPG.

LUCKOMBE, Philip (d1803) writer.
R R.H.LAURIE, after T.Kearsley, hl seated, mezz, oval, BM, NPG. H.MUTLOW, hs, line, oval, NPG.

LUDLAM, William (1717-1788) mathematician.
D LEWIS VASLET, 1785, hl, profile, pastel, oval, Queen's College, Oxford.

LUMISDEN, Andrew (1720-1801) Jacobite.
C JAMES TASSIE, 1784, paste medallion, SNPG 135.
R W.RIDLEY, hs, stipple, oval, for *European Mag*, 1798, BM, NPG.

LUNARDI, Vincenzo (1759-1806) aeronaut.
R F.BARTOLOZZI, after R.Cosway, hl, stipple, oval, for his *Account of the first Aerial Voyage in England*, 1784, BM, NPG. UNKNOWN, after Duché de Vaney, hl, etch, oval, pub 1784, BM.
C J.KAY, wl in his balloon, etch, BM.

LUPTON, Thomas Goff (1791-1873) engraver.
P GEORGE CLINT, hl, NPG 1619.
D N.O.LUPTON, after a bust by Scipio Clint, hs, pen and ink, BM.
G GEORGE CLINT, the last scene in *A New Way to Pay Old Debts*, oil, 1820, Garrick Club, London.

LUSHINGTON, Stephen (1782-1873) judge.
P WILLIAM HOLMAN HUNT, 1862, hl seated, NPG 1646. G.F.WATTS, 1867, Trinity House, London.
G SIR G.HAYTER, 'The Trial of Queen Caroline, 1820', oil, NPG 999. B.R.HAYDON, 'The Anti-Slavery Society Convention, 1840', oil, NPG 599.
R T.WRIGHT, after A.Wivell, hs, profile, stipple, pub 1821, NPG. W.WALKER, after W.J.Newton, tql seated, mezz, pub 1834, BM, NPG.
H UNKNOWN, hs, albumen, NPG Twist Album. MAULL and POLYBLANK, wl seated, carte, NPG.

LUSHINGTON, Stephen Rumbold (1776-1868) Indian official.
P JAMES PENELL, tql, Corporation of the City of Canterbury.
PR M.O'CONNOR, wl, lith, BM.

LUTTRELL, Henry Lawes, see 2nd Earl of Carhampton.

LUTTRELL, James (1751?-1788) captain in the navy.
PR W.ANGUS, after J.Millar, hs, line, circle, for *European Mag*, 1783, BM, NPG.

LUXBOROUGH, Henrietta Knight, Lady (d1756) friend of the poet Shenstone.
PR E.BOCQUET, hl, stipple, pub 1807, BM, NPG.

LUXMOORE, John (1756-1830) bishop of St Asaph.
G SIR GEORGE HAYTER, 'The Trial of Queen Caroline, 1820', oil, NPG 999.

LYALL, Robert (1790-1831) botanist and traveller.
PR M.GAUCI, hl, lith, BM, NPG.

LYALL, William Rowe (1788-1857) dean of Canterbury.
P UNKNOWN, tql, The Deanery, Canterbury.
PR T.H.MAGUIRE, after W.Buckler, tql seated, lith, pub 1857, BM, NPG.

LYELL, Sir Charles, 1st Bart (1797-1875) geologist.
P LOWES DICKINSON, 1883, replica of his portrait of 1870, tql, NPG 1387. UNKNOWN, Geological Society, London.
D GEORGE RICHMOND, c1853, head, chalk, NPG 1064.
SC Two busts by WILLIAM THEED, Westminster Abbey, London and Royal Society, London.
PR T.H.MAGUIRE, tql seated, lith, for *Ipswich Museum Portraits*, 1852, BM, NPG.
PH ELLIOTT and FRY, hs, carte, NPG Cunnington Collection. MAYALL, wl seated, carte, NPG Album of Photographs 1949. UNKNOWN, wl seated, albumen, NPG Twist Album.

LYNAM, Robert (1796-1845) miscellaneous writer.
PR H.ADLARD, after Hervé, hs, stipple and line, NPG.

LYNDHURST, John Singleton Copley, 1st Baron (1772-1863) lord chancellor.
P JOHN SINGLETON COPLEY, 1793, wl, 'The Red Cross Knight', National Gallery of Art, Washington DC, USA. THOMAS PHILLIPS, 1836, wl in chancellor's robes, NPG 472. H.W.PICKERSGILL, c1839, wl seated in chancellor's robes, Lincoln's Inn, London. G.F.WATTS, 1862, hs, NPG 683. COUNT A.D'ORSAY, assisted by Sir E.Landseer, tql, Hughenden Manor (NT), Bucks.
D F.ROFFE, c1836, hl, w/c, NPG 4121. GEORGE RICHMOND, 1851, hs, chalk, NPG 2144.
G J.S.COPLEY, 'The Copley Family', oil, 1776–77, National Gallery of Art, Washington DC. SIR G.HAYTER, 'The Trial of Queen Caroline, 1820', oil, NPG 999. SIR G.HAYTER, 'The House of Commons, 1833', oil, NPG 54. SIR DAVID WILKIE, 'The First Council of Queen Victoria', oil, 1837, Royal Coll. JOHN PARTRIDGE, 'The Fine Arts Commissioners, 1846', NPG 342, 3.
SC WILLIAM BEHNES, 1844, bust, Trinity College, Cambridge.
PH Two photographs (same pose) by J.E.MAYALL, 1861, wl, albumen carte, wl, albumen, NPG.

LYNEDOCH, Thomas Graham, 1st Baron (1748-1843) general.
P POMPEO BATONI, 1772, wl seated, Yale Center for British Art, New Haven, USA. SIR THOMAS LAWRENCE, 1817, wl, Wellington Museum, Apsley House, London. SIR T.LAWRENCE, c1820, wl, formerly United Service Club, London (c/o The Crown Commissioners). SIR GEORGE

HAYTER, hl, NPG 1037.

SC After THOMAS WEBB, plaster medallion, SNPG 69.

PR S.W.REYNOLDS, after J.Hoppner, hl in uniform, mezz, pub 1802, BM, NPG.

LYNN, George (1707-1758) barrister.

SC L.F.ROUBILIAC, relief medallion on marble monument, St Mary Church, Southwick, Northants.

LYON, George Francis (1795-1832) captain in the navy and arctic explorer.

PR M.GAUCI, after E.Allingham, tql in uniform, lith, BM. R.J.LANE, wl in oriental dress, lith, NPG.

LYON, Hart, or **Hirsch Löbel** or **Lewin (1721-1800)** chief rabbi.

PR E.FISHER, after J.Turner, tql seated, mezz, BM.

LYON, John (1737-1776), see 9th Earl of Strathmore.

LYONS, Edmund Lyons, 1st Baron (1790-1858) admiral.

P LOWES DICKINSON, 1855, wl, Arundel Castle, W.Sussex. G.F.WATTS, 1856–57, hl, NPG 685. MARGARET THOMAS, Admiralty House, Portsmouth.

M UNKNOWN, enamel, Arundel Castle.

SC MATTHEW NOBLE, 1856, marble bust, Arundel Castle. M.NOBLE, 1860, marble statue, St Paul's Cathedral, London.

PR J.H.LYNCH, hs, lith, pub 1854, BM, NPG. G.ZOBEL, after R.Buckner, tql in uniform, mezz, pub 1856, BM, NPG. D.J.POUND, after a photograph by Kilburn, tql, stipple and line, NPG.

LYSONS, Daniel (1727-1800) physician.

P TILLY KETTLE, hl, Courtauld Institute Galleries (Lee Coll), London.

LYSONS, Daniel (1762-1834) topographer.

D GEORGE DANCE, 1793, hs profile, pencil, BM.

LYSONS, Samuel (1763-1819) antiquary.

D SIR THOMAS LAWRENCE, 1790s, head, pencil, NPG 5078. GEORG▢ DANCE, 1793, hs profile, pencil, BM.

PR S.W.REYNOLDS, after T.Lawrence, hl, mezz, oval, pub 18C▢ BM, NPG. W.BOND, after W.J.Newton, tql seated, stipple, p▢ 1823, BM, NPG.

LYTE, Henry Francis (1793-1857) hymn-writer.

P UNKNOWN, called Lyte, 1840, hl, Montclair Art Museum, N▢ Jersey, USA.

PR G.H.PHILLIPS, after J.King, hl, mezz, BM.

LYTTELTON, Charles (1714-1768) antiquary and bishop Carlisle.

PR J.WATSON, after F.Cotes, tql seated, engr for Society Antiquaries and pub in *Vetusta Monumenta*, vol ii, mezz, BM, NF▢

LYTTELTON, George Lyttelton, 1st Baron (1709-177▢ chancellor of the exchequer and man of letters.

P UNKNOWN, hl, NPG 128.

PR R.DUNKARTON, after B.West, hl in peer's robes, mezz, ov▢ pub 1774, BM. G.H.EVERY, after J.Reynolds, hl, mezz, BM, NF▢

C GEORGE TOWNSHEND, wl, drg, NPG 4855 (49).

LYTTELTON, Thomas Lyttelton, 2nd Baron (1744-177▢ politician and profligate.

P After T.GAINSBOROUGH, hl, NPG 1446. PRINCE HOAR▢ Stourhead (NT), Wilts.

PR C.TOWNLEY, after R.Cosway, hl, mezz, pub 1781, B▢ UNKNOWN, hs, stipple, oval, for Park's ed of Walpole's *Ro▢ and Noble Authors*, 1806, BM, NPG.

LYTTELTON, William Henry Lyttelton, 1st Bar▢ (1724-1808) governor of South Carolina.

P BENJAMIN WILSON, tql with map of South Carolina, Anto▢ House (NT), Cornwall.

LYTTELTON, William Henry Lyttelton, 3rd Bar▢ (1782-1837) politician.

D SIR GEORGE HAYTER, hl, a study for a miniature, NPG 883 (1▢

M

McADAM, John Loudon (1756-1836) the 'macadamiser' of roads.
P UNKNOWN, wl seated, NPG 3686.
SL AUGUSTIN EDOUART, 1827, wl, SNPG 823.
PR C.TURNER, hl, mezz, pub 1825, BM, NPG.

McALL, Robert Stephens (1792-1838) congregational minister.
PR W.WARD, after J.Bostock, tql, mezz, pub 1837, NPG. WOOLNOTH, after H.Bostock, hl, stipple, pub 1843, NPG.

MACARDELL, James (1729-1765) mezzotint engraver.
P SIR JOSHUA REYNOLDS, 1756-60, hl, NPG 3123.
PR R.EARLOM, after J.McArdell of 1765, hl, mezz, pub 1771, BM.

McARTHUR, John (1755-1840) writer.
P GEORGE ROMNEY, 1794, hl, SNPG 1584.

MACARTNEY, George Macartney, 1st Earl (1737-1806) diplomat and colonial governor.
P SIR JOSHUA REYNOLDS, exhib 1764, hl, Petworth (NT), W.Sussex. L.F.ABBOTT, 1784, hl with Sir George Staunton, NPG 329. UNKNOWN, wl, Scone Palace, Tayside region, Scotland.
D G.S.BARTOLOZZI, after H.Edridge, hs, chalk, BM. GUSTAV LUNDBERG, hs, pastel, Ulster Museum.
G K.A.HICKEL, 'The House of Commons, 1793', oil, NPG 745.
R H.HUDSON, after M.Brown, hl, mezz, pub 1790, BM. C.TOWNLEY, after S. de Koster, wl in Bath robes, mezz, pub 1793, BM. J.HALL, after T.Hickey, tql seated, line, for vol II of his *Embassy to China*, 1796, BM, NPG. J.SINGLETON, after O.Humphry, hl, stipple, for *European Mag*, 1796, BM, NPG.
C JAMES GILLRAY, 'The Reception of the Diplomatique and his Suite at the Court of Peking', etch, pub 1792, NPG.

MACARTNEY, James (1770-1843) anatomist.
SC After R.J.H.TROY, 1832, plaster bust, Department of Anatomy, Cambridge University.

MACAULAY, Catharine, née Sawbridge (1731-1791) historian.
P UNKNOWN, hs, NPG 1357.
G RICHARD SAMUEL, 'The Nine Living Muses of Great Britain', oil, exhib 1779, NPG 4905.
SC J.F.MOORE, c1778, marble statue, Reference Library, Warrington.
PR J.SPILSBURY, after C.Read, hl holding *Magna Charta*, mezz, oval, pub 1764, BM, NPG. J.BASIRE, after G.B.Cipriani, head, medallion, line, for vol III of her *Hist of England*, 1767, BM. UNKNOWN, wl, line, BM, NPG.

MACAULAY, Zachary (1768-1838) philanthropist.
C HENRY WEEKES, 1838, bust, Westminster Abbey, London.
R UNKNOWN, hs, medallion, one of set 'Heroes of the Slave Trade Abolition', NPG.

McAULEY, Catharine (1787-1841) foundress of the Order of Mercy.
P UNKNOWN, Convent of Mercy, Dublin.

MACBRIDE, David (1726-1778) medical writer.
PR J.T.SMITH, after Reynolds (of Dublin), tql, stipple and line, pub 1797, BM, NPG.

MACBRIDE, John (d1800) admiral.

PR H.R.COOK, after Smart of 1760, hl stipple, oval, pub 1808, NPG. J.FITTLER, after J.Northcote, tql, line, BM, NPG.

MACBRIDE, John David (1778-1868) principal of Magdalen College, Oxford.
P W.SALTER, tql seated, Hertford College, Oxford.

McCAUL, Alexander (1799-1863) divine.
PR W.T.DAVEY, after E.J.Fisher, tql, mezz, BM.

MACCULLOCH, John (1773-1835) geologist.
P B.R.FAULKNER, hl, Royal Society, London, engr C.E.Wagstaff, mezz, pub 1837, BM.

McCULLOCH, John Ramsay (1789-1864) statistician and economist.
P SIR DANIEL MACNEE, 1840, tql, NPG 677.
D WILLIAM BEWICK, chalk, SNPG 543.
PR UNKNOWN, hs, lith, BM, NPG. UNKNOWN, after a photograph by J. & C.Watkins, tql, woodcut, for *Illust London News*, 1864, NPG.

McCRACKEN, Henry Joy (1767-1798) Irish nationalist.
G UNKNOWN, 'The United Irish Patriots of 1798', coloured lith, NPG.

McCRIE, Thomas (1772-1835) Scottish seceding divine and ecclesiastical historian.
P SIR JOHN WATSON GORDON, hl, SNPG 197.

M'DIARMID, John (1790-1852) journalist.
P WILLIAM MENZIES TWEEDIE, 1852, tql, SNPG 2200.

MACDONALD, Sir Archibald, 1st Bart (1747-1826) chief baron of the exchequer.
P GEORGE ROMNEY, 1793-95, tql in robes, Christ Church, Oxford. UNKNOWN, Harvard Law Library, Cambridge, USA.
SC SIR FRANCIS CHANTREY, 1818, marble bust, V & A.
C J.GILLRAY, 'Ancient Music', etch, pub 1787, NPG.

MACDONALD, Flora (1722-1790) Jacobite heroine.
P RICHARD WILSON, 1747, hl, SNPG 1162. ALLAN RAMSAY, 1749, hl, Bodleian Library, Oxford, engr J.McArdell, 1749, NPG. ALLAN RAMSAY, called Flora Macdonald but does not agree with known types, hl, NGS 1884. After ALLAN RAMSAY, hl, SNPG 947. JOSEPH HIGHMORE, hl, North Carolina Museum of Art, Raleigh, USA.
D ALLAN RAMSAY, chalk, SNPG 1665.
PR UNKNOWN, after I.Markluin, tql seated with miniature of Prince Charles, mezz, pub 1747, BM. J.FABER jun, after T.Hudson, (1747), tql with portrait of the Prince, mezz, BM, NPG.

MACDONALD, John (1779-1849) dissenting minister, called the 'Apostle of the North'.
PR W.T.FRY, tql seated, stipple, for *Evangelical Mag*, 1823, BM. J.SINCLAIR, hl, mezz, pub 1850, NPG.
C J.KAY, hl, etch, 1813, NPG.

MACDONALD, Sir John (d1850) soldier.
PR UNKNOWN, hs, stipple, NPG.

MACDONALD, Lawrence (1799-1878) sculptor.
SC JOHN HUTCHISON, 1860, bust, Royal Scottish Academy, Edinburgh.

MACDONALD, Patrick (1729-1824) collector of Gaelic music.

SL UNKNOWN, SNPG 1429.

MACDONELL, Alexander (1762-1840) first Roman Catholic bishop of Upper Canada.
PR C.TURNER, after M.A.Shee, tql seated in robes, mezz, pub 1825, BM.

MACDONELL, Sir James (d 1857) general.
P WILLIAM SALTER, tql study for 'Waterloo Banquet', NPG 3753. Attrib F.R.SAY, tql, SNPG 1465.
M UNKNOWN, tql, oval, NPG 2656.
G W.SALTER, 'Waterloo Banquet at Apsley House', oil, 1836, Wellington Museum, Apsley House, London.

MACDOUGALL, Sir Duncan (1787-1862) soldier, served in Peninsula, Canada, and again in Spain, 1835.
SC G.G.ADAMS, 1862, bust? on monument, St Paul's Cathedral, London.

MACDOWELL, Patrick (1799-1870) sculptor.
PR UNKNOWN, hs, woodcut, for *Art Journal*, 1850, BM, NPG. UNKNOWN, after a photograph, hs, woodcut, for *Illust London News*, 1870, BM.
PH MAULL & POLYBLANK, wl, carte, NPG Album of Photographs 1949.

MACERONI, Francis (1788-1846) aide-de-camp to Murat, King of Naples, and mechanical inventor.
PR C.PICART, after A.Wivell, hl, stipple, pub 1822, BM.

MACFARLAN, Walter (d 1767) antiquary.
P JOHN THOMAS SETON, 1757, SNPG L34.

MACFARLANE, Charles (d 1858) historian.
D WILLIAM BROCKEDON, 1832, hs, chalk, NPG 2515 (60).

M'GAVIN, William (1773-1832) controversialist.
PR S.FREEMAN, after J.Campbell, hl, for Chambers's *Dict of Eminent Scotsmen*, 1835, BM, NPG.

MACGOWAN, John (1726-1780) baptist minister and controversialist.
PR R.HOUSTON, after J.Russell, hl, mezz, oval, pub 1774, BM, NPG.

MACGREGOR, Sir Gregor (1786-1845) adventurer.
P GEORGE WATSON, hl, SNPG 2201.
PR S.W.REYNOLDS, after J.S.Rochard, hl, mezz, BM, NPG.

McGRIGOR, Sir James, 1st Bart (1771-1858) army surgeon.
D THOMAS HEAPHY, hs, w/c, NPG 1914 (8).
SC UNKNOWN, 1858, plaster bust, SNPG 1310. MATTHEW NOBLE, c1865, bronze statue, Royal Army Medical College, Millbank, London. WILLIAM THEED jun, bust, Royal Military Academy, Sandhurst, Camberley, Surrey.
PR J.HOLL, after H.Room, hl, stipple and line, pub 1839, NPG.

MACHALE, John (1791-1881) archbishop of Tuam.
P ALESSANDRO CAPALTI, 1855, tql in robes, NGI 406.
G UNKNOWN, 'The Illustrious Sons of Ireland', coloured lith, NPG.
SC SIR THOMAS FARRELL, statue, The Square, Tuam, Galway, Eire. J.H.FOLEY, bronze statue, Tuam.

MACINTOSH, Charles (1766-1843) chemist and inventor.
PR E.BURTON, after J.G.Gilbert, tql seated, mezz, BM.

MACKAY, Andrew (1760-1809) mathematician.
PR J.HEATH, after A.Roberton, hs, stipple, NPG.

MACKENZIE, Sir Alexander (1755?-1820) North American explorer.
P SIR THOMAS LAWRENCE, c1800, hl, National Gallery of Canada, Ottawa, Canada.
PR P.CONDÉ, after T.Lawrence, hs, stipple, oval, for his *Voyages*, 1801, BM.

MACKENZIE, Colin (1753?-1821) colonel in the Madr[as] engineers.
P THOMAS HICKEY, 1816, wl with three Brahmin assistants, Ind[ia] Office, London.

MACKENZIE, Henry (1745-1831) novelist and essayist.
P WILLIAM STAVELY, 1795, hl, SNPG 318. COLVIN SMITH, tql, SNP[G] 1032. SIR HENRY RAEBURN, hl, NPG 455.
D WILLIAM BEWICK, 1824, hs, chalk, SNPG 1047.
SC SAMUEL JOSEPH, c1822, marble bust, SNPG 254.
PR R.RHODES, after A.Geddes, wl seated, line, pub 1822, BM, NP[G] S.FREEMAN, after J.W.Gordon, hl, stipple, for Chambers's *Dict* [of] *Eminent Scotsmen*, 1835, BM, NPG.

MACKENZIE, James Archibald Stuart-Wortley, see [1st] Baron Wharncliffe.

MACKENZIE, Maria Elizabeth Frederica Stewart, s[ee] Lady Hood.

MACKENZIE, William Lyon (1795-1861) leader [of] Canadian insurgents.
P J.W.L.FORSTER, tql, Public Archives of Canada, Ottaw[a] Canada.

MACKINNON, William Alexander (1789-1870) legislato[r] and author.
PR UNKNOWN, hl, lith, BM, NPG.

MACKINTOSH, Sir James (1765-1832) philosopher.
P SIR THOMAS LAWRENCE, RA 1804, hl, NPG 45. COLVIN SMIT[H] tql, SNPG 248.
D F.W.WILKIN, 1824, chalk, SNPG 938.
M ANN SPARROW, after F.W.Wilkin, 1837, hs, oval, Ashmole[an] Museum, Oxford.
PR W.RIDLEY, after J.Opie, hs, stipple, oval, for *Monthly Mirro[r]* 1804, BM, NPG. J.THOMSON, after W.Derby, hl, stipple, fo[r] *European Mag*, 1824, BM, NPG. I.W.SLATER, after J.Slater, hs, lit[h] pub 1832, BM, NPG. C.TURNER, after H.B.Burlowe, from a bus[t] mezz, BM, NPG.
C WILLIAM HEATH, 'Keeping the Child Quiet', coloured etch, pu[b] 1829, V & A.

MACKLIN, Maria (d 1781) actress.
D JAMES ROBERTS, 1778, as Camillo in Vanbrugh's *The Mistak[e]* BM.
G JOHAN ZOFFANY, with her father in a scene from *The Merchant* [of] *Venice*, oil, 1767-68, TATE 6005.
PR Theatrical prints, BM.

MACLAINE, Archibald (1722-1804) divine.
PR C.H.HODGES, hl, mezz, 1796, BM.

MACLAREN, Charles (1782-1866) editor and geologist.
SC WILLIAM BRODIE, 1861, marble bust, Museum of Science an[d] Art, Edinburgh. JOHN HUTCHISON, after William Brodi[e] marble bust, SNPG 281.

McLEAN, Archibald (1733-1812) baptist minister.
P GEORGE WATSON, hl, SNPG 1993.
PR UNKNOWN, hl, stipple, pub 1815, V & A.

MACLEAY, Alexander (1767-1848) entomologist an[d] Australian statesman.
P SIR THOMAS LAWRENCE, c1825, hl, Linnean Society, Londo[n] engr C.Fox, line, BM, NPG.

MACLEAY, William Sharp (1792-1865) zoologist.
SC C.SUMMERS, 1870, marble bust, Linnean Society, London.

MACLEHOSE, Mrs Agnes, née Craig (1759-1841) 'Clarinda', friend and correspondent of Robert Burns.
L JOHN MIERS, 1788, hs, SNPG 567.

McLELLAN, Archibald (1797-1854) coachbuilder and art collector.
P R.C.CRAWFORD, after J.Graham-Gilbert of 1839, wl, Glasgow City Art Gallery.

MACMICHAEL, William (1784-1839) physician.
D WILLIAM HAINES, 1823, hs, w/c, Royal College of Physicians, London.

MACNAGHTEN, Sir William Hay, 1st Bart (1793-1841) diplomat and orientalist.
D JAMES ATKINSON, 1841, hl, w/c, NPG 749.
R L.DICKINSON, hs, lith, for *Portraits of the Cabul Prisoners*, 1843, NPG.

McNEILE, Hugh (1795-1879) dean of Ripon.
C G.G.ADAMS, marble statue, St George's Hall, Liverpool.
R H.COUSINS, after T.C.Thompson, tql seated, mezz, pub 1838, BM. T.LUPTON, after S.Hawksett, tql, mezz, BM. D.J.POUND, after a photograph by J.T.Foard, tql, stipple and line, NPG.

McNEILL, Duncan (1793-1874), see 1st Baron COLONSAY and Oronsay.

MACNEILL, Hector (1746-1818) Scottish poet.
C JOHN HENNING, 1802, porcelain medallion, SNPG 2357.
R P.THOMSON, after Willam, hl seated, line, for his *Works*, 1801, BM.

McNEILL, Sir John (1795-1883) diplomatist.
P UNKNOWN, SNPG 1503. G.F.WATTS, hs, Inveraray Castle, Strathclyde region, Scotland.
C SIR JOHN STEELL, 1859, marble bust, SNPG 149.

MACNEVEN, William James (1783-1841) Irish nationalist.
G UNKNOWN, 'The United Irish Patriots of 1798', coloured lith, NPG.

MACONOCHIE, Allan, see 1st Lord Meadowbank.

MACONOCHIE-WELWOOD, Alexander, see 2nd Lord Meadowbank.

MACPHERSON, James (1736-1796) poet.
P SIR JOSHUA REYNOLDS, RA 1772, hl, Petworth (NT), W.Sussex.
R After G.ROMNEY, tql seated, photogravure, BM.

MACPHERSON, Sir John (1745-1821) governor-general of India.
P SIR JOSHUA REYNOLDS, RA 1781, hs, SNPG 647.
G R.EARLOM, after J.Zoffany of c1795, 'The Death of the Royal Tyger', mezz, pub 1802, India Office, London.
R S.W.REYNOLDS, hl, mezz, pub 1796, BM.

MACQUEEN, Robert, see Lord Braxfield.

MACREADY, William Charles (1793-1873) actor.
P JOHN JACKSON, 1821, hl as Henry IV, NPG 1503. GEORGE CLINT, 1821, hl as Macbeth, V & A. HENRY INMAN, c1827, hs as William Tell, Metropolitan Museum of Art, New York. H.P.BRIGGS, 1844, hs, Garrick Club, London. DANIEL MACLISE, c1849-50, wl as Werner, V & A. JOHN BOADEN, wl as Orestes in *The Distressed Mother*, Garrick Club. DANIEL MACLISE, tql, Drury Lane Theatre, London.
D Attrib DANIEL MACLISE, wl, w/c, NPG 3329. G.WIGHTWICK, 1869, hs profile, NPG. UNKNOWN, after a photograph, c1870, hs, w/c, NPG 3017.
C WILLIAM BEHNES, 1843-44, marble bust, NPG 1504.
R Numerous theatrical prints, BM, NPG.
M MASON, wl, NPG.

MADAN, Martin (1726-1790) divine and writer.
PR J.WATSON, after G.James, wl with C.E. de Coetlogon, mezz, pub 1774, BM, NPG. UNKNOWN, hs, line, oval, pub 1784, NPG. R.HOUSTON, after Jenkin, tql seated, mezz, BM. MANWARING, tql, mezz, BM.

MADAN, Spencer (1729-1813) bishop of Peterborough.
PR T.CHEESMAN, after J.Barry, hs, stipple, pub 1794, BM, NPG.

MADDEN, Richard Robert (1798-1886) miscellaneous writer.
P J.P.HAVERTY, hs, NGI 493.
D COUNT ALFRED D'ORSAY, 1828, hl, profile, pencil and chalk, NPG 4026 (41).
SL UNKNOWN, wl, NGI.
G B.R.HAYDON, 'The Anti-Slavery Society Convention, 1840', oil, NPG 599.
PR R.J.HAMERTON, wl in Turkish dress, lith, NPG. T.W.HUFFAM, after a daguerreotype by Claudet, hs, mezz, NPG.

MADOCKS, William Alexander (1774-1828) philanthropist.
PR C.TURNER, after J.Ramsay, tql, mezz, pub 1812, BM, NPG.

MAGEE, William (1766-1831) archbishop of Dublin.
P H.D.HAMILTON, hs, Deanery, Cork. HENRY WYATT, RA 1828, wl, Trinity College, Dublin.
SC THOMAS KIRK, exhib 1840, marble bust, Trinity College.

MAGINN, William (1793-1842) writer.
G D.MACLISE, 'The Fraserians', lith, for *Fraser's Mag*, 1835, BM.
PR D.MACLISE, wl seated, lith, for *Fraser's Mag*, 1831, BM, NPG.

MAGUIRE, Rochfort (d1867) naval commander.
G STEPHEN PEARCE, wl, 'The Arctic Council planning a search for Sir John Franklin', oil, 1851, NPG 1214.

MAGUIRE, Thomas (1792-1847) Roman Catholic controversialist.
PR H.BROCAS, after C.O'Donel, tql, line, BM.

MAIDMENT, James (c1795-1879) antiquary.
D WILLIAM GREENLEES, 1850, hs, oval, w/c, SNPG 754.

MAITLAND, James (1759-1839), see 8th Earl of Lauderdale.

MAITLAND, Sir Peregrine (1777-1854) general and colonial governor.
P WILLIAM SALTER, tql study for 'Waterloo Banquet', NPG 3736.
G W.SALTER, 'The Waterloo Banquet at Apsley House', oil, 1836, Wellington Museum, Apsley House, London.
SC W.THEED jun, bust, Royal Military Academy, Sandhurst, Camberley, Surrey.

MAITLAND, Sir Thomas (1759?-1824) lieutenant-general.
SC BERTEL THORVALDSEN, 1818, plaster bust, Thorvaldsen Museum, Copenhagen.
PR T.LUPTON, after J.Hoppner, tql, mezz, NPG.

MAITLAND, Thomas (1792-1851), see Lord Dundrennan.

MAJENDIE, Henry William (1754-1830) bishop of Bangor.
D SIR GEORGE HAYTER, study for NPG 999, NPG 1695 (n).
SL AUGUSTE EDOUART, Christ's College, Cambridge.
G SIR GEORGE HAYTER, 'The Trial of Queen Caroline, 1820', oil, NPG 999.
PR C.TURNER, after W.Beechey, tql, mezz, pub 1823, BM, NPG.

MAJOR, John Henniker, see 2nd Baron Henniker.

MAJOR, Thomas (1720-1799) engraver.
PR T.MAJOR, hs, line, 1759, BM.

MALCOLM, Sir John (1769-1833) diplomat and writer on India.
P SAMUEL LANE, wl, Oriental Club, London. S.LANE, hs, SNPG 439.

D SIR FRANCIS CHANTREY, hs, pencil, NPG 316a (81). WILLIAM BEWICK, 1824, chalk, SNPG 1051.

SC SIR FRANCIS CHANTREY, RA 1837, marble statue, Westminster Abbey, London. SIR F.CHANTREY, bust, Ashmolean Museum, Oxford.

PR J.PORTER, tql, mezz, pub 1827, BM, NPG.

MALCOLM, Sir Pulteney (1768-1838) admiral.

P SAMUEL LANE, hl, SNPG 2050.

SC E.H.BAILY, 1842, statue, St Paul's Cathedral, London.

PR W.J.WARD, after S.Lane, hl, mezz, pub 1836, BM.

MALCOLM, Sarah (1710?-1733) criminal.

P WILLIAM HOGARTH, c1732-33, tql in Newgate, NGS 838.

MALKIN, Benjamin Heath (1769-1842) historian and writer.

D SIR FRANCIS CHANTREY, hs, pencil, NPG 316a (82).

SC SIR FRANCIS CHANTREY, medallion on monument, St James's Church, Bury St Edmunds.

MALKIN, Sir Benjamin Heath (1797-1837) judge.

PR M.GAUCI, after A.E.Chalon, tql seated, lith, BM.

MALMESBURY, James Harris, 1st Earl of (1746-1820) diplomatist.

M C.BESTLAND, after T.Lawrence, 1807, hs, NPG L152 (29).

SC SIR FRANCIS CHANTREY, marble statue, Salisbury Cathedral.

PR C.WATSON, after J.Reynolds, tql, stipple, pub 1786, BM, NPG. B.GRANGER, after R.Corbould, hs, stipple, for *English Mag*, 1797, BM, NPG. C.PICART, after H.Edridge, hl, stipple, for *Contemporary Portraits*, 1814, BM, NPG.

MALONE, Anthony (1700-1776) chancellor of the exchequer in Ireland.

PR J.R.SMITH, after J.Reynolds, tql in chancellor's robes, mezz, pub 1779, BM, NPG.

MALONE, Edmund (1741-1812) critic and editor of Shakespeare.

P SIR JOSHUA REYNOLDS, 1778, hl, NPG 709.

MALONE, Richard, see Baron Sunderlin.

MALTBY, Edward (1770-1859) bishop of Durham.

P SIR WILLIAM BEECHEY, 1832, tql, Bishop Auckland Palace, Durham. H.P.BRIGGS, University College, Durham. UNKNOWN, Pembroke College, Cambridge.

D HENRY EDRIDGE, hl, w/c, BM.

SC WILLIAM BEHNES, c1844, marble bust, Fitzwilliam Museum, Cambridge.

PR G.T.PAYNE, after H.P.Briggs, tql, mezz, BM. MRS D.TURNER, after J.S.Cotman, hs, etch, BM. R.COOPER, after H.Edridge, hl, stipple, BM, NPG.

MALTHUS, Thomas Robert (1766-1834) political economist.

P JOHN LINNELL, hl, Haileybury College, Herts.

MALTON, Thomas (1748-1804) water-colour painter.

PR W.W.BARNEY, after G.Stuart, hl, mezz, pub 1806, BM, NPG.

MANBY, George William (1765-1854) inventor of apparatus for saving life from shipwreck.

P SIR THOMAS LAWRENCE, c1790s, tql, Royal Society, London.

PR T.BLOOD, after S.Lane, hl, stipple, for *European Mag*, 1813, BM, NPG. MRS D.TURNER, after S. de Koster, hs, etch, BM, NPG. J.M.JOHNSON, after T.Wageman, tql, lith, BM, NPG.

MANCHESTER, George Montagu, 4th Duke of (1737-1788) lord chamberlain.

P Attrib A.R.MENGS, wl, Kimbolton Castle, Cambs.

D JOHN SINGLETON COPLEY, head, chalk, Metropolitan Museum of Art, New York.

PR J.JONES, after G.Stuart, hl in peer's robes with chamberlain's

wand, mezz, pub 1790, BM, NPG. W.LENEY, after W.Peters, hl in peer's robes, stipple, oval, pub 1796, BM.

MANCHESTER, William Montagu, 5th Duke of (1771-1843) governor of Jamaica.

D SIR GEORGE HAYTER, hs, pencil, BM.

MANGIN, Edward (1772-1852) miscellaneous writer.

PR W.SAY, after J.Saxon, hl, mezz, BM, NPG.

MANGNALL, Richmal (1769-1820) schoolmistress.

D JOHN DOWNMAN, 1814, hl, w/c, NPG 4377.

MANN, Sir Horace, 1st Bart (1701-1786) British envoy at Florence.

G JOHAN ZOFFANY, 'The Tribuna of the Uffizi', oil, 1772-78, Royal Coll. THOMAS PATCH, a caricature group, oil, The Royal Albert Memorial Museum, Exeter.

PR W.GREATBATCH, after Astley, hs, line, pub 1857, NPG.

MANN, Theodore Augustus (1735-1809) Abbé Mann, scientist, historian and antiquary.

PR R.ROGERS, after C.H.Jones, hs, stipple, oval, BM.

MANNERS, Charles (1754-1787), see 4th Duke of Rutland

MANNERS, John (1721-1770), see Marquess of Granby.

MANNERS, Lord Robert (1758-1782) captain.

P THOMAS HUDSON, wl as a child, with dog, Winton House, Lothian region, Scotland. SIR JOSHUA REYNOLDS, c1781, wl, Belvoir Castle, Leics. T.STOTHARD, his death scene, Belvoir Castle.

M 'P.C.', hs, Winton. R.COSWAY, hs, Belvoir Castle.

SC JOSEPH NOLLEKENS, c1782-84, marble bust, Belvoir Castle.

PR A.N.SANDERS, after T.Gainsborough, tql in Vandyck dress, mezz, BM. Several prints of his death scene, NPG.

MANNERS SUTTON, Charles (1755-1828) archbishop of Canterbury.

P JOHN HOPPNER, c1794, tql, Royal Coll. After T.LAWRENCE, tql, Lambeth Palace, London.

D STEPHANOFF, study for 'Coronation of George IV', w/c, V & A. SIR FRANCIS CHANTREY, hs profile, pencil, NPG 316a (121). SIR GEORGE HAYTER, study for NPG 999, NPG 1695 (t).

G SIR GEORGE HAYTER, 'The Trial of Queen Caroline, 1820', oil, NPG 999.

SC SIR FRANCIS CHANTREY, bust, Ashmolean Museum, Oxford.

PR W.HOLL, afrer T.Wageman, tql seated, stipple, pub 1828, BM, NPG.

MANNERS SUTTON, Charles (1780-1845), see 1st Viscount Canterbury.

MANNERS, Thomas Manners-Sutton, 1st Baron (1756-1842) lord chancellor of Ireland.

P W.BURRELL, King's Inns, Dublin.

PR A.CARDON, after J.Comerford, hl in chancellor's robes, stipple, pub 1811, BM, NPG.

C JOHN DOYLE, several satirical drgs, BM.

MANSEL, William Lort (1753-1820) bishop of Bristol.

P THOMAS KIRKBY, wl, Trinity College, Cambridge, engr W.Say, mezz, pub 1812, BM, NPG.

PR MRS D.TURNER, after G.H.Harlow, hl, etch, BM, NPG.

MANSFIELD, David Murray, 2nd Earl of (1727-1796) diplomatist and statesman.

P POMPEO BATONI, 1768, hl, Scone Palace, Tayside region, Scotland. GEORGE ROMNEY, 1783, tql in robes with Thistle Star, Christ Church, Oxford. M.BUCCARELLI, hl, Scone Palace. Attrib M.BUCCARELLI, hs, Scone Palace. Attrib DAVID MARTIN, hl seated, Scone Palace.

D S.HARDING, tql, w/c, BM.

R UNKNOWN, hs, profile, line, oval, for *London Mag*, 1780, BM, NPG.

C JAMES SAYERS, wl, 'Razor's Levée', etch, pub 1783, NPG. J.SAYERS, wl, etch, pub 1784, NPG.

MANSFIELD, Sir James (1733-1821) chief justice of the common pleas.

R C.TURNER, after H.Edridge, wl seated, mezz, pub 1825, BM, NPG.

C JAMES SAYERS, 'The Master of the Inn confers the order of knighthood on Don Quixote', aquatint, NPG.

MANSFIELD, William Murray, 1st Earl of (1705-1793) judge.

P J.B.VAN LOO, 1732, hl seated, Scone Palace, Tayside region, Scotland; version NPG 474. J.B.VAN LOO, c1738, tql in turban, Royal College of Physicians, London. DAVID MARTIN, 1770, wl seated in peer's robes, Christ Church, Oxford; versions, Scone Palace and 1777, SNPG 598. SIR JOSHUA REYNOLDS, c1776, tql, Scone Palace. JOHN SINGLETON COPLEY, 1783, wl, NPG 172 (chalk study, BM).

D FRANCESCO BARTOLOZZI, hs, chalk, Metropolitan Museum of Art, New York. JOHN SINGLETON COPLEY, head, sketch, Boston, Athenaeum, USA. DAVID MARTIN, hs, red chalk, oval, SNPG 1445.

G JOHAN ZOFFANY, 'Charles Macklin as Shylock', a scene from *The Merchant of Venice*, oil, 1767–68, TATE 6005. J.S.COPLEY, 'The Collapse of the Earl of Chatham in the House of Lords, 7 July 1778', oil, TATE 100, on loan to NPG.

C J.M.RYSBRACK, 1743, marble bust, Scone Palace. JOSEPH NOLLEKENS, 1779, marble bust, Kenwood House, London. J.NOLLEKENS, 1790, marble bust, Belvoir Castle, Leics. NOLLEKENS, bust, Trinity Hall, Cambridge. JAMES TASSIE, 1779, Wedgwood medallion, BM, JOHN FLAXMAN, 1801, statue on monument, Westminster Abbey, London. E.H.BAILEY, 1855, marble statue, Palace of Westminster, London.

R J.JONES, after W.Grimaldi, tql seated, stipple, pub 1791, BM.

MANT, Richard (1776-1848) bishop of Down and Connor and Dromore.

P E.K., 1831, tql, Oriel College, Oxford.

R R.SMITH, tql seated, line, pub 1840, BM, NPG. G.R.WARD, after M.Cregan, tql, mezz, pub 1843, BM.

MANTELL, Gideon Algernon (1790-1852) geologist.

P J.J.MASQUERIER, hl, Royal Society, London.

R W.T.DAVEY, after Senties, hl, mezz, oval, BM, NPG.

MARA, Mrs Gertrude Elizabeth, née Schmeling (1749-1833) singer.

D J.HUTCHINSON, hs, pastel, Garrick Club, London.

R J.COLLYER, after P.Jean, tql as Armida, stipple, oval, pub 1794, BM, NPG. W.RIDLEY, after J.L.David, hl, stipple, oval, for *Monthly Mirror*, 1800, BM.

C JAMES SAYERS, wl, 'The Charmers of the Age', etch, pub 1786, NPG. J.GILLRAY, 'Ancient Music', etch, pub 1787, NPG.

MARCET, Alexander John Gaspard (1770-1822) physician.

P SIR HENRY RAEBURN, hs, Royal Society of Medicine, London.

MARCH, Samuel, see Samuel March PHILLIPPS.

MARCHANT, Nathaniel (1739-1816) gem engraver.

P Attrib JOHN JACKSON, Sir John Soane's Museum, London.

D GEORGE DANCE, hs, profile, Royal Academy, London.

R W.DANIELL, after G.Dance, hs, profile, soft-ground etch, BM.

MARCHI, Giuseppe Filippo Liberati (1735?-1808) painter, assistant to Sir Joshua Reynolds.

P SIR JOSHUA REYNOLDS, 1753–54, hl in turban, Royal Academy, London.

MARCHMONT, Hugh Hume, 3rd Earl of (1708-1794) politician.

P PIERRE FALCONET, 1769, hs, SNPG 1184.

SC UNKNOWN, marble bust, Stowe, Bucks.

MARIA Clementina Sobieska (1702-1735) wife of Prince James Francis Edward Stuart, the 'Old Pretender'.

P UNKNOWN (Italian), c1719, hl, oval, NPG 1262. F.TREVISANI, hl, Prado, Madrid (on loan to the Spanish Embassy, Lima, Peru). By or after TREVISANI, hl holding fan, SNPG 886. Attrib GIROLAMO PESCI, c1721, hl on copper, Bodleian Library, Oxford. GIROLAMO PESCI, c1722, tql with her son, Stanford Hall, Leics. UNKNOWN, c1722, hl, Lennoxlove, Lothian region, Scotland; version, Versailles. After LOUIS GABRIEL BLANCHET, SNPG 1837. ANTONIO DAVID type, tql, Lambeth Palace, London.

SC OTTO HAMERANI, 1719, hl, bronze medal, NPG 1686. Various medals, SNPG.

PR PIERRE DREVET, after Antonio David, tql, line, BM. ANDREW MILLER, after F.Trevisani, tql, with rose, mezz, BM. F.CHEREAU, after F.Trevisani, hl, line, BM.

MARKHAM, William (1719-1807) archbishop of York.

P SIR JOSHUA REYNOLDS, c1759–61, tql, Christ Church Oxford. BENJAMIN WEST, c1771, hs, NPG 4495. JOHN HOPPNER, RA 1799, tql, Royal Coll.

G JOHN SINGLETON COPLEY, 'The Collapse of the Earl of Chatham in the House of Lords, 7 July 1778', oil, TATE 100, on loan to NPG.

SC JOHN BACON jnr, RA 1804, marble bust, Christ Church.

PR J.WARD, after G.Romney, tql seated, mezz, pub 1800, BM, NPG.

MARLBOROUGH, Charles Spencer, 3rd Duke of (1706-1758) soldier.

P STEPHEN SLAUGHTER, 1737, wl in classical dress, Althorp, Northants. SIR JOSHUA REYNOLDS, 1757, hl, Wilton House, Wilts. J.B. VAN LOO, wl, Blenheim Palace, Oxon. UNKNOWN, tql, DoE (British Embassy, Bonn).

G WILLIAM HOGARTH, sometimes called 'The Holland House Group', oil, c1737, Ickworth (NT), Suffolk. THOMAS HUDSON, c1754, with his family, Blenheim in the background, Blenheim Palace.

SC J.M.RYSBRACK, 1750, marble bust, Blenheim Palace.

MARLBOROUGH, George Spencer, 4th Duke of (1739-1817) soldier.

P SIR JOSHUA REYNOLDS, 1762, hl, Blenheim Palace, Oxon. SIR JOSHUA REYNOLDS, 1764, tql, Wilton House, Wilts. R.COSWAY, hs, oval, Blenheim Palace.

G THOMAS HUDSON, in family group of the 3rd Duke of Marlborough, oil, c1754, Blenheim Palace. SIR JOSHUA REYNOLDS, wl seated with his family, oil, 1778, Blenheim Palace.

PR J.OGBORNE, after F.Bartolozzi, hs with badge and collar of the Garter, stipple, oval, pub 1795, BM, NPG.

MARLBOROUGH, George Spencer, 5th Duke of (1766-1840) politician.

G SIR JOSHUA REYNOLDS, The Marlborough Family, oil, 1778, Blenheim Palace, Oxon.

PR J.S.AGAR, after R.Cosway, wl in fancy dress, stipple, BM, NPG.

MARRYAT, Frederick (1792-1848) naval captain and novelist.

P JOHN SIMPSON, c1835, hl, NPG 1239. E.DIXON, RA 1839, hl, NMM, Greenwich.

PR H.COOK, after W.Behnes, wl, stipple, BM, NPG. R.J.LANE, after A.D'Orsay, hs, lith, NPG. UNKNOWN, hl, line, pub 1826, BM.

MARSDEN, Samuel (1764-1838) apostle of New Zealand.

P UNKNOWN, Old Colonists' Museum, Auckland, New Zealand.

PR UNKNOWN, hs, stipple, NPG.

MARSDEN, William (1754-1836) orientalist and numismatist.
P UNKNOWN, c1805-10, hl, DoE (Admiralty House, London).
D GEORGE DANCE, 1794, hs, pencil and wash, NPG 4410. SIR FRANCIS CHANTREY, hs and hs profile, pencil, NPG 316a (85, 86).
PR MRS D.TURNER, after T.Phillips, hs, etch, BM, NPG.

MARSDEN, William (1796-1867) surgeon.
P UNKNOWN, wl, Royal Free Hospital, London.

MARSH, Sir Henry, 1st Bart (1790-1860) physician.
SC JOHN HENRY FOLEY, 1866, statue, Royal College of Physicians, Dublin. JOSEPH R.KIRK, monument, Mount Jerome Cemetery, Dublin. J.R.KIRK, marble bust, Royal College of Surgeons, Dublin.

MARSH, Herbert (1757-1839) bishop of Peterborough.
P UNKNOWN, St John's College, Cambridge.
PR J.COCHRAN, after J.W.Wright, hl, stipple, for Jerdan's *Nat Portrait Gallery*, 1831, BM, NPG. S.W.REYNOLDS, after J.Ponsford, tql seated, mezz, pub 1835, BM.

MARSH, William (1775-1864) divine and writer.
PR C.TURNER, after J.G.Strutt, in pulpit, preaching, mezz, pub 1818, BM. J.LINNELL, after M.R.S., tql seated, mixed, pub 1831, BM, NPG.

MARSHALL, Benjamin (1767?-1835) painter of sporting subjects.
P LAMBERT MARSHALL, (his son), hs, NPG 2671. Self-portrait, with a gun and two dogs, Yale Center for British Art, New Haven, USA.
D Attrib I.R.CRUIKSHANK, wl, pencil, NPG 2787.
PR UNKNOWN, hl, stipple, for *Sporting Mag*, 1826, BM, NPG.

MARSHALL, Henry (1775-1851) physician and military hygienist.
P SIR DANIEL MACNEE, hl, SNPG 552.

MARSHALL, William (1748-1833) violinist and composer.
PR C.TURNER, after J.Moir, tql, mezz, pub 1817, BM.

MARSHMAN, Joshua (1768-1837) orientalist and missionary.
P Attrib GEORGE CHINNERY, hl, Serampore College, West Bengal, India.

MARTIN, Benjamin (1704-1782) optician and compiler.
PR UNKNOWN, hl, line, oval, for *Gent Mag*, 1785, BM, NPG.

MARTIN, David (1737-1798) portrait painter.
P Self-portrait, hs, SNPG 194. Self-portrait, c1760, hs, NGS 569.

MARTIN, Sir George (1764-1847) admiral of the fleet.
P CHARLES LANDSEER, after Sir Thomas Lawrence (c1821-25), hl with Bath ribbon and star, NMM, Greenwich.
G WORTHINGTON & PARKER, after R.Smirke, 'Naval Victories', 'Commemoration of 14th February 1797', line, pub 1803, BM, NPG.

MARTIN, Sir James Ronald (1793-1874) surgeon.
PH ERNEST EDWARDS, wl, for vol II of *Men of Eminence*, ed L.Reeve, 1863, NPG.

MARTIN, John (1741-1820) baptist minister.
PR J.LINNELL, tql seated, etch, pub 1813, BM, NPG.

MARTIN, John (1789-1854) painter of Biblical subjects.
P HENRY WARREN, c1839, hl, NPG 958.
D C.R.LESLIE, 1822, hs, pencil, chalk, pen and ink, BM. WILLIAM BROCKEDON, 1826, hl, chalk, NPG 2515 (13). CHARLES MARTIN (his son), 1854, hs, Laing Art Gallery, Newcastle. CARL VOGEL, Küpferstichkabinett, Staatliche Kunstsammlungen, Dresden.
PR J.THOMSON, after W.Derby, hl, stipple, for *European Mag*, 1822,

BM, NPG. C.WAGSTAFF, after T.Wageman, wl seated, for Arnold's *Mag of Fine Arts*, 1834, BM, NPG. SEAR & CO, hl, stipple, pub 1828, BM.

MARTIN, Jonathan (1782-1838) lunatic who set fire to York Minster in 1829.
P ROBERT WOODLEY BROWN, 1829, hl, Dean and Chapter, York, on loan to York City Art Gallery.
D GEORGE CRUIKSHANK, at his trial, Laing Art Gallery, Newcastle.
PR W.WALTON, after T.Kilby, tql, lith, BM.

MARTIN, Matthew (1748-1838) naturalist and philanthropist.
M JAMES SCOULER, 1770, hs?, V & A.

MARTIN, Richard (1754-1834) politician, known as 'Humanity Martin'.
P UNKNOWN, hl, RSPCA, London.
D UNKNOWN, sketch, Ashmolean Museum, Oxford.
PR S.DRUMMOND, hl, lith, BM.

MARTIN, Sir Thomas Byam (1773-1854) admiral of the fleet.
P T.W.MACKAY, 1852, tql, formerly United Service Club, London (c/o The Crown Commissioners).

MARTIN, William (1772-1851) inventor and eccentric.
M GEORGE PATTEN, hs, NPG 1576.
PR Two engr, Laing Art Gallery, Newcastle. COLLARD, after H.P.Parker, hl, line, NPG.

MARTINDALE, Miles (1756-1824) Wesleyan minister.
PR RIDLEY, hs, stipple, oval, for *Methodist Mag*, NPG.

MARTYN, Henry (1781-1812) missionary.
P THOMAS HICKEY, 1810, hl, Henry Martyn Hall, Cambridge; copy, W.H.Hay, 1865, St John's College, Cambridge.

MARTYN, Thomas (1735-1825) botanist.
PR J.FARN, after S.Drummond, hs, stipple, oval, for *European Mag* 1795, BM, NPG. UNKNOWN, hs, coloured stipple, oval, NPG.

MARY, Princess of Hesse (1723-1772) 4th daughter of George II.
G WILLIAM HOGARTH, 'The Family of George II', oil, c1731-32 Royal Coll; smaller version, NGI 126. Attrib PHILIPPE MERCIER the children of George II, Chatsworth, Derbyshire. UNKNOWN 'The Royal Family of Great Britain', line, BM.
SC JOHN SIGISMUND TANNER, gold, silver and copper medal, BM CHRISTIAN SCHIRMER, wl, silver medal, BM.
PR J.SIMON, wl when young, with coronet, BM, NPG. J.FABER jun after A.Pond, hl, mezz, BM, NPG. UNKNOWN, one of a set o medallion portraits of the Royal Family, mezz, BM, NPG J.SIMON, after E.Seeman, tql, mezz, NPG.

MARY, Princess, Duchess of Gloucester and Edinburgh (1776-1857) fourth daughter of George III.
P THOMAS GAINSBOROUGH, 1782, hs, Royal Coll. JOHN HOPPNER, RA 1785, hl, Royal Coll. SIR WILLIAM BEECHEY, RA 1797, hl, Royal Coll. SIR THOMAS LAWRENCE, RA 1824, tql Royal Coll.
D HENRY EDRIDGE, wl, Royal Coll.
M RICHARD COSWAY, hs, Royal Coll.
G JOHN SINGLETON COPLEY, wl with Princess Amelia and Princess Sophia, oil, 1785, Royal Coll.
PR T.H.MAGUIRE, after F.X.Winterhalter, hl, lith, pub 1851, BM NPG.

MARYBOROUGH, William Wellesley-Pole, 1st Baron see 3rd Earl of Mornington.

MASERES, Francis (1731-1824) mathematician, historian and

reformer.
PR P.AUDINET, after C.Hayter, tql, aged 83, line, BM, NPG.

MASKELYNE, Nevil (1732-1811) Astronomer Royal.
P JOHN DOWNMAN, 1779, hl, NMM, Greenwich. L.F.VANDER
PUYL, tql, Royal Society, London.
G J.F.SKILL, J.GILBERT, W. and E.WALKER, 'Men of Science
Living in 1807-8', pencil and wash, NPG 1075.
PR UNKNOWN, hl, stipple, oval, for *European Mag*, 1804, BM.

MASON, John Monck (1726-1809) Shakespearean
commentator.
G FRANCIS WHEATLEY, 'The Irish House of Commons', oil, 1780,
Leeds City Art Galleries, Lotherton Hall.
R C.KNIGHT, after S.Harding, hl, stipple, for Harding's *Shakespeare
Illustrated*, 1791, BM, NPG.

MASON, Sir Josiah (1795-1881) pen manufacturer and
philanthropist.
SC FRANCIS JOHN WILLIAMSON, bronze statue, Orphanage Road
and Chester Road, Erdington, Birmingham.
PH UNKNOWN, hs, albumen, for John Thackray Bunce's *Josiah
Mason: A Biography*, 1882, NPG.

MASON, William (1725-1797) poet and biographer of
Thomas Gray.
P SIR JOSHUA REYNOLDS, 1774, hl, Pembroke College,
Cambridge. WILLIAM DOUGHTY, 1778, hl, York City Art
Gallery; version, NPG 4806.
M Attrib JOHN PLOTT, hl, NPG 1393.
SL FRANCIS MAPLETOFT, c1765, wl seated, at his easel, Pembroke
College.
SC JOHN BACON snr, relief medallion on monument, Westminster
Abbey, London.
PR R.PAGE, after L.Vaslet, (1771), hl, stipple, oval, pub 1815, NPG.

MASSEY, Eyre, see 1st Baron Clarina.

MASSIE, James William (1799-1869) independent minister.
G S.BELLIN, after J.R.Herbert, 'The Meeting of the Council of the
Anti Corn Law League', mixed engr, pub 1850, BM, NPG.
R UNKNOWN, hl, stipple and line, NPG.

MASSON, Francis (1741-1805) gardener and botanist.
P G.GERRARD, hl, Linnean Society, London.

MASTERS, Robert (1713-1798) historian.
PR FACIUS, after T.Kerrich, hl, stipple, pub 1795, BM, NPG.

MATHEW, Theobald (1790-1856) apostle of temperance.
P J.P.HAVERTY, RA 1844, receiving a repentant pledge breaker,
NGI 4035. E.D.LEAHY, 1846, hs, NPG 199.
G UNKNOWN, 'The Illustrious Sons of Ireland', coloured lith, NPG.
SC J.H.FOLEY, 1863, bronze statue, Patrick Street, Cork. WILLIAM
WOODHOUSE, bronze medal, National Museum of Ireland.
R R.J.LANE, after R.G.A.Levinge, hl, pub 1845, NPG.
W.O.GELLER, after S.West, tql, mezz, BM. E.J.HARDING, tql
seated, etch, BM. UNKNOWN, tql, etch, BM.
C JOHN DOYLE, drg, BM.

MATHEWS, Charles (1776-1835) comedian.
P The following paintings are all at the Garrick Club, London: by
SAMUEL DE WILDE, 1810, wl as Dick Cypher in *Hit or Miss*; 1810,
wl as Sir Fretful Plagiary in *The Critic*; 1812, hl in character; RA
1813, wl as Somno in *The Sleepwalker*, by G.H.HARLOW, RA
1814, seated, looking at himself in four different characters; by
JAMES LONSDALE, RA 1827, hs; by GEORGE CLINT, RA 1832, wl
as Monsieur Mallet. A painting by G.Clint, hs, NPG 1734.
D Three w/c drgs by DE WILDE, in character, Garrick Club,
G.H.HARLOW, hl, pencil, NPG 3097a.
G GEORGE CLINT, RA 1830, wl as Flexible in a scene from *Love,
Law, and Physic*, Garrick Club.

SC SAMUEL JOSEPH, 1822, plaster bust, NPG 1710.
PR Various theatrical prints, BM, NPG.
C SIR EDWIN LANDSEER, hl, pen and ink, NPG 3097 (2-4).

**MATHEWS, Mrs Lucia Elizabeth, née Bartolozzi (1797-
1856)** actress.
P R.W.BUSS, after G.Clint, hl, Garrick Club, London.
D SAMUEL LOVER, c1826, wl as Mistress Ford in *The Merry Wives of
Windsor*, w/c, NPG 2786. Attrib LOUISA SHARPE, wl, w/c,
Garrick Club. HENRY SINGLETON, as Zelmira, chalk and w/c,
BM.
M ALFRED EDWARD CHALON, oval, Royal Shakespeare
Theatre Picture Gallery, Stratford-upon-Avon. J.W.CHILDE, hs,
Garrick Club.
G G.CLINT, in *Paul Pry*, with other characters, V & A, engr
T.Lupton, mezz, pub 1828, NPG.
PR Various theatrical prints, BM, NPG.
PH Two cartes by Mayall, wl, NPG.

MATHIAS, Benjamin Williams (1772-1841) divine.
PR C.TURNER, after Mrs Taylor, tql seated, mezz, pub 1821, BM.
UNKNOWN, hl, stipple, pub 1825, NPG.

MATON, William George (1774-1835) physician.
P MARGARET CARPENTER, c1820?, hl, Royal College of
Physicians, London. UNKNOWN, hl, Royal College of
Physicians.
D T.RACHETT, hs, profile, pencil, The Wellcome Historical
Medical Museum and Library, London. 'R.W.P.', hs, profile,
chalk, BM. UNKNOWN, hs, pencil, Library of the Botanic Garden,
Oxford.
SC WILLIAM BEHNES, bust, Linnean Society, London.

MATTHEWS, Henry (1789-1828) judge and traveller.
PR UNKNOWN, hs, lith, BM, NPG.

MATTHEWS, John (1755-1826) physician and poet.
SC UNKNOWN, called Matthews, Wedgwood medallion, c1790,
Wedgwood Museum, Barlaston, Staffs.

MATTOCKS, Isabella (1746-1826) actress.
P GAINSBOROUGH DUPONT, c1793-94, hs, as Louisa in *The
Duenna*, Garrick Club, London. SAMUEL DE WILDE, wl, as Lady
Restless in *All in the Wrong*, Garrick Club.
D SAMUEL DE WILDE, wl, pencil and chalk, BM. JAMES ROBERTS, as
Catherine in Shakespeare's *Henry V*, BM.
PR Various theatrical prints, BM, NPG.

MATURIN, Charles Robert (1782-1824) novelist and
dramatist.
P WILLIAM BROCAS, hl, National Library of Ireland, engr
H.Meyer, stipple, for *New Monthly Mag*, 1819, BM, NPG.

MATY, Matthew (1718-1776) physician, writer and principal
librarian at the British Museum.
P BARTHOLOMEW DUPAN, hl, BM.
PR F.BARTOLOZZI, hs, stipple, BM.

MATY, Paul Henry (1745-1787) assistant-librarian of the
British Museum.
SC After JAMES TASSIE, plaster medallion, SNPG 384.

MAUDSLAY, Henry (1771-1831) engineer.
G J.F.SKILL, J.GILBERT, W. and E.WALKER, 'Men of Science Living
in 1807-08', pencil and wash, NPG 1075.
SC HENRY WEEKES, after Sir Francis Chantrey, marble bust,
Institute of Mechanical Engineers, London; related plaster bust,
Science Museum, London.
PR H.GREVEDON, 1827, hs, lith, NPG.

MAUDUIT, Israel (1708-1787) political pamphleteer.
PR T.HOLLOWAY, after M.Chamberlin, hs, line, oval, for *European*

Mag, 1787, BM, NPG.

MAULE, Sir William Henry (1788-1858) judge.
D GEORGE RICHMOND, 1862, copy of drawing of 1852, hs, Lincoln's Inn, London.
SC J.BAILEY, 1858, bust, Lincoln's Inn.

MAULE, William Ramsay, see Baron Panmure.

MAUNDER, Samuel (1785-1849) compiler.
PR E.FINDEN, after J.Waugh, tql seated, stipple, BM.

MAURICE, Thomas (1754-1824) oriental scholar and historian.
D THOMAS UWINS, hs, chalk and pencil, BM.
PR W.RIDLEY, after Plimer, hs, stipple, oval, for *Monthly Mirror*, 1799, BM, NPG. W.RIDLEY, after S.Drummond, hs, stipple, oval, for *European Mag*, 1801, BM, NPG.

MAVOR, William Fordyce (1758-1837) compiler of educational works.
PR UNKNOWN, hs, line, oval, pub 1796, NPG. C.TURNER, after J.Saxon, hl seated, mezz, for his *Miscellanies*, 1829, BM, NPG.

MAWBEY, Sir Joseph, 1st Bart (1730-1798) politician.
PR J.DIXON, after R.E.Pine, tql seated, mezz, NPG. T.HOLLOWAY, after R.E.Pine, hs, line, oval, for *European Mag*, 1787, BM, NPG. J.NEWTON, after J. de Fleury, hs, profile, line, oval, NPG.
C J.GILLRAY, hl, etch, pub 1787, BM.

MAXWELL, Jane, see Duchess of Gordon.

MAXWELL, Sir Murray (1775-1831) naval captain.
PR T.WAGEMAN, 1817, hs, stipple, NPG.
C R.DIGHTON, wl, etch, BM, V & A.

MAXWELL, William Hamilton (1792-1850) Irish novelist.
D CHARLES GRAY, tql, pen, NGI 2591.
PR W.GREATBACH, after S.Lover, hs, line, for *Bentley's Miscellany*, 1840, BM, NPG. J.KIRKWOOD, after C.Grey, tql seated with dog, etch, NPG.

MAYNE, Sir Richard (1796-1868) police commissioner.
PR T.LANGER, after a photograph by J.Watkins, hs, line, NPG. UNKNOWN, after a photograph by J.Watkins, hs, woodcut, for *Illust London News*, 1869, NPG.

MAYO, John (1761-1818) physician.
SL JOHN MIERS, hs profile, oval, on plaster, NPG 4878.

MAYO, Thomas (1790-1871) president of the Royal College of Physicians.
D GEORGE RICHMOND, 1862, hs, chalk, Royal College of Physicians, London.

MEADE, Richard Charles Francis, see 3rd Earl of Clanwilliam.

MEADOWBANK, Alexander Maconochie-Welwood, 2nd Lord (1777-1861) judge.
P SIR MARTIN ARCHER SHEE, SNPG 1424.
SC SIR FRANCIS CHANTREY, bust, Ashmolean Museum, Oxford.
C R.DIGHTON, tql, coloured etch, NPG. J.KAY, hs, etch, NPG.

MEADOWBANK, Allan Maconochie, 1st Lord (1748-1816) judge.
P SIR HENRY RAEBURN, hs, SNPG 2188.
D JOHN BROWN, c1780, hs, pencil, National Museum of Antiquities, Scotland.
SC JAMES TASSIE, 1791, paste medallion, SNPG 164.
C J.KAY, hs, etch, line, 1799, NPG.

MEADOWS, Drinkwater (1799-1869) actor.
P HENRY MEYER, wl as Raubvogel, in *Returned Killed*, Garrick Club, London.

PR W.MEADOWS, hs, lith, NPG. Several R.J.LANE liths, and two engr in character, NPG.

MEADOWS, Joseph Kenny (1790-1874) artist.
P L.B.SMITH, tql, National Museum of Wales 59, Cardiff.

MEDLEY, Samuel (1738-1799) baptist minister and hymn-writer.
PR UNKNOWN, hl, line, oval, for *Gospel Mag*, 1776, BM, NPG. J.FITTLER, after S.Medley, tql seated, line, pub 1793, BM, NPG.

MEDOWS, Sir William (1738-1813) general.
PR ORME, after Smart, hs, stipple, oval, pub 1794, NPG. H.R.COOK, after W.Haines, hl, stipple, for *Royal Military Panorama*, 1814, BM, NPG.

MEDWYN, John Hay Forbes, Lord (1776-1854) Scottish judge.
M ANDREW ROBERTSON, hl, NGS 1992.

MEE, Anne, née Foldsone (1775?-1851) miniature painter.
PR H.MEYER, after Anne Mee, tql, stipple, for her *Gallery of Beauties*, 1812, BM, NPG.

MEIKLE, Andrew (1719-1811) millwright and inventor of the thrashing-machine.
P A.REDDOCK, 1811, tql, NPG 5001.

MEILAN, Mark Anthony (fl 1812) miscellaneous writer.
PR UNKNOWN, hs, line, oval, NPG.

MELBOURNE, Frederick James Lamb, 3rd Viscount (1782-1853) diplomat.
P JOHN PARTRIDGE, 1846, tql, NPG 3894.
G F.BARTOLOZZI, after J.Reynolds (1785), 'The Lamb Family', stipple, pub 1791, BM.

MELBOURNE, William Lamb, 2nd Viscount (1779-1848) prime-minister.
J JOHN HOPPNER, 1796, in Montem dress, hl, Royal Coll. SIR THOMAS LAWRENCE, c1805, hl, NPG 5185. SIR EDWIN LANDSEER, 1836, tql, NPG 3050. JOHN PARTRIDGE, 1844, tql seated, NPG 941. G.H.HARLOW, tql, NGI 255.
D SIR GEORGE HAYTER, 1837, wl, pencil, NPG 4342. SIR FRANCIS CHANTREY, 1838, hs and hs profile, pencil, NPG 316a (87). SAMUEL DIEZ, 1841, hl, pencil and wash, NPG 3103.
G F.BARTOLOZZI, after J.Reynolds (1785), 'The Lamb Family', stipple, pub 1791, BM. SIR GEORGE HAYTER, 'The Trial of Queen Caroline, 1820', oil, NPG 999. SIR GEORGE HAYTER, 'The House of Commons, 1833', oil, NPG 54. SIR FRANCIS GRANT, 'Party at Ranton Abbey', 1837, Shugborough House (NT), Staffs. SIR DAVID WILKIE, 'Queen Victoria's First Council', oil, 1837, Royal Coll. SIR G.HAYTER, 'Queen Victoria's Coronation', oil, 1838, Royal Coll. C.R.LESLIE, 'The Queen Receiving the Sacrament after her Coronation', oil, 1838, Royal Coll. SIR F.GRANT, 'Queen Victoria Riding at Windsor Castle', 1839, Royal Coll. JOHN PARTRIDGE, 'The Fine Arts Commissioners, 1846', NPG 342, 3.
SC R.MOODY, 1838, bust, Royal Coll. JOHN FRANCIS, 1838, bust, Royal Coll. SIR FRANCIS CHANTREY, 1841, marble bust, Royal Coll.
C JOHN DOYLE, numerous political satires, drgs, BM.

MELDOLA, Raphael (1754-1828) Jewish theologian.
PR J.LOPEZ, after F.B.Barlin, tql, stipple, pub 1806, NPG.

MELLON, Harriot, see Duchess of St Albans.

MELMOTH, Courtney, see Samuel Jackson PRATT.

MELVILL, Henry (1798-1871), canon of St Paul's.
PR C.TURNER, after J.Rand, tql seated, mezz, pub 1835, BM. R.ARTLETT, after Rand, tql seated, stipple, NPG.

MELVILL, Hester Jean Frances, Lady (*d* 1864) wife of Sir James Cosmo Melvill.
P JOHN JAMES NAPIER, *c*1858, tql seated, NPG 4825a.

MELVILL, Sir James Cosmo (1792-1861) civil servant in India.
P JOHN JAMES NAPIER, exhib 1858, tql seated, NPG 4825.

MELVILLE, Henry Dundas, 1st Viscount (1742-1811) statesman.
P SIR THOMAS LAWRENCE, 1810, hs, NPG 746. SIR HENRY RAEBURN, wl in robes, National Bank of Scotland. SIR HENRY RAEBURN, hs in robes, Buccleuch Estates, Selkirk, Scotland. Attrib SIR JOSHUA REYNOLDS, hs, Arniston House, Lothian region, Scotland. JOHN RISING, tql, SNPG L123. GEORGE ROMNEY, wl, in robes, Arniston House.
D ARCHIBALD SCIRVING, after David Martin, hs, pastel, Arniston House.
G SIR JOSHUA REYNOLDS, 'The Society of Dilettanti', oil, 1777-79, Society of Dilettanti, Brooks's Club, London. K.A.HICKEL, 'The House of Commons, 1793', oil NPG 745. HILL and PUGIN, after Nattes, 'The Trial of Henry Lord Viscount Melville in Westminster Hall', coloured aquatint, pub 1806, Palace of Westminster, London.
SC SIR FRANCIS CHANTREY, statue, Parliament House, Edinburgh. SIR F.CHANTREY, busts, The Admiralty, London and Ashmolean Museum, Oxford. JAMES TASSIE, paste medallion, SNPG 1267.
C Several JOHN KAY etchs, BM, NPG.

MELVILLE, Robert (1723-1809) soldier and antiquary.
P SIR HENRY RAEBURN, SNPG 1852.
SC After JAMES TASSIE, 1791, plaster medallion, SNPG 497.

MELVILLE, Robert Saunders Dundas, 2nd Viscount (1771-1851) statesman.
P COLVIN SMITH, *c*1831, tql, with Thistle Star, SNPG 252.
G SIR GEORGE HAYTER, 'The Trial of Queen Caroline, 1820', oil, NPG 999.
PR C.TURNER, after T.Lawrence, tql seated, mezz, pub 1827, BM, NPG.

MENDES, Moses (*d* 1758) poet and dramatist.
PR W.BROMLEY, hs, stipple and line, oval, for *European Mag*, 1792, NPG.

MENDIP, Welbore Ellis, Baron (1713-1802) politician.
P K.A.HICKEL, 1793, hs, NPG 3993. THOMAS GAINSBOROUGH, *c*1769, tql, Christ Church, Oxford.
G K.A.HICKEL, 'The House of Commons, 1793', oil, NPG 745.
SC After JAMES TASSIE, 1780, plaster medallion, SNPG 479.
PR J.WHESSELL, after Gainsborough, 1763, tql, line, BM. C.WATSON, after J.Meyer, hs, stipple, oval, pub 1791, BM, NPG.

MENDOZA, Daniel (1764-1836) pugilist.
PR H.KINGSBURY, after J.Robineau, wl in fighting attitude, mezz, pub 1789, BM.
C J.GILLRAY, wl in fighting attitude, etch, BM.

MENZIES, Archibald (1754-1842) botanical collector.
P E.U.EDDIS, Linnean Society, London.
PR MISS TURNER, after E.U.Eddis, hs, lith, BM, NPG.

MERCER, Hugh (1726?-1777) American brigadier-general.
D JOHN TRUMBULL, 1791, hs study for 'Death of General Mercer', Fordham University, New York, USA; hs sketch, Metropolitan Museum of Art, New York. 5 sketches, studies for 'Death of General Mercer', Princeton University Library, USA.

MEREDITH, Sir William, 3rd Bart (1725?-1790) politician.
PR T.WATSON, after D.Gardner, hl seated, mezz, oval, pub 1773, BM, NPG.

MEREWETHER, Henry Alworth (1780-1864) serjeant-at-law.
PR MISS TURNER, after J.Lucas, hs, lith, BM, NPG.

MEREWETHER, John (1797-1850) dean of Hereford.
PR C.BAUGNIET, tql, lith, 1848, BM.

MERIVALE, John Herman (1779-1844) scholar.
PR J.POSSELWHITE, after E.U.Eddis, hs, stipple, pub 1844, NPG.

MERRIMAN, Samuel (1731-1818) physician.
PR J.CORNER, after T.Richmond, hl aged 84, line, oval, BM.

MERRIMAN, Samuel (1771-1852) physician.
PR UNKNOWN, hl, stipple, BM.

MERRY, Robert (1755-1798) dilettante.
PR J.COLLYER, after H.D.Hamilton, hl, line, for *British Album*, 1789, BM, NPG. UNKNOWN, hs, stipple, oval, for *European Mag*, 1793, BM.

MERYON, Charles Lewis (1783-1877) physician and biographer.
P ARMINIUS MEYER, *c*1846, hs, Royal College of Physicians, London.
PH UNKNOWN, tql as an old man, BM (Engr Ports Coll).

METCALF, John (1717-1810) commonly known as 'Blind Jack of Knaresborough'.
PR UNKNOWN, after J.R.Smith, tql aged 79, line, for his *Life*, BM, NPG.

METCALFE, Charles Theophilus Metcalfe, 1st Baron (1785-1846) Indian and colonial governor.
P J.J.MASQUERIER, *c*1800, hs, a leaving portrait, Eton College, Berks. F.R.SAY, wl seated, Oriental Club, London. Attrib CORNELIUS KRIEGHOFF, hl, Château de Ramezay, Montreal, Canada. UNKNOWN, Royal Commonwealth Society, London.
SC E.H.BAILY, 1843, plaster bust, India Office, London.
PR A.MAURIN, after A.Duperly, wl seated, lith, BM.

METCALFE, Philip (1733-1818) collector and patron of the arts.
P POMPEO BATONI, hs, NPG 2001.
PR W.EVANS, after E.Scott, 1801, hs, stipple, NPG.

METHUEN, David Smythe, Lord (1746-1806) judge.
SC JAMES TASSIE, 1794, paste medallion, SNPG 1254.

MEYER, Jeremiah (1735-1789) miniaturist.
D GEORGE DANCE, hs, profile, Royal Academy, London, etched by W.Daniell, NPG.
G JOHAN ZOFFANY, 'The Royal Academicians, 1772', oil, Royal Coll.
SC Relief, Kew Parish Church.
PR W.PETHER, after N.Dance, hl, mezz, BM. D.P.PARISET, after P.Falconet, hs, stipple, BM, same plate altered by B.Reading, BM, NPG.

MEYRICK, Sir Samuel Rush (1783-1848) antiquary.
D WILLIAM BROCKEDON, *c*1830, hs, chalk, NPG 2515 (62).
PR J.SKELTON, after H.P.Briggs, tql, line, BM.

MICHELL, Henry (1714-1789) scholar.
PR E.SCOTT, after C.Sherriff, hs, stipple, oval, BM, NPG.

MICKLE, William Julius (1735-1788) poet, translator of the Lusiad.
D OZIAS HUMPHRY, head, chalk, BM.
PR C.BESTLAND, after O.Humphry, hl seated, stipple, for *European Mag*, 1789, BM, NPG. W.SKELTON, after S.Taylor, hl, line, oval, BM. W.H.WORTHINGTON, after J.Thurston, hs, line, pub 1821, NPG.

MIDDLETON, Charles (1726-1813), see 1st Baron Barham.

MIDDLETON, Erasmus (1739-1805) author.
PR UNKNOWN, hs, line, oval, for *Gospel Mag*, 1778, BM, NPG.
W.RIDLEY, hs, stipple, for *Evangelical Mag*, 1805, BM, NPG.
ANKER SMITH, tql seated, line, pub 1821, NPG.

MIDDLETON, Thomas Fanshaw (1769-1822) bishop of
Calcutta.
SC J.G.LOUGH, *c*1832, marble statue on monument, St Paul's
Cathedral, London.
PR H.MEYER, after J.Jackson, tql seated, stipple, for *Contemporary
Portraits*, 1815, BM, NPG.

MILL, William Hodge (1792-1853) orientalist.
D SIR FRANCIS CHANTREY, hs and hs profile, pencil, NPG 316a (88).
SC SIR FRANCIS CHANTRY, RA 1840, marble bust, Asiatic Society of
Bengal; plaster model, Ashmolean Museum, Oxford. J.B.PHILIP,
1860, recumbent effigy, Ely Cathedral.

MILLAR, James (1762-1827) physician and author.
D JOHN HENNING, head, crayon, SNPG 879.

MILLAR, John (1735-1801) professor of law.
SC JAMES TASSIE, 1796, paste medallion, SNPG 158.

MILLER, Anna, Lady, née Riggs (1741-1781) poet.
SC JOHN BACON snr, medallion on monument, Bath Abbey.

MILLER, Edward (1731-1807) organist and historian of
Doncaster.
PR T.HARDY, hl, stipple, BM, NPG.

MILLER, George (1764-1848) divine.
SC THOMAS KIRK, marble bust, Trinity College, Dublin.
PR J.KIRKWOOD, tql, etch, NPG.

MILLER, Patrick (1731-1815) pioneer of steam navigation.
P SIR GEORGE CHALMERS, hs, NPG 2009.
G J.F.SKILL, J.GILBERT, W and E.WALKER, 'Men of Science Living
in 1807–08', pencil and wash, NPG 1075.
SC After JAMES TASSIE, 1789, plaster medallion, SNPG 385.

MILLER, Ralph Willett (1762-1799) naval captain.
G WORTHINGTON & PARKER, after R.Smirke, 'Naval Victories',
'Commemoration of the 14th February 1797', and
W.BROMLEY, J.LANDSEER & LENEY, after R.Smirke, 'Victors
of the Nile', line, pub 1803, BM, NPG.
SC JOHN FLAXMAN, medallion on monument, St Paul's Cathedral,
London.

MILLER, Sir Thomas (1717-1789), see Lord Glenlee.

MILLER, Thomas (1731-1804) bookseller.
PR E.SCRIVEN, after H.Edridge, hl, stipple, oval, BM, NPG.

MILLER, Sir William (1755-1846), see Lord Glenlee.

MILLER, William (1769-1845) publisher.
PR J.D.ENGLEHEART, tql, aged 57, lith, BM, NPG. E.SCRIVEN, after
T.Phillips, tql seated, stipple, BM, NPG. MRS D.TURNER, after
T.Phillips, hs, etch, BM, NPG.

MILLER, William (1795-1861) general in the Peruvian army.
PR C.TURNER, after Sharpe, wl, mezz, for his *Memoirs*, 1829, BM,
NPG.

MILLER, William (1796-1882) landscape engraver.
PR UNKNOWN, after a photograph, hs, woodcut, BM.

MILLER, William Henry (1789-1848) book collector.
G SIR GEORGE HAYTER, 'The House of Commons, 1833', oil, NPG
54.

MILLES, Jeremiah (1714-1784) antiquary.
P NATHANIEL DANCE, hl, Society of Antiquaries, London.
D JOHN DOWNMAN, 1785, hl, w/c, NPG 4590.
SC JOHN BACON sen, 1785, marble bust, Society of Antiquaries.

MILMAN, Henry Hart (1791-1868) poet and historian.

P G.F.WATTS, *c*1863, hs, NPG 1324.
D THOMAS UWINS, 1813, reciting the Latin prize poem, pencil, BM.
SC F.J.WILLIAMSON, 1876, monument with recumbent figure, St
Paul's Cathedral, London.
PR W.WALKER, after T.A.Woolnoth, tql seated, mezz, pub 1852,
BM, NPG.

MILNE, Colin (1743?-1815) divine and botanist.
D JOHN RUSSELL, 1803, hl, pastel, NPG 5180.

MILNE, Sir David (1763-1845) admiral.
P G.F.CLARKE, after Sir Henry Raeburn, *c*1818, wl with Bath star,
NMM, Greenwich.
PR UNKNOWN, hl, stipple, for Brenton's *Naval History*, 1837, BM,
NPG.

MILNE, William (1785-1822) missionary to China.
PR UNKNOWN, hl, stipple, for *Evangelical Mag*, 1823, BM, NPG.

MILNER, Isaac (1750-1820) mathematician and divine.
P JOHN OPIE, tql seated, Queen's College, Cambridge.
D THOMAS UWINS, w/c and pencil, BM.
PR FACIUS, after T.Kerrich, hl, stipple, pub 1811, BM, NPG.
H.MEYER, after J.Jackson, hl, stipple, for *Contemporary
Portraits*, 1815, BM, NPG.

MILNER, John (1752-1826) bishop of Castabala and author.
PR W.RADCLYFFE, after J.V.Barber, tql, line, pub 1819, BM, NPG.
C.B.FOX, after G.A.Keman, hl, line, pub 1822, BM. W.ROFFE,
hl, stipple, NPG. T.WYATT, after a bust by G.Clarke, lith, pub
1826, NPG.

MILNER, Joseph (1744-1797) evangelical divine.
PR UNKNOWN, silhouette profile with representation of his monument, line, pub 1809, BM, NPG.

MILTON, John (1759-1805) assistant engraver to the Royal
Mint.
M JOHN BOYLE, 1788, V & A.

MINTO, Gilbert Elliott, 1st Earl of (1751-1814) governor-
general of India.
P ROBERT HOME, *c*1811, wl with maps, papers and writing
materials, Rashtrapati Bhavan, New Delhi. ROBERT HOME,
1812, wl seated at desk, Victoria Memorial Hall, Calcutta.
GEORGE CHINNERY 1812–13, wl in peer's robes, with map of
Java, SNPG L301. GEORGE CHINNERY, *c*1813, wl seated in peer's
robes, Rijksmuseum, Amsterdam. JAMES ATKINSON, hl, NPG
836.
D JAMES ATKINSON, 1813, hs, ink and pencil, SNPG 335.

MINTO, Gilbert Elliot, 2nd Earl of (1782-1859) diplomat.
P BUTLER, after Sir Francis Grant, tql, with Bath Ribbon, DoE
(Foreign Office, London).
SC UNKNOWN, plaster medallion, SNPG 931.
PR G.ZOBEL, after F.Grant, tql seated, mezz, pub 1851, BM, NPG.

MITCHELL, Alexander (1780-1868) civil engineer.
P UNKNOWN, hl, Belfast Harbour Commissioners.

MITCHELL, Sir Andrew (1708-1771) diplomat.
P After ALLAN RAMSAY, (type of 1766), hl, with Bath star, NPG
2514.

MITCHELL, Sir Andrew (1757-1806) admiral.
P L.F.ABBOTT, wl, Dunfermline Town Council; hl copy, NMM
Greenwich.
PR J.CHAPMAN, hs, stipple, oval, pub 1800, NPG. H.R.COOK, after
R.Bowyer, hs in uniform, stipple, oval, for *Naval Chronicle*
1806, BM, NPG.

MITFORD, John Freeman, see 1st Baron Redesdale.

MITFORD, Mary Russell (1787-1855) novelist an

dramatist.

P B.R.HAYDON, 1824, hs, Reading Museum and Art Gallery; copy by John Lucas, c1853, NPG 404.

D A.R.BURT, 1832, hl, w/c, Folger Shakespeare Library, Washington DC. JOHN LUCAS, 1852, hs, chalk, NPG 4045.

PR J.B.HUNT, after J.Plott, hs as a child, stipple, oval, pub 1852, NPG. W.READ, after Miss Drummond, hl, stipple, for *La Belle Assemblée*, 1823, NPG. J.BROMLEY, after J.Lucas (1828), tql seated, mezz, pub 1830, BM. D.MACLISE, wl seated, lith, for *Fraser's Mag*, 1831, BM, NPG (pencil study V & A).

MITFORD, William (1744-1827) historian.

D After H.EDRIDGE, hl, pencil, NPG 1760a.

PR C.PICART, after H.Edridge, hl seated, stipple, for *Contemporary Portraits*, 1811, BM, NPG.

MOFFAT, Robert (1795-1883) missionary in South Africa.

P WILLIAM SCOTT, 1842, hs, NPG 3774.

D C.BELL, 1835, 'Visit to Moselekatze', with Dr A.Smith, University of Witwatersrand, South Africa.

PR J.COCHRAN, after H.Room, hl, stipple, NPG. J.C.ARMYTAGE, after E.Heaphy, hs, stipple, pub 1842, NPG. G.BAXTER, 1843, tql, colour print, NPG.

PH ELLIOTT & FRY, hs, carte, NPG Cunnington album.

MOIR, David Macbeth (1798-1851) physician and author.

P SIR JOHN WATSON GORDON, 1850, hl, SNPG L284.

D JOHN FAED, hs, w/c, SNPG 2179.

G DANIEL MACLISE, 'The Fraserians', lith, for *Fraser's Mag*, 1835, BM.

SC A.F.RITCHIE, 1853, statue, Musselburgh, Scotland.

PR DANIEL MACLISE, wl seated, lith, for *Fraser's Mag*, NPG.

MOIRA, Francis Rawdon-Hastings, 2nd Earl of, see 1st Marquess of Hastings.

MOLESWORTH, John Edward Nassau (1790-1877) vicar of Rochdale.

PR H.COOK, hl, stipple, BM, NPG.

MONBODDO, James Burnett, Lord (1714-1799), judge and author.

D JOHN BROWN, hs, pencil, SNPG 362.

M UNKNOWN, V & A.

C JOHN KAY, several etch, NPG.

MONCKTON, Mary, see Countess of CORK and Orrery.

MONCKTON, Robert (1726-1782) general in North America.

P UNKNOWN, (called Robert Monckton), tql, Public Archives of Canada, Ottawa, Canada.

SC JAMES TASSIE, paste medallion, SNPG 1256.

PR J.McARDELL, after T.Hudson, tql, mezz, BM, NPG. J.WATSON, after B.West, wl with cannon, mezz, BM.

MONCRIEFF, Sir James Wellwood Moncrieff, Lord (1776-1851) Scottish judge.

P SIR JOHN WATSON-GORDON, hl, Faculty of Advocates, Parliament Hall, Edinburgh.

SC SAMUEL JOSEPH, 1823, plaster bust, SNPG L51. WILLIAM BRODIE, 1863, marble bust, Faculty of Advocates, Parliament Hall, Edinburgh.

PR C.HOLL, after Sir H.Raeburn, hl, stipple, NPG.

MONCRIEFF, William Thomas (1794-1857) dramatist and theatrical manager.

PR J.K.MEADOWS, tql seated, lith, BM. UNKNOWN, hs, aged 25, stipple, BM.

MONCRIEFF-WELLWOOD, Sir Henry, Bart (1750-1827) Scottish divine.

PR E.SCRIVEN, after H.Raeburn, hl seated, stipple, for *Contemporary Portraits*, 1812, BM, NPG.

C J.KAY, in pulpit, preaching in gown and bands, open bible before him, etching, oval, 1793, BM.

MONK, James Henry (1784-1856) bishop of Gloucester and Bristol.

PR G.PARKER, after J.Moore, tql, stipple, for Jerdan's *Nat Portrait Gallery*, 1832, BM, NPG. F.BACON, after W.Gush, tql, mezz, pub 1843, BM.

MONRO, Alexander (1733-1817) anatomist.

P EDWARD CALVERT, tql, Edinburgh University.

SC UNKNOWN, plaster bust, SNPG 232.

PR J.HEATH, after H.Raeburn, hl, stipple, pub 1800, BM, NPG.

C J.KAY, wl, etch, BM, NPG.

MONRO, Alexander (1773-1859) anatomist.

P KENNETH MACLEAY, hs, Royal College of Surgeons, Edinburgh. SIR JOHN WATSON-GORDON, hl, Edinburgh University.

SL AUGUSTIN EDOUART, SNPG 782.

C B.W.CROMBIE, 1848, wl, coloured etch, reprinted in *Modern Athenians*, 1882, NPG.

PH D.O.HILL, tql seated, carbon print, NPG; daguerreotype, BM (Engr Ports Coll).

MONRO, Henry (1791-1814) portrait and subject painter.

PR Self-portrait, 1813, hs, etch, BM.

MONRO, John (1715-1791) physician.

P NATHANIEL DANCE, 1769, hl, Royal College of Physicians, London. UNKNOWN, Bethlem Royal Hospital, Beckenham, Kent.

MONRO, Thomas (1759-1833) physician and connoisseur.

D HENRY MONRO, c1810, hl, pastel, Royal College of Physicians, London. H.MONRO, 1813, hs, pencil, BM. H.MONRO, head, pencil and wash, NPG 3117. JOHN HENDERSON, hs, pen and ink, BM.

MONTAGU, Edward Wortley (1713-1776) author and traveller.

P M.W.PETERS, hl in Arab dress, NPG 4573. GEORGE ROMNEY, tql in Arab dress, Warwick Castle, Warwicks.

SC PETER SCHEEMAKERS, 1766, bust, Trinity College, Cambridge.

C J.PILLEMENT, wl, etch, NPG.

MONTAGU, Mrs Elizabeth, née Robinson (1720-1800) writer and leader of society.

G RICHARD SAMUEL, 'The Nine Living Muses of Great Britain', oil, exhib 1779, NPG 4905.

SC UNKNOWN, 1775, Wedgwood medallion, Wedgwood Museum, Barlaston, Staffs.

PR J.R.SMITH, after J.Reynolds, tql seated, mezz, pub 1776, BM, NPG. C.TOWNLEY, after F.Reynolds, tql seated, stipple, BM, NPG. W.RIDLEY, after Rivers, hl, stipple, oval, for *Lady's Monthly Museum* 1800, BM, NPG. R.COOPER, after C.F.Zincke, hl in character of Anne Boleyn, stipple, oval, for Wraxall's *Memoirs*, 1809, BM.

MONTAGU, George (1737-1788), see 4th Duke of Manchester.

MONTAGU, Sir George (1750-1829) admiral.

P UNKNOWN, c1782-83, wl before seascape, NMM, Greenwich.

MONTAGU, George Brudenell, 4th Earl of Cardigan and Duke of (1712-1790) privy councillor.

P HERMAN VAN DER MYN, 1732, hl, Deene Park, Northants. THOMAS GAINSBOROUGH, before 1768, tql with Garter star, Buccleuch Estates, Selkirk, Scotland. Attrib ENOCH SEEMAN, wl, Buccleuch Estates. THOMAS HUDSON, hl, Buccleuch Estates.

UNKNOWN, hl, Beaulieu Abbey, Hants. SIR WILLIAM BEECHEY, 1789–90, hs with Garter star, Hatfield House, Herts.
D THOMAS GAINSBOROUGH, hs, pastel, BM.
SL JOHN MIERS, hs profile, on plaster, Royal Coll.

MONTAGU, James (1752-1794) naval captain.
D JOHN BACON, design for a monument, ink, BM.
G BARTOLOZZI, LANDSEER, RYDER & STOW, after R.Smirke, 'Naval Victories', 'Commemoration of the victory of June 1st 1794', line, pub 1803, BM.
SC JOHN FLAXMAN, statue on monument, Westminster Abbey.
PR H.R.COOK, after Maynard, after statue on monument, stipple, pub 1805, BM.

MONTAGU, John (1718-1792), see 4th Earl of Sandwich.

MONTAGU, William (1771?-1843), see 5th Duke of Manchester.

MONTAGU-Dunk, George (1716-1771), see 2nd Earl of Halifax.

MONTEAGLE, Thomas Spring-Rice, 1st Baron (1790-1866) chancellor of the exchequer.
P WILLIAM TURNER DE LOND, 'The chairing of Thomas Spring Rice', Limerick Chamber of Commerce.
G SIR GEORGE HAYTER, 'The House of Commons, 1833', oil, NPG 54.
PR J.LINNELL, tql seated by table, holding book, mixed, pub 1836, BM, NPG. F.HOLL, after G.Richmond, hs, stipple, NPG.
C Several drawings by J.Doyle, BM.

MONTEFIORE, Sir Moses Haim, 1st Bart (1784-1885) philanthropist.
P HENRY WEIGALL, 1881, hs, NPG 2178.
PR R.BLIND, hs, lith, NPG E.KRUGER, two portraits, as he appeared in Alexandria in 1840 and Petersburg in 1846, lith, BM. LUNOIS, hs aged 99, lith, BM. UNKNOWN, tql seated, lith, BM.
C RICHARD DIGHTON, 1818, wl, coloured etch, NPG, V & A.
PH ELLIOTT & FRY, hs, cabinet, NPG.

MONTGOMERIE, Archibald (1726-1796), see 11th Earl of Eglinton.

MONTGOMERIE, Hugh (1739-1819), see 12th Earl of Eglinton.

MONTGOMERY, Henry (1788-1865) founder of the remonstrant synod of Ulster.
P J.P.KNIGHT, RA 1846, tql, Royal Belfast Academical Institution.

MONTGOMERY, James (1771-1854) poet.
SC EDWIN SMITH, 1843, marble bust, Cutler's Hall, Sheffield. WILLIAM ELLIS, 1852, bronze medallion, Sheffield City Art Gallery.
PR RIDLEY and BLOOD, after F.Chantrey, hl, stipple, for *Monthly Mirror*, 1807, BM. C.TURNER, after J.R.Smith, tql seated, mezz, pub 1819, BM, NPG. H.MEYER, after T.Westoby, hl seated, stipple, pub 1819, BM, NPG. H.ADLARD, after J.Jackson, hl aged 55, stipple, for his *Memoirs*,IV, by Holland and Everett, BM, NPG. F.A.ROBERTS, after T.H.Illidge, tql seated, stipple, NPG. ROFFE, after Pickering, hl, stipple and line, for his *Poetical Works*, NPG.

MONTGOMERY, Sir James William, 1st Bart (1721-1803) Scottish judge.
P SIR HENRY RAEBURN, 1801, wl seated, and George Willison, tql, both Kinross House, Tayside region, Scotland.
D JOHN BROWN, hs, pencil, SNPG L87.
C JOHN KAY, hs with David Stuart Moncrief, etch, 1788, NPG.

MONTRESOR, John (1736-1799) major, Royal Engineers.
P JOHN SINGLETON COPLEY, 1771, hl, Detroit Institute of Arts, USA.

MONTROSE, James Graham, 3rd Duke of (1755-183.) statesman.
G SIR DAVID WILKIE, 'The entrance of George IV at Holyroodhouse', oil, 1822–29, Royal Coll.
C JOHN KAY, wl in Highland dress with 6th Earl of Buchan, etc. 1784, BM, NPG.

MONTROSE, James Graham, 4th Duke of (1799-187.) statesman.
P UNKNOWN, hl, a leaving portrait, Eton College, Berks.
PR W.J.EDWARDS, after Sir W.C.Ross, hl, stipple, BM, NPG.

MOODY, John (1727?-1812) actor.
P BENJAMIN VANDERGUCHT, RA 1775, wl as Teague in Howard The Committee, SAMUEL DE WILDE, as Commodore Flip in T. Fair Quaker, and SAMUEL DRUMMOND, hs as Jobson in *The Devil to Pay*, all at the Garrick Club, London. B.VANDERGUCHT, with John Hayman Packer in the farce *The Register Office*, Leicester Museum and Art Gallery.
D JAMES ROBERTS, as Teague, BM. UNKNOWN, gouache, Garrick Club.
PR Numerous theatrical prints, BM, NPG.

MOON, Sir Francis Graham, 1st Bart (1796-1871) print-seller and publisher.
PR UNKNOWN, hs, line, NPG.

MOOR, Edward (1771-1848) writer on Hindoo mythology.
PR MRS D.TURNER, 1810, tql seated with figure of Hindoo deity, etch, BM, NPG.

MOORCROFT, William (1765?-1825) veterinary surgeon and traveller.
D HYDER YOUNG HEARSEY, 1812, with the artist, w/c, India Office Library and Records, London.

MOORE, Ann, née Pegg (fl 1813) the 'fasting woman of Tutbury'.
PR A.CARDON, after C.Linsell, wl aged 58, sitting in bed in a garret, stipple, pub 1812, BM. UNKNOWN, hl, stipple and line, pub 181. NPG. J.WARD, hl, etch, BM.

MOORE, Charles (1730-1822), see 6th Earl and 1st Marquess of Drogheda.

MOORE, Edward (1712-1757) poet and dramatist.
PR J.NEAGLE, after T.Worlidge, hs, line, oval, for his *Dramatic Works*, 1787, BM, NPG.

MOORE, Sir Graham (1764-1843) admiral.
P SIR THOMAS LAWRENCE, RA 1792, hl, NPG 1129.

MOORE, Henry (1751-1844) Wesleyan minister and biographer.
PR UNKNOWN, hs aged 32, line, for *Arminian Mag*, 1785, BM, NPG. W.RIDLEY, hs aged 44, stipple, oval, for *Methodist Mag*, 1797, BM, NPG. W.T.FRY, hl, stipple, NPG.

MOORE, John (1729-1802) physician and writer.
P SIR THOMAS LAWRENCE, hs, SNPG 571. ANTOINE VESTIER, hs, Musée Carnavelet, Paris.
D GEORGE DANCE, 1794, hl profile, pencil, NPG 1148.
G GAVIN HAMILTON, tql with 8th Duke of Hamilton and Ensign John Moore, Toronto Art Gallery, Canada.
SC UNKNOWN, Wedgwood medallion, Wedgwood Museum, Barlaston, Staffs.
PR W.BROMLEY, after S.Drummond, hs, line, oval, for *European Mag*, 1790, BM, NPG. W.LIZARS, after G.Hamilton, tql seated, line, for his *Life*, by R.Anderson, 1820, BM, NPG. J.COCHRAN, after W.Cochrane, hl, stipple, BM, NPG.

MOORE, John (1730-1805) archbishop of Canterbury.
P GEORGE ROMNEY, 1783, tql, Lambeth Palace, London. SIR

THOMAS LAWRENCE, RA 1794, tql, Southampton Art Gallery. Attrib G.HAMILTON, wl, Lambeth Palace, London.
c R.DIGHTON, wl, coloured etch, pub 1803, NPG.

MOORE, Sir John (1761-1809) general.
P SIR THOMAS LAWRENCE, c1800, hl, NPG 1128; version, c1805, with Bath star, National Army Museum, London. JAMES NORTHCOTE, tql (fragment of the Death of Abercromby), SNPG 1301.
G GAVIN HAMILTON, hl, with 8th Duke of Hamilton, and Dr John Moore, Toronto Art Gallery, Canada.
sc JOHN BACON, jun, monument, St Paul's Cathedral, London.
R J.TISCHBEIN, j., hs as a boy, soft-ground etch, oval, BM. A.CARDON, after A.J.Oliver, hs, stipple, oval, pub 1809, BM. C.TURNER, after J.J.Halls, hl, mezz, pub 1811, BM.

MOORE, Sir John Henry, 2nd Bart (1756-1780) poet.
R P.CONDÉ, after R.Cosway, hl seated, stipple, oval, BM, NPG.

MOORE, Thomas (1779-1852) poet and biographer of Byron.
P JOHN JACKSON, 1818, hl, NGI 257. SIR MARTIN ARCHER SHEE, 1818, hl, NPG 3327; version NGI 775. GEORGE MULVANY, 1835, NGI 1097. DANIEL MACLISE, 1837, wl seated, NGI 4054. GILBERT S.NEWTON, hs, oval, Bowood, Wilts. UNKNOWN, m, NPG 1340.
D EDWARD HAYES, 1815, tql, pencil, NGI 2713. GEORGE RICHMOND, 1843, head, chalk, NGI 2251. DANIEL MACLISE, pencil and w/c, for 'Gallery of Illustrious Literary Characters', V & A.
sc CHRISTOPHER MOORE, 1842, marble bust, NPG 117; version, NGI 8067. C.MOORE, statue, College St., Dublin. JOHN HOGAN, plaster statuette, NGI 8061.

MOORSOM, Constantine Richard (1792-1861) vice-admiral.
G B.R.HAYDON, 'The Anti-Slavery Society Convention, 1840', oil, NPG 599.

MORE, Hannah (1745-1833) religious writer and poet.
P H.W.PICKERSGILL, 1822, tql, NPG 412. SIR HENRY RAEBURN, called Hannah More, hl, Louvre, Paris. FRANCES REYNOLDS, tql, Bristol City Art Gallery.
D JOHN JACKSON, hl, pencil, BM.
SL AUGUSTE EDOUART, 1827, wl seated, NPG 4501. AUGUSTE EDOUART, 1831, SNPG 2280.
G RICHARD SAMUEL, 'The Nine Living Muses of Great Britain', oil exhib 1779, NPG 4905.
R J.HEATH, after J.Opie, tql seated, stipple and line, for Lord Orford's *Works*, 1798, BM. J.GODBY, after E.Bird, tql seated, stipple, for *Contemporary Portraits*, 1809, BM, NPG. E.SCRIVEN, after J.Slater, tql aged 63, stipple, pub 1814. BM, NPG.

MORE, Jacob (1740-1793) landscape painter.
P Self-portrait, 1782, wl seated in landscape, Uffizi Gallery, Florence.

MORELL, Thomas (1703-1784) classical scholar.
R J.BASIRE, after W.Hogarth, seated by table, in front of organ, line, for his *Thesaurus*, 1762, BM, NPG.

MORES, Edward Rowe (1731-1778) antiquary.
R J.MYNDE, after R.v.Bleeck, hs, line, BM.

MORESBY, Sir Fairfax (1786-1877) admiral of the fleet.
P E.A.GIFFORD, 1870, tql seated with Bath star and ribbon, NMM, Greenwich.

MORGAN, Sydney, Lady, née Owenson (1783?-1859) novelist.
P R.T.BERTHON, 1818, tql, NGI 133.
D WILLIAM BEHNES, wl reclining, pen and ink, NPG 1177. CHARLES MARTIN, 1844, wl, pencil, BM. SIR THOMAS LAWRENCE, hl,

Wellington Museum, Apsley House, London.
sc DAVID D'ANGERS: c1830, marble bust, Bethnal Green Museum, London; plaster bust and bronze medallion, Musée des Beaux Arts, Angers, France.
PR H.MEYER, after T.Wageman, hl, stipple, pub 1818, NPG. R.COOPER, after S.Lover, tql seated, stipple, 1825, BM, NPG. D.MACLISE, wl, lith for *Fraser's Mag*, 1835, NPG. J.H.LYNCH, after S.Gambardella, tql, lith, pub 1855, NPG.

MORGAN, Sir Thomas Charles (1783-1843) physician and philosophical writer.
PR J.CLARKE, hl seated, lith, pub 1841, BM, NPG.

MORGAN, William (1750-1833) actuary.
PR C.TURNER, after T.Lawrence, tql seated, mezz, pub 1830, BM, NPG.

MORI, Nicolas (1797-1839) violinist.
PR UNKNOWN, wl, aged 8, stipple, BM.

MORIER, David Richard (1784-1877) diplomatist.
PR F.C.LEWIS, after J.Slater, hs, stipple, for 'Grillion's Club' series, BM, NPG.

MORIER, James Justinian (1780?-1849) traveller and author.
PR D.MACLISE, wl, lith, for *Fraser's Mag*, 1833, BM. S.W.REYNOLDS, after W.Boxall, hl, mezz, pub 1850, NPG.

MORISON, Sir Alexander (1779-1866) physician.
PR M.GAUCI, after J.Irvine, hl seated, lith, pub 1830, BM.

MORISON, James (1770-1840) empiric.
PR UNKNOWN, wl, coarse woodcut, BM.

MORISON, John (1791-1859) congregational minister.
PR J.BLOOD, hs, stipple, for *Evangelical Mag*, 1818, BM, NPG. J.THOMSON, after Wilson, hl seated, stipple, for *Evangelical Mag*, 1828, BM, NPG. J.WHITEHEAD, after H.Room, hl, mezz, NPG.

MORISON, Thomas (d1824) army surgeon.
PR W.WARD, after W.Nicholson, hl, mezz, NPG.

MORLAND, George (1763-1804) painter.
P Self-portrait, c1802-03, in his studio with his man Gibbs, Castle Museum, Nottingham. Self-portrait, hs, NPG 422.
D Self-portrait, hs, chalk, NPG 1196. SOPHIA JONES, 1805, hl, pencil and chalk, NPG 4370.
PR T.GAUGAIN, after G.Morland, wl seated, chalk manner, pub 1804, BM. W.WARD, after R.Muller, hl, mezz, pub 1805, BM, NPG. J.R.SMITH, tql seated, mezz, pub 1805, BM, NPG.
C THOMAS ROWLANDSON, three wl drgs, BM.

MORLAND, Henry Robert (1730?-1797) portrait painter.
D GEORGE MORLAND (his son), head, pencil, NPG 2905. UNKNOWN, wl seated, pencil and w/c, BM (Engr Ports Coll).

MORLEY, John Parker, 1st Earl of (1772-1840) statesman.
P SIR JOSHUA REYNOLDS, RA 1773, as a baby, with his mother, Saltram House (NT), Devon. SIR JOSHUA REYNOLDS, 1781, wl with his sister, Theresa, Saltram House. JAMES NORTHCOTE, c1781, hl, Melford Hall (NT), Suffolk. GILBERT STUART, hl as a boy, Saltram House.
D DANIEL GARDNER, wl as a child, gouache, Saltram House. JOHN DOWNMAN, 1805, wl, chalk and wash, Saltram House.
G SIR GEORGE HAYTER, 'The Trial of Queen Caroline, 1820', oil, NPG 999.
sc JOSEPH NOLLEKENS, bust, Saltram House.
PR W.SAY, after F.R.Say, hl seated, mezz, pub 1831, BM.

MORNINGTON, Anne, née Hill, Countess of (1742-1831) mother of 1st Duke of Wellington.
P WILLIAM OWEN, tql seated, Stratfield Saye, Hants.
D ROBERT HEALY, 1760, wl feeding peacocks, chalk, oval,

Stratfield Saye. SIR THOMAS LAWRENCE, hs, pencil and sanguine, NPG 2665. JOHN RUSSELL, hl, pastel, Badminton House, Avon. Attrib ROCHARD, hl, w/c, Stratfield Saye.
M Attrib GEORGE CHINNERY, NGI 2695.

MORNINGTON, Garrett Wellesley (or Wesley), 1st Earl of (1735-1781) professor of music.
P UNKNOWN, c1760, tql, Stratfield Saye, Hants. UNKNOWN, hl, at the harpsicord, Stratfield Saye.

MORNINGTON, William Wellesley-Pole, 3rd Earl of and 1st Baron Maryborough (1763-1845) statesman.
P JOHN HOPPNER, hl, Stratfield Saye, Hants. UNKNOWN, hl, Stratfield Saye. UNKNOWN, hs, Wellington Museum, Apsley House, London.
D DANIEL GARDNER, hs, oval, gouache, Badminton House, Avon.
SC JOSEPH NOLLEKENS, 1811, marble bust, NPG 5060.
PR C.PICART, after W.Owen, hl, stipple, for *Contemporary Portraits*, 1815, BM, NPG.

MORPETH, George Howard, Viscount, see 6th Earl of Carlisle.

MORRIS, Charles (1745-1838) song-writer.
P JAMES LONSDALE, hl, NPG 739.
PR T.HODGETTS, after A.J.Oliver, hl, mezz, pub 1808, BM. UNKNOWN, hs, stipple, oval, for *The Busy Bee*, 1790, BM.

MORRISON, James (1790-1857) merchant and politician.
D SIR FRANCIS CHANTREY, hs, pencil, NPG 316a (90).
SC SIR F.CHANTREY, c1842, plaster bust, Ashmolean Museum, Oxford.

MORRISON, Sir Richard (1767-1849) architect.
P UNKNOWN, hl, Royal Institute of the Architects of Ireland, Dublin.

MORRISON, Robert (1782-1834) missionary in China.
P Attrib GEORGE CHINNERY, head, profile, NPG 3943.
D WILLIAM NICHOLSON, pencil and w/c, SNPG 1237.
PR T.BLOOD, after J.Wildman, tql, stipple, for *Evangelical Mag*, 1827, BM, NPG. C.TURNER, after G.Chinnery, translating bible into Chinese with two Chinese assistants, mezz, pub 1830, BM, NPG.

MORRITT, John Bacon Sawrey (1772?-1843) traveller and classical scholar.
P SIR MARTIN ARCHER SHEE, 1832, hl, The Society of Dilettanti, Brooks's Club, London.

MORTIMER, Cromwell (d1752) physician.
C RIGOU, after W.Hogarth, wl with figure of Folly, line, BM.

MORTIMER, John Hamilton (1740-1779) history painter.
P Self-portrait, c1765, with Joseph Wilton and a student, Royal Academy, London; similar portrait, with artist and student only, NPG 234. RICHARD WILSON, hl, Royal Academy.
D By or after J.H.MORTIMER, hs in character, pen and ink, V & A, engr R.Blyth, 1782, BM, V & A.
G Called a self-portrait, and said to be with his father, brother and two dogs, Yale Center for British Art, New Haven, USA.
PR A. VAN ASSEN, after J.H.Mortimer, hs, etch, pub 1810, BM, NPG, V & A.
C JAMES GILLRAY, sketch for 'Connoisseurs examining a Collection of George Morland's', drg, V & A.

MORTIMER, Thomas (1730-1810) writer.
PR W.RIDLEY, after W.Beechey, hl, stipple, oval, for *European Mag*, 1799, BM, NPG.

MORTON, James Douglas, 14th Earl of (c1702-1768) keeper of the Records of Scotland and president of the Royal Society.

G JEREMIAH DAVISON, 1740, with his family, SNPG 2233.

MORTON, Thomas (1764?-1838) dramatist.
P SIR MARTIN ARCHER SHEE, exhib 1835, TATE 368.
D J.R.SMITH, hl, chalk, NPG 1540.
PR W.RIDLEY, after W.Naish, hl, stipple, oval, for *Monthly Mirror*, 1796, BM, NPG. J.HOPWOOD, after S. de Wilde, hl, stipple, pub 1806, BM.

MOSELEY, Benjamin (1742-1819) physician to Chelsea Hospital.
PR M.A.BOURLIER, after R.M.Paye, tql seated, stipple, BM, NPG.

MOSER, George Michael (1704-1783) enameller.
D GEORGE DANCE, hs, Royal Academy, London. UNKNOWN, hs, oval, w/c, for Northcote's *Life of Reynolds*, vol II, NPG.
G JOHAN ZOFFANY, 'The Royal Academicians, 1772', oil, Royal Coll.
C THOMAS ROWLANDSON, hs, pen and ink, BM.

MOSER, Joseph (1748-1819) writer.
PR W.RIDLEY, after S.Drummond, hl, stipple, oval, for *European Mag*, 1803, BM, NPG.

MOSER, Mary (d1819) flower painter.
G JOHAN ZOFFANY, 'The Royal Academicians, 1772', oil, Royal Coll. HENRY SINGLETON, 'The Royal Academicians, 1793', oil, Royal Academy, London.

MOSS, Charles (1711-1802) bishop of St David's and of Bath and Wells.
P GEORGE ROMNEY, Bishop's Palace, Wells.
PR UNKNOWN, hs, line, oval, pub 1783, NPG. S.W.REYNOLDS, after J.Hoppner, tql, mezz, pub 1801, BM, V & A.

MOSS, Charles (1763-1811) bishop of Oxford.
P GEORGE ROMNEY, 1782, hl, leaving portrait, Eton College, Berks. L.HOPPNER (?), tql seated, Christ Church, Oxford.

MOSSE, Bartholomew (1712-1759) philanthropist.
P UNKNOWN, c1745, tql, The Rotunda Hospital, Dublin.

MOSSOP, Henry (1729?-1774?) actor.
P NATHANIEL HONE, hs, Garrick Club, London. UNKNOWN, NGI 557.
D THOMAS HICKEY, hl, chalk, NGI.
PR W.RIDLEY, after J.H.Mortimer, hl, stipple, oval, for *Monthly Mirror*, 1799, BM, NPG. Several theatrical prints, BM.

MOSTYN, Savage (d1757) vice-admiral.
PR T.WORLIDGE, tql, etch, BM, NPG.

MOTHERWELL, William (1797-1835) poet.
P ANDREW HENDERSON, hs, SNPG 313.
SL AUGUSTIN EDOUART, SNPG 790.
SC JOHN FILLANS, 1833, wax medallion, SNPG 235. JAMES FILLANS, plaster bust, SNPG 236.

MOUNTAIN, Jacob (1749-1825) first bishop of Quebec.
D JOHN DOWNMAN, 1778, hl, chalk, Fitzwilliam Museum, Cambridge.
PR C.TURNER, after H.Edridge, tql seated, mezz, pub 1820, BM, NPG.

MOUNTAIN, Mrs Rosoman, née Wilkinson (1768?-1841) actress and singer.
P GEORGE ROMNEY, hs sketch, Garrick Club, London.
D SAMUEL DE WILDE, wl, as Matilda in Burgoyne's *Richard Coeur de Lion*, w/c, Garrick Club.
M 'SG', 1806, hl, NPG 760.
PR T.CHEESMAN, after A.Buck, tql with guitar, stipple, pub 1804, BM, NPG. C.TURNER, after J.Masquerier, hl, mezz, pub 1804, BM, NPG. K.MACKENZIE, after R.Dighton, hl, stipple, oval, BM, NPG.

MOUNT-EDGCUMBE, George Edgcumbe, 1st Earl of (1721-1795) navy lieutenant.
P Several portraits by SIR JOSHUA REYNOLDS: 1748, tql, NMM, Greenwich; c1755-6, hs, Exeter City Museum and Art Gallery; 1758, Mount Edgcumbe, Cornwall; exhib 1761, tql, Mount Edgcumbe; NGI 137.
G JOHN SINGLETON COPLEY, 'The Collapse of the Earl of Chatham in the House of Lords, 7 July 1778', oil, TATE 100, on loan to NPG.

MOUNT-EDGCUMBE, Richard Edgcumbe, 2nd Earl of (1764-1839) politician.
P SIR JOSHUA REYNOLDS, RA 1774, as a boy, Mount Edgcumbe, Cornwall.
G JOHAN ZOFFANY, 'The Tribuna of the Uffizi', oil, 1772-78, Royal Coll. J.JONES, after J.Roberts, 'Marlborough Theatricals' pl III, as Young Clackitt in Kelly's *The Guardian*, mezz, pub 1788, BM, NPG.

MOYLAN, Francis (1735-1815) bishop of Cork.
SC PETER TURNERELLI, portrait? on monument, St Anne's, Shandon, Cork, Eire.

MUDFORD, William (1782-1848) journalist.
G SIR GEORGE HAYTER, 'The Trial of Queen Caroline, 1820', oil, NPG 999.

MUDGE, John (1721-1793) physician.
PR W.DICKINSON, after J.Reynolds, hl, mezz, BM, same picture engraved S.W.Reynolds, mezz, pub 1820, BM, NPG.

MUDGE, Thomas (1717-1794) chronometer maker.
P NATHANIEL DANCE, Clockmakers' Company Guildhall, London.
PR C.TOWNLEY, after N.Dance, hl seated, mezz, oval, 1772, BM.

MUIR, Thomas (1765-1798) parliamentary reformer.
D DAVID MARTIN, wl, chalk, SNPG 1668.
PR T.HOLLOWAY, after a bust by T.Banks, hs profile, line, oval, pub 1795, NPG. F.BONNEVILE, hs with patch on eye, line, oval, NPG.
C J.KAY, hs, profile, oval, etch, BM, 1793, NPG. J.KAY, wl, etch, pub 1793, BM.

MUIR, William (1787-1869) Scottish divine.
PR C.TURNER, after J.Graham, tql seated, mezz, pub 1822, BM, NPG.

MULGRAVE, Sir Constantine Henry Phipps, see 1st Marquess of Normanby.

MULGRAVE, Constantine John Phipps, 2nd Baron (1744-1792) naval commander.
P THOMAS GAINSBOROUGH, c1786, wl, Smithsonian Institution, Washington DC, USA. OZIAS HUMPHRY, c1779, hl, oval, NMM, Greenwich. By or after T.GAINSBOROUGH, Cincinnati Art Museum, USA. Attrib JOHAN ZOFFANY, wl, NPG 1094.
D JOHN DOWNHAM, 1782, hl, w/c, NPG 966.
G SIR JOSHUA REYNOLDS, 'The Society of Dilettanti', oil, 1777-79, Brooks's Club, London. J.ZOFFANY, with five friends, Ickworth (NT), Suffolk.
PR UNKNOWN, hl, mezz, oval, pub 1774, BM. UNKNOWN, hs, line, pub 1782, NPG.

MULGRAVE, Sir Henry Phipps, 1st Earl of (1755-1831) soldier and statesman.
P SIR THOMAS LAWRENCE, c1790, Neue Pinakothek, Munich, West Germany.
M Attrib RICHARD COSWAY, wl, NPG 2630.
G J.G.MURRAY, after J.Stephanoff, 'The Trial of Queen Caroline, 1820', stipple, pub 1823, BM. W.J.WARD, after J.Jackson, with Sir George Beaumont, Hon A.Phipps, and E.Phipps, mezz, BM, NPG.

PR S.W.REYNOLDS, after J.Hoppner, wl, mezz, pub 1801, BM. W.SKELTON, after W.Beechey, hl, line, pub 1808, BM, NPG. H.MEYER, after J.Jackson, hl, stipple, pub 1811, BM, NPG.

MULREADY, William (1786-1863) painter and illustrator.
P JOHN LINNELL, 1833, hl, NPG 1690; unfinished version, NGI 843. Self-portrait, c1835, hs, NPG 4450.
D THOMAS BRIDGFORD, c1842, tql seated, pencil, NGI. CHARLES MARTIN, 1844, tql, pencil, BM. C.H.LEAR, 1846, hs, chalk, NPG 1456 (22).
G SIR D.WILKIE, 'The Refusal', Mulready is portrayed as Duncan Gray, 1814, V & A.
SC HENRY WEEKES, 1866, marble bust, Tate 2076.
PH CUNDALL & DOWNES & CO, c1860, hl, carte, V & A. UNKNOWN, tql seated, NPG.

MUNCASTER, Sir John Pennington, 1st Baron (1737-1814) politician.
P UNKNOWN, hl, Muncaster Castle, Cumbria.

MUNDEN, Joseph Shepherd (1758-1832) comedian.
P GEORGE CLINT, hl, NPG 1283. SAMUEL DRUMMOND, head, Garrick Club, London. J.P.KNIGHT, hs, Garrick Club. JOHN OPIE, hl, Garrick Club. SIR M.A.SHEE, hs, Garrick Club.
D GEORGE DANCE, 1798, hl profile, pencil, NPG 1149. J.LONSDALE, hs, charcoal and sanguine, Garrick Club. Several w/c, SAMUEL DE WILDE, Garrick Club.
G JOHAN ZOFFANY, in a scene from *Speculation*, oil c1795-96, and G.CLINT, the last scene in *A New Way to Pay Old Debts*, oil, 1820, both Garrick Club.
PR Various theatrical prints, BM, NPG.

MUNRO, Sir Hector (1726-1805) general.
P 'IWP', 1785, wl by cannon, troops beyond, NPG 1433.
SC After JAMES TASSIE, 1796, plaster medallion, SNPG 468.

MUNRO, Sir Thomas, 1st Bart (1761-1827) administrator in India.
P SIR MARTIN ARCHER SHEE, hs, NPG 3124. R.R.REINAGLE, wl in Indian landscape, Oriental Club, London.
SC SIR FRANCIS CHANTREY, 1838, equestrian statue, Madras, India. SIR F.CHANTREY, c1840, bust, Ashmolean Museum, Oxford.

MUNSTER, George Augustus Frederick Fitzclarence, 1st Earl of (1794-1842) illegitimate son of William IV, major-general.
PR T.WRIGHT, after A.Wivell, hs, stipple, pub 1820, NPG. W.H.COOK, after J.Atkinson, hl in uniform and robes, stipple, for Jerdan's *Nat Portrait Gallery*, 1833, BM, NPG. A.R.ARTLETT, after T.Phillips, tql, stipple, for *Eminent Conservative Statesmen*, 1839, BM, NPG. D.MACLISE, wl, lith, for *Fraser's Mag*, BM, NPG.

MUNTZ, George Frederick (1794-1857) political reformer.
C JOHN DOYLE, several political satires, drgs, BM.

MURCHISON, Sir Roderick Impey, 1st Bart (1792-1871) geologist.
P STEPHEN PEARCE, c1850-56, hs, NPG 906. H.W.PICKERSGILL, hl, Edinburgh University.
SC SIR RICHARD WESTMACOTT, 1848, plaster bust, SNPG 747. HENRY WEEKES, 1871, bust, Geological Museum, London.
PR W.DRUMMOND, hs, lith, for *Athenaeum Portraits*, No 41, BM. T.H.MAGUIRE, tql, lith, for *Ipswich Museum Portraits*, BM, NPG.
C SIR LESLIE WARD, 'Spy', 1868, wl, pencil and wash, NPG. CARLO PELLEGRINI, 'Ape', wl, chromo litho, for *Vanity Fair*, 1870, NPG.
PH C.SILVY, wl, carte, NPG Album of Photographs, 1939. UNKNOWN, wl, carte, NPG Twist Album. UNKNOWN, hs, carte, NPG Cunnington Collection.

MURDOCK, William (1754-1839) inventor of gas-lighting.
P JOHN GRAHAM GILBERT, City Art Gallery, Birmingham.

D SIR FRANCIS CHANTREY, hs and hs profile, pencil, NPG 316a (91, 92).
G J.F.SKILL, J.GILBERT, W. and E.WALKER, 'Men of Science Living in 1807–08', pencil and wash, NPG 1075.
SC SIR F.CHANTREY, 1839, marble bust, St Mary Church, Handsworth, Birmingham. After CHANTREY, plaster bust, SNPG 808. WILLIAM BLOYE, 20th century bronze group, Broad Street, Birmingham.

MURLIN, John (1722-1799) methodist preacher.
PR RIDLEY, hs, stipple, oval, for *Arminian Mag*, NPG.

MURPHY, Arthur (1727-1805) author and actor.
P NATHANIEL DANCE, tql, NPG 10. N.DANCE, NGI 959.
PR W.RIDLEY, after S.Drummond, hs, stipple, oval, for *Monthly Mirror*, 1798, BM, NPG. P,CONDÉ, after T.R.Poole, hs aged 72, stipple, for his *Life*, by J.Foot, 1811, BM. E.SCRIVEN, after P.Turnerelli, from marble bust, stipple, oval, BM, pub 1807, NPG.

MURPHY, James Cavanah (1760-1814) architect and antiquary.
PR W.I.NEWTON, after M.A.Shee, hl, line, NPG.

MURRAY, Alexander (1712-1778) Jacobite.
P ALLAN RAMSAY, 1742, hl, oval, SNPG L26.

MURRAY, Alexander (1736-1795), see Lord Henderland.

MURRAY, Alexander (1775-1813) linguist.
D ANDREW GEDDES, 1812, hs, pencil, SNPG 196.

MURRAY, Charles (1754-1821) actor and dramatist.
P GAINSBOROUGH DUPONT, hl as Baron Wildenheim in *Lover's Vows*, Garrick Club, London.
D SAMUEL DE WILDE, 1815, as Tobias in *The Stranger*, w/c, Garrick Club.
PR Theatrical prints, BM.

MURRAY, Daniel (1768-1852) archbishop of Dublin.
P N.J.CROWLEY, NGI 1756. Attrib CROWLEY, St Vincent's Hospital, Dublin.
SC SIR THOMAS FARRELL, 1855, statue, Marlborough Street Church, Dublin. JOHN HOGAN, marble bust, NGI 8034.
PR PISTRUCCI, after P.Turnerelli bust, lith, NPG.

MURRAY, David (1727-1796), see 2nd Earl of Mansfield.

MURRAY, Lord George (1700?-1760) Jacobite general.
P JEREMIAH DAVISON, hs, oval, Blair Castle, Tayside region, Scotland. UNKNOWN, wl in Highland dress, Blair Castle.

MURRAY, Sir George (1759-1819) vice-admiral.
PR H.R.COOK, hs, stipple, oval, pub 1807, NPG. W.SAY, after C.Woolcott, hl, mezz, pub 1819, BM.

MURRAY, Sir George (1772-1846) general and statesman.
P JOHN PRESCOTT KNIGHT, RA 1843, hl, Wellington Museum, Apsley House, London. H.W.PICKERSGILL, wl, SNPG 639.
D JOHN LINNELL, 1836, head, chalk, NPG 1818. JOHN LINNELL, 1836, chalk, SNPG 889. THOMAS HEAPHY, tql, pencil and w/c, NPG 4319.
PR H.MEYER, after T.Lawrence, hl, stipple, for Jerdan's *Nat Portrait Gallery*, 1831, BM, NPG.

MURRAY, George (1784-1860) bishop of Rochester.
P B.R.FAULKNER, RA 1829, tql seated, Christ Church, Oxford. SAMUEL LANE, exhib 1849, hl, NPG 4964. UNKNOWN, Blair Castle, Tayside region, Scotland.
PR F.C.LEWIS, after J.Slater, hs, stipple, for 'Grillion's Club' series, BM, NPG.

MURRAY, James (1719-1794) general and governor of Canada.

P ALLAN RAMSAY, 1742, hs, oval, SNPG 2215. UNKNOWN, tql, NPG 3122.
PR UNKNOWN, after J.Gillray, hl in uniform, stipple, oval, pub 1782, BM, NPG. UNKNOWN, hl, line, oval, for *Universal Mag*, 1783, NPG.

MURRAY, James (1732-1782) divine and author.
PR POLLARD, after Van Cook, hs, line, NPG. UNKNOWN, hs, stipple, NPG.

MURRAY, John (1729-1774), see 3rd Duke of Atholl.

MURRAY, John (1732-1809), see 4th Earl of Dunmore.

MURRAY, Sir John, 8th Bart of Clermont (1768?-1827) general.
P P.C.WONDER, 1826, wl, study for a large group, NPG 792.

MURRAY, John (1778-1843) publisher.
D WILLIAM BROCKEDON, 1837, hs, pencil and chalk, NPG 2515 (83). DANIEL MACLISE, pencil, NG, on loan to V & A.
PR T.LUPTON, after J.W.Gordon, tql, mezz, pub 1840, BM, NPG. E.FINDEN, after H.Pickersgill, tql seated, stipple, for Finden's *Illustrations of Life and Works of Byron*, 1833, BM, NPG.

MURRAY, Sir John Archibald Murray, Lord (1779-1859) Scottish judge.
P SIR JOHN WATSON-GORDON, 1856, tql seated, SNPG 1066.
G SIR GEORGE HAYTER, 'The House of Commons, 1833', oil, NPG 54.
PR W.WALKER, after H.Raeburn, hl, mezz, pub 1835, BM.

MURRAY, Lindley (1745-1826) grammarian.
PR T.A.DEAN, after E.Westoby, hl, stipple, for his *Memoirs*, by E.Frank, 1826, BM, NPG.

MURRAY, William (1705-1793), see 1st Earl of Mansfield.

MURRAY, William Henry (1790-1852) actor and manager of Theatre Royal, Edinburgh.
P SIR WILLIAM ALLAN, 1843, SNPG 904. SIR WILLIAM ALLAN, 1848, hs, SNPG 190. SIR JOHN WATSON-GORDON, hs, Garrick Club, London. UNKNOWN, hs, oval, Garrick Club.
C B.W.CROMBIE, as 'Paul Pry', pencil, SNPG 2306.

MURRAY-PULTENEY, Sir James, 7th Bart of Clermont, Fifeshire (1751?-1811) general.
P UNKNOWN, tql, SNPG 638.

MUSGRAVE, Sir Thomas (1737-1812) general.
PR G.S.FACIUS, after L.Abbott, tql in uniform, stipple, 1797, BM.

MUSGRAVE, Thomas (1788-1860) archbishop of York.
P F.R.SAY, 1850, tql in convocation robes, Bishop's Palace, Hereford; versions, 1863, Trinity College, Cambridge, Bishopthorpe Palace, York.
M SIR W.C.ROSS, RA 1842, tql, Bishopthorpe Palace.
SC MATTHEW NOBLE, 1860, recumbent figure on monument, York Minster.

MYLNE, Robert (1734-1811) architect and civil engineer.
D GEORGE DANCE, 1795, hl profile, pencil, NPG 1150.
G J.F.SKILL, J.GILBERT, W. and E.WALKER, 'Men of Science Living in 1807–08', pencil and wash, NPG 1075.
PR V.VANGELISTI, after profile drawing of 1757 by R.Brompton, line, pub 1783, NPG.
C Two satirical prints, BM.

MYLNE, William Chadwell (1781-1863) engineer.
PR H.ADLARD, after H.W.Phillips, hl, stipple and line, oval, pub 1860, BM.

MYTTON, John (1796-1834) sportsman and eccentric.
PR UNKNOWN, after W.Webb, hs, profile, oval, NPG.

N

NAGLE, Sir Edmund (1757-1830) admiral.
D Sir Hilgrove Turner, tql seated, w/c, NPG 4858.
PR W.J.Ward, after W.Corden, tql seated, mezz, pub 1830, BM, NPG. E.Scriven, after P.Stephanoff, wl in Bath robes, stipple and aquatint, for Sir G.Nayler's work on the Coronation of George IV, BM.

NAGLE, Nano or Honora (1728-1784) foundress of the Presentation order of nuns.
PR C.Turner, tql seated instructing three girls, BM.

NAIRNE, Carolina, née Oliphant, Baroness (1766-1845) songwriter.
P Sir John Watson-Gordon, hs, SNPG 1125. Sir John Watson-Gordon, with her son W.M.Nairne, SNPG 610.

NAIRNE, Margaret Mercer Elphinstone, Baroness, see Viscountess Keith.

NAIRNE, Sir William (1731?-1811), see Lord Dunsinane.

NAPIER, Sir Charles (1786-1860) admiral.
P John Simpson, c1835, tql, SNPG 7. T.M.Joy, 1847, wl, NMM, Greenwich. T.M.Joy, tql, formerly United Service Club, London (c/o The Crown Commissioners). E.W.Gill, 1854, hl, NPG 1460.
SC After John Henning, 1811, plaster medallion, SNPG 539. G.G.Adams, 1868, bust in relief, St Paul's Cathedral, London. Unknown, memorial with medallion, Victoria Park, Portsmouth.
PR C.Baugniet, tql, lith, pub 1854, BM, NPG. Skelton, after A.H.Taylor, hl, coloured lith, pub 1854, BM, NPG.

NAPIER, Sir Charles James (1782-1853) conqueror of Sind.
P S.Gambardella, c1827, hs, Wellington Museum, Apsley House, London. Edwin Williams, 1849, hl, NPG 1369. George Jones, 1851, hs, NPG 333. Attrib S.P.Smart, tql seated, NPG 3964.
SC G.G.Adams, several sculptures: 1853, bronze bust, SNPG 586; 1853, plaster cast of bust, NPG 1198; 1856, bronze statue, Trafalgar Square, London; 1860, marble statue, St Paul's Cathedral, London.
PR R.J.Lane, after Count Pierlas, hs, lith, pub 1849, NPG. T.W.Hunt, after a photograph by Kilburn, tql, stipple, NPG.
C John Doyle, several drgs, BM.

NAPIER, David (1790-1869) marine engineer.
SC Matthew Noble, 1870, plaster bust, SNPG 587.

NAPIER, Francis Napier, 7th Baron (1758-1823) soldier.
C John Kay, wl, etch, one of the 'Edinburgh Portraits', 1795, BM, NPG.

NAPIER, George (1751-1804) colonel.
PR Walker and Cockerell, hs, photogravure, BM.

NAPIER, Sir George Thomas (1784-1855) general and governor of the Cape of Good Hope.
M F.J.J.Sieurac, 1814, hs, oval, V & A.

NAPIER, Macvey (1776-1847) editor of the 'Edinburgh Review'.
D P.Sclater, ink and wash, SNPG 1689.

NAPIER, Mark (1798-1879) historical biographer.
P Colvin Smith, 1867, SNPG 1388.

NAPIER, Robert (1791-1876) marine engineer.
SL Auguste Edouart, 1832, SNPG 791.
PR E.Burton, after J.G.Gilbert, tql seated, mezz, 1847, BM.

NAPIER, Sir William Francis Patrick (1785-1860) general and military historian.
P S.Gambardella, c1845, hs, Wellington Museum, Apsley House, London. Unknown, c1845, tql, Wellington Museum.
G F.Bromley, after J.P.Knight, 'The Peninsular Heroes', mixed, coloured engr, pub 1847, BM.
SC G.G.Adams, 1855, marble bust, NPG 1197. G.G.Adams, 1863, statue, St Paul's Cathedral, London.
PR Unknown, after a miniature by Miss E.Jones, hl as a young man in uniform, stipple, NPG. W.H.Egleton, after W.F.P.Napier, head, profile, stipple, NPG. Unknown, after G.F.Watts, hs, stipple and line, for *Life of W.F.P.Napier*, 1864, NPG. Unknown, after a photograph by Kilburn, hl, woodcut, for *Illust London News*, 1860, NPG.

NAPLETON, John (1738?-1817) chancellor of Hereford.
PR C.Picart, after T.Leeming, hl, stipple, BM, NPG.

NARES, Sir George (1716-1786) judge.
PR W.Dickinson, after N.Hone, tql in robes, mezz, pub 1776, BM, NPG.

NARES, James (1715-1783) composer of church music.
PR T.Hardy, hs, stipple, oval, for *European Mag*, 1795, BM, NPG.

NARES, Robert (1753-1829) philologist.
PR S.Freeman, after J.Hoppner, hl, stipple, for Jerdan's *Nat Portrait Gallery*, 1830, BM, NPG.

NASH, Frederick (1782-1856) painter of architectural subjects.
D Jules Nogués, 1839, hs, w/c, NPG 2688.

NASH, John (1752-1835) architect.
P Sir Thomas Lawrence, tql, RIBA, London.
SC J.A.Couriguer, c1820, hs, NPG 2778. William Behnes, 1830, marble bust, RIBA.
C Sir Edwin Landseer, pen and ink, NPG 3097 (7).

NASH, Treadway Russell (1725-1811) historian of Worcestershire.
PR J.Caldwall, after D.Gardner, hs, line, for vol iii of his edition of Butler's *Hudibras*, 1793, BM, NPG.

NASMITH, David (1799-1839) originator of town and city missions.
PR J.C.Armytage, hl, stipple, NPG.

NASMYTH, Alexander (1758-1840) painter and scientist.
P Andrew Geddes, hl, Royal Scottish Academy, Edinburgh.
G J.F.Skill, J.Gilbert, W. and E.Walker, 'Men of Science Living in 1807-08', pencil and wash, NPG 1075.

NASMYTH, Patrick (1787-1831) landscape painter.
D William Bewick, hs, pencil, NPG 350.

NATTER, Lorenz (1705-1763) gem-engraver.
PR F.Bartolozzi, after L.Natter, hs, line, circle, for *Memoirs of Thomas Hollis*, 1780, BM.

NAYLER, Sir George (1764?-1831) garter king-of-arms.
PR E.SCRIVEN, after W.Beechey, hl wearing orders, stipple, BM.

NEALE, Sir Harry Burrard, 2nd Bart (1765-1840) admiral.
PR C.TURNER, after M.Brown, hl in uniform, mezz, pub 1812, BM. J.B.LANE, after W.Beechey, hl in uniform, stipple, for *Contemporary Portraits*, 1822, BM. G.CHILDS, after C.S. Le Bailly, hl, lith, BM.

NEEDHAM, John Tuberville (1713-1781) Roman Catholic divine and man of science.
M JEAN BAPTISTE GARAND, 1755, hs, oval, NPG 4889. HENRY EDRIDGE, after Sir Joshua Reynolds, hs, Holburne of Menstrie Museum, Bath.

NEELE, Henry (1798-1828) poet and miscellaneous writer.
PR H.MEYER, tql seated, stipple, for Britton's *Autobiography*, 1849, BM, NPG.

NEILD, James (1744-1814) philanthropist.
P SAMUEL DE WILDE, 1804, hl, seated, NPG 4160.
M F.PULHAM, hs, oval, Royal Coll.
PR UNKNOWN, hs profile, silhouette, line, for *Gent Mag*, 1817, NPG.

NEILL, Patrick (1776-1851) naturalist.
PR R.M.HODGETTS, after J.Syme, hl, mezz, pub 1837, BM.
C B.W.CROMBIE, wl, coloured etch, 1847, reprinted for *Modern Athenians*, 1882, NPG.

NEILSON, Samuel (1761-1803) Irish nationalist.
P UNKNOWN, hs, Ulster Museum, Belfast.
G UNKNOWN, 'The United Irish Patriots of 1798', coloured lith, NPG.

NELSON, Frances Herbert Nelson, née Woodward, Viscountess (1761-1831) wife of Viscount Horatio Nelson.
P UNKNOWN, c1800, tql, NMM, Greenwich.

NELSON, Horatio Nelson, Viscount (1758-1805) victor of Trafalgar.
P J.F.RIGAUD, 1781, tql, NMM, Greenwich. L.F.ABBOTT, several portraits with variations, 1797-98: hl, NMM; 1798, hl, NMM; hl with hat and several medals, NMM; hl, NPG 394; SNPG 965. GUY HEAD, 1798-1800, wl with midshipman, NPG 5101. LEONARDO GUZZARDI, 1799, wl, Museo di San Martino, Naples; versions, DoE (The Admiralty, London); NMM. HEINRICH FÜGER, 1800, hs in civilian dress, NPG 73. UNKNOWN, c1800, hl wounded at the Nile, NMM. SIR WILLIAM BEECHEY, 1801, wl, St Andrew's Hall, Norwich; related sketch of head, NPG L129. JOHN HOPPNER, 1800, hl, NMM. J.HOPPNER, c1801-05, wl, Royal Coll. JOHN RISING, 1801, wl, NMM. M.H.KEYMER, 1801, hl, NMM. SIMON DE KOSTER, 1801-03, hs profile, NMM. A.W.DEVIS, 1805-07, wl, NMM.
D CUTHBERT COLLINGWOOD, c1785, profile, NMM. HENRY SINGLETON, 1798, hl, pencil, NMM. CHARLES GRIGNION, 1799, tql seated, Royal United Services Institution, London. JOHANN SCHMIDT, 1800, hs, pastel, NMM. HENRY EDRIDGE, 1802, wl, w/c, NPG 879. WILLIAM GOLDSMITH, c1802, with Lady Hamilton in the grounds of Merton House, w/c, DoE (Lord Privy Seal). UNKNOWN, pastel, SNPG 863.
G A.W.DEVIS, 'The Death of Nelson', oil, NMM. DANIEL MACLISE, 'The Death of Nelson', fresco, Palace of Westminster, London; oil study, Walker Art Gallery, Liverpool.
SC JOHN DE VAERE, 1798, Wedgwood medallion, Wedgwood Museum, Barlaston, Staffs. THALLOR and RANSOM, 1801, marble bust, NMM. LAURENCE GAHAGAN, 1804, bust, Victoria Art Gallery, Bath. CATHERINE ANDRAS, 1806, wax effigy, Westminster Abbey, London. JOHN FLAXMAN, 1809, statue on monument, St Paul's Cathedral, London. A.S.DAMER, 1827, bust, Royal Coll. SIR FRANCIS CHANTREY, 1835, marble busts,

Royal Coll, and NPG 4309. E.H.BAILY, 1839-43, statue on Nelson's Column, Trafalgar Square, London. SIR RICHARD WESTMACOTT, bronze statue, The Bull Ring, Birmingham.
PR S.W.REYNOLDS, after J.P.Knight, wl with the Duke of Wellington, coloured engr, Wellington Museum, Apsley House, London.
C JAMES GILLRAY, 'Extirpation of the Plagues of Egypt', etch, pub 1798, NPG.

NELSON, William Nelson, 1st Earl (1757-1835) brother of Horatio, Viscount Nelson.
G SIR GEORGE HAYTER, 'The Trial of Queen Caroline, 1820', oil, NPG 999.

NELSON, Wolfred (1792-1863) Canadian insurgent.
P UNKNOWN, hs, oval, McCord Museum, McGill University, Montreal, Canada.

NEPEAN, Sir Evan, 1st Bart (1751-1822) secretary of the admiralty.
P UNKNOWN, c1800, hs, DoE (Admiralty House, London).

NESBITT, Robert (1700-1761) physician.
P JOHN NESBITT, wl seated, Royal College of Surgeons, London.

NEVILLE, George, afterwards **Grenville (1789-1854)** master of Magdalene College, Cambridge.
PR EDWARD SCRIVEN, after H.Legge, tql, stipple, NPG.

NEVILLE, Richard Aldworth Griffin (1750-1825), see 2nd Baron Braybrooke.

NEVILLE, Richard Griffin (1783-1858), see 3rd Baron Braybrooke.

NEVILLE, Richard Neville Aldworth (1717-1793) statesman.
P JOHN VANDERBANK, 1739, wl, DoE (Audley End House, Essex). JOHAN ZOFFANY, 1761, hl, DoE (Audley End).

NEWCASTLE-under-Lyme, Henry Clinton, 2nd Duke of (1720-1794) cofferer of the household.
P SIR GODFREY KNELLER, c1721, with 1st Duke of Newcastle, NPG 3215. WILLIAM HOARE, replica, wl in Garter robes, NPG 2504.
G F.BARTOLOZZI and S.ALKEN, after F.Wheatley, wl equestrian, 'The Return from Shooting', stipple, pub 1792, BM.
PR C.WARREN, after W.H.Brown, hs, line, for *The Senator*, 1792, NPG.

NEWCASTLE-under-Lyme, Henry Clinton, 4th Duke of (1785-1851) politician.
P H.W.PICKERSGILL, c1835, tql seated, Palace of Westminster, London.
G Attrib ISAAC CRUIKSHANK, 'Members of the House of Lords, c1835', pencil and wash, NPG 2789.
SC JOSEPH NOLLEKENS, RA 1815, marble, Newark Town Hall, Lincs. WILLIAM BEHNES, 1843, bust, Eton College, Berks.
PR C.TURNER, after T.Lawrence, wl in uniform, mezz, pub 1830, BM, NPG. S.W.REYNOLDS, tql in Garter robes, mezz, BM.
C JOHN DOYLE, 'Newcastle versus Newark', pencil, 1829, BM. J.DOYLE, wl, equestrian, pencil, 1840, BM.

NEWCOME, William (1729-1800) archbishop of Armagh.
P H.D.HAMILTON, 1798, hl, Pembroke College, Oxford.

NEWDIGATE, Sir Roger, 5th Bart (1719-1806) antiquary.
P ARTHUR DEVIS, wl, Arbury Hall, Warwicks. GEORGE ROMNEY, wl, Arbury Hall.

NEWELL, Edward John (1771-1798) Irish informer.
PR UNKNOWN, after a self-portrait sketch, wl, mezz, NPG.

NEWENHAM, Sir Edward (1732-1814) Irish politician.
G FRANCIS WHEATLEY, 'The Volunteers in College Green', oil,

1779, NGI 125; similar w/c group, V & A.

NEWLAND, Abraham (1730-1807) chief cashier at the Bank of England.
P SAMUEL DRUMMOND, hl, Bank of England, London. GEORGE ROMNEY, tql, Bank of England.

NEWPORT, Sir John, 1st Bart (1756-1843) Irish politician.
PR R.COOPER, after S.Catterson Smith, hl, seated, stipple, pub 1826, NPG. T.LUPTON, after J.Ramsay, tql, with 'Corn Intercourse Act', mezz, pub 1828, BM, NPG.

NEWTON, Charles Hay, Lord (1740?-1811) Scottish judge.
P SIR HENRY RAEBURN, hs in robes, SNPG L302.
D JOHN CLERK, wl, pen and ink, SNPG 668.
C J.KAY, 1806, wl, etch, NPG. J.KAY, 1814, hl in robes, etch, NPG.

NEWTON, Francis Milner (1720-1794) portrait painter.
D GEORGE DANCE, 1793, hs profile, Royal Academy, London.
G JOHAN ZOFFANY, 'Royal Academicians, 1772', oil, Royal Coll.

NEWTON, Gilbert Stuart (1794-1835) painter.
PR S.J.FERRIS, after G.S.Newton, 1821, hs profile, etch, BM, NPG.

NEWTON, John (1725-1807) divine and friend of the poet Cowper.
PR J.COLLYER, after J.Russell, hl, line, pub 1808, BM, NPG.

NEWTON, Robert (1780-1854) methodist minister.
P JOHN JACKSON, hl, Methodist Publishing House, London. WILLIAM GUSH, tql seated, Methodist Publishing House.
PR J.ELLINGWORTH, hs, lith, BM.

NEWTON, Thomas (1704-1782) bishop of Bristol.
P BENJAMIN WEST, tql, Trinity College, Cambridge, engr R.Earlom, mezz, pub 1767, BM. SIR JOSHUA REYNOLDS, RA 1774, tql, Lambeth Palace, London.

NEWTON, William (1735-1790) architect.
D Self-portrait, hs, indian ink, BM.
PR J.NEWTON, after R.Smirke, profile head in oval medallion, stipple, for his ed of *Vitruvius*, 1791, BM, NPG. J.NEWTON, after A.Cozens, profile head in medal, stipple, BM.

NEWTON, Sir William John (1785-1869) miniature painter.
D Self-portrait, hs, chalk, BM.

NIAS, Sir Joseph (1793-1879) admiral.
P After a photograph by MAULL & CO, hand-coloured in oil, tql, NPG 2437.
PH UNKNOWN, hl, ambrotype, NPG P2.

NICHOLAS, William (1785-1812) major in the royal engineers.
PR E.SCRIVEN, after B.Pym, hs, stipple, for *Military Chronicle*, 1813, NPG.

NICHOLL, Sir John (1759-1838) judge.
P WILLIAM OWEN, RA 1814, tql, St John's College, Oxford.
D SIR FRANCIS CHANTREY, hs, and hs profile, pencil, NPG 316a (95, 96).
PR P.W.TOMKINS, after M.A.Shee, hl, stipple, pub 1806, BM, NPG.

NICHOLLS, Sir George (1781-1865) poor law reformer and administrator.
P R.R.REINAGLE, 1834, hl seated, NPG 4807.

NICHOLS, John (1745-1826) printer and antiquarian author.
PR T.COOK, after F.Towne, hs profile, aged 37, line, oval, for *Collections for Leicestershire*, BM. H.MEYER, after J.Jackson, tql, aged 66, mezz, for *Hist of Leicestershire*, 1795, BM, NPG. C.HEATH, after J.Jackson, tql seated, line, for *Literary Anecdotes*, 1812, BM, NPG. A.CARDON, after H.Edridge, hl seated, stipple, for *Contemporary Portraits*, 1814, BM, NPG. H.MEYER, tql seated, stipple, for *Gent Mag*, 1827, BM, NPG.

C JAMES SAYERS, wl, etch, pub 1797, NPG. UNKNOWN, wl etch, NPG.

NICHOLS, John Bowyer (1779-1863) printer and antiquary.
PR J.H.LYNCH, after S.Laurence, hs, lith, from a chalk drawing, BM, NPG.

NICHOLSON, Charles (1795-1837) flautist and composer.
PR T.WAGEMAN, after G.Hargreaves, hs, stipple, circle, BM. M.GAUCI, hs, lith, for *Flutists' Mag*, BM.

NICHOLSON, Francis (1753-1844) landscape painter.
PR M.GAUCI, after J.Green, hs, lith, BM, NI .

NICHOLSON, George (1787-1878) painter and Yorkshire topographer.
P THOMAS ELLERBY, 1828, hl with palette, York City Art Gallery.

NICHOLSON, John (1730-1796) bookseller at Cambridge.
P PHILIP REINAGLE, 1788, wl, University Library, Cambridge.

NICHOLSON, John (1790-1843) 'the Airedale poet'.
P W.O.GELLER, City of Bradford Art Gallery and Museums.
PR W.O.GELLER, tql seated, mezz, for *Poems*, 1844, BM, NPG.

NICHOLSON, Margaret (1750?-1828) assailant of George III.
PR T.TAYLOR, hs, line, oval, for *New Lady's Mag*, 1786, BM, NPG. UNKNOWN, hl, line, oval, pub 1786, BM, NPG. J.T.SMITH, hl when old, etch, BM. Popular prints, NPG.

NICHOLSON, Peter (1765-1844) mathematician and architect.
P JAMES GREEN, 1816?, hs, NPG 4225.
PR C.ARMSTRONG, after T.Heaphy, hl seated with compasses, line, for *Builder and Workman's New Director*, 1824, BM, NPG. H.ADLARD, hl, with compasses, stipple, for *Mechanics' Mag*, 1825, BM, NPG. J.COCHRAN, after W.Derby, tql seated with compasses and rule, stipple, for *Practical Builder*, 1825, BM, NPG.

NICHOLSON, William (1753-1815) scientist.
PR T.BLOOD, after S.Drummond, hl, stipple, for *European Mag*, 1812, BM, NPG.

NICHOLSON, William (1781-1844) portrait-painter and etcher.
P Self-portrait, hl, SNPG 1202. Self-portrait, hl, Royal Scottish Academy, Edinburgh.

NICOLAS, Sir John Toup (1788-1851) rear-admiral.
PR BLOOD, hs, stipple, pub 1818, BM, NPG.

NICOLL, Alexander (1793-1828) orientalist.
SC UNKNOWN, relief medallion, Christ Church Chapel, Oxford.

NICOLLS, Sir Jasper (1778-1849) lieutenant-general.
P UNKNOWN, hl with Bath star, National Army Museum, Sandhurst, Camberley, Surrey.

NIMMO, Alexander (1783-1832) civil engineer.
SC JOHN EDWARD JONES, bust, Royal Dublin Society.

NIMROD, see Charles James Apperley.

NOBBS, George Hunn (1799-1884) missionary and chaplain of Pitcairn Island.
PR H.ADLARD, from a daguerreotype by McKilburn, tql seated, stipple, NPG.

NOBLE, Mark (1754-1827) biographer.
PR J.HANCOCK, hl, oval, for *Memoirs of House of Cromwell*, 1784, BM. J.K.SHERWIN, hl, stipple, oval, NPG.

NOEL, Baptist Wriothesley (1798-1873) divine.
PR W.HARLAND, after A.Wivell, hl, stipple, pub 1842, NPG. W.J.EDWARDS, after G.Richmond, hs, stipple, from a drawing, pub 1851, BM, NPG. G.B.SHAW, after H.Anelay, hs, stipple, from

a drawing, BM, NPG. D.J.POUND, tql seated, from a photograph, stipple and line, for *Drawing Room Portrait Gallery*, BM, NPG.

PH MAULL and POLYBLANK, tql seated, carte, NPG Album of Photographs 1949.

NOEL, Gerard Thomas (1782-1851) divine.

PR W.SAY, after J.Cooper, tql seated, mezz, BM, NPG.

NOEL-HILL William, see 3rd Baron Berwick.

NOLLEKENS, Joseph (1737-1823) sculptor.

P SIR WILLIAM BEECHEY, exhib 1812, hs, TATE 120. L.F.ABBOTT, hl with bust, NPG 30. JAMES LONSDALE, hs, NPG 360. Attrib MARY MOSER, tql modelling a Bacchus, Yale Center for British Art, New Haven, USA. JAMES NORTHCOTE, hs, Fitzwilliam Museum, Cambridge.

D HENRY EDRIDGE, 1807, hs, pencil and w/c, BM. ALFRED CHALON, wl, ink, V & A. GEORGE DANCE, hs, profile, Royal Academy, London. JOHN JACKSON, hl, black lead and w/c, BM.

G JOHAN ZOFFANY, 'Royal Academicians, 1772', oil, Royal Coll.

SC Busts by SIR FRANCIS CHANTREY: 1817, marble, Woburn Abbey, Beds; 1818, marble, BM; original models, Ashmolean Museum, Oxford. L.A.GOBLET, 1821, marble bust, V & A.

NORBURY, John Toler, 1st Earl of (1745-1831) chief-justice of the common pleas.

PR UNKNOWN, hs, stipple, oval, BM. UNKNOWN, wl, coloured etch, NPG.

NORDEN, Frederick Lewis (1708-1742) traveller and artist.

PR BARRETT, hs, line, pub 1793, NPG. UNKNOWN, hl, line, oval, NPG.

NORFOLK, Bernard Edward Howard, 12th Duke of (1765-1842) privy councillor.

P THOMAS GAINSBOROUGH, c1788, wl, Arundel Castle, W.Sussex. HENRY PICKERSGILL, RA 1830, tql seated in robes, Arundel Castle. By or after PICKERSGILL, hl in robes, Arundel Castle.

D JOHN DOYLE, wl equestrian, pen and chalk, BM. F.P.STEPHANOFF, study for the Coronation of George IV, w/c, V & A.

SC JOHN FRANCIS, 1842, marble bust, Arundel Castle.

NORFOLK, Charles Howard, 10th Duke of (1720-1786) writer.

P UNKNOWN, wl in robes, Arundel Castle, W.Sussex. R.E.PINE, RA 1784, tql seated, Arundel Castle.

M British School, hs, oval, Arundel Castle.

NORFOLK, Charles Howard, 11th Duke of (1746-1815) Whig politician.

P THOMAS GAINSBOROUGH, c1784-86, wl, Arundel Castle, W.Sussex. SIR THOMAS LAWRENCE, RA 1799, tql, Arundel Castle. JAMES LONSDALE, 1815, tql seated, Arundel Castle.

D DANIEL GARDNER, hs profile, oval, pastel, (unfinished), BM.

PR T.WILLIAMSON, after W.C.Ross, hl seated with miniature, stipple, pub 1813, BM, NPG. UNKNOWN, after J.Hoppner, tql seated in robes, stipple, BM, NPG.

C JAMES SAYERS, wl, etch, pub 1782, NPG. R.DIGHTON, wl, 'A view of Norfolk', coloured etch, pub 1796, BM, NPG.

NORFOLK, Henry Charles Howard, 13th Duke of (1791-1856) lord steward.

P SIR GEORGE HAYTER, wl in robes, as a page at the Coronation of George IV, Arundel Castle, W.Sussex. Attrib ARCHER JAMES OLIVER, tql, Arundel Castle. D.DALBEY, wl equestrian, Arundel Castle.

D HOPE JAMES STEWART, 1849, wl, pencil and w/c, SNPG 1167.

G SIR GEORGE HAYTER, 'The House of Commons, 1833', oil, NPG 54.

NORFORD, William (1715-1793) surgeon and physician.

PR J.SINGLETON, after G.Ralph, tql with dog, stipple, oval, pub 1788, BM.

NORIE, John William (1772-1843) writer on navigation.

D ADAM BUCK, after a miniature by Williams, tql, w/c, NPG 113

NORMAN, George Warde (1793-1882) writer on finance

P FRANK WILKIN, hl, Bank of England, London.

NORMANBY, Constantine Henry Phipps, 1st Marques of (1797-1863) statesman.

P JOHN JACKSON, RA 1813, or RA 1819, Hardwick Hall Derbyshire. N.J.CROWLEY, c1839, study for a portrait, NGI 202

D DANIEL MACLISE, 1835, wl, pen and ink, NPG 3139. COUNT ALFRED D'ORSAY, 1840, hl, DoE (British Embassy, Paris). SIR THOMAS LAWRENCE, hs, chalk, Royal Coll.

G SIR GEORGE HAYTER, 'The Coronation of Queen Victoria 1838', oil, Royal Coll.

SC GEORGE BROWN and BERNARD MULRENIN, 1837, bronze medallion, National Museum of Ireland, Dublin.

PR H.THOMSON, after F.R.Say, hs, 'The Author of Matilda' stipple, for *New Monthly Mag*, 1831, BM, NPG. C.TURNER, after H.P.Briggs, tql, mezz, 1836, BM, NPG.

C JOHN DOYLE, several drgs, BM.

NORRIS, Antony (1711-1786) antiquary.

PR W.C.EDWARDS, after T.Bardwell, hl, line, BM, NPG.

NORRIS, Catherine Maria, see Kitty Fisher.

NORRIS, Charles (1779-1858) artist.

P JOHN LINNELL, 1837, hl, National Museum of Wales 958 Cardiff.

NORRIS, John (1734-1777) benefactor.

PR W.C.EDWARDS, after Smissen, tql, line, BM, NPG.

NORRIS, Thomas (1741-1790) musician and singer.

PR J.TAYLOR, hl, profile, mezz, oval, pub 1777, BM, NPG.

NORTH, Brownlow (1741-1820) bishop of Winchester.

P TILLY KETTLE, 1762, Baltimore Museum of Art, USA. GEORGE ROMNEY, 1776, tql, The Deanery, Canterbury. HENRY HOWARD, RA 1818, tql seated in robes of prelate of the order of the Garter, All Souls College, Oxford.

SC SIR FRANCIS CHANTREY, 1825, monument, kneeling figure profile, Winchester Cathedral.

NORTH, Christopher, see John Wilson.

NORTH, Dudley Long (1748-1829) politician.

G WILLIAM LANE, 'Whig Statesmen and their Friends, c1810' chalk, NPG 2076.

NORTH, Francis (1761-1817), see 4th Earl of Guilford.

NORTH, Frederick (1732-1792), see 2nd Earl of Guilford.

NORTH, Frederick (1766-1827), see 5th Earl of Guilford.

NORTHAMPTON, Spencer Joshua Alwyne Compton 2nd Marquess of (1790-1851) president of the Royal Society

P JOHN SINGLETON COPLEY, RA 1803, with his father, Castle Ashby, Northants. THOMAS PHILLIPS, (completed by H.W.Phillips), RA 1847, tql, Royal Society, London. SIR HENRY RAEBURN, tql, Castle Ashby.

PR C.COOK, after a daguerreotype by Claudet, tql seated, profile stipple, BM, NPG.

PH D.O.HILL and ROBERT ADAMSON, hl seated, NPG P6(3).

NORTHBROOK, Francis Thornhill Baring, 1st Baron (1796-1866) statesman.

P SIR GEORGE HAYTER, c1833, hs, NPG 1257.

G SIR G.HAYTER, 'The House of Commons, 1833', oil, NPG 54 J.PHILLIP, 'The House of Commons, 1860', oil, Palace of Westminster, London.

PR W.HOLL, after G.Richmond, hs, stipple, for 'Grillion's Club', series, BM, NPG.

C JOHN DOYLE, several political sketches, drgs, BM.

NORTHCOTE, James (1746-1831) painter and writer.

P Self-portrait, 1779, hl, Uffizi Gallery, Florence. Self-portrait, 1784, hl with palette, NPG 3253. Self-portrait, exhib 1812, Walker Art Gallery, Liverpool. Self-portrait, 1823, tql with hawks, Royal Albert Memorial Museum, Exeter. Self-portrait, 1827, hl, NPG 147. Self-portrait, 1828, painting Sir Walter Scott, Royal Albert Memorial Museum. Self-portrait, hl, Frans Halsmuseum, Haarlem, The Netherlands. G.H.HARLOW, tql seated as an older man, NPG 969. Self-portrait, hl aged 81, Royal Albert Memorial Museum.

D GEORGE DANCE, 1793, hs profile, Royal Academy, London. PRINCE HOARE, 1813, hs, pencil and crayon, Victoria Art Gallery, Bath. WILLIAM BROCKEDON, 1825, hs, pencil and chalk, NPG 2515 (5). G.H.HARLOW, hl seated, pencil and chalk, BM. PRINCE HOARE, as an old man, pencil and w/c, V & A. Self-portrait, hs, pencil, NPG 3026. Self-portrait, pencil and w/c, V & A. GEORGE SHEPHEARD, wl profile, pencil, NPG 4206.

G HENRY SINGLETON, 'The Royal Academicians, 1793', oil, Royal Academy.

SC SIR FRANCIS CHANTREY, RA 1812, original model for bust, Ashmolean Museum, Oxford. SIR F.CHANTREY, RA 1840, marble statue, seated, Exeter Cathedral.

NORTHESK, William Carnegie, 7th Earl of (1758-1831) admiral.

PR RIDLEY and HOLL, hs, stipple, oval, pub 1806, BM. H.COOK, after H.Patterson, tql seated, stipple, for Jerdan's *Nat Portrait Gallery*, 1831, BM, NPG. J.HIBBERT, jun, wl standing near sea, etch and aquatint, BM.

NORTHINGTON, Robert Henley, 1st Earl of (1708?-1772) lord chancellor.

P THOMAS HUDSON, exhib 1761, tql with Chancellor's purse, All Souls College, Oxford. Studio of THOMAS HUDSON, tql seated, NPG 2166.

NORTHINGTON, Robert Henley, 2nd Earl of (1747-1786) lord-lieutenant of Ireland.

P SIR JOSHUA REYNOLDS, RA, 1785, tql in robes, NGI 217.

NORTHMORE, Thomas (1766-1851) miscellaneous writer and inventor.

PR C.TURNER, after W.Brockedon, hl, mezz, pub 1818, BM, NPG.

NORTHUMBERLAND, Sir Algernon Percy, 4th Duke of and 1st Baron Prudhoe (1792-1865) admiral and scholar.

P UNKNOWN, Alnwick Castle, Northumberland.

PR S.COUSINS, after F.Grant, wl seated in peer's robes, mezz, BM. UNKNOWN, tql, woodcut, for *Illust London News*, 1845–46, NPG. UNKNOWN, hs, woodcut, for *Illust London News*, 1865, NPG.

NORTHUMBERLAND, Sir Hugh Percy, 2nd Duke of (1742-1817) soldier and politician.

P POMPEO BATONI, hl, Alnwick Castle, Northumberland. NATHANIEL DANCE, 1762, wl seated with Rev Jonathon Lippyatt, Syon House, Middx. A. VAN RYMSDYKE, 1776, after Pompeo Batoni, hl, Syon House. GILBERT STUART, 1785, Syon House. THOMAS PHILLIPS, RA 1801, tql in robes, Petworth (NT), W.Sussex. T.PHILLIPS, after Reynolds, tql, Eton College, Berks.

PR L.S.STADLER, after C.Rosenberg & Son, wl seated, coloured lith, pub 1814, NPG.

NORTHUMBERLAND, Sir Hugh Percy, 3rd Duke of (1785-1847) lord-lieutenant of Ireland.

P THOMAS PHILLIPS, as a young boy, Alnwick Castle, Northumberland. T.PHILLIPS, hl, a leaving portrait, Eton

College, Berks. T.PHILLIPS, 1803, hl, Fitzwilliam Museum, Cambridge. MARTIN CREGAN, Dublin Castle.

D SIR GEORGE HAYTER, study for NPG 999, NPG 1695 (u). JOHN DOWNMAN, 1811, chalk and w/c, Syon House, Middx.

G SIR G.HAYTER, 'The Trial of Queen Caroline, 1820', oil, NPG 999. UNKNOWN, 'The Coronation of George IV', oil, Royal Coll.

SC J.G.LOUGH, 1843, bust, Alnwick Castle.

PR R.GRAVES, after Mrs Robertson, tql in peer's robes, line, pub 1825, BM, NPG. W.HOLL, after G.Ward, hl, stipple, for *Eminent Conservative Statesmen*, 1838, BM, NPG.

NORTHUMBERLAND, Sir Hugh Percy Smithson, 1st Duke of (1715-1786) lord lieutenant of Ireland.

P Attrib SIR JOSHUA REYNOLDS, c1760, tql in peer's robes, Alnwick Castle, Northumberland. R.E.PINE, 1761, wl laying the foundation stone for Middlesex Hospital, Middlesex Hospital, London. SIR JOSHUA REYNOLDS, c1762, The Mansion House, Dublin. THOMAS GAINSBOROUGH, RA 1783, wl in Garter robes, The Middlesex Guildhall, London. T.GAINSBOROUGH, c1783, hl with Garter star, Albury Park, Surrey; version NGI 129. JAMES BARRY, c1784, wl in Garter robes, Syon House, Middx. ALLAN RAMSAY, Aldbury Park. JOHAN ZOFFANY, wl with Mr Henry Selby, Albury Park.

D H.D.HAMILTON, hl, pastel, Alnwick Castle, engr J.Finlaison, mezz, pub 1771, BM.

M THOMAS BEWICK, indian ink, BM.

G Attrib PHILLIPS, 'The Henry V Club', Royal Coll.

SC JAMES TASSIE, 1780, paste medallion, NPG 4954. UNKNOWN, marble bust, Syon House.

NORTON, Fletcher, see 1st Baron Grantley.

NOTT, Sir William (1782-1845) major-general.

P THOMAS BRIGSTOCKE, wl with Bath ribbon and star, Oriental Club, London. B.R.FAULKNER, tql with Bath ribbon and star, India Office, London. J.D.FRANCIS, hl, National Museum of Wales 49, Cardiff.

SC EDWARD DAVIS, 1851, bronze statue, Carmarthen.

NOURSE, Edward (1701-1761) surgeon.

P JOSEPH HIGHMORE, c1750, hl, Royal College of Surgeons, London.

NOVELLO, Vincent (1781-1861) musical composer and publisher.

PR UNKNOWN, after E.P.Novello, hl, etch, 1834, NPG. WILLIAM HUMPHRYS, after E.P.Novello, hl, line, NPG.

NOWELL, Thomas (1730-1801) divine.

P UNKNOWN, hs, Oriel College, Oxford.

NUGENT, Sir Charles Edmund (1759?-1844) admiral of the fleet.

PR W.RIDLEY, after R.Cosway, hl in uniform, stipple, oval, BM, pub 1803, NPG.

NUGENT, Christopher (c1715-1807) physician.

P JAMES BARRY, hs profile, Victoria Art Gallery, Bath.

NUGENT, Sir George, 1st Bart (1757-1849) field-marshal.

PR R.WOODMAN, after J.Downman, hl, stipple, NPG.

NUGENT, George Nugent Grenville, Baron (1788-1850) writer.

P SIR THOMAS LAWRENCE, c1813, wl, on loan to DoE (Home Office).

PR W.WARD, after T.Lawrence, wl, mezz, pub 1822, BM. B.P.GIBSON, after Rochard, hs, line, oval, pub 1830, BM, NPG.

C R.DIGHTON, wl 'A noble student at Oxford', coloured lith, BM, pub 1808, NPG. R.DIGHTON, 'A view of Nugent', coloured etch, pub 1822, V & A. JOHN DOYLE, 'Auction Extraordinary', pen and pencil, 1830, BM.

NUGENT, Robert Nugent, Earl (1702-1788) statesman and writer.

P THOMAS GAINSBOROUGH, 1760, tql, Bristol Town Hall.

PR UNKNOWN, hl, line, oval, for *European Mag*, 1784, BM, NPG.

C JAMES SAYERS, wl, etch, pub 1782, NPG.

NUGENT, Thomas (1700?-1772) miscellaneous writer.

PR UNKNOWN, tql seated, stipple, oval, BM.

NUTHALL, Thomas (d1775) politician and public official.

P FRANCIS HAYMAN, c1748, wl seated with Hambleton Custance and 2 dogs, TATE T.52. NATHANIEL DANCE, wl with dog and gun, TATE T.53. FRANCIS HAYMAN, wl with Hambleton Custance and a dog, Upton House (NT), Warwicks.

NUTTALL, Thomas (1786-1859) naturalist.

PR J.THOMSON, after W.Derby, hl, stipple, pub 1825, BM, NPG. UNKNOWN, hs profile, etch, NPG.

O

OAKELEY, Sir Charles, 1st Bart (1751-1826) governor of Madras.
R S.W.REYNOLDS, after T.Barber, hl, mezz, BM, NPG.

OAKES, Sir Hildebrand, 1st Bart (1754-1822) lieutenant-general.
R W.NICHOLLS, hl in uniform, stipple, for *Military Chronicle*, 1813, BM, NPG.

OASTLER, Richard (1789-1861) reformer.
C J.B.PHILIP, 1866, statue, Rawson Square, Bradford, Yorks.
R UNKNOWN, wl seated, lith, 1840, NPG. E.MORTON, after W.P.Frith, hl, lith, BM. J.POSSELWHITE, after B.Garside, tql seated, stipple and line, NPG. W.BARNARD, after T.H.Illidge, tql, mezz, NPG.

O'BRIEN, Donat Henchy (1785-1857) rear-admiral.
R J.BROWN, after J.Pelham, hl, stipple, for *Adventures during the late War*, 1839, BM.

O'BRIEN, Nelly (d1768) courtesan.
P SIR JOSHUA REYNOLDS, c1762, tql with dog, Wallace Collection, London. SIR JOSHUA REYNOLDS, c1766, tql seated, Glasgow University.

O'BRIEN, Patrick, see Patrick COTTER.

O'BRIEN, William (d1815) actor.
G W.J.WARD, after 'W.Hogarth', 'Garrick in the Green Room', mezz, BM.
R J.WATSON, after F.Cotes, hl, mezz, oval, BM, NPG.

O'BRYEN, Edward (1754?-1808) admiral.
G G.NOBLE and J.PARKER, after J.Smart, 'Naval Victories', 'Commemoration of 11th Oct 1797', line, pub 1803, BM, NPG.
R W. and J.SKELTON, after J.Smart, hs, line, pub 1809, BM.

OCHTERLONY, Sir David, 1st Bart (1758-1825) general.
P R.R.REINAGLE, wl in uniform, Oriental Club, London.
D Called Ochterlony, by a Delhi artist, c1820, gouache, India Office Library and Records, London.
M UNKNOWN, hl, NPG 1266.
G SHEKH ALAM, 'A Darbar at Delhi', oil, c1820, India Office, London. Delhi Artist, c1820, 'Durbar at Delhi of Akbar II', w/c, India Office Library and Records.
R H.MEYER, after A.W.Devis, hl in uniform, mezz, pub 1816, BM, NPG.

O'CONNELL, Daniel (1775-1847) Irish nationalist leader.
P SIR GEORGE HAYTER, 1834, hs, NPG 4582. SIR DAVID WILKIE, 1838, wl, National Bank of Ireland. G.F.MULVANEY, hl, NGI 207.
D DANIEL MACLISE, sketch, w/c, V & A.
M BERNARD MULRENIN, 1836, hl, NPG 208. JOHN COMERFORD, head, NGI 2924.
G J.P.HAVERTY, with his contemporaries, the Clare election, 1828, oil, NGI 1183. SIR GEORGE HAYTER, 'The House of Commons, 1833', oil, NPG 54. B.R.HAYDON, 'The Anti-Slavery Society Convention, 1840', oil, NPG 599.
C J.P.DANTAN, 1834, group with William Cobbett, Musée Carnavelet, Paris. J.E.JONES, 1843, marble bust, NGI 8071. COUNT ALFRED D'ORSAY, 1847, bronze, NGI 8142. JOHN

HENRY FOLEY, 1866, memorial statue, O'Connell St, Dublin. Irish school, wax death mask, NGI 8229. Several medals, National Museum of Ireland, Dublin.
PR Numerous popular prints, BM, NPG. W.HOLL, after T.Carrick, tql seated, stipple, pub 1844, BM, NPG.
C W.HEATH, 'Paul Pry', 'Keeping the Child Quiet', with others, coloured etch, pub 1829, V & A. Numerous JOHN DOYLE, drgs, BM.

O'CONNOR, Arthur (1763-1852) Irish rebel.
G UNKNOWN, 'The United Irish Patriots of 1798', coloured lith, NPG.
PR JOHN GODEFROY, after F.Gerard, hl, stipple, NPG.

O'CONNOR, Feargus (1794-1855) chartist leader.
SC UNKNOWN, stone statue. The Arboretum, Nottingham.
PR UNKNOWN, hl, stipple and line, NPG. W.READ, wl, stipple, NPG.
C JOHN DOYLE, 'Extremes Meet', pencil, 1848, BM.

O'CONNOR, Roger (1762-1834) Irish nationalist.
PR A.WIVELL, 1822, hl with coronet, mezz, pub 1830, NPG.

O'CONOR, Charles (1710-1791) Irish antiquary.
D BERNARD MULRENIN, after a portrait, w/c, NGI 2196.
PR MAGUIRE, hs, surrounded by clouds, stipple, NPG.

O'CONOR, Charles (1764-1828) Irish antiquary, librarian at Stowe.
PR LORD NUGENT, wl seated, lith, BM.

O'FERRALL, Richard More (1797-1880) governor of Malta.
G SIR GEORGE HAYTER, 'The House of Commons, 1833', oil, NPG 54.
C JOHN DOYLE, 'A Good Man Struggling with Difficulties', chalk, 1841, BM.

OFFOR, George (1787-1864) editor and topographer.
PR T.GILKS, hl, woodcut, BM, NPG.

OGDEN, Samuel (1716-1778) divine.
P UNKNOWN, hl, St John's College, Cambridge.
PR G.SCOTT, after F. vr Myn, hs, stipple, oval, for Harding's *Biographical Mirror*, 1793, BM, NPG.

OGILVIE, John (1733-1813) Scottish divine and poet.
PR J.HEATH, after A.Robertson, hs, stipple, oval, for *Britannia, a Poem*, 1801, BM, NPG.

OGILVY, David, see 6th titular Earl of Airlie.

OGLE, Esther Jane, see Mrs Esther Jane Sheridan.

OGLE, George (1742-1814) Irish politician.
G FRANCIS WHEATLEY, 'The Irish House of Commons, 1780', oil, Leeds, City Art Galleries, Lotherton Hall, West Yorks.
SC JOHN SMYTH, statue, St Patrick's Cathedral, Dublin.
PR UNKNOWN, wl, line, BM, NPG.

O'HARA, Kane (1714?-1782) Irish playwright.
PR E.DORRELL, hs profile, etch, circle, pub 1802, BM.

O'KEEFFE, John (1747-1833) dramatist.
P THOMAS LAWRANSON, 1786, hl seated, NPG 165.

O'KELLY, Dennis (1720?-1787) horse-owner and horse-breeder.

C 'R. ST G.MANSERGH', wl equestrian, 'The Eclipse Macarony', etch, pub 1773, NPG.

OKES, Richard (1797-1888) provost of King's College, Cambridge.
P SIR H. VON HERKOMER, 1881, hl, King's College, Cambridge.

OLDHAM, Nathaniel (fl 1740) virtuoso.
G JOSEPH HIGHMORE, 'Mr Oldham and his Guests', oil, *c*1750, TATE 5864.

O'LEARY, Arthur (1729-1802) Irish priest and politician.
PR W.BOND, after Murphy, hs, stipple, pub 1822, NPG.

OLIPHANT, Carolina, see Baroness Nairne.

OLIVER, George (1782-1867) topographer and freemason.
PR J.HARRIS, tql with masonic insignia, lith, BM.

OLIVER, Richard (1734?-1784) alderman and politician.
PR F.ALIAMET, after R.E.Pine, hs, lith, pub 1771, BM, NPG. W.DICKINSON, after the same portrait, hl, mezz, pub 1773, BM. UNKNOWN, wl, with Mayor of London, stipple and line, NPG.

OLIVER, Thomas (1734-1815) lieutenant-governor of Massachusetts.
P JOSEPH BLACKBURN, hs, Boston Museum of Fine Arts, USA.

OLIVER, Tom (1789-1864) pugilist.
PR UNKNOWN, hs, woodcut, NPG.

OLLIVANT, Alfred (1798-1882) bishop of Llandaff.
PR UNKNOWN, hs, woodcut, NPG.

O'LOGHLEN, Sir Michael, 1st Bart (1789-1842) Irish judge.
P G.F.MULVANY, 1843, NGI 932.

O'MALLEY, George (d1843) major-general.
P WILLIAM SALTER, tql study for 'Waterloo Banquet', NPG 3741.
G W.SALTER, 'Waterloo Banquet at Apsley House', oil, 1836, Wellington Museum, Apsley House, London.

OMMANNEY, Sir John Acworth (1773-1855) admiral.
PR R.J.LANE, after B.R.Faulkner, hl, lith, 1851, BM, NPG.

O'NEILL, Charles Henry St John O'Neill, 2nd Viscount and 1st Earl (1779-1841) grand master of Irish Orangemen.
P PHILIP JEAN, hl, Eton College, Berks.
PR J.BROWN, after T.Phillips, tql seated, stipple, BM, NPG.

O'NEILL, Eliza, see Lady WRIXON Becher.

ONSLOW, George (1731-1792) politician.
C JAMES SAYERS, wl, etch, 1782, NPG.

ONSLOW, George(s) (1784-1853) musical composer.
PR VIGNERON, hl, lith, NPG.

ONSLOW, George Onslow, 1st Earl of (1731-1814) politician.
P THOMAS STEWARDSON, hl, Clandon Park (NT), Surrey.
G JOHN SINGLETON COPLEY, 'The Collapse of the Earl of Chatham in the House of Lords, 7 July 1778', oil, TATE 100, on loan to NPG.
SL JOHN FIELD, hs profile, NPG 5212.

ONSLOW, Sir Richard, 1st Bart (1741-1817) admiral.
P Attrib THOMAS PHILLIPS, 1797-99, hl with Bath ribbon and star, NMM, Greenwich. JOHN RUSSELL, wl, Guildhall, Guildford.
G P.ROBERTS, 'British Admirals', set of medallion portraits, stipple, pub 1800, BM. G.NOBLE and J.PARKER, after J.Smart, 'Naval Victories', 'Commemoration of 11th Oct 1797', line, pub 1803, BM, NPG.
PR D.ORME, hs, stipple, oval, pub 1799, BM, NPG.

ONSLOW, Thomas Onslow, 2nd Earl of (1755-1827) politician.
P Attrib W.HOGARTH (sometimes attrib T.Hudson), tql as a child,

Clandon Park (NT), Surrey. UNKNOWN, hl, Clandon Park.
D DANIEL GARDNER, watching 7th Viscount Fitzwilliam and E of Pembroke playing chess, pastel, Clandon Park.

OPIE, Amelia, née Alderson (1769-1853) novelist and po wife of John Opie.
P JOHN OPIE, 1798, hl, NPG 765.
D H.P.BRIGGS, 1834, hl, Staatliche Kunstsammlungen, Dresde
G B.R.HAYDON, 'The Anti-Slavery Society Convention, 184 oil, NPG 599.
SC P.D.D'ANGERS, 1829, bronze medallion, NPG 1081.
PR W.RIDLEY, after J.Opie, hl, stipple, oval, for *European M* 1803, BM, NPG. J.HOPWOOD, after J.Opie, hs, stipple, for *T Cabinet*, 1807, BM, NPG.

OPIE, John (1761-1807) portrait and history painter.
P Self-portraits: 1785, hl, NPG 47; 1789, hs with palette, NGS 9 *c*1790, TATE 1826; *c*1790, hs, Royal Institution of Cornwall; i 1801-02, hs, Royal Academy, London; Dulwich College Pictu Gallery; SNPG L89; Victoria Art Gallery, Bath; Yale Center i British Art, New Haven, USA.
D GEORGE DANCE, hs profile, Royal Academy.
G HENRY SINGLETON, 'The Royal Academicians 1793', oil, Ro Academy.

ORAM, Edward (fl 1770-1800) landscape painter.
D JOHN FLAXMAN, head, pencil, NPG 3112.

ORDE, Sir John, 1st Bart (1751-1824) admiral.
PR S.W.REYNOLDS, after G.Romney, hl in uniform, mezz, BM

ORDE, Thomas Powlett, see 1st Baron Bolton.

ORFORD, Horace Walpole, 4th Earl of (1717-1797) wri and collector.
P JOHN GILES ECCARDT, 1754, hl, NPG 988. SIR JOSH REYNOLDS, *c*1756-7, The Art Gallery of Toronto, Cana versions, Bowood, Wilts; Ragley Hall, Warwicks.
D ROSALBA CARRIERA, 1741, hl, pastel, Houghton Hall, Norfo UNKNOWN, 1788, 3 wl sketches, Huntington Library and A Gallery, San Marino, USA. GEORGE DANCE, 1793, hl, pen NPG 1161. After J.G.ECCARDT, copy of an unfinished painti hl, pen and wash, Huntington Library and Art Gallery. S THOMAS LAWRENCE, hs, pencil, NPG 3631.
PR W.GREATBACH, after G.P.Harding, after Muntz of *c*1755, seated, line, pub 1842, NPG. DEAN, after a miniature C.F.Zincke of 1745, hs, stipple and line, pub 1834, N D.P.PARISET, after P.Falconet, hs profile, stipple, BM, NPG.

ORGER, Mrs Mary Ann, née Ivers (1788-1849) actress.
G GEORGE CLINT, in the last scene of *A New Way to Pay Old Del* oil, 1820, Garrick Club, London. GEORGE CLINT, as Fanny i scene from *Lock and Key*, oil, RA 1821, Garrick Club.
PR H.R.COOK, after Walton, wl, as Lorenza, stipple, for *T Theatrical Inquisitor*, 1815, NPG. R.W.SIEVIER, af M.Haughton, hl, as Mrs Lovemore in Murphy's *The Way to ke him*, stipple and line, for Oxberry's *New English Drama*, 1818, B NPG. UNKNOWN, hl, stipple, BM, NPG.

ORIEL, John Foster, 1st Baron (1740-1828) speaker of t Irish House of Commons.
P After GILBERT STUART, hl, NGI 867. H.D.HAMILTON, Mans House, Dublin. R.L.WEST, Royal Dublin Society.
PR M.GAUCI, after T.Lawrence, hs, lith, BM, NPG. F.BARTOLOZ hl, stipple, BM, NPG. UNKNOWN, hl in speaker's robes, line, o in broadside, *List of Members who voted for a Legislative Uni* 1799, BM.

ORME, Robert (1728-1801) writer on India.
PR UNKNOWN, hs, line, oval, for *European Mag*, 1801, BM, NPC

ORME, William (1787-1830) congregational minister.

R J.THOMSON, after J.R.Wildman, hl, stipple, for *Evangelical Mag*, 1830, BM.

ORMEROD, George (1785-1873) topographer.

D JOHN JACKSON, 1817, tql seated, w/c, The Bodleian Library, Oxford.

ORONSAY, Duncan McNeill, Baron, see Baron COLONSAY and Oronsay.

ORRERY, Mary Monckton, Countess of Cork and, see CORK.

ORTON, Job (1717-1783) dissenting minister.

R UNKNOWN, hl, line, oval, BM, NPG.

OSBALDESTON, George (1787-1866) sportsman.

R T.C.WILSON, wl profile, lith, from pen drawing, for Wildrake's *Cracks of the Day*, BM, NPG. P.W.MAYKING, tql with cricket bat, Marylebone Cricket Club, London. ROFFE, after Woodhouse, hl, stipple, NPG. J.BROWN, after a photograph by J.Watkins, hs, stipple, NPG.

OSBORNE, Francis (1751-1799), see 5th Duke of Leeds.

O'SULLIVAN, Mortimer (1791?-1859) Irish protestant divine.

R J.KIRKWOOD, after C.Grey, wl, etch, NPG.

OSWALD, James (1715-1769) politician.

R W.H.LIZARS, probably Oswald, hs, line, NPG.

OTTER, William (1768-1840) bishop of Chichester.

SC JOSEPH TOWNE, 1844, bust, Chichester Cathedral.

R J.LINNELL, tql seated, mezz, BM.

OTTLEY, William Young (1771-1836) writer on art, and amateur artist.

R F.C.LEWIS, after Pellegrini, hl seated, stipple, BM. F.C.LEWIS, after W.Riviere, head, stipple, BM.

OTWAY, Caesar (1780-1842) writer.

R J.KIRKWOOD, after W.Stevenson, wl seated, etch, pub 1839, NPG.

OTWAY, Sir Robert Waller, 1st Bart (1770-1846) admiral.

P UNKNOWN, 1843–46, tql with ribbon and star of the Bath, NMM, Greenwich.

R M.GAUCI, after J.Masquerier, hl, lith, BM, NPG.

OUGHTON, Sir James Adolphus Dickenson (1720-1780) lieutenant-general.

P Attrib JOHN DOWNMAN, SNPG 1846.

R UNKNOWN, hs profile, a silhouette shade, BM.

OUSELEY, Gideon (1762-1839) methodist.

R T.A.DEAN, after J.Jackson, hl seated, stipple, for *Methodist Mag*, BM, NPG.

OUSELEY, Sir Gore, 1st Bart (1770-1844) diplomatist and oriental scholar.

R W.RIDLEY, after S.Drummond, hs, stipple, for *European Mag*,

1810, BM, NPG. H.COOK, after R.Rothwell, hl, stipple, for Jerdan's *Nat Portrait Gallery*, 1833, BM, NPG.

OUSELEY, Sir William (1767-1842) orientalist.

PR H.R.COOK, after S.Drummond, hs, stipple, oval, for *European Mag*, 1811, BM, NPG.

OUSELEY, Sir William Gore (1797-1866) diplomat.

P Self-portrait, wl, DoE (Montevideo Legation).

OVERSTONE, Samuel Jones Loyd, 1st Baron (1796-1883) banker and economist.

P FRANK HOLL, 1880, tql seated, University of Reading.

OWEN, Sir Edward Campbell Rich (1771-1849) admiral.

P H.W.PICKERSGILL, 1849, tql with Bath ribbon and star, NMM, Greenwich; copy, National Museum of Wales 728, Cardiff.

OWEN, Henry (1716-1795) divine and scholar.

PR W.BROMLEY, after S.Drummond, hs, mezz, oval, for *European Mag*, 1795, BM, NPG. J.T.SMITH, hl, line, pub 1797, BM.

OWEN, Hugh (1784-1861) soldier in service of Portugal.

M ANDREW ROBERTSON, 1808, NPG 975.

OWEN, John (1766-1822) secretary of British and Foreign Bible Society.

P UNKNOWN, Corpus Christi College, Cambridge.

PR H.R.COOK, after W.Foster, hs, stipple, pub 1812, NPG. E.SCRIVEN, after J.Slater, hl, seated, stipple, pub 1823, BM, NPG.

OWEN, Robert (1771-1858) pioneer of practical socialism.

P W.H.BROOKE, 1834, hl, NPG 943. W.H.BROOK, hs, National Museum of Wales 129, Cardiff.

D AUGUSTUS HERVIEU, 1829, hs, w/c, NPG 2507. EBENEZER MORLEY, 1834, hl, w/c, NPG 4521. FREDERICK CRUIKSHANK, 1839, tql seated, w/c, Manchester City Art Gallery. 'SB', 1851, hs, chalk, NPG 328. MARY ANN KNIGHT, w/c, SNPG 1606. UNKNOWN, wl, w/c, Fabian Society, London.

SC JULIAN LEVEROTTI, bronze medallion after a life-mask, NPG 602.

OWEN, Samuel (1769-1857) water-colourist.

D T.MONTAGUE, 1794–95, tql, w/c, NPG 3129.

OWEN, William (1769-1825) portrait-painter.

P Self-portrait, *c*1805, hs, Royal Academy, London.

PR H.MEYER, after J.Wright, hs, stipple, for *The Cabinet*, 1809, BM, NPG.

OWEN, William Fitzwilliam (1774-1857) vice-admiral.

PR UNKNOWN, hl, stipple and line, BM.

OWENSON, Sydney, see Lady Morgan.

OXBERRY, William (1784-1824) actor.

D SAMUEL DE WILDE, 1811, as Leo Luminati in *Oh! This Love*, w/c, Garrick Club, London.

G GEORGE CLINT, in the last scene of *A New Way to Pay Old Debts*, oil, 1820, Garrick Club.

PR Several theatrical prints, BM, NPG.

P

PACK, Sir Denis (1772?-1823) major-general.
SC WILLIAM THEED, jun, bust, Royal Military Academy, Sandhurst, Camberley, Surrey. SIR FRANCIS CHANTREY, bust, Ashmolean Museum, Oxford.
PR C.TURNER, after G.L.Saunders, hl, mezz, pub 1834, BM, NPG.

PACKER, John Hayman (1730-1806) actor.
P UNKNOWN, hs, Garrick Club, London. BENJAMIN VANDERGUCHT, wl in *The Register Office*, Leicester Museum and Art Gallery.
G J.CALDWALL and S.SMITH, after G.Carter, 'Immortality of Garrick', line, pub 1783, BM.

PAGET, Sir Arthur (1771-1840) diplomatist.
P JOHN HOPPNER, wl in Bath robes, Plas Newydd, Gwynedd.
D COUNT ALFRED D'ORSAY, 1840, hl profile, pen and chalk, NPG 4026 (43).
SC SAMUEL PERCY, wax model, V & A.

PAGET, Sir Charles (1778-1839) vice-admiral.
P T.C.THOMPSON, RA 1823, with 1st Marquess of Anglesey, Army and Navy Club, London.

PAGET, Sir Edward (1775-1849) general.
P UNKNOWN, tql in uniform, Plas Newydd, Gwynedd.
D HENRY EDRIDGE, 1810, w/c, V & A.
M ROBERT HOME, hl, NPG 3247.

PAGET, Henry (1744-1812), see 3rd Earl of Uxbridge.

PAGET, Henry William (1768-1854), see 1st Marquess of Anglesey.

PAINE, James (1725-1789) architect.
P SIR JOSHUA REYNOLDS, 1764, hl seated with his son, Ashmolean Museum, Oxford.
PR D.P.PARISET, after P.Falconet 1769, hs, profile, stipple, oval, pub 1795, BM, NPG.

PAINE, James (d1829) architect.
P SIR JOSHUA REYNOLDS, 1764, hl with his father, Ashmolean Museum, Oxford.
PR DANIEL BERGER, after Reynolds, head, line, 1773, NPG.

PAINE, Thomas (1737-1809) author of the 'Rights of Man'.
P AUGUSTE MILLIÈRE, after an engraving by G.Romney, hl, NPG 897.
PR W.ANGUS, after C.W.Peale, tql seated, line, pub 1791, BM, NPG. BARLOW, after S.Collings, tql, line, pub 1792, BM. W.SHARP, after G.Romney, hl, line, pub 1793, BM, NPG. Several popular prints, BM, NPG.

PAINTER, Edward (1784-1852) pugilist.
PR W.M.FELLOWS, after G.Sharples, tql, aquatint, NPG.

PAKENHAM, Sir Edward Michael (1778-1815) major-general.
D THOMAS HEAPHY, hs, w/c, NPG 1914 (9).
SC SIR RICHARD WESTMACOTT, 1823, statue and monument, with General Walsh, St Paul's Cathedral, London.

PAKENHAM, Sir Hercules Robert (1781-1850) general.
PR UNKNOWN, hs, woodcut, for *Illust London News*, 1846-47, NPG.

PAKENHAM, Sir Thomas (1757-1836) admiral.
G BARTOLOZZI, LANDSEER, RYDER and STOW, after R.Smirke,

'Naval Victories', 'Commemoration of the victory of June 1794', line, pub 1803, BM, NPG.

PAKINGTON, Sir John Somerset, see 1st Baron Hampto[n]

PALEY, William (1743-1805) theological writer.
P GEORGE ROMNEY, 1789, tql, NPG 3659. SIR WILLIAM BEECHE[Y] after Romney, hl, NPG 145.
PR W.RIDLEY, after S.Drummond, hs, stipple, oval, for *Europe[an] Mag*, 1805, BM, NPG.

PALGRAVE, Sir Francis (1788-1861) historian.
SC THOMAS WOOLNER, 1861, plaster cast of medallion, NPG 20[6]
PR MRS D.TURNER, after T.Phillips, hl, profile, etch, 1823, N[PG]

PALLISER, Sir Hugh, 1st Bart (1723-1796) admiral.
P NATHANIEL DANCE, tql, Los Angeles County Museum of A[rt] USA. Attrib GEORGE DANCE, after Nathaniel Dance, wl, NM[M] Greenwich.
PR J.R.SMITH, tql, mezz, pub 1787, BM. E.ORME, after D.Orme, [hs] stipple, oval, for *European Mag*, 1796, BM.

PALMER, John (1742?-1798) actor.
P ARROWSMITH, tql, as Colonel Cohenberg in *The Siege [of] Belgrade*, Garrick Club, London. HENRY WALTON, wl character, NPG 2086. UNKNOWN, hs, Garrick Club.
D JAMES ROBERTS, as Stukeley, drg, BM. J.RUSSELL, hs, past[el] oval, Garrick Club.
G THOMAS PARKINSON, wl as Iachimo in a scene from Act V [of] *Cymbeline*, oil, 1778, Garrick Club. JAMES ROBERTS, as Jose[ph] Surface in a scene from *The School for Scandal*, oil, RA 17[ ] Garrick Club. JOHAN ZOFFANY, in a scene from *The Alchem[ist]* oil, Castle Howard, North Yorks.
PR Numerous theatrical prints, BM, NPG.

PALMER, John (1742-1818) originator of mail coaches.
P THOMAS GAINSBOROUGH, hl, Pennsylvania Museu[m] Philadelphia, USA. Attrib WILLIAM HOARE, hl, The Guildha[ll] Bath.
D GEORGE DANCE, 1793, hs profile, pencil, NPG 4929.

PALMER, Robert (1757-1805?) actor.
P SAMUEL DE WILDE portraits at the Garrick Club, London: [RA] 1797, as Tag in *The Spoiled Child*; wl as Tom in *Conscious Love[rs]*
PR RIDLEY, after Spicer, hs, stipple, oval, for Parson's *Minor Theat[re]* 1794, NPG. W.RIDLEY, after S.Drummond, hl, stipple, oval, f[or] *European Mag*, 1802, BM, NPG. Several theatrical prints, BM, NP[G]

PALMER, Samuel (1741-1813) independent minister.
PR H.MEYER, after A.W.Devis, hl seated, mezz, pub 1814, BM, NP[G]

PALMER, Thomas Fyshe (1747-1802) unitarian minister.
C JOHN KAY, hl, seated, etch, oval, BM.

PALMERSTON, Emily Mary Temple, Viscounte[ss] (1787-1869) Whig hostess.
D Attrib E.B.MORRIS, hs, chalk and w/c, NPG 3954.
PR M.GAUCI, after J.Lucas, tql seated, lith, BM. F.HOLL, aft[er] J.R.Swinton, hs, stipple, oval, BM.
PH H.HERING, wl, carte, NPG 'Album of Photographs 1939'.

PALMERSTON, Henry John Temple, 3rd Viscou[nt] (1784-1865) prime minister.
P JOHN PARTRIDGE, c1844-5, hl, NPG 1025. J.PARTRIDGE, 18[ ]

wl, on loan to the Palace of Westminster. FREDERICK CRUIKSHANK, c1855, wl addressing House of Commons, on loan to the Palace of Westminster. F.CRUIKSHANK, c1855, hl, on loan to NPG (3953). SIR FRANCIS GRANT, 1862, tql, DoE (Foreign Office). E.B.MORRIS, 1863, wl as Lord Warden of the Cinque Ports, Town Hall, Dover. JOHN LUCAS, 1866, wl as Master of Trinity House, Trinity House, London.

D THOMAS HEAPHY, 1802, wl seated in landscape, w/c, NPG 751. THOMAS HEAPHY, 1804, Buscot Park (NT), Oxon.

G SIR DAVID WILKIE, 'Queen Victoria's First Council, 1837', oil, Royal Coll. JOHN PARTRIDGE, 'Fine Art Commissioners, 1846', oil, NPG 342, 3. SIR JOHN GILBERT, 'Coalition Ministry, 1854', pencil and wash, NPG 1125. JOHN PHILLIP, 'House of Commons, 1860', oil, Palace of Westminster.

C R.C.LUCAS, 1856, wax relief, NPG 2226. MATTHEW NOBLE, 1860, marble bust, Reform Club, London. ROBERT JACKSON, 1865, marble statue, in garter robes, Westminster Abbey, London. THOMAS WOOLNER, 1876, bronze statue, Parliament Square, London.

PANIZZI, Sir Anthony (1797-1879) principal librarian of the British Museum.

P G.F.WATTS, c1847, hl, NPG 1010.

C R.C.LUCAS, 1850, wax medallion, NPG 2187. UNKNOWN, marble bust, BM Reading Room.

C CARLO PELLEGRINI, 'Ape', 1874, wl, w/c, for Vanity Fair, NPG 2736.

H ERNEST EDWARDS, wl seated, for Men of Eminence, ed L.Reeve, vol II, 1864, NPG. Several photographs, BM, NPG.

PANMURE, William Ramsay Maule, 1st Baron (1771-1852) parliamentarian.

P COLVIN SMITH, hl, SNPG 2177.

R H.COUSINS, after T.M.Joy, wl aged 67, seated, with bust of C.J.Fox, mezz, BM.

C JOHN KAY, wl with horse 'Generous Sportsman', etch, 1795, BM, NPG.

PAOLI, Pascal (1725-1807) Corsican general and patriot.

P RICHARD COSWAY, hs, Uffizi Gallery, Florence.

D GEORGE DANCE, 1797, hs profile, pencil, BM.

M GIUSEPPE MACPHERSON, hs?, Burghley House, Northants.

G UNKNOWN, wl seated with soldiers and a dog, Wilton House, Wilts.

C JOHN FLAXMAN, bust, Westminster Abbey, London.

R UNKNOWN, after H.Bembridge, wl, mezz, pub 1769, BM, NPG. R.HOUSTON, after P.Gheradi, wl, battle in background, mezz, pub 1769, BM. R.BROOKSHAW, after Gambalini, tql, battle in background, mezz, BM, NPG.

PAPINEAU, Louis Joseph (1786-1871) Canadian rebel.

R UNKNOWN, hl, photogravure, NPG.

PAPWORTH, John Buonarotti (1775-1847) architect and designer.

D WILLIAM BROCKEDON, c1829, hs, chalk, NPG 2515 (53).

R J.GREEN, after W.Say, hl, mezz, BM.

PARIS, John Ayrton (1785-1856) physician.

P C.SKOTTOWE, c1838, tql seated, Royal College of Physicians, London.

C Attrib ISAAC JACKSON, plaster bust, Royal College of Physicians.

R W.DRUMMOND, after E.U.Eddis, hl, lith, for Athenaeum Portraits, 1836, BM, NPG.

PARISH, Sir Woodbine (1796-1882) diplomatist.

R I.W.SLATER, after T.Phillips, hl, lith, BM, NPG.

PARK, Sir James Alan (1763-1838) judge.

R W.J.WARD, after W.J.Newton, tql seated, mezz, pub 1833, BM.

PARK, Mungo (1771-1806) explorer.

D THOMAS ROWLANDSON, c1805, hs, w/c, NPG 4924.

M After HENRY EDRIDGE, hl, NPG 1104.

SC ANDREW CURRIE, 1839, statue, Selkirk, Scotland.

PARK, Thomas (1759-1834) antiquary and bibliographer.

PR I.T.WEDGWOOD, hl, stipple, pub 1820, NPG.

PARKE, Sir James, see Baron Wensleydale.

PARKE, John (1745-1829) oboist.

G G.H.HARLOW, 'Court for the Trial of Queen Catherine' (Henry VIII), oil, c1817, Royal Shakespeare Memorial Theatre Museum, Stratford-on-Avon.

PARKER, Sir Charles Christopher, 5th Bart (1792-1869) admiral.

P THOMAS UWINS, 1826, hl, NMM, Greenwich.

PARKER, George (1732-1800) actor, lecturer, soldier.

PR UNKNOWN, hl, stipple and line, oval, for his Life's Painter of variegated Characters, 1789, BM, NPG.

PARKER, Henry Perlee (1795-1873) painter.

P RAPHAEL HYDE PARKER, hl, oval, NPG 4972.

D UNKNOWN, Sheffield City Museum.

PR UNKNOWN, after a photograph, hs, woodcut, for Illust London News, 1874, BM, NPG.

PARKER, Sir Hyde, 5th Bart (1714-1782) vice-admiral.

P JAMES NORTHCOTE, 1781, hl, Saltram House (NT), Devon. GEORGE ROMNEY, c1782-83, tql, Melford Hall (NT), Suffolk; version, NMM, Greenwich. Attrib SIR JOSHUA REYNOLDS, Melford Hall.

PARKER, Sir Hyde (1739-1807) admiral.

P GEORGE ROMNEY, 1779, wl, Melford Hall (NT), Suffolk.

PARKER, John (d1765?) painter.

P Attrib MARCO BENEFIAL, hs, Accademia di S Luca, Rome.

PARKER, John (1772-1840), see 1st Earl of Morley.

PARKER, John William (1792-1870) publisher.

PR UNKNOWN, tql seated, from a daguerreotype, lith, BM, NPG.

PARKER, Sir Peter, 1st Bart (1721-1811) admiral of the fleet.

P L.F.ABBOTT, 1795-99, wl, NMM, Greenwich.

PR I.JONES, hs, stipple, oval, pub 1793, NPG. RIDLEY, after V.Green, hs, stipple, oval, pub 1804, NPG.

PARKER, Sir Peter, 2nd Bart (1785-1814) naval captain.

P JOHN HOPPNER, 1808-09, hl, NMM, Greenwich.

SC CHRISTOPHER PROSPERI, relief showing his death, St Margaret's, Westminster, London.

PARKER, Richard (1767?-1797) mutineer.

PR SANSON, after Bailey, hl, stipple, oval, pub 1797, BM, NPG. HARRISON & CO, after W.Chamberlaine, wl with drawn cutlass, line, pub 1797, BM. G.MURRAY, after I.Cruikshank, hs, line, oval, pub 1797, NPG. W.BROMLEY, after S.Drummond, hl, stipple, oval, pub 1797, BM.

PARKER, Thomas Lister (1779-1858) antiquary.

PR J.YOUNG, after J.Northcote, tql with dog, for Young's Leicester Gallery, etch, BM.

PARKER, Sir William, 1st Bart (1743-1802) admiral.

G WORTHINGTON and PARKER, after R.Smirke, 'Naval Victories', 'Commemoration of the 14th February 1797', line, pub 1803, BM, NPG.

PARKER, Sir William, 1st Bart (1781-1866) admiral of the fleet.

P Attrib MARGARET THOMAS, 1882, tql, HMS Mercury.

PARKES, David (1763-1833) artist and antiquarian.
M UNKNOWN, hl, Shrewsbury Borough Museums.

PARKES, Samuel (1761-1825) chemist.
PR PARKER, after A.Wivell, hl seated, stipple, for *Imperial Mag*, 1822, BM.

PARKHURST, John (1728-1797) biblical lexicographer.
M JOHN SMART, 1765, V & A.

PARNELL, Sir John, 2nd Bart (1744-1801) chancellor of the Irish exchequer.
P POMPEO BATONI, *c*1770, hl, Castle Ward (NT), Co Down, N.Ireland. Irish School, NGI 660.
G FRANCIS WHEATLEY, 'The Irish House of Commons, 1780', oil, Leeds City Art Galleries, Lotherton Hall, West Yorks.

PARR, Samuel (1747-1825) teacher.
P JOHN OPIE, RA 1807, hl, Holkham Hall, Norfolk. JAMES LONSDALE, *c*1823, hl, Fitzwilliam Museum, Cambridge. GEORGE DAWE, hl, NPG 9. T.KIRKBY, hl, Harrow School, Middx. GEORGE ROMNEY, hl, Emmanuel College, Cambridge.
PR W.SAY, after W.Artaud, tql seated, mezz, pub 1804, BM, NPG. A.CHISHOLM, wl seated, lith, BM, NPG.
C JAMES SAYERS, hl, 'Preface to Bellendenus', etch, pub 1787, NPG.

PARRIS, Edmund Thomas (1793-1873) painter.
PR UNKNOWN, wl repainting Sir James Thornhill's pictures in St Paul's, woodcut, for *Illust London News*, 1856, NPG. UNKNOWN, after a photograph, hl, woodcut, for *Illust London News*, 1873, BM, NPG.

PARRY, Caleb Hillier (1755-1822) physician.
SC LUCIUS GAHAGAN, bust, Victoria Art Gallery, Bath.
PR UNKNOWN, hl, line, NPG.

PARRY, John (*d*1782) blind musician.
PR UNKNOWN, wl profile, seated with harp, line, BM. W.PARRY, small wl with harp, etch, BM.

PARRY, John (1776-1851) musician and composer.
P UNKNOWN, hl, Royal Society of Musicians, London.
D ABRAHAM WIVELL, 1830, hl, pencil, NPG 5152. 'AW', 1847, hl, pencil, Royal Society of Musicians.
SC UNKNOWN, plaster bust, Royal Society of Musicians.
PR E.MORTON, after C.Durham, tql seated, from a miniature, lith, for *Welsh Harper*, 1839, BM.

PARRY, Joseph (1744-1826) painter.
PR J.PARRY, tql with palette, etch, BM.

PARRY, Sir William Edward (1790-1855) rear-admiral and explorer.
P SIR WILLIAM BEECHEY, 1819, tql, NMM, Greenwich. CHARLES SCOTTOWE, RA 1838, hl, NMM. STEPHEN PEARCE, 1850, hs, (study for NPG 1208), NPG 912. SAMUEL DRUMMOND, hl, NPG 5053.
G S.PEARCE, 'The Arctic Council planning a search for Sir John Franklin', oil, 1851, NPG 1208.
PR S.W.REYNOLDS, after W.Haines, hl, mezz, pub 1827, BM. H.PERRY, hs, lith, BM.

PARSONS, Edward (1762-1833) congregational minister at Leeds.
PR J.OGBORNE, after H.Singleton, in pulpit preaching, stipple, pub 1789, BM, NPG. T.LUPTON, after J.Northcote, hl, mezz, pub 1819, BM, NPG. PARKER, after J.R.Wildman, hl, stipple, for *Evangelical Mag*, 1827, BM, NPG. J.THOMSON, after W.Derby, hl, stipple, pub 1829, BM, NPG.

PARSONS, Edward (1797-1844) dissenting minister.
PR UNKNOWN, hl, stipple, for *Evangelical Mag*, 1826, BM.

PARSONS, James (1705-1770) physician and antiquary.

P BENJAMIN WILSON, 1762, hl, NPG 560.

PARSONS, James (1799-1877) congregational minister at York.
P Attrib PHILIP WESTCOTT, City of York Art Gallery.
PR W.J.WARD, after G.Marshall, hl, mezz, pub 1825, BM. T.BLOOD, after J.R.Wildman, hl, stipple, for *Evangelical Mag*, 1825, BM, NPG. J.COCHRAN, after a photograph by S.Haggard, tql, stipple and line, NPG.

PARSONS, John (1761-1819) bishop of Peterborough.
P WILLIAM OWEN, RA 1818, tql, Balliol College, Oxford; copy by Thomas Kirkby, Wadham College, Oxford.

PARSONS, Sir Lawrence (1758-1841), see 2nd Earl of Rosse.

PARSONS, William (1736-1795) actor.
P Several paintings at the Garrick Club, London: BENJAMIN VANDERGUCHT, RA 1775, wl in a scene from *The Committee*; SAMUEL DE WILDE, 1791, wl as Dumps in *The Natural Son*; S. DE WILDE, 1793, wl as Sheepface in *The Village Lawyer*; S. DE WILDE, wl as Colonel Oldboy in *Lionel and Clarissa*; JOHAN ZOFFANY, wl as Sheepface in *The Village Lawyer*. JOHAN ZOFFANY, *c*1766-70, as Old Man in *Lethe*, Birmingham City Art Gallery.
D UNKNOWN, *c*1793, gouache, Garrick Club. ROBERT DIGHTON, wl as Moneytrap in *The Confederacy*, Garrick Club. Attrib NOAD, wl as Lope Tocho in *The Mountaineers*, Garrick Club.
PR Numerous theatrical prints, BM, NPG.

PARSONS, Sir William (1746?-1817) professor of music and magistrate.
P CHARLES WILKIN, *c*1790, hs, Examination Schools, Oxford. UNKNOWN, hl, Royal Society of Musicians, London.
PR RIDLEY and BLOOD, after F.Wilkins, hs, stipple, for *European Mag*, 1808, NPG.

PARTINGTON, Miles (*b*1751) apothecary and pioneer of electricity.
D GEORGE DANCE, 1800, hl, pencil, NPG 4205.

PARTRIDGE, John (1790-1872) portrait-painter.
G JOHN PARTRIDGE, 'A Meeting of the Sketching Society', ink and wash, BM.

PASCO, John (1774-1853) rear-admiral.
P UNKNOWN, hl, NMM, Greenwich.

PASLEY, Sir Charles William (1780-1861) general.
P UNKNOWN, 1812, hl, Royal Engineers Museum, Chatham, Kent. E.U.EDDIS, tql, Royal Engineers Museum.

PASLEY, Sir Thomas, 1st Bart (1734-1808) admiral.
P L.F.ABBOTT, 1795, NMM, Greenwich.
G BARTOLOZZI, LANDSEER, RYDER and STOW, after R.Smirke, 'Naval Victories', 'Commemoration of the victory of June 1st 1794', line, pub 1803, BM, NPG.
PR C.TOWNLEY, after W.Beechey, tql, mezz, pub 1795, BM. W.RIDLEY, after M.Brown, hl, stipple, oval, for *European Mag*, 1805, BM, NPG.

PASQUIN, Anthony, see John WILLIAMS.

PATCH, Richard (1770?-1806) criminal.
PR UNKNOWN, after G.Simpson, hl, stipple, pub 1806, BM. UNKNOWN, hs, etch and aquatint, pub 1806, NPG. UNKNOWN, hs, profile, etch, BM.

PATCH, Thomas (*d*1782) painter and engraver.
D Self-portrait, Royal Albert Memorial Gallery, Exeter, Devon.
M UNKNOWN, hs, NPG 4081.
G JOHAN ZOFFANY, 'The Tribuna of the Uffizi', oil, 1772-8, Royal Coll.
C Self-portrait, group of beasts with human heads, in pictures on

the wall, oil, Royal Albert Memorial Museum, Exeter. Self-portrait, wl seated, measuring mask with compasses, etch, for his *Caricature*, 1768, BM. Self-portrait, wl, caricatured as a bullock in a field, etch, for his *Caricature*, 1769, BM.

PATERSON, John (1776-1855) missionary.
R JENKINS, after Jarvis, hl, stipple, NPG.

PATON, George (1721-1807) antiquary.
D JOHN BROWN, hl, pencil, SNPG 200. JOHN BROWN, hs, profile, pencil, SNPG L66.
C JOHN KAY, one of a set of 'Edinburgh Portraits', etch, BM.

PATTESON, Sir John (1790-1861) justice of the King's bench.
P MARGARET CARPENTER, tql, King's College, Cambridge.
R S.COUSINS, after M.Carpenter, tql in judicial robes, mezz, BM, NPG.

PATTISON, William (1706-1727) poet.
R R.FOURDRINIER, after J.Saunders, hl, line, for *Cupid's Metamorphoses*, 1728, NPG.

PATTRICK, George (1746-1800) divine.
R J.COLLYER, after J.Russell, hl, line, oval, BM.

PAUL, Sir George Onesiphorus, 2nd Bart (1746-1820) philanthropist.
SC R.W.SIEVIER, 1828, bust on monument, Gloucester Cathedral.

PAUL, Hamilton (1773-1854) poet and humorist.
SL UNKNOWN, ink, SNPG 2185.

PAULET, Harry, see 6th Duke of Bolton.

PAULET, Lavinia, see Duchess of Bolton.

PAULL, James (1770-1808) politician.
D JAMES GILLRAY, head, pencil, BM.
R HOPWOOD, hs, stipple, oval, pub 1808, BM, NPG.
C JAMES GILLRAY, 'Political Mathematicians Shaking the Broad bottom'd Hemispheres', etch, pub 1807, BM, NPG. J.GILLRAY, several political satires, BM.

PAYE, Richard Morton (d1821) painter.
P Self-portrait, painting by candlelight, Upton House (NT), Warwicks.
R R.DAGLEY, after R.M.Paye, hs, stipple, for *Library of the Fine Arts*, 1832, BM, NPG. UNKNOWN, hs, line, oval, NPG.

PAYNE, George (1781-1848) congregational divine.
PR FREEMAN, hs, stipple, pub 1822, NPG. J.COCHRAN, hl, stipple and line, NPG.

PAYNE, John Willett (1752-1803) rear-admiral.
P JOHN HOPPNER, c1795–1806, tql, Royal Coll; version, hl, Weston Park, Salop.
G BARTOLOZZI, LANDSEER, RYDER and STOW, after R.Smirke, 'Naval Victories', 'Commemoration of the victory of June 1st 1794', line, pub 1803, BM, NPG.
R ORME, jun, hs, stipple, oval, BM.

PAYNE, Roger (1739-1797) bookbinder.
R S.HARDING, wl putting book in a press, etch, BM.

PEABODY, George (1795-1869) philanthropist.
P H.W.PICKERSGILL, RA 1863, Corporation of London.
C W.W.STORY, bronze statue, Royal Exchange Buildings, London.
R T.L.ATKINSON, after H.W.Pickersgill, tql seated, mezz, pub 1869, NPG. J.C.BUTTRE, after a photograph by Brady, hs, line, NPG. D.J.POUND, after a photograph by H.N.King, tql, stipple and line, NPG.
H DISDERI, tql, carte, NPG 'Album of Photographs 1939'. UNKNOWN, hs, carte, NPG 'Cunnington Coll'.

PEACOCK, George (1791-1858) mathematician, dean of Ely.
P D.Y.BLAKISTON, tql seated, Royal Society, London.
PR UNKNOWN, hs profile, woodcut, BM.

PEACOCK, Thomas Love (1785-1866) novelist and poet.
P HENRY WALLIS, 1858, head, NPG 1432.
M ROGER JEAN, c1805, hs, NPG 3994.

PEARCE, Samuel (1766-1799) hymn-writer.
PR D.ORME, after S.Medley, hs, stipple, oval, pub 1800, NPG.

PEARMAN, William (fl 1810-1824) singer.
PR Several theatrical prints, BM, NPG.

PEARSALL, Robert Lucas de (1795-1856) composer.
P PHILIPPA S.HUGHES (his daughter), 1849, hs, NPG 1785.
D UNKNOWN, as a boy, w/c, Bristol Art Gallery.

PEARSON, Edward (1756-1811) controversialist.
PR W.C.EDWARDS, after W.M.Bennett, hl, line, BM, NPG.

PEARSON, George (1751-1828) physician and chemist.
D SIR FRANCIS CHANTREY, hs profile, pencil, NPG 316a (98).
PR J.S., hs, from a pen drawing, lith, pub 1829, BM, NPG. UNKNOWN, hs, silhouette, line, BM. UNKNOWN, hl, line, oval, NPG.

PEARSON, Sir Richard (1731-1806) naval captain, lieutenant governor of Greenwich Hospital.
P CHARLES GRIGNION, 1780, tql, NMM, Greenwich.
PR J.WATSON, after C.Grignion, tql, mezz, pub 1780, BM. H.R.COOK, hs, stipple, oval, for *Naval Chronicle*, 1810, BM, NPG.

PEARSON, Richard (1765-1836) physician and medical writer.
PR UNKNOWN, hl, stipple, for *Gentleman's Mag*, 1836, NPG. E.J.POSSELWHITE, after Miss Bracken, hl, stipple, BM.

PEARSON, William (1767-1847) astronomer.
P THOMAS PHILLIPS, tql demonstrating an orrery to his wife and daughter, Royal Astronomical Society, London.

PEASE, Edward (1767-1858) railway projector.
PR W.MILLER, hl, line, NPG.

PEASE, Joseph (1772-1846) reformer.
G B.R.HAYDON, 'The Anti-Slavery Society Convention, 1840', oil, NPG 599.

PEASE, Joseph (1799-1872) railway projector.
P H.J.WRIGHT, 1874, wl, Museum of British Transport, York.
G SIR GEORGE HAYTER, 'The House of Commons, 1833', oil, NPG 54.
PR T.L.ATKINSON, wl, mezz, NPG. UNKNOWN, hl seated, lith, presented with the *British Liberator*, BM.

PECKARD, Peter (1718?-1797) whig divine.
P RALPH, Magdalene College, Cambridge.

PECKWELL, Henry (1747-1787) divine.
PR R.HOUSTON, after J.Russell, tql seated, mezz, pub 1774, BM. J.FITTLER, after R.Bowyer, tql seated, line, pub 1787, BM, NPG. T.TROTTER, preaching in pulpit of Westminster Chapel, line, pub 1787, BM, NPG.

PEDDIE, James (1758-1845) presbyterian divine.
PR RIDLEY, after Branwhite, hs, stipple, oval, pub 1809, NPG. J.RAMAGE, after G.Watson, hl, line, NPG.
C J.KAY, three hl etchs, two dated 1791, one dated 1810, BM, NPG.

PEEL, Jonathan (1799-1879) general, politician and sportsman.
P SIR FRANCIS GRANT, wl seated, Huntingdon Town Hall.
PR S.W.REYNOLDS, after Wilson, hl, mezz, pub 1825, NPG. T.C.WILSON, wl profile, from a pen sketch, lith, for Wildrake's

Cracks of the Day, 1841, BM, NPG.

PEEL, Sir Robert, 1st Bart (1750-1830) manufacturer.
PR HOPWOOD, hs, stipple, pub 1815, NPG. W.DICKINSON, after J.Northcote, tql, seated, mezz, pub 1818, BM. H.ROBINSON, after T.Lawrence, tql seated, line, for Jerdan's *Nat Portrait Gallery*, 1834, BM, NPG.

PEEL, Sir Robert, 2nd Bart (1788-1850) statesman.
P JOHN LINNELL, 1838, tql seated, NPG 772. F.X.WINTERHALTER, c1844, wl with the Duke of Wellington, Royal Coll. H.W.PICKERSGILL, wl, NPG 3796; version, DoE (Home Office).
D SIR FRANCIS CHANTREY, c1833, 2 hs drgs, one in profile, NPG 316a (99).
G P.C.WONDER, c1826, wl, with David Wilkie and Lord Egremont, oil, NPG 795. SIR GEORGE HAYTER, 'The House of Commons, 1833', oil, NPG 54. SIR DAVID WILKIE, 'The Queen's First Council', oil, 1837, Royal Coll. F.X.WINTERHALTER, 'Queen Victoria Receiving Louis Philippe at Windsor Castle, 1844', oil, Musée de Versailles, France. JEMIMA WEDDERBURN, 1844, with Lord Brougham and others, pencil and w/c, NPG 2772. JOHN PARTRIDGE, 'The Fine Arts Commissioners, 1846', NPG 342, 3.
SC SIR FRANCIS CHANTREY, 1835, marble bust, Royal Coll. MATTHEW NOBLE, 1851, marble bust, NPG 596. E.H.BAILY, 1851, bronze statue, Bury, Lancs. JOHN GIBSON, 1852, statue, Westminster Abbey, London. M.NOBLE, 1852-4, marble statue, St George's Hall, Liverpool. M.NOBLE, 1876-77, bronze statue, Parliament Square, London.
C JOHN DOYLE, numerous political sketches, drgs, BM.

PEGGE, Sir Christopher (1765-1822) physician.
D THOMAS UWINS, wl, w/c and pencil, BM.
M ANDREW PLIMER, V & A.

PEGGE, Samuel (1704-1796) prebendary of Lincoln, antiquary.
PR J.BASIRE, after A.W.Devis, hl, aged 81, line, oval, for *Forme of Cury*, 1780, BM, NPG. P.AUDINET, after E.Needham, hl, line, pub 1818, NPG, for Nichols's *Literary Illustrations*, 1822, BM.

PEIRSON, Francis (1757-1781) soldier.
D JOHN SINGLETON COPLEY, c1783, wl, study for TATE 733, TATE 4984.
G JOHN SINGLETON COPLEY, 'The Death of Major Peirson, 6 January 1781', oil, TATE 733.
PR R.MARCUARD, after Hays, hs, stipple, oval, pub 1781, NPG.

PELHAM, George (1766-1827) bishop of Lincoln.
PR I.W.SLATER, after J.Slater, hl, lith, BM, NPG.

PELHAM, Thomas (1728-1805), see 1st Earl of Chichester.

PELHAM, Thomas (1756-1826), see 2nd Earl of Chichester.

PELL, Sir Watkin Owen (1788-1869) admiral.
P JOHN LUCAS, 1849-50, tql, NMM, Greenwich.

PELLATT, Apsley (1791-1863) glass-manufacturer.
PR UNKNOWN, hl, woodcut, NPG.

PELLEW, Sir Edward, see 1st Viscount Exmouth.

PELLY, Sir John Henry, 1st Bart (1777-1852) governor of the Hudson's Bay Company.
P H.P.BRIGGS, tql, Hudson's Bay Company, London.

PEMBERTON, Charles Reece (1790-1840) actor, writer and lecturer.
PR C.E.WAGSTAFF, after O.Oakley, tql seated, stipple, pub 1840, BM, NPG.

PEMBERTON, Christopher Robert (1765-1822) physician.
P After SIR THOMAS LAWRENCE (type of c1810), hl, Royal College of Physicians, London.

PEMBERTON (-LEIGH), Thomas, see Baron Kingsdown.

PEMBROKE, George Augustus Herbert, 11th Earl of (1759-1827) general.
P Portraits at Wilton House, Wilts: SIR JOSHUA REYNOLDS, c1764-7, tql with his mother; SIR JOSHUA REYNOLDS, c1765-7, wl with his father and a dog; DAVID MORIER, c1765-7, equestrian, with his father, a horse and dogs; POMPEO BATONI, 1779, hl, oval; WILLIAM OWEN, 1821, hs.
G DANIEL GARDNER, with 7th Viscount Fitzwilliam, playing chess, 2nd Earl of Onslow standing behind them, pastel, Clandon Park (NT), Surrey.
SC SIR RICHARD WESTMACOTT, 1827, relief bust on marble monument, Wilton Church, Wilts.

PEMBROKE, Henry Herbert, 10th Earl of (1734-1794) general.
P Portraits at Wilton House, Wilts: POMPEO BATONI, 1754, tql; SIR JOSHUA REYNOLDS, c1762, tql; DAVID MORIER, c1764-5, wl equestrian with groom and dogs; D.MORIER, c1764-5, wl with his son George, a horse, and dogs; SIR J.REYNOLDS, c1765-7, wl seated with his son George and a dog.
D WILLIAM HOARE, 1744, hs, chalk, Wilton House.
G DAVID MORIER, with his regiment, the Royal Dragoon Guards, oil, Wilton House; version, Royal Coll.

PENN, Granville (1761-1844) writer.
G C.TURNER, after J.Reynolds, 'Penn Family, 1764', as a child, mezz, pub 1819, BM.

PENN, John (1760-1834) writer, last proprietor of Pennsylvania.
G C.TURNER, after J.Reynolds, 'Penn Family, 1764', as a child, mezz, pub 1819, BM.
PR L.SCHIAVONETTI, after J.Deare, from a bust, stipple, pub 1802, BM, NPG. R.DUNKARTON, after W.Beechey, wl in uniform, mezz, pub 1809, BM.

PENN, Richard (1784-1863) humorist.
PR M.GAUCI, after E.U.Eddis, hs, lith, 1834, NPG.

PENN, Thomas (1702-1775) colonist.
PR D.MARTIN, after Davis, hl, mezz, BM.

PENNANT, Richard, see Baron Penrhyn.

PENNANT, Thomas (1726-1798) naturalist and topographer.
P By or after THOMAS GAINSBOROUGH, c1776, hl, National Museum of Wales 860.
SC UNKNOWN, Wedgwood medallion, Wedgwood Museum, Barlaston, Staffs.
PR UNKNOWN, hl, line, oval, BM, NPG. UNKNOWN, hl, etch, NPG.

PENNEFATHER, Edward (1774?-1847) chief justice of the Queen's bench.
PR UNKNOWN, hs, woodcut, for *Illust London News*, 1843-44, NPG.

PENNEFATHER, Richard (1773-1859) Irish judge.
PR J.H.LYNCH, after P.W.Burton, wl, lith, NPG.

PENNINGTON, Sir Isaac (1745-1817) physician.
P UNKNOWN, St John's College, Cambridge.
PR UNKNOWN, wl, stipple and line, NPG.

PENNINGTON, Sir John (1737-1813), see 1st Baron Muncaster.

PENNY, Edward (1714-1791) portrait and historical painter.
P Self-portrait, 1759, hl, Royal Academy, London.
G JOHAN ZOFFANY, 'Royal Academicians, 1772', oil, Royal Coll.

PENRHYN, Richard Pennant, Baron (1737?-1808) Whig

politician.

P Attrib SIR JOSHUA REYNOLDS, c1760, hs, Penrhyn Castle (NT), Gwynedd. HENRY THOMSON, wl, and GEORGE ROMNEY, tql seated, both Penrhyn Castle.

PENROSE, Sir Charles Vinicombe (1759-1830) Vice-admiral.

PR R.J.LANE, hs, lith, NPG. UNKNOWN, hl in uniform, lith, NPG.

PENROSE, John (1778-1859) divine.

R W.SHARP, hl, lith, NPG.

PENROSE, Thomas (1742-1779) poet.

PR W.BROMLEY, after N.Farrer, hl, line, for *Effigies Poeticae*, 1823, BM, NPG.

PENSHURST, Percy Clinton Sidney Smythe, 1st Baron (1780-1855) diplomatist and poet.

D COUNT A.D'ORSAY, 1841, hl profile, pencil, DoE.

M UNKNOWN, hs, Society of Antiquaries, London.

PR UNKNOWN, hs in uniform, stipple, BM. UNKNOWN, hs in plain coat, with orders, BM.

PEPYS, Sir Charles Christopher, see 1st Earl of Cottenham.

PEPYS, Henry (1783-1860) bishop of Worcester.

P UNKNOWN, hl, Hartlebury Castle, Worcs.

PEPYS, Sir Lucas, 1st Bart (1742-1830) physician.

PR J.GODBY, after H.Edridge, hl, stipple, for *Contemporary Portraits*, 1809, BM, NPG.

PEPYS, William Hasledine (1775-1856) scientific inventor.

PR UNKNOWN, after Walter, hl, lith, for *Athenaeum Portraits*, 1836, BM, NPG.

PERCEVAL, Alexander (1787-1858) serjeant-at-arms.

G SIR GEORGE HAYTER, 'The House of Commons, 1833', oil, NPG 54.

PR JENKINSON, hl, stipple, BM, NPG.

PERCEVAL, Sir John (1711-1770), see 2nd Earl of Egmont.

PERCEVAL, Spencer (1762-1812) prime-minister.

P Several portraits by G.F.JOSEPH, taken from a death mask by Nollekens: 1812, tql seated, NPG 1031; 1812, hl, Trinity College, Cambridge; 1816, hl, DoE (10 Downing St); hl seated, NPG 4.

SC JOSEPH NOLLEKENS, 1813, marble bust, Wellington Museum, Apsley House, London. NOLLEKENS, 1818, marble bust, Belton House, Lincs. SIR FRANCIS CHANTREY, 1818, statue, Northampton Town Hall. UNKNOWN, marble bust, NPG 1657.

PR UNKNOWN, hs, stipple, for *Trial between the Duke of York and Col Wardle*, 1809, BM, NPG. A.CARDON, after Miles, hs, stipple, oval, from a miniature, pub 1812, BM, NPG. GODBY and DUBOURG, wl seated, lith, pub 1812, NPG. W.SKELTON, after W.Beechey, hl seated, holding 'Regency Bill', line, pub 1813, BM, NPG.

PERCY, Sir Algernon (1792-1865), see 4th Duke of Northumberland.

PERCY, Sir Hugh (1715-1786), see 1st Duke of Northumberland.

PERCY, Sir Hugh (1742-1817), see 2nd Duke of Northumberland.

PERCY, Hugh (1784-1856) bishop of Rochester and Carlisle.

P THOMAS PHILLIPS, hl seated, Eton College, Berks. JOHN OPIE, hl, The Deanery, Canterbury.

PERCY, Sir Hugh (1785-1847), see 3rd Duke of Northumberland.

PERCY, Thomas (1729-1811) bishop of Dromore, editor of *Reliques of Ancient Poetry*.

P After SIR JOSHUA REYNOLDS, (1773), hl, Art Institute, Chicago,

USA.

G Attrib THOMAS ROBINSON, wl, a political group at the Bishop's Palace at Dromore, oil, c1801-08, Castle Ward (NT), Co Down, N.Ireland.

PR W.DICKINSON, after J.Reynolds, hl, mezz, pub 1775, BM, NPG. J.OGBORNE, after L.Abbott, tql seated, line and stipple, for Harding's *Biographical Mirrour*, 1802, BM, NPG. AUDINET, hl profile, line, NPG.

PERRIN, Louis (1782-1864) Irish judge.

SC CHRISTOPHER MOORE, 1843, marble bust, NGI 8108.

PERROTT, Sir Richard, 2nd Bart (d1796) soldier and diplomatist.

PR V.GREEN, hl, mezz, pub 1770, BM, NPG.

PERRY, George (1793-1862) musical composer.

PR J.ROMNEY, after J.A.Sluce, hl seated with sheet of music, line, pub 1837, BM.

PERRY, James (1756-1821) journalist.

D JOHN JACKSON, tql seated, pencil and w/c, BM.

PR J.THOMSON, after A.Wivell, hl, stipple, for *European Mag*, 1818, BM, NPG.

C RICHARD DIGHTON, wl, 'The Morning Chronicle', coloured etch, NPG.

PERRY, Sampson (1747-1823) surgeon and political writer.

PR MADDAN, after R.Cosway, hs, stipple, oval, BM, NPG.

PERRYN, Sir Richard (1723-1803) baron of the exchequer.

PR G.DUPONT, after Gainsborough, tql seated in robes, mezz, pub 1779, BM, NPG.

PERTH, James Drummond, 6th Earl and 3rd titular Duke of (1713-1746) Jacobite.

P After FRANCOIS DE TROY, wl in Scots dress, Floors Castle, Borders region, Scotland.

D JOHN SOBIESKI STUART, (copy), with Lord Seaforth, ink, SNPG 1662.

PERTH, John Drummond, 7th Earl and 4th titular Duke of (1714-1747) Jacobite.

P DOMENICO DUPRA, 1739, SNPG 1597.

PERY, Edmund Henry, see 1st Earl of Limerick.

PERY, Edmund Sexton, Viscount (1719-1806) Irish politician.

P GILBERT STUART, NGI 822.

G FRANCIS WHEATLEY, 'Entry of the speaker into the Irish House of Commons, 1782', w/c, NGI 2930. FRANCIS WHEATLEY, 'The Irish House of Commons, 1780', oil, Leeds City Art Galleries, Lotherton Hall, West Yorks.

SC J.C.F.ROSSI, 1807, marble bust, Trinity College, Dublin. WILLIAM MOSSOP, silver medal, National Museum of Ireland, Dublin.

PETER, 'The Wild Boy' (1712-1785) a protégé of George I.

PR J.SIMON, after W.Kent, hl, mezz, BM. V.GREEN, after P.Falconet, wl as an old man, mezz, BM, NPG.

PETERS, Matthew William (1742-1814) painter and chaplain to the Prince Regent.

D Self-portrait, 1758, hs profile, with Robert West, charcoal, NPG 2169.

PR W.LENEY, after M.W.Peters, hs, stipple, pub 1795, BM.

PETHER, William (1738?-1821) mezzotint engraver.

PR Self-portrait?, hl, mezz, BM.

PETIT, John Lewis (1736-1780) physician.

P JAMES LONSDALE, Queen's College, Cambridge.

PETRIE, George (1789-1866) artist and archaeologist.

P JOHN SLATTERY, 1857, Royal Irish Academy, Dublin. BERNARD MULRENIN, hs, oval, NGI 408.

M JAMES PETRIE, hs, as a young man, NGI.

SC Irish school, plaster death mask, NGI 8154.

PR J.KIRKWOOD, wl, etch, pub 1839, NPG.

PETTIGREW, Thomas Joseph (1791-1865) surgeon, antiquary and writer.

PR MISS TURNER, after E.U.Eddis, hs, aged 40, lith, BM, NPG. W. and F.HOLL, after H.Room, tql seated, stipple, for *Medical Portrait Gallery*, 1840, BM, NPG.

PETTY, Sir William, see 1st Marquess of Lansdowne.

PETTY-FITZMAURICE, Sir Henry, see 3rd Marquess of Lansdowne.

PHILIDOR, François André Danican (1726-1795) chessplayer and composer.

P UNKNOWN, Musée de Versailles, France.

PR A. ST AUBIN, after C.H.Cochin, 1772, hs, profile, line, oval, NPG.

PHILIP, Alexander Philip Wilson (1772-1851?) physician.

PR H.COOK, after Mrs Robinson, tql seated, stipple, for Pettigrew's *Medical Portrait Gallery*, 1839, BM.

PHILIP, John (1775-1851) missionary to South Africa.

G R.WOODMAN, after H.Room, wl in a group giving evidence to the House of Commons, line, pub 1844, NPG.

PR THOMPSON, after J.R.Wildman, hl, stipple, for *Evangelical Mag*, pub 1829, BM, NPG. UNKNOWN, hl, stipple, pub 1829, NPG.

PHILIP, Robert (1791-1858) divine.

PR R.WOODMAN, hs, stipple, pub 1828, NPG. BLOOD, after J.R.Wildman, hs, stipple, for *The Evangelical Mag*, 1832, NPG.

PHILIP(S), see PHILIPP(S), PHILLIP(S), and PHILLIPP(S).

PHILIPPS, Thomas (1774-1841) singer.

D SAMUEL DE WILDE, 1809, wl as Hartwell, Garrick Club, London.

PR T.L.BUSBY, after W.Foster, hl, stipple, BM.

PHILLIP, Arthur (1738-1814) vice-admiral, first governor of New South Wales.

P FRANCIS WHEATLEY, 1786, wl, NPG 1462. FRANCIS WHEATLEY, hl with map, Mitchell Library, Sydney, New South Wales, Australia.

PR W.SHERWIN, after F.Wheatley, hl, stipple, oval, pub 1789, NPG.

PHILLIPPS, Samuel March (1780-1862) legal writer.

PR F.C.LEWIS, after J.Slater, hs, profile, stipple, for 'Grillion's Club' series, BM, NPG.

PHILLIPPS, Sir Thomas, 1st Bart (1792-1872) antiquary and bibliophile.

D SIR HENRY DRYDEN, 1853, 2 hs profile, w/c, NPG 3094.

PHILLIPS, Charles (1787?-1859) barrister and writer.

PR H.MEYER, after S.Drummond, hs, stipple, for *European Mag*, 1816, BM, NPG. S.WATTS, after W.Yellowlees, hs, line, pub 1819, BM, NPG. T.WOOLNOTH, after T.Wageman, tql, stipple, pub 1821, BM. R.NEWTON, after W.T.Newton, hl in toga, line, pub 1827, NPG.

PHILLIPS, Molesworth (1755-1832) soldier.

D WILLIAM BROCKEDON, 1825, hs, pencil and chalk, NPG 2515 (4).

G G.NOBLE and J.PARKER, after J.Smart, 'Naval Victories', 'Commemoration of 11th Oct 1797', line, pub 1803, BM, NPG.

PR A.GEDDES, tql, etch, BM.

PHILLIPS, Sir Richard (1767-1840) author, bookseller and publisher.

P JAMES SAXON, 1806, hl, NPG 944.

PHILLIPS, Richard (1778-1851) chemist.

PR UNKNOWN, after a daguerreotype by Claudet, hl woodcut, NPG.

PHILLIPS, Teresia Constantia (1709-1765) courtesan.

PR J.FABER, jun, after J.Highmore, tql with date 1748, mezz, BM, NPG.

PHILLIPS, Thomas (1760-1851) surgeon and benefactor.

P UNKNOWN, St David's University College, Lampeter.

PHILLIPS, Thomas (1770-1845) portrait-painter.

P Self-portrait, 1802, hs, NPG 1601. Self-portrait, c1830, hl, oval, Royal Academy, London.

D WILLIAM BROCKEDON, 1834, hs, pencil and chalk, NPG 2515 (70).

M WILLIAM SHERLOCK, 1795, V & A.

SC SIR FRANCIS CHANTREY, c1821, original model for bust, Ashmolean Museum, Oxford.

PR T.LUPTON, after T.Phillips of c1844, hl, mezz, pub 1845, BM, NPG. MRS D.TURNER, after T.Phillips, hs, etch, BM, NPG.

PHILLIPS, William (1731?-1781) major-general of the royal artillery.

SC UNKNOWN, called Phillips, Wedgwood medallion, BM.

PHILLPOTTS, Henry (1778-1869) bishop of Exeter.

P JOHN PRESCOTT KNIGHT, RA 1852, tql, Magdalen College, Oxford. T.A.WOOLNOTH, tql, The Bishop's Palace, Exeter. HASTINGS, tql, University College, Durham. UNKNOWN, tql, Corpus Christi College, Oxford.

M ANDREW ROBERTSON, 1841, hs, Ashmolean Museum, Oxford.

C JOHN DOYLE, chalk, BM.

PH UNKNOWN, wl seated, carte, NPG 'Twist Album'. Attrib MAULL and POLYBLANK, wl seated, NPG.

PHIPPS, Sir Constantine Henry, see 1st Marquess of Normanby.

PHIPPS, Constantine John, see 2nd Baron Mulgrave.

PHIPPS, Edmund (1760-1837) general.

D COUNT A.D'ORSAY, 1832, hl profile, NPG 4026 (44).

M RICHARD COSWAY, hs?, V & A.

G W.J.WARD, after J.Jackson, wl with Lord Mulgrave, Sir G.Beaumont and A.Phipps, mezz, BM, NPG.

PR C.TURNER, after J.Jackson, hl in uniform, mezz, pub 1824, BM. A.D'ORSAY, hl, profile, lith, BM.

C SIR EDWIN LANDSEER, c1835, tql, pen and wash, NPG 4918.

PHIPPS, Sir Henry, see 1st Earl of Mulgrave.

PICKERSGILL, Henry William (1782-1875) painter.

D CARL VOGEL, 1837, hs, Staatliche Kunstsammlungen, Dresden. C.H.LEAR, 1848, head, pencil, NPG 1456 (23). C.W.COPE, c1862, head, sketch, NPG 3182 (9).

C SIR EDWIN LANDSEER, tql, pen and ink, NPG 3097 (1).

PH MAULL and POLYBLANK, wl, carte, NPG, 'Album of Photographs 1949'. UNKNOWN, carte, NPG 'Album of Artists', vol III.

PICTON, Sir Thomas (1758-1815) general.

P SIR MARTIN ARCHER SHEE, hl, NPG 126. SIR WILLIAM BEECHEY, 1815, hl with Bath star, Wellington Museum, Apsley House, London.

SC SEBASTIAN GAHAGAN, 1816, marble bust on monument, St Paul's Cathedral, London.

PR W.DANIELL, after G.Dance, hs, profile, soft-ground etch, pub 1809, BM, NPG. UNKNOWN, wl equestrian, line, for Kelly's *Hist of the French Revolution*, 1815, BM, NPG.

PIERCE, Samuel Eyles (1746-1829) Calvinist divine.

PR W.GOUL, after W.Irving, tql, stipple, NPG.

PIGOT, David Richard (1797-1873) chief baron of the exchequer.

PR FRANK REYNOLDS, King's Inns, Dublin.

PIGOT, Sir George Pigot, Baron (1719-1777) governor of Madras.
P GEORGE WILLISON, 1777, hs, NPG 3837.
PR B.GREEN, after G.Stubbs, wl on horseback, mezz, pub 1769, BM, NPG. SCAWEN, after Powell, hl, mezz, oval, BM, NPG.

PIKE, John Deodatus Gregory (1784-1854) baptist minister.
PR W.HOLL, after James, tql seated, stipple, BM, NPG.

PIKE, Samuel (1717?-1773) independent minister.
PR J.HOPWOOD, after an unknown artist, hl, stipple, pub 1809, NPG.

PILKINGTON, Laetitia, née Van Lewen (1712-1750) adventuress.
PR R.PURCELL, after N.Hone, hl, mezz, oval, for *Story of John Carteret Pilkington*, 1760, BM, NPG. UNKNOWN, hl, mezz, for her *Memoirs*, BM.

PILKINGTON, Mary, née Hopkins (1766-1839) writer.
PR J.HOPWOOD, after J.Slater, hl seated, stipple, for *Lady's Monthly Museum*, 1812, BM, NPG.

PILLANS, James (1778-1864) educational reformer.
D UNKNOWN, ink and pencil, SNPG 2268.
PR C.TURNER, after H.Raeburn, tql seated, mezz, pub 1823, BM. T.WOOLNOTH, after Warren, hl, stipple, BM, pub 1829, NPG.

PINCHBECK, Christopher (1710?-1783) mechanician and inventor.
PR W.HUMPHREY, after Cunningham, hl, mezz, oval, pub 1783, BM.

PINCKARD, George (1768-1835) physician.
P UNKNOWN, hl seated, St Giles-in-the-Fields, London.

PINDAR, Peter, see John Wolcot.

PINKERTON, John (1758-1826) antiquary and historian.
SC JAMES TASSIE, 1798, paste medallion, SNPG 2237.
PR W.N.GARDINER, after S.Harding, hl seated, stipple, for *Hist of Scotland*, 1796, BM, NPG. RIDLEY, HALL and BLOOD, hl, stipple, oval, for *European Mag*, 1807, BM, NPG.

PINNOCK, William (1782-1843) publisher and educational writer.
PR W.H.MOTE, after W.Beard, tql, stipple and line, pub 1844, NPG.

PINTO, George Frederic (1787-1806) violinist and musical composer.
PR A.R.BURT, after Robertson, hs, stipple, pub 1806, NPG.

PINTO, Thomas (1710?-1773) violinist.
PR P.REINAGLE, hl, mezz, oval, pub 1777, BM.

PIOZZI, Gabriel (1741-1809) musician, married Mrs Thrale.
D GEORGE DANCE, 1793, hs profile, pencil, NPG 1152.

PIOZZI, Hester Lynch (1741-1821) (Mrs Thrale) writer and friend of Dr Johnson.
P WILLIAM HOGARTH, c1758-9, (called Mrs Thrale), 'The Lady's Last Stake', wl, Buffalo Fine Arts Academy, USA. SIR JOSHUA REYNOLDS, 1777-8, wl with her daughter Helena, Beaverbrook Art Gallery, Fredericton, Canada. Italian School, c1785, hl, NPG 4942.
D GEORGE DANCE, 1793, hs profile, pencil, NPG 1151.
M UNKNOWN, 1811, hl, Johnson Birthplace Museum, Lichfield. S.T.ROCHE, 1817, hl, National Museum of Wales, Cardiff.
PR T.HOLLOWAY, as after J.Reynolds (but in fact by R.E.Pine), hl, line, oval, for *European Mag*, 1786, BM, NPG. H.MEYER, after J.Jackson, tql seated wearing hat and cloak, stipple, for *Contemporary Portraits*, 1811, BM, NPG.
C JAMES SAYER, 'The Biographers', hl with Boswell and Courtenay, etch, pub 1786, NPG. JAMES SAYERS, wl seated with Johnson's Ghost, for the 2nd edition of Dr Johnson's *Letters*, etch,

pub 1788, NPG.

PISTRUCCI, Benedetto (1784-1855) gem-engraver.
SC UNKNOWN, hs, shell cameo, V & A.

PITCAIRN, David (1749-1809) physician.
P JOHN HOPPNER, c1800, hl, Royal College of Physicians, London.
M H.P.BONE, c1809, after J.Hoppner, Royal College of Physicians.

PITCAIRN, Robert (1793-1855) lawyer and antiquary.
M UNKNOWN, SNPG 1242.

PITCAIRN, William (1711-1791) physician.
P SIR JOSHUA REYNOLDS, RA 1777, hl with gown, Royal College of Physicians, London; copy, c1850, St Bartholomew's Hospital, London.
G THOMAS ROWLANDSON, 'The Dissecting Room', drg, Royal College of Physicians.

PITT, Ann (1720?-1799) actress.
P UNKNOWN, wl, Garrick Club, London.
PR WALKER, after D.Dodd, wl as Lady Wishfor't in Congreve's *Way of the World*, line, for Lowndes's *New English Theatre*, 1776, BM.

PITT, George (1722?-1803), see 1st Baron Rivers.

PITT, Sir John, see 2nd Earl of Chatham.

PITT, Thomas (1737-1793), see 1st Baron Camelford.

PITT, Thomas (1775-1804), see 2nd Baron Camelford.

PITT, William (1708-1778), see 1st Earl of Chatham.

PITT, William (1759-1806) statesman.
P By or after THOMAS GAINSBOROUGH, 1788, tql, Lincoln's Inn, London; versions or copies, Kenwood House, London; Burrell Collection, Glasgow. GAINSBOROUGH DUPONT, 1796, wl, Trinity House, London. JOHN HOPPNER, 1805, tql, Merchant Taylor's Hall, London; versions, NPG 697; Trinity College, Cambridge; Inner Temple, London. SIR THOMAS LAWRENCE, RA 1808, tql, Royal Coll.
D HENRY EDRIDGE, c1800, wl seated, pencil, BM.
G JOHN SINGLETON COPLEY, 'The Collapse of the Earl of Chatham in the House of Lords, 7 July 1778', oil, TATE 100, on loan to NPG. K.A.HICKEL, 'The House of Commons, 1793', oil, NPG 745.
SC Attrib JOHN FLAXMAN, jun, c1787, Wedgwood medallion, Wedgwood Museum, Barlaston, Staffs. Numerous busts by JOSEPH NOLLEKENS, taken from a death mask; 1806, Fitzwilliam Museum, Cambridge; 1807, Royal Coll; 1810, Belton House, Lincs; NPG 120. J.NOLLEKENS, 1812, marble statue, Senate House, Cambridge. RICHARD WESTMACOTT, 1813, statue, Westminster Abbey, London. SIR FRANCIS CHANTREY, 1831, bronze statue, Hanover Square, London.
C Numerous political caricatures and satires, by JAMES GILLRAY, JAMES SAYERS, and others, BM, NPG.

PLACE, Francis (1771-1854) political and social reformer.
P SAMUEL DRUMMOND, 1833, hl seated, NPG 1959.
D DANIEL MACLISE, original drg for 'Gallery of Illustrious Literary Characters', *Fraser's Magazine*, V & A.
G S.BELLIN, after J.R.Herbert, 'The Anti-Corn Law League', mixed engr, pub 1850, BM, NPG.
PR D.MACLISE, wl, lith, for *Fraser's Mag*, NPG. WALKER and BOUTALL, after G.P.Healy (1843), hs, photogravure, NPG.

PLAMPIN, Robert (1762-1834) vice-admiral.
M ADAM BUCK, 1803, hs, NGI.

PLANCHÉ, James Robinson (1796-1880) dramatist.
P H.P.BRIGGS, RA 1835, tql, Garrick Club, London.
PR BUTTERWORTH and HEATH, after Portch, hs, wood engr, oval,

for *The Critic*, 1859, NPG.

PLANTA, Joseph (1744-1827) librarian.
D GEORGE DANCE, 1794, hs profile, pencil, BM. WILLIAM SHARP, after Benedetto Pistrucci, head, profile, from a medallion, sepia, BM.
G A.ARCHER, 'The Temporary Elgin Room', oil, 1819, BM.
PR C.PICART, after H.Edridge, tql seated, stipple, for *Contemporary Portraits*, 1812, BM, NPG. H.HUDSON, after F.Engleheart, hl, mezz, oval, BM.

PLANTA, Joseph (1787-1847) under-secretary of state.
PR S.W.REYNOLDS, after T.Phillips, hl, mezz, pub 1835, BM, NPG. R.J.LANE, after J.Salter, hs, lith, for 'Grillion's Club' series, BM, NPG.

PLAYFAIR, Sir Hugh Lyon (1786-1861) Indian officer and provost of St Andrews.
P JAMES WILSON, tql, Royal and Ancient Golf Club, St Andrews, Scotland.
PR UNKNOWN, after a photograph, hs, woodcut, for *Illust London News*, 1861, NPG.

PLAYFAIR, John (1748-1819) mathematician and geologist.
P SIR HENRY RAEBURN, tql, NPG 840; version, Edinburgh University.
D WILLIAM NICHOLSON, hs, pencil, SNPG 1688. WILLIAM NICHOLSON, hl, pencil and w/c, SNPG L44.
G J.F.SKILL, J.GILBERT, W. and E.WALKER, 'Men of Science Living in 1807-08', pencil and wash, NPG 1075.
SC SIR FRANCIS CHANTREY, plaster bust, SNPG 244. SIR F.CHANTREY, *c*1814, original model for bust, Ashmolean Museum, Oxford.

PLAYFAIR, William Henry (1789-1857) architect.
PR J.T.SMYTH, after J.W.Gordon, hs, stipple, BM, NPG.

PLEASANTS, Thomas (1728-1818) philanthropist.
P SOLOMON WILLIAMS, Royal Dublin Society, Dublin.

PLEYDELL-Bouverie, William, see 3rd Earl of Radnor.

PLIMER, Andrew (1763-1837) miniature-painter.
P ANDREW GEDDES, 1815, tql seated, NGS 847.

PLIMER, Nathaniel (1751-1822) miniature painter.
PR A.GEDDES, head, 'Give the Devil his due', drypoint, BM.

PLOWDEN, Francis Peter (1749-1829) writer.
PR W.BOND, after S.Woodforde, hl, stipple, for his *Review of the State of Ireland*, 1803, BM, NPG. KING, after R.Cosway, hs, stipple, BM, NPG.

PLUMER, Sir Thomas (1753-1824) master of the rolls.
P SIR THOMAS LAWRENCE, *c*1810, hl in robes, Lincoln's Inn, London; version, University College, Oxford. UNKNOWN, Harvard University Law School, Cambridge, USA.

PLUMPTRE, Anna or Anne (1760-1818) author.
PR H.MEYER, after J.Northcote, hl, stipple, pub 1817, NPG. UNKNOWN, hs, stipple, oval, for *The Lady's Monthly Museum*, 1817, BM.

PLUMPTRE, John (1753-1825) dean of Gloucester.
PR W.SAY, after H.Pickersgill, hl, mezz, pub 1821, BM, NPG.

PLUMPTRE, Robert (1723-1788) president of Queen's College, Cambridge.
P Attrib CHRISTOPHER SHARP, Queen's College, Cambridge.

PLUMRIDGE, Sir James Hanway (1787-1863) vice-admiral.
G M.ALOPHE, 'Les Défenseurs du Droit et de la Liberté de l'Europe', lith, pub 1854, BM.
PR UNKNOWN, hs, woodcut, for *Illust London News*, 1854, NPG.

PLUNKET, William Conyngham Plunket, 1st Baron (1764-1854) lord chancellor of Ireland.
P MARTIN CREGAN, King's Inns, Dublin.
SC CHRISTOPHER MOORE, 1841, marble sculpture, NGI 8066; 1841, plaster bust, NGI 8187.
PR J.HEATH, after H.D.Hamilton, hs, stipple, for Sir J.Barrington's *Historic Memoirs*, BM, NPG. J.KIRKWOOD, after C.Grey, hl, lith, pub 1840, NPG. D.LUCAS, after R.Rothwell, tql seated, mixed, pub 1844, BM.

PLUNKETT, Elizabeth, née Gunning (1769-1823) novelist.
PR F.BARTOLOZZI, after R.Saunders, hl, stipple, oval, for *Memoirs of Mad de Barneveldt*, 1796, BM.

POCOCK, Sir George (1706-1792) admiral.
P After THOMAS HUDSON, (type *c*1761), hs, NPG 1787.
SC PETER SCHEEMAKERS, 1764, marble statue, India Office, London. JOHN BACON, sen, 1792, medallion on monument, Westminster Abbey, London.

POCOCK, Nicholas (1741?-1821) marine painter.
PR E.SCRIVEN, after I.Pocock, hl, stipple, BM, NPG.

POLE, Sir Charles Morice (1757-1830) admiral.
P Attrib GILBERT STUART, hl, Saltram House (NT), Devon.
D Attrib MATHER BROWN, chalk, SNPG 2242.
PR W.RIDLEY, after J.Northcote, hl, stipple, oval, for *European Mag*, 1805, BM, NPG. C.TURNER, after W.Beechey, hl, mezz, for Brenton's *Naval History*, 1823, BM, NPG.

POLE, William Wellesley, see 3rd Earl of Mornington.

POLIDORI, John William (1795-1821) physician and author.
P F.G.GAINSFORD, hl, NPG 991.

POLKEMMET, William Baillie, Lord (*d*1816) Scottish judge.
C J.KAY, hl, etch, oval, 1789, BM, 1799, NPG. J.KAY, 'Last Sitting of the Old Court of Session', etch, 1808, NPG.

POLLARD, Robert (1755-1838) painter and engraver.
P RICHARD SAMUEL, 1784, tql, NPG 1020.

POLLOCK, Sir George, 1st Bart (1786-1872) field-marshal.
P SIR FRANCIS GRANT, 1856, India Office, London. SAMUEL LANE, RA 1848, wl, Oriental Club, London. H.VALDA, *c*1867, hl, Royal Artillery Institution, London.
D MISS BEADELL, 1870, Victoria Memorial Hall, Calcutta, India. COLONEL L.G.FAWKES, 1872, hl, pencil, NPG 2459.
SC JOSEPH DURHAM, 1870, marble bust, NPG 364.

POLLOCK, Sir Jonathan Frederick, 1st Bart (1783-1870) judge.
P SAMUEL LAURENCE, *c*1842, tql, NPG 758 (on loan to Law Courts). SIR FRANCIS GRANT, 1848, wl, Corporation of Huntingdon.
D SAMUEL LAURENCE, 1863, head, profile, NPG 732.
G SIR GEORGE HAYTER, 'The House of Commons, 1833', oil, NPG 54.
SC WILLIAM BEHNES, 1842, bust, Inner Temple, London. THOMAS WOOLNER, *c*1870, bust, Inner Temple.
PR H.ROBINSON, after T.Phillips, hl, stipple, for *Eminent Conservative Statesmen*, 1838, BM, NPG.
C A.THOMPSON, wl, lith, for *Vanity Fair*, 2 April 1870, NPG.
PH JOHN and CHARLES WATKINS, hs, carte, NPG.

POLLOK, Robert (1798-1827) poet.
D SIR DANIEL MACNEE, hs, chalk, SNPG 293.
SL UNKNOWN, SNPG 1231.

POLWHELE, Richard (1760-1838) miscellaneous writer.
PR UNKNOWN, hs, line, oval, for *European Mag*, 1795, BM, NPG.

P.AUDINET, after J.Opie, hs, line, for Nichols's *Illustrations of Literature*, 1816, BM.

POMFRET, Henrietta Louisa Fermor, née Jeffreys (1703-1761) letter-writer.

P THOMAS BARDWELL, wl with her husband, 1st Earl of Pomfret, Ashmolean Museum, Oxford.

SC UNKNOWN, marble bust, Ashmolean Museum.

R C.WATSON, hl, stipple, oval, from *Correspondence with the Countess of Hertford*, 1805, BM.

POMFRET, Thomas William Fermor, 4th Earl of (1770-1833) general.

R M.GAUCI, after Mrs Ansley, hl in uniform, lith, BM.

POND, Arthur (1705?-1758) painter and engraver.

R A.POND, hl, etch, BM.

PONSONBY, Caroline, see Lady Caroline Lamb.

PONSONBY, Sir Frederic Cavendish (1783-1837) major-general.

P J.W.PIENEMAN, hs, Wellington Museum, Apsley House, London. Attrib THOMAS HEAPHY, c1819, wl, Royal Lancers Officers' Mess, Market Harborough.

D THOMAS HEAPHY, hs, w/c, NPG 1914 (10).

SC UNKNOWN, marble bust, Wellington Museum.

PONSONBY, George (1755-1817) lord chancellor of Ireland.

R J.GODBY, after A.Pope, hl seated, stipple, for *Contemporary Portraits*, 1811, BM, NPG.

PONSONBY, John (1713-1787) speaker of the Irish House of Commons.

P By or after GEORGE KNAPTON, hs, oval, Hardwick Hall (NT), Derbyshire. Attrib GEORGE GAVEN, tql, NGI 399.

PONSONBY, Sir John Ponsonby, Viscount and 2nd Baron (1770?-1855) ambassador.

D J.F.LEWIS, tql seated, w/c, DoE (British Embassy, Vienna).

C JOHN DOYLE, wl equestrian, 'The New Pasha of Egypt', pencil, BM.

PONSONBY, John William, see 4th Earl of Bessborough.

PONSONBY, Sarah (1755?-1831) one of the 'Ladies of Llangollen'.

R R.J.LANE, after Lady Leighton, with Lady Eleanor Butler, hl seated, lith, BM; related lith, NPG. J.H.LYNCH, wl in walking dress, with Lady Eleanor Butler, lith, NPG.

PONSONBY, William (1704-1793), see 2nd Earl of Bessborough.

PONSONBY, Sir William (1772-1815) major-general.

R G.MAILE, hl in uniform, stipple, pub 1817, BM.

PONSONBY, William Brabazon Ponsonby, 1st Baron (1744-1806) politician.

P SIR THOMAS LAWRENCE, c1805, tql, Leicester Museum and Art Gallery.

POOLE, John (1786?-1872) dramatist.

P H.W.PICKERSGILL, c1826, hs, NPG 3807.

D WILLIAM BROCKEDON, 1830, hs, chalk, NPG 2515 (25).

POOLE, Robert (1708-1752) physician and philanthropist.

R J.FABER, jun, after A.Armstrong, hl mezz, oval, for *Journey from London to France*, 1750, BM.

POPE, Alexander (1763-1835) actor and miniature painter.

P GAINSBOROUGH DUPONT, hl as Hamlet in Vandyck dress, Garrick Club, London. M.W.SHARP, wl as Henry VIII, Garrick Club. SIR MARTIN ARCHER SHEE, wl, Garrick Club.

G MATHER BROWN, a scene from *The Gamester*, oil, RA 1787, Garrick Club.

PR Various theatrical prints, BM, NPG.

POPE, Clara Maria, née Leigh (d1838) artist.

PR R.STANIER, after F.Wheatley, tql reclining, stipple, oval, pub 1788, BM.

POPE, Elizabeth, née Younge (1740-1797) actress.

P GAINSBOROUGH DUPONT, 1793-4, hs, as Queen Katharine in Henry VIII, Garrick Club, London.

D JAMES ROBERTS, several drgs, in character, BM.

G MATHER BROWN, a scene from *The Gamester*, oil, RA 1787, Garrick Club.

PR Various theatrical prints, BM, NPG.

POPE, Jane (1742-1818) actress.

P JAMES ROBERTS, wl as Mrs Page in *The Merry Wives of Windsor*, Garrick Club, London.

D JAMES ROBERTS, four drgs in character, BM.

PR R.LAURIE, after R.Dighton, hl, mezz, oval, pub 1780, BM, NPG. P.ROBERTS, after A.Buck, wl with her sister and niece, coloured stipple, BM. Theatrical prints, BM, NPG.

POPE, Maria Ann, née Campion (1775-1803) actress, 2nd wife of Alexander Pope, the actor.

P SIR MARTIN ARCHER SHEE, c1803, tql as Juliet, Garrick Club, London.

PR W.RIDLEY, after A.Pope, hs, stipple, oval, for *Monthly Mirror*, 1798, BM, NPG.

POPHAM, Sir Home Riggs (1762-1820) rear-admiral.

P MATHER BROWN, wl, NPG 811.

PR J.HOPWOOD, after Hastings, hs, stipple, oval, BM, NPG.

POPHAM, William (d1821) lieutenant-general.

P SIR MARTIN ARCHER SHEE, tql, NPG 812.

PORSON, Richard (1759-1808) Greek scholar.

P JOHN HOPPNER, 1796, Old Schools, Cambridge. THOMAS KIRKBY, tql, Trinity College, Cambridge. J.BROOKS, 1844, after J.Opie, c1796, hs, Trinity College.

M GEORGE ENGLEHEART, hs, Trinity College.

SC SIR FRANCIS CHANTREY, 1808, marble bust, Trinity College. By or after G.D.GIANELLI, 1808, plaster bust, Classical Faculty Board Library, Cambridge. G.D.GIANELLI, bust, Eton College, Berks. WILLIAM BEHNES, marble bust, Eton College. G.D.GIANELLI, plaster bust from a death mask, NPG 673.

PORTEOUS, Beilby, see Porteus.

PORTER, Anna Maria (1780-1832) novelist.

D G.H.HARLOW, hl, pencil, NPG 1109.

PR J.THOMSON, after G.H.Harlow, hl with guitar, stipple, pub 1823, NPG.

PORTER, Jane (1776-1850) novelist.

D G.H.HARLOW, hl, pencil, NPG 1108.

SL AUGUSTE EDOUART, SNPG 824.

PR S.FREEMAN, after G.H.Harlow, hl, stipple, pub 1811, BM, NPG. UNKNOWN, wl in landscape, stipple, BM, NPG.

PORTER, Sir Robert Ker (1777-1842) painter and traveller.

SL AUGUSTE EDOUART, SNPG 824.

PR A.CARDON, after J.Wright, hs, stipple, oval, pub 1806, BM. T.WOOLNOTH, after G.H.Harlow, wl in Russian uniform, stipple, for *Ladies' Monthly Museum*, 1822, BM, NPG.

PORTEUS, Beilby (1731-1808) bishop of London.

P Attrib JOHN HOPPNER, 1787, tql seated, Fulham Palace, London. I.POCOCK, 1807, tql, Bishop's House, Chester.

D ADAM BUCK, wl, chalk and w/c, NPG 735.

PORTLAND, William Henry Cavendish Bentinck, 3rd Duke of (1738-1809) prime-minister.

P SIR THOMAS LAWRENCE, 1792, wl in robes, Bristol Corporation. GEORGE ROMNEY, c1794–7, wl, Christ Church, Oxford. BENJAMIN WEST, 1814, wl seated in Chancellor's robes, Examination Schools, Oxford. MATTHEW PRATT, hl, National Gallery of Art, Washington DC, USA.

D JOHN SINGLETON COPLEY, hs, Metropolitan Museum of Art, New York, USA.

G JOHN SINGLETON COPLEY, 'The Collapse of the Earl of Chatham in the House of Lords, 7 July 1778', oil, TATE 100, on loan to NPG.

PR J.R.SMITH, after B.West, wl in peer's robes with his brother, mezz, pub 1774, BM, NPG. J.MURPHY, after J.Reynolds, tql seated, mezz, pub 1785, BM, NPG.

C JAMES SAYERS, wl, 'Razors' Levée', etch, pub 1783, NPG. Several political satires, BM, NPG.

PORTLOCK, Nathaniel (1747-1817) captain in the navy.

P UNKNOWN, c1788, hl, NMM, Greenwich.

PR MAZELL, after Dodd, hs, line, oval, pub 1789, NPG.

PORTMAN, Edward Berkeley Portman, 1st Viscount (1799-1888) politician.

G SIR GEORGE HAYTER, 'The House of Commons, 1833', NPG 54.

PR S.W.REYNOLDS, jun, after R.Ansdell, wl, mezz, pub 1846, BM. UNKNOWN, after a photograph by John and Charles Watkins, hl, woodcut, for *Illust London News*, 1862, NPG.

C UNKNOWN, wl, 'A view in Portman Square', coloured etch, pub 1823, NPG.

POST, Jacob (1774-1855) quaker.

G BENJAMIN ROBERT HAYDON, 'The Anti-Slavery Society Convention, 1840', oil, NPG 599.

POSTLETHWAITE, Thomas (1731-1798) master of Trinity College, Cambridge.

P After D.P.MURPHY, hs, oval, Trinity College, Cambridge.

POTT, Joseph Holden (1759-1847) archdeacon and author.

PR J.PORTER, after W.Owen, tql seated, mezz, pub 1843, BM, NPG.

POTT, Percival (1714-1788) surgeon.

P SIR JOSHUA REYNOLDS, RA 1784, tql seated, St Bartholomew's Hospital, London. GEORGE ROMNEY, c1781–6, hl, Royal College of Surgeons, London. NATHANIEL DANCE, hl, Royal College of Surgeons.

SC PETER HOLLINS, marble bust, Royal College of Surgeons.

POTTER, Richard (1778-1842) politician.

G SIR GEORGE HAYTER, 'The House of Commons, 1833', oil, NPG 54.

PR S.W.REYNOLDS, tql seated, mezz, BM, NPG.

POTTER, Robert (1721-1804) poet and politician.

PR MRS D.TURNER, after A.Payne, head, etch, BM, NPG.

POTTINGER, Sir Henry, 1st Bart (1789-1856) soldier and diplomatist.

P SIR FRANCIS GRANT, 1845, wl, DoE (Foreign Office, London); version, Oriental Club, London.

PR L.DICKINSON, after S.Laurence, hs, lith, BM, NPG.

POUNDS, John (1766-1839) teacher and friend of poor children.

PR H.ANELAY, wl with a group of children, woodcut, NPG.

POWELL, Foster (1734-1793) established records for long distance walking.

PR UNKNOWN, wl, etch, pub 1771, NPG. S.HARDING, wl, etch, pub 1786, BM. UNKNOWN, hl, oval, etch, NPG.

POWELL, Richard (1767-1834) physician.

P UNKNOWN, as an older man, St Bartholomew's Hospital, London.

PR J.JENKINS, after J.Lonsdale, hl, stipple, pub 1839, BM, NPG.

POWELL, William (1735-1769) actor.

P R.PYLE, tql, Garrick Club, London.

M UNKNOWN, hs in character, Garrick Club.

G BENJAMIN WILSON, wl with his wife and daughters, Garric Club. J.H.MORTIMER, wl in a scene from *King John*, Garric Club, London.

PR Theatrical prints, BM, NPG.

POWELL, Mrs (d1831) actress.

P SAMUEL DE WILDE, three paintings in character, Garrick Clu London: wl as Boadicea; wl in male dress as Douglas; wl as Mar Queen of Scots in *The Albion Queens*.

D S. DE WILDE, 1808, as Adelgitha, w/c, Garrick Club.

PR Theatrical prints, BM, NPG.

POWER, Marguerite, see Countess of Blessington.

POWER, Tyrone (1797-1841) Irish actor.

PR C.TURNER, after J.Simpson, hl, mezz, pub 1833, B A.D'ORSAY, hl, lith, BM, NPG. Theatrical prints, BM, NPG.

POWIS, Edward Clive, 1st Earl of (1754-1839) governor Madras.

P THOMAS GAINSBOROUGH, early 1760s, wl, Powis Castle (N Powys. WILLIAM HOARE, hs, Eton College, Berks.

POWIS, Edward Herbert, 2nd Earl of (1785-1848) To politician.

P SIR THOMAS LAWRENCE, c1803, Eton College, Berks. S FRANCIS GRANT, 1843, tql, Powis Castle (NT), Powys. S F.GRANT, 1848, wl, Powis Castle.

D ANNA TONELLI, 1794, hs, pastel, Powis Castle.

G SIR GEORGE HAYTER, 'The House of Commons, 1833', oil, N 54.

SC EDWARD RICHARDSON, 1856, bust, Powis Castle. EDWAR RICHARDSON, recumbent effigy, St Mary's Church, Welshpo

PR F.C.LEWIS, after J.Slater, hs, stipple, for 'Grillion's Club' seri BM, NPG.

POWLETT, Thomas Orde-, see 1st Baron Bolton.

POYNTER, William (1762-1827) Roman catholic bisho

PR H.MEYER, after J.Ramsay, hl, stipple, pub 1818, B UNKNOWN, hs, stipple, NPG.

PRATT, Sir Charles (1714-1794), see 1st Earl and 1st Bar Camden.

PRATT, Sir John Jeffreys, see 2nd Earl and 1st Marquess Camden.

PRATT, John Tidd (1797-1870) registrar of friendly societi

PR C.BAUGNIET, hl, lith, BM, NPG.

PRATT, Josiah (1768-1844) evangelical divine.

PR S.W.REYNOLDS, after H.Wyatt, hl seated, mezz, pub 1826, B NPG. H.TURNER, after E.U.Eddis, hl, lith, BM.

PRATT, Samuel Jackson (1749-1814) poet and novelist.

PR C.TURNER, after J.Masquerier, hl, mezz, pub 1802, BM, NP W.RIDLEY, after T.Beach, hl, stipple, oval, for *Monthly Mirr* 1803, BM, NPG. C.WATSON, after T.Lawrence, hl seated, stipp pub 1805, BM, NPG.

PRESCOTT, Robert (1725-1816) governor of Canada.

M JOHN BOGLE, 1776, hs, NPG 3963.

PRESTON, William (1742-1818) writer on freemasonry.

PR J.THOMSON, after S.Drummond, hl with masonic badge, li pub 1794, BM.

PRESTONGRANGE, William Grant, Lord (c1701-176 judge.

P ALLAN RAMSAY, 1751, hl, SNPG 1509.

PRETYMAN, Sir George, see Sir George Pretym

TOMLINE.

PREVOST, Sir George, 1st Bart (1767-1816) soldier and governor-general of Canada.
P ROBERT FIELD, hl, McCord Museum, McGill University, Montreal, Canada. R.FIELD, 1808, hl, Musée du Séminaire de Quebec, Canada. UNKNOWN, wl, Public Archives of Canada, Ottawa.
R UNKNOWN, wl equestrian, coloured etch, BM.

PRICE, Francis (c1704-1753) architect.
P GEORGE BEARE, 1747, hl, NPG 1960.

PRICE, James (1752-1783) chemist.
D JOHN RUSSELL, hs, chalk, NPG 1942.

PRICE, John (1734-1813) librarian of Bodleian, Oxford.
R J.C.BROMLEY, after H.H.Baber, hs, line, pub 1814, BM. UNKNOWN, hl profile, line, BM.

PRICE, Richard (1723-1791) nonconformist minister and political writer.
P By or after BENJAMIN WEST, hl seated, Royal Society, London.
C JAMES SAYERS, 'The Repeal of the Test Act. A Vision', etch, pub 1790, NPG. UNKNOWN, hl standing in tub, 'Tale of a Tub', etch, pub 1791, NPG. UNKNOWN, wl, 'The Mystical Divine', etch, NPG.

PRICE, Sir Uvedale, 1st Bart (1747-1829) writer on 'the picturesque'.
P SIR THOMAS LAWRENCE, RA 1799, Museum of Fine Arts, Boston, USA.

PRIESTLEY, Joseph (1733-1804) theologian and scientist.
P HENRY FUSELI, 1783, hl seated, Dr Williams's Library, London. WILLIAM ARTAUD, RA 1794, hl seated, Dr Williams's Library. JOHN OPIE, hs, Brompton Hospital, London. UNKNOWN, after Gilbert Stuart, City Museum and Art Gallery, Birmingham. UNKNOWN, hl, Royal Society, London. J.MILLAR, hl, Royal Society.
D MOSES HAUGHTON, jun, tql, wash over pencil and chalk, BM. ELLEN SHARPLES, hs, pastel, NPG 2904; related drgs, NPG 175 and Bristol City Art Gallery.
SC PHIPSON, c1795, medallion, NPG 175a. From a model by GIUSEPPE CERACCHI, 1779, Wedgwood medallion, Brooklyn Museum, USA. THOMAS HALLIDAY, medallion, NPG 175b. After HOLLINS, plaster medallion, Dr Williams's Library. GILBERT BAYES, 20th cent statue, wl seated, Russell Square, London.
C JAMES GILLRAY, 'A Birmingham Toast, as given on the 14th of July, by the — Revolution Society', etch, pub 1791, BM. JAMES SAYERS, several etchings, NPG.

PRIESTLEY, Timothy (1734-1814) independent minister.
R T.HOLLOWAY, hl, mezz, pub 1792, BM.

PRIMROSE, Archibald, see 4th Earl of Rosebery.

PRINGLE, Andrew, see Lord Alemoor.

PRINGLE, Sir John, Bart (1707-1782) physician.
P SIR JOSHUA REYNOLDS, c1774, hl, Royal Society, London.

PRINSEP, James (1799-1840) orientalist.
PR C.G., wl, lith, BM.

PRIOR, Sir James (1790?-1869) naval surgeon and author.
D WILLIAM BROCKEDON, 1832, hs, chalk, NPG 2515 (43).
PR W.DRUMMOND, after E.U.Eddis, hs, lith, for *Athenaeum Portraits*, 1835, BM, NPG.

PRITCHARD, George (1796-1883) missionary and consul at Tahiti.
PR C.BAUGNIET, tql, lith, BM, NPG. G.BAXTER, tql seated, coloured Baxter print, BM.

PRITCHARD, Hannah, née Vaughan (1711-1768) actress.
P FRANCIS HAYMAN, 1747, wl with David Garrick in *The Suspicious Husband*, Garrick Club, London; version, Museum of London. F.HAYMAN, wl with bust of Shakespeare, Garrick Club. F.HAYMAN, hs, Garrick Club. JOHAN ZOFFANY, wl as Lady Macbeth, with Garrick as Macbeth, Garrick Club.

PRITCHARD, John Langford (1799-1850) actor.
PR Theatrical prints, BM, NPG.

PROBY, Sir John Joshua, see 1st Earl of and 2nd Baron Carysfort.

PROCTER, Bryan Waller (1787-1874) poet and biographer of Charles Lamb, 'Barry Cornwall'.
D WILLIAM BROCKEDON, 1830, hs, chalk, NPG 2515 (23). COUNT ALFRED D'ORSAY, 1841, hl, pencil and chalk, NPG 4026 (48). CHARLES MARTIN, 1844, wl, pencil, BM. R.LEHMANN, 1869, BM.
G DANIEL MACLISE, 'The Fraserians', lith, pub 1835, BM; 2 pencil studies for this, V & A.
SC JOHN HENRY FOLEY, marble bust, NPG 788.
PR B.HOLL, after A.Wivell, pub 1832, Harvard Theatre Collection, Cambridge, USA. UNKNOWN, after a photograph by H.Watkins, woodcut, for *Illust London News*, 1874, NPG.

PROUT, Samuel (1783-1852) water-colour painter.
P UNKNOWN, as a boy, City Museum and Art Gallery, Plymouth. JOHN JACKSON, 1823, hl, NPG 1618.
D WILLIAM BROCKEDON, 1826, hs, chalk, NPG 2515 (12). CHARLES TURNER, c1836, tql, chalk, NPG 1245. WILLIAM HUNT, hs, w/c, City Museum and Art Gallery, Plymouth. Self-portrait, pencil, SNPG 1724.
M UNKNOWN, Royal Coll.
PR UNKNOWN, after Sir W.C.Ross, hs, woodcut, oval, for *Art Journal*, 1849, BM, NPG.

PROUT, William (1784-1850) physician and chemist.
P H.M.PAGET, after John Hayes (type c1835-40), hs, oval, Royal College of Physicians, London; version, Edinburgh University. H.W.PHILLIPS, after a miniature by an unknown artist, c1855, hs, Royal College of Physicians.

PRYCE, William (1725?-1790) surgeon and antiquary.
PR J.BASIRE, after Clifford, hs, line, oval, for *Mineralogia Cornubiensis*, 1778, BM, NPG.

PUGHE, William Owen (1759-1835) Welsh antiquary and lexicographer.
PR C.PICART, after E.Jones, tql, stipple, BM, NPG. UNKNOWN, hl, woodcut, NPG. UNKNOWN, hl seated, line, BM.

PUGIN, Augustus Charles (1762-1832) architect.
P JAMES GREEN, hl, RIBA, engr E.Scriven, stipple, for *Library of the Fine Arts*, 1833, BM, NPG.
PR 'A.F.R.'?, hl, etch, 1844, NPG.

PULLER, Sir Christopher (1774-1824) barrister-at-law.
P UNKNOWN, hl, a leaving portrait, Eton College, Berks.
PR F.C.LEWIS, after J.Slater, hl, stipple, BM, NPG.

PULTENEY, Richard (1730-1801) physician and botanist.
P THOMAS BEACH, 1788, hl, Linnean Society, London. THOMAS BEACH, 1788, (different type), hl, Leicester City Art Gallery.

PURCELL, Peter (1788-1846) founder of the Royal Agricultural Society of Ireland.
P STEPHEN CATTERSON SMITH, hl, NGI 308.

PUSEY, Philip (1799-1855) agriculturist.
PR F.C.LEWIS, after G.Richmond, hs, stipple, for 'Grillion's Club' series, BM, NPG.

PYE, Henry James (1745-1813) poet laureate.
P S.J.ARNOLD, c1801, hl, NPG 4253, engr B.Pym, mezz, pub 1801,

BM, NPG.

PR J.CHAPMAN, after S.Drummond, hl, stipple, oval, for *European Mag*, 1796, BM.

PYE, John (1782–1874) engraver.

SC H.B.BURLOWE, 1831, plaster cast of bust, NPG 2190.

PR J.H.ROBINSON, after W.Mulready, head, with Charles Warren, etch, for his *Patronage of British Art*, 1845, BM. UNKNOWN, hs, from a photograph, woodcut, for *Illust London News*, 1874, BM, NPG.

Q

QUEENSBERRY, Catherine, née Hyde, Duchess of (*c*1701-1777) eccentric and patron of writers.

P Attrib CHARLES JERVAS, tql, NPG 238; versions, Petworth (NT), West Sussex; Penicuick House, Midlothian, Scotland. UNKNOWN, hl seated, Buccleuch Estates, Selkirk, Scotland; version, Scone Palace, Tayside region, Scotland. UNKNOWN, hs as an old woman, Buccleuch Estates.

D Attrib CATHERINE READ, hl as an old woman, pastel, Buccleuch Estates.

M C.F.ZINCKE, hs, Buccleuch Estates.

G Attrib studio of VANLOO, wl with her husband and children, Buccleuch Estates.

QUEENSBERRY, Henry Scott, 5th Duke of, see 3rd Duke of Buccleuch.

QUEENSBERRY, William Douglas, 4th Duke of (1724-1810) rake and patron of the turf.

P ALLAN RAMSAY, 1742, tql, Buccleuch Estates, Selkirk, Scotland. SIR JOSHUA REYNOLDS, 1759, hl, Wallace Collection, London. Attrib JOHN OPIE, hl, NPG 4849.

PR UNKNOWN, hs profile, stipple, (with hs of Sir Robert Peel), pub 1803, NPG.

C JAMES SAYERS, 'The Comet', etch, pub 1789, NPG. UNKNOWN, tql, 'Quizzing a Filly', stipple and line, pub 1795, NPG. R.DIGHTON, wl 'Old Q-uiz the Old Goat of Piccadilly', wl, etch, pub 1796, NPG. UNKNOWN, wl seated on his balcony, with umbrella, line, BM, pub 1807, NPG. JAMES GILLRAY, hs, coloured stipple, pub 1811, NPG. Various caricatures, BM.

QUICK, John (1748-1831) comedian.

P GAINSBOROUGH DUPONT, RA 1794, hl as Spado in *The Castle of Andalusia*, Garrick Club, London. SAMUEL DE WILDE, 1805, hl as Old Doiley in *Who's the Dupe*, Garrick Club. THOMAS LAWRANSON, hl, NPG 1355. UNKNOWN, hs as Isaac Mendoza in *The Duenna*, Garrick Club.

D ROBERT DIGHTON, wl as Isaac Mendoza, w/c, Garrick Club. JAMES ROBERTS, as Judge Gripus, in Dryden's *Amphytrion*, BM.

G JOHAN ZOFFANY, in a scene from *Speculation*, oil, Garrick Club.

PR Numerous theatrical prints, BM, NPG.

QUIN, Frederic Hervey Foster (1799-1878) the first homeopathic physician in England.

PR A.D'ORSAY, hl seated, lith, BM.

R

RADCLIFFE, William (1760-1841) inventor of the cotton-dressing machine.
PR T.O.BARLOW, after Huquaire, hl, mezz, oval, pub 1862, BM.

RADNOR, William Pleydell-Bouverie, 3rd Earl of (1779-1869) Whig politician.
D DANIEL MACDONALD, 1847, hs, pen and ink, BM.
G S.BELLIN, after J.R.Herbert, 'Anti Corn Law League', mixed engr, pub 1850, BM, NPG.

RADSTOCK, Granville George Waldegrave, 2nd Baron (1786-1857) admiral.
PR F.HOLL, after G.Richmond, hl seated, stipple, pub 1848, BM, NPG.

RADSTOCK, William Waldegrave, 1st Baron (1753-1825) admiral.
G WORTHINGTON and PARKER, after R.Smirke, 'Naval Victories', 'Commemoration of the 14th February 1797', line, pub 1803, BM, NPG.
PR RIDLEY, after Northcote, hs, stipple, oval, pub 1803, NPG. C.WILKIN, after F.W.Wilkin, hl, stipple, for *Contemporary Portraits*, 1810, BM, NPG. T.LANDSEER, after G.Hayter, hl seated, line, pub 1820, BM, NPG.

RAE, Alexander (1782-1820) actor.
D SAMUEL DE WILDE, 1807–1816, three w/c, Garrick Club, London: hl; as Ranald in *The Tale of Mystery*; wl as Hamlet. J.TURMEAU, hl as Cassius in *Julius Caesar*, w/c, Garrick Club.
PR Theatrical prints, BM, NPG.

RAE, Sir David, 1st Bart, see Lord Eskgrove.

RAE, James (1716-1791) surgeon.
C J.KAY, wl carrying young boy, etch, BM, NPG.

RAEBURN, Sir Henry (1756-1823) portrait painter.
P Self-portrait, c1815, hl, NGS 930.
D SIR FRANCIS CHANTREY, 1818, hs, profile, pencil, SNPG 601.
SC THOMAS CAMPBELL, 1822, marble bust, SNPG 1037. JAMES TASSIE, 1792, two paste medallions (modelled by Sir Henry Raeburn), SNPG 936, 1968.

RAFFALD, Elizabeth (1733-1781) cook and writer.
PR UNKNOWN, after P.McMorland, hl, line, oval, for *Experienced English Housekeeper*, 1782, BM, NPG.

RAFFLES, Thomas (1788-1863) independent minister at Liverpool.
SC ISAAC JACKSON, marble bust, Walker Art Gallery, Liverpool.
PR T.BLOOD, hl, stipple, for *Evangelical Mag*, 1812, BM, NPG. J.THOMSON, after Mosses, hl, stipple, for *Imperial Mag*, 1822, BM, NPG. D.J.POUND, tql seated, stipple, for *Illust London News*, BM, NPG.

RAFFLES, Sir Thomas Stamford Bingley (1781-1826) colonial governor and zoologist.
P G.F.JOSEPH, 1817, wl, NPG 84. UNKNOWN, hs, Zoological Society, London.
SC SIR FRANCIS CHANTREY, 1826, marble statue, Westminster Abbey, London; plaster cast, Ashmolean Museum, Oxford.

RAGLAN, Lord Fitzroy James Henry Somerset, 1st Baron (1788-1855) field marshal.

P SIR FRANCIS GRANT, 1853, wl, formerly United Service Club, London, (c/o The Crown Commissioners). After SIR FRANCIS GRANT, c1858, Army and Navy Club, London. J.W.PIENEMAN, hs study for 'Battle of Waterloo', Wellington Museum, Apsley House, London. WILLIAM SALTER, tql study for 'Waterloo Banquet at Apsley House', NPG 3743.
D T.HEAPHY, 1813–14, hs, w/c, NPG 1914 (11).
G T.JONES BARKER, Duke of Wellington writing for reinforcements at the bridge at Sauroren, oil, Stratfield Saye, Hants. WILLIAM SALTER, 'The Waterloo Banquet at Apsley House', oil, 1836, Wellington Museum. J.W.PIENEMAN, 'The Battle of Waterloo', oil, Rijksmuseum, Amsterdam.
PH ROGER FENTON, 1855, wl seated, NPG P19. ROGER FENTON, 1855, wl with Omar Pasha and Marshal Pelissier, NPG P49.

RAIKES, Henry (1782-1854) divine.
PR J.ROMNEY, hs, lith, NPG.

RAIKES, Robert (1735-1811) promoter of Sunday schools.
P GEORGE ROMNEY, 1785-8, tql seated, NPG 1551.
SC WILLIAM TASSIE, paste medallion, NPG 2548. THOMAS BROCK, 1880, bronze statue, Victoria Embankment, London.
PR W.BROMLEY, after S.Drummond, hs, line, for *European Mag*, 1788, BM, NPG.

RAIKES, Thomas (1777-1848) dandy and diarist.
C R.DIGHTON, wl, 'One of the Rakes of London', coloured etch, pub 1818, BM, V & A.

RAIMBACH, Abraham (1776-1843) engraver.
P SIR DAVID WILKIE, 1818, hl, NPG 775.

RAINE, Matthew (1760-1811) schoolmaster and divine.
P JOHN HOPPNER, 1799, hs, Trinity College, Cambridge.

RAINIER, Peter (1741?-1808) admiral.
P THOMAS HICKEY, c1799–1804, hl, NMM, Greenwich.

RAINY, Harry (1792-1876) physician.
PR C.HOLL and F.A.ROBERTS, after G.Richmond, hl, stipple, NPG.
PH THOMAS ANNAN, hl, carte, NPG.

RAMBERG, Johann Heinrich (1763-1840) painter.
PR BARON DOMINIQUE VIVONT DENON, tql, etch, V & A.

RAMSAY, Allan (1713-1784) portrait painter.
P Self-portrait, c1739, hs, NPG 3311. ALEXANDER NASMYTH, 1781, after Allan Ramsay, (NPG 3311) hs, SNPG 189.
D Self-portraits: c1733, as a young man, NGS D223; 1755, tql, chalk, NGS; hs, pastel, SNPG 727; hs, chalk, SNPG L10; Huntington Library and Art Gallery, San Marino, USA; 1776, hs, chalk, NPG 1660.
SC MICHAEL FOYE, 177?, marble bust, SNPG 641.
PR A.WIVELL, after A.Ramsay, hl with easel, mezz, pub 1820, BM, NPG.

RAMSAY, Edward Bannerman (1793-1872) dean of Edinburgh.
P SIR JOHN WATSON GORDON, SNPG 950.
SL AUGUSTIN EDOUART, SNPG 783.
SC SIR JOHN STEELL, plaster bust, SNPG 176.
PR O.LEYDE, head, lith, BM.

RAMSAY, James (1733-1789) divine and philanthropist.

P C.F. VON BREDA, 1789, hl, NPG 2559.

RAMSDEN, Jesse (1735-1800) optician and mechanician.
P ROBERT HOME, tql seated, with large wheel, Royal Society, London.
PR C.TURNER, after H.Edridge, tql, mezz, pub 1801, BM.

RANDALL, John (1715-1799) organist, professor of music at Cambridge.
PR R.CLAMP, after S.Harding, hl in robes, stipple, oval, pub 1794, BM.

RANDOLPH, Francis (1752-1831) divine.
D JOHN DOWNMAN, 1777, hl, chalk, Fitzwilliam Museum, Cambridge.

RANDOLPH, John (1749-1813) bishop of Oxford, Bangor and London.
P WILLIAM OWEN, 1811-12, tql seated, Christ Church, Oxford. W.OWEN, 1812, hl, Fulham Palace, London.
PR C.TURNER, after J.Hoppner, tql, mezz, pub 1810, BM, NPG.

RANDOLPH, Thomas (1701-1783) president of Corpus Christi College, Oxford.
PR J.K.SHERWIN, after J.Taylor, tql seated, line, for *Posthumous Works*, 1784, BM, NPG.

RANSOME, James (1782-1849) agricultural implement maker.
PR T.H.MAGUIRE, tql seated, lith, 1849, for *Ipswich Museum Portraits*, BM, NPG.

RANSON, Thomas Frazer (1784-1828) engraver.
PR T.RANSON, wl seated in cell in Cold-Bath-Fields prison, where he was unlawfully confined, line, pub 1818, BM, NPG.

RASBOTHAM, Dorning (1730-1791) author.
PR H.ROBINSON, after H.Pickering, hl in Vandyck dress, stipple and line, pub 1833, BM, NPG.

RASHLEIGH, Philip (1729-1811) antiquary and politician.
M H.J.STUBBLE, 1786, tql, w/c, oval, V & A.

RASPE, Rudolf Eric (1737-1794) author, antiquary and mineralogist.
SC JAMES TASSIE, 1784, paste medallion, SNPG 258.

RATHBONE, William (1757-1809) merchant.
PR E.SMITH, after J.Allen, hl, line, BM, NPG.

RATHBONE, William (1787-1868) philanthropist.
SC EDWARD DAVIS, 1855, marble bust, Walker Art Gallery, Liverpool. J.H.FOLEY, marble statue, Sefton Park, Liverpool.
PR W.HOLL, hs, line, BM.

RAUZZINI, Venanzio (1747-1810) musical composer and teacher.
P JOSEPH HUTCHINSON, hs, Victoria Art Gallery, Bath.
PR R.HANCOCK, after J.Hutchinson, hl seated, stipple, pub 1800, BM. S.FREEMAN, after Bennett, hl, stipple, for *Monthly Mirror*, 1807, BM, NPG.

RAVENET, Simon François (1721?-1774) engraver.
PR S.F.RAVENET, after J.Zoffany, hl, line, oval, 1763, BM, NPG.

RAVENSWORTH, Sir Henry Thomas Liddell, 2nd Baron and 1st Earl of (1797-1878) politician and writer.
PR W.WALKER, after R.Buckner, tql, mezz, pub 1855, BM, NPG. UNKNOWN, tql, woodcut, for *Illust London News*, 1878, NPG.

RAWDON, Christopher (1780-1858) unitarian benefactor.
SC UNKNOWN, bust, marble relief, Unitarian Church, Ullet Road, Liverpool.

RAWDON, Francis Hastings, see 1st Marquess of Hastings.

RAWLINSON, Sir Thomas (d1769) lord mayor of London.

G THOMAS HUDSON, 'Benn's Club', oil, 1782, Goldsmith's Hall, London.

RAY, Martha (c1745-1779) mistress of the Earl of Sandwich.
P UNKNOWN, 1770-75, hl seated, DoE (Admiralty House, London).
PR V.GREEN, after N.Dance, tql seated, mezz, pub 1779, BM, NPG.

RAYMOND, James Grant (1771-1817) actor.
D SAMUEL DE WILDE, wl as Frederick the Great, w/c, Garrick Club, London.
PR Theatrical prints, BM, NPG.

RAYNER, Lionel Benjamin (1788?-1855) actor.
PR Theatrical prints, BM, NPG.

READ, David Charles (1790-1851) painter and etcher.
SC R.C.LUCAS, 1840, plaster bust, Ashmolean Museum, Oxford.

REDDISH, Samuel (1735-1785) actor.
P THOMAS PARKINSON, 1778, wl as Posthumus, with John Palmer as Iachimo, in *Cymbeline*, Garrick Club, London.
D THOMAS PARKINSON, as Edgar in *King Lear*, ink and w/c, BM. JAMES ROBERTS, as Young Beville, in Steele's *Conscious Lovers*, BM.
PR Numerous theatrical prints, BM, NPG.

REDESDALE, John Freeman-Mitford, 1st Baron (1748-1830) speaker of the House of Commons.
P SIR THOMAS LAWRENCE, 1803-04, hs, Palace of Westminster, London. SIR MARTIN ARCHER SHEE, tql in Lord Chancellor's gown, NPG 1265. SIR M.A.SHEE, tql in Lord Chancellor's gown, Palace of Westminster.
G K.A.HICKEL, 'The House of Commons, 1793', oil, NPG 745.
C JOHN DOYLE, 'The Prophecy', pencil, 1829, BM. J.DOYLE, 'A small tea party of superannuated politicians', pen over pencil, 1829, BM.

REED, Andrew (1787-1862) independent minister and philanthropist.
PR J.PARKER, after Wildman, tql seated, line, BM, NPG. D.J.POUND, after a photograph by Mayall, tql seated, stipple and line, NPG.

REED, Isaac (1742-1807) critic.
PR C.KNIGHT, after S.Harding, hl, stipple, for Harding's *Shakespeare Illustrated*, 1791, BM, NPG. S.FREEMAN, after G.Romney, hl, stipple, for *Monthly Mirror*, 1807, BM, NPG.

REES, Abraham (1743-1825) encyclopaedist.
P JOHN OPIE, RA 1796, tql seated, Dr Williams's Library, London. JAMES LONSDALE, hl, NPG 564.
PR W.DANIELL, after G.Dance of 1794, hs, profile, etch, NPG.
C J.SAYERS, 'A Repeal of the Test Act', etch, pub 1790, BM, NPG.

REES, Henry (1798-1869) Calvinistic methodist leader.
PR SCHENCK and McFARLANE, tql, lith, from a photograph, BM.

REES, William Jenkins (1772-1855) Welsh antiquary.
P HUGH HUGHES, hl, National Museum of Wales 325, Cardiff.

REEVE, Clara (1729-1807) novelist.
PR T.BLOOD, tql, stipple, for *La Belle Assemblée*, 1824, BM, NPG.

REEVE, John (1799-1838) actor.
P C.AMBROSE, hs, Garrick Club, London. JAMES NORTHCOTE, as Henry Alias in *One, two, three, four, five*, Art Gallery and Museum, Brighton.
PR Theatrical prints, BM, NPG.

REEVE, William (1757-1815) actor and musician.
PR J.HOPWOOD, after E.Smith, hl, stipple, for *The Cabinet*, 1807, BM, NPG.

REEVES, John (1752-1829) King's printer.
P UNKNOWN, tql, NPG 2633.

PR J.CHAPMAN, after S.Drummond, hs, stipple, oval, for *European Mag*, 1798, BM, NPG. THOMSON, after S.Drummond, hl, stipple, for *European Mag*, 1818, NPG.

REID, John (1721-1807) general, musical composer.
P UNKNOWN, *c*1745, hl, Edinburgh University. UNKNOWN, *c*1782, hl, Edinburgh University. Attrib GEORGE WATSON, 1806, tql, Edinburgh University.

REID, Thomas (1710-1796) philosopher.
P SIR HENRY RAEBURN, hs, Art Gallery of Ontario, Toronto, Canada.
D JAMES TASSIE, 1789, wash, SNPG 120.
SC J.TASSIE, 1791, paste medallion, SNPG 2144.

REID, Sir William (1791-1858) major-general.
P After J.LANE, Royal Engineers Mess, Chatham, Kent.
PR R.J.LANE, tql, lith, 1859, NPG. UNKNOWN, hs, woodcut, for *Illust London News*, 1851, NPG.

REINAGLE, Ramsay Richard (1775-1862) painter.
D Self-portrait?, identity doubtful, tql, chalk, NPG 3025. Self-portrait, BM.
G P.REINAGLE, (their father), as a child with his sisters, oil, RA 1788, Upton House (NT), Warwicks. A.E.CHALON, 'Students at the British Institution, 1807', w/c, BM.
SC Plaster death mask, Bodleian Library, Oxford.

REINHOLD, Charles Frederick (1737-1815) actor and singer.
P JOHAN ZOFFANY, wl as Hawthorn in *Love in a Village*, Garrick Club, London.
PR UNKNOWN, wl with Mrs Farrell in *Artaxerxes*, line, BM.

RELLY, James (1722?-1778) universalist.
PR S.HARDING, hl seated, etch, BM, NPG.

RENDEL, James Meadows (1799-1856) engineer.
PR S.BELLIN, after J.Opie, tql seated, mezz, pub 1866, BM, NPG.

RENNELL, James (1742-1830) geographer.
D GEORGE DANCE, 1794, hl, NPG 1153.
SC T.HAGBOLT, bust, Westminster Abbey, London. UNKNOWN, marble bust, NPG 896. UNKNOWN, wax medallion, V & A.
PR A.CARDON, after Scott, hl, stipple, oval, pub 1799, BM, NPG.

RENNELL, Thomas (1787-1824) divine.
PR S.W.REYNOLDS and W.BRETT, after T.Foster, hl, mezz, pub 1824, BM, NPG.

RENNIE, George (1791-1866) civil engineer.
M JOHN LINNELL, 1824, hl, NPG 3683.

RENNIE, John (1761-1821) civil engineer.
P SIR HENRY RAEBURN, hs, SNPG 1840.
D GEORGE DANCE, 1803, hl, NPG 1154. SIR FRANCIS CHANTREY, head, profile, pencil, NPG 316a (100).
G J.F.SKILL, J.GILBERT, W. and E.WALKER, 'Men of Science Living in 1807-8', pencil and wash, NPG 1075.
SC SIR FRANCIS CHANTREY, 1818, marble bust, NPG 649; plaster cast, Ashmolean Museum, Oxford. W.BAIN, bronze medallion, NPG 679.
PR J.THOMSON, after W.Behnes, hl, stipple, for *European Mag*, 1821, BM, NPG. E.SCRIVEN, after S.Kirven, hs, profile, stipple and line, NPG.

RENNIE, John (1794-1874) civil engineer.
P JAMES ANDREWS, RA 1853, tql seated, Institute of Civl Engineers, London.
M SIMON J.ROCHARD, 1831, hs, V & A.

REPTON, Humphry (1752-1818) landscape gardener.
PR W.HOLL, after S.Shelley, hl, stipple, pub 1802, BM, NPG.

REVETT, Nicholas (1720-1804) architect.
P Attrib THOMAS HUDSON, hl, RIBA, London.
D GEORGE DANCE, 1800, hl, pencil, BM.
PR W.C.EDWARDS, after 'A.Ramsay', hl seated as a young man, line, BM.

REYNOLDS, Frances (1729-1807) painter, sister of Sir Joshua Reynolds.
P SIR JOSHUA REYNOLDS, *c*1746, hs, Cottonian Coll, City Museum and Art Gallery, Plymouth.

REYNOLDS, Frederic (1764-1841) dramatist.
PR W.RIDLEY, after W.Nash, hs, stipple, oval, from a miniature, for *Monthly Mirror*, 1796, BM, NPG. T.WILLIAMSON, after J.R.Smith, hl, stipple, oval, for *European Mag*, 1804, BM, NPG. H.MEYER, after G.H.Harlow, hl seated, stipple, for his *Life*, 1826, BM, NPG.

REYNOLDS, Henry Revell (1745-1811) physician.
P After L.ABBOTT, 1798?, hl, Royal College of Physicians, London.

REYNOLDS, John Hamilton (1796-1852) poet, close friend and correspondent of Keats.
M JOSEPH SEVERN, 1818, hs, NPG 5052.
SL UNKNOWN artist, Keats House, London.

REYNOLDS, Sir Joshua (1723-1792) painter.
P Self-portrait, *c*1747, hl, NPG 41. Self-portrait, *c*1755-60, TATE 889. Self-portrait, *c*1766-1773, hl, Society of Dilettanti, Brooks's Club, London. Self-portrait, 1769, hs, Woburn Abbey, Beds. ANGELICA KAUFFMANN, 1767, tql seated, Saltram House (NT), Devon. Self-portrait, *c*1773, hl, TATE 306. Self-portrait, *c*1773, tql with bust of Michaelangelo, Royal Academy, London. Self-portrait, 1775, hl, Uffizi Gallery, Florence. Self-portrait, *c*1775, hs as a deaf man, TATE 4505. Self-portrait, *c*1788, hl in spectacles, Royal Coll. GILBERT STUART, tql, National Gallery of Art, Washington DC, USA.
D Self-portrait, 1760, hs, chalk, BM. NATHANIEL DANCE, *c*1767, wl seated, talking to Angelica Kauffmann, pencil, Harewood House, Leeds, W.Yorks. Self-portrait, *c*1784, as a figure of horror, chalk, TATE 1834.
M OZIAS HUMPHREY, hs, oval, Corsham Court, Wilts.
G JOHAN ZOFFANY, 'Royal Academicians, 1772', oil, Royal Coll. JOHN FRANCIS RIGAUD, hl with Sir William Chambers and Joseph Wilton, oil, 1782, NPG 987.
SC GIUSEPPE CERACCHI, 1778, marble bust, Royal Academy. JOHN FLAXMAN, 1813, statue, St Paul's Cathedral, London. Attrib J.FLAXMAN, Wedgwood medallion, Nottingham Museum and Art Gallery.

REYNOLDS, Richard (1735-1816) philanthropist and industrialist.
SC SAMUEL PERCY, *c*1817, wax bust in frame, NPG 4674.
PR W.SHARP, after W.Hobday, hl seated, line, pub 1817, BM, NPG.

REYNOLDS, Samuel William (1773-1835) mezzotint engraver.
P Self-portrait, *c*1820-5, hs, NPG 4989. JOHN OPIE, hs, NPG 1320.
M ELIZABETH WALKER (his daughter), hs, NPG 2123.
PR E.BELL, head, etch, BM.

RHODES, Ebenezer (1762-1839) topographer.
P N.POOLE, 1830, tql, Cutler's Hall, Sheffield. SIR FRANCIS CHANTREY, Graves Art Gallery, Sheffield.

RICARDO, David (1772-1823) political economist.
PR T.HODGETTS, after T.Phillips, tql seated, mezz, pub 1822, BM, NPG.

RICE, Thomas Spring, see 1st Baron Monteagle.

RICH, Claudius James (1787-1820) traveller.

P THOMAS PHILLIPS, hs, BM.

RICHARDS, George (1767-1837) poet.
PR C.TURNER, after C.Ross, tql seated, mezz, pub 1832, BM, NPG.

RICHARDS, John Inigo (d1810) landscape and scene painter.
D GEORGE DANCE, hs profile, Royal Academy, London.
G JOHAN ZOFFANY, 'Royal Academicians, 1772', oil, Royal Coll. HENRY SINGLETON, 'Royal Academicians, 1793', oil, Royal Academy, London.

RICHARDS, William (1749-1818) historian of King's Lynn.
PR HOPWOOD, hs, stipple, oval, NPG.

RICHARDSON, Sir John (1771-1841) judge.
P THOMAS PHILLIPS, 1829, tql seated, University College, Oxford.
PR B.HOLL, after W.Allingham, hl, stipple, pub 1826, BM, NPG.

RICHARDSON, Sir John (1787-1845) explorer and naturalist.
P THOMAS PHILLIPS, RA 1829, hs, Royal Naval Hospital, Gosport, Hants. STEPHEN PEARCE, 1850, hl, profile, study for NPG 1208, NPG 909.
G STEPHEN PEARCE, 'The Arctic Council, 1851', oil, NPG 1208.
SC BERNARD SMITH, 1842, plaster medallion, NPG 888.

RICHARDSON, Joseph (1755-1803) journalist and author.
PR W.RIDLEY, after M.A.Shee, hl, stipple, oval, for *Monthly Mirror*, 1800, BM, NPG.

RICHARDSON, Robert (1779-1847) traveller and physician.
D WILLIAM BROCKEDON, 1826, hs, chalk, NPG 2515 (26).

RICHARDSON, Thomas (1771-1853) quaker and financier.
C RICHARD DIGHTON, wl, 'A friend in Lombard Street', coloured etch, NPG.

RICHARDSON, William (1743-1814) professor at Glasgow and writer.
P SIR HENRY RAEBURN, tql seated, Dunedin Art Gallery, New Zealand.
PR W.RIDLEY, hl stipple, oval, for *Monthly Mirror*, 1799, BM, NPG.

RICHMOND AND LENNOX, Sir Charles Lennox, 2nd Duke of (1701-1750) lieutenant-general.
P Attrib SIR GODFREY KNELLER, wl as a young man, seated with dog, Goodwood, W.Sussex. UNKNOWN, as a young man, tql in armour, Deene Park, Northants. Attrib KNELLER, tql in armour, with his wife, Goodwood. Attrib MICHAEL DAHL, tql, Goodwood. W.SMITH, hl with Garter star, Goodwood; version, Lennoxlove, Lothian, Scotland. J.B. VAN LOO, hl with Garter ribbon, in armour, Goodwood. UNKNOWN, 1740, wl, Goodwood.

RICHMOND AND LENNOX, Charles Lennox, 3rd Duke of (1735-1806) soldier, diplomat and politician.
P Portraits at Goodwood, W.Sussex: UNKNOWN, c1740, hl as a child; SIR JOSHUA REYNOLDS, RA 1758, tql as young man with dog; attrib POMPEO BATONI, tql as a young man with dog; GEORGE ROMNEY, tql with Garter star; CHEVALIER MENGS, tql in Vandyck dress. GEORGE ROMNEY, 1776, hl, NPG 4877; version, Goodwood.
G GEORGE STUBBS, c1762, wl equestrian in hunting party, oil, Goodwood. JOHN SINGLETON COPLEY, 'The Collapse of the Earl of Chatham in the House of Lords, 7 July 1778', oil, TATE 100, on loan to NPG. G.STUBBS, equestrian with Mary, his Duchess, at race-horse training, Goodwood.

RICHMOND AND LENNOX, Charles Lennox, 4th Duke of (1764-1819) soldier, governor general of British North America.
P GEORGE ROMNEY, wl as a boy with dog, Beaverbrook Art

Gallery, Fredericton, New Brunswick, Canada. UNKNOWN, wl as a boy, sketch, Goodwood, W.Sussex. JOHN HOPPNER, (sometimes attrib John Jackson), 1809, hl, Goodwood. UNKNOWN, hs, Goodwood.
M Attrib S.J.ROCHARD, hs, oval, NPG 4943.
SC JOSEPH NOLLEKENS, probably 4th Duke, bust, Goodwood. W.THEED, jun, bust, Royal Military Academy, Sandhurst, Camberley, Surrey.
PR J.KAY, wl, etch, BM, NPG.

RICHMOND AND LENNOX, Charles Gordon-Lennox, 5th Duke of (1791-1860) soldier and politician.
P WILLIAM SALTER, tql study for 'Waterloo Banquet at Apsley House', NPG 3746; version, Goodwood, W.Sussex. SAMUEL LANE, RA 1842, wl in Garter robes, Goodwood. Attrib F.WILKIN, hl in robes, Goodwood. UNKNOWN, tql as an old man, Goodwood.
D THOMAS HEAPHY, hs, w/c, NPG 1914 (12).
G SIR GEORGE HAYTER, 'The Trial of Queen Caroline, 1820', oil, NPG 999. SIR G.HAYTER, 'The House of Commons, 1833', oil, NPG 54. W.SALTER, 'Waterloo Banquet at Apsley House', oil, 1836, Wellington Museum, Apsley House, London. UNKNOWN, wl equestrian, shooting party, Goodwood.
SC HENRY WEEKES, 1845, bust, Goodwood.

RICHMOND, Legh (1772-1827) evangelical divine.
PR W.FINDEN, after Slater, hs, line, pub 1828, NPG. J.COLLYER, after R.Livesay, hl, line, BM.

RICKMAN, John (1771-1840) statistician.
P SAMUEL LANE, c1831, tql seated, Palace of Westminster, London.
G SIR GEORGE HAYTER, 'The House of Commons, 1833', oil, NPG 54.

RICKMAN, Thomas, 'CLIO' (1761-1834) bookseller and reformer.
PR J.HOLMES, after W.Hazlitt, hl, stipple, pub 1800, BM, NPG. S.SPRINGSGUTH, jun, wl, line, pub 1814, NPG.

RIDDELL, Henry Scott (1798-1870) Scottish poet.
PR UNKNOWN, hs, lith, BM.

RIDDLE, Edward (1788-1854) mathematician and astronomer.
PR UNKNOWN, woodcut, after a bust, for *Illust London News*, 1852, NPG.

RIDLEY, Glocester (1702-1774) miscellaneous writer.
PR J.HALL, after J.Scouler, hl, line, oval, for *Melampus*, 1781, BM, NPG.

RIGAUD, John Francis (1742-1810) painter.
D GEORGE DANCE, 1793, hs profile, Royal Academy, London.
G HENRY SINGLETON, 'Royal Academicians, 1793', oil, Royal Academy.

RIGAUD, Stephen Peter (1774-1839) mathematical historian and astronomer.
SL UNKNOWN, hs, profile, Exeter College, Oxford. UNKNOWN, hs, profile, Radcliffe Observatory, Oxford.

RIGBY, Edward (1747-1821) physician.
PR MRS D.TURNER, after M.Sharp, hl, etch, BM.

RIGBY, Richard (1722-1788) politician.
C JAMES SAYERS, wl, etch, pub 1782, NPG.

RIGGS, Anna, see Lady Miller.

RING, John (1752-1821) surgeon.
PR J.ROGERS, after S.Drummond, hl, stipple, pub 1821, BM, pub 1824, NPG. R.J.LANE, hl, lith, NPG.

RINTOUL, Robert Stephen (1787-1858) journalist.

PH DAVID OCTAVIUS HILL, hl, NPG P6/79.

RIOU, Edward (1758?-1801) captain in the navy.
P UNKNOWN, 1776, hl, on loan to the NMM, Greenwich.
SC J.C.ROSSI, monument with Captain Rosse, St Paul's Cathedral, London.
PR J.HEATH, after S.Shelley, hl in uniform, stipple, BM.

RIPON, Frederick John Robinson, 1st Earl of (1782-1859) prime-minister.
P SIR THOMAS LAWRENCE, c1824, hl, NPG 4875. WILLIAM ROBINSON, on loan to Ripon Town Hall, North Yorks.
G S.W.REYNOLDS, after Sir J.Reynolds, with 2nd Lord Grantham, and Hon Philip Robinson, wl as children, with dogs in landscape, mezz, BM, NPG. J.C.BROMLEY, after B.R.Haydon, 'Reform Banquet, 1832', mezz, BM. SIR GEORGE HAYTER, 'The House of Commons, 1833', oil, NPG 54.
C UNKNOWN, 'A View near Ripon', wl, coloured etch, pub 1823, NPG. JOHN DOYLE, 'Sparring', pen and pencil, 1846, BM.

RIPPINGILLE, Edward Villiers (1798?-1859) painter and writer on art.
P Self-portrait, 1822, wl seated, with a sitter, Clevedon Court (NT), Avon.
G E.V.RIPPINGILLE, 'The Travellers' Breakfast', oil, c1824, Clevedon Court.

RIPPON, John (1751-1836) baptist divine.
PR R.DUNKARTON, in pulpit preaching, mezz, oval, pub 1775, BM. J.FITTLER, after R.Bowyer, hs, line, oval, pub 1790, NPG. W.J.ALAIS, hl, in old age, stipple, BM, NPG.

RIPPON, Thomas (1761-1835) chief cashier of the bank of England.
P UNKNOWN, hl, Bank of England, London.

RITSON, Jonathan (1776?-1846) wood-carver.
P GEORGE CLINT, hl, Petworth (NT), W.Sussex.

RITSON, Joseph (1752-1803) antiquary and critic.
C J.SAYER, wl in room filled with books and vegetables, etch, BM, pub 1803, NPG.

RIVERS, George Pitt, 1st Baron (1722?-1803) diplomat.
P THOMAS GAINSBOROUGH, 1768-9, wl, Cleveland Museum of Art, USA.
D T.GAINSBOROUGH, hs, chalk, V & A.

RIVINGTON, James (1724-1803) publisher.
D FRANCIS COTES, 1756, hs, pastel, The New York Historical Society, New York, USA.

ROBERTS, Sir Abraham (1784-1873) general.
P UNKNOWN, hl, NPG 3928.

ROBERTS, Barré Charles (1789-1810) antiquary.
PR UNKNOWN, head, stipple, BM, NPG.

ROBERTS, David (1796-1864) painter.
P SIR DANIEL MACNEE, hl seated, Royal Scottish Academy, Edinburgh. SIR JOHN WATSON GORDON, Royal Scottish Academy.
D THOMAS BRIDGFORD, RA 1843, Royal Hibernian Academy, Dublin. CLARKSON STANSFIELD, RA 1843, hs, pen, Royal Academy, London. CHARLES WEST COPE, c1862, head, pencil sketch, NPG 3182 (7). Self-portrait, pencil, Newport Museum and Art Gallery, Monmouthshire. UNKNOWN, hs, chalk, NPG 1371.
SC GEORGE T.MORGAN, 1875, bronze medal, for the Art Union, SNPG 599, NPG.
PH DAVID OCTAVIUS HILL and ROBERT ADAMSON, wl profile, NPG P6/90. Several photographs, NPG.

ROBERTS, John (1712?-1772) politician.

P JOHN SHACKLETON, hl with Rt Hon Henry Pelham, DoE (The Treasury, London).

ROBERTS, Richard (1789-1864) improver of the spinning mule.
D J.STEPHENSON, Science Museum, London.
SC UNKNOWN, bronze head, University College of Wales, Aberystwyth.
PR T.O.BARLOW, after T.Rippingille, hl, mezz, oval, for *Portraits of Inventors*, 1862, BM.

ROBERTS, Samuel (1763-1848) author and pamphleteer.
PR H.ADLARD, wl silhouette profile, line, for vol 2 of Holland and Everett, *Memoirs of James Montgomery*, 1854, BM.

ROBERTSON, Andrew (1777-1845) miniature-painter.
M Self-portrait, w/c, Aberdeen Art Gallery.

ROBERTSON, James (1714-1795) orientalist.
SC After JAMES TASSIE, plaster medallion, SNPG 388.

ROBERTSON, Patrick Robertson, Lord (1794-1855) judge.
P SIR JOHN WATSON GORDON, wl seated, Faculty of Advocates, Parliament Hall, Edinburgh.
SC JOHN HENNING, paste medallion, SNPG 1277.
PR E.BURTON, after T.Duncan, tql seated, mezz, pub 1844, BM.
C BENJAMIN WILLIAM CROMBIE, pencil study for 'Modern Athenians', SNPG 2306.
PH D.O.HILL and ROBERT ADAMSON, hl seated, NPG P6/74.

ROBERTSON, Robert (1742-1829) physician.
PR J.HEATH, after E.Smith, hl, stipple, oval, BM.

ROBERTSON, William (1721-1793) historian.
P SIR JOSHUA REYNOLDS, 1772, tql seated, SNPG 1393. SIR HENRY RAEBURN, 1792, tql, Edinburgh University.
SC JAMES TASSIE, 1791, paste medallion, SNPG 185.
PR J.KAY, etch, 1790, NPG.

ROBINS, George Henry (1778-1847) auctioneer.
PR G.E.MADELEY, hl seated, lith, BM. UNKNOWN, hl conducting an auction, etch, NPG.

ROBINSON, Sir Christopher (1766-1833) lawyer.
D SIR GEORGE HAYTER, pen, pencil, wash, study for NPG 999, NPG 1695(h).
G SIR G.HAYTER, 'The Trial of Queen Caroline, 1820', oil, NPG 999.

ROBINSON, Frederick John, see 1st Earl of Ripon.

ROBINSON, Henry Crabb (1775-1867) journalist and diarist.
P HENRY DARVALL, tql, NPG 1347.
D GEORGE SCHARF, 1860, hl seated, pencil, BM.
M GEORGE SCHARF, after Herve 1811, hs profile, BM. UNKNOWN, after Herve?, The Times Newspapers Ltd, London.
SC G.E.EWING, 1831, marble bust, Dr Williams's Library, London; plaster cast of Ewing bust, Dr Williams's Library.
PR W.HOLL, hl seated, stipple, for his *Diary*, 1869, BM, NPG.

ROBINSON, John (1727-1802) politician.
PR W.BOND, after G.F.Joseph, tql, stipple, BM, NPG.

ROBINSON, John (1774-1840) divine.
PR R.SMITH, hl, stipple, BM, NPG.

ROBINSON, John Henry (1796-1871) engraver.
PR UNKNOWN, hs, woodcut, oval, BM. UNKNOWN, hs, woodcut, for *Illust London News*, 1867, NPG.

ROBINSON, Mary, née Darby (1758-1800) 'Perdita', actress.
P THOMAS GAINSBOROUGH, 1781, wl seated with dog, Wallace

Collection, London; sketch, Royal Coll, related hs portrait, Waddesdon Manor (NT), Bucks. GEORGE ROMNEY, 1781, hl, Wallace Collection. SIR JOSHUA REYNOLDS, RA 1782, hl, Waddesdon Manor. SIR J.REYNOLDS, 1784, hl, Wallace Collection. SIR J.REYNOLDS, 1784, hl, Taft Museum, Cincinnati, USA. JOHN HOPPNER, hl, National Gallery of Victoria, Melbourne, Australia. WILLIAM OWEN, wl with dog, Petworth (NT), W.Sussex. Attrib JOHAN ZOFFANY, hs as Rosaline in *As You Like It*, Garrick Club, London.

D JAMES ROBERTS, 1778, as Amanda in Cibber's *Love's Last Shift*, BM. GEORGE DANCE, hl, pencil, NPG 1254. JOHN HOPPNER, hl, chalk, BM.

M MRS MEE, *c*1790, hs, oval, Garrick Club.

ROBINSON, Mary (fl 1802) known as the 'Beauty of Buttermere'.

PR J.GILLRAY, wl serving in her father's inn, coloured etch, pub 1802, BM. UNKNOWN, wl seated, coloured etch and mezz, pub 1803, BM. MACKENZIE, after W.Bennet, hl, stipple, oval, pub 1803, NPG.

ROBINSON, Richard (1709-1794), see 1st Baron Rokeby.

ROBINSON, Robert (1735-1790) baptist minister and hymn-writer.

PR T.TROTTER, hs, stipple, oval, pub 1785, NPG. J.WOODING, after J.Paxton, hs, line, BM.

ROBINSON, Sir Thomas, 1st Bart (1700?-1777) colonial governor.

G WILLIAM HOGARTH, probably represented in 'The Beggar's Opera, Act III, Scene 2', oil, 1729-31, Yale Center for British Art, New Haven, USA; version, TATE 2437.

SC UNKNOWN, portrait? on monument, Westminster Abbey, London.

ROBINSON, Thomas (1738-1786), see 2nd Baron Grantham.

ROBINSON, Thomas (1749-1813) divine.

PR W.SAY, after J.Slater, hl, mezz, pub 1814, BM, NPG.

ROBINSON, Thomas Romney (1792-1882) astronomer and physicist.

P MAUDE HUMPHREY, 1893, from a photograph, Royal Irish Academy.

PR R.COOPER, wl as a boy, holding lyre and scattering flowers on the tomb of Romney the painter, stipple, for Hayley's *Life of Romney*, 1809, BM, NPG.

ROBINSON, William (1777-1848) topographer and solicitor.

PR I.MILLS, after F.Simoneau, hl, stipple, 1820, BM, NPG.

ROBINSON-Montagu, Henry, see 6th Baron Rokeby.

ROBINSON-Morris, Matthew, see 2nd Baron Rokeby.

ROBISON, John (1739-1805) mathematician and scientist.

P SIR HENRY RAEBURN, *c*1798, tql, Edinburgh University.

SC After JAMES TASSIE, 1791, plaster medallion, SNPG 389.

ROBSON, George Fennell (1788-1833) water-colour painter.

G JOHN PARTRIDGE, 'A Meeting of the Sketching Society', pen, ink, wash, BM.

PR H.ADLARD, after J.T.Smith, hl, stipple, for Arnold's *Mag of the Fine Arts*, 1834, BM, NPG.

ROBY, John (1793-1850) organist and author.

PR UNKNOWN, tql seated, stipple, for his *Traditions of Lancashire*, 1840, BM.

ROBY, William (1766-1830) congregational minister and

religious writer.

PR FREEMAN, after Stephens, hl, stipple, pub 1817, NPG. S.W.REYNOLDS, after W.H.Parry, wl seated, mezz, pub 1829, BM, NPG.

ROCHE, Eugenius (1786-1829) journalist and poet.

D WILLIAM HOME CLIFT, 1824, hl, Royal College of Surgeons, London.

ROCHFORD, William Henry Zuylestein, 4th Earl of (1717-1781) diplomatist and secretary of state.

P CHARLES JERVAS, 1738, tql in coronation robes, Brodick Castle (NT), Strathclyde region, Scotland. THOMAS BARDWELL, 1741, wl with racehorse and groom, Brodick Castle.

PR R.HOUSTON, after D.Dupra, hl, mezz, BM, NPG. V.GREEN, after J.B.Perroneau, hl, mezz, BM, NPG.

ROCKINGHAM, Charles Watson Wentworth, 2nd Marquess of (1730-1782) prime-minister.

P SIR JOSHUA REYNOLDS, 1766-8, tql seated with Edmund Burke (unfinished), Fitzwilliam Museum, Cambridge. After REYNOLDS of 1766-8, wl in Garter robes, Royal Coll. Studio of REYNOLDS (after portrait of 1768), hl, NPG 406. Studio of REYNOLDS, *c*1781-2, wl, Mansion House, York.

G JOHN SINGLETON-COPLEY, 'The Collapse of the Earl of Chatham, in the House of Lords, 7 July 1778', oil, TATE 100, on loan to NPG.

SC JOSEPH NOLLEKENS, marble bust, Althorp, Northants. J.NOLLEKENS, marble bust, Goodwood, W.Sussex. JAMES TASSIE, hs, oval, Ickworth. J.TASSIE, paste medallion, SNPG 301.

C JAMES SAYERS, wl, etch, pub 1782, NPG.

RODD, Thomas (1763-1822) printseller.

PR B.READING, after A.Wivell, hs, profile, soft-ground etch, BM, NPG.

RODDAM, Robert (1719-1808) admiral.

P LEMUEL FRANCIS ABBOTT, *c*1778-83, hl, NMM, Greenwich.

RODEN, Robert Jocelyn, 1st Earl of (1731-1797) auditor-general of Ireland.

PR JAMES HEATH, after John Oldham, hs with star of St Patrick, stipple, pub 1815, NPG.

RODEN, Robert Jocelyn, 3rd Earl of (1788-1870) grand master of the Orange Society.

PR JOHN KIRKWOOD, tql, etch, pub 1840, NPG. T.LUPTON, after F.R.Say, tql, mezz, NPG.

C JOHN DOYLE, 'Dentatus', black chalk, 1839, BM.

PH CAMILLE SILVY, 1860, wl seated, carte, NPG Distinguished Persons Album, vol V.

RODNEY, George Brydges Rodney, 1st Baron (1719-1792) admiral.

P SIR JOSHUA REYNOLDS, RA 1761, tql, Petworth (NT), W.Sussex. ROBERT EDGE PINE, RA 1784, wl with his Officers, Historical Institute, Kingston, Jamaica. SIR JOSHUA REYNOLDS, RA 1789, wl wearing ribbon and star of the Bath, Royal Coll. JEAN LAURENT MOSNIER, 1791, tql seated, NMM, Greenwich. After REYNOLDS, hl, NPG 1398.

M WILLIAM GRIMALDI, hl, oval, Royal Coll.

SC J.C.ROSSI, 1815, statue on monument, St Paul's Cathedral, London.

PR G.DUPONT, after Gainsborough, wl, mezz, pub 1788, BM.

ROGERS, Charles (1711-1784) art collector.

P SIR JOSHUA REYNOLDS, RA 1777, hl, Cottonian Collection, City Museum and Art Gallery, Plymouth.

ROGERS, Robert (1727-1800) colonel.

PR UNKNOWN, tql with American Indians, mezz, pub 1776, NPG.

ROGERS, Samuel (1763-1855) poet, banker and connoisseur.
P SIR GEORGE HAYTER, 1821, hl, Woburn Abbey, Beds. JOHN LINNELL, 1833-5, hl, TATE 5117. J.LINNELL, sketch after the portrait, 1846, NG 4142. CHESTER HARDING, c1847, hl, Harvard University, Cambridge, USA. THOMAS PHILLIPS, hl, NPG 763.
D GEORGE DANCE, 1795, hl seated, profile, NPG 1155. GEORGE RICHMOND, 1848, hl, chalk, NPG 1044. THOMAS LAWRENCE, hs, chalk, NPG 400. T.LAWRENCE, hl, chalk, BM. JEMIMA WEDDERBURN, hs, w/c, NPG 2772.
G CHARLES MOTTRAM, 'Breakfast party given by Mr. Samuel Rogers', engr 1815, V & A. FRANK STONE, c1845, wl seated with the Hon Caroline Norton and Mrs Phipps, oil, unknown. JOHN PARTRIDGE, 'The Fine Arts Commissioners, 1846', NPG 342, 3.
SC J.P.DANTAN, 1833, plaster caricature bust, NPG 3888.
C SIR EDWIN LANDSEER, c1835, 3 pen and wash drgs, NPG 4919-21. Several caricatures, BM.
PH PAINE (his valet), hl, NPG 'Distinguished Persons' album.

ROGERS, William Gibbs (1792-1875) wood-carver.
PR R. and E.TAYLOR, hl from a photograph, woodcut, for *Illust London News*, 1875, BM.

ROGET, Peter Mark (1779-1869) physician, author of 'Thesaurus of English Words and Phrases'.
D WILLIAM BROCKEDON, 1835, hs, pencil and chalk, NPG 2515 (79).
PR W.DRUMMOND, after E.U.Eddis, hs, lith, for *Athenaeum Portraits*, BM, NPG.

ROKEBY, Henry Robinson-Montagu, 6th Baron (1798-1883) general.
PR G.ZOBEL, after Sir F.Grant, hl, mezz, pub 1858, BM, NPG. UNKNOWN, tql, lith, BM, NPG.

ROKEBY, Matthew Robinson-Morris, 2nd Baron (1713-1800) politician.
PR J.CHAPMAN, hl with long hair and beard, stipple, oval, BM, pub 1801, NPG.

ROKEBY, Richard Robinson, 1st Baron (1709-1794) primate of Armagh.
P SIR JOSHUA REYNOLDS, c1763, tql seated, Christ Church, Oxford. SIR J.REYNOLDS, 1775, tql, Barber Institute of Fine Arts, Birmingham University.
SC JOHN BACON, sen, marble bust, Christ Church, Oxford. After JAMES TASSIE, plaster medallion, SNPG 473. WILLIAM MOSSOP, bronze medal, National Museum of Ireland.

ROKEWODE, John Gage (1786-1842) antiquary.
PR T.HODGETTS, after M.Carpenter, hl, mezz, pub 1824, BM, NPG.

ROLFE, Robert Monsey, see Baron Cranworth.

ROLLE of Stevenstone, John Rolle, Baron (1750-1842) politician.
P Attrib RICHARD COSWAY, wl, Torrington Town Hall, Devon.
G SIR GEORGE HAYTER, 'The Trial of Queen Caroline, 1820', oil, NPG 999.
SC E.B.STEPHENS, statue, Bicton, Devon.
PR C.TURNER, after T.Lawrence, wl seated in peer's robes, mezz, pub 1826, BM, NPG. H.T.RYALL, after F.Cruikshank, hl, stipple and line, BM, NPG.

ROMAINE, William (1714-1795) evangelical divine.
P FRANCIS COTES, 1758, tql, NPG 2036.
PR R.HOUSTON, after J.Russell, hl, mezz, oval, pub 1775, BM.

ROMILLY, Joseph (1791-1864) divine.
M MISS HERVÉ, 1836, hl, w/c, The Registry, Cambridge University.

ROMILLY, Sir Samuel (1757-1818) solicitor-general and law reformer.

P JOHN HOPPNER, hl, NPG 3325. SIR THOMAS LAWRENCE, hl, NPG 1171; copy, Grays Inn, London (on loan from the National Gallery).
SC After JOHN HENNING, 1813, hs, Wedgwood medallion, Wedgwood Museum, Barlaston, Staffs.
PR S.W.REYNOLDS, jun, after M.Cregan, hl seated, mezz, pub 1818, BM, NPG. J.T.WEDGWOOD, after W.Behnes, hl, line, pub 1819, BM, NPG.

ROMNEY, George (1734-1802) portrait-painter.
P Self-portrait, c1765, hs, Uffizi Gallery, Florence. Self-portrait, 1782, hl, NPG 959. Self-portrait, hl, Metropolitan Museum of Art, New York, USA.
D Self-portrait, hs, pencil, NPG 2814.
M MISS M.BARRETT, hs, NPG 1881.
G GEORGE ROMNEY, 'The Four Friends', oil, 1796, Abbot Hall Art Gallery, Kendal, Westmorland.
PR W.BOND, after M.A.Shee, tql, stipple, for Britton's *Fine Arts of the English School*, 1810, BM, NPG.

ROMNEY, Peter (1743-1777) painter.
M GEORGE ROMNEY (his brother), hs, NPG 1882.

RONALDS, Sir Francis (1788-1873) electrician and meteorologist.
P HUGH CARTER, c1870, hl, NPG 1095.
G J.F.SKILL, J.GILBERT, W. and E.WALKER, 'Men of Science Living in 1807-8', pencil and wash, NPG 1075.
SC EDWARD DAVIS, RA 1871, marble bust, Royal Society, London. E.DAVIS, 1876, marble bust, Institution of Electrical Engineers, London.

ROOKE, Sir Giles (1743-1808) judge.
P JOHN HOPPNER, RA 1795, tql, Merton College, Oxford.
D LEWIS VASLET, 1780, hs, Merton College, Oxford. GEORGE DANCE, hl profile, pencil, Merton College, engr W.Daniell, soft ground etch, pub 1809, BM, NPG.

ROOKER, Michael Angelo (1743-1801) painter and engraver.
D GEORGE DANCE, 1793, hs, pencil, BM.

ROSCOE, William (1753-1831) banker, historian and collector.
P RICHARD CADDICK, hs as a young man, Walker Art Gallery, Liverpool. SIR MARTIN ARCHER SHEE, 1822, wl, Walker Art Gallery. JAMES LONSDALE, 1825, Liverpool Royal Institution. Attrib J.WILLIAMSON, hl, NPG 963.
M MOSES HAUGHTON, 1811, w/c, Walker Art Gallery. THOMAS HARGREAVES, hs, oval, Walker Art Gallery.
SC SIR FRANCIS CHANTREY, RA 1840, marble statue, Liverpool Royal Institution. SIR FRANCIS CHANTREY, bust, Ashmolean Museum, Oxford. JOHN GIBSON, marble relief bust, Unitarian Church, Ullet Road, Liverpool. Attrib WILLIAM SPENCE, marble bust, NPG 4147. JOHN GIBSON, bust, Liverpool Royal Institution.
C DANIEL MACLISE, wl, lith, for *Fraser's Mag*, 1832, BM, NPG.

ROSE, George (1744-1818) statesman.
P SIR WILLIAM BEECHEY, 1802, hl, NPG 367.
PR T.BLOOD, after A.Wivell, hs, from a medallion, stipple, oval, for *European Mag*, 1818, BM, NPG. J.S.AGAR, after R.Cosway, hs, stipple, oval, pub 1819, BM, NPG.

ROSE, Samuel (1767-1804) barrister and editor.
PR H.ROBINSON, after T.Lawrence, tql seated, stipple, for Cowper's *Works*, 1836, ed by Southey, BM, NPG.

ROSEBERY, Archibald John Primrose, 4th Earl of (1783-1868) politician.
G SIR GEORGE HAYTER, 'The Trial of Queen Caroline, 1820', oil

NPG 999.

PR E.BURTON, after J.R.Swinton, wl seated, with ribbon and star of the Thistle, mezz, BM.

ROSENHAGEN, Philip (1737?-1798) divine.
C JAMES SAYERS, wl with Lord Shelburne, etch, NPG.

ROSS, David (1728-1790) actor.
P JOHAN ZOFFANY, wl as 'Hamlet', Garrick Club, London. UNKNOWN, hs as Kitely in *Every Man in his Humour*, Garrick Club.
R J.THORNTHWAITE, after Roberts, wl as Essex, line, pub 1776, NPG.

ROSS, Sir Hew Dalrymple (1779-1868) field-marshal.
P WILLIAM SALTER, tql study for 'Waterloo Banquet at Apsley House', NPG 3748. SIR FRANCIS GRANT, 1868, wl, Royal Artillery Mess, Woolwich.
D THOMAS HEAPHY, hs, pencil and w/c, NPG 1914 (13).
G W.SALTER, 'Waterloo Banquet at Apsley House', oil, 1836, Wellington Museum, Apsley House, London.

ROSS, John (1719-1792) bishop of Exeter.
P UNKNOWN, hl, Longleat House, Wilts. Attrib L.F.ABBOTT, hl, The Bishop's Palace, Exeter.

ROSS, Sir John (1777-1856) rear-admiral and arctic explorer.
P JAMES GREEN, 1833, hl, NPG 314. B.R.FAULKNER, hl, SNPG 8. UNKNOWN, hl, Royal Geographical Society, London. UNKNOWN, c1833, tql, NMM, Greenwich.
D UNKNOWN, hs, w/c, Royal Geographical Society.
SC DAVID D'ANGERS, 1836, bronze medallion, Musée des Beaux Arts, Angers, France.
PR H.GOULDSMITH, hs, lith, pub 1833, NPG. W.WATKINS, after T.H.Shepherd, hl, stipple, pub 1835, NPG.

ROSS, Sir John Lockhart (1721-1790) Vice-admiral.
P Attrib JOHAN ZOFFANY, 1767-74, wl, NMM, Greenwich.
M SAMUEL COTES, 1758, w/c, SNPG 1287.
PR J.MCARDELL, after J.Reynolds, tql in uniform, mezz, BM.

ROSS, Robert (1766-1814) soldier.
P UNKNOWN, Regimental Museum, Headquarters Lancashire Fusiliers.
SC J.J.P.KENDRICK, c1820, monument, St Paul's Cathedral, London.

ROSS, Sir William Charles (1794-1860) miniaturist.
M Self-portrait, 1827, hs, V & A. HUGH ROSS (his brother), c1843, hs, NPG 1946. MRS DALTON, Royal Coll.
PR UNKNOWN, after T.Illidge, hs, woodcut, oval, for *Art Journal*, 1849, BM. UNKNOWN, 'Members of the Royal Academy in 1857', woodcut, one of eight ovals, for *Illust London News*, 2 May 1857, BM. UNKNOWN, after a photograph by John Watkins, tql, woodcut, for *Illust London News*, 1860, NPG.

ROSSE, Sir Lawrence Parsons, 2nd Earl of (1758-1841) statesman.
PR J.HEATH, after J.Comerford, hs, stipple, for Sir J.Barrington's *Memoirs*, BM, NPG.

ROSSLYN, Alexander Wedderburn, 1st Earl of (1733-1805) lord chancellor.
P SIR JOSHUA REYNOLDS, 1785, tql seated in wig and gown, Lincoln's Inn, London. WILLIAM OWEN, hl seated, NPG 392 (on loan to the Law Courts). MATHER BROWN, wl seated in wig and gown, Walker Art Gallery, Liverpool.
D HENRY EDRIDGE, 1795, tql, pencil, BM.
G J.S.COPLEY, 'The Collapse of the Earl of Chatham in the House of Lords, 7 July 1778', TATE 100, on loan to NPG.
PR H.MEYER, after J.Northcote, hl, stipple, for *Contemporary Portraits*, 1812, BM, NPG.

C R.DIGHTON, 'A Chance Seller, with a capital prize in the State Lottery', coloured etch, pub 1797, NPG. Several etchings by SAYERS, GILLRAY, KAY, etc, BM, NPG.

ROSSLYN, Sir James St Clair Erskine, 2nd Earl of (1762-1837) general.
G SIR GEORGE HAYTER, 'The Trial of Queen Caroline, 1820', oil, NPG 999. SIR G.HAYTER, 'The House of Commons, 1833', oil, NPG 54.

ROTHSCHILD, Nathan Meyer (1777-1836) financier and merchant.
SC J.P.DANTAN, 1833, caricature plaster statuette, Musée Carnavelet, Paris.
PR UNKNOWN, after C.Penny, hl seated, stipple, pub 1827, NPG. STANDIDGE & LEMON, after Edouart, wl silhouette, lith, pub 1836, NPG.
C R.DIGHTON, wl, 'A view from the Royal Exchange', coloured etch, pub 1817, NPG, V & A.

ROUPELL, George Leith (1797-1854) physician.
PR UNKNOWN, tql, line, BM.

ROUS, Henry John (1795-1877) admiral and sportsman.
P HENRY WEIGALL, RA 1866, wl, Jockey Club, London. G.THOMPSON, tql profile, with George Payne, NPG 2957.
D COUNT A.D'ORSAY, 1842, hl, pencil, DoE.
SC M.RAGGI, RA 1878, marble bust, Jockey Club, London.
PR J.BROWN, hs, stipple, pub 1860, NPG. UNKNOWN, hs, lith, for Cassells' *National Portrait Gallery*, 1877, NPG.
C A.THOMPSON, wl, chromo-lith, for *Vanity Fair*, 7 May 1870, NPG.

ROUS, John Edward Cornwallis, see 2nd Earl of Stradbroke.

ROUTH, Martin Joseph (1755-1854) divine.
P T.C.THOMPSON, RA 1843, tql, Magdalen College, Oxford; copy 1851, Bodleian Library, Oxford. KARL HARTMANN, 1850, hl, Magdalen College. J.KENNEDY, 1850, hl, Magdalen College. H.W.PICKERSGILL, 1850, tql, Magdalen College.
D H.W.PICKERSGILL, head, study for the portrait, pastel, Magdalen College.

ROUTH, Sir Randolph Isham (1785?-1858) commissary-general in the army.
PR F.JOUBERT, after E.U.Eddis, wl seated, mezz, BM.

ROWAN, Archibald Hamilton (1751-1834) Irish nationalist.
G UNKNOWN, 'The United Irish Patriots of 1798', coloured lith, NPG.
PR UNKNOWN, silhouette profile, lith, from set of 'Irish Politicians', BM.

ROWAN, Sir Charles (1782?-1852) soldier and chief commissioner of police.
P WILLIAM SALTER, tql study for 'Waterloo Banquet at Apsley House', NPG 3749.
G WILLIAM SALTER, 'Waterloo Banquet at Apsley House', oil, 1836, Wellington Museum, Apsley House, London.

ROWE, Harry (1726-1800) showman.
PR UNKNOWN, hs profile, line, pub 1787, NPG. UNKNOWN, hl, oval, etch, pub 1798, NPG. R.THEW, after J.England, hl profile, stipple, and line, BM.

ROWLANDS, Daniel (1713-1790) Welsh methodist.
M ROBERT BOWYER, hs, oval, National Library of Wales, Aberystwyth, Dyfed.
PR UNKNOWN, hl, line, oval, for *Gospel Mag*, 1778, BM.

ROWLANDSON, Thomas (1757-1827) satirical draughtsman.
D THOMAS ROWLANDSON, 1784, wl talking with a lady outside

The Angel, Lymington, pen and w/c over pencil, Huntington Library and Art Gallery, San Marino, USA. T.ROWLANDSON, 1784, wl breakfasting at Egham, pen and w/c, Huntington Library and Art Gallery. T.ROWLANDSON, 1784, wl at dinner, pen and w/c, Huntington Library and Art Gallery. J.R.SMITH, c1795, hs, pencil, chalk and wash, BM. G.H.HARLOW, 1814, hl, pencil and chalk, NPG 2813. J.T.SMITH, 1824, hs, pen and wash, Metropolitan Museum of Art, New York, USA. JOHN JACKSON, hs, pencil, NPG 2198.

ROWLEY, Sir Charles, Bart (1770-1845) admiral.
P FRANK S.EASTMAN, after an unknown artist, The Admiralty, Portsmouth.
PR J.R.JACKSON, after G.Sanders, hl in uniform, mezz, pub 1848, BM, NPG.

ROWLEY, Sir Joshua, Bart (1734-1790) vice-admiral.
P GEORGE ROMNEY, 1787-8, hl, NMM, Greenwich.

ROWLEY, Sir Josias, Bart (1765-1842) vice-admiral.
P ANDREW MORTON, 1832-3, tql in uniform with orders, NMM, Greenwich.
C JOHN KIRKWOOD, wl, etch, NPG.

ROWLEY, Thomas, see Thomas CHATTERTON.

ROWLEY, William (1742-1806) surgeon.
M PETER PAILLOU jun, hl, oval, V & A.

ROXBURGH(E), James Innes-Ker, 5th Duke of (1738-1823) soldier.
P Attrib SIR JOSHUA REYNOLDS, hs, Floors Castle, Borders region, Scotland, engr V.Green, mezz, pub 1807, BM.

ROXBURGH(E), John Ker, 3rd Duke of (1740-1804) bibliophile.
P POMPEO BATONI, 1761, wl in peer's robes, Floors Castle, Borders region, Scotland. THOMAS PATCH, wl caricature, NPG 724. UNKNOWN, hs, SNPG 288. UNKNOWN, hl with star of the thistle, Floors Castle.
PR W.SAY, after W.Beechey, hl, mezz, for vol iv of Dibdin's ed of Ames's *Typographical Antiquities*, 1819, BM, NPG. C.E.WAGSTAFF, after W.Hamilton, tql, stipple, for Jerdan's *Nat Portrait Gallery*, 1832, BM, NPG.

ROXBURGH, William (1751-1815) botanist.
PR C.WARREN, tql seated, from a miniature, line, for *Transactions of the Society of Arts*, 1815, BM.

ROY, John (1700-1752) see John STEWART.

ROYLE, John Forbes (1799-1858) surgeon and naturalist.
D UNKNOWN, tql seated, drg or lith, Royal Botanic Gardens, Kew.

RUDING, Rogers (1751-1820) coin-collector.
D LEWIS VASLET, hs, pastel, Merton College, Oxford.

RUMBOLD, Sir Thomas, 1st Bart (1736-1791) governor of Madras.
PR W.ANGUS, after T.Stothard, hs, line, for *European Mag*, 1782, BM.

RUMFORD, Sir Benjamin Thomson, Count von (1753-1814) scientist and founder of the Royal Institution.
P THOMAS GAINSBOROUGH, hs, Fogg Art Museum, Cambridge, USA. M.KELLERHOVEN, hs, Royal Institution, London. After M.KELLERHOVEN, hs, NPG 1332. REMBRANDT PEALE, hs, American Academy of Arts and Sciences, Boston, USA. J.R.SMITH, tql seated, The Royal Society, London.
G J.F.SKILL, J.GILBERT, W. and E.WALKER, 'Men of Science Living in 1807-8', pencil and wash, NPG 1075.
SC After JAMES TASSIE, 1796, plaster medallion, SNPG 390.
PR J.RAUSCHMAYER, after G.Dillis, hs, stipple, oval, 1797, BM, NPG.
G JAMES GILLRAY, 1802, 'Scientific Researches', etch, NPG. JAMES

GILLRAY, wl, entitled 'The Comforts of a Rumford Stove', etch, Royal Institution, London.

RUNCIMAN, Alexander (1736-1785) painter.
P Self-portrait, 1784, hs with John Brown, SNPG L31.
D JOHN BROWN, 1785, hl, pencil, SNPG L88. J.RUNCIMAN, wl, pencil, NGS. JOHN BROWN, hs, pencil, NGS.
PR J.STEWART, after J.Brown, hl, stipple, oval, pub 1802, BM.

RUNCIMAN, John (1744-1768) artist.
P Self-portrait, 1767, hs, SNPG L32.

RUNNINGTON, Charles (1751-1821) legal-writer.
PR T.BLOOD, hs, stipple, for *European Mag*, 1817, BM, NPG.

RUSHTON, Edward (1756-1814) poet and bookseller.
PR E.SMITH, hs, line, oval, pub 1815, BM.

RUSHTON, Edward (1796-1851) printer and stationer.
P SPIRIDIONE GAMBARDELLA, hl, Walker Art Gallery, Liverpool.

RUSSELL, Alexander (1715?-1768) physician.
PR TROTTER, after N.Dance, hs, stipple, oval, NPG.

RUSSELL, Francis (1765-1802), see 5th Duke of Bedford.

RUSSELL, Lord George William (1790-1846) major-general.
P SIR GEORGE HAYTER, RA 1820, wl equestrian, attending the 1st Duke of Wellington, Woburn Abbey, Beds.
G SIR GEORGE HAYTER, 'The Trial of Queen Caroline, 1820', oil, NPG 999.
SC SIR RICHARD WESTMACOTT, 1843, bust, Woburn Abbey.

RUSSELL, Sir Henry, Bart (1751-1836) Indian judge.
SC SIR FRANCIS CHANTREY, 1822, bust, Ashmolean Museum, Oxford.
PR S.W.REYNOLDS, after G.Chinnery, wl in robes, mezz, BM, NPG.

RUSSELL, James (1754-1836) surgeon.
P DAVID MARTIN, 1769, wl with his father, SNPG 2014.

RUSSELL, James (1790-1861) barrister and law reporter.
PR T.LUPTON, after E.Coleman, tql seated, mezz, BM, NPG.

RUSSELL, John (1710-1771), see 4th Duke of Bedford.

RUSSELL, John (1745-1806) portrait-painter and pastelist.
D Self-portrait, head, chalk, NPG 3907. GEORGE DANCE, hl, Royal Academy, London.
G H.SINGLETON, 'The Royal Academicians, 1793', oil, Royal Academy.
PR UNKNOWN, hs when young, process block, oval, BM.

RUSSELL, John (1766-1839), see 6th Duke of Bedford.

RUSSELL, John (1787-1863) divine.
PR W.SAY, after B.R.Faulkner, tql, mezz, pub 1829, BM, NPG.

RUSSELL, John (1795-1883) 'the sporting parson'.
PR UNKNOWN, after S.J.Carter, wl, process block, NPG. JOSEPH BROWN, after a photograph by Britton and Sons, wl, stipple, pub 1870, NPG.

RUSSELL, Lord John Russell, 1st Earl (1792-1878) prime-minister.
P SIR WILLIAM BEECHEY, as a boy, Woburn Abbey, Beds. SIR GEORGE HAYTER, c1815, hs, Longleat House, Wilts. SIR GEORGE HAYTER, 1832, Woburn Abbey. G.F.WATTS, c1851, hs, NPG 895. SIR FRANCIS GRANT, 1853, wl, NPG 1121.
D DANIEL MACLISE, 1831, wl seated, pencil, V & A. G.F.WATTS, c1852, hs, chalk, NPG 2635. S.F.DIEZ, tql, drg, Staatliche Kupferstichkabinett, Berlin.
G SIR G.HAYTER, 'The Trial of Queen Caroline, 1820', oil, NPG 999. SIR G.HAYTER, 'The House of Commons, 1833', oil, NPG 54. SIR DAVID WILKIE, 'The First Council of Queen Victoria

1837', oil, Royal Coll. JOHN PARTRIDGE, 'The Fine Arts Commissioners, 1846', NPG 342, 3. H.W.PHILLIPS, 'The Royal Commissioners for the Great Exhibition, 1851', oil, V & A. SIR JOHN GILBERT, 'The Coalition Ministry, 1854', pencil and wash, NPG 1125. J.PHILLIP, 'The Marriage of the Princess Royal, 1858', oil, Royal Coll. J.PHILLIP, 'The House of Commons, 1860', oil Palace of Westminster, London. T.J.BARKER, 'Queen Victoria Presenting a Bible in the Audience Chamber at Windsor', oil, c1861, NPG 4969.

SC JOHN FRANCIS, 1832, marble bust, NPG 678, on loan to the House of Lords. J.FRANCIS, 1838, bust, Royal Coll. RICHARD WESTMACOTT jun, c1843, bust, Woburn Abbey. SIR J.E.BOEHM, 1880, statue, Palace of Westminster, London; related marble bust, Westminster Abbey, London; study, terracotta head, NPG 4291.

C C.PELLEGRINI, ('Ape'), wl seated, coloured lith, for Vanity Fair, 5 June 1869, NPG. JOHN DOYLE, numerous political drgs, BM.

PH WINDOW and BRIDGE, tql, carte, NPG.

RUSSELL, Patrick (1727-1805) physician and naturalist.
D After GEORGE DANCE, 1794, hs, profile, pencil, Royal College of Physicians, London.
PR W.DANIELL, after G.Dance, hl profile, soft-ground etch, pub 1811, BM, NPG. W.RIDLEY, after L.Vaslet, hs in turban, stipple, oval, for European Mag, 1811, BM, NPG.

RUSSELL, Samuel Thomas (1769?-1845) actor.
D SAMUEL DE WILDE, wl as Jerry Sneak in Foote's The Mayor of Garratt, w/c, Garrick Club, London.
G S. DE WILDE, RA 1810, wl in The Mayor of Garratt, Garrick Club.

RUSSELL, Thomas (1767-1803) Irish Nationalist.
G UNKNOWN, 'The United Irish Patriots of 1798', coloured lith, NPG.

RUSSELL, Thomas (1781?-1846), see CLOUTT.

RUTHERFORD, Andrew, see Rutherfurd.

RUTHERFORD, Daniel (1749-1819) physician and botanist.
P After SIR HENRY RAEBURN, hl, Royal College of Physicians, Edinburgh.
G J.F.SKILL, J.GILBERT, W. and E.WALKER, 'Men of Science Living in 1807-8', pencil and wash, NPG 1075.
PR HOLL, after Reaburn, hl, stipple, oval, 1804, NPG.

RUTHERFURD, Andrew Rutherfurd, Lord (1791-1854) Scottish judge.

P SIR JOHN WATSON GORDON, wl, SNPG 710. COLVIN SMITH, wl, Faculty of Advocates, Parliament Hall, Edinburgh.
D SIR J.W.GORDON, wl, chalk, SNPG 1727. B.W.CROMBIE, w/c, SNPG L40.
G SIR GEORGE HARVEY, with the Marquess of Breadalbane, the Earl of Dahousie and Lord Cockburn, oil, SNPG 1497.
SC WILLIAM BRODIE, marble bust, Faculty of Advocates, Parliament Hall, Edinburgh.

RUTLAND, Charles Manners, 4th Duke of (1754-1787) lord-lieutenant of Ireland.
P By of after THOMAS GAINSBOROUGH, tql in Vandyke dress, Belvoir Castle, Leics; version, Eton College, Berks. Attrib SIR JOSHUA REYNOLDS, hs, oval, Belvoir Castle. M.W.PETERS, tql, Belvoir Castle.
M HORACE HONE, 1805, hs with Garter star, enamel, oval, NGI.
PR W.DICKINSON, after J.Reynolds, wl in Garter robes, holding white wand, mezz, pub 1791, BM. W.LANE, after R.Cosway, hs, stipple, oval, NPG.

RYAN, Sir Edward (1793-1875) judge.
P FREDERICK, LORD LEIGHTON, c1872, hl, Society of Dilettanti, Brooks's Club, London.

RYDER, Dudley (1762-1847), see 1st Earl of and 2nd Baron Harrowby.

RYDER, Dudley (1798-1882), see 2nd Earl of Harrowby.

RYDER, Henry (1777-1836) bishop of Gloucester, of Lichfield, and of Coventry.
SC SIR FRANCIS CHANTREY, 1841, statue, kneeling figure, Lichfield Cathedral; model for statue, Ashmolean Museum, Oxford.
PR R.W.SIEVIER, after W.Behnes, hl profile, stipple, pub 1817, NPG. T.WOOLNOTH, after H.Pickersgill, tql seated, stipple, for Christian Keepsake, 1836, BM, NPG.

RYDER, Thomas (1735-1790) actor.
D JAMES ROBERTS, head, profile, Garrick Club, London.
PR Various theatrical prints, BM.

RYLAND, John Collett (1723-1792) divine.
PR R.HOUSTON, after J.Russell, hl, mezz, oval, for Witsen's Oeconomia, 1775, BM.

RYLAND, William Wynne (1732-1783) engraver.
PR D.P.PARISET, after P.Falconet, hs profile, stipple, BM, NPG.

RYVES, Mrs Lavinia Janetta Horton de Serres, née Serres (1797-1871) claimed to be Princess of Cumberland and Duchess of Lancaster.
PR UNKNOWN, hs, woodcut, for Illust London News, 1861, NPG.

S

SABINE, Sir Edward (1788-1883) soldier and scientist.
P STEPHEN PEARCE, 1850, hs, study for 'The Arctic Council', NPG 907; tql version, 1855, Royal Society, London. G.F.WATTS, 1874, hl in uniform, Royal Artillery Mess, Woolwich.
G STEPHEN PEARCE, 'The Arctic Council, 1851', oil, NPG 1208.
SC JOSEPH DURHAM, 1859, bust, Royal Society.
PR T.H.MAGUIRE, tql seated, lith, for *Ipswich Museum Portraits*, 1851, BM, NPG.
PH W.WALKER, NPG.

SABINE, Joseph (1770-1837) horticulturist.
PR W.DRUMMOND, after E.U.Eddis, hl, lith, for *Athenaeum Portraits*, BM, NPG. MISS TURNER, after E.Rigby, hl, lith, BM.

SACKVILLE, Charles (1711-1769), see 2nd Duke of Dorset.

SACKVILLE, George Sackville Germain, 1st Viscount (c1716-1785) soldier and politician.
P THOMAS GAINSBOROUGH, tql, Knole (NT), Kent.
M NATHANIEL HONE, 1760, hs, oval, NPG 4910.
G JOHN SINGLETON COPLEY, 'The Collapse of the Earl of Chatham in the House of Lords, 7 July 1778', oil, TATE 100, on loan to NPG.
SC After JAMES TASSIE, plaster medallion, SNPG 499.
PR J.JACOBÉ, after G.Romney, tql, mezz, pub 1780, BM, NPG. J.MCARDELL, after J.Reynolds, tql, mezz, BM, NPG.

SACKVILLE, John Frederick, see 3rd Duke of Dorset.

SADLER, James (1753-1828) aeronaut.
P UNKNOWN, tql, NPG 4955.
PR B.TAYLOR, hl seated, stipple, pub 1812, BM, NPG. E.SCOTT, after J.Roberts, hl, stipple, oval, BM.

SADLER, Michael Thomas (1780-1835) social reformer.
P WILLIAM ROBINSON, before 1830, hl, NPG 2907.
D JOHN DOYLE, two wl, pencil, BM.
PR UNKNOWN, wl, lith, pub 1829, NPG. D.MACLISE, wl in House of Commons, lith, for *Fraser's Mag*, 1835, BM.
C JOHN DOYLE, wl in 'Newcastle versus Newark', BM.

ST ALBANS, Harriot, née Mellon, Duchess of (1777?-1837) actress.
P SIR WILLIAM BEECHEY, wl in landscape, NPG 1915.
PR W.RIDLEY, after C.Allingham, tql seated, stipple, oval, for *Monthly Mirror*, pub 1803, BM. W.SAY, after J.Masquerier, wl as Mrs Page in *Merry Wives of Windsor*, mezz, pub 1804, BM. J.HOPWOOD, after S.J.Stump, hs, from a miniature, stipple, pub 1813, BM, NPG.

ST AUBYN, Sir John, 5th Bart (1758-1839) politician.
P SIR JOSHUA REYNOLDS, 1757-59, Pencarrow House, Cornwall. NATHANIEL HONE, 1778, St Michaels Mount (NT), Cornwall. Portraits by JOHN OPIE, and one by Opie's son, St Michaels Mount. J.OPIE, after Reynolds of c1786-90, St Michaels Mount. J.OPIE, c1785, City Art Gallery, Plymouth.
M UNKNOWN, V & A.
PR S.W.REYNOLDS, after J.Opie, wl in landscape, mezz, BM.

ST GERMANS, Edward Granville Eliot, 3rd Earl of (1798-1877) lord-lieutenant of Ireland.
P STEPHEN CATTERSON SMITH, Dublin Castle.
PR W.J.EDWARDS, after S.Bendixen, hl, line, BM. W.HOLL, after G.Richmond, hs, stipple, for 'Grillion's Club' series, BM, NPG.

ST HELENS, Alleyne Fitzherbert, Baron (c1753-1839) diplomat.
G SIR GEORGE HAYTER, 'The Trial of Queen Caroline, 1820', oil NPG 999.
PR W.WARD, after J.W.Chandler, tql in uniform, mezz, pub 1795 BM, NPG. UNKNOWN, after H.Edridge, tql, stipple, BM, NPG.

ST LEGER, John Hayes (1756-1800) general, friend of the Prince of Wales.
P SIR JOSHUA REYNOLDS, 1778, wl, Waddesdon Manor (NT) Bucks. THOMAS GAINSBOROUGH, 1782, wl, Royal Coll.
PR P.ROBERTS, after R.Cosway, hs in uniform, stipple, oval, for *European Mag*, 1795, BM, NPG.

ST LEONARDS, Edward Burtenshaw Sugden (1781-1875) lord chancellor.
P E.U.EDDIS, c1853, tql in robes, Lincoln's Inn, London.
PR E.SCRIVEN, after J.Moore, hl seated, stipple, for *Eminent Conservative Statesman*, 1837, BM, NPG. FRANCIS HOLL, after C.Sugden, hs, stipple, 1859, NPG. T.WOOLNOTH, after C.Penny, hl, stipple, BM, NPG.

ST VINCENT, John Jervis, 1st Earl of (1735-1823) admiral of the fleet.
P FRANCIS COTES, 1769, tql, NPG 2026. GILBERT STUART 1782-7, hs in uniform with Bath, unfinished sketch, NMM Greenwich. SIR WILLIAM BEECHEY, 1792-3, hl with Bath, oval NMM. DOMENICO PELLIGRINI, 1806, wl in uniform, with Bath and St Vincent medal, NMM. JOHN HOPPNER, 1809, wl in uniform, with orders as above, Royal Coll. Studio of L.F.ABBOTT, hs, NPG 936. SIR WILLIAM BEECHEY, tql, Guildhall Art Gallery, London. W.BEECHEY, hs, NPG 3310. UNKNOWN, c1822-3, hl seated, in old age, NMM.
D BOUCH, hs, pencil, NPG 167a.
SC JOHN DE VAERE, 1798, Wedgwood medallion, BM. SIR FRANCIS CHANTREY, bust on monument, St Michael Church, Stone Staffs. SIR FRANCIS CHANTREY, bust, Ashmolean Museum Oxford.

SALE, Florentina, Lady, née Wynch (1790?-1853) wife of Sir Robert Sale.
PR R.J.LANE, after H.Moseley, hl, lith, pub 1845, NPG. W.J.WARD after T.Lawrence, hl seated, mezz, BM.

SALE, Sir Robert Henry (1782-1845) colonel.
PR THOMAS LUPTON, after G.Clint, tql, mezz, pub 1845, NPG R.J.LANE, hs in uniform, lith, pub 1846, BM, NPG. F.HOLL, after H.Moseley, tql in uniform, stipple, BM, NPG.

SALISBURY, James Cecil, 7th Earl and 1st Marquess of (1748-1823) lord chamberlain.
P GEORGE ROMNEY, c1781-3, wl holding lord chamberlain's staff Hatfield House, Herts. UNKNOWN, c1790-3, tql holding staff Hatfield House. SIR WILLIAM BEECHEY, RA 1805, wl in Garter robes, holding staff, Hatfield House.
M SAMUEL COTES, 1775, hs, oval, Hatfield House. Two portraits attrib ADAM BUCK, one c1795-1800, the other 1823, both hs oval, Hatfield House.
SL UNKNOWN, c1785, hs, oval, Hatfield House.
PR A.CARDON, after H.Edridge, wl in official dress, with staff and key, stipple, BM.

SALISBURY, Mary Amelia Hill, 1st Marchioness of (1750-1835) peeress, burnt to death at Hatfield.
P Sir JOSHUA REYNOLDS, RA 1781, wl in garden with dog, Hatfield House, Herts.
M GEORGE ENGELHEART, c1790, hs, oval, Hatfield House.
G ARTHUR DEVIS, '1st Marquess of Downshire and family', oil, c1760, NPG L160.

SALISBURY, Richard Anthony (1761-1829) botanist.
D W.J.BURCHELL, 1817, hs, oval, Royal Botanic Gardens, Kew.

SALOMON, Johann Peter (1745-1815) musician.
P Sir WILLIAM BEECHEY, 1784, hl, Faculty of Music, Oxford. THOMAS HARDY, RA 1792, hl, Royal College of Music, London. Attrib T.LAWRENCE, wl, Garrick Club, London.
G WILLIAM LANE, study for a group of musical performers, chalk, Royal Coll.
PR G.FACIUS, after W.Owen, hl, stipple, pub 1807, NPG. W.DANIELL, after G.Dance, hl profile, soft-ground etch, pub 1810, BM, NPG.

SALOMONS, Sir David, 1st Bart (1797-1873) lord mayor of London.
PR C.TURNER, after Mrs C.Pearson, tql in sheriff robes, mezz, pub 1837, BM, NPG. Two woodcuts by unknown artists, one pub 1844, NPG.

SALT, Henry (1780-1827) draughtsman and traveller.
PR UNKNOWN, after J.J.Halls, tql, stipple, BM, NPG.

SALTOUN, Alexander George Fraser, 16th Baron (1785-1853) lieutenant-general.
P Sir THOMAS LAWRENCE, c1809, wl, formerly United Service Club, London (c/o The Crown Commissioners). WILLIAM SALTER, tql study for 'Waterloo Banquet', oil, c1834-40, NPG 3750.
G WILLIAM SALTER, 'Waterloo Banquet at Apsley House', oil, 1836, Wellington Museum, Apsley House, London.
PR C.BAUGNIET, tql seated, lith, BM, NPG. G.ZOBEL, after T.Lawrence, wl in uniform, mezz, BM.

SAMS, Joseph (1784-1860) orientalist.
G BENJAMIN ROBERT HAYDON, 'The Anti-Slavery Society Convention, 1840', oil, NPG 599.

SANCHO, Ignatius (1729-1780) writer.
P THOMAS GAINSBOROUGH, hs, National Gallery of Canada, Ottawa, Canada.

SANDBY, Paul (1730/1-1809) water-colourist and engraver.
P FRANCIS COTES, 1761, hl, TATE 1943. Sir WILLIAM BEECHEY, 1789, hl, NPG 1379. Sir WILLIAM BEECHEY, Royal Academy, London.
D PIERRE-ETIENNE FALCONET, 1768, hs, chalk with wash, BM. GEORGE DANCE, 1794, hs profile, w/c, Royal Academy, London.
G JOHAN ZOFFANY, 'Royal Academicians, 1772', oil, Royal Coll. HENRY SINGLETON, 'Royal Academicians, 1793', oil, Royal Academy.
PR R.DAGLEY, after R.Cosway, hl, stipple, for Arnold's *Library of the Fine Arts*, 1831, BM, NPG. P.SANDBY, wl with his wife and children, etch, BM.

SANDBY, Thomas (1723-1798) draughtsman and architect.
P Sir WILLIAM BEECHEY, 1792, hl seated, NPG 1380.
D GEORGE DANCE, 1794, hs profile, Royal Academy, London.
G JOHAN ZOFFANY, 'Royal Academicians, 1772', oil, Royal Coll. HENRY SINGLETON, 'Royal Academicians, 1793', oil, Royal Academy.

SANDERS, George (1774-1846) portrait-painter.

P ANDREW GEDDES, 1816, wl, NGS 416.

SANDFORD, Daniel (1766-1830) bishop of Edinburgh.
PR W.WALKER and S.COUSINS, after J.W.Gordon, tql seated, mezz, pub 1829, BM, NPG.

SANDFORD, Sir Daniel Keyte (1798-1838) professor of Greek at Glasgow University.
SL AUGUSTIN EDOUART, 1830, SNPG 793.

SANDON, Dudley Ryder, Viscount, see 1st Earl of and 2nd Baron Harrowby.

SANDWICH, John Montagu, 4th Earl of (1718-1792) statesman and rake.
P JOSEPH HIGHMORE, 1740, tql with turban, NPG 1977. GEORGE KNAPTON, 1745, hl with turban, Society of Dilettanti, Brooks's Club, London. THOMAS GAINSBOROUGH, 1783, wl with plan of Greenwich Infirmary, NMM, Greenwich. J.E.LIOTARD, wl, on loan to DoE (Foreign Office, London). After ZOFFANY, hl, NPG 182.
G JOHN SINGLETON COPLEY, 'The Collapse of the Earl of Chatham in the House of Lords, 7 July 1778', oil, TATE 100, on loan to NPG.
SC Wedgwood medallion, hs, BM.
C GEORGE TOWNSHEND, wl, pencil, ink, w/c, NPG 4855 (23). JAMES SAYERS, wl, etch, pub 1782, NPG.

SASS, Henry (1788-1844) painter.
D CHARLES HUTTON LEAR, c1845, hs, pencil, NPG 1456 (24).
PR E.STALKER, tql by table with bust, skull, etc, line, pub 1822, BM, NPG.

SAUMAREZ, James, Baron de (1757-1834), see Baron DE Saumarez.

SAUMAREZ, Philip (1710-1747) captain in the navy.
SC Sir HENRY CHEERE, monument, Westminster Abbey, London.

SAUNDERS, Sir Charles (1713?-1775) admiral.
P Sir JOSHUA REYNOLDS, c1765, tql in uniform, NMM, Greenwich. RICHARD BROMPTON, 1772-3, tql with Bath, NMM.
PR J.CHAPMAN, hs in uniform, stipple, oval, pub 1800, BM, NPG. UNKNOWN, from a bust, stipple and line, for Hervey's *Naval History*, NPG.

SAUNDERS, George (1762-1839) architect.
D Sir FRANCIS CHANTREY, two sketches, one hs, one hs profile, pencil, NPG 316a (106).
SC Sir FRANCIS CHANTREY, bust, RIBA, London.

SAUNDERS, John Cunningham (1773-1810) opthalmic surgeon.
PR A.CARDON, after A.W.Devis, hl, stipple, for his *Works*, 1811, BM, NPG.

SAUNDERS, William (1743-1817) physician.
P H.ASHBY, 1809, tql, seated, Royal College of Physicians, London.
PR C.TOWNLEY, after L.Abbott, hl, mezz, pub 1792, BM. J.R.SMITH, tql seated, mezz, pub 1803, BM. H.MEYER, after R.W.Satchwell, hl, stipple, for *European Mag*, 1817, BM.

SAVAGE, Samuel Morton (1721-1791) divine.
PR UNKNOWN, hl, line, oval, pub 1796, BM.

SAVILE, Sir George, 8th Bart (1726-1784) whig politician.
SC JOHN FISHER, 1784, statue, York Minster. JOSEPH NOLLEKENS, 1784, bust, Fitzwilliam Museum, Cambridge; replica, V & A.
PR B.WILSON and J.BASIRE, after B.Wilson, wl, etch and line, pub 1770, BM.

SAWBRIDGE, John (1732?-1795) lord mayor of London.
G R.HOUSTON, tql with Alderman Beckford MP, and Alderman James Townsend, MP, mezz, pub 1769, BM, NPG. B.SMITH, after

W.Miller, 'Lord Mayor Newnham taking the oaths, 1782', stipple, pub 1801, BM.

PR T.WATSON, after B.West, wl in dress of a Roman tribune, mezz, pub 1772, BM, NPG. RIDLEY, hs, stipple, oval, pub 1798, NPG. J.HOPWOOD, hs, stipple, oval, pub 1805, BM.

C JAMES SAYERS, wl with Burke and Powys, entitled '. . . on the Sublime and Beautiful', etch, pub 1785, NPG. JAMES SAYERS, wl, etch, pub 1788, NPG. JAMES SAYERS, entitled 'The Comet', etch, pub 1789, NPG.

SAXTON, Sir Charles, Bart (1732-1808) captain in the navy.

PR S.W.REYNOLDS, after J.Northcote, tql in uniform, mezz, pub 1795, BM.

SAY, William (1768-1834) mezzotint engraver.

P JAMES GREEN, hs, NPG 1836.

SAYERS, Frank (1763-1817) poet and archaeologist.

PR W.C.EDWARDS, after J.Opie, hl, line, for his *Works*, 1823, BM, NPG.

SAYERS, James (1748-1823) caricaturist.

PR M.GAUCI, after J.Sayers, hs, aged 65, lith, BM.

SCARLETT, James (1769-1844), see 1st Baron Abinger.

SCARLETT, Sir James Yorke (1799-1871) general.

D EDWIN HAVELL, 1868, hl, Towneley Hall Art Gallery, Burnley. E.GOODWYN LEWIS, tql in uniform, pastel, Towneley Hall Art Gallery.

SC MATTHEW NOBLE, 1873, marble bust, Towneley Hall Art Gallery; related plaster cast, NPG 807.

PR UNKNOWN, hl, oval, woodcut, for *Illust Times*, 1871, NPG.

PH Two, both anonymous, wl and hs, Towneley Hall Art Gallery.

SCHANCK, John (1740-1823) admiral.

P UNKNOWN, c1795–1805, hl, NMM, Greenwich. JOHN JAMES MASQUERIER, hl, NPG 1923, engr C.Turner, mezz, pub 1799, BM.

SCHETKY, John Christian (1778-1874) marine painter.

PR UNKNOWN, hl, woodcut, for *Illust London News*, 1874, BM.

SCHIAVONETTI, Luigi (1765-1810) line-engraver.

PR A.CARDON, after H.Edridge, hl, stipple, pub 1811, BM, NPG.

SCHIMMELPENNINCK, Mrs Mary Anne (1778-1856) author.

PR H.ADLARD, after Fisher, hl, stipple, NPG.

SCHMELING, Gertrude Elizabeth, see Mrs Mara.

SCHOLEFIELD, James (1789-1853) classical scholar.

PR J.B.HUNT, after G.F.Joseph, tql, mezz, NPG.

SCHOMBERG, Sir Alexander (1720-1804) captain in the navy.

P WILLIAM HOGARTH, 1763, hl, NMM, Greenwich.

SCHOMBERG, Isaac (1714-1780) physician.

P THOMAS HUDSON, hl, Huntington Library and Art Gallery, San Marino, USA.

SCHOMBERG, Isaac (1753-1813) captain in the navy.

G BARTOLOZZI, LANDSEER, RYDER & STOW, after R.Smirke, 'Naval Victories', 'Commemoration of the victory of June 1st 1794', line engr, pub 1803, BM.

SCHOMBERG, Ralph (1714-1792) physician.

P THOMAS GAINSBOROUGH, wl, NG 684.

SCHWANFELDER, Charles Henry (1773-1837) painter.

P WILLIAM FREDERICK, 1825, hl, Leeds City Art Gallery. Self-portrait, wl seated in landscape, Leeds City Art Gallery. Self-portrait, hs, Leeds City Art Gallery.

SCHWEICKHARDT, Heinrich Wilhelm (1746-1797) landscape painter.

P Self-portrait, hs, Bilderdijk-Museum, Amsterdam.

SCORESBY, William (1760-1829) arctic navigator.

PR J.THOMSON, after A.Wivell, hl, stipple, for *Imperial Mag*, 1822, BM, NPG. H.ADLARD, hl, stipple, NPG.

SCORESBY, William (1789-1857) Minister, arctic explorer and man of science.

P EDWIN COCKBURN, hl, Whitby Museum, North Yorks.

D J.S.COTMAN, 1824, hs, pencil, V & A.

PR E.SMITH, after A.Mosses, hl in lay dress, line, for *Imperial Mag*, 1821, BM, NPG. J.B.HUNT, after a photograph by M.Claudet, hl, stipple and line, NPG.

SCOTT, Caroline Lucy, Lady, née Douglas (1784-1857) novelist.

PR W.SAY, after C.L.Douglas, wl standing on the battlements of a castle, mezz, BM.

SCOTT, Henry (1746-1812), see 3rd Duke of Buccleuch.

SCOTT, John (1730-1783) poet.

PR J.HALL, after J.Townsend, hs, line, oval, for his *Works*, 1782, BM, NPG.

SCOTT, John (1739-1798), see 1st Earl of Clonmell.

SCOTT, John (1747-1819), see John Scott WARING.

SCOTT, John (1751-1838), see 1st Earl of Eldon.

SCOTT, John (1774-1827), animal engraver.

PR W.T.FRY, after J.Jackson, tql seated, stipple, pub 1825, NPG, pub 1826, BM.

SCOTT, John (1783-1821) journalist.

D SEYMOUR KIRKUP, 1819, pencil, SNPG 1969.

SCOTT, Michael (1789-1835) author.

SL AUGUSTIN EDOUART, SNPG 794.

SCOTT, Samuel (1702?-1772) painter.

P T.HUDSON, c1730, tql, NPG L144. UNKNOWN, called Scott, hs, NPG 1683.

D JAMES DEACON, hs, profile, pencil and wash, BM.

SCOTT, Thomas (1747-1821) divine.

PR J.COLLYER, after L.Cossé, tql seated, line, pub 1820, BM, NPG. UNKNOWN, hs, stipple, for *New Baptist Mag*, 1826, NPG.

SCOTT, Sir Walter (1771-1832) novelist and poet.

P JAMES SAXON, c1805, tql seated with dog, SNPG 628. SIR HENRY RAEBURN, c1808, hs, Buccleuch Estates, Selkirk, Scotland. SIR HENRY RAEBURN, c1822, hs, SNPG 1286. SIR EDWIN LANDSEER, c1824, hl, NPG 391. SIR THOMAS LAWRENCE, 1826, tql seated, Royal Coll. SIR JOHN WATSON GORDON, 1830, hs, SNPG 575. SIR FRANCIS GRANT, 1831, SNPG 103. SIR WILLIAM ALLAN, 1832, wl seated in his study, NPG 321.

D ANDREW GEDDES, 1823, hs, pencil and chalk, SNPG 95. DANIEL MACLISE, 1825, hs profile, BM. WILLIAM BROCKEDON, 1830, hs, pencil and chalk, NPG 2515 (30). Several drgs, MICHAELANGELO GAETANI, 1832, SNPG 1105 and 1204. SIR WILLIAM ALLAN, head, pencil and chalk, NPG 2646. SIR EDWIN LANDSEER, 2 drgs, head, pen and ink, NPG 2811. SIR EDWIN LANDSEER, 2 drgs, one with Lady Scott, pencil, SNPG 140.

M UNKNOWN, 1775, hs as a child, w/c, SNPG L41.

SL AUGUSTE EDOUART, wl profile, NPG 1638.

G SIR DAVID WILKIE, 'The Abbotsford Family', oil, 1817, SNPG 1303. THOMAS FAED, Scott with his friends, SNPG 825.

SC SAMUEL JOSEPH, 1824, marble bust, Preston Hall, Lothian region, Scotland. SIR FRANCIS CHANTREY, 1828, marble bust, SNPG 662. JOHN GREENSHIELD, statue, Faculty of Advocates, Parliament Hall, Edinburgh. Death mask, plaster, after Chantrey, SNPG 180. SIR JOHN STEELL, c1865, statue on monument, Edinburgh.

SCOTT, William (1745-1836), see Baron Stowell.

SCOTT, William (1797-1848) jockey.

P HARRY HALL, wl equestrian, led by Sir Tatton Sykes, Yale Center for British Art, New Haven, USA. J.F.HERRING, wl equestrian on Memnon at Doncaster, Yale Center for British Art.

SCOVELL, Sir George (1774-1861) general.

P WILLIAM SALTER, tql study for 'Waterloo Banquet', NPG 3752.

D THOMAS HEAPHY, hs, w/c, NPG 1914 (14).

G W.SALTER, 'Waterloo Banquet at Apsley House', oil, 1836, Wellington Museum, Apsley House, London.

SCRIVEN, Edward (1775-1841) engraver.

D WILLIAM MULREADY, hs, V & A.

PR B.P.GIBBON, after A.Morton, hs, line and etch, BM, NPG. B.P.GIBBON, after W.Mulready, head, with another of G.Clint, etch, for Pye's *Patronage of British Art*, 1845, BM.

SCROPE, George Julius Poullett (1797-1876) geologist and political economist.

PR J.S.TEMPLETON, after E.U.Eddis, tql seated, lith, pub 1848, BM.

SEAFORD, Charles Rose Ellis, 1st Baron (1771-1845) politician.

P SIR THOMAS LAWRENCE, c1829, tql, Ickworth (NT), Suffolk.

SEAFORTH and MACKENZIE, Francis Mackenzie Humberston, Baron (1754-1815) soldier and governor of Barbados.

D JOHN SOBIESKA STUART, after unknown artist, with the 3rd titular Duke of Perth, ink, SNPG 1662. BERTEL THORVALDSEN, hs, pencil, Thorvaldsen Museum, Copenhagen.

SEATON, Sir John Colborne, 1st Baron (1778-1863) field marshal.

P J.W.PIENEMAN, 1821, hs, Wellington Museum, Apsley House, London. WILLIAM FISHER, 1862, wl, formerly United Service Club, London (c/o The Crown Commissioners). GEORGE JONES, 1860-3, hs, NPG 982b. UNKNOWN, Regimental Museum of the Oxford and Berkshire Light Infantry, Oxford.

SC GEORGE GAMMON ADAMS, 1863, marble bust, formerly United Service Club, London (c/o The Crown Commissioners); related plaster cast, NPG 1205.

PR W.J.EDWARDS, after G.Richmond, hs, stipple, pub 1855, BM, pub 1866, NPG.

SEBRIGHT, Sir John Saunders, 7th Bart (1767-1846) politician and agriculturalist.

G SIR GEORGE HAYTER, 'The House of Commons, 1833', oil, NPG 54.

PR S.W.REYNOLDS, after P.Boileau, hs, mezz, pub 1834, BM.

SEDGWICK, Adam (1785-1873) geologist.

P THOMAS PHILLIPS, c1832, tql, SAMUEL LAURENCE, c1844, hl, and R.B.FARREN, 1870, hl, all in Department of Geology, Cambridge. SIR W.BOXALL, 1851, hs, Trinity College, Cambridge.

D H.W.JUKES, tql as a young man, pencil, and LOWES DICKINSON, 1867, hs, both in Department of Geology, Cambridge.

SL AUGUSTE EDOUART, 1828, wl profile, NPG 4502; version, Sedgwick Museum, Cambridge.

SC HENRY WEEKES, 1846, marble bust, Geological Society, London. THOMAS WOOLNER, 1860, marble bust, Trinity College, Cambridge; related plaster cast, NPG 1669.

PR T.H.MAGUIRE, 1850, tql seated, lith, for *Ipswich Museum Portraits*, 1850, BM, NPG.

SEED, Jeremiah (1700-1747) divine.

PR S.F.RAVENET, after Hayman, hs, line, oval, BM, NPG.

SÉGUIER, William (1771-1843) first keeper of the National

Gallery, artist.

P JOHN JACKSON, 1830, hs, NG 6022. Attrib J.JACKSON, hs, NPG 2644.

PR MISS TURNER, after E.H.Baily, from marble bust, lith, BM.

SELBY, Prideaux John (1788-1867) naturalist.

PR T.H.MAGUIRE, tql seated, lith, for *Ipswich Museum Portraits*, BM, NPG.

SELWYN, George Augustus (1719-1791) wit and politician.

P SIR JOSHUA REYNOLDS, c1770, with Frederick, 5th Earl of Carlisle, Castle Howard, North Yorks.

D H.D.HAMILTON, 1770, hs, pastel, Castle Howard, North Yorks.

G SIR JOSHUA REYNOLDS, 'The Committee of Taste', oil, c1759, City Art Gallery, Bristol.

SEMPLE, James George (fl 1799) adventurer.

PR HARDING, hl, stipple, oval, pub 1799, NPG.

SENIOR, Nassau William (1790-1864) economist.

PR W.DRUMMOND, after W.Behnes, from a bust, lith, for *Athenaeum Portraits*, 1836, BM.

SEPPINGS, Sir Robert (1767-1840) surveyor of the navy.

P WILLIAM BRADLEY, c1833, tql, NMM, Greenwich.

SERRES, Dominic (1722-1793) marine painter.

D UNKNOWN, 1792, wl, pencil and wash, NPG 650a. GEORGE DANCE, 1793, hs, profile, Royal Academy, London.

M PHILIP JEAN, 1788, hl, NPG 1909.

G JOHAN ZOFFANY, 'Royal Academicians, 1772', oil, Royal Coll.

PR MRS D.TURNER, after O.Humphry, hl, etch, BM, NPG.

SERRES, Mrs Lavinia Janetta Horton de, see Mrs Ryves.

SERRES, Olivia, née Wilmot (1772-1834) artist and author.

PR MACKENZIE, after G.F.Joseph, hl, stipple, oval, BM.

SEVERN, Joseph (1793-1879) painter and friend of Keats.

D Self-portrait, c1820, hs, pencil, NPG 3091. JOHN PARTRIDGE, 1825, pencil, (probably Joseph Severn), NPG 3944 (20).

SEWARD, Anna (1742-1809) writer.

P TILLY KETTLE, 1762, hs, NPG 2017.

PR W.RIDLEY, after G.Romney, hl, stipple, oval, for *Monthly Mirror*, 1797, BM, NPG. J.CHAPMAN, hl, stipple, oval, for *Lady's Monthly Museum*, 1821, BM, NPG. H.LANDSEER, after John Downman, hl, stipple, NPG.

SEWARD, Thomas (1708-1790) canon of Lichfield.

PR R.H.CROMEK, after J.Wright, hl, line, for vol ii of Anna Seward's *Letters*, 1811, BM.

SEWARD, William (1747-1799) writer.

D GEORGE DANCE, 1793, hl profile, NPG 1157.

PR W.HOLL, after J.G.Wood, hl, stipple, pub 1799, BM, NPG.

SEYER, Samuel (1757-1831) divine.

PR WILLIAM WALKER, after N.Branwhite (1824), tql seated, stipple, NPG.

SEYMOUR, Edward Adolphus, see 11th Duke of Somerset.

SEYMOUR, Francis Ingram, see 2nd Marquess of Hertford.

SEYMOUR, Sir George Francis (1787-1870) admiral.

P JOHN LUCAS, tql in uniform, Ragley Hall, Northants.

PR F.HOLL, after J.Harrison, hl in uniform, stipple, pub 1852, BM, NPG.

SEYMOUR, Sir George Hamilton (1797-1880) diplomat.

P UNKNOWN, hs with Bath and Guelphic Order, Merton College, Oxford.

PR C.BAUGNIET, hl, lith, 1842, BM.

SEYMOUR, Lord Hugh (1759-1801) vice-admiral.

P JOHN HOPPNER, 1799, hl in uniform, NMM, Greenwich; versions,

Althorp, Northants, Ragley Hall, Warwicks. JOHN HOPPNER, hl, Weston Park, Salop.
D JOHN DOWNMAN, 1785, hl profile, w/c, Ragley Hall.
PR BARTOLOZZI, LANDSEER, RYDER & STOW, after R.Smirke, 'Naval Victories', 'Commemoration of the victory of June 1st 1794', line, pub 1803, BM.

SEYMOUR, James (1702-1752) painter of hunting subjects.
D Self-portrait, pen and ink, Yale Center for British Art, New Haven, USA.

SEYMOUR, Sir Michael, 1st Bart (1768-1834) admiral.
P UNKNOWN, tql, Rockingham Castle, Northants.
PR H.R.COOK, after J.Northcote, hl in uniform, stipple, oval, pub 1809, NPG.

SEYMOUR-CONWAY, Francis, see 1st Marquess of Hertford.

SEYMOUR-CONWAY, Francis Charles, see 3rd Marquess of Hertford.

SHADWELL, Sir Lancelot (1779-1850) last vice-chancellor of England.
P THOMAS PHILLIPS, RA 1840, tql seated in robes, Lincoln's Inn, London.
PR UNKNOWN, tql seated, lith, BM, NPG.

SHARP, Granville (1735-1813) scholar and philanthropist.
P JAMES HAYLLAR, rescuing a slave from the hands of his master, V & A, on loan to Wilberforce House, Hull.
D GEORGE DANCE, 1794, hl, pencil, NPG 1158.
G JOHAN ZOFFANY, 'The Sharp Family', oil 1779–81, NPG L169.
SC After CATHERINE ANDRAS, plaster medallion SNPG 455. SIR FRANCIS CHANTREY, bust, Ashmolean Museum, Oxford. UNKNOWN, portrait medallion, Westminster Abbey, London.
PR C.TURNER, after L.Abbott, hl, mezz, for *The Claims of the People of England*, 1805, BM. S.COUSINS, after F.Chantrey, from a bust, mezz, pub 1827, BM.

SHARP, Thomas (1770-1841) antiquary.
PR MRS D.TURNER, after J.S.Cotman, hs, etch, BM.

SHARP, William (1749-1824) engraver.
P JAMES LONSDALE, tql, NPG 25. SIR MARTIN ARCHER SHEE, hl seated, Petworth House, (NT), West Sussex.
D Attrib MATHER BROWN, chalk, SNPG 2258. B.R.HAYDON, head, BM.
SC SIR FRANCIS CHANTREY, bust, Ashmolean Museum, Oxford.
PR W.SHARP, after G.F.Joseph, hl, line, pub 1817, BM, NPG. MISS TURNER, after B.R.Haydon, head, lith, BM.

SHARPE, Charles Kirkpatrick (c1781-1851) antiquary.
P THOMAS FRASER, hs, SNPG L35. JOHN IRVINE, hs, oval, SNPG 193.
D C.K.SHARPE, after T.Fraser, wash, SNPG 1677.

SHARPE, Gregory (1713-1771) divine.
PR V.GREEN, after R.Crosse, hl, mezz, pub 1770, BM, NPG.

SHARPE, Samuel (1799-1881) egyptologist.
P MISS MATILDA SHARPE, 1868, hl, NPG 1476.

SHAW, Sir Frederick, 2nd Bart (1799-1876) Irish politician.
P FRANK REYNOLDS, King's Inns, Dublin.
D JOHN DOYLE, wl, in 'The Wandering Minstrel', pen and pencil, 1840, BM.
G SIR GEORGE HAYTER, 'The House of Commons, 1833', oil, NPG 54.
PR E.SCRIVEN, after F.Cruikshank, tql seated, stipple, for *Eminent Conservative Statesmen*, 1836, BM, NPG.

SHAW, George (1751-1813) naturalist.
PR W.HOLL, after J.Russell, hl, stipple, oval, with view of British Museum below, for Thornton's *Sexual System of Linnaeus*, 1803, BM, NPG.

SHAW, Sir James (1764-1843) Chamberlain of London.
P JAMES TANNOCK, RA 1817, Kilmarnock Town Hall. MRS CHARLES PEARSON, Corporation of London.
SC JAMES FILLANS, 1848, statue, Kilmarnock, Scotland.
PR RIDLEY & HOLL, after S.Drummond, hs, stipple, for *European Mag*, 1806, BM, NPG. H.MEYER, after J.Hoppner, hl, holding 'The King's Warrant of Precedence', mezz, pub 1806, BM. R.DIGHTON, 1819, wl, etch, pub 1824, NPG.

SHAW, Stebbing (1762-1802) topographer.
PR UNKNOWN, hl, line, pub 1844, BM, NPG.

SHAW-LEFEVRE, Charles, see Viscount Eversley.

SHAW-LEFEVRE, Sir John George (1797-1879) civil service commissioner.
P SIR JOHN WATSON GORDON, tql seated, SNPG 732.
D CARLO PELLEGRINI ('Ape'), hs, w/c, for *Vanity Fair*, 1871, NPG 2741.

SHEAFFE, Sir Roger Hale (1763-1851) general.
P MATHER BROWN, wl, Albury Park, Surrey.

SHEBBEARE, John (1709-1788) political writer.
PR W.BROMLEY, hl, line, oval, for *European Mag*, 1788, BM, NPG.

SHEE, Sir Martin Archer (1769-1850) portrait painter.
P Self-portrait, 1794, hl, NPG 1093.
D JOHN JACKSON, c1815, hs, chalk and w/c, NPG 3153. THOMAS BRIDGFORD, c1841, NGI. C.VOGEL, Küpferstichkabinett, Staatliche Kunstsammlungen, Dresden.
PR UNKNOWN, wl seated, etch, for Arnold's *Mag of Fine Arts*, 1834, BM, NPG. H.GRIFFITHS, hs, stipple, pub 1846, NPG.

SHEEPSHANKS, John (1787-1863) art amateur.
P WILLIAM MULREADY, wl seated with maidservant, V & A; pen and wash study, BM.

SHEEPSHANKS, Richard (1794-1855) astronomer.
PR L.STOCKS, hl, line, BM.

SHEFFIELD, Anne North, Countess of (1764-1832) 3rd wife of 1st Earl.
D HENRY EDRIDGE, 1798, wl, pencil, NPG 2185a.

SHEFFIELD, John Baker Holroyd, 1st Earl of (1735-1821) statesman.
D HENRY EDRIDGE, 1798, wl, pencil, NPG 2185.
PR J.R.SMITH, after Angelica Kauffman, wl, mezz, pub 1777, NPG. J.JONES, after J.Reynolds, hl in robes, stipple, pub 1789, BM. NPG. UNKNOWN, hs, line, for *European Mag*, 1784, BM, NPG. J.JONES, after J.Downman, hl, stipple, oval, BM.

SHEIL, Richard Lalor (1791-1851) politician and dramatist.
P J.P.HAVERTY, hl, NGI 1304.
D WILLIAM BEWICK, chalk, SNPG 1719.
G SIR GEORGE HAYTER, 'The House of Commons, 1833', oil, NPG 54.
SC CHRISTOPHER MOORE, 1847, marble bust, NGI 8065. THOMAS FARRELL, plaster, NGI 8183.
PR R.COOPER, after J.C.Smith, hs, stipple, pub 1825, BM, NPG.
C DANIEL MACLISE, wl with O'Connell, lith, for *Fraser's Mag*, 1834; preliminary sketch, V & A.

SHELBURNE, William Petty, see 1st Marquess of Lansdowne.

SHELDON, John (1752-1808) anatomist.
P JOHN KEENAN, Devon and Exeter Hospital.
D GEORGE DANCE, c1793, hl, profile, pencil and crayon. Royal College of Surgeons, London.
PR S.FREEMAN, after A.W.Devis, hl, stipple, for *Monthly Mirror*, 1809, BM.

SHELLEY, Mary Wollstonecraft (1797-1851) novelist.
P RICHARD ROTHWELL, 1841, hl, NPG 1235.
M REGINALD EASTON, hl, (posthumous), Bodleian Library, Oxford.

SHELLEY, Percy Bysshe (1792-1822) poet.
P AMELIA CURRAN, 1819, hl, NPG 1234. ALFRED CLINT, after Amelia Curran and E.E.Williams, hl, NPG 1271.
SC MARIANNE LEIGH HUNT, 1836, bust, Eton College, Berks. Attrib M.LEIGH HUNT, head, plaster cast of medallion, (posthumous), NPG 2683.

SHENSTONE, William (1714-1763) poet and landscape gardener.
P THOMAS ROSS, 1738, hl, NPG 4386; replica, or copy, Pembroke College, Oxford. EDWARD ALCOCK, 1760, wl with dog, NPG 263. Attrib E.ALCOCK, hs, City Museum and Art Gallery, Birmingham.
PR UNKNOWN, a bust on a pedestal, with lyre etc, line, for his *Works*, 1764, BM.

SHEPHERD, Antony (1721-1796) professor of astronomy.
P L.F.G. VAN DER PUYL, 1784, wl, Old Schools, Cambridge.
SC JOHN BACON, 1796, marble bust, Trinity College, Cambridge.

SHEPHERD, Sir Samuel (1760-1840) chief baron of the exchequer in Scotland.
SC UNKNOWN, wax medallion, SNPG 1279.
PR J.R.JACKSON, after T.Lawrence, tql, mezz, pub 1846, BM, NPG.

SHEPHERD, William (1768-1847) unitarian minister and political reformer.
P T.H.ILLIDGE, Walker Art Gallery, Liverpool.
PR R.W.SIEVIER, after Moses Haughton, hl, stipple, pub 1817, NPG. J.THOMSON, hl, stipple, for *Imperial Mag*, 1821, BM, NPG. J.DICKSON, hl seated, lith, pub 1841, BM, NPG.

SHEPPARD, John (1702-1724) criminal.
D Attrib JAMES THORNHILL, 1724, tql, chalk, pencil and wash, NPG 4313. UNKNOWN, tql, pen and wash, Museum of London.
PR G.WHITE, after J.Thornhill, tql in cell, handcuffed, mezz, BM. UNKNOWN, wl, line, BM. UNKNOWN, after J.Thornhill, head, lith, BM.

SHERIDAN, Elizabeth Ann, née Linley (1754-1792) singer, first wife of R.B.Sheridan.
P THOMAS GAINSBOROUGH, 1768, hl with her brother Thomas, Sterling and Francine Clark Art Institute, Williamstown, Mass, USA. T.GAINSBOROUGH, 1772, with her sister Mary, Dulwich College Art Gallery, London. SIR JOSHUA REYNOLDS, RA 1775, wl as St. Cecilia, Waddesdon Manor (NT), Bucks. T.GAINSBOROUGH, 1785-6, wl in landscape, National Gallery of Art, Washington DC, USA. T.GAINSBOROUGH, hs, oval, Pennsylvania Museum, Philadelphia, USA.
G RICHARD SAMUEL, 1779, 'The Nine Living Muses of Great Britain', oil, NPG 4905.

SHERIDAN, Esther Jane (1776-1817) 2nd wife of R.B.Sheridan.
P JOHN HOPPNER, wl with her son Charles on her back, Metropolitan Museum of Art, New York, USA, engr T.Nugent, stipple, pub 1800, BM, NPG.

SHERIDAN, Frances, née Chamberlaine (1724-1766) author, mother of R.B.Sheridan.
PR UNKNOWN, hl, stipple, for *La Belle Assemblée*, 1824, BM, NPG.

SHERIDAN, Richard Brinsley (1751-1816) dramatist and MP.
P Studio of SIR JOSHUA REYNOLDS, c1789, hl, Garrick Club, London. K.A.HICKEL, 1793, hs, oval, study for 'House of Commons', Royal Coll. JOHN HOPPNER, called Sheridan, hl, The Hermitage, Leningrad.
D JOHN RUSSELL, called Sheridan, hl, oval, pastel, NPG 651.
G FRANCIS WHEATLEY, 'Interior of the Shakespeare Gallery, 1790', w/c, V & A. K.A.HICKEL, 'The House of Commons, 1793', oil, NPG 745.
SC Attrib JOHN LOCHÉE, c1790, called Sheridan, marble bust, V & A. GEORGE GARRARD, 1813, plaster cast of bust, Sir John Soane's Museum, London. THOMAS KIRK, 1824, marble bust, NGI 8000.
C JAMES SAYERS, several etch and caricatures, NPG. UNKNOWN, wl 'Citizen Bardolph refused admittance at Prince Hal's', etch, pub 1794, NPG. JAMES GILLRAY, with the Duke of Norfolk, etch, pub 1809, V & A. Various caricatures, BM.

SHERIDAN, Thomas (1719-1788) actor, father of R.B.Sheridan.
P JOHN LEWIS, NGI 1132. After GILBERT STUART, hs, oval, Garrick Club, London.
PR Various theatrical prints, BM.

SHERMAN, James (1796-1862) dissenting divine.
PR W.SAY, after F.Lake, tql, mezz, pub 1829, BM, NPG. C.BAUGNIET, tql, lith, BM. R.WOODMAN, after E.B.Morris, tql seated, stipple, NPG.

SHERWIN, John Keyse (1751?-1790) engraver.
PR UNKNOWN, after J.K.Sherwin, hl, stipple, oval, pub 1794, BM, NPG.

SHERWOOD, Mary Martha (1775-1851) writer.
PR M.MASKALL, hl, lith, BM.

SHIELD, William (1748-1829) composer.
P Attrib THOMAS HARDY, hl, Royal College of Music, London.
D GEORGE DANCE, 1798, hl, profile, NPG 1159. WILLIAM BROCKEDON, 1826, hs, pencil and chalk, NPG 2515 (11). JOHN JACKSON, hl, w/c, NPG 5221.
PR R.DUNKARTON, after J.Opie, hl, mezz, pub 1788, BM. T.HARDY, hl, stipple, pub 1796, BM, NPG. T.WOOLNOTH, after J.Jackson, hl, stipple, for *Contemporary Portraits*, 1822, BM, NPG.

SHILLITOE, Thomas (1754-1836) quaker.
PR UNKNOWN, hs, after death, lith, NPG.

SHIPLEY, Sir Charles (1755-1815) general.
PR H.COOK, after J.Eckstein, tql in uniform, stipple, for Jerdan's *Nat. Portrait Gallery*, 1833, BM, NPG.

SHIPLEY, Jonathan (1714-1788) bishop of St Asaph.
P SIR JOSHUA REYNOLDS, Bodrhyddan Hall, Clwyd.
SC UNKNOWN, Wedgwood medallion, hs, Wedgwood Museum, Barlaston, Staffs.
PR J.R.SMITH, after J.Reynolds, hl, mezz, oval, pub 1777, BM, NPG.

SHIPLEY, William (1714-1803) founder of the Society of Arts.
P RICHARD COSWAY, 1759, hl, Royal Society of Arts, London.
M W.HINKS, hs, oval, Royal Society of Arts.

SHIPLEY, William Davies (1745-1826) dean of St Asaph.
P SIR WILLIAM BEECHEY, Bodrhyddan Hall, Clwyd.
SC JOHN TERNOUTH, 1829, statue, St Asaph's Cathedral, Clwyd.

SHIPP, John (1784-1834) soldier and author.
PR W.T.FRY, after J.Buchanan, tql, stipple, BM, NPG.

SHIRLEY, Laurence, see 4th Earl Ferrers.

SHIRLEY, Walter (1725-1786) hymn-writer.
PR J.DIXON, after R.E.Pine, hl, mezz, oval, pub 1773, BM. UNKNOWN, hl, line, oval, for *Gospel Mag*, 1775, BM.

SHIRLEY, Walter Augustus (1797-1847) bishop of Sodor

and Man.
PR H.B.HALL, after O.Oakley, tql, seated, stipple, NPG.

SHORE, John, see 1st Baron Teignmouth.

SHORT, James (1710-1768) optician and mathematician.
P Attrib BENJAMIN WILSON, c1758, hl, Museum of the History of Science, Oxford.
D 11TH EARL OF BUCHAN, pencil and chalk, SNPG 1644.

SHORT, Thomas Vowler (1790-1872) bishop of St Asaph.
P SIR MARTIN ARCHER SHEE, RA 1842, hl, Christ Church, Oxford.
PR E.DENT, after T.Bridgford, c1841, tql, mezz, BM. D.J.POUND, after a photograph by Mayall, tql seated, stipple and line, NPG.

SHORTLAND, John (1769-1810) captain in the navy.
PR H.R.COOK, after R.Field, hl in uniform, stipple, oval, for *Naval Chronicle*, 1810, BM, NPG.

SHRAPNEL, Henry (1761-1842) inventor of the Shrapnel shell.
P Attrib THOMAS ARROWSMITH, 1817, hl, Royal Artillery Institution, Woolwich.

SHRUBSOLE, William (1729-1797) author and minister.
PR RIDLEY, hs, stipple, oval, for *Evangelical Mag*, pub 1797, NPG.

SHULDHAM, Molyneux Shuldham, Baron (1717?-1798) admiral.
PR W.DICKINSON, after N.Dance, tql in uniform, mezz, pub 1780, BM.

SHUTER, Edward (1728?-1776) actor.
P Attrib B.DOWNES, hl, as Scapin in *The Rival Queens*, Garrick Club, London.
D THOMAS PARKINSON, wl as Falstaff in *Henry IV*, ink and w/c, BM. JAMES ROBERTS, as Lovegold, BM. ISAAC TAYLOR sen, as Obadiah Prim, ink and w/c, BM.
PR Various theatrical prints, BM, NPG.

SHUTTLEWORTH, Philip Nicholas (1782-1842) bishop of Chichester.
P THOMAS KIRKBY, hl, New College, Oxford, engr S.W.Reynolds, mezz, pub 1826, BM, NPG. THOMAS PHILLIPS, 1842, tql, New College, Oxford.

SIBBALD, James (1745-1803) bookseller and author.
P UNKNOWN, hs, oval, SNPG 322.
G J.KAY, 'Connoisseurs', etch, BM.

SIBLY, Manoah (1757-1840) philosopher.
PR W.WISE and W.HUTIN, after J.Clover, hl, stipple, BM.

SIBTHORP, Charles de Laet Waldo (1783-1855) politician.
C Various drawings by JOHN DOYLE, BM. A.FORRESTER, one of set of satirical statuettes, entitled 'Will any one give this a name', lith, BM.

SIBTHORP, Humphry (1713-1797) botanist.
M UNKNOWN, hs, NPG 4408.

SIBTHORP, John (1758-1796) botanist.
P UNKNOWN, hs, Library of the Botanic Garden, Oxford.
M UNKNOWN, hs, NPG 4409.

SIBTHORP, Richard Waldo (1792-1879) divine.
PR J.SCOTT, after E.Turtle, hl, mezz, pub 1839, BM, NPG.

SIDDONS, Mrs Harriet (1783-1844) actress.
P After R.SMIRKE, hl, Dundee City Art Gallery. JOHN WOOD, hs, oval, SNPG 214.
PR W.RIDLEY, hl, stipple, oval, for *Monthly Mirror*, 1801, BM.

SIDDONS, Henry (1774-1815) actor, son of Sarah Siddons.
P WILLIAM HAMILTON, SNPG 1487.

M SAMUEL JOHN STUMP, 1807, hs, oval, NPG 4879. UNKNOWN, hs, wash, Garrick Club, London.
PR W.RIDLEY, after H.Edridge, hl, stipple, oval, for *Monthly Mirror*, 1802, BM.

SIDDONS, Sarah, née Kemble (1755-1831) actress.
P SIR JOSHUA REYNOLDS, 1784, wl as the Tragic Muse, Huntington Library and Art Gallery, San Marino, USA; copy Dulwich College Art Gallery, London. THOMAS GAINSBOROUGH, c1785, tql seated, NG 683. SIR THOMAS LAWRENCE, 1786, TATE 2222. Attrib GILBERT STUART, hl seated, NPG 50. SIR WILLIAM BEECHEY, 1793, wl with the emblems of tragedy, NPG 5159. SIR THOMAS LAWRENCE, c1797, hl, NPG L143. SIR THOMAS LAWRENCE, 1804, hl, TATE 188. G.H.HARLOW, wl as Lady Macbeth, Garrick Club, London. RICHARD WESTALL, wl as Lady Macbeth, Garrick Club, London.
D JOHN DOWNMAN, 1787, hl, chalk, NPG 2651. JOHN HAYTER, 1826, hs, profile, chalk, BM. SIR THOMAS LAWRENCE, hs, pencil, Garrick Club. G.H.HARLOW, hl, pencil, Bowood, Wilts. G.H.HARLOW, hl, pencil and wash, Brodie Castle, Grampian region, Scotland.
M HORACE HONE, 1784, hs, oval, w/c, NGI 7318. RICHARD CROSSE, hl, oval, V & A.
G G.H.HARLOW, 'Court for the Trial of Queen Catherine' (*Henry VIII*) oil, 1817, Royal Shakespeare Memorial Theatre Museum, Stratford-upon-Avon.
SC JOHN FLAXMAN, 1784, Wedgwood medallion, Wedgwood Museum, Barlaston, Staffs. SIR FRANCIS CHANTREY, 1831, statue, Westminster Abbey, London. THOMAS CAMPBELL, marble relief, hl, NPG 642. L.F.CHAVALLIAUD, marble statue, Paddington Green, London.
PR Various theatrical prints, BM, NPG.

SIDMOUTH, Henry Addington, 1st Viscount (1757-1844) prime-minister.
P JOHN SINGLETON COPLEY, 1797, wl in robes, City Art Museum St Louis, USA. THOMAS PHILLIPS, after J.S.Copley, wl, Speaker's House, Palace of Westminster, London.
D GEORGE RICHMOND, 1833, wl, w/c, NPG 5.
G K.A.HICKEL, 'The House of Commons, 1793', oil, NPG 745.
SC WILLIAM BEHNES, 1831, marble bust, NPG 3917.
PR J.PARKER, after W.Beechey, tql seated, line, pub 1803, BM. S.W.Reynolds and S.Cousins, after T.C.Thompson, tql, mezz, pub 1823, BM, NPG.
C Drawings by JOHN DOYLE, BM.

SIMCOE, John Graves (1752-1806) first governor of Upper Canada.
P UNKNOWN, hl, Public Archives of Canada, Ottawa, Canada.

SIMEON, Charles (1759-1836) divine.
P JAMES NORTHCOTE, 1810, hl, King's College, Cambridge.
SL AUGUSTE EDOUART, 1828, twelve silhouettes, eight of him preaching, King's College, Cambridge.
SC SAMUEL MANNING jun, 1855, marble bust, Old Schools, Cambridge.
PR W.FINDEN, after W.Beechey, hl, stipple, BM. W.SAY, after J.Jackson, tql, mezz, BM, NPG.
C J.KAY, in pulpit preaching, etch, BM.

SIMMONS, Samuel (1777?-1819) actor.
P SAMUEL DE WILDE, hl as Master Matthew in *Every Man in his Humour*, and wl as Baron Mordecai in *Love à la Mode*, Garrick Club, London.
D SAMUEL DE WILDE, wl as Jonathan Oldskirt in *Who Wants a Guinea?*, w/c, Garrick Club. JOHN TURMEAU, two hs drawings, pencil and w/c, Garrick Club. SAMUEL DE WILDE, wl as Simkin in

Dibdin's *Deserter*, pencil and w/c, Royal Coll.
PR Various theatrical prints, BM, NPG.

SIMPSON, David (1745-1799) divine.
PR J.COLLYER, after J.Russell, hs, stipple, oval, NPG.

SIMPSON, Sir George (1792-1860) administrator of Hudson's Bay Company's territory.
PR SCOTT, after S.Pearce, tql, mezz, NPG. UNKNOWN, hl, profile, stipple, for *Narrative of a Journey round the World*, 1847, BM.

SIMPSON, Sir James (1792-1868) general.
PR J.W.HUNT, after a photograph by R.Fenton, tql, stipple and line, NPG.

SIMS, James (1741-1820) president of Medical Society of London.
D Attrib GEORGE DANCE, 1796, hs, profile, pencil, Royal College of Physicians, London.
G N.BRANWHITE, after S.Medley, 'Institutors of the Medical Society of London', stipple, pub 1801, BM.
PR N.C.BRANWHITE, after S.Medley, hl, stipple, pub 1799, BM, NPG. R.PAGE, tql, stipple, pub 1823, NPG.

SIMS, John (1749-1831) physician and botanist.
PR MRS D.TURNER, after B.Pistrucci, head, from a medallion, 1817, etch, BM.

SINCLAIR, Sir George (1790-1868) politician and author.
P SIR HENRY RAEBURN, wl as a boy, Kenwood House, London.
G SIR GEORGE HAYTER, 'The House of Commons, 1833', oil, NPG 54.

SINCLAIR, Sir John, 1st Bart (c1754-1835) president of the Board of Agriculture.
P SIR HENRY RAEBURN, c1794-5, wl, NGS 2301. SIR HENRY RAEBURN, tql, NPG 454.
SC After JAMES TASSIE, 1797, plaster medallion, SNPG 459.
PR W.SKELTON, after T.Lawrence, hl seated, line, pub 1790, BM, NPG. W.BROMLEY, after S.Drummond, hs, line, oval, for *European Mag*, 1791, BM, NPG. J.KAY, wl, 'The Scottish Patriot', etch, 1791, NPG. W.BOND, after A.Robertson, hl, stipple, pub 1817, BM, NPG.

SINCLAIR, John (1791-1857) tenor opera singer.
P G.H.HARLOW, hs, Royal Society of Musicians, London.
D SAMUEL DE WILDE, 1812, two drawings, as Apollo in different scenes from *Midas*, w/c, Garrick Club, London.

SIRR, Henry Charles (1764-1841) chief of Dublin police.
PR UNKNOWN, hl in uniform, process block, BM. UNKNOWN, after W.Ewing, head, profile, from an ivory relief, process block, BM.

SIRR, Joseph D'Arcy (1794-1868) author.
PR UNKNOWN, tql, from a photograph, process block, BM.

SKEFFINGTON, Sir Lumley St George, Bart (1771-1850) dramatist.
PR RIDLEY and HOLL, after J.T.Barber, hl, stipple, oval, for *Monthly Mirror*, 1806, BM.

SKELTON, William (1763-1848) line-engraver.
PR W.SKELTON, after Sir William Beechey, hl, lith, BM, NPG.

SKENE, James (1775-1864) antiquarian, artist and friend of Scott.
D UNKNOWN, wash, SNPG 2051.

SKINNER, James (1778-1841) commander of Skinner's Horse.
D GHULANS ALI KHAN, c1827-8, 'Returning from the Review', equestrian, w/c, National Army Museum, London.
G GHULANS ALI KHAN, 'The Durbar', with his son, holding a regimental durbar at Hansi, w/c, c1827-8, National Army Museum.

SKINNER, John (1721-1807) song-writer, minister of Longside.
PR T.WOOLNOTH, hl, stipple, for Chambers's *Dict of Eminent Scotsmen*, BM, NPG.

SKINNER, John (1744-1816) bishop of Aberdeen.
PR C.TURNER, after A.Robertson, hl, mezz, pub 1810, BM.

SKINNER, William (1700-1780) chief engineer of Great Britain.
P THOMAS BEACH, hl with his daughter, Firle Place, East Sussex.

SKIRVING, Adam (1719-1803) Jacobite song-writer.
P ARCHIBALD SKIRVING, SNPG 596.

SKIRVING, Archibald (1749-1819) artist.
P ANDREW GEDDES, hs, SNPG L313. SIR HENRY RAEBURN, hl, Smithsonian Institution, Washington DC, USA. GEORGE WATSON, hl, SNPG 713.
D Self-portrait, hs, chalk, SNPG 595.

SKYNNER, Sir John (1723-1805) chief-baron of the exchequer.
P THOMAS GAINSBOROUGH, c1785, tql seated, Christ Church, Oxford; version, Lincoln's Inn, London.

SLADE, Felix (1790-1868) art-collector and scholar.
D MARGARET CARPENTER, 1851, hs, chalk and w/c, BM.

SLADE, Sir John, 1st Bart (1762-1859) general.
SC WILLIAM THEED jun, terracotta bust, Royal Military Academy, Sandhurst, Camberley, Surrey.

SLEATH, John (1767-1847) high-master of St Paul's school.
PR I.W.SLATER, after J.Slater, hl, lith, pub 1834, BM, NPG.

SMALL, John (1726-1796) major-general and lieutenant-governor of Guernsey.
D UNKNOWN, chalk, SNPG 671.
M PHILIP JEAN, c1783-87, hs, R.W.Norton Art Gallery, Shreveport, Louisiana, USA.

SMART, Christopher (1722-1771) poet.
P UNKNOWN, c1745, hs, NPG 3780. UNKNOWN, tql seated, Pembroke College, Cambridge.
PR H.MEYER, hs, stipple, oval, for *Poems*, 1791, BM.

SMART, Sir George Thomas (1776-1867) musician.
P WILLIAM BRADLEY, 1829, hl, NPG 1326. CHARLES HODGSON, hs, Royal Society of Musicians, London. JOHN CAWSE, hl, Thomas Coram Foundation for Children, London.

SMART, John (1741-1811) miniaturist.
P Attrib L.F.ABBOTT, hl, NPG 3817. Attrib GILBERT STUART, c1783, hs, Joslyn Art Museum, Omaha, USA.
D Attrib MATHER BROWN, chalk, SNPG 2254.
M Self-portrait, 1786, Museum of Fine Arts, Boston, USA. Self-portrait, 1797, hs, V & A. Self-portrait, 1802, hl, oval, Cleveland Museum of Art, USA.

SMEATON, John (1724-1792) civil engineer.
P GEORGE ROMNEY, after Rhodes, hl, NPG 80. J.RICHARDSON, tql seated, Royal Society, London. MATHER BROWN, hl, Royal Society.
PR UNKNOWN, after T.Gainsborough, hl, lith, NPG.

SMELLIE, William (1740-1795) printer, naturalist and antiquary.
P GEORGE WATSON, tql seated, SNPG L29.
D JOHN BROWN, hs, pencil, SNPG L64.
SC R.CUMMINS, plaster bust, SNPG L52.
PR J.KAY, wl conversing with Andrew Bell, etch, 1787, BM.

SMIRKE, Robert (1752-1845) painter and illustrator.

D GEORGE DANCE, 1793, hs, Royal Academy, London. J.JACKSON, after Miss Smirke, hl, w/c, NPG 2672.

G HENRY SINGLETON, 'Royal Academicians, 1793', oil, Royal Academy, London.

SC E.H.BAILY, 1828, plaster bust, NPG 4525.

SMIRKE, Sir Robert (1781-1867) architect.

D GEORGE DANCE, 1809, hs, profile, Royal Academy, London.

SC THOMAS CAMPBELL, 1845, bust, BM.

SMIRKE, Sydney (1798-1877) architect.

PR UNKNOWN, hl, woodcut, for *Illust London News*, 1859, BM, NPG. UNKNOWN, hs, for *Illust London News*, 1877, NPG.

SMITH, Adam (1723-1790) political economist.

P UNKNOWN, called Adam Smith, SNPG 1472. T.COLLOPY, called Adam Smith, National Museum of Antiquities, Scotland.

SC JAMES TASSIE, 1787, plaster medallion, NPG 1242. JAMES TASSIE, 1787, paste medallion, NPG 3237. Various medals, SNPG. P.PARK, 1845, bust, City Art Gallery, Glasgow.

PR J.KAY, wl, etch, 1787, NPG. J.KAY, wl, etch, 1790, NPG.

SMITH, Alexander (1764-1829), see John Adams.

SMITH, Benjamin (d1833) engraver.

D UNKNOWN, hl, w/c, BM (Engraved Portraits Coll).

SMITH, Charles (1749?-1824) painter to the Great Mogul.

PR C.SMITH, hl holding portfolio, etch, 1776, BM.

SMITH, Charles Hamilton (1776-1859) soldier and naturalist.

D WILLIAM BROCKEDON, 1830, hs, pencil and chalk, NPG 2515 (22).

PR J.SCOTT, after E.Opie, tql seated, mezz, pub 1841, BM, NPG.

SMITH, Charlotte, née Turner (1749-1806) poet and novelist.

PR RIDLEY, hs, stipple, oval, pub 1799, NPG. S.FREEMAN, after G.Romney (said to be after J.Opie), hl, stipple, oval, for *Monthly Mirror*, 1808, BM, NPG. UNKNOWN, hl, stipple, BM.

SMITH, Elizabeth (1774-1806) oriental scholar.

PR W.RIDLEY, hl, stipple, oval, for *European Mag*, 1809, BM. T.WOOLNOTH, hl with book, stipple, for *Ladies Monthly Museum*, 1822, BM.

SMITH, George (1713-1776) landscape painter.

P Self-portrait, wl with his brother, in a landscape, NPG 4117.

G W.PETHER, 'The Smiths of Chichester', mezz, pub 1765, BM.

PR J.HOPWOOD, after W.Pether, hl, stipple, oval, for *Pastorals*, 1811, BM.

SMITH, George Charles (1782-1863) 'Boatswain Smith', baptist minister and philanthropist.

PR A.WIVELL, hl with book, mezz, pub 1819, BM.

SMITH, Sir Harry George Wakelyn, 1st Bart (1787-1860) general.

M UNKNOWN, c1846, hl, NPG 1945.

SC G.G.ADAMS, c1849, marble, St Mary's Church, Whittlesea; plaster cast, NPG 1255.

PR T.FAIRBANK, after H.Moseley (1847), India Office Library, London. E.DALTON, hl in uniform, lith, BM. UNKNOWN, woodcut, for *Illust London News*, 1846, NPG. E.DALTON, hl in uniform, lith, BM. D.J.POUND, after a photograph by John Eastham, tql seated, stipple and line, NPG.

SMITH, Horatio (1779-1849) poet and novelist.

D E.M.WARD, 1835, wl, pencil and wash, NPG 4578. UNKNOWN, hl seated, w/c, NPG 2200.

PR E.FINDEN, after G.H.Harlow, hl with his brother James, stipple, for *Rejected Addresses*, 1833, BM. FINDEN, after J.Masquerier, hl, stipple and line, pub 1835, BM, NPG.

SMITH, James (1775-1839) writer and humorist.

P JAMES LONSDALE, tql seated, NPG 1415.

PR E.FINDEN, after G.H.Harlow, hl with his brother, Horatio, stipple, for *Rejected Addresses*, 1833, BM.

SMITH, James (1782-1867) geologist and man of letters.

P SIR HENRY RAEBURN, The Royal Technical College, Glasgow.

SMITH, Sir James Edward (1759-1828) botanist.

D SIR FRANCIS CHANTREY, two hs sketches, pencil, NPG 316a (108, 109).

PR MRS D.TURNER, after T.Worlidge, hl, aged 4, etch, oval, BM. W.RIDLEY, after J.Russell, hl, stipple, for Thornton's *Sexual System of Linnaeus*, 1800, BM, NPG. F.C.LEWIS, after W.Lane, tql seated, chalk manner, pub 1816, BM, NPG.

SMITH, John (1717-1764) landscape painter.

P Self-portrait, wl with his brother in a landscape, NPG 4117.

G W.PETHER, 'The Smiths of Chichester', mezz, pub 1765, BM.

SMITH, John Christopher (1712-1795) musician, Handel's amanuensis.

PR E.HARDING, after Johan Zoffany, hl seated, stipple, pub 1799, NPG.

SMITH, John Pye (1774-1851) nonconformist divine.

P THOMAS PHILLIPS, tql seated, Dr Williams's Library, London.

SC UNKNOWN, plaster bust, Dr Williams's Library.

PR C.BAUGNIET, tql, lith, BM. T.BLOOD, hs, stipple, oval, for *Evangelical Mag*, 1812, BM.

SMITH, John Raphael (1752-1812) portrait painter, engraver and pastelist.

D Self-portrait, hl, pastel, NPG 981. Self-portrait, hl, chalk and wash, BM. GEORGE MORLAND, hl, chalk, BM.

G UNKNOWN, after P.Sandby, 'Sketches taken at Print Sales', line engr, pub 1798, BM. Self-portrait, with others, 'A Promenade at Carlisle House, Soho Square', crayon, oval, V & A.

SC SIR FRANCIS CHANTREY, 1825, marble bust, V & A. SIR F.CHANTREY, c1811, plaster bust, Ashmolean Museum, Oxford.

SMITH, John Stafford (1750-1836) musical composer.

PR T.ILLMAN, after W.Behnes, hl, stipple, for *Harmonist in Miniature*, BM, NPG.

SMITH, John Thomas (1766-1833) draughtsman and antiquary.

D W.BROCKEDON, 1832, hs, pencil and chalk, NPG 2515 (34).

PR W.SKELTON, after J.Jackson, hs, line, pub 1833, BM.

SMITH, Pleasance, Lady, née Reeve (1773-1877) centenarian.

PR MISS TURNER, after J.Opie, tql as a gipsy, aged 24, lith, BM. Same picture, with another representing her at the age of 94, woodcut, from a newspaper, 1877, BM.

SMITH, Richard John (1786-1855) actor, called O.Smith.

P E.M.WARD, hs, Garrick Club, London.

PR Various theatrical prints, BM, NPG.

SMITH, Robert (1752-1838), see 1st Baron Carrington.

SMITH, Sarah (1783-1850), see Bartley.

SMITH, Sir Sidney (1764-1840), see Sir William Sidney Smith.

SMITH, Sydney (1771-1845) famous wit and Canon of St Paul's.

P H.P.BRIGGS, tql seated, NPG 1475. E.U.EDDIS, hl, New College, Oxford.

SL 'S.A.D.', 1839, BM Ms Loan 60/4: 139/2.

G MISS ROLINDA SHARPLES, 'The Trial of Colonel Brereton', oil, 1831, Bristol City Art Gallery.

PR S.FREEMAN, after J.Wright, hl, stipple, for *Contemporary Portraits*, 1817, BM. W.DRUMMOND, after R.Westmacott, from marble bust, lith, for *Athenaeum Portraits*, 1836, BM. E.MORTON, after Arthur Cookenden, hs, lith, pub 1839, NPG. D.MACLISE, wl, lith, for *Fraser's Mag*, BM.

C SIR EDWIN LANDSEER, c1835, with allegorical figures of the Church and the Devil, pen and wash, NPG 4917. JOHN DOYLE, 1840, wl, entitled 'Dives and Lazarus', pen and pencil, BM.

SMITH, Thomas (d1762) admiral.

P RICHARD WILSON, tql, NMM, Greenwich.

SMITH, Thomas Assheton (1776-1858) sportsman.

P SIR WILLIAM BEECHEY, hs, a leaving portrait, Eton College, Berks.

SMITH, Thomas Southwood (1788-1861) physician and sanitary reformer.

SC J.HART, 1856, marble bust, NPG 339. UNKNOWN, bust, Highgate Literary and Scientific Institute, London.

PR J.C.ARMYTAGE, for R.Horne's *A New Spirit of the Age*, 1844, NPG.

SMITH, William (1707-1764) painter.

G W.PETHER, 'The Smiths of Chichester', mezz, pub 1765, BM.

SMITH, William (1730?-1819) actor.

P JOHN HOPPNER, c1788, hl seated, TATE 133.

G JAMES ROBERTS, as Charles Surface with others in *School for Scandal*, oil, RA 1779, Garrick Club, London.

PR Various theatrical prints, BM, NPG.

SMITH, William (1756-1835) politician.

P T.C.THOMPSON, St Andrew's Hall, Norwich.

PR V.GREEN, after J.Opie, hl, mezz, pub 1800, BM. W.C.EDWARDS, after H.Thomson, tql holding 'Bill for Abolition of Slave Trade', line, BM.

SMITH, Sir William, 2nd Bart (1766-1836) Irish judge.

SC E.LYON, c1834, wax bust, V & A.

SMITH, William (1769-1839) geologist and engineer.

P H.FOURAU, Geological Society, London, engr T.A.Dean, hl, stipple, BM, NPG.

D JOHN JACKSON, 1831, hs, pencil, BM.

G W.WALKER and G.ZOBEL, after J.F.Skill, J.Gilbert, W. and E.Walker, 'Men of Science Living in 1807–8', engr, NPG 1075a.

SC MATTHEW NOBLE, 1848, marble bust, University Museum, Oxford. MATTHEW NOBLE, marble bust, St Peter's Church, Northampton.

SMITH, Sir William Sidney (1764-1840) admiral.

P JOHN OPIE, 1783, hl, NMM, Greenwich. JOHN ECKSTEIN, 1800–2, wl, NPG 832, on loan to the National Maritime Museum. After PHILLIPPE HÉNNEQUIN (of 1796), tql, NMM, Greenwich.

D THOMAS STOTHARD, hs profile, pencil, BM.

G THOMAS SUTTON, the siege of St Jean at D'Acre, Penicuik House, Midlothian, Scotland.

SC THOMAS KIRK, 1845, statue, NMM, Greenwich.

PR E.BELL, after Chandler, hl, mezz, pub 1803, NPG.

SMITHSON, Sir Hugh Percy, see 1st Duke of Northumberland.

SMOLLETT, Tobias George (1721-1771) novelist.

P UNKNOWN (Italian), c1770, hl, NPG 1110.

PR F.ALIAMET, after Sir Joshua Reynolds, hs, line, oval, for *Hist of England*, BM. J.COLLYER, hs, line, oval, pub 1790, NPG.

SMYTH, Edward (1749-1812) sculptor.

PR H.MEYER, after J.Comerford, hs, stipple, NPG.

SMYTH, Sir James Carmichael, 1st Bart (1779-1838) soldier and governor of British Guiana.

SC SIR FRANCIS CHANTREY, bust, Georgetown Cathedral Church, Demerara, Guyana.

PR THOMAS HODGETTS, after E.H.Latilla, hl, mezz, pub 1841, NPG.

SMYTH, William (1765-1849) professor of modern history at Cambridge.

P UNKNOWN, Peterhouse, Cambridge.

SC E.H.BAILY, 1851, marble bust, Fitzwilliam Museum, Cambridge.

PR I.W.SLATER, after J.Slater, hl seated, lith, 1831, BM, NPG.

SMYTH, William Henry (1788-1865) admiral and scientific writer.

D WILLIAM BROCKEDON, 1838, hs, pencil and chalk, NPG 2515 (85).

PR R.J.LANE, after E.U.Eddis, hl, with his wife, lith, BM, NPG. UNKNOWN, after E.U.Eddis (c1861), woodcut, for *Illust London News*, 1865, NPG.

SMYTHE, David (1746-1806), see Lord Methuen.

SMYTHE, Percy Clinton Sidney, see 1st Baron Penshurst.

SNELL, Hannah (1723-1792) female soldier.

PR J.FABER jnr, after R.Phelps, hl in male attire, mezz, 1750, BM, NPG. J.JOHNSON, after J.Wardell, hl, mezz, BM, NPG.

SNELLING, Thomas (1712-1773) numismatist.

PR J.THANE, hs, profile, etch, 1770, BM, NPG. C.HALL, after J.Pingo, hs, profile, line, for *English Medals*, 1776, BM.

SOANE, George (1790-1860) miscellaneous writer.

P WILLIAM OWEN, c1805, with his brother, Sir John Soane's Museum, London.

SC THOMAS BANKS, c1804, bust, Sir John Soane's Museum.

SOANE, Sir John (1753-1837) architect.

P C.W.HUNNEMAN, 1779, Sir John Soane's Museum, London. WILLIAM OWEN, 1804, Soane Museum. JOHN JACKSON, hl, NPG 701. JOHN JACKSON, 1828, tql, Soane Museum. SIR THOMAS LAWRENCE, RA 1829, tql, Soane Museum. THOMAS PHILLIPS, hs, Bank of England, London.

D N.DANCE, 1774, pencil, Soane Museum. GEORGE DANCE, 1795, pencil, Soane Museum. THOMAS COOLEY, 1810, four studies, hs, NPG 4913 (3). WILLIAM BROCKEDON, 1835, hs, pencil and chalk, NPG 2515 (76). SIR FRANCIS CHANTREY, hs sketch, pencil, NPG 316a (111). DANIEL MACLISE, V & A.

SC SIR FRANCIS CHANTREY, 1830, marble bust, Soane Museum.

SOBIESKA, Maria Clementina, see Maria.

SOLANDER, Daniel Charles (1736-1782) botanist.

P UNKNOWN, wl, Linnean Society, London.

SC JOHN FLAXMAN, 1775, Wedgwood medallion, Wedgwood Museum, Barlaston, Staffs.

PR J.NEWTON, after J.Sowerby, hl, seated, stipple, pub 1784, BM, NPG.

C UNKNOWN, wl entitled 'The Simpling Macaroni', line, pub 1772, NPG.

SOMERSET, Edward Adolphus Seymour, 11th Duke of (1775-1855) mathematician.

G SIR GEORGE HAYTER, 'The Trial of Queen Caroline, 1820', oil, NPG 999.

D JAMES STEPHANOFF, c1821, for 'Coronation of George IV', w/c, V & A.

SOMERSET, Lord Fitzroy James Henry, see 1st Baron Raglan.

SOMERSET, Lord Granville Charles Henry (1792-1848) politician.

G SIR GEORGE HAYTER, 'The House of Commons, 1833', oil, NPG 54.

PR F.C.LEWIS, after J.Slater, hs, stipple, for 'Grillion's Club' series,

BM, NPG.

C Two pencil drawings by JOHN DOYLE, BM.

SOMERSET, Henry (1792-1853), see 7th Duke of Beaufort.

SOMERSET, Lord Robert Edward Henry (1776-1842) general.

P J.W.PIENEMAN, 1821, hs study for 'Battle of Waterloo', Wellington Museum, Apsley House, London. W.SALTER, tql study for 'Waterloo Banquet', NPG 3754.

D THOMAS HEAPHY, hs, w/c, NPG 1914 (15).

G J.W.PIENEMAN, 'Battle of Waterloo', oil, 1824, Rijksmuseum, Amsterdam. W.SALTER, 'The Waterloo Banquet at Apsley House', oil, 1836, Wellington Museum, Apsley House, London.

SOMERVILLE, John Southey Somerville, 15th Baron (1765-1819) agriculturalist.

PR R.RHODES, after S.Woodforde, hs in uniform, line, for *Memoirs of the Somervilles*, 1815, BM, NPG.

SOMERVILLE, Mary (1780-1872) scientific writer.

P JOHN JACKSON, hs, Somerville College, Oxford. THOMAS PHILLIPS, hl, SNPG 1115. UNKNOWN, Somerville College.

D SIR FRANCIS CHANTREY, 1832, two hs sketches, pencil, NPG 316a (114, 115). SAMUEL LAURENCE, 1836, Girton College, Cambridge. JAMES RANNIE SWINTON, 1848, hs, chalk, NPG 690. C.VOGEL, Küpferstichkabinett, Staatliche Kunstsammlungen, Dresden.

SC LAWRENCE MACDONALD, 1844, bronze cast of medallion, Somerville College, Oxford; reduced plaster version, SNPG 279. DAVID D'ANGERS, bronze medallion, Musée des Beaux Arts, Angers.

SOMERVILLE, William (1771-1860) physician.

D SIR FRANCIS CHANTREY, hs sketches, pencil, NPG 316a (112, 113).

SOTHEBY, William (1757-1833) poet and classicist.

D THOMAS LAWRENCE, hs, chalk, NPG 3955.

SOUTH, John Flint (1797-1882) surgeon.

SC HENRY WEEKES, 1872, bust, St Thomas's Hospital, London.

SOUTHAMPTON, Charles Fitzroy, 1st Baron (1737-1797) general.

P SIR JOSHUA REYNOLDS, 1760, hl, Royal Coll.

SOUTHCOTT, Joanna (1750-1814) religious fanatic.

D WILLIAM SHARP, 1812, hl, pencil, NPG 1402.

PR A.FLAT, after G.L., wl seated, entitled 'The Cunning Woman', etch, pub 1814, BM.

SOUTHEY, Robert (1774-1843) poet.

P PETER VANDYKE, 1795, hs, NPG 193. SAMUEL LANE, RA 1824, hl, Balliol College, Oxford. SIR THOMAS LAWRENCE, RA 1829, tql seated in landscape, National Gallery, Cape Town.

D R.HANCOCK, 1796, hl, pencil and w/c, NPG 451. H.EDRIDGE, 1804, wl seated, pencil and chalk, NPG 119. DIONYSIUS AGUIRRE, head, NPG 4071.

M M.BETHAM, 1809, called Southey, hs, City Art Gallery, Bristol. UNKNOWN, hl seated, NPG 4028.

SC SIR FRANCIS CHANTREY, 1832, marble bust, NPG 3956. .E.W.WYON, 1835, wax medallion, NPG 2681. J.G.LOUGH, 1845, marble bust, NPG 841. J.G.LOUGH, 1846, marble recumbent effigy, Crossthwaite Church, Westmorland. E.H.BAILY, bust, Bristol Cathedral. HENRY WEEKES, bust, Westminster Abbey, London.

PR W.H.EGLETON, after J.Opie, hl, stipple, for his *Life and Correspondence*, ed by his son, 1849, BM, NPG.

SOUTHGATE, Richard (1729-1795) numismatist.

PR T.TROTTER, hl, oval, line, for *Museum Southgatianium*, 1795, BM.

SOWERBY, James (1757-1822) naturalist and artist.

PR MRS D.TURNER, after T.Heaphy, hs, etch, BM, NPG.

SPENCE, Elizabeth Isabella (1768-1832) writer.

PR T.WOOLNOTH, after T.Wageman, tql seated, stipple, for *Ladies' Monthly Museum*, 1824, BM.

SPENCE, George (1787-1850) jurist.

PR T.BRAGG, after A.J.Oliver, hl, line, BM, NPG.

SPENCE, William (1783-1860) entomologist.

PR W.RADDON, after J.Masquerier, hl seated, line, pub 1839, BM, NPG. T.H.MAGUIRE, tql seated, lith, for *Ipswich Museum Portraits*, 1849, BM, NPG.

SPENCER, Aubrey George (1795-1872) first bishop of Newfoundland.

P UNKNOWN, hl, Hertford College, Oxford.

PR M.GAUCI, after F.Rochard, tql, lith, BM.

SPENCER, Charles (1706-1758), see 3rd Duke of Marlborough.

SPENCER, Lord Charles (1740-1820) politician.

P SIR JOSHUA REYNOLDS, c1759, hl, Blenheim Palace, Oxon. SIR JOSHUA REYNOLDS, c1762, tql, Wilton House, Wilts.

G THOMAS HUDSON, 'The Family of the Duke of Marlborough', oil, c1754, Blenheim Palace.

SPENCER, George (1739-1817), see 4th Duke of Marlborough.

SPENCER, George (1766-1840), see 5th Duke of Marlborough.

SPENCER, George John Spencer, 2nd Earl (1758-1834) first lord of the admiralty.

P SIR JOSHUA REYNOLDS, RA 1776, wl in landscape in Vandyke dress, Althorp, Northants. JOHN SINGLETON COPLEY, c1800, wl in Garter robes, Althorp. MARTIN ARCHER SHEE, RA 1802, tql in Garter robes, Althorp. JOHN HOPPNER, c1807-08, hl, Althorp. THOMAS PHILLIPS, 1810, tql seated, Althorp. JOHN SINGLETON COPLEY, hs, NPG 1487. GEORGE CLINT, tql seated in Garter robes, Althorp.

D SIR FRANCES CHANTREY, hs, sketch, pencil, NPG 316a (116). JOHN DOWNMAN, hl, chalk, Fitzwilliam Museum, Cambridge. HENRY EDRIDGE, wl with book, pencil and w/c, BM. CATHERINE READ, three pastel drgs, one with his sisters, Althorp.

M SIR HENRY RAEBURN, hs, ivory, Althorp.

G ANGELICA KAUFFMANN, wl with the Duchess of Devonshire and the Countess of Beesborough, oil, 1771-74, Althorp. JOHN SINGLETON COPLEY, The Collapse of the Earl of Chatham in the House of Lords, 7 July 1778', oil, 1779-80, TATE 100, on loan to NPG.

SPENCER, Georgiana, see Duchess of Devonshire.

SPENCER, Lord Henry John (1770-1795) diplomat.

P SIR JOSHUA REYNOLDS, c1775, with Lady Charlotte Spencer, 'The Fortune Tellers', Huntington Library and Art Gallery, San Marino, USA.

SPENCER, John Charles Spencer, 3rd Earl (1782-1845) Whig statesman.

P SIR JOSHUA REYNOLDS, 1786, wl as a child in landscape, Althorp, Northants. SIR JOSHUA REYNOLDS, 1783-84, with his mother, Huntington Library and Art Gallery, San Marino, USA. MARTIN ARCHER SHEE, RA 1801, hs, Althorp. SIR GEORGE HAYTER, 1816, wl standing in landscape by classical urn, Althorp. THOMAS PHILLIPS, wl in landscape, Althorp.

D CHARLES TURNER, tql, chalk, NPG 1318.

G SIR GEORGE HAYTER, 'The House of Commons, 1833', oil, NPG

54. RICHARD ANDSELL, wl with his bailiff and two herdsmen, oil, 1843, Althorp.

SPENCER, Sir Robert Cavendish (1791-1830) captain in the navy.
P THOMAS PHILLIPS, hl holding telescope, Althorp, Northants. CHARLES ALLINGHAM, seated at desk, Althorp.
D H.EDRIDGE, wl in uniform, Althorp.
SC SIR FRANCIS CHANTREY, marble bust, Althorp.
PR M.GAUCI, after T.Phillips, tql standing in uniform, lith, BM, NPG.

SPENCER, Thomas (1791-1811) independent divine.
PR E.SCRIVEN, after N.Branwhite, hl seated, stipple, for *Life*, 1812 by T.Raffles, BM.

SPODE, Josiah (1733-1797) potter.
M UNKNOWN, hl, oval, NPG 4586.

SPODE, Josiah (1754-1827) potter to George III.
P WILLIAM McCALL, hl, City Museum, Stoke-on-Trent, Staffs. UNKNOWN, wl in riding dress, City Museum, Stoke-on-Trent.
M UNKNOWN, hl, oval, NPG 4587.

SPRING, Thomas, see Thomas WINTER.

SPRING-RICE, Thomas, see 1st Baron Monteagle.

SPURGIN, John (1797-1866) medical writer.
P JANE SUTHERLAND, 1858, hl, Royal College of Physicians, London.

STACKHOUSE, John (1742-1819) botanist.
PR UNKNOWN, hl seated holding paper with drawing of a plant, stipple, BM, NPG.

STAFFORD, Granville Leveson-Gower, 1st Marquess of (1721-1803) politician.
P GEORGE ROMNEY, c1776-8, wl in robes, Dunrobin Castle, Highland region, Scotland.
SC Attrib HACKWOOD, Wedgwood medallion, Wedgwood Museum, Barlaston, Staffs.
PR C.WARREN, after W.H.Brown, hs, profile, line, oval, for the *Senator*, pub 1792, BM. E.FISHER, after J.Reynolds, tql standing in peers robes, hand on purse of privy seal, mezz, BM, NPG.

STAIR, John Hamilton Macgill Dalrymple, 8th Earl of (1771-1853) general.
G SIR GEORGE HAYTER, 'The House of Commons, 1833', oil, NPG 54.

STANFIELD, Clarkson (1793-1867) marine and landscape painter.
P Attrib JOHN SIMPSON, c1829, hl, NPG 2637. SIR DANIEL MACNEE, RA 1859, hl, Royal Scottish Academy, Edinburgh.
D WILLIAM BROCKEDON, 1833, hs, pencil and chalk, NPG 2515 (40). DAVID ROBERTS, hl, pen, Royal Academy, London.
G JOHN PARTRIDGE, 'The Sketching Society, 1836', pen, ink and wash, BM. Self-portrait, 1842, with Maclise, Dickens and Forster in Cornwall, drg, V & A. C.R.LESLIE, tql with J.J.Chalon and A.E.Chalon in fancy dress, on twelfth night, wash over pencil, BM.
PH J. and C.WATKINS, 1864, hs, carte, NPG. MAULL and POLYBLANK, tql, NPG.

STANFIELD, James Field (d1824) actor and author.
PR G.ADCOCK, after C.Stanfield, hl, stipple, BM.

STANGER, Christopher (1759-1834) physician.
P Attrib GEORGE WATSON, hl seated with books on table, Thomas Coram Foundation for Children, London.

STANHOPE, Charles (1753-1829), see 3rd Earl of Harrington.

STANHOPE, Charles (1780-1851), see 4th Earl of Harrington.

STANHOPE, Charles Stanhope, 3rd Earl (1753-1816) politician and scientist.
P JOHN OPIE, hl, NPG 3324. A. or J.PRUD'HOMME, c1774, wl, Mellerstain, Borders region, Scotland.
D OZIAS HUMPHRY, 1796, hl, chalk, NPG 380.
G J.F.SKILL, J.GILBERT, W. and E.WALKER, 'Men of Science Living in 1807-8', pencil and wash, NPG 1075.
PR H.RICHTER, hl profile, stipple, oval, pub 1798, BM, NPG.
C JAMES SAYERS, wl, etch, NPG. JAMES SAYERS, hl entitled 'Anacharsis Cloots', etch, BM.

STANHOPE, Lady Hester Lucy (1776-1839) eccentric.
PR R.J.HAMERTON, wl in oriental dress with hookah, lith, BM.

STANHOPE, Leicester Fitzgerald Charles, see 5th Earl of Harrington.

STANHOPE, Philip (1755-1815), see 5th Earl of Chesterfield.

STANHOPE, Philip Henry Stanhope, 4th Earl (1781-1855) man of affairs.
PR S.W.REYNOLDS, after W.Haines, wl in peer's robes, mezz, BM, NPG.

STANLEY, Edward (1779-1849) bishop of Norwich.
P JAMES GREEN, 1803, hl, NPG 4242.
PR T.H.MAGUIRE, tql seated, lith, for *Ipswich Museum Portraits*, 1849, BM, NPG. NEGELEN, after G.Richmond, hl, lith, BM, NPG.

STANLEY, Edward (1793-1862) surgeon.
SC J.G.LOUGH, 1861, bust, St Bartholomew's Hospital, London.

STANLEY, Edward George, see 14th Earl of Derby.

STANLEY, Edward Smith (1775-1851), see 13th Earl of Derby.

STANLEY, John (1714-1786) musician.
PR UNKNOWN, hl playing organ, line, for *European Mag*, 1784, BM, NPG. M.A.RIGG, after T.Gainsborough, hl, stipple, oval, pub 1781, BM, NPG. J.McARDELL, after J.Williams, tql seated playing organ, mezz, BM, NPG.

STANNARD, Joseph (1797-1830) landscape painter.
PR S.V.HUNT, after G.Clint, head, etch, 1831, BM.

STAPLETON, Gregory (1748-1802) Roman Catholic prelate.
PR UNKNOWN, silhouette profile, hs, oval, woodcut, BM.

STARK, James (1794-1859) landscape painter.
D H.B.LOVE, 1830, hl, w/c, NPG 1562. UNKNOWN, hl, pen and ink, BM.
PR UNKNOWN, hs, lith, BM.

STAUNTON, Sir George Leonard, 1st Bart (1737-1801) diplomat.
P L.F.ABBOTT, 1784, hl with George, Earl Macartney, NPG 329.
PR C.PICART, after G.Engleheart, hs, stipple, oval, BM.

STAUNTON, Sir George Thomas, 2nd Bart (1781-1859) writer on China.
G SIR GEORGE HAYTER, 'The House of Commons, 1833', oil, NPG 54.
PR W.GELLER, after G.Swandale, tql, mezz, pub 1839, BM.

STEBBING, Henry (1799-1883) editor of the *Athenaeum*.
PR C.BAUGNIET, tql, lith, pub 1845, BM.

STEDMAN, John Gabriel (1744-1797) soldier and author.
D UNKNOWN, wl, w/c, The Marylebone Cricket Club, London.

STEELE, Joshua (1700-1791) author.
G JAMES BARRY, 'The Society for the Encouragement of Arts', oil, 1777-82, Royal Society of Arts, London.

STEEVENS, George (1736-1800) commentator on Shakespeare.
D GEORGE DANCE, 1793, hl, pencil, NPG 1160.
PR W.EVANS, after J.Zoffany, tql seated with dogs, stipple, BM, NPG. G.COOKE, after J.Flaxman, wl seated, with bust of Shakespeare, outline, for *European Mag*, 1812, BM, NPG. J.SAYER, hs, etch, BM.

STENNETT, Samuel (1728-1795) baptist minister.
PR UNKNOWN, hs, line, oval, pub 1796, BM. T.HOLLOWAY, hl, line, NPG. ROFFE, hl seated, stipple, BM.

STEPHEN, James (1758-1832) master in chancery.
PR J.LINNELL, hl, mezz, pub 1834, NPG.

STEPHEN, Sir James (1789-1859) colonial under-secretary and historian.
SC BARON CARLO MAROCHETTI, 1858, marble bust, NPG 1029. ALEXANDER MUNRO, plaster bust, Colonial Office Library, London.

STEPHENS, Catherine, see Countess of Essex.

STEPHENS, Sir Philip, 1st Bart (1725-1809) secretary of the admiralty.
P SIR WILLIAM BEECHEY, RA 1796, hl, DoE (Admiralty House, London).
PR J.COLLYER, after Sir William Beechey, hl seated, stipple, oval, for Colnett's *Voyage Round Cape Horn*, 1798, BM.

STEPHENSON, George (1781-1848) inventor of the railway-engine.
P H.P.BRIGGS, hl seated, Institution of Mechanical Engineers, London. WILLIAM DANIELLS, V & A. JOHN LUCAS, wl standing, train in background, Institution of Civil Engineers, London. H.W.PICKERSGILL, hl, NPG 410. UNKNOWN, hl, National Railway Museum, York. JOHN LUCAS, with his son Robert, Institution of Civil Engineers.
G UNKNOWN, oil, Science Museum, London.
SC JOSEPH PITTS, 1846, marble bust, NPG 261. JOHN GIBSON, 1851, statue, St George's Hall, Liverpool. J.G.LOUGH, 1862, statue, Newcastle.

STERNE, Laurence (1713-1768) writer.
P SIR JOSHUA REYNOLDS, 1760, tql, NPG 5019; copy, City Art Gallery, York. THOMAS PATCH, 1765, wl looking at the hand of death, with an hour glass, Jesus College, Cambridge. UNKNOWN, tql, NPG 2022.
D LOUIS DE CARMONTELLE, 1762, wl, w/c, Musée Condé, Chantilly, France. Attrib LOUIS DE CARMONTELLE, c1762, wl, w/c, NPG 2785.
SC JOSEPH NOLLEKENS, c1766, marble bust, NPG 1891.
C THOMAS PATCH, wl, etch, pl 20 of his *Caricature*, 1769, BM, V & A.

STEVENSON, Sir John Andrew (1760?-1833) musical composer.
P G.F.JOSEPH, hl, NGI 416.
M WILLIAM SHERLOCK, 1805, hs, on ivory, oval, V & A.
PR A.CARDON, after C.Robertson, tql seated with music, stipple, pub 1825, BM, NPG.

STEVENSON, Robert (1772-1850) lighthouse engineer.
P JOHN SYME, hl, SNPG 657.
SC After SAMUEL JOSEPH, plaster bust, SNPG 272.

STEVENSON, William (1749?-1821) antiquary and publisher.
PR W.SHARP, after W.Hilton, hl holding coin, lith, BM.

STEWARDSON, Thomas (1781-1859) portrait painter.
PR W.W.BARNEY, after J.Opie, hl, mezz, BM, NPG.

STEWART, Anthony (1773-1846) miniature-painter.

P ANDREW GEDDES, 1812, hs, SNPG 430.

STEWART, Prince Charles Edward, see Prince CHARLES.

STEWART, Charles James (1775-1837) bishop of Quebec.
P Attrib JOHN JACKSON, tql, All Souls College, Oxford.

STEWART, Charles William Vane, see 3rd Marquess of Londonderry.

STEWART, David (of Garth) (1772-1829) general.
PR J.B.SHAW, after J.Watson Gordon, hl in uniform, stipple, for Chamber's *Dict of Eminent Scotsmen*, 1835, BM, NPG. S.W.REYNOLDS, after J.Scrymgeour, wl in uniform, mezz, BM.

STEWART, Dugald (1753-1828) philosopher.
P SIR HENRY RAEBURN, hl, SNPG 821.
D J.HENNING, 1811, hs, profile, pencil, NPG 1428. SIR DAVID WILKIE, 1824, chalk, SNPG 1985. ARCHIBALD SKIRVING, chalk, SNPG L36.
SC JAMES TASSIE, 1797, paste medallion, SNPG 266. JOHN HENNING, 1811, Wedgwood medallion, SNPG 1542. SAMUEL JOSEPH, bronze bust, SNPG 209.

STEWART, Helen D'Arcy Cranstoun (1765-1838) song writer.
SC After JOHN HENNING, plaster medallion, SNPG 417.

STEWART, Henry Benedict Maria Clement, see Cardinal York.

STEWART or STUART, Louisa, see Countess of Albany.

STEWART or STUART, Princess Maria Clementina, see MARIA.

STEWART, Robert (1769-1822), see 2nd Marquess of Londonderry.

STEWART, see Stuart.

STILLINGFLEET, Benjamin (1702-1771) botanist.
PR VALENTINE GREEN, after Johan Zoffany, c1762, tql seated, mezz, oval, 1782, BM, NPG.

STIRLING, Sir James, 1st Bart (1740?-1805) lord provost of Edinburgh.
C J.KAY, with Henry Dundas, 'Patent for Knighthood', etch, 1792, BM. J.KAY, wl with Mr Hay, etch, 1796, BM.

STIRLING, Sir James (1791-1865) admiral and first governor of Western Australia.
P Attrib THOMAS PHILLIPS, tql, Public Library of New South Wales, (Mitchell and Dixson Galleries), Sydney, Australia.

STIRLING, Sir Walter (1718-1786) naval captain.
P JAMES NORTHCOTE, c1780, hl in uniform with telescope, NMM, Greenwich.

STOCK, Joseph (1741-1813) Irish bishop.
P UNKNOWN, hl, Trinity College, Dublin.

STOCKDALE, John (1749?-1814) bookseller.
C T.ROWLANDSON, wl as a blacksmith hammering a book, etch, BM.

STOCKDALE, Percival (1736-1811) author.
PR J.FITTLER, after J.Downman, hl, line, oval, for his *Sermons to Seamen*, 1784, BM, NPG.

STOKES, Whitley (1763-1845) professor of medicine.
D CHARLES GREY, pencil, NGI 2596.

STONE, Andrew (1703-1773) under-secretary of state.
PR C.BESTLAND, after I.Gosset, hs, stipple, oval, for *Works of R.O.Cambridge*, 1803, BM, NPG.

STONE, George (1708-1764) archbishop of Armagh.
P Attrib ALLAN RAMSAY, tql, Christ Church, Oxford.

STOPFORD, Sir Robert (1768-1847) admiral.
P SIR WILLLAIM BEECHEY, c1790-01, hl in uniform, oval, NMM, Greenwich. UNKNOWN, 1840, hl seated, NPG 1774. FREDERICK RICHARD SAY, tql in uniform, NMM.

STORACE, Anna Selina (1766-1817) singer and actress.
P M.W.SHARP, hl, Garrick Club, London.
PR P.BETTELINI, hl wearing hat, stipple, oval, pub 1788, BM. J.CONDÉ, after Samuel de Wilde, wl, as Euphrosyne in Milton's *Comus*, holding cup, stipple, pub 1791, BM, NPG.

STORER, Anthony Morris (1746-1799) collector.
P SIR MARTIN ARCHER SHEE, wl, Prado, Madrid; version (attrib John Hoppner), Baltimore Museum of Art, USA.

STORMONT, Viscount David Murray (1727-1796), see 2nd Earl of Mansfield.

STOTHARD, Charles Alfred (1786-1821) antiquarian draughtsman.
PR R.COOPER, after A.Chalon, hl, stipple and line, for *Memoirs* by Mrs Stothard, 1823, BM, NPG.

STOTHARD, Thomas (1755-1834) printer and illustrator.
P JAMES GREEN, 1830, hl, NPG 2. JOHN JACKSON, hl, Manchester City Art Gallery. JOHN JACKSON, hl, Fitzwilliam Museum, Cambridge. JOHN WOOD, 1833, tql, Dulwich College Art Gallery, London.
D GEORGE DANCE, 1794, hs, profile, Royal Academy, London. HENRY EDRIDGE, tql by easel, pencil, BM. JOHN FLAXMAN, hs, pencil, NPG 1096. JOHN FLAXMAN, hs, profile, chalk, BM.
G HENRY SINGLETON, 'The Royal Academicians, 1793', oil, Royal Academy, London.
SC SIR FRANCIS CHANTREY, c1812, bust, Ashmolean Museum, Oxford. E.H.BAILY, 1825, marble bust, Royal Academy. HENRY WEEKES, bust TATE 2075.
PR W.WORTHINGTON, after G.H.Harlow, hl standing, his 'Canterbury Pilgrims' in background, line, pub 1818, BM, NPG.

STOW, David (1793-1864) educational writer.
SC A.H.RITCHIE, 1852, bust, Glasgow City Art Gallery.

STOWELL, William Scott, Baron (1745-1836) judge.
P JOHN HOPPNER, c1806, tql seated in robes, University College, Oxford. WILLIAM OWEN, c1811-16, wl seated, Convocation House, Oxford. THOMAS PHILLIPS, tql in robes, Corpus Christi College, Oxford.
D GEORGE DANCE, 1803, hl seated, NPG 1156.
G SIR GEORGE HAYTER, 'The Trial of Queen Caroline, 1820', oil, NPG 999.
SC WILLIAM BEHNES, 1824, marble bust, NPG 125. M.L.WATSON and G.NELSON, c1843-7, marble group with 1st Earl of Eldon, University College, Oxford.

STRADBROKE, John Edward Cornwallis Rous, 2nd Earl of (1794-1886) soldier and politician.
PR T.C.WILSON, wl in hunting dress, lith, for Wildrake's *Cracks of the Day*, 1841, BM. J.J.CHANT, after Sir F.Grant, wl with dog, mezz, pub 1863, NPG. JOSEPH BROWN, after a photograph by Mayall, hs, stipple, pub 1861, NPG. C.W.WALTON, from a photograph by B.W.Bentley, hs, aged 90, lith, NPG.
C C.PELLEGRINI, 'Ape', wl, w/c, for *Vanity Fair*, 31 July 1875, NPG 4744.

STRAFFORD, John Byng, 1st Earl of (1772-1860) field-marshal.
P WILLIAM SALTER, c1834-40, tql, study for 'Waterloo Banquet', NPG 3757.
G SIR GEORGE HAYTER, 'The House of Commons, 1833', oil, NPG 54. W.SALTER, 'The Waterloo Banquet at Apsley House', oil, 1836, Wellington Museum, Apsley House, London.

STRAHAN, William (1715-1785) printer and publisher.
P SIR JOSHUA REYNOLDS, 1783, tql, NPG 4202.

STRANGE, Sir Robert (1721-1792) line engraver.
P JOSEPH SAMUEL WEBSTER, 1750, SNPG 1992.
D JEAN BAPTISTE GREUZE, wash, SNPG L296.
PR Copper plate, engraved by Sir Robert Strange, after Jean Baptiste Greuze, engraved 1791, SNPG 1847.

STRANGE, Sir Thomas Andrew Lumisden (1756-1841) Indian jurist.
P BENJAMIN WEST, 1799, hl, SNPG 1991. SIR THOMAS LAWRENCE, 1820, Government House, Madras. SIR MARTIN ARCHER SHEE, tql, Christ Church, Oxford.
M UNKNOWN, on ivory, oval, SNPG L295.

STRANGFORD, Percy Clinton Sidney Smythe, 6th Viscount, see 1st Baron Penshurst.

STRATFORD, Edward, see 2nd Earl of Aldborough.

STRATFORD de Redcliffe, Stratford Canning, Viscount (1786-1880) diplomat.
P GEORGE FREDERICK WATTS, 1856-7, hl, NPG 684. H.R.GRAVES, RA 1865, Eton College, Berkshire. SIR H.HERKOMER, 1879, hl, King's College, Cambridge.
D GEORGE RICHMOND, 1853, hs, chalk, NPG 1513. R.LEHMANN, 1859, hs, BM.
SC SIR JOSEPH EDGAR BOEHM, 1864, marble bust, DoE (British Embassy, Istanbul); plaster cast, NPG 791.
PH G.GRANVILLE, hl seated in his study, NPG.

STRATHEARN, Henry Frederick, Duke of, see Duke of Cumberland.

STREATFIELD, Thomas (1777-1848) topographer.
PR H.L.SMITH, seated with *Hist of Kent*, lith, BM.

STRICKLAND, Agnes (1796-1874) historian.
P JOHN HAYES, 1846, tql, NPG 403.
D CHARLES L.GOW, 1846, hl, chalk, NPG 2923.
PH SOUTHWOOD BROS, wl seated, carte, NPG.

STRUTT, Jedediah (1726-1797) cotton spinner and improver of the stocking-frame.
P JOSEPH WRIGHT, c1790, tql seated, Derby Museum and Art Gallery.

STRUTT, Joseph (1749-1802) engraver and antiquary.
D OZIAS HUMPHRY, hl, pastel, NPG 323.
G UNKNOWN, after P.Sandby, 'Sketches taken at Print Sales', line engr, pub 1798, BM.

STUART, Andrew (d1801) lawyer.
PR T.WATSON, after Sir J.Reynolds, hl, mezz, oval, BM, NPG.

STUART, Sir Charles (1753-1801) general.
P GEORGE ROMNEY, tql, City Museum and Art Gallery, Glasgow, engr J.Grozer, mezz, pub 1794, BM, NPG.
SC After JAMES TASSIE, plaster medallion, SNPG 458.

STUART, Prince Charles Edward, see Prince CHARLES.

STUART, Gilbert (1742-1786) historian.
PR UNKNOWN, after J.Donaldson, hl, aged 35, line, for *European Mag*, 1780, BM, NPG.

STUART, Gilbert (1755-1828) portrait-painter.
P Self-portrait, 1778, hs, Redwood Library, Newport, Rhode Island, USA. Self-portrait, c1785, hs, oval, TATE 5612. JOHN NEAGLE, 1825, Boston Museum of Fine Arts, Boston, USA. Self-portrait, head, sketch, Metropolitan Museum of Art, New York, USA. CHARLES WILSON PEALE, New York Historical Society, New York, USA.
D BENJAMIN WEST, tql painting a portrait of West, pen and wash,

BM.

SC J.H.I.BROWERE, 1825, bust, Redwood Library.

STUART, Henry Benedict Maria Clement, see Cardinal York.

STUART, James (1713-1788) painter and architect.
D Self-portrait, chalk, RIBA, London. JOHN HENNING?, after George Dance, hl, V & A.
M Attrib PHILIP JEAN, hs, NPG 55.
SC Wedgwood medallion, SNPG 364.
PR C.KNIGHT, from death mask, stipple, for *Antiquities of Athens*, 1789, BM, NPG. J.BASIRE, tql seated, line, for *Rudiments of Ancient Architecture*, 1794, BM. S.W.REYNOLDS, after Sir Joshua Reynolds, hl in turban and cloak, etch, pub 1795, BM.

STUART, James (b1728) wandering minstrel and centenarian, known as 'The Last of the Stuarts'.
PR T.C.HOGARTH, aged 115, wl with fiddle, etch, BM, NPG.

STUART, James (c1735-1793) commander-in-chief in Madras.
P GEORGE ROMNEY, SNPG 1832, engr C.H.Hodges, mezz, pub 1789, BM.

STUART, James (1741-1815) general.
D T.HICKEY, 1799, hs, Stratfield Saye, Hants.
PR G.CLINT, after Sir Thomas Lawrence, tql in uniform, mezz, pub 1802, BM.

STUART, James (1775-1849) duellist and pamphleteer.
P SIR DANIEL MACNEE, hl, SNPG 1143.

STUART, John (1713-1792), see 3rd Earl of Bute.

STUART, Sir John (1759-1815) general, the 'hero of Maida'.
PR A.CARDON, after W.Wood, hl in uniform, stipple, pub 1806, BM, NPG.

STUART, William (1755-1822) archbishop of Armagh.
SC SIR FRANCIS CHANTREY, 1828, marble bust, V & A; plaster cast, Ashmolean Museum, Oxford.
PR S.W.REYNOLDS, after William Owen, tql, holding 'a Bill', mezz, pub 1816, BM.

STUART DE ROTHESAY, Sir Charles Stuart, Baron (1779-1845) general.
PR DE FREY, hl, line, NPG.

STUART-WORTLEY-MACKENZIE, James Archibald, see 1st Baron Wharncliffe.

STUART, see Stewart.

STUBBS, George (1724-1806) animal painter.
P Self-portrait, 1781, hl, enamel on Wedgwood plaque, oval, NPG 4575. Self-portrait, wl on horseback, enamel on china tablet, Lady Lever Art Gallery, Port Sunlight.
D GEORGE DANCE, 1794, hs, pencil and chalk, Royal Academy, London. OZIAS HUMPHRY, hl, w/c, NPG 1399. OZIAS HUMPHRY, hs, pastel, Walker Art Gallery, Liverpool. Self-portrait, hl, plumbago, study for NPG 4575, Yale Center for British Art, New Haven, USA.
PR BRETHERTON, after T.Orde, tql painting, etch, BM, NPG.

STUMP, Samuel John (1778-1863) painter and miniaturist.
M Self-portrait, hl, Guildhall Art Gallery, London.
G JOHN PARTRIDGE, 'A Meeting of the Sketching Society', pen, ink and wash, BM.

STURGE, Joseph (1793-1859) Quaker and philanthropist.
P JERRY BARRET, 1855, City Museum and Art Gallery, Birmingham.
G BENJAMIN ROBERT HAYDON, 'The Anti-Slavery Society Convention, 1840', oil, NPG 599.

SC JOHN THOMAS, marble statue, Five Ways, Edgbaston, Birmingham.
PR M.GAUCI, after A.Rippingille, tql with negro child, lith, BM. D.J.POUND, after a photograph by Whitlock, tql seated, stipple and line, BM, NPG.

STURT, Charles (1795-1869) Australian explorer.
P JOHN MICHAEL CROSSLAND, c1853, tql, Art Gallery of South Australia, Adelaide, Australia; replica, tql, NPG 3302.
SC C.SUMNERS, bust, Art Gallery of South Australia.

SUCKLING, Maurice (1725-1778) comptroller of the navy.
P THOMAS BARDWELL, 1764, wl seated, NPG 2010.
PR W.RIDLEY, hl in uniform, stipple, oval, for *Naval Chronicle*, 1805, BM, NPG.

SUETT, Richard (1755-1805) actor.
P Various portraits by SAMUEL DE WILDE, mostly in character, Garrick Club, London, Ashmolean Museum, Oxford and V & A. JOHN GRAHAM, wl as Bayes in Duke of Buckingham's *The Rehearsal*, V & A.
PR Various theatrical prints, BM, NPG.

SUFFIELD, Edward Harbord, 3rd Baron (1781-1835) philanthropist.
G SIR FRANCIS GRANT, 'The Melton Hunt going to draw Ram's Head Cover', oil, Stratfield Saye, Hants.
PR UNKNOWN, after A.Wivell, hl, stipple, pub 1823, BM. S.W.REYNOLDS, after H.Edridge, wl in uniform, mezz, BM.

SUGDEN, Edward Burtenshaw, see Baron St Leonards.

SUMBEL, Mary, see Mrs Wells.

SUMNER, Charles Richard (1790-1874) bishop of Winchester.
PR C.BAUGNIET, nearly wl seated, lith, BM. S.COUSINS, after M.A.Shee, nearly wl seated, mezz, BM, NPG. D.J.POUND, after a photo by Mayall, tql seated, stipple and line, NPG.

SUMNER, John Bird (1780-1862) archbishop of Canterbury.
P E.U.EDDIS, c1851, Lambeth Palace, London. MARGARET SARAH CARPENTER, c1852, hl, NPG 3975. E.U.EDDIS, 1853, King's College, Cambridge.
D GEORGE RICHMOND, 1849, hs, chalk, NPG 2467.
G J.PHILLIP, 'The Marriage of the Princess Royal, 1858', oil, Royal Coll.
SC G.G.ADAMS, 1863, plaster bust, NPG 1207. HENRY WEEKES, marble statue, Canterbury Cathedral.

SUNDERLAND, Charles Spencer, 5th Earl of, see 3rd Duke of Marlborough.

SUNDERLIN, Richard Malone, Baron (1738-1816) Irish peer.
P SIR JOSHUA REYNOLDS, NGI 1734.

SUSSEX, Augustus Frederick, Duke of (1773-1843) son of George III.
P THOMAS GAINSBOROUGH, hs, as a child, oval, Royal Coll. G.HEAD, 1798, hl, NPG 648. JAMES LONSDALE, 1817, wl seated, Trinity College, Cambridge. SIR DAVID WILKIE, c1833, wl in Scots costume, with dog, Royal Coll. THOMAS PHILLIPS, 1840, tql seated, Royal Society, London. SIR WILLIAM BEECHEY, hl, with Garter star, Smithsonian Institution, Washington DC, USA. DOMENICO PELLEGRINI, wl, Galleria dell'Accademia di San Luca, Rome.
D COUNT D'ORSAY, 1843, hs, pencil and chalk, NPG 4026 (54). SIR FRANCIS CHANTREY, two hs sketches, pencil, NPG 316a (119, 120). BENJAMIN WEST, chalk, V & A.
M RICHARD COLLINS, 1789, V & A. ANDREW ROBERTSON, 1807, Aberdeen Art Gallery. RICHARD COSWAY, hs, oval, Royal Coll.

SC CHRISTOPHER PROSPERI, 1811, bust, Woburn Abbey, Beds. SIR FRANCIS CHANTREY, c1832, plaster bust, Ashmolean Museum, Oxford. W.THEED, 1879, bust, Royal Coll.

SUTHERLAND, George Granville Leveson-Gower, 1st Duke of (1758-1833) diplomat and magnate.

P THOMAS PHILLIPS, 1805, hl, NPG 1298. P.C.WONDER, c1826, wl, study for a group, NPG 794.

D SIR FRANCIS CHANTREY, two hs sketches, pencil, NPG 316a (117, 118).

G SIR GEORGE HAYTER, 'The Trial of Queen Caroline, 1820', oil, NPG 999.

SC JOSEPH NOLLEKENS, 1805, plaster bust, Dunrobin Castle, Highland region, Scotland. JAMES FRANCIS, 1834, bust, Dunrobin Castle. SIR FRANCIS CHANTREY, 1838, statue, Parish Church, Trentham, Staffs.

PR H.MEYER, after W.Owen, hl, stipple, for *Contemporary Portraits*, 1811, BM, NPG.

SUTHERLAND, George Granville-Sutherland-Leveson-Gower, 2nd Duke of (1786-1861) collector and connoisseur.

P SIR THOMAS LAWRENCE, c1824, Dunrobin Castle, Highland region, Scotland. JOHN PARTRIDGE, 1850, tql, study for 'Fine Art Commissioners', Dunrobin Castle.

D HUET VILLIERS, 1811, hs, w/c, Dunrobin Castle.

G SIR GEORGE HAYTER, 'The Trial of Queen Caroline, 1820', oil, NPG 999. JOHN PARTRIDGE, 'Fine Art Commissioners, 1846', NPG 342, 343.

SC JOSEPH NOLLEKENS, 1810, marble bust, Dunrobin Castle. BERTEL THORVALDSEN, 1817, bust, Thorvaldsen Museum, Copenhagen. J.FRANCIS, 1838, marble bust, Royal Coll. MATTHEW NOBLE, 1861, statue, Dunrobin Castle. SIR FRANCIS CHANTREY, plaster bust, Ashmolean Museum, Oxford.

SUTTON, Charles Manners (1755-1828), see Manners.

SWAIN, Joseph (1761-1796) hymn-writer and preacher.

P UNKNOWN, hs, stipple, oval, for *Evangelical Mag*, 1795, NPG.

SWAINSON, William (1789-1855) naturalist.

PR E.FINDEN, after Mosses, hl seated, stipple, for *Taxidermy, with the Biography of Zoologists and notices of their works*, 1840, NPG.

SWINBURNE, Henry (1743?-1803) traveller.

P POMPEO BATONI, 1779, hs, Laing Art Gallery, Newcastle-upon-Tyne.

D HUGH DOUGLAS HAMILTON, 1771, hl, pastel, Fonman Castle, South Glamorgan.

SC Attrib CHRISTOPHER HEWETSON, c1779, bronze bust, Lotherton Hall, West Yorks.

PR W.ANGUS, hs, line, oval, for *European Mag*, pub 1785, BM, NPG. M.BOVI, after R.Cosway, hl, stipple, for *Journey from Bayonne*, 1787, BM, NPG.

SYDENHAM, Charles Edward Poulett Thomson, Baron (1799-1841) governor-general of Canada.

G SIR GEORGE HAYTER, 'The House of Commons, 1833', oil, NPG 54.

PR S.REYNOLDS jun, tql, mezz, pub 1833, BM, NPG. W.H.MOTE, after Sir George Hayter, hl, stipple, for Saunders's *Political Reformers*, 1840, BM, NPG. T.C.WILSON, tql holding paper, lith, NPG.

SYDNEY, John Thomas Townshend, 2nd Viscount (1764-1831) politician.

G SIR GEORGE HAYTER, 'The House of Lords, 1820', oil, NPG 999.

PR J.YOUNG, after G.Stuart, hl seated, mezz, BM.

SYDNEY, Thomas Townshend, 1st Viscount (1733-1800) statesman.

PR J.SCOTT, after Sir Joshua Reynolds, wl with Colonel Acland, with bows and arrows, mezz, BM, NPG. JAMES SAYERS, wl, etch, 1784, NPG.

SYKES, Sir Mark Masterman, 3rd Baronet (1771-1823) book-collector.

PR R.GRAVE, after P.Rouw, profile, from a wax model, line, BM, NPG.

SYKES, Sir Tatton, 4th Bart (1772-1863) sportsman.

P SIR FRANCIS GRANT, 1847, wl equestrian, Sledmere House, Humberside. HARRY HALL, c1845-50, wl leading horse with jockey, Yale Center for British Art, New Haven, USA. UNKNOWN, hs, NPG 3102.

PR J.BROWN, hl, stipple, for *Baily's Mag*, 1861, BM.

SYME, James (1799-1870) surgeon.

P GEORGE RICHMOND, SNPG 768. 'G.R.', 1875, hs, Royal College of Surgeons, Edinburgh.

D GEORGE RICHMOND, 1857, hs, chalk, SNPG 616.

SYME, John (1795-1861) artist.

P Self-portrait, SNPG 1544. Self-portrait, SNPG 1545. Self-portrait, hl, Royal Scottish Academy.

SYMINGTON, Andrew (1785-1853) Scottish divine.

PR W.H.EGLETON, after Henry Anelay, hs, stipple, NPG. SCHENCK and McFARLANE, tql seated in armchair holding book, lith, BM.

SYMINGTON, William (1763-1831) engineer.

G J.F.SKILL, J.GILBERT, W. and E.WALKER, 'Men of Science Living in 1807-08', pencil and wash, NPG 1075.

PR T.O.BARLOW, after D.O.Hill, hl, oval, mixed, BM. ROFFE, hs, stipple, from a bust, pub 1834, NPG.

SYMINGTON, William (1795-1862) divine.

PR J.G.MURRAY, after A.Craig, tql seated, mezz, NPG. SCHENCK and McFARLANE, tql seated, lith, oval, BM.

SYMMONS, Charles (1749-1826) man of letters.

PR R.GRAVES, hl, BM.

SYMONDS, John (1729-1807) professor of modern history at Cambridge.

PR J.SINGLETON, after G.Ralph, hl, stipple, pub 1788, BM, NPG.

SYMONDS, Sir William (1782-1856) rear-admiral.

PR E.MORTON, after H.W.Phillips, nearly wl, in uniform, holding compasses, lith, pub 1850, BM, NPG.

SYMONS, Benjamin Parsons (1785-1878) warden of Wadham College, Oxford.

P H.W.PICKERSGILL, c1835, tql, Wadham College, Oxford.

T

TALBOT, Catherine (1721-1770) author.
PR C.HEATH, hl, stipple, for *Works*, 1812, BM, NPG.

TALBOT, Mary Anne (1778-1808) female soldier and sailor.
PR G.SCOTT, after J.Green, hl in sailor's dress, stipple, for Kirby's *Wonderful Museum*, 1804, BM, NPG. G.SCOTT, wl, aged 26, in female attire, stipple, for Kirby's *Wonderful Museum*, 1804, BM, NPG.

TALBOT, Thomas (1771-1853) colonist.
P Attrib J.B.WANDESFORD, wl, University of Western Ontario, London, Canada.

TALBOT OF HENSOL, Sir Charles Chetwynd, 2nd Earl (1777-1849) lord lieutenant of Ireland.
PR S.W.REYNOLDS, after T.C.Thompson, wl in robes of St Patrick with page, mezz, pub 1822, BM.

TALFOURD, Sir Thomas Noon (1795-1854) judge and author.
P JOHN LUCAS, hl seated holding paper, Garrick Club, London. H.W.PICKERSGILL, tql seated in judge's robes, NPG 417 (on loan to Law Courts). H.W.PICKERSGILL, hl, Middle Temple, London. UNKNOWN, Law Library, Harvard University, Cambridge, USA.
SC J.G.LOUGH, 1855, bust, Crown Court, Stafford.
PR W.HOLL, after K.Meadows, hl, stipple, for Saunders's *Political Reformers*, 1840, BM, NPG. J.C.ARMYTAGE, hl, stipple, NPG. ROFFE, after B.R.Haydon, hl, stipple, BM, NPG.

TALSARN (1796-1857), see John JONES.

TANDY, James Napper (1740-1803) Irish nationalist.
P Irish School, NGI 429.
G FRANCIS WHEATLEY, 'The Volunteers in College Green, 1779', oil, NGI 125; version, w/c, V & A. UNKNOWN, 'The United Irish patriots of 1798', coloured lith, NPG.
PR J.HEATH, after J.Petrie, hs in uniform, stipple, for Sir J.Barrington's *Historic Memoirs*, 1815, BM, NPG.
C JAMES GILLRAY, hs, etch, pub 1799, NPG.

TANNAHILL, Robert (1774-1810) Scottish song-writer.
PR S.FREEMAN, after A.Blair, hl, stipple, for Chambers's *Dict of Eminent Scotsmen*, 1835, BM, NPG.

TANS'UR, William (1706-1783) teacher of psalmody.
PR UNKNOWN, wl, oval, woodcut, for *Heaven on Earth*, 1738, BM. B.COLE, wl seated, oval, line, for *Works*, 1748, BM. UNKNOWN, 1760, hs, oval, line, NPG. E.NEWTON, hl, oval, line, for *Melodia Sacra*, 1772, BM.

TARLETON, Sir Banastre, Bart (1754-1833) general.
P SIR JOSHUA REYNOLDS, 1782, wl, with horse and cannon, NG 5985.
PR C.TOWNLEY, after R.Cosway, hs in uniform, stipple, BM.

TASSIE, James (1735-1799) modeller.
P DAVID ALLAN, hl, SNPG 576. JOHN PAXTON, SNPG L33.
SL UNKNOWN, 1776, SNPG 1225.
SC WILLIAM TASSIE, two paste medallions, SNPG 259 and 260.

TATE, James (1771-1843) schoolmaster and author.
PR S.COUSINS, after H.Pickersgill, tql seated, mezz, BM, NPG.

TATHAM, Charles Heathcote (1772-1842) architect.

D BENJAMIN ROBERT HAYDON, 1823, hs, pastel, BM.
SC FREDERICK TATHAM, 1837, bust, Lord Northampton's Almshouses, Greenwich.

TATHAM, Edward (1749-1834) controversialist.
P UNKNOWN, wl with books, Lincoln College, Oxford.

TATTERSALL, Richard (1724-1795) horse-auctioneer.
D 'JCB', 1788, hs, ink and wash, NPG 2357.
PR J.JONES, after T.Beach, tql with stud-book, mezz, pub 1787, BM.

TAUNTON, Henry Labouchere, Baron (1798-1869) statesman.
G SIR GEORGE HAYTER, 'The House of Commons, 1833', oil, NPG 54.
SC BERTEL THORVALDSEN, 1828, plaster bust, Thorvaldsen Museum, Copenhagen.
PR C.W.WASS, after Sir Thomas Lawrence, wl, as a child with his brother, stipple, BM, NPG. F.C.LEWIS, after J.Slater, hs, stipple, for 'Grillion's Club' series, BM, NPG.
PH UNKNOWN, wl, NPG, 'Twist Album'. CAMILLE SILVY, wl seated, carte, NPG 'Silvy Photographs 1860', vol I.

TAUNTON, Sir William Elias (1773-1835) justice of the King's bench.
P UNKNOWN, c1795, hl, Town Hall, Oxford. H.P.BRIGGS, c1833, tql, Christ Church, Oxford.
C R.DIGHTON, wl, etch, pub 1807, NPG.

TAYLER, John James (1797-1869) professor and ecclesiastical historian.
P JOHN PRESCOTT KNIGHT, c1862, tql, Manchester College, Oxford.

TAYLOR, Ann (Mrs Gilbert) (1782-1866) children's poet.
P I.TAYLOR, 1791, wl with her sister Jane, NPG 1248.

TAYLOR, Sir Brook (1776-1846) diplomatist.
PR C.BAUGNIET, hl seated, star on coat, lith, 1843, BM.

TAYLOR, Charles (1781-1847) actor and singer.
P SAMUEL DE WILDE, 1805, hs, Garrick Club, London. THOMAS ELLERBY, hs, Garrick Club, London.
D SAMUEL DE WILDE, as Noodle in *Tom Thumb*, w/c, Garrick Club, London. SAMUEL DE WILDE, as Lubin in *The Quaker*, w/c, Garrick Club, London, engr R.Cooper, stipple, for Cawthorn's *Minor Theatre*, 1805, BM.

TAYLOR, Edgar (1793-1839) solicitor and author.
PR C.TURNER, after E.U.Eddis, tql seated, mezz, pub 1841, BM, NPG.

TAYLOR, Edward (1784-1863) musician.
D GEORGE HARLOW WHITE, hs, ink and pencil, NPG 4217.
PR H.E.DAWE, after T.S.Tait, hl, mezz, BM.

TAYLOR, George Watson (d 1841) collector.
P P.C.WONDER, c1826, wl study for a group, NPG 792.
SC SIR FRANCIS CHANTREY, c1820, plaster bust, Ashmolean Museum, Oxford.
PR J.THOMSON, after A.Wivell, hl, stipple, No 2 of set of plates of persons present at trial of Queen Caroline, pub 1821, BM, NPG.

TAYLOR, Sir Herbert (1775-1839) lieutenant-general.
P UNKNOWN, hl, NPG 2878.

PR W.J.WARD, after W.J.Newton, tql in uniform, mezz, pub 1836, BM.

TAYLOR, Isaac (1759-1829) engraver.
PR T.BLOOD, after I.Taylor, hl, stipple, for *Evangelical Mag*, pub 1818, BM, NPG. J.ANDREWS, hs, stipple, pub 1832, NPG.

TAYLOR, Isaac (1787-1865) author and artist.
D JOSIAH GILBERT, 1862, head, chalk, NPG 884.
PR UNKNOWN, hl, woodcut, for the *Illust London News*, 1865, NPG.

TAYLOR, James (1753-1825) engineer.
SC WILLIAM TASSIE, 1801, paste medallion, SNPG 1259.

TAYLOR, Jane (1783-1824) children's poet.
P I.TAYLOR, 1791, wl with her sister Ann, NPG 1248.

TAYLOR, John (1703-1772) oculist.
SC ANDREAS VESTNER, silver medal, BM.
PR P.ENDLICH, hl, line, oval, 1735, BM. R.COOPER, after W. De Nune, hl, line, oval, with ornaments and inscriptions, BM. J.FABER jun, after P.Ryche, tql standing, mezz, BM, NPG.

TAYLOR, Sir John, Bart (d1786?) connoisseur.
G JOHAN ZOFFANY, 'The Tribuna of the Uffizi', oil, c1772-8, Royal Coll. SIR JOSHUA REYNOLDS, 'The Society of Dilettanti', oil, 1777-9. The Society of Dilettanti, Brooks's Club, London.
PR W.DICKINSON, after R.E.Pine, tql in fancy dress, mezz, oval, BM, NPG. J.DIXON, after J.Smart, hl, mezz, BM, NPG.

TAYLOR, John (1711-1788) friend of Dr Johnson.
P JOHN OPIE, hl, on loan to the Johnson Birthplace Museum, Lichfield.

TAYLOR, John (1757-1832) writer.
PR UNKNOWN, hl, stipple, for his *Records of my Life*, 1832, BM.

TAYLOR, John (1779-1863) mining engineer.
PR C.TURNER, after Sir Thomas Lawrence, tql seated, mezz, pub 1831, BM, NPG.

TAYLOR, John (1781-1864) publisher and writer.
SC UNKNOWN, paste medallion, NPG 1808A.

TAYLOR, John Sydney (1795-1841) barrister and journalist.
PR J.THOMSON, after C.Moore, hs, from a medallion, stipple, BM.

TAYLOR, Michael Angelo (1757-1834) politician.
G SIR GEORGE HAYTER, 'The House of Commons, 1833', oil, NPG 54.
PR S.W.REYNOLDS, after J.Lonsdale, hl seated, mezz, pub 1822, BM, NPG.
C JAMES GILLRAY, entitled 'End of the Irish Invasion', etch, pub 1797, NPG.

TAYLOR, Richard (1781-1858) printer and naturalist.
PR R.HICKS, after E.U.Eddis, hs, oval, stipple, 1845, NPG. T.H.MAGUIRE, tql seated, lith, for *Ipswich Museum Portraits*, BM, NPG.

TAYLOR, Sir Robert (1714-1788) architect.
P After REYNOLDS, tql RIBA, London. UNKNOWN, tql holding scroll, Taylor Institution, Oxford.
D UNKNOWN, hl, w/c, NPG 1323.
PR E.SCOTT, after W.Miller, hl wearing sheriff's gown, stipple, oval, pub 1789, BM.

TAYLOR, Thomas (1738-1816) methodist preacher.
PR W.RIDLEY, hs, aged 58, stipple, oval, for *Arminian Mag*, 1797, BM.

TAYLOR, Thomas (1758-1835) platonist.
P SIR THOMAS LAWRENCE, RA 1812, tql seated, National Gallery of Canada, **Ottawa. R.EVANS, after** Lawrence, tql seated, NPG 374.

TAYLOR, William (1765-1836) man of letters.
PR T.LUPTON, after J.Barwell, hl seated, aged 69, mezz, BM, NPG.

TEIGNMOUTH, John Shore, 1st Baron (1751-1834) governor-general of India.
D GEORGE RICHMOND, 1832, tql seated, w/c, NPG 5145.
SC THOMAS R.POOLE, 1818, wax medallion, hs, NPG 4986. THEODORE PHYFFERS, c1867, statue, India Office, London.
PR H.DAWE, after H.P.Briggs, nearly wl seated, mezz, pub 1823, BM, NPG. T.CHEESMAN, after M.Keeling, hl, stipple, BM, NPG.

TELFORD, Thomas (1757-1834) engineer.
P SAMUEL LANE, wl seated, Institute of Civil Engineers, London. GEORGE PATTEN, hl seated holding plans, Art Gallery and Museum, Glasgow. HENRY RAEBURN, hs, Lady Lever Art Gallery, Port Sunlight. UNKNOWN, hl as a young man, Shrewsbury Borough Museums, Salop.
D WILLIAM BROCKEDON, 1834, hs, pencil and chalk, NPG 2515 (67).
G J.F.SKILL, J.GILBERT, W. and E.WALKER, 'Men of Science Living in 1807-8', pencil and wash, NPG 1075.
SC PETER HOLLINS, RA 1832, bust, Institute of Civil Engineers. E.H.BAILY, 1839, statue, Westminster Abbey, London.

TEMPLE, Ann Chambers, Countess (1709-1777) poet.
D HUGH DOUGLAS HAMILTON, 1770, hl, pastel, NPG 246.

TEMPLE, Emily Mary, see Viscountess Palmerston.

TEMPLE, Henry (1739-1802), see 2nd Viscount Palmerston.

TEMPLE, Henry John, see 3rd Viscount Palmerston.

TEMPLE, Richard Grenville Temple, 2nd Earl of (1711-1779) statesman.
P WILLIAM HOARE, 1760, tql seated with Garter ribbon and star, NPG 258. ALLAN RAMSAY, c1762, wl in Garter robes, National Gallery of Victoria, Melbourne, Australia.
G JOHN SINGLETON COPLEY, 'The Collapse of the Earl of Chatham in the House of Lords, 7 July 1778', oil, TATE 100 (on loan to NPG).
SC PETER SCHEEMAKERS, 1740, bust, Stowe School, Bucks.
PR W.DICKINSON, after Sir Joshua Reynolds, tql in Garter robes, mezz, pub 1778, BM, NPG.

TEMPLEMAN, Peter (1711-1769) physician.
P RICHARD COSWAY, hl holding quill, Royal Society of Arts, London.

TENNANT, Charles (1768-1838) manufacturing chemist.
G J.F.SKILL, J.GILBERT, W. and E.WALKER, 'Men of Science Living in 1807-08', pencil and wash, NPG 1075.
SC PATRIC PARK, 1841, bust, Glasgow Necropolis.
PR J.G.MURRAY, after Andrew Geddes, tql, mezz, NPG.

TENNANT, William (1784-1848) poet and linguist.
P UNKNOWN, SNPG 1156.
D UNKNOWN, pencil and w/c, SNPG 124.
PR F.CROLL, hs, stipple and line, for Hogg's *Weekly Instructor*, NPG.

TENNYSON D'Eyncourt, Charles, see D'EYNCOURT.

TENTERDEN, Charles Abbott, 1st Baron (1762-1832) lord chief justice.
P WILLIAM OWEN, c1819, tql in robes, Corpus Christi College, Oxford. JOHN HOLLINS, after William Owen, tql seated, NPG 481 (on loan to Law Courts). JOHN WOOD, hl, Middle Temple, London.
D J.W.WRIGHT, 1830, tql, w/c, Inner Temple, London.
SC P.SARTI, 1883, marble bust, Middle Temple, London.
PR C.PICART, after J.Northcote, tql in robes, stipple, pub 1804, NPG. H.R.COOK, after S.H.Gimber, hl seated in robes, stipple, BM, NPG. H.MEYER, after C.Penny, hl seated on bench, stipple, BM,

NPG.

TERRICK, Richard (1710-1777) bishop of Peterborough and of London.

P NATHANIEL DANCE, 1764, tql seated, Lambeth Palace, London. STEWART, after Dance, hs, Fulham Palace.

TERROT, Charles Hughes (1790-1872) bishop of Edinburgh.

PH UNKNOWN, tql seated, carte, NPG.

TERRY, Daniel (1780-1829) actor.

P J.P.KNIGHT, hs, Garrick Club, London.

D WILLIAM NICHOLSON, hs, w/c, SNPG 1082. SAMUEL DE WILDE, wl as Barford in 'Who Wants a Guinea?', w/c, Garrick Club, London.

PR Various theatrical prints, BM, NPG.

THACKERAY, Frederick Rennell (1775-1860) general.

P F.BARSWELL, tql, Royal Engineers H.Q. Mess, Chatham, Kent.

THACKERAY, George (1777-1850) provost of King's College, Cambridge.

P F.JOSEPH, hl, King's College, Cambridge.

PR R.J.LANE, after F.Joseph, tql, lith, BM, NPG.

THACKWELL, Sir Joseph (1781-1859) lieutenant-general.

P UNKNOWN, hl in uniform, National Army Museum, London.

PR T.H.WILSON, tql in uniform, lith, BM.

THANE, John (1748-1818) printseller.

G UNKNOWN, after P.Sandby, 'Sketches taken at Print Sales', line, pub 1798, BM.

PR J.OGBORNE, after W.R.Bigg, tql seated at a table, holding a print and a coin, line, BM, NPG.

THANET, Sackville Tufton, 9th Earl of (1769-1825) gambler.

P SIR JOSHUA REYNOLDS, 1777, wl as a boy, with his brother and a large dog, Petworth (NT), West Sussex.

G SIR GEORGE HAYTER, 'The Trial of Queen Caroline, 1820', oil, NPG 999.

THELWALL, John (1764-1834) reformer and elocutionist.

P Attrib WILLIAM HAZLITT, hs, NPG 2163.

PR H.RICHTER, hs, stipple, pub 1794, NPG. UNKNOWN, hl holding scroll, stipple, oval, for Baxter's Hist of England, BM.

THESIGER, Frederick, see 1st Baron Chelmsford.

THICKNESSE, Ann, née Ford (1737-1824) musician and dancer.

P THOMAS GAINSBOROUGH, c1760, wl, Cincinnati Art Museum, USA; study for portrait, BM.

THICKNESSE, Philip (1719-1792) author and eccentric.

P THOMAS GAINSBOROUGH, c1750-5, wl, City Art Museum, St Louis, USA.

D WILLIAM HOARE, tql, chalk, BM.

M NATHANIEL HONE, 1757, hl, enamel, NPG 4192.

PR J.GILLRAY, hs, etch, oval, for Curious Facts not to be found in Memoirs of P.T., 1790, BM, NPG.

C J.GILLRAY, 'Lieut Gover Gall-stone', etch, pub 1790, NPG. UNKNOWN, wl, entitled 'The Monstrous Assassin or the Coward turn'd Bill Sticker', etch, NPG.

THIRLWALL, Connop (1797-1875) historian and bishop of St Davids.

P FRANK HOLL, c1865, tql, Abergwili Palace (The Bishop of St David), Wales. UNKNOWN, St David's University College, Lampeter, Wales.

SC EDWARD DAVIS: 1876, bust, Westminster Abbey, London; marble bust, Trinity College, Cambridge.

PH H.WATKINS, c1865, hs, NPG, in album, 'Portraits and

Autographs'. E.EDWARDS, c1864, wl, for Men of Eminence, ed L.Reeve, NPG.

THISTLEWOOD, Arthur (1770-1820) Cato Street conspirator.

G W.HOLL, after G.Scharf, 'Spa Fields Rioters', stipple, pub 1817, BM.

PR UNKNOWN, after A.Wivell, hs, stipple, pub 1820, BM, NPG. UNKNOWN, hs, lith, pub 1820, BM. Several popular prints, NPG.

THOM, John Nichols, see John Nichols TOM.

THOMAS, Honoratus Leigh (1769-1846) surgeon.

P JAMES GREEN, tql, Royal College of Surgeons, London.

THOMAS, John (1712-1793) bishop of Rochester.

P After SIR JOSHUA REYNOLDS, tql in robes, City Museum and Art Gallery, Birmingham. UNKNOWN, The Deanery, Westminster.

SC JOHN BACON, 1793, statue, Westminster Abbey.

PR J.BAKER, after R.Corbould, hs in robes, line, oval, for The Senator, 1791, BM, NPG. J.SWAINE, after B. Van der Gucht, hs with Bath badge, line, pub 1822, BM, NPG.

THOMAS, Joshua (1719-1797) Welsh writer.

PR RIDLEY, hs, stipple, oval, for Evangelical Mag, 1798, NPG.

THOMAS, Matthew Evan (1787/8-1830) architect.

G SIR GEORGE HAYTER, 'The Trial of Queen Caroline, 1820', oil, NPG 999.

THOMAS, Sir Noah (1720-1792) physician.

P Attrib JOHN ROMNEY, 1781, tql, St John's College, Cambridge.

THOMASON, Sir Edward (1769-1849) manufacturer and inventor.

P UNKNOWN, City Museum and Art Gallery, Birmingham.

D WILLIAM BROCKEDON, 1834, hs, pencil and chalk, NPG 2515(73).

PR C.E.WAGSTAFF, tql seated holding medal, mezz, BM, NPG.

THOMPSON, Benjamin (1753-1814) see Count von RUMFORD.

THOMPSON, Benjamin (1776?-1816) dramatist.

PR J.R.SMITH, tql seated, mezz, pub 1799, BM.

THOMPSON, Charles (1740?-1799) vice-admiral.

G WORTHINGTON and PARKER, after R.Smirke, 'Naval Victories', 'Commemoration of the 14th February 1797', line engr, pub 1803, BM, NPG.

THOMPSON, Edward (1738?-1786) commodore and writer.

P UNKNOWN, Trinity House, Hull.

PR A.McKENZIE, after a miniature by Hardy, hl, stipple, oval, pub 1783, BM.

THOMPSON, Sir Thomas Boulden, 1st Bart (1766?-1828) admiral.

G W.BROMLEY, J.LANDSEER and LENEY, after R.Smirke, 'Victors of the Nile', line, pub 1803, BM, NPG.

PR F.ENGLEHEART, after G.Engleheart, hl in uniform, stipple, pub 1799, BM.

THOMPSON, Thomas Perronet (1783-1869) reformer.

G S.BELLIN, after J.R.Herbert, 'Anti-Corn Law League', mixed, pub 1850, BM, NPG.

PR W.H.MOTE, after B.Duppa, hl, stipple, for Saunders's Political Reformers, 1840, BM, NPG.

THOMPSON, William (1712?-1766) poet.

PR UNKNOWN, hl aged 47, line, BM.

THOMPSON, William (1793-1854) politician.

P H.W.PICKERSGILL, 1840, wl, Christ's Hospital, Sussex.

PR T.L.BUSBY, hs, line, pub 1826, BM.

THOMSON, Sir Alexander (1744-1817) chief baron of the exchequer.

PR H.MEYER, after W.Owen, hl in robes, mezz, 1812, BM, NPG.

C THOMAS ROWLANDSON, 'We three Logger Heads be', Laing Art Gallery, Newcastle-upon-Tyne.

THOMSON, Andrew Mitchell (1779-1831) Scottish divine.

SC ALEXANDER HANDYSIDE RITCHIE, 1837, bust, Presbyterian Hall, Edinburgh.

PR W.WALKER, after H.Raeburn, hl, stipple, pub 1827, BM, NPG. T.HODGETTS, after G.Watson, wl with bible, mezz, pub 1834, BM.

THOMSON, Charles Edward Poulett, see Baron Sydenham.

THOMSON, George (1757-1851) collector of Scottish music.

P WILLIAM SMELLIE WATSON, tql seated in armchair, SNPG 273. After SIR HENRY RAEBURN, hl, SNPG 961.

D WILLIAM NICHOLSON, hs, w/c, SNPG 1061.

THOMSON, Henry (1773-1843) painter and illustrator.

D JOHN JACKSON, c1817, hl seated, w/c, NPG 3156.

THOMSON, James (1700-1748) poet.

P WILLIAM AIKMAN, 1720, hs, SNPG 331. By or after AIKMAN, hs, Huntington Library and Art Gallery, San Marino, USA. STEPHEN SLAUGHTER, 1736, hl holding paper, Yale Center for British Art, New Haven, USA. After JOHN PATOUN, c1746, hs, NPG 11.

SC M.H.SPRANG, c1760, monument, Westminster Abbey, London. UNKNOWN, posthumous marble medallion, oval, NPG 4896.

PR J.BASIRE, after W.Aikman, hl wearing cap, line, oval, for vol i of Works, 1762, BM.

THOMSON, John (1765-1846) physician and surgeon.

P ANDREW GEDDES, c1818, tql seated, Royal College of Surgeons, Edinburgh.

THOMSON, John (1778-1840) landscape-painter.

P WILLIAM WALLACE, SNPG 1069. WILLIAM WALLACE, SNPG L14.

D WILLIAM BEWICK, 1824, chalk, SNPG 1049. SIR THOMAS DICK LAUDER, 1831, wl with dog, pencil, SNPG 1285.

THOMSON, Thomas (1768-1852) lawyer and legal antiquary.

P ROBERT SCOTT LAUDER, hs, SNPG 211.

D WILLIAM BEWICK, chalk, SNPG 1050.

SC SIR JOHN STEELL, marble bust, Faculty of Advocates, Parliament Hall, Edinburgh; plaster bust, SNPG 224.

THOMSON, Thomas (1773-1852) chemist.

P UNKNOWN, SNPG 1148.

G J.F.SKILL, J.GILBERT, W. and E.WALKER, 'Men of Science Living in 1807-8', pencil and wash, NPG 1075.

THORBURN, Grant (1773-1863) author, original of Galt's 'Lawrie Todd'.

PR UNKNOWN, wl, line, NPG.

THORNBROUGH, Sir Edward (1754-1834) admiral.

P SAMUEL LANE, c1817, tql in uniform, NMM, Greenwich.

PR W.T.FRY, after A.Huey, hs in uniform, stipple, NPG.

THORNTON, Bonnell (1724-1768) writer and wit.

PR RIVERS, hl, line, oval, pub 1802, NPG. ROGERS, hl seated, stipple, pub 1826, BM, NPG.

THORNTON, Henry (1760-1815) philanthropist.

P SAMUEL JENNINGS, 1792, 'Liberty displaying the arts and sciences', with ? a bust of Henry Thornton, Winterthur Museum, Delaware, USA.

PR J.WARD, after J.Hoppner, tql, mezz, BM, NPG.

THORNTON, John (1720-1790) merchant and philanthropist.

P THOMAS GAINSBOROUGH, c1782, wl seated, Marine Society, London.

G J.HALL, after E.Edwards, 'The Marine Society', line engr, pub 1774, BM.

THORNTON, Robert John (1768?-1837) botanist.

PR F.BARTOLOZZI, after J.Russell, hl with book, stipple, oval, for Sexual System of Linnaeus, 1799, BM, NPG. B.SMITH, after G.H.Harlow, hl, stipple, pub 1808, BM.

THORNTON, Samuel (1755-1838) director of the Bank of England.

P A.HICKEL, 1794, hs, oval, Bank of England, London.

PR C.TURNER, after T.Phillips, tql seated with letter, mezz, pub 1827, BM.

THORNTON, Thomas (1757-1823) sportsman.

PR W.N.BATE, after Capon and R.Reinagle, shooting roebuck in Glenmore forest, with sporting emblems, stipple, pub 1810, BM. UNKNOWN, hl in racing cap with horse race below, stipple, pub 1823, BM. MACKENZIE, after Reinagle, hl in hat, holding falcon, stipple, oval, BM.

THORNTON, William (1763-1841) general.

PR MADELEY, tql in uniform, lith, pub 1812, NPG. C.TURNER, after Me.Varillat, tql in uniform, mezz, pub 1818, BM. UNKNOWN, wl standing in battlefield, coloured stipple, NPG.

THORP, Charles (1783-1862) archdeacon and prebendary of Durham, warden of Durham University.

P J.R.SWINTON, tql with cap and scroll, University College, Durham, engr G.R.Ward, mezz, pub 1846, BM.

THORPE, John (1715-1792) antiquary.

PR T.COOK, after W.Hardy, hl seated, aged 72, line, for Nichols's Illustrations of Literary History, 1822, BM. W.RADCLIFFE, after W.Hardy, same picture, NPG.

THRALE, Henry (1728-1781) brewer, friend of Dr Johnson.

PR E.SCRIVEN, after J.Reynolds, hl, stipple, BM, NPG.

THRALE, Hester Lynch, see Piozzi.

THRALE, Hester Maria, see Viscountess Keith.

THROSBY, John (1740-1803) antiquary.

PR W. and J.WALKER, after J.Walker, aged 50, hl seated with book, line, oval, for Hist of Leicester, 1791, BM, NPG.

THURLOW, Edward Thurlow, 1st Baron (1731-1806) lord chancellor.

P SIR JOSHUA REYNOLDS, c1781, tql seated in robes, Longleat, Wilts. GEORGE ROMNEY, c1780-4, wl in robes, Inner Temple, London. SIR THOMAS LAWRENCE, c1803, tql seated, Royal Coll. THOMAS PHILLIPS, 1806, tql seated, NPG 1264 (on loan to Law Courts). THOMAS PHILLIPS, 1806, hl, seated, NPG 249. THOMAS PHILLIPS, 1807, tql, Palace of Westminster, London. Attrib R.EVANS, hs, NPG 395. GEORGE ROMNEY, wl seated, Palace of Westminster.

SC J.C.F.ROSSI, 1801, marble bust, Royal Coll; plaster replica, Inner Temple, London. J.C.F.ROSSI, 1809, bust, NPG 5238. After CATHERINE ANDRAS, plaster medallion, SNPG 498.

C J.GILLRAY, 'The Wierd Sisters', coloured etch, pub 1791, NPG. J.SAYERS, several caricatures, NPG.

THURLOW, Thomas (1737-1791) bishop of Durham.

PR UNKNOWN, hl, line, BM.

THURTELL, John (1794-1824) murderer.

G H.WHITE, hl, with his associates, Joseph Hunt and William Probert, woodcut, BM. UNKNOWN, hs with Hunt and Probert, etch, BM, NPG.

PR T.MEDLAND, hl, from a sketch made in court, stipple, pub 1823, BM.

THYER, Robert (1709-1781) Chetham librarian and editor of Butler's *Remains*.
PR W.H.WORTHINGTON, after G.Romney, hs, line, BM, NPG.

THYNNE, Thomas (1734-1796), see 1st Marquess of Bath.

THYNNE, Thomas (1765-1837), see 2nd Marquess of Bath.

TICKELL, Mary, née Linley (1756?-1787) vocalist.
P THOMAS GAINSBOROUGH, c1772, wl seated holding music, with her sister Elizabeth Ann, Dulwich College Picture Gallery, London.
PR JOHN CONDÉ, after R.Cosway, wl, stipple, NPG. T.RYDER, after R.Westall, tql in landscape, lyre hanging on tree, stipple, oval, pub 1785, BM, NPG.

TIERNEY, George (1761-1830) statesman.
P SIR GEORGE HAYTER, 1823, tql, NGI 559.
G SIR GEORGE HAYTER, 'The Trial of Queen Caroline, 1820', oil, NPG 999.
SC WILLIAM BEHNES, 1822, marble bust, NPG 173. RICHARD WESTMACOTT, jun, 1830, bust, Westminster Abbey.
PR W.NUTTER, after L.Abbott, tql holding petition, stipple, pub 1798, BM, NPG. R.J.LANE, after W.Hunt, hl, lith, 1830, NPG.

TIERNEY, Sir Matthew John, 1st Bart (1776-1845) physician.
D UNKNOWN, hl seated, w/c, NPG 2175a.
SC SIR FRANCIS CHANTREY, plaster bust, Ashmolean Museum, Oxford.

TIGHE, Mary, née Blachford (1770-1810) poet.
M ANDREW ROBERTSON, after Romney, hs, NPG 1629.
PR J.HOPWOOD, jun, after E.Drummond, hl, stipple, BM, NPG. E.SCRIVEN, after G.Romney, hl, from a miniature by Comerford, stipple, for *Psyche*, 1812, BM, NPG.

TILLOCH, Alexander (1759-1825) printer, inventor of stereotyping.
D UNKNOWN, 1815, pencil, SNPG 336.
PR J.THOMSON, after Frazer, hl, stipple, pub 1821, NPG.

TINDAL, Sir Nicholas Conyngham (1776-1846) chief justice of the common pleas.
P THOMAS PHILLIPS, 1840, tql seated, NPG 482 (on loan to the Law Courts).
D JOHN DOYLE, entitled 'A Joinder of the Pleas', pencil, BM.
PR T.WRIGHT, after A.Wivell, hl when counsel for Queen Caroline, stipple, pub 1821, BM, NPG. W.J.WARD, after W.J.Newton, tql seated with book, mezz, pub 1834, BM. J.LUCAS, tql seated in robes, mezz, pub 1835, BM.

TITE, Sir William (1798-1873) architect.
P JOHN PRESCOTT KNIGHT, hl, RIBA, London.
SC WILLIAM THEED, jun, 1869, bust, Guildhall, Bath.

TOD, James (1782-1835) colonel and Indian diplomatist.
D Unknown Udaipur artist, travelling through Rajasthan on an elephant, copy of an original, c1820, gouache, V & A.

TODD, Henry John (1763-1845) editor of Milton and writer.
P JOSEPH SMITH, c1840-53, hs, Magdalen College, Oxford.

TOFTS, Mary (1701?-1763) 'the rabbit breeder'.
PR UNKNOWN, tql seated with rabbit, line, pub 1810, NPG. MADDOCKS, after J.Laguerre, tql seated with rabbit, stipple, for Caulfield's *Remarkable Persons*, 1819, BM, NPG.

TOLER, John, see 1st Earl of Norbury.

TOLLET, George (1725-1779) Shakespearean critic.
PR S.W.REYNOLDS, jun, after R.Ansdell, wl in landscape, mezz,

pub 1844, BM, NPG.

TOM, John Nichols (1799-1838) impostor and madman.
PR Various anonymous prints, NPG.

TOMKINS, Thomas (1743-1816) calligrapher.
P SIR JOSHUA REYNOLDS, c1790, hl with quill and paper, Guildhall Art Gallery, London.
SC SIR FRANCIS CHANTREY, 1816, marble bust, BM; plaster cast, Ashmolean Museum, Oxford.
PR L.SCHIAVONETTI, after G.Engleheart, hl, line, oval, for *Rays of Genius*, 1806, BM.

TOMLINE, Sir George Pretyman, Bart (1750-1827) bishop of Winchester and tutor to the younger Pitt.
PR C.THOMAS, after W.H.Brown, hs, line, oval, for *The Senator*, 1791, BM. R.COOPER, after H.Edridge, hl stipple, for *Contemporary Portraits*, 1814, BM, NPG. H.MEYER, after J.Jackson, hl in robes, stipple, BM, NPG.

TOMLINSON, Nicholas (1765-1847) vice-admiral.
PR PAGE, hs in uniform, stipple, oval, for *Naval Chronicle*, 1811, BM, NPG.

TOMS, Peter (d1777) painter and herald.
G JOHAN ZOFFANY, 'Royal Academicians, 1772', oil, Royal Coll.

TONE, Theobald Wolfe (1763-1798) Irish nationalist.
P UNKNOWN, NGI 1784.
G UNKNOWN, 'The Illustrious Sons of Ireland', coloured lith, NPG. UNKNOWN, 'The United Irish Patriots of 1798', coloured lith, NPG.
SC TERENCE FARRELL, marble bust, Trinity College, Dublin. JAMES PETRIE, cast from a death mask, NGI.
PR C.HULLMANDEL, after C.S.Tone, hs in French uniform, lith, pub 1827, BM.

TONNA, Charlotte Elizabeth, née Browne (1790-1846) miscellaneous writer.
PR F.CROLL, hl, stipple and line, oval, for Hogg's *Instructor*, NPG.

TOOKE, John Horne (1736-1812) radical politician and philologist.
P RICHARD BROMPTON, tql seated with winged helmet of Mercury, Manchester City Art Gallery, engr J.Corner, line, for *European Mag*, 1791, BM.
D SIR FRANCIS CHANTREY, head, pencil sketch, NPG 316a (122).
G R.HOUSTON, hl seated with John Glynn and John Wilkes, oil c1768, NPG 1944.
SC After JAMES TASSIE, 1793, plaster medallion, SNPG 460. SIR FRANCIS CHANTREY, 1811, terracotta bust, Sheffield City Museum. SIR FRANCIS CHANTREY, 1811, marble bust, Fitzwilliam Museum, Cambridge.
C J.GILLRAY, wl seated painting, entitled 'Two Pair of Portraits', etch, pub 1798, NPG.

TOOKE, Thomas (1774-1858) economist.
PR R.DIGHTON, wl, coloured etch, pub 1823, NPG, V & A.

TOOKE, William (1744-1820) historian of Russia.
PR J.COLLYER, after M.A.Shee, hl, line, for *Lucian*, 1820, BM, NPG.

TOOKE, William (1777-1863) president of the Society of Arts.
G SIR GEORGE HAYTER, 'The House of Commons, 1833', oil, NPG 54.
PR C.TURNER, after J.White, tql with book, mezz, pub 1836, BM. UNKNOWN, hl seated, woodcut, for *Illust London News*, 1863, BM.

TOPHAM, Edward (1751-1820) journalist and play-writer.
PR P.W.TOMKINS, after J.Russell, hl, stipple, oval, pub 1790, NPG, BM (pub date given as 1780). UNKNOWN, head, **with Mr**

Cosway, stipple, pub 1803, NPG, for *Public Characters*, 1805, BM.

TOPHAM, Thomas (1710?-1749) strong man.
PR W.H.TOMS, after C.Leigh, wl lifting three hogsheads of water on a scaffold, line, pub 1741, BM.

TOPLADY, Augustus Montague (1740-1778) divine and hymn writer.
D After J.R.SMITH, tql seated, pencil and gouache, NPG 3138.
Pr C.BLACKBERD, after C.R.Ryley, tql with book, line, for *Memoirs*, 1794, BM, NPG.

TORRENS, Sir Henry (1779-1828) major-general.
P SIR THOMAS LAWRENCE, RA 1816, wl in uniform, Londonderry Town Hall, engr C.Turner, mezz, pub 1817, BM.

TOULMIN, Joshua (1740-1815) dissenting historian and biographer.
PR G.CLINT, after R.Bonington, hl, mezz, pub 1810, BM. J.PARTRIDGE, hs, stipple, NPG.

TOWERS, John (1747?-1804) independent preacher.
PR TERRY and BATLEY, after Fisher, tql seated with book, mezz, oval, pub 1770, BM. UNKNOWN, hl, mezz, BM.

TOWERS, Joseph (1737-1799) biographer and dissenting minister.
PR FARN, after S.Drummond, hs, stipple, oval, for *European Mag*, 1796, BM, NPG. B.DUTERREAU, after C.Borckhardt, hs, stipple, oval, pub 1796, NPG.

TOWGOOD, Michaijah (1700-1792) dissenting minister.
P JOHN OPIE, 1783, tql seated with book, Dr Williams's Library, London.

TOWNE, Charles (d1850?) artist.
PR UNKNOWN, hl with crayon, stipple, pub 1824, BM, NPG.

TOWNELEY, Charles (1737-1805) collector of classical antiquities.
D JOHN BROWN, hl profile, seated, pencil, National Gallery of Scotland, Edinburgh.
G JOHAN ZOFFANY, wl seated in his Library with 'Marbles' and friends, oil, c1781-3, Towneley Hall Museum and Art Gallery, Burnley.
SC JOSEPH NOLLEKENS, 1802 or 1812?, marble bust, BM; version, 1807, Towneley Hall, Burnley. Attrib TASSIE, c1780?, Wedgwood medallion, hs, Wedgwood Museum, Barlaston, Staffs.

TOWNLEY, James (1714-1778) author of 'High Life below Stairs'.
PR C.TOWNLEY, tql seated, stipple, oval, pub 1794, BM. H.D.THIELCKE, hl, stipple, NPG.

TOWNLEY, James (1774-1833) Wesleyan divine.
PR J.THOMSON, after J.Jackson, hl, stipple, for *Methodist Mag*, BM.

TOWNSEND, George (1788-1857) author, prebendary of Durham.
P EDWARD HASTINGS, hl, University College, Durham.
SC TOMMASO SAULINI, 1850, hs, copper electrotype medallion, BM.
PR W.DRUMMOND, hs, lith, for *Athenaeum Portraits*, 1836, BM, NPG.

TOWNSEND, John (1757-1826) founder of the asylum for the deaf and dumb.
PR UNKNOWN, hs, stipple, oval, pub 1795, NPG. R.H.DYER, after W.Behnes, bust, stipple, pub 1827, BM. UNKNOWN, hl, as an old man, stipple, NPG.

TOWNSEND, Joseph (1739-1816) geologist.
PR MILTON, after J.Townsend, hl with book, stipple, oval, NPG.

TOWNSHEND, Charles (1725-1767) chancellor of the exchequer.

P UNKNOWN, c1750, tql with Ms and classical bust, Buccleuch Estates, Selkirk, Scotland.
SC Attrib I.GOSSETT, hs, wax medallion, NPG 1756.
PR J.DIXON, after Sir Joshua Reynolds, hl in gown, mezz, oval, pub 1770, BM, NPG.

TOWNSHEND, Charles (1728-1810), see 1st Baron Bayning.

TOWNSHEND, Charles Fox (1795-1817) M.P. for Yarmouth.
SC SIR FRANCIS CHANTREY, marble monument, St John's College Chapel, Cambridge.
PR UNKNOWN, head, stipple, BM.

TOWNSHEND, Charles Townshend, 3rd Viscount (1700-1764) statesman.
PR JOHN SMITH, after G.Kneller, tql as a boy with parrot, mezz, BM, NPG. W.C.EDWARDS, tql standing beside table with books, line, BM.

TOWNSHEND, Chauncey Hare (1798-1868) poet.
P JOHN BOADEN, RA 1828, V & A. SAMUEL WOODHOUSE, as a child, with his sister Charlotte, V & A.
D JOHN RAPHAEL SMITH, c1805, as a boy, crayon, V & A.

TOWNSHEND, George Townshend, 1st Marquess (1724-1807) field-marshal.
P THOMAS HICKEY, 1769, Mansion House, Dublin. SIR JOSHUA REYNOLDS, 1779, wl in armour, Art Gallery of Ontario, Toronto, Canada. MATHER BROWN, hl in uniform, Public Archives of Canada, Ottawa, Canada.
D COUNT DE LIPPE, hl, pen and ink, BM.
PR J.McARDELL, after T.Hudson, tql holding militia bill, mezz, BM, NPG.

TOWNSHEND, George Townshend, 2nd Marquess (1755-1811) president of the Society of Antiquaries.
G JOHN SINGLETON COPLEY, 'The Collapse of the Earl of Chatham in the House of Lords, 7 July 1778', oil, TATE 100, on loan to NPG. WILLIAM LANE, 'Whig Statesmen and their Friends', chalk, c1810, NPG 2076.
PR F.BROMLEY, after Sir Joshua Reynolds, wl in uniform in landscape, mezz, BM.

TOWNSHEND, John, Lord (1757-1833) politician.
SC JOHN EDWARD CAREW, 1831, bust, Woburn Abbey, Beds; replica, Petworth (NT), West Sussex.
PR JOHN JONES, after Sir Joshua Reynolds, hl, mezz, pub 1789, BM, NPG.

TOWNSHEND, John Thomas, see 2nd Viscount SYDNEY.

TOWNSHEND, John Townshend, 4th Marquess (1798-1863) rear admiral.
PR S.W.REYNOLDS, jun, after E. La Critel, tql seated, mezz, BM.

TOWNSHEND, Thomas (1701-1780) teller of the exchequer.
PR E.HARDING, hl, stipple, oval, for Adolphus's *British Cabinet*, 1799, BM.

TOWNSHEND, Thomas (1733-1800), see 1st Viscount SYDNEY.

TOWRY, George Henry (1767-1809) naval captain.
PR W.RIDLEY, after P.Jean, hs in uniform, stipple, oval, for *European Mag*, 1797, BM, NPG.

TRAILL, Thomas Stewart (1781-1862) professor of medical jurisprudence.
P JAMES LONSDALE, 1833, University of Liverpool, (Liverpool Royal Institution).

TRAVERS, Benjamin (1783-1858) surgeon.
P CHARLES ROBERT LESLIE, tql seated with book, Royal College of Surgeons, London.
SC WILLIAM BEHNES, 1858, marble bust, Royal College of Surgeons.
PR R.J.LANE, after W.Behnes, hl seated, lith, BM, NPG. T.H.MAGUIRE, tql, lith, BM.

TRAVERS, Sir Eaton Stannard (1782-1858) rear-admiral.
P UNKNOWN, c1815, hl in uniform, NMM, Greenwich.

TREDGOLD, Thomas (1788-1829) engineer.
PR UNKNOWN, hs, line, BM, NPG.

TRELAWNY, Edward John (1792-1881) author and adventurer.
D JOSEPH SEVERN, 1838, head, pen and ink, NPG 2132. B.E.DUPPA, two hs pencil sketches, NPG 2882-3. SIR EDWIN LANDSEER, head, pencil, NPG 2886.
G SIR JOHN EVERETT MILLAIS, 'The North-West Passage', oil, 1874, TATE 1509.
PR COUNT A.D'ORSAY, hl, lith, pub 1842, BM. SEYMOUR KIRKUP, hs profile, lith, NPG. D.LUCAS, hs, mezz, BM.

TRENCH, Sir Frederick William (1775-1859) general.
D JOHN DOYLE, equestrian, pen and chalk, BM.
PR J.H.ROBINSON, after J.Robson, hl in uniform, stipple, for *Eminent Conservative Statesmen*, 1839, BM, NPG.
C JOHN DOYLE, wl as Leporella in 'A scene from Don Giovanni', political cartoon, chalk and ink, BM. JOHN DOYLE, study for the 'Great Moth', pencil, BM.

TRENCH, Melesina, née Chenevix (1768-1827) author.
PR F.HOLL, after G.Romney, hl with paper, stipple, NPG.

TRENCH, Power le Poer (1770-1839) archbishop of Tuam.
G SIR GEORGE HAYTER, 'The Trial of Queen Caroline, 1820', oil, NPG 999.

TRESHAM, Henry (1749?-1814) painter.
D GEORGE DANCE, profile head, Royal Academy, London.
PR S.FREEMAN, after J.Opie, hl, stipple, oval, for *Monthly Mirror*, 1809, BM. A.CARDON, after A.Pope, hl, stipple, for *Contemporary Portraits*, 1814, BM, NPG. MRS D.TURNER, after G.Chinnery, tql seated in armchair, etch, BM.

TREVELYAN, Raleigh (1781-1865) writer.
M SILVESTER HARDING, called Trevelyan, but possibly his brother Walter, hl, oval, Fitzwilliam Museum, Cambridge.

TREVELYAN, Sir Walter Calverley, 6th Bart (1797-1879) naturalist.
P W.B.SCOTT, tql seated, Wallington Hall (NT), Northumberland.
PR G.B.BLACK, hs, lith, 1819, NPG.

TREVITHICK, Richard (1771-1833) engineer and inventor.
P JOHN LINNELL, 1816, hl, Science Museum, London.
M UNKNOWN, Science Museum, London.
G J.F.SKILL, J.GILBERT, W. and E.WALKER, 'Men of Science Living in 1807-8', pencil and wash, NPG 1075.

TREVOR, Arthur Hill-, see 3rd Viscount Dungannon.

TREVOR, Richard (1707-1771) bishop of Durham.
P THOMAS HUDSON, 1756, tql, Bishop Auckland Palace, Durham. Attrib THOMAS HUDSON, 1756, tql, Christ Church, Oxford. UNKNOWN, hl, All Souls College, Oxford.
SC JOSEPH NOLLEKENS, c1775, marble statue, Bishop Auckland Palace, Durham. JOHN BACON, sen, marble bust, Christ Church, Oxford.
PR J.COLLYER, after R.Hutchinson, hs, line, oval, for *Life*, 1776, BM.

TREVOR, Robert Hampden-Trevor, 4th Baron, see 1st Viscount Hampden.

TRIMMER, Sarah, née Kirby (1741-1810) writer.
P H.HOWARD, hl seated with quill and books, NPG 796, engr W.Bond, stipple, pub 1799, BM, NPG.
PR T.CHAPMAN, hs, stipple, oval, for *Ladies' Monthly Museum*, 1798, BM, NPG.

TROLLOPE, Arthur William (1768-1827) headmaster of Christ's Hospital, London.
Pr AUGUSTUS FOX, after Tannock, hl, line, NPG.

TROLLOPE, Frances, née Milton (1780-1863) novelist.
M AUGUSTE HERVIEU, c1832, hl, NPG 3906. MISS LUCY ADAMS, w/c copy, BM, engr W.Holl, stipple, for Taylor's *National Portrait Gallery*, 1845, BM, NPG.
PR J.BROWN, hl wearing cap, stipple, for *New Monthly Mag*, 1839, BM. W.GREATBACH, hl with book, line, for *The Domestic Manners of Americans*, 1839, NPG.

TROLLOPE, Sir Henry (1756-1839) admiral.
G G.NOBLE and J.PARKER, after J.Smart, 'Naval Victories', 'Commemoration of 11th Oct 1797', line engr, pub 1803, BM, NPG.
PR J.CHAPMAN, hs, stipple, oval, pub 1801, NPG. D.ORME, hl in uniform, stipple, oval, for *European Mag*, 1802, BM, NPG. H.R.COOK, after R.Bowyer, hl in uniform, stipple, oval, for *Naval Chronicle*, 1807, BM, NPG.

TROTTER, Thomas (1760-1832) physician to the fleet and author.
PR D.ORME, hl, stipple, oval, 1796, BM, NPG.

TROUBRIDGE, Sir Thomas, 1st Bart (1758?-1807) rear-admiral.
P SIR WILLIAM BEECHEY, c1804-5, tql in uniform, NMM, Greenwich. SAMUEL DRUMMOND, wl in uniform beside cannon, formerly United Service Club, London (c/o Crown Commissioners), engr H.R.Cook, stipple, for *Naval Chronicle*, 1810, BM.
G WORTHINGTON and PARKER, after R.Smirke, 'Naval Victories', 'Commemoration of the 14th February 1797', line engr, pub 1803, BM, NPG. W.BROMLEY, J.LANDSEER and LENEY after R.Smirke, 'Victors of the Nile', line engr, pub 1803, BM, NPG.

TROUGHTON, Edward (1753-1835) scientific instrument maker.
D SIR FRANCIS CHANTREY, 1822, hs pencil studies, NPG 316a 123-4.
G W.WALKER and G.ZOBEL, after J.F.Skill, J.Gilbert, W. and E.Walker, 'Men of Science living in 1807-8', engr, NPG 1075a.
SC SIR FRANCIS CHANTREY, bust, Royal Observatory, Greenwich.

TROY, John Thomas (1739-1823) archbishop of Dublin.
P THOMAS CLEMENT THOMPSON, 1821, NGI 229.
SC PETER TURNERELLI, 1816, plaster, NGI 8199.

TRUMAN, Sir Benjamin (1711-1780) brewer.
P THOMAS GAINSBOROUGH, c1770-75, wl in landscape, TATE T 2261.

TRURO, Thomas Wilde, 1st Baron (1782-1855) lord chancellor.
P SIR FRANCIS GRANT, 1850, tql seated, St Paul's School, London. Copy, THOMAS YOUNGMAN GOODERSON, NPG 483, (on loan to the Law Courts) and copy Palace of Westminster, London.
G SIR GEORGE HAYTER, 'The Trial of Queen Caroline, 1820', oil, NPG 999. SIR GEORGE HAYTER, 1820, with Sir Robert Gifford, Lord Lyndhurst, Dr Stephen Lushington, Spinetti and others, study for NPG 999, pen, pencil and wash, NPG 1695 (i). SIR GEORGE HAYTER, 1820, hs profile, with second profile visible, pencil, pen and wash (study for the same), NPG 1695(o).

SC HENRY WEEKES, marble bust, Palace of Westminster, London. H.WEEKES, bust, Middle Temple, London.

PR T.WRIGHT, after A.Wivell, hl, when counsel for Queen Caroline, stipple, pub 1821, BM, NPG. H.LINTON, after Thomas, woodcut, NPG.

TRUSLER, John (1735-1820) eccentric divine.
PR DENT, hs in wig and gown, line, small medallion, for his *Hogarth Moralized*, 1768, BM. L.LEGOUX, after Bonmaison, aged 60, hl seated at table, line, pub 1807, BM.

TUCKER, Abraham (1705-1774) philosopher.
P ENOCH SEEMAN, 1739, hl, NPG 3942.

TUCKER, Joseph (fl 1820) surveyor of the navy.
P UNKNOWN, c1815, hl, NMM, Greenwich.

TUCKER, Josiah (1712-1799) dean of Gloucester.
PR R.CLAMP, tql seated in wig and gown, stipple, oval, for Harding's *Biographical Mirrour*, 1793, BM, NPG. UNKNOWN, hs in hat and wig, line, oval, for *European Mag*, 1799, BM, NPG.

TUCKER, Thomas Tudor (1775-1852) rear-admiral.
P UNKNOWN, c1790, hl seated, Bermuda Historical Monuments Trust, Bermuda.

TUFTON, Sackville, see 9th Earl of Thanet.

TUNSTALL, Marmaduke (1743-1790) naturalist.
PR LAMBERT, hl, line, oval, BM.

TURMEAU, John (1777-1846) miniature-painter.
M Self-portrait, hs, on ivory, Walker Art Gallery, Liverpool.

TURNER, Charles (1774-1857) engraver.
D WILLIAM BROCKEDON, 1832, hs, pencil and chalk, NPG 2515(59). Self-portrait, 1850, hl seated, chalk, NPG 1317.
R C.TURNER, after J.Lonsdale, hl, mezz, NPG.

TURNER, Dawson (1775-1858) botanist and antiquary.
R W.DRUMMOND, hs, lith, for *Athenaeum Portraits*, 1837, BM. MISS TURNER, after J.P.Davis, head, lith, BM. A.FOX, after M.W.Sharp, hl, line, oval, BM, NPG.

TURNER, Sir Edward, Bart (1719-1766) MP for Oxfordshire.
P THOMAS GAINSBOROUGH, 1762, wl standing, Wolverhampton Art Gallery.

TURNER, Sir George James (1798-1867) lord justice of appeal in chancery.
R F.HOLL, after G.Richmond, hs, stipple, BM, NPG.

TURNER, Joseph Mallord William (1775-1851) landscape painter.
P Self-portrait, c1793, called Turner as a boy, Indianapolis Museum of Art, Indiana, USA. Self-portrait, c1798, hs, TATE 458. JOHN LINNELL, 1838, hl, NPG L157. WILLIAM PARROTT, c1846, wl on varnishing day, Reading University, Berks. Attrib J.T.SMITH, wl holding palette, with canvas and easel, TATE 2728.
D Self-portrait, (so-called), 1792, hl, w/c, NPG 1314. GEORGE DANCE, 1800, hs profile, pencil and chalk, Royal Academy, London. EDWARD BIRD, 1815, hs profile, pencil, BM. C.R.LESLIE, 1816, hs, pencil, NPG 4084. EDWARD BELL, 1828, hs sketch, BM. J.T.SMITH, 1830–32, hl, examining print, w/c, BM. CHARLES TURNER, 1841, hl, chalk and w/c, BM; copy, Charles Turner, 1842, hl profile, chalk, NPG 1182. CHARLES MARTIN, 1844, wl, pencil, NPG 1483. JOHN GILBERT, 1846, Witt Collection, Courtauld Institute Galleries, London.
SC PATRICK MACDOWELL, 1851, statue, St Paul's Cathedral, London. Attrib THOMAS WOOLNER, 1851, plaster cast of death mask, NPG 1664.

TURNER, Sharon (1768-1847) historian.

P M.A.SHEE, hs, NPG 1848.

TURNER, William (1761-1859) dissenting divine.
PR WILLIAM COLLARD, after A.Morton, hs, line, NPG. T.RONSON, after W.Nicholson, tql, line, NPG. W.J.WARD, after T.Carrick, tql seated, mezz, pub 1838, BM, NPG.

TURNER, William (1789-1862) artist.
P Self-portrait, hl, Ashmolean Museum, Oxford.

TURNER, William (1792-1867) diplomatist and author.
PR H.S.TURNER, after T.Phillips, hs, lith, BM, NPG.

TURNERELLI, Peter (1774-1839) sculptor.
PR J.THOMSON, after S.Drummond, tql modelling bust of George III, stipple, for *European Mag*, 1821, BM, NPG.

TURPIN, Richard (1706-1739) highwayman.
PR R.GRAVE, wl in a cave, line, for Caulfield's *Remarkable Persons*, 1820, BM, NPG.

TURTON, Thomas (1780-1864) bishop of Ely.
P H.W.PICKERSGILL, hl seated, St Catharine's College, Cambridge.
SC R.W.SIEVIER, 1831, marble bust, St Catharine's College.

TUSSAUD, Marie (1760-1850) modeller in wax.
D PAUL FISCHER, hl seated in her gallery, aged 85, w/c, Madame Tussaud's, London. Attrib F.TUSSAUD, hs, chalk, NPG 2031.
SC MARIE TUSSAUD, 1842, wl wax model, Madame Tussaud's.

TWEDDELL, John (1769-1799) classical scholar.
PR UNKNOWN, hs, a silhouette, stipple and line, for his *Remains*, 1815, BM, NPG.

TWEEDDALE, George Hay, 8th Marquess of (1787-1876) pioneer in agriculture.
P SIR FRANCIS GRANT, wl in uniform, SNPG 1571. SIR JOHN WATSON GORDON, hl, formerly United Service Club, London (c/o The Crown Commissioners).

TWEEDIE, Alexander (1794-1884) physician.
P ENRICO BELLI, c1870, hl with book, Royal College of Physicians, London.

TWINING, Richard (1749-1824) director of the East India Company.
PR C.TURNER, after J.J.Halls, tql seated, mezz, pub 1812, BM, NPG.

TWINING, Richard (1772-1857) tea-merchant.
PR DAY and SON, after M.Carpenter, hl seated, lith, BM.

TWINING, Thomas (1735-1804) translator of Aristotle.
PR C.TURNER, after J.J.Halls, hl, mezz, pub 1805, BM, NPG.

TWISS, Frances, née Kemble (1759-1822) actress.
PR J.JONES, after J.Downman, hl, stipple, oval, pub 1784, BM. J.JONES, after J.Reynolds, hl, mezz, pub 1784, BM, NPG.

TWISS, Horace (1787-1849) wit and politician.
PR C.MARTIN, wl seated at desk, tinted pencil sketch, 1844, for *Twelve Victorian Celebrities*, NPG.

TWISS, Richard (1747-1821) writer.
PR UNKNOWN, 1814, hl seated, NPG. MRS D.TURNER, after G.H.Harlow, hl seated, etch, BM, NPG.

TYERMAN, Daniel (1773-1828) missionary.
PR T.BLOOD, hs, stipple, oval, for *Evangelical Mag*, BM, NPG.

TYERS, Thomas (1726-1787) author.
G Called Thomas Tyers by FRANCIS HAYMAN, c1740–45, wl with his sisters, Yale Center for British Art, New Haven, USA.
PR J.HALL, after I.Taylor, hs, profile, line, oval, BM, NPG.

TYLER, James Endell (1789-1851) divine.
P GEORGE CLINT, tql in gown, St Giles-in-the-Field, London, engr T.Lupton, mezz, pub 1833, BM. UNKNOWN, hl, Oriel College,

Oxford.

TYLER, William (d1801) sculptor and architect.
D GEORGE DANCE, 1796, hl, pencil, Royal Academy, London.
G JOHAN ZOFFANY, 'Royal Academicians, 1772', oil, Royal Coll.

TYRREL, Richard (1716/17-1766) admiral.
P THOMAS HUDSON, c1759–62, tql in uniform with telescope, NMM, Greenwich.
PR T.WORLIDGE, hs, in uniform, profile, oval, with account of his exploit when commanding the *Buckingham*, etch, BM.

TYRWHITT, Thomas (1730-1786) literary critic.
P UNKNOWN, hl, NPG 2942.
G T.HOLLOWAY, 'Shakespearean Critics', line engr, for Malone's ed of *Shakespeare*, BM.

PR J.JONES, after B.Wilson, hl, mezz, pub 1788, BM, NPG.

TYTLER, Alexander Fraser, see Lord Woodhouselee.

TYTLER, James (1747?-1805) chemist and author.
G JOHN KAY, with others, saying farewell to Lunardi, the aeronaut, etch, BM.

TYTLER, Patrick Fraser (1791-1849) Scottish historian.
P MARGARET SARAH CARPENTER, c1845, hl seated with book, NPG 226. SIR JOHN WATSON GORDON, SNPG 666; study of reduced replica of this, SNPG 187.
PR W.DRUMMOND, hl seated, lith, for *Athenaeum Portraits*, 1836, BM. R.J.LANE, hs, lith, NPG.

TYTLER, William (1711-1792) Scottish historian.
PR J.JONES, after H.Raeburn, hl in hat, mezz, pub 1790, BM.

U

UNWIN, Mary, née Cawthorne (1724-1796) friend of the poet Cowper.
PR R.COOPER, after A.Devis, aged 26, hl in cap, stipple, for vol ii of *Correspondence of W.Cowper*, 1824, BM, NPG. H.ROBINSON, after W.Harvey, wl seated, stipple, pub 1836, NPG.

UNWIN, William Cawthorne (1745?-1786) correspondent of the poet Cowper.
PR H.ROBINSON, after W.Harvey, from a painting by Gainsborough, hl, stipple, pub 1836, NPG.

UPCOTT, William (1779-1845) antiquary and autograph collector.
PR T.BRAGG, after W.Behnes, tql seated in armchair, holding book, line, 1818, BM, NPG. UNKNOWN, after L.Schmid, hs, lith, 1835, BM, NPG. G.P.HARDING, hl, lith, pub 1837, BM, NPG.

UPTON, John (1707-1760) editor of Spenser and Shakespeare.
PR UNKNOWN, after J.Collyer, hl, oval, stipple, for Harding's *Shakespeare Illustrated*, 1793, BM.

URE, Andrew (1778-1857) chemist and scientific writer.
P SIR DANIEL MACNEE, V & A, engr R.Roffe, stipple, pub 1837, NPG.
D UNKNOWN, hs, w/c, NPG 2876.
PR T.BRIDGFORD, hs, lith, BM. C.COOK, hl seated, stipple, from a photograph, BM.

URWICK, Thomas (1727-1807) independent divine.

D UNKNOWN, hs, pastel, oval, Dr Williams's Library, London.

USSHER, Sir Thomas (1779-1848) rear-admiral.
P UNKNOWN, c1830-33, hl in uniform, NMM, Greenwich.

UTTERSON, Edward Vernon (1776?-1856) scholar and antiquary.
PR J.POSSELWHITE, after J.Jackson, hl seated, stipple, BM.

UWINS, Thomas (1782-1857) painter.
P J.PARTRIDGE, 1836, small tql seated, study for 'Sketching Society', NPG 4231.
D J.PARTRIDGE, 1825, hs, pencil, NPG 3944(14). C.H.LEAR, 1845, head, chalk, NPG 1456(12). G.H.WHITE, c1845, hs, pencil, NPG 4218.
G J.PARTRIDGE, 'A Meeting of the Sketching Society', pen, ink and wash, BM.
PR J.SMYTH, after T.H.Illidge, tql seated, line, for the *Art Union*, 1847, BM, NPG.

UXBRIDGE, Henry Paget, 3rd Earl of (1744-1812) landowner.
P POMPEO BATONI, c1765, tql seated, Plas Newydd (NT), Gwynedd. GEORGE ROMNEY, tql seated holding a sample of copper in his hand, Plas Newydd.
M GEORGE ENGLEHEART, hs, Plas Newydd. J.SMART, hs, Plas Newydd.

UXBRIDGE, Henry William Paget, Earl of (1768-1854), see 1st Marquess of Anglesey.

V

VALLANCEY, Charles (1721-1812) antiquary.
P GEORGE CHINNERY, *c*1800, tql, Royal Irish Academy, Dublin.

VALPY, Richard (1754-1836) schoolmaster.
P JOHN OPIE, wl seated by table, Reading Corporation, Berks, engr C.Turner, mezz, pub 1811, BM.
SC SAMUEL NIXON, 1838, statue, St Lawrence's Church, Reading, engr J.H.Nixon, lith, BM.

VANCOUVER, George (1758-1798) explorer.
P Called George Vancouver, by an unknown artist, tql seated with globe, NPG 503.
C JAMES GILLRAY, 'The Caneing in Conduit Street', wl with Lord Camelford, coloured etch, pub 1796, NPG.

VANDELEUR, Sir John Ormsby (1763-1849) general.
P WILLIAM SALTER, *c*1834-40, tql study for 'Waterloo Banquet', NPG 3762.
G W.SALTER, 'The Waterloo Banquet at Apsley House', oil, 1836, Wellington Museum, Apsley House, London.

VANDENHOFF, John (1790-1861) actor.
PR Various theatrical prints, BM, NPG.

VANE, Anne (1705-1736) mistress of Frederick, Prince of Wales.
PR UNKNOWN, wl, pointing to a portrait of the Prince of Wales, line, for *Secret Hist of Vanella*, 1732, BM. J.FABER, jun, after J.Vanderbank, tql seated, mezz, BM.

VANE, Frances Anne Vane, Viscountess, née Hawes (1713-1788) infamous for gambling and profligacy.
PR UNKNOWN, tql in walking dress, line, BM.

VANE, William Harry, see 1st Duke of Cleveland.

VANE-STEWART, Charles William, see 3rd Marquess of Londonderry.

VAN MILDERT, William (1765-1836) bishop of Durham.
P SIR THOMAS LAWRENCE, 1829, tql seated in rochet and bands, (finished by R.Evans), Bishop Auckland Palace, Durham.
G SIR GEORGE HAYTER, 'The Trial of Queen Caroline, 1820', oil, NPG 999.
SC JOHN GIBSON, 1836, statue, Durham Cathedral.

VANSITTART, Henry (1732-1770) governor of Bengal.
P SIR JOSHUA REYNOLDS, 1768-69, hl, Fitzwilliam Museum, Cambridge, engr S.W.Reynolds, mezz, pub 1822, BM, NPG.

VANSITTART, Henry (1777-1843) vice-admiral.
PR M.GAUCI, after C.R.Bone, hl in uniform, lith, BM.

VANSITTART, Nicholas, see 1st Baron Bexley.

VARLEY, Cornelius (1781-1873) painter.
PR UNKNOWN, hs, from a photograph, woodcut, for *Illust London News*, 1873, BM.

VARLEY, John (1778-1842) landscape painter.
P JOHN LINNELL, hl, Ashmolean Museum, Oxford. WILLIAM MULREADY, hs, NPG 1529.
D WILLIAM BLAKE, hs, pencil, NPG 1194. JOHN LINNELL, hs, w/c, V & A. JOHN LINNELL, 1821, hl seated with William Blake, pencil, Fitzwilliam Museum, Cambridge. WILLIAM MULREADY, hs

profile, chalk, BM.

VASHON, James (1742-1827) admiral.
PR J.YOUNG, after G.Watson, tql seated, in uniform, mezz, pub 1809, BM.

VASSALL, Spencer Thomas (1764-1807) soldier.
PR E.SCRIVENS, hl in uniform, oval, stipple, BM.

VAUGHAN, Benjamin (1751-1835) politician.
P FRANCIS COTES, 1765, tql seated, Museum of Fine Arts, Boston, USA.

VAUGHAN, Sir Charles Richard (1774-1849) diplomatist.
P SIR THOMAS LAWRENCE, after 1820, hl seated, All Souls College, Oxford, engr S.Cousins, mezz, 1832, BM, NPG.

VAUGHAN, Henry (1766-1844), see Sir Henry Halford.

VAUGHAN, Sir John (1769-1839) judge.
P School of SIR THOMAS LAWRENCE, tql in robes of Baron of exchequer, Lamport Hall, Northants.

VAUGHAN, Robert (1795-1868) congregational divine.
PR R.WOODMAN, hl, stipple, pub 1825, NPG. W.HOLL, after J.R.Wildman, hl, stipple, for *Evangelical Mag*, pub 1830, BM, NPG. S.BELLIN, after P.Westcott, nearly wl seated in gown, mezz, pub 1830, BM, NPG.

VAUGHAN, William (1752-1850) merchant and author.
SC SIR FRANCIS CHANTREY, 1811, marble bust, NPG 4934.

VEITCH, William (1794-1885) classical scholar.
P JAMES IRVINE, tql seated with book, SNPG 150.

VENN, Henry (1725-1797) evangelical divine.
D J.RUSSELL, 1787, hs, oval, chalk, NPG 3161.
PR G.ADCOCK, hs, stipple, pub 1834, NPG.

VENN, Henry (1796-1873) secretary of the Church Missionary Society.
PR S.COUSINS, after G.Richmond, nearly wl seated, mezz, BM.

VENN, John (1759-1813) rector of Clapham.
PR E.SCRIVEN, after J.Slater, hl, stipple, pub 1813, BM, NPG.

VERE, Sir Charles Broke (1779-1843) major-general.
P WILLIAM SALTER, *c*1834-40, tql seated in uniform, study for 'Waterloo Banquet', NPG 3763.
G W.SALTER, 'The Waterloo Banquet at Apsley House', oil, 1836, Wellington Museum, Apsley House, London.
PR T.LUPTON; after G.Patten, hl in uniform, mezz, pub 1839, BM. R.J.LANE, after C.Patten, hl in uniform, lith, NPG.

VEREKER, Charles, see 2nd Viscount Gort.

VERNON, Sir Edward (1723-1794) admiral.
P Attrib FRANCIS HAYMAN, *c*1755, wl in uniform, NMM, Greenwich. HENRY SINGLETON, *c*1791, wl in uniform, NMM.
SC After JAMES TASSIE, 1785, plaster medallion, SNPG 480.

VERNON, Edward Venables, see Edward Venables HARCOURT.

VERNON, Joseph (1738?-1782) actor.
G J.CALDWALL and S.SMITH, after G.Caster, 'Immortality of Garrick', line engr, pub 1783, BM.
PR Various theatrical prints, BM, NPG.

VERNON, Robert (1774-1849) art patron and collector.
P G.JONES and H.COLLEN, 1848, wl seated, NPG 4513.
H.W.PICKERSGILL, c1846, tql seated with dog, TATE 416.
SC WILLIAM BEHNES, 1849, bust, TATE 2237.

VESEY, Elizabeth (1715?-91) 'blue-stocking' and hostess.
D UNKNOWN, hl, chalk, NPG 3131.

VESTRIS, Gaetano Apollino Baldassare (1729-1808) ballet-master.
PR F.BARTOLOZZI, wl as Jason in a satire on tragic poses in dancing, etch and aquatint, oval, pub 1781, V & A. J.MILLER, hs, line, for *London Mag*, 1781, BM, NPG. THORNTHWAITE, after J.Roberts, as the Prince in the pantomime ballet *Ninette*, wl, line, for Bell's *British Theatre*, 1781, BM.

VESTRIS, Lucia Elizabeth, see Mrs Mathews.

VESTRIS, Marie Auguste (1760-1842) dancer.
P Attrib GAINSBOROUGH DUPONT, c1780-85, hs, TATE 1271.
D G? or N?DANCE, wl dancing, w/c, Fitzwilliam Museum, Cambridge, engr F.Bartolozzi and Pastorini, line and aquatint, pub 1781, BM, NPG.
SC JEAN-PIEERE DANTAN, 1834, as Zéphir in Gardel's *Psyche*, bronze statue, Musée Carnavelet, Paris.
PR THORNTHWAITE, after J.Roberts, wl in *Les Amans Supris*, line, for Bell's *British Theatre*, 1781, BM. C.RUOTTE, after G.Scorodomoff, as Colas in the ballet *Minette à la Cour*, wl standing, stipple, oval, pub 1781, BM. H.MEYER, after J.F.Godelet, hs, stipple and line, pub 1809, NPG.

VIDLER, William (1758-1816) universalist.
PR J.PARTRIDGE, after T.Millichap, hs in spectacles, stipple, BM.

VIGNOLES, Charles Blacker (1793-1875) engineer.
PR UNKNOWN, hs, stipple, NPG. UNKNOWN, hl seated, woodcut, for *The Builder*, 1870, NPG. UNKNOWN, hs, profile, woodcut, for the *Illust London News*, 1875, NPG.

VIGORS, Nicholas Aylward (1785-1840) zoologist.
G SIR GEORGE HAYTER, 'The House of Commons, 1833', oil, NPG 54.

VILLETTES, William Anne (1754-1808) general, lieutenant-governor.

PR C.HEATH, hs in uniform, stipple for a *Memoir* of him by T.Bowdler, BM.

VILLIERS, George Bussy, see 4th Earl of Jersey.

VILLIERS, George Child, see 5th Earl of Jersey.

VILLIERS, Thomas (1709-1786), see 1st Earl of Clarendon.

VILLIERS, Thomas (1753-1824), see 2nd Earl of Clarendon.

VINCE, Samuel (1749-1821) mathematician and astronomer.
PR R.COOPER, after T.Wageman, tql seated in gown, holding spectacles, stipple, pub 1821, BM, NPG.

VINCENT, George (1796-1836?) landscape-painter.
D JOHN JACKSON, hl, w/c, NPG 1822.

VINCENT, Richard Budd (1770?-1831) captain in the navy.
PR H.R.COOK, hs in uniform, stipple, oval, pub 1807, NPG.

VINCENT, William (1739-1815) Dean of Westminster.
P UNKNOWN, The Deanery, Westminster Abbey, London.
D H.EDRIDGE, hs, pencil and w/c, NPG 1434, engr C.Picart, stipple, for *Contemporary Portraits*, pub 1810, BM, NPG.
PR H.MEYER, after W.Owen, nearly wl seated, with Bath star, stipple, for Ackermann's *Hist of Westminster Abbey*, 1812, BM, NPG.

VINT, William (1768-1834) congregational divine.
PR UNKNOWN, hs, stipple, for *Evangelical Mag*, 1819, BM. FRY, hs, stipple, pub 1819, NPG.

VIVARES, François (1716-1780) landscape-engraver.
PR F.VIVARES and J.CALDWALL, hs holding graver and plate, line, oval, pub 1776, BM, NPG.

VIVIAN, Sir Richard Hussey Vivian, 1st Baron (1775-1842) general.
P WILLIAM SALTER, tql study for 'Waterloo Banquet', NPG 3764.
G SIR GEORGE HAYTER, 'The House of Commons, 1833', oil, NPG 54. W.SALTER, 'The Waterloo Banquet at Apsley House', oil, 1836, Wellington Museum, Apsley House, London.
PR J.BROWN, hs in uniform, stipple, pub 1840, BM.

VULLIAMY, Benjamin Lewis (1747-1811) clockmaker.
P UNKNOWN, hl seated drawing designs, Guildhall Art Gallery, London (on loan from the Clockmakers Company).

W

WADD, William (1776-1829) surgeon.
P JOHN JACKSON, hl, Royal College of Surgeons, London.

WADDILOVE, Robert Darley (1736-1828) dean of Ripon.
PR W.J.WARD, after G.Marshall, hl, mezz, pub 1827, BM, NPG.

WADDINGTON, Samuel (1736-1758) painter.
PR S.WADDINGTON, tql aged 21, holding palette and knife, etch, BM.

WAITHMAN, Robert (1764-1833) politician, lord mayor of London.
P WILLIAM PATTEN, tql seated in alderman's gown, Guildhall Art Gallery, London, engr E.Scriven, stipple, pub 1821, BM, NPG.
PR R.COOPER, after C.Holroyd, hs, stipple, for *Aurora Borealis*, 1821, BM. C.S.TAYLOR, hl, in lord mayor's robes, stipple, for *New European Mag*, 1823, BM, NPG.
C R.DIGHTON, wl, coloured etch, pub 1818, BM, NPG, V & A.

WAKEFIELD, Daniel (1776-1846) writer on political economy.
PR F.C.LEWIS, after A.Wivell, hl, stipple, BM, NPG.

WAKEFIELD, Edward Gibbon (1796-1862) colonial statesman.
P E.J.COLLINS, 1850 (dogs by R.Ansdell), Christ Church Museum, New Zealand.
M UNKNOWN, c1820, hs, NPG 1561.
SC J.DURHAM, 1875, marble bust, DoE (Foreign and Commonwealth Office, London).
PR B.HOLL, after A.Wivell, 1826, engr, Mitchell Library, Sydney, Australia.

WAKEFIELD, Gilbert (1756-1801) scholar and controversial writer.
P WILLIAM ARTAUD, tql seated, Dr Williams's Library, London, engr R.Dunkarton, mezz, pub 1802, BM, NPG.
D JOHN DOWNMAN, 1778, hl, chalk, Fitzwilliam Museum, Cambridge.
PR W.RIDLEY, after Green, hl, stipple, oval, for *Monthly Mirror*, 1798, BM, NPG.

WAKEFIELD, Mrs Priscilla (1751-1832) writer and philanthropist.
PR J.THOMSON, after T.Wageman, tql seated, stipple, pub 1818, NPG.

WAKLEY, Thomas (1795-1862) medical reformer, founder of 'The Lancet'.
PR G.E.MADELEY, wl standing, lith, NPG. W.H.EGLETON, after K.Meadows, hl, stipple, for Saunders's *Political Reformers*, 1840, BM, NPG.
C Various drgs by JOHN DOYLE, BM.

WALDEGRAVE, George Granville, see 2nd Baron Radstock.

WALDEGRAVE, James Waldegrave, 2nd Earl of (1715-1763) statesman.
PR J.THOMSON, after J.Reynolds, hs profile with Garter ribbon and star, stipple, pub 1821, NPG. J.MCARDELL, after same picture, mezz, BM, NPG.

WALDEGRAVE, Lady Maria, Countess, see Duchess of Gloucester.

WALDEGRAVE, William, see 1st Baron Radstock.

WALDEN, John Griffin, see 4th Baron HOWARD de Walden.

WALDRON, Francis Godolphin (1744-1818) writer and actor.
G SAMUEL DE WILDE, wl with Mrs Henry in *All the World's a Stage*, 1803, National Theatre, London.
PR W.N.GARDINER, after S.Harding, as Sir Christopher Hatton in *The Critic*, hl, stipple, pub 1788, NPG.

WALE, Samuel (1720-1786) painter.
G JOHAN ZOFFANY, 'Royal Academicians, 1772', oil, Royal Coll.

WALHOUSE, Edward John, see 1st Baron Hatherton.

WALKER, Adam (1731?-1821) author and inventor.
G GEORGE ROMNEY, hs with his family, looking at diagrams, oil, NPG 1106.
SC After JAMES TASSIE, 1795, plaster medallion, SNPG 392.
PR S.DRUMMOND, hs, stipple, oval, for *European Mag*, 1792, BM, NPG. H.HUMPHREY, hl in laboratory, etch, pub 1796, NPG.

WALKER, George (1734?-1807) dissenting minister and mathematician.
PR G.CLINT, after R.Bonington, hl seated, mezz, pub 1805, BM.

WALKER, Sir George Townshend, Bart (1764-1842) general.
D THOMAS HEAPHY, hs, w/c, NPG 1914(16).
SC WILLIAM THEED, jun, 1860, plaster bust, Royal Military Academy, Sandhurst, Camberley, Surrey.

WALKER, James (1764-1831) rear-admiral.
G G.NOBLE and J.PARKER, after J.Smart, 'Naval Victories', 'Commemoration of 11th Oct 1797', line, pub 1803, BM, NPG.

WALKER, John (1731-1803) botanist.
C JOHN KAY, wl profile, etch, 1789, BM.

WALKER, John (1732-1807) actor and lexicographer.
M JOHN BARRY, hs, V & A.
PR R.HICKS, after J.Barry, tql seated, stipple, pub 1825, BM, NPG.

WALKER, Sayer (1748-1826) physician.
G N.BRANWHITE, after S.Medley, 'Institutors of the Medical Society of London', stipple, pub 1801, BM.

WALKER, Thomas (1749-1817) merchant at Manchester, tried for treason 1794.
SC JAMES TASSIE, 1798, paste medallion, SNPG 651.
PR W.SHARP, after G.Romney, hl, line, pub 1794, BM, NPG.

WALKER, William (1767?-1816) astronomer.
M MISS M.BARRATT, hs?, V & A.
PR W.RIDLEY, after Miss Barratt, hl, stipple, oval, for *Monthly Mirror*, 1798, BM, NPG.

WALKINSHAW, Clementina Maria Sophia (1726?-1802) mistress of Prince Charles Edward, the Young Pretender.
P UNKNOWN, SNPG, 1102.

WALL, Joseph (1737-1802) governor of Goree.
PR CHAPMAN, hs, profile, stipple, pub 1804, NPG. UNKNOWN, wl, seated in prison, etch, NPG.

WALL, Martin (1747-1824) physician.
P UNKNOWN, tql seated, New College, Oxford.

WALLACE, Robert (1773-1855) postal reformer.
SC UNKNOWN, bust, Greenock Town Hall, Strathclyde.

WALLACE, Thomas Wallace, Baron (1768-1844) Master of the Mint.
P GEORGE ROMNEY, hl, leaving portrait, Eton College, Berks.
PR C.BESTLAND, after W.Beechey, hl, stipple, pub 1795, NPG. C.TURNER, after T.Clarke, hl, mezz, pub 1801, BM, NPG. W.HOLL, after A.Wivell, hs, one of set of portraits of persons at trial of Queen Caroline, stipple, pub 1823, BM, NPG. J.BROWN, hl, stipple, for *Eminent Conservative Statesmen*, 1823, BM, NPG.

WALLACE, William (1768-1843) mathematician.
P JOHN THOMSON of Duddington, *c*1825, hl, Edinburgh University.
D ANDREW GEDDES, pencil and chalk, SNPG 195.

WALLACK, James William (1791?-1864) actor.
P S.J.STUMP, hl holding sword, as Hotspur?, Garrick Club, London. GEORGE CLINT, hs seated, Garrick Club, London.
M SAMUEL JOHN STUMP, hs, oval, Metropolitan Museum of Art, New York, USA.
PR Various theatrical prints, BM, NPG.

WALLICH, Nathaniel (1786-1854) botanist.
P JOHN LUCAS, Linnean Society, London.
PR T.H.MAGUIRE, tql seated, holding a plant and spectacles, lith, for *Ipswich Museum Portraits*, BM. M.GAUCI, after A.Robertson, hl, lith, BM.

WALLIS, Sir Provo William Parry (1791-1892) admiral.
PR R.TAYLOR, aged 19, wl standing in uniform, woodcut, for *Illust London News*, 1890, BM.

WALLIS, Miss, afterwards Mrs Campbell (fl 1789-1814) actress.
PR Various theatrical prints, BM.

WALLMODEN, Amalie Sophie Marianne, see Countess of Yarmouth.

WALMESLEY, Charles (1722-1797) Roman catholic prelate and mathematician.
P UNKNOWN, English College, Rome.

WALMSLEY, Sir Joshua (1794-1871) politician.
P WILLIAM DANIELS, V & A.
PR UNKNOWN, tql seated, lith, NPG.

WALPOLE, Horace (1717-1797), see 4th Earl of Orford.

WALPOLE, Maria (1739-1807), see Duchess of Gloucester.

WALSINGHAM, William de Grey, 1st Baron (1719-1781) judge.
SC UNKNOWN, Wedgwood medallion, Wedgwood Museum, Barlaston, Staffs.

WALTER, Henry (1785-1859) divine and antiquary.
D GEORGE RICHMOND, 1821, hs, black lead, BM.

WALTER, John (1739-1812) chief proprietor of *The Times*.
P UNKNOWN, *c*1783-4, hl, The Times Newspapers Ltd, London.

WALTER, John (1776-1847) chief proprietor of *The Times*.
P UNKNOWN, hl, The Times Newspapers Ltd, London.
M UNKNOWN, w/c, The Times Newspapers Ltd.
G SIR GEORGE HAYTER, 'The House of Commons, 1833', oil, NPG 54.

WANSEY, Henry (1752?-1827) antiquary.
P SAMUEL WOODFORDE?, hl, Stourhead (NT), Wilts.

WARBURTON, Henry (1784?-1858) radical.

G SIR GEORGE HAYTER, 'The House of Commons, 1833', oil, **NPG** 54.
PR W.H.MOTE, after Sir George Hayter, hl, stipple, for Saunders's *Political Reformers*, 1840, BM, NPG.

WARD, Sir Henry George (1797-1860) colonial governor.
G SIR GEORGE HAYTER, 'The House of Commons, 1833', oil, NPG 54.
PR W.H.MOTE, after J.Holmes, hl seated, stipple, pub 1842, BM, NPG.

WARD, James (1769-1859) animal and landscape painter.
P GILBERT STUART, 1779, tql, Institute of Arts, Minneapolis, USA. Self-portrait, 1834, hs with spectacles, NPG 1684. Self-portrait, 1848, hl with long beard, NPG 309.

WARD, John (1704-1773) actor and manager, grandfather of Mrs Siddons.
P UNKNOWN, *c*1770, hl, Garrick Club, London. UNKNOWN, hs, Garrick Club, London.

WARD, John William, see 1st Earl of Dudley.

WARD, Nathaniel Bagshaw (1791-1868) botanist.
P A.ACKLAND HUNT, 1867, tql surrounded by vegetation, Apothecaries' Hall, London. J.P.KNIGHT, 1856, tql, Linnean Society, London, engr R.J.Lane, lith, 1859, NPG.

WARD, Robert Plumer (1765-1846) novelist and politician.
D SIR THOMAS LAWRENCE, hs, chalk and wash, Royal Coll.
PR J.THOMSON, after F.R.Say, hs in furred cloak, stipple, for *New Monthly Mag*, 1831, BM, NPG.

WARD, Mrs Sarah (d1786) actress, wife of John Ward.
P SAMUEL DE WILDE, as Octavia in *All for Love*, wl, Garrick Club, London, engr P.Audinet, line, for Bell's *British Theatre*, 1792, BM.
PR Two theatrical prints, BM.

WARD, William (1769-1823) baptist missionary.
PR UNKNOWN, hl, stipple, pub 1817, NPG. H.MEYER, after J.Jackson, baptising a Hindoo in the Ganges, stipple, pub 1821, BM. E.SCRIVEN, after T.Overton, nearly tql seated, stipple, pub 1823, BM.

WARDE, James Prescott (1792-1840) actor.
PR R.J.LANE, hs, as Cassius, lith, pub 1839, NPG.

WARDLAW, Ralph (1779-1853) Scottish congregationalist.
P SIR DANIEL MACNEE, wl seated holding spectacles, Glasgow Art Gallery and Museum.
PR JAMES ANDREWS, hl seated, stipple, NPG.

WARDLE, Gwyllym Lloyd (1762?-1833) soldier and politician.
P A.W.DEVIS, 1809, tql, NPG 4265.
PR J.HOPWOOD, after Armstrong, hl holding scroll, stipple, for a report of the trial of the Duke of York, pub 1809, BM, NPG. C.TURNER, after P.Turnerelli, sculptured bust, mezz, pub 1809, BM, NPG.

WARDROP, James (1782-1869) surgeon.
P ANDREW GEDDES, hl, Royal College of Surgeons, Edinburgh, engr J.Thomson, stipple, for Pettigrew's *Medical Portrait Gallery*, 1840, BM, NPG. THOMAS MUSGROVE JOY, SNPG 1113.

WARE, James (1756-1815) surgeon.
G N.BRANWHITE, after S.Medley, 'Institutors of the Medical Society of London', stipple, pub 1801, BM.
PR W.RIDLEY, after Mather Brown, hl with spectacles, stipple, oval, for the *European Mag*, 1804, BM.

WARING, John Scott (1747-1819) politician.
PR C.TURNER, after J.Masquerier, tql seated, mezz, pub 1802, BM.

WARNEFORD,   Samuel   Wilson   (1763-1855)

philanthropist.
SC PETER HOLLINS, 1840, statue, Warneford Hospital, Oxford.

WARNER, Joseph (1717-1801) surgeon.
P SAMUEL MEDLEY, hl, Royal College of Surgeons, London, engr
W.Branwhite, stipple, pub 1801, BM, NPG.

WARNER, Richard (1763-1857) divine.
PR S.HARDING, after J.Williams, hl, stipple, for his *Hist of Bath*,
1801, BM, NPG. L.HAGHE, after S.C.Smith, tql seated, lith, BM.

WARREN, Charles (1767-1823) engraver.
D JAMES BROMLEY, after William Behnes, hs, pencil, BM.
PR S.W.REYNOLDS, after W.Behnes, from a marble bust, mezz, BM,
NPG.

WARREN, Frederick (1775-1848) vice-admiral.
PR R.J.LANE, tql seated in uniform, holding sword, lith, NPG.

WARREN, John (1730-1800) bishop of Bangor.
P THOMAS GAINSBOROUGH, tql seated, Lambeth Palace, London.
PR V.GREEN, after G.Romney, nearly wl seated, mezz, BM.

WARREN, Sir John Borlase (1753-1822) admiral.
P JOHN OPIE, 1794, hl in uniform, Ulster Museum, Belfast. MARK
OATES, *c*1799, hl in uniform, NMM, Greenwich. After JOHN
OPIE, Sudbury Hall (NT), Derbys.
D FRANCIS PHILIP STEPHANOFF, study for 'The Coronation of
George IV', w/c, V & A.
PR J.STOW, after S.Drummond, wl on sea-shore in uniform, stipple,
BM.

WARREN, Pelham (1778-1835) physician.
P JOHN LINNELL, 1835, tql with book, Royal College of
Physicians, London.

WARREN, Sir Peter (1703-1752) vice-admiral.
P THOMAS HUDSON, *c*1747, tql in uniform, NPG 5158; version
NMM, Greenwich.
SC L.F.ROUBILIAC, bust, Westminster Abbey, London.
UNKNOWN, brass medal, BM.

WARREN, Richard (1731-1797) physician.
P THOMAS GAINSBOROUGH, tql, Royal College of Physicians,
London.
PR G.BARTOLOZZI, after G.Stuart, hl, stipple, for *Contemporary
Portraits*, 1810, BM.

WARREN, Samuel (1781-1862) methodist minister and
rector of Ancoats.
PR W.T.FRY, after J.Jackson, hl, stipple, for *Methodist Mag*, 1824,
BM, NPG. J.THOMSON, after R.W.Warren, hl, stipple, pub 1834,
BM.

WARTON, Joseph (1722-1800) critic.
D JOSEPH FISHER, after J.Reynolds, hl in gown and cassock, w/c,
Trinity College, Oxford, engr J.R.Smith, mezz, pub 1777, BM,
NPG.
SC JOHN FLAXMAN, tomb effigy, Winchester Cathedral.

WARTON, Thomas (1728-1790) poet laureate.
P SIR JOSHUA REYNOLDS, *c*1784, hl, Trinity College, Oxford.

WATERS, Sir John (1774-1842) lieutenant-general.
P WILLIAM SALTER, *c*1834-40, tql study for 'Waterloo Banquet at
Apsley House', NPG 3765.
G WILLIAM SALTER, 'The Waterloo Banquet at Apsley House', oil,
1836, Wellington Museum, Apsley House, London.

WATERTON, Charles (1782-1865) naturalist.
P CHARLES WILSON PEALE, 1824, hl, holding bird, cat's head and
book on table, NPG 2014.
D P.H.FITZGERALD, 1860, wl, pen and ink, NPG 1621.

SC W.HAWKINS, 1865, bust, Linnean Society, London.

WATHEN, James (1751?-1828) traveller.
PR T.BRAGG, after A.J.Oliver, tql seated, line, BM, NPG.

WATKINS, Charles Frederick (1793-1873) writer.
D HERBERT L.SMITH, 1862, hl w/c, oval, Northamptonshire
Record Office, Delapre Abbey, Northants.

WATKINS, John (fl 1792-1831) miscellaneous writer.
PR W.LENEY, hl, stipple, oval, pub 1794, BM, NPG.

WATSON, Sir Brook, 1st Bart (1735-1807) merchant and
official.
P JOHN SINGLETON COPLEY, 1778, wl 'Brook Watson and the
Shark', National Gallery of Art, Washington DC, USA. JOHN
SINGLETON COPLEY, tql seated in lord mayor's robes, John
Herron Art Museum, Indianapolis, USA.
C R.DIGHTON, 1803, wl, coloured etch, NPG.

WATSON, Charles (1714-1757) rear-admiral.
P School of SIR GODFREY KNELLER, 1725, hl as a boy, NMM,
Greenwich. THOMAS HUDSON, wl with his son, Victoria
Memorial Hall, Calcutta.
PR E.FISHER, after T.Hudson, tql, holding telescope, mezz, NPG.
SC PETER SCHEEMAKERS, 1757, statue, Westminster Abbey,
London.

WATSON, David (1713?-1761) major general.
P ANDREA SOLDI, 1756, tql with map, Arniston House, Lothian
region, Scotland.

WATSON, George (1767-1837) portrait-painter.
P Self-portrait, hl with palette and brushes, SNPG 714.

WATSON, Henry (1737-1786) engineer.
PR T.PRATTENT, hs, line, oval, for *European Mag*, 1787, BM.

WATSON, Henry George (1796-1879) Founder of the
Watson Gordon Chair of Fine Arts.
P WILLIAM SMELLIE WATSON, tql, Edinburgh University.

WATSON, James (1766?-1838) agitator.
G W.HOLL, after G.Scharf, 'Spa Fields Rioters', hs profile, stipple,
pub 1817, BM.
PR I.R.CRUIKSHANK, hl, etch, for Fairburn's report of trial of Spa
Field rioters, BM.

WATSON, John (1725-1783) rector of Stockport, antiquary.
PR J.BASIRE, after D.Stringer, hl, line, for his *Hist of the Earls of
Warren and Surrey*, 1785, BM, NPG. W.WILLIAMS, hl in gown,
etch, NPG.

WATSON, Joshua (1771-1855) philanthropist.
PR W.O.GELLER, after Sir W.Ross, hl seated, stipple, NPG.

WATSON, Richard (1737-1816) cleric and chemist.
P GEORGE ROMNEY, tql, Trinity College, Cambridge.
G W.WALKER and G.ZOBEL, after drawing by J.F.Skill, J.Gilbert,
W. and E.Walker, 'Men of Science Living in 1807-8', engr, NPG
1075a.
C J.SAYERS, wl, etch, pub 1787, NPG. J.SAYERS, entitled 'The
Comet', one of several head sketches, etch, pub 1789, NPG.

WATSON, Richard (1781-1833) methodist divine.
P UNKNOWN, hl, Methodist Publishing House, London.
PR T.BLOOD, after J.Renton, hl seated, stipple, for *Methodist Mag*,
1824, BM.

WATSON, Robert (1746-1838) adventurer.
P CARL CHRISTIAN VOGEL, hl, SNPG L38.

WATSON, Sir Thomas, 1st Bart (1792-1882) physician.
P GEORGE RICHMOND, tql seated with book, Royal College of
Physicians, London.
SC HENRY WEEKES, 1839, bust, Royal Infirmary, Sheffield.

WATSON, Sir William (1715-1787) physician.
P L.F.ABBOTT, hl, Royal Society, London.

WATSON-WENTWORTH, Charles, see 2nd Marquess of Rockingham.

WATT, James (1736-1819) engineer.
P C.F. VON BREDA, 1792, tql seated with diagrams, NPG 186a. SIR WILLIAM BEECHEY, 1801, hl, City of Birmingham Art Gallery. JOHN GRAHAM-GILBERT, hl, University of Glasgow. HENRY HOWARD, hs, NPG 663. SIR HENRY RAEBURN, hl, Huntington Library and Art Gallery, San Marino, USA. Unknown artist, SNPG 636.
D GEORGE DAWE, pencil and wash, SNPG 126.
SC P.ROUW, 1802, hs, wax, NPG 183. SIR FRANCIS CHANTREY, 1825, marble statue, St Mary Church, Handsworth, Birmingham. SIR FRANCIS CHANTREY, marble bust, SNPG 1186. SIR FRANCIS CHANTREY, marble statue, University of Glasgow.
PR C.TURNER, after T.Lawrence, wl seated, mezz, pub 1815, BM.

WATTS, Alaric Alexander (1797-1864) poet.
D WILLIAM BROCKEDON, 1825, hs, chalk, NPG 2515(51).
PR D.MACLISE, wl carrying a picture under each arm, lith, for *Fraser's Mag*, 1835, BM.

WAUGH, Alexander (1754-1827) minister of the Secession Church.
SC JAMES and WILLIAM TASSIE, several paste medallions, SNPG.

WAY, Lewis (1772-1840) advocate of conversion of the Jews.
D LEWIS VASLET, 1796, hs, pastel, Merton College, Oxford.

WAYLETT, Mrs Harriett, née Cooke (1798-1851) actress.
PR T.WOOLNOTH, after T.Wageman, tql, stipple, for *Ladies Monthly Museum*, 1823, BM, NPG. T.HODGETTS, after F.Meyer, hs, paint over print, oval, pub 1830, NPG. J.ROGERS, after R.Cruikshank, wl, stipple, for *Dramatic Mag*, BM, NPG. UNKNOWN, wl with basket, as Davie Gellitley, in boy's dress, stipple, BM, NPG.
C SIR E.LANDSEER, c1825-35, wl, as the 'Butterfly', pen and ink, NPG 3097(9).

WEAVER, Robert (1773-1852) congregational divine and antiquary.
PR UNKNOWN, after J.Cochran, hl, stipple, and line, NPG.

WEBB, Francis (1735-1815) writer.
PR C.TOWNLEY, after L.Abbott, hs, mezz, pub 1793, NPG.

WEBB, Mrs, née Child (d1793) actress.
P SAMUEL DE WILDE, as Lady Dove in *The Brothers*, wl, Garrick Club, London, engr P.Audinet, line, for Bell's *British Theatre*, 1792, BM, NPG.
C JAMES SAYERS, wl in a scene from 'The Beggar's Opera', etch, pub 1786, NPG.

WEBB, Sir John (1772-1852) director-general, ordnance medical department.
PR HUNTER, after Escazana, tql seated, mezz, NPG.

WEBB, Philip Barker (1793-1854) botanist.
P LALAGERO DI BERNARDIS, 1820, wl seated, in Arabic dress, NPG 4327. MARTINI, after a portrait by Roemer of 1847, Botanical Institute, Florence.
SC GIOVANNI LUSINI, 1874, marble bust, Botanical Institute, Florence.

WEBBE, Samuel (1770?-1843) teacher and composer.
PR W.SKELTON, after W.Behnes, hl, (or his father?), line, for *European Mag*, pub 1820, NPG.

WEBBER, John (1750?-1793) landscape painter of Swiss extraction.
PR H.MEYER, after J.Webber, 1820, hs, line, oval, NPG.

WEBSTER, Alexander (1707-1784) Scots writer and minister.
P DAVID MARTIN, SNPG 812.
C D.LIZARS, hs, line, oval, pub 1784, NPG. J.KAY, 1785, in pulpit, etch, BM, NPG.

WEBSTER, Benjamin Nottingham (1797-1882) actor and dramatist.
P PHILIP HOYOLL, hl seated, Garrick Club, London. UNKNOWN, hs, oval, Garrick Club.
D T.H.WILSON, 1840, two w/cs, as Stanislas De Fonblanche in *The Roused Lion*, Garrick Club, London.
PR T.HOLLIS, as Tartuffe, wl, stipple and line, from a daguerreotype by Mayall, for Tallis's *Drawing Room Table Book*, BM, NPG. D.J.POUND, after a photograph by Mayall, tql, for 'Drawing Room Portrait Gallery', BM, NPG. Several theatrical prints, NPG.
PH UNKNOWN, hs, carte, NPG.

WEDDERBURN, Alexander, see 1st Earl of Rosslyn.

WEDGWOOD, Josiah (1730-1795) potter.
P SIR JOSHUA REYNOLDS, 1782, hl, Wedgwood Museum, Barlaston, Staffs. GEORGE STUBBS, hs, enamel, oval, Wedgwood Museum.
G GEORGE STUBBS, 'The Wedgwood Family', oil, wl in the grounds of Etruria Hall, Wedgwood Museum.
SC JOACHIM SMITH, c1773, Wedgwood medallion, Manchester City Art Galleries. W.HACKWOOD, 1779, Wedgwood medallion, NPG 1948. W.HACKWOOD, 1782, Wedgwood medallion, Wedgwood Museum. JOHN FLAXMAN, 1795, medallion on monument, St Peter ad Vincula, Stoke on Trent.

WEDGWOOD, Thomas (1771-1805) son of Josiah Wedgwood, pioneer of photography.
D UNKNOWN, profile, chalk, Wedgwood Museum, Barlaston, Staffs.

WELD, Thomas (1773-1837) cardinal.
P JAMES RAMSAY, hl, Ugbrooke Park, Devon. UNKNOWN, English College, Rome.

WELLBELOVED, Charles (1769-1858) unitarian divine and archaeologist.
P Attrib CHESTER EARLES, after James Lonsdale, 1859, City Art Gallery, York.
PR H.COUSINS, after J.Lonsdale, hl seated, mezz, BM, NPG.

WELLESLEY, Arthur, see 1st Duke of Wellington.

WELLESLEY, Henry (1773-1847), see 1st Baron Cowley.

WELLESLEY, Henry (1791-1866) scholar.
PR F.C.LEWIS, after J.Slater, head, stipple, for 'Grillion's Club' series, BM, NPG. UNKNOWN, hl, imitation of a drawing, BM.

WELLESLEY, Richard Colley Wellesley, 1st Marquess (1760-1842) governor general of India.
P GEORGE ROMNEY, 1781, a leaving portrait, hl seated, Eton College, Berks. K.A.HICKEL, 1793, hs, oval, study for NPG 745, Stratfield Saye, Hants. ROBERT HOME, c1805, wl in robes of order of St Patrick, Wellington Museum, Apsley House, London. SIR THOMAS LAWRENCE, RA 1813, tql seated, Royal Coll. C.FORTESCUE BATES, wl in Garter robes, Christ Church, Oxford. J.P.DAVIS, hs, NPG 846. THOMAS HICKEY, wl seated, Apsley House. S.CATTERSON SMITH, tql in robes of order of St Patrick, Apsley House. Attrib MATHER BROWN, hs with star of order of St Patrick, Stratfield Saye.
D DANIEL GARDNER, aged 15, hs, gouache, oval, Badminton, Avon. J.P.DAVIS, head, w/c, NPG 847. JOHN DOWNMAN, tql, pencil and w/c, Stratfield Saye.
G K.A.HICKEL, 'The House of Commons, 1793', oil, NPG 745.
SC JOSEPH NOLLEKENS, 1808, marble bust, Royal Coll. JOHN

BACON, jun, marble bust, NPG 992. JOHN BACON, jun, 1809, statue, Calcutta.

WELLESLEY-POLE, Priscilla Anne, Countess of, see Westmorland.

WELLESLEY-POLE, William (1763-1845), see 3rd Earl of Mornington.

WELLINGTON, Arthur Wellesley, 1st Duke of (1769-1852) field-marshal and prime-minister.
P JOHN HOPPNER, c1795, hl, Stratfield Saye, Hants. ROBERT HOME, 1804, hl, NPG 1471. ROBERT HOME, c1805, wl beside tent, Royal Coll. DOMENICO PELLEGRINI, 1809, hl, National Museum of Fine Arts, Lisbon. FRANCISCO GOYA, c1812, hl, NG 6322. GOYA, wl, equestrian, Wellington Museum, Apsley House, London. THOMAS PHILLIPS, 1814, hl in uniform, Stratfield Saye. SIR THOMAS LAWRENCE, 1814, hl, Wellington Museum. SIR THOMAS LAWRENCE, 1814-15, wl with sword of state, Royal Coll. P.E.STRÖHLING, c1815, hl in cloak, National Army Museum, London. SIR DAVID WILKIE, 1835, hl, Hatfield, Herts. JOHN LUCAS, 1838, wl, Trinity House, London. B.R.HAYDON, 1839, wl, NPG L152(3). F.X.WINTERHALTER, 1843, wl with Sir Robert Peel, Royal Coll. BARON GERARD, wl in landscape, DoE (British Embassy, Paris). H.W.PICKERSGILL, wl, Oriental Club, London. SIR DAVID WILKIE, wl seated writing despatches, Aberdeen Art Gallery, Scotland.
D FRANCISCO GOYA, 1812, hs, chalk, BM. THOMAS HEAPHY, c1813, wl in landscape, w/c, NPG 4176. T.HEAPHY, two sketches, 1813-14, hs and hl, w/c, NPG 1914(17) (18). SIR THOMAS LAWRENCE, c1816, hs, chalk, NPG 4670.
M UNKNOWN, 1804, hs, NPG 741. RICHARD COSWAY, c1806, V & A. J.B.ISABEY, 1818, Wallace Collection, London.
G SIR GEORGE HAYTER, 'The Trial of Queen Caroline', oil, 1820, NPG 999. GEORGE JONES, 'The Battle of Vittoria', oil, 1822, Royal Coll. J.W.PIENEMAN, 'The Battle of Waterloo', oil, 1824, Rijksmuseum, Amsterdam. SIR GEORGE HAYTER, 'The House of Commons, 1833', oil, NPG 54. WILLIAM SALTER, 'Waterloo Banquet at Apsley House', oil, 1836, Wellington Museum. DAVID WILKIE, 'The First Council of Queen Victoria', oil, 1838, Royal Coll. F.X.WINTERHALTER, '1st of May 1851', with Queen Victoria and Prince Albert, presenting a casket to his godson, oil, Royal Coll. ROBERT THORBURN, wl seated with his grandchildren, Stratfield Saye.
SC PETER TURNERELLI, 1815, marble bust, Foreign Office, (DoE), London. SIR FRANCIS CHANTREY, 1824, marble bust, Petworth (NT), West Sussex. SIR FRANCIS CHANTREY, 1828, marble bust, Royal Coll. SIR JOHN STEELL, 1845, marble bust, SNPG 967. Plaster cast of death mask, NPG 2155a.
C Numerous JOHN DOYLE drgs, BM.

WELLS, Mary, née Davies, afterwards Mrs Sumbel (1759?-1826?) actress.
P SAMUEL DE WILDE, as Anne Lovely in Centlivre's *Bold Stroke for a Wife*, Garrick Club, London, engr W.Leney, line, for Bell's *British Theatre*, 1791, BM. MATHER BROWN, in *The Gamester*, with Alexander Pope and others, wl, Garrick Club, London.
D J.H.RAMBERG, 1785, as Lavinia in *Titus Andronicus*, indian ink, oval, BM. J.H.RAMBERG, as Imogen in *Cymbeline*, 1785, indian ink, oval. J.DOWNMAN, 1792, hl wearing hat, chalk and w/c, BM.
PR EDMUND SCOTT, after J.Singleton, wl with Mr Edwin, entitled 'Lingo and Cowslip', stipple, pub 1788, NPG. J.R.SMITH, hl, wearing hat, holding a bowl of milk, with title 'Cowslip', mezz, pub 1802, BM.

WELSH, David (1793-1845) Scottish divine.
PR F. ANGELO ROBERTS, after George Harvey, hl, stipple, NPG.

WELWOOD, Alexander Maconochie, see Lord MEADOWBANK.

WEMYSS, David (1721-1787), see Lord Elcho.

WEMYSS, David Douglas (1760-1839) general.
PR H.R.COOK, after J. or T.Stewardson, hl in uniform, stipple, for *Royal Military Panorama*, pub 1814, BM, NPG.

WENSLEYDALE, Sir James Parke, Baron (1782-1868) judge.
P THOMAS PHILLIPS, tql standing, Inner Temple, London. G.F.WATTS, Castle Howard, North Yorks.
D 9TH EARL OF CARLISLE, (his grandson), c1863, hs, pencil, NPG 2028.
G SIR GEORGE HAYTER, 'The Trial of Queen Caroline, 1820', oil, NPG 999, study, NPG 1695(h).
PH WALKER & SONS, wl, NPG.

WENTWORTH, Charles Watson, see 2nd Marquess of Rockingham.

WENTWORTH, Sir John (1737-1820) colonial governor.
P JOHN SINGLETON COPLEY, hl, New York Public Library, New York, USA. ROBERT FIELD, c1808, tql, Governor's Residence, Halifax, Canada.

WENTWORTH, William Charles (1793-1872) advocate of colonial self-government.
P UNKNOWN, Parliament building, Sydney, Australia.
SC THOMAS WOOLNER, c1854, bronze medallion, NPG 1671. PIETRO TENERANI, 1861, statue, Sydney University, Australia.

WESLEY, Charles (1707-1788) divine.
P WILLIAM GUSH, 185?, hl in wig and gown, standing at pulpit with open book before him, Kingswood School, Bristol. UNKNOWN, tql in wig and gown, Methodist Publishing House, London.
PR J.SPILSBURY, from life, tql at pulpit, stipple, pub 1786, NPG.

WESLEY, John (1703-1791) Methodist leader.
P J.M.WILLIAMS, 1742, Didsbury College, Manchester; version, Lincoln College, Oxford. ROBERT HUNTER, c1765, hl, Wesley's Chapel, London. NATHANIEL HONE, c1766, tql in gown, NPG 135. JOHN RUSSELL, 1773, Kingswood School, Bristol. THOMAS HORSLEY, c1784, hl, Richmond College, Surrey. WILLIAM HAMILTON, 1788, hl in wig at pulpit, NPG 317. GEORGE ROMNEY, 1789, tql, Philadelphia Museum of Art, USA.
D HENRY BONE, pencil and chalk, SNPG 2113.
SC UNKNOWN, 1793, coade-ware bust, Methodist Archives and Research Centre, London. UNKNOWN, marble bust, NPG 271. ENOCH WOOD, pottery bust, Methodist Archives and Research Centre.
PR J.W.TINNEY, c1750, hl, mezz, oval, NPG. W.RIDLEY, after an unknown artist, after death, stipple, oval, pub 1791, BM.

WESLEY, Samuel (1766-1837) composer and organist.
P JOHN JACKSON, hs, NPG 2040.
PR W.DICKINSON, after J.Russell, aged 11, wl, mezz, pub 1778, BM, NPG.

WEST, Benjamin (1738-1820) painter.
P MATTHEW PRATT, 1765, hl, Pennsylvania Academy of Fine Arts, Philadelphia, USA. Self-portrait, c1771, hl wearing hat, National Gallery of Art, Washington DC, USA. GILBERT STUART, c1785, hl, NPG 349. GILBERT STUART, c1785, hl, TATE 229. Self-portrait, 1793, hl seated, Royal Academy, London. Self-portrait, c1806, hs painting a portrait of his wife, Pennsylvania Academy of Fine Arts. SIR THOMAS LAWRENCE, RA 1811, hl, Yale Center for British Art, New Haven, USA. GEORGE WATSON, RA 1816, hl, NGS 319. Self-portrait, 1818, hs, Society of Dilettanti, Brooks's Club, London. Self-portrait,

1819, hl, Smithsonian Institution, Washington DC, USA. SIR THOMAS LAWRENCE, RA 1821, wl pointing to 'The Death of Ananias', Wadsworth Athenaeum, Hertford, Connecticut, USA; replica, TATE 144. Self-portrait, hs with his son, Yale Center for British Art.

M Self-portrait, c1758, hs, Yale University Art Gallery, New Haven, USA. JOHN DOWNMAN, hl with self-portrait, oval, NPG L152 (2).

D ANGELICA KAUFFMANN, 1763, hs, chalk, NPG 1649. GEORGE DANCE, hl profile, pencil, Royal Academy.

G MATTHEW PRATT, 'The American School, 1765', oil, Metropolitan Museum of Art, New York, USA. BENJAMIN WEST, with his family, oil, 1772, Yale Center for British Art. JOHAN ZOFFANY, 'Royal Academicians, 1772', oil, Royal Coll. HENRY SINGLETON, 'Royal Academicians, 1793', oil, Royal Academy.

SC SIR FRANCIS CHANTREY, 1811, bust, New York Historical Society, USA. JOSEPH NOLLEKENS, 1812, marble bust, Royal Horticultural Society, London. SIR FRANCIS CHANTREY, 1818, bust, Royal Academy. SIR FRANCIS CHANTREY, 1819, marble bust, NPG 607.

WEST, George John Sackville, see 5th Earl DE la Warr.

WEST, Gilbert (1703-1756) author.
PR E.SMITH, after W.Walker, hl, line, pub 1824, NPG.

WEST, James (1704?-1772) politician and antiquary.
PR THOMAS HODGETTS, tql in Vandyke costume, mezz, pub 1819, NPG.

WEST, John (1729-1777), see 2nd Earl DE la Warr.

WEST, Raphael Lamar (1769-1850) painter and book-illustrator.
P BENJAMIN WEST, c1770, hl as a child with his mother. Cleveland Museum of Art, USA.

WEST, Robert (d1770) Irish painter.
D M.W.PETERS, 1758, hs with the artist, charcoal, NPG 2169.

WEST, Robert Lucius (1774-1849) painter.
P Self-portrait, 1816, NGI 418.

WEST, Mrs, née Cooke (1790-1876) actress.
PR H.R.COOK, after W.Foster, tql seated, stipple, pub 1813, BM. H.COOPER, after R.Drummond, hl, stipple, for *The Drama or Theatrical Pocket Mag*, BM. C.BAUGNIET, tql, lith, 1843, NPG.

WESTALL, Richard (1765-1836) historical painter.
P Self-portrait, 1793, nearly hl, Royal Academy, London.
D GEORGE DANCE, hs profile, Royal Academy.
G H.SINGLETON, 'Royal Academicians 1793', oil, Royal Academy.

WESTALL, William (1781-1850) topographical painter.
PR G.K.CHILDS, hs, woodcut, cutting from *Art Journal*, 1850, BM. UNKNOWN, hs, profile, lith, NPG.

WESTCOTT, George Blagdon (1745?-1798) captain in the navy.
G BARTOLOZZI, LANDSEER, RYDER and STOW, after R.Smirke, 'Naval Victories', 'Commemoration of the victory of June 1st 1794', line engr, pub 1803, BM, NPG. W.BROMLEY, J.LANDSEER and LENEY, after R.Smirke, 'Victors of the Nile', hs, line engr, pub 1803, BM, NPG.
PR E.BELL, hl in uniform, oval, mezz, pub 1799, BM.

WESTERN, Charles Callis, Baron (1767-1844) politician and agriculturalist.
P JOHN SINGLETON COPLEY, tql with his brother Shirley as children, Huntington Library and Art Gallery, San Marino, USA.

PR S.W.REYNOLDS, jun, after R.Ansdell, when old, wl in landscape, mezz, pub 1844, BM.

WESTMACOTT, Sir Richard (1775-1856) sculptor.
D WILLIAM BROCKEDON, 1844, hs, pencil and chalk, NPG 2515(95). C.H.LEAR, c1845, pencil, NPG 1456(27). CHARLES BENAZECH, hs, chalk, NPG 731.

WESTMACOTT, Richard (1799-1872) sculptor.
D JOHN PARTRIDGE, hs, 1825, pencil, NPG 3944(4). COUNT A.D'ORSAY, 1831, nearly hl, pencil and chalk, NPG 4026(59).
PH J.WATKINS, NPG.

WESTMINSTER, Richard Grosvenor, 2nd Marquess of (1795-1869) landowner and MP.
D THOMAS UWINS, wl, w/c and pencil, BM.
SC THOMAS THORNYCROFT, 1869, statue, Grosvenor Park, Chester.
PR C.TURNER, after W.Jones, tql, mezz, pub 1833, BM, NPG.

WESTMINSTER, Robert Grosvenor, 1st Marquess of (1767-1845) statesman.
D SIR FRANCIS CHANTREY, hs sketches, pencil, NPG 316(a) (60, 61).
G SIR GEORGE HAYTER, 'The Trial of Queen Caroline, 1820', oil, NPG 999. P.C.WONDER, 'Patrons and Lovers of Art, 1826', study for a large group, NPG 794.
SC SIR FRANCIS CHANTREY, bust, Ashmolean Museum, Oxford.
PR H.MEYER, after J.Hoppner, hl in peer's robes, stipple, for *Contemporary Portraits*, 1811, BM, NPG.

WESTMORLAND, John Fane, 10th Earl of (1759-1841) Lord lieutenant of Ireland.
P GEORGE ROMNEY, c1770, wl as a boy, with dog in landscape, DoE (10 Downing St, London). GEORGE ROMNEY, 1789, tql in peer's robes, Emmanuel College, Cambridge. SIR THOMAS LAWRENCE, c1806, wl, Prado, Madrid.
G SIR G.HAYTER, 'The Trial of Queen Caroline, 1820', oil, NPG 999.
PR C.WARREN, hs, line, oval, pub 1792, BM. S.W.REYNOLDS and S.COUSINS, after Sir T.Lawrence, hl, mezz, BM, NPG.
C R.DIGHTON, 1821, coloured etch, for *West End Characters*, V & A, NPG.

WESTMORLAND, John Fane, 11th Earl of (1784-1859) diplomat and general.
D UNKNOWN, after Sir T.Lawrence, hs, pencil and wash, NPG 3886.
PR S.W.REYNOLDS, after Sir J.Reynolds, as a child, mezz, pub 1820, BM. J.BULL, after Sir T.Lawrence, hs, stipple, BM.
C R.DIGHTON, 1822, wl, coloured etch, BM, NPG.

WESTMORLAND, Priscilla Anne Fane, Countess of (1793-1879) artist.
PR J.THOMSON, after Sir T.Lawrence, with her sisters, stipple, pub 1827, BM. G.LONGHI, after Sir T.Lawrence, hl with child, entitled 'Le Delizie Materne', line, BM. Unknown artist, tql seated, lith, BM.

WESTON, Stephen (1747-1830) antiquary.
P UNKNOWN, tql in Vandyck dress, Exeter College, Oxford.

WESTON, Thomas (1737-1776) actor.
P JOHAN ZOFFANY, in character in Foote's *Devil Upon Two Sticks*, Castle Howard, North Yorks. THOMAS PARKINSON, wl as Billy Button in the *Maid of Bath*, Garrick Club, London.
D ROBERT DIGHTON, wl as Costard, ink and w/c, BM.
PR Various theatrical prints, BM, NPG.

WETHERELL, Sir Charles (1770-1846) politician.
PR H.B.HALL, after Moore, hl seated, stipple, for Ryall's *Eminent Conservative Statesmen*, 1837, BM, NPG.
C J.DOYLE, wl, entitled 'The man wot prefers his character to his place', pencil, BM. WILLIAM HEATH, coloured etch, pub 1831, V & A. UNKNOWN, hl, holding candlestick and burning a map

of Bristol, etch, NPG.

WEWITZER, Ralph (1748-1825) comedian.
D SAMUEL DE WILDE, 1808, as Dr Caius in *The Merry Wives of Windsor*, w/c, Garrick Club, London.

WEYMOUTH, Thomas Thynne, 3rd Viscount, see 1st Marquess of Bath.

WHALLEY, Peter (1722-1791) author and editor.
PR W.RIDLEY, after Harding, hl, stipple, for Harding's *Shakespeare Illustrated*, 1791, BM, NPG.

WHALLEY, Thomas Sedgwick (1746-1828) poet and traveller.
PR J.BROWN, after Sir J.Reynolds, tql with dog, line, pub 1862, NPG.

WHARNCLIFFE, James Archibald Stuart-Wortley-Mackenzie, 1st Baron (1776-1845) statesman.
PR H.T.RYALL, after H.P.Briggs, hl, stipple, for Ryall's *Eminent Conservative Statesmen*, 1836, BM.
C J.DOYLE, 'Coroner's Inquest upon the Late Administration', pen and chalk, BM. Attrib I.CRUIKSHANK, 'Members of the House of Lords', pencil and wash, c1835, NPG 2789.

WHATELY, Richard (1787-1863) archbishop of Dublin.
P UNKNOWN, hl, Oriel College, Oxford.
SC WILLIAM BEHNES, 1833, plaster bust, Oriel College, Oxford. SIR THOMAS FARRELL, tomb effigy, St Patrick's Cathedral, Dublin.
PR H.MEYER, after C.Grey, tql, stipple, BM.
PH UNKNOWN, tql seated, NPG/'Photographs-Portraits' Album 44.

WHEATLEY, Francis (1747-1801) painter.
D WILLIAM HAMILTON, hl, pencil and w/c, oval, NPG 5037. GEORGE DANCE, hs profile, Royal Academy, London.
G H.SINGLETON, 'The Royal Academicians, 1793', oil, Royal Academy.

WHEELER, Thomas (1754-1847) botanist.
P HENRY BRIGGS, tql seated, Apothecaries' Hall, London.

WHEWELL, William (1794-1866) mathematician and philosopher.
P JAMES LONSDALE, 1825, hl, Trinity College, Cambridge. G.F.JOSEPH, 1836, tql, Trinity College. SAMUEL LAURENCE, 1845, hl, Trinity College.
M MARGARET CARPENTER, 1842, wl with bust, Trinity College.
SC E.H.BAILY, 1851, marble bust, Trinity College; plaster cast NPG 1390. THOMAS WOOLNER, 1872, marble statue, Trinity College. UNKNOWN, plaster death mask, Trinity College.
PH ERNEST EDWARDS, wl seated, for *Men of Eminence*, 1863, ed L.Reeve, vol I, NPG. J.RYLANDS, wl, carte, NPG Cunnington Collection.

WHITAKER, John (1735-1808) historian of Manchester.
PR G.F.STORM, after H.Bone, hs, stipple, for Britton's *Autobiography*, 1850, BM, NPG.

WHITAKER, John (1776-1847) organist and composer.
PR N.HANHART, after F.Y.Hurlstone, nearly wl, lith, BM, NPG.

WHITAKER, Thomas Dunham (1759-1821) topographer.
SC C.R.SMITH, recumbent figure on monument, Whalley?, Yorks.
PR W.MADDOCKS, after W.D.Fryer, hl, stipple, pub 1805, NPG. P.AUDINET, after J.Northcote, hs, line, for Nichols's *Literary Illustrations*, IV, 1822, BM, NPG.

WHITBREAD, Samuel (1720-1796) brewer.
D H.P.BONE, after Sir W.Beechey, hs, pencil, NPG 'Bone's Drawings'.
SC JOHN BACON, sen, 1799, marble monument, St Mary's Church, Cardington, Beds.
PR W.WARD, after W.Beechey, hl, mezz, pub 1797, BM, NPG.

S.W.REYNOLDS, after J.Reynolds, tql seated, mezz, pub 1803, BM.

WHITBREAD, Samuel (1764-1815) politician.
P GEORGE ROMNEY, 1781, hl, a leaving portrait, Eton College, Berks.
SC JOSEPH NOLLEKENS, 1814, marble bust, Drury Lane Theatre, London.
PR S.W.REYNOLDS, after J.Opie, wl seated, mezz, pub 1804, BM. NPG. S.W.REYNOLDS, after J.Opie, hl, mezz, pub 1806, BM. NPG. W.DAY, after J.Northcote, wl with 'Magna Carta', lith, pub 1831, BM.
C JAMES SAYERS, wl, 'The Brewer and the Thistle', aquatint, pub 1805, NPG. Various political satires, BM.

WHITE, Anthony (1782-1849) surgeon.
P UNKNOWN, c1815, Westminster Hospital, London. T.F.DICKSEE, 1843, tql, Royal College of Surgeons, London.

WHITE, Charles (1728-1813) surgeon.
P JOSEPH ALLEN, hl, Manchester City Art Gallery, engr W.Ward, mezz, pub 1809, BM.

WHITE, Gilbert (1720-1793) 'White of Selborne', naturalist and writer.
D Two sketches in White's copy of 1st ed (1720) of Pope's trans of 'The Iliad', BL Add Mss 38875-80; THOMAS CHAPMAN, hs, pen and ink, BL Add Ms 38877. UNKNOWN, hs profile, pen, BL Add Ms 38879.

WHITE, Henry Kirke (1785-1806) poet.
P SYLVANUS REDGATE, after an unknown artist, hl profile, NPG 3248. Three portraits by THOMAS BARBER, F.C.COOPER and JOHN HOPPNER, Castle Art Gallery, Nottingham.
D UNKNOWN, hl profile, pencil, NPG 493.
M UNKNOWN, V & A.
SC SIR FRANCIS CHANTREY, medallion, NPG 93.

WHITE, Joseph (1745-1814) orientalist and theologian.
PR J.THOMSON, after W.Peters, hs in gown, oval, stipple, for *European Mag*, 1796, BM, NPG.

WHITE, Joseph Blanco (1775-1841) theological writer.
D JOSEPH SLATER, 1812, head, pencil and wash, NPG 3788.
SC UNKNOWN, marble relief bust, Unitarian Church, Liverpool.
PR F.C.LEWIS, after W.Behnes, hl seated, stipple, pub 1836, BM, NPG.

WHITEFIELD, George (1714-1770) leader of Calvinistic methodists.
P JOHN WOLLASTON, c1742, hl in pulpit, NPG 131. JOHN RUSSELL, 1770(?), hs, pub 1792. UNKNOWN, hs, Pembroke College, Oxford. UNKNOWN, hs, Whitefield Memorial Church, London.
PR J.WATSON, after J.Russell, preaching in Moorfields, mezz, pub 1772, BM. J.FABER, jun, after G.Beard, hl, oval, mezz, BM, NPG. J.GREENWOOD, after N.Hone, tql in pulpit with both arms raised, mezz, BM, NPG. J.FABER, jun, after F.Kyte, 1743, wl, mezz, BM.

WHITEFOORD, Caleb (1734-1810) diplomatist.
P Studio of SIR JOSHUA REYNOLDS, 1773-74, hl, NPG 1400. GILBERT STUART, 1782, Montclair Art Museum, New Jersey, USA. UNKNOWN, c1800, hl, Royal Society of Arts, London.
PR W.DANIELL, after G.Dance of 1795, hl, etch, pub 1809, BM. P.CONDÉ, after R.Cosway, hs, stipple, oval, for *European Mag*, 1810, BM, NPG, V & A.
C JAMES GILLRAY, 'Connoisseurs examining a Collection of George Morland's', sitter represented in two of six sketches, V & A.

WHITEHEAD, Paul (1710-1774) satirist.
PR J.COLLYER, after T.Gainsborough, hl, line, oval, for his *Poems*,

1777, BM.

WHITEHEAD, William (1715-1785) poet laureate.
P WILLIAM DOUGHTY, 1776, hs, oval, V & A.

WHITEHURST, John (1713-1788) horologer.
P JOSEPH WRIGHT, c1783, John Smith & Sons, Midland Clock Works, Derby.
PR J.HALL, after J.Wright, hl, line, pub 1786, BM.

WHITELOCKE, John (1757-1833) general.
PR UNKNOWN, wl at his trial, etch, BM. UNKNOWN, hs, stipple, BM.

WHITLOCK, Mrs Elizabeth (1761-1836) actress.
P SAMUEL DE WILDE, as Margaret of Anjou in *The Earl of Warwick*, wl, Garrick Club, London, engr P.Audinet, line, for Bell's *British Theatre*, 1792, BM.

WHITSHED, Sir James Hawkins, 1st Bart (1762-1849) admiral of the fleet.
D H.P.BONE, after J.Northcote, 1799, hl in uniform, pencil, NPG, 'Bone's Drawings'.
G WORTHINGTON and PARKER, after R.Smirke, 'Commemoration of a Naval Victory, 14th February, 1797', line engr, pub 1803, BM, NPG.

WHITWELL, John Griffin, see 4th Baron HOWARD de Walden.

WHITWORTH, Charles, 1st Earl of (1752-1825) diplomatist.
P SIR THOMAS LAWRENCE, 1807, Louvre, Paris.
D HENRY EDRIDGE, 1801, Knole (NT), Kent.
G SIR GEORGE HAYTER, 'The Trial of Queen Caroline, 1820', oil, NPG 999.
PR R.LAURIE, after A.Graff, hl in uniform, mezz, BM.

WHYTE, Samuel (1733-1811) schoolmaster and author.
PR BROCAS, after H.Hamilton, hs, oval, stipple, for his *Poems*, 1795, BM.

WHYTT, Robert (1714-1766) physician.
P After ANTONIO BELLUCCI, 1863 after portrait of 1738, hs, Royal College of Physicians, Edinburgh.

WICKLOW, Ralph Howard, Viscount, see 1st Baron Clonmore.

WIFFEN, Jeremiah Holmes (1792-1836) translator of Tasso.
D SIR GEORGE HAYTER, 1824, hs, pen and sepia, BM. WILLIAM BROCKEDON, 1830, hs, pencil and chalk, NPG 2515(18).
PR J.THOMSON, after A.Wivell, hl, stipple, pub 1824, BM, NPG.

WIGHT, Robert (1796-1872) botanist.
D SIR DANIEL MACNEE, hl, crayon, Royal Botanic Gardens, Kew.

WIGHTMAN, Sir William (1784-1863) judge.
P UNKNOWN, hl in robes, Queen's College, Oxford.

WIGRAM, Sir James (1793-1866) vice-chancellor.
D GEORGE RICHMOND, hl, crayon, Trinity College, Cambridge.
PR W.WALKER, after J.W.Gordon, hl, mezz, oval, pub 1849, BM.

WILBERFORCE, William (1759-1833) philanthropist and reformer.
P JOHN RUSSELL, 1770, hs as a child, NPG 759. JOHN RUSSELL, c1801, Leeds City Art Gallery. SIR THOMAS LAWRENCE, 1828, hl, NPG 3. GEORGE RICHMOND, 1833, hl, St John's College, Cambridge. JOHN RISING, Wilberforce House, Hull. A.HICKEL, Wilberforce House, Hull.
D GEORGE RICHMOND, 1833, wl seated, w/c, NPG 4997. UNKNOWN, pastel, Wilberforce House, Hull.
G K.A.HICKEL, 'The House of Commons, 1793', oil, NPG 745.
SC SAMUEL JOSEPH, 1833, marble bust, City Art Gallery, York. SAMUEL JOSEPH, 1838, marble statue, Westminster Abbey,

London.
C C.WILLIAMS, with the Bishop of Rochester, Lord Hawkesbury and William Pitt, etch, V & A.

WILCOCKS, Joseph (1724-1791) antiquary.
PR S.PHILLIPS, after B.West, hl, oval, stipple, for his *Roman Conversations*, 1797, BM, NPG.

WILDE, Thomas, see 1st Baron Truro.

WILDERSPIN, Samuel (1792?-1866) founder of the infant school system.
P G.T.PAYNE, tql, BM.
PR G.T.PAYNE, after J.R.Herbert, tql seated, mezz, BM, NPG.

WILKES, John (1727-1797) politician and agitator.
P R.E.PINE, 1768, hl, Palace of Westminster, London.
D RICHARD EARLOM, wl, pencil, NPG 284.
G RICHARD HOUSTON, with Glyn and Tooke, oil, c1768, NPG 1944.
SC UNKNOWN, hs, silver medal, NPG 1702. DAVID D'ANGERS, bronze medallion, Musée des Beaux Arts, Angers, France. L.F.ROUBILIAC, bust, Guildhall Art Gallery, London.
PR WILLIAM HOGARTH, wl seated holding cap of liberty on a pole, etch, pub 1763, BM, NPG.

WILKIE, Sir David (1785-1841) painter.
P Self-portrait, 1813, hl, NPG 53. ANDREW GEDDES, 1816, wl, SNPG 1443. THOMAS PHILLIPS, 1829, hl, SNPG 719. Various self-portraits, hl, SNPG 573, 584 and 2197.
D JOHN JACKSON, 1807, hs, black lead, BM. B.R.HAYDON, 1816, hs, pencil, NPG 2423. W.H.HUNT, hs, w/c, NPG 2770. JOHN JACKSON, hs, w/c, NPG 3154.
G P.C.WONDER, 'Patrons and Lovers of Art, 1826', one of several studies for a large group, NPG 795.
SC 'Smith a Phrenologist', plaster life mask, SNPG 181.

WILKINS, William (1778-1839) architect.
SC E.H.BAILY, 1830, marble bust, Trinity College, Cambridge.

WILKINSON, John (1728-1808) ironmaster.
P UNKNOWN, hl, Wolverhampton Art Gallery. L.F.ABBOTT, hs, NPG 3785.

WILKINSON, Sir John Gardiner (1797-1875) explorer and egyptologist.
D WILLIAM BROCKEDON, 1838, hs, chalk, NPG 2515(86). COUNT ALFRED D'ORSAY, 1839, hs profile, pencil and chalk, NPG 4026(28).

WILKINSON, Tate (1739-1803) actor and theatrical manager.
P Attrib STEPHEN HEWSON, tql seated, York City Art Gallery. STEPHEN HEWSON, 1791, hs, Garrick Club, London.
PR W.RIDLEY, after F.Atkinson, hl, oval, stipple, for *Monthly Mirror*, 1799, BM, NPG. M.U.SEARS, tql seated, mezz, pub 1829, NPG.

WILLAN, Robert (1757-1812) physician and dermatologist.
M Probably JOSEPH ROBINSON, hs, oval, Royal College of Physicians, London. MARY HOWELL, posthumous, hl, Royal College of Physicians.

WILLETT, Ralph (1719-1795) book-collector.
PR UNKNOWN, after P.Sandby, 'Sketches Taken at Print Sales', line, pub 1798, BM.

WILLIAM IV (1765-1837) reigned 1830-37.
P ALLAN RAMSAY, c1767, wl with drum, Royal Coll. JOHAN ZOFFANY, c1770, wl with Princess Charlotte, Royal Coll. SIR BENJAMIN WEST, 1778, wl with Duke of Kent, Royal Coll. THOMAS GAINSBOROUGH, 1782, hs with Garter, Royal Coll. SIR THOMAS LAWRENCE, 1793, Upton House (NT), Warwicks. SIR

M. ARCHER SHEE, 1800, wl in naval uniform with Garter, NPG 2199. SIR THOMAS LAWRENCE, c1827, wl with Garter, Royal Coll. SIR DAVID WILKIE, 1832, wl in Garter robes, Royal Coll. SIR M.A.SHEE, 1833, wl in Garter robes, Royal Coll. SIR DAVID WILKIE, 1833, wl in uniform with Garter, Wellington Museum, Apsley House, London.

D SIR FRANCIS CHANTREY, 1830, hs in profile, pencil, NPG 316a (142). UNKNOWN, after a portrait by Henry Dawe, c1830, hl with Garter, w/c, NPG 1163. REGINALD EASTON, hl with Garter, w/c, NPG 4703.

M RICHARD COSWAY, 1791, oval, Royal Coll.

G JOHAN ZOFFANY, 'George III, Queen Charlotte and their six eldest children', oil, 1770, Royal Coll. SIR GEORGE HAYTER, 'The Trial of Queen Caroline, 1820', oil, NPG 999. GEORGE JONES, 'Banquet at the Coronation of George IV', oil, 1821, Royal Coll. R.B.DAVIS, 'The Coronation Procession of William IV', oil, 1831, Royal Coll.

SC SIR FRANCIS CHANTREY, 1837, marble bust, Royal Coll. JOHN DE VEAUX, red wax medallion, NPG 2920.

C J.GILLRAY, entitled 'Naval Eloquence', etch, pub 1795, NPG.

WILLIAM Augustus, Duke of Cumberland, see CUMBERLAND.

WILLIAM Frederick, 2nd Duke of Gloucester, see GLOUCESTER.

WILLIAM Henry, 1st Duke of Gloucester, see GLOUCESTER.

WILLIAMS, Anna (1706-1783) poet and friend of Dr Johnson.

P Attrib FRANCES REYNOLDS, hl, Dr Johnson's House, London.

PR E.STALKER, after F.Reynolds, hs, line, pub 1817, NPG.

WILLIAMS, Sir Charles Hanbury (1708-1759) satirical writer and diplomat.

P Attrib J.G.ECCARDT, c1746, hl seated, holding paper inscribed 'An Ode/To the Honble Henry Fox', NPG 383.

PR W.N.GARDINER, after S.Harding, hl with the Bath, stipple, pub 1794, NPG. R.RHODES, after J.Thurston, hl, holding letter, line, pub 1820, NPG.

WILLIAMS, David (1738-1816) founder of Royal Literary Fund.

P Attrib JOHN HOPPNER, hl, National Museum of Wales, 93, Cardiff.

PR UNKNOWN, hs, engraved silhouette, for *Gentleman's Magazine*, July 1816, NPG. THORNTHWAITE, after S.F.Rigaud, tql with pen, line, BM, NPG.

WILLIAMS, Edward (1746-1826) Welsh bard.

PR R.CRUIKSHANK, after E.Waring, tql seated, etch, for E.Waring, *Recollections of Edward Williams*, 1850, BM.

WILLIAMS, Edward (1750-1813) nonconformist divine.

PR RIDLEY and HOLL, hs, stipple, for *Evangelical Mag*, 1806, BM.

WILLIAMS, Edward Ellerker (1793-1822) friend of Shelley.

D Self-portrait, hl seated with pen, w/c over pencil, BM.

M UNKNOWN, hs, Bodleian Library, Oxford.

WILLIAMS, George James (1719-1805) wit.

G SIR JOSHUA REYNOLDS, 'The Committee of Taste', oil, c1759, Bristol City Art Gallery.

WILLIAMS, Helen Maria (1762-1827) writer.

PR J.SINGLETON, after O.Humphry, hl, from a miniature, stipple, BM. H.LIPS, hs, from a medallion, stipple, oval, BM.

WILLIAMS, Hugh William (1773-1829) landscape painter.

P SIR HENRY RAEBURN, hl, NPG 965. WILLIAM NICHOLSON, hl, SNPG 716.

SC SIR JOHN STEELL, marble medallion, NGS 524.

WILLIAMS, John (1761-1818) 'Anthony Pasquin', satirist.

P After GEORGE ROMNEY, John Henderson as Macbeth, one of the witches said to be John Williams, Garrick Club, London.

D SIR M. ARCHER SHEE, tql seated with pen, w/c, BM. UNKNOWN, wl, pencil and wash, NPG 4204.

PR F.BARTOLOZZI, hl seated, stipple, oval, BM, NPG.

WILLIAMS, Sir John (1777-1846) judge.

G SIR GEORGE HAYTER, 'The Trial of Queen Caroline, 1820', oil, NPG 999.

PR T.WRIGHT, after A.Wivell, when counsel for Queen Caroline, hs, stipple, pub 1820, BM, NPG.

WILLIAMS, John (1792-1858) archdeacon of Cardigan.

SC JOSEPH EDWARDS, marble bust, Balliol College, Oxford.

WILLIAMS, John (1796-1839) missionary.

PR GEORGE BAXTER, 1843, tql seated, Baxter colour print, NPG 4956.

WILLIAMS, William (1781-1840) Welsh preacher, known as 'Williams of Wern'.

PR J.THOMSON, after J.R.Wildman, hl, for *Evangelical Mag*, stipple, BM, NPG.

WILLIAMS afterwards **Williams-Freeman, William Peere (1742-1832)** admiral of the fleet.

P GEORGE ROMNEY, tql in uniform, Manchester City Art Gallery.

WILLIAMSON, Peter (1730-1799) author and publisher.

PR UNKNOWN, wl in dress of Delaware Indian, for the *Grand Magazine*, 1759, NPG.

C JOHN KAY, wl with James Bruce, etch, pub 1791, BM.

WILLIS, Francis (1718-1807) physician, attended George III.

D JOHN RUSSELL, 1789, hs, pastel, NPG 2186. J.RUSSELL, 1799, pastel, Burghley, Northants.

SC GEORGE GARRARD, 1803, plaster bust, Burghley, Northants.

PR J.FITTLER, after R.Bowyer, hs, oval, line, pub 1789, BM, NPG.

WILLIS, Robert (1799-1878) medical writer.

PR UNKNOWN, aged 79, hs in skull-cap reading, etch, BM.

WILLISON, George (1741-1797) portrait-painter.

SC JAMES TASSIE, after Guilliobe, paste medallion, SNPG 2134.

PR Engraving, said to be by his son, hl in profile, SNPG.

WILLOUGHBY, Sir Nesbit Josiah (1777-1849) rear-admiral.

PR UNKNOWN, after Barber, almost tql in uniform, NPG.

WILLS, John (1741-1806) benefactor of Wadham College, Oxford.

P JOHN HOPPNER, c1792-6, tql, Wadham College, Oxford.

D LEWIS VASLET, 1790, hs in gown, pastel, Bodleian Library, Oxford.

WILLS, Thomas (1740-1802) evangelical preacher.

PR T.HOLLOWAY, after T.Lawrence, hl, line, pub 1790, NPG. W.RIDLEY, hs, stipple, for *Evangelical Mag*, 1799, BM, NPG.

WILLSHIRE, Sir Thomas, Bart (1789-1862) general.

M UNKNOWN, hs, NPG 2008.

WILMOT, Sir John Eardley (1709-1792) the lord chief justice of the common pleas.

P NATHANIEL DANCE, c1766-71, wl in robes, Thomas Coram Foundation for Children, London; version, DoE (Royal Courts of Justice, London). Attrib JOSEPH WRIGHT, hl, Inner Temple, London.

PR F.BARTOLOZZI, after Sir J.Reynolds, hl, stipple, for his *Memoirs*, 1802, BM, NPG.

WILMOT, John Eardley (1750-1815) politician.

D GEORGE DANCE, 1802, hs, pencil, All Souls College, Oxford.

PR W.DANIELL, after G.Dance, hs, soft-ground etch, pub 1811, BM, NPG.

WILSON, Alexander (1714-1786) astronomer.

P UNKNOWN, oil on card, SNPG 750.

WILSON, Alexander (1766-1813) ornithologist.

SL UNKNOWN, SNPG 282.

SC After A.J.STOTHARD, plaster medal, SNPG 76.

WILSON, Anthony (fl 1793) cataloguer of engraved British portraits, 'Henry Bromley'.

PR BARRETT, hs, oval in scroll, with heads of Van Dyck, Lely, Faithorne and Hollar, line, BM.

WILSON, Benjamin (1721-1788) painter.

P Self-portrait, hl with crayon, Althorp, Northants, etch Wilson, BM, NPG.

WILSON, Caroline, née Fry (1787-1846) author.

P SIR THOMAS LAWRENCE, 1827, TATE 1307.

WILSON, Christopher (1714-1792) bishop of Bristol.

PR J.JONES, after G.Romney, nearly wl, mezz, pub 1788, BM, NPG. C.WARREN, after C.Corbould, hs in oval, line, pub 1791, NPG.

WILSON, Daniel (1778-1858) bishop of Calcutta.

P UNKNOWN, hl, Bodleian Library, Oxford. UNKNOWN, hs, St Edmund Hall, Oxford.

SC WILLIAM BEHNES, 1846, bust, St Paul's Cathedral, Calcutta.

PR J.COLLYER, after J.Jackson, hl in pulpit, stipple, pub 1821, BM. J.COCHRAN, after F.Howard, hl, stipple, for Jerdan's *Nat Portrait Gallery*, 1830, BM, NPG. W.HOLL, after Claxton, hl, line, NPG. J.BROWN, after Colesworthy Grant, wl, mezz, NPG.

WILSON, George (b1765) pedestrian.

PR WILLIAMS, aged 50, as he appeared on 12th day of his feat of walking 1000 miles in twenty days, wl, coloured etch, pub 1815, BM. G.WOODWARD, on 9th day of same feat, etch, pub 1815, BM, NPG.

WILSON, Harriette (1789-1846) woman of fashion.

PR UNKNOWN, wl, lith, pub 1825, BM.

WILSON, Horace Hayman (1786-1860) orientalist.

P UNKNOWN, hl, NPG 2748. ROBERT HOME, hl, Asiatic Society, Calcutta.

D JAMES ATKINSON, 1821, hs, w/c, NPG 826. UNKNOWN, 1808, w/c, Victoria Memorial Hall, Calcutta. SIR FRANCIS CHANTREY, c1837, hs profile and full-face, pencil, NPG 316a (143).

SC SIR FRANCIS CHANTREY, c1837, marble bust, Asiatic Society, Calcutta; plaster cast, Ashmolean Museum, Oxford.

PR W.WALKER, after J.W.Gordon, nearly wl seated, mezz, pub 1851, BM, NPG.

WILSON, James Arthur (1795-1882) physician.

PR W.WALKER, after E.Walker, hl seated by table holding eyeglass, mezz, pub 1852, BM. R.J.LANE, after Count A.D'Orsay, hl, lith, NPG.

WILSON, Sir John (1741-1793) judge.

PR J.MURPHY, after G.Romney, hl in wig and gown, 1792, mezz, BM. NPG.

WILSON, John (1785-1854) author and essayist, 'Christopher North'.

P SIR JOHN WATSON-GORDON, c1829-33, two similar hl portraits, SNPG 646, NPG 187. SIR HENRY RAEBURN, 1829, wl with horse, SNPG 708. THOMAS DUNCAN, wl with gun, SNPG 1369. ROBERT SCOTT LAUDER, wl seated with book, Edinburgh University.

D WILLIAM NICHOLSON, 1817, Abbotsford, Borders region, Scotland.

SC JAMES FILLANS, 1845, marble bust, County Hall, Paisley; plaster cast, SNPG 604. SIR JOHN STEELL, 1865, statue, Dean Cemetery, Edinburgh.

C B.W.CROMBIE, pencil and w/c, a study for 'Modern Athenians', SNPG 2306.

WILSON, Patrick (1743-1811) astronomer.

SC JAMES TASSIE, 1796, plaster medallion, oval, SNPG 2236.

WILSON, Richard (1714-1782) landscape painter.

P ANTON R.MENGS, hl with palette, National Museum of Wales, 637, Cardiff. After A.R.MENGS, hl, NPG 1803. Self-portrait, Royal Academy, London.

D ANTON R.MENGS, hs, chalk, BM. JOSEPH FARINGTON, painting from nature in Moor Park, 1765, V & A.

G JOHAN ZOFFANY, 'Royal Academicians 1772', oil, Royal Coll.

WILSON, Richard (fl 1774-1792) actor.

P Attrib SAMUEL DE WILDE, 1790, wl, as Sir Francis Wronghead in *The Provok'd Husband*, Somerset Maugham Coll, National Theatre, London. Attrib GEORGE ROMNEY, hl as Polonius in *Hamlet*, with John Henderson as Hamlet, Garrick Club, London.

D J.ROBERTS, head, wearing cocked hat, pencil, Garrick Club, London.

PR Various theatrical prints, BM, NPG.

WILSON, Sir Robert Thomas (1777-1849) general and governor of Gibraltar.

D COUNT ALFRED D'ORSAY, 1837, hl profile, DoE.

G A.J.BLANCHARD, after A.Neveu, hs with Sir John Hely Hutchinson and Michael Bruce, line, BM.

PR W.HOLL, after R.Cosway, hl in armour, stipple, pub 1805, BM, NPG. W.WARD, after H.Pickersgill, tql in uniform, with orders, mezz, pub 1819, NPG, BM.

C R.DIGHTON, entitled 'A Good Soldier, but no General', in 'West End Characters', 1821, coloured etch, NPG, V & A.

WILSON, Thomas (1703-1784) divine.

P UNKNOWN, tql pointing to 'Magna Carta, Bill of Rights', Oriel College, Oxford.

PR J. and C.SHERWIN, after J.Wright, tql seated, line, for his father's *Works*, 1782, BM, NPG.

WILSON, Thomas (1747-1813) schoolmaster.

PR W.WARD, after J.Allen, tql seated in wig and gown, mezz, BM.

WILSON, Thomas (1764-1843) nonconformist benefactor.

PR H.DAWE, after S.Dawe, hs, Dr Williams's Library, London.

WILSON, Thomas (1767-1852) merchant, alias 'Buckskin' Wilson.

C R.DIGHTON, 1824, coloured etch, NPG, V & A.

WILSON, Mrs, née Adcock (d1786) actress.

PR W.N.GARDINER, after S.Harding, as Harriet in Holcroft's *Seduction*, hl, coloured stipple, pub 1787, BM.

WILTON, Joseph (1722-1803) sculptor.

P SIR JOSHUA REYNOLDS, 1752, hl, NPG 4810. Attrib J.H.MORTIMER, c1779(?), wl with the artist and a student, Royal Academy, London.

D CHARLES GRIGNION, jun, c1773, hs, chalk, NPG 4314. GEORGE DANCE, 1793, hs, profile, Royal Academy.

G JOHAN ZOFFANY, 'Royal Academicians, 1772', oil, Royal Coll. J.F.RIGAUD, 'Sir Joshua Reynolds, Sir William Chambers and Joseph Wilton, 1782', oil, NPG 987.

SC L.F.ROUBILIAC, 1760, terracotta bust, Royal Academy.

C JOHN CAWSE, 1793, wl, pen and ink, BM.

WINCHESTER, Harry Poulet, 11th Marquess of, see 6th Duke of Bolton.

WINCHILSEA, George William Finch Hatton, 10th Earl of (1791-1858) politician of reactionary views.
PR H.ROBINSON, after T.Phillips, tql, stipple, for *Eminent Conservative Statesmen*, pub 1839, BM, NPG.

WINDHAM, William (1717-1761) colonel.
P JOHN SHACKLETON, wl in uniform, Felbrigg Hall (NT), Norfolk.
SC JEAN DASSIER, copper medal, BM.

WINDHAM, William (1750-1810) statesman.
P SIR JOSHUA REYNOLDS, 1788, hl, NPG 704. SIR THOMAS LAWRENCE, 1803, hl, NPG 38. JOHN HOPPNER, wl, Strangers Hall, Norwich.
D HENRY EDRIDGE, two pencil sketches, BM.
M UNKNOWN, c1795, two portraits, V & A.
SC JOSEPH NOLLEKENS, marble monument, Felbrigg Church, Norfolk. JOSEPH NOLLEKENS, marble bust, Holkham Hall, Norfolk.

WINSOR, Frederick Albert (1763-1830) pioneer of gas lighting.
PR M.GAUCI, after G.Dupont, hl, lith, BM. J.A.VINTER, hl, with plans, lith, BM.

WINT, Peter de, see DE Wint.

WINTER, Thomas (1795-1851) pugilist, styled 'Tom Spring'.
PR J.W.GEAR, after C.Ambrose, tql with cup, lith, BM.

WINTERBOTHAM, William (1763-1829) dissenting minister and political prisoner.
PR W.GRAINGER, after Taylor, hs in oval, line, pub 1795, BM, NPG.

WINTRINGHAM, Sir Clifton, Bart (1710-1794) physician.
SC THOMAS BANKS, marble statue, Westminster Abbey, London.

WITHERING, William (1741-1799) physician.
P CARL F. VON BREDA, 1792, tql, National Museum, Stockholm, engr W.Ridley and E.Bond, NPG, BM.

WITHERINGTON, William Frederick (1785-1865) painter.
D C.W.COPE, c1862, two pencil sketches, NPG. 3182 (6 and 9).

WITHERSPOON, John (1723-1794) presbyterian divine and statesman.
P C.W.PEALE, Princeton University, New Jersey, USA.
SC After JAMES TASSIE, 1784, plaster medallion, SNPG 481.
PR T.TROTTER, hl in gown, line, pub 1785, BM.

WIVELL, Abraham (1786-1849) portrait-painter.
PR W.HOLL, after A.Wivell, hs, stipple, oval, BM.

WODHULL, Michael (1740-1816) book-collector and translator.
PR E.HARDING, after W.N.Gardiner, hl in gown, stipple, BM, NPG.

WOFFINGTON, Margaret (1714?-1760) actress.
P JOHN LEWIS, 1753, hl with hat, NGI 579. UNKNOWN, called Peg Woffington, a sick-bed portrait, NPG 650.
PR J.BROOKS, hl, line, pub 1740, eight lines below, 'Roll on fair Sun', etc, BM. J.FABER, jun, after J.E.Eccardt, tql with volume, mezz, BM, NPG. P. VAN BLEEK, hl in hat, with title, 'Phebe', mezz, 1747, BM, NPG. J.FABER, jun, after E.Haytley, as Mrs Ford in *Merry Wives of Windsor*, wl, mezz, 1751, BM, NPG. J.FABER, jun, after H.Pickering, tql seated, mezz, BM.

WOIDE, Charles Godfrey (1725-1790) oriental scholar.
PR F.BARTOLOZZI, hl in wig, stipple, pub 1791, BM, NPG.

WOLCOT, John (1738-1819) 'Peter Pindar', physician and satirist.
P JOHN OPIE, hl, NPG 830. JOHN OPIE, c1785, Royal Institution of Cornwall, Truro. JOHN OPIE, hl, City Art Gallery, Auckland,

New Zealand.
D GEORGE DANCE, 1793, hs, pencil, BM.
M HENRY BONE, 1793, V & A. W.S.LETHBRIDGE, hl with book, NPG 156.

WOLFE, Arthur (1739-1803), see Viscount Kilwarden.

WOLFE, Charles (1791-1823) poet.
PR H.MEYER, after J.J.Russell, nearly hl, profile, stipple, pub 1826, NPG.

WOLFE, James (1727-1759) general.
P JOSEPH HIGHMORE, hl, Public archives of Canada, Ottawa, Canada. Attrib J.S.C.SHAAK, hl profile, NPG 48. UNKNOWN, hl, NPG IIII.
D VISCOUNT DILLON, after H.Smith, head, tracing, NPG 713a. LADY ELIZABETH FOSTER, hs, pencil and w/c, NPG 688. GEORGE TOWNSEND, hs, w/c, McCord Museum, McGill University, Montreal, Canada.
G BENJAMIN WEST, 'The Death of Wolfe', oil, 1770, National Gallery of Canada, Ottawa; version, Royal Coll.
SC JOSEPH WILTON, c1759, plaster bust, in armour, NPG 4415. JOSEPH WILTON, monument, Westminster Abbey, London.

WOLFF, Joseph (1795-1862) missionary.
P UNKNOWN, probably the sitter, hl, Lambeth Palace, London.
PR H.MEYER, after E.Fancourt, hl with book, mezz, pub 1827, BM. UNKNOWN, hs in profile, lith, NPG.

WOLLASTON, William Hyde (1766-1828) physiologist, chemist and physicist.
P JOHN JACKSON, tql, Royal Society, London.
D JOHN JACKSON, tql, pencil, NPG 1703. WILLIAM BROCKEDON, hs, pencil and chalk, NPG 2515(10). SIR FRANCIS CHANTREY, hs, pencil, NPG 316a (144). SIR THOMAS LAWRENCE, hs, Althorp, Northants.
G J.F.SKILL, J.GILBERT, W. and E.WALKER, 'Men of Science Living in 1807-8', pencil and wash, NPG 1075.
SC SIR FRANCIS CHANTREY, plaster bust, Ashmolean Museum, Oxford.

WOLLSTONECRAFT, Mary, see Godwin.

WOOD, Alexander (1725-1807) surgeon.
P D.ALISON, SNPG 1368.
C J.KAY, wl in profile with umbrella, etch, BM.

WOOD, Sir George (1743-1824) baron of the exchequer.
PR T.HODGETTS, after J.Lonsdale, wl in robes, mezz, pub 1819, BM, NPG.

WOOD, Sir George Adam (1767-1831) general.
P Attrib S.COLE, c1815, hl in uniform, NPG 3990. UNKNOWN, hl in uniform, Royal Artillery Mess, Woolwich. H.W.PICKERSGILL, c1825, tql in uniform, with orders, Royal Coll.

WOOD, James (1760-1839) mathematician.
P JOHN JACKSON, 1824, hs, St John's College, Cambridge.
SC E.H.BAILY, 1843, marble monument, St John's College Chapel, Cambridge.
C R.DIGHTON, wl, coloured etch, pub 1809, NPG.

WOOD, Sir James Athol (1756-1829) rear admiral.
PR H.R.COOK, hs in uniform, stipple, pub 1810, NPG.

WOOD, Sir Matthew, 1st Bart (1768-1843) municipal and political reformer, lord mayor of London.
P A.W.DEVIS, almost hl, NPG 1481.
G SIR GEORGE HAYTER, 'The Trial of Queen Caroline, 1820', oil, NPG 999.
C R.DIGHTON, 1819, hl, 'A View in the Justice Room, Guildhall', coloured etch, pub 1824, NPG. UNKNOWN, head of sitter, with an owl's body, entitled 'Absolute Wisdom or Queen's Owl',

coloured etch, NPG.

WOOD, Robert (1716-1771) classical archaeologist and politician.
P ALLAN RAMSAY, 1755, hl with papers, NPG 4868.
PR J.HALL, 1773, after G.Hamilton (1758), 'James Dawkins and Robert Wood Esqrs First Discovering Sight of Palmyra', NPG. P.W.TOMKINS, after R.Mengs, hl, stipple and line, for Ottley's *Stafford Gallery*, 1818, BM.

WOODD, Basil (1760-1831) hymn-writer.
PR R.W.SIEVIER, after J.Barry, hl in gown, from a miniature, stipple, oval, pub 1817, BM, NPG.

WOODFALL, William (1746-1803) parliamentary reporter and dramatic critic.
P THOMAS BEACH, 1782, hl, NPG 169.
PR UNKNOWN, hs, stipple, oval, for his 'An Impartial Report-of-the-Debates in the Two Halves of Parliament in the year 1797', pub 1797, NPG.

WOODFORD, Sir Ralph James, Bart (1784-1828) governor of Trinidad.
P SIR THOMAS LAWRENCE, RA 1830, wl in uniform, Legislative Chamber, Red House, Port of Spain, Trinidad, engr C.Turner, hl, mezz, pub 1829, BM, NPG.
M GEORGE ENGLEHEART, hs, oval, Metropolitan Museum of Art, New York, USA.

WOODHOUSE, James (1735-1820) shoemaker and poet.
PR UNKNOWN, wl, line, pub 1765, NPG. H.COOK, after W.Hobday, hs, line, pub 1818, BM, NPG.

WOODHOUSELEE, Alexander Fraser Tytler, Lord (1747-1813) historian.
PR C.PICART, after H.Raeburn, hs, stipple, for *Contemporary Portraits*, 1813, BM, NPG.

WOODVILLE, William (1752-1805) physician and botanist.
P L.F.ABBOT, hl, Royal College of Physicians, London.
G N.BRANWHITE, after S.Medley, 'Institutors of the Medical Society of London', stipple, pub 1801, BM.

WOODWARD, Francis (1721-1785) physician.
P THOMAS BEACH, hl, Victoria Art Gallery, Bath.

WOODWARD, George Moutard (1760?-1809) caricaturist.
PR T.CHEESMAN, after A.Buck, hl, stipple, for his *Literary Works*, 1805, BM, NPG.

WOODWARD, Henry (1714-1777) actor.
P BENJAMIN VANDERGUCHT, 1775, as Petruchio, in *Catherine and Petruchio*, tql, Garrick Club, London. SAMUEL DE WILDE, after Johan Zoffany, as Razor in *The Upholsterer*, hs, Garrick Club. THOMAS WORLIDGE, as Bran in *The Confederacy*, hl, Garrick Club. SIR JOSHUA REYNOLDS, hl in Vandyke dress, Petworth (NT), West Sussex.
D JAMES ROBERTS, 1776, as Bobadil, in *Every Man in his Humour*, BM. FRANCIS HAYMAN, wl, pencil, as the Fine Gentleman in Garrick's farce *Lethe*, Fitzwilliam Museum, Cambridge. JAMES ROBERTS, as Captain Brazen in Farquhar's *Recruiting Officer*, BM.
PR Various theatrical prints, BM, NPG.

WOODWARD, Samuel (1790-1838) geologist and antiquary.
PR MISS TURNER, hs, lith, BM.

WOOLER, Thomas Jonathan (1786?-1853) journalist and politician.
PR UNKNOWN, after C.Landseer, hs, etch, pub 1817, BM, NPG. S.FREEMAN, after T.Smith, hl, stipple, BM, NPG. UNKNOWN, hl, holding copy of 'The Black Dwarf', NPG.

WOOLL, John (1767-1833) schoolmaster.

PR C.TURNER, after T.Lawrence, tql, mezz, pub 1813, BM, NPG.

WOOLLETT, William (1735-1785) draughtsman and line engraver.
P GILBERT STUART, exhib 1783, hl, TATE 217.
D WILLIAM JEFFERYS, hl, pastel, Maidstone Art Gallery, Kent. Self-portrait, hl, Maidstone Art Gallery. Self-portrait (?), hl, chalk, BM.
PR J.K.SHERWIN, hl, line, pub 1784, BM, NPG.

WORDSWORTH, William (1770-1850) poet.
P WILLIAM SHUTER, 1798, hs, Cornell University, Ithaca, New York. RICHARD CARRUTHERS, hl, replica of his portrait of 1817, Municipal Art Gallery, East London, South Africa. SIR WILLIAM BOXALL, 1831, hs, NPG 4211. BENJAMIN ROBERT HAYDON, 1842, tql on Hellvelyn, NPG 1857. BENJAMIN ROBERT HAYDON, 1843, unfinished, Dove Cottage, Cumbria. SAMUEL CROSTHWAITE, 1844, hl, Dove Cottage. HENRY INMAN, 1844, hs, University of Pennsylvania, Philadelphia. H.W.PICKERSGILL, wl (replica), NPG 104. H.W.PICKERSGILL, tql, St John's College, Cambridge.
D ROBERT HANCOCK, 1798, hl profile seated, pencil and chalk, NPG 450. BENJAMIN ROBERT HAYDON, 1818, hs, pencil and chalk, NPG 3687. H.W.PICKERSGILL, 1832, head, chalk, St John's College, Cambridge. BENJAMIN ROBERT HAYDON, 1843, chalk and pencil, Dove Cottage. SIR FRANCIS CHANTREY, head, profile, pencil, NPG 316a (146).
M MARGARET GILLIES, 1839, hl seated, Dove Cottage, Cumbria.
G JAMES STEPHANOFF, 'The Trial of Queen Caroline, 1820', w/c, Palace of Westminster, London.
SC BENJAMIN ROBERT HAYDON, 1815, plaster cast of life mask, NPG 2020. SIR FRANCIS CHANTREY, 1820, marble bust, Indiana University, Bloomington, USA. FREDERICK THRUPP, marble statue, Westminster Abbey, London.

WORLINGHAM, Sir Archibald Acheson, 1st Baron, see 2nd Earl of Gosford.

WORSLEY, Sir Richard, 7th Bart (1751-1805) antiquary and traveller.
M GEORGE ENGLEHEART, 1800, oval, V & A.
PR A.CARDON, hs in oval, stipple, BM, NPG.

WORTHINGTON, Hugh (1752-1813) Arian divine.
PR HARDING, after W.Read, in pulpit, line, oval, BM.

WORTLEY-Montagu, Edward, see MONTAGU.

WOULFE, Stephen (1787-1840) Irish judge.
PR S.CATTERSON SMITH, after M.Cregan, King's Inns, Dublin.

WRANGHAM, Francis (1769-1842) classical scholar and miscellaneous writer.
M E.WESTOOY, hl with book, Trinity College, Cambridge.
PR R.HICKS, after J.Jackson, hl, stipple, for Jerdan's *Nat Portrait Gallery*, 1829, BM, NPG.

WRAXALL, Sir Nathaniel William, 1st Bart (1751-1831) author of historical memoirs.
PR T.CHEESMAN, after J.Wright, hl, stipple, for *Contemporary Portraits*, 1813, BM, NPG. R.COOPER, after J.Jackson, hl, stipple, for his *Historical Memoirs*, 1815, BM, NPG.

WRAY, Sir Cecil, 13th Bart (1734-1805) politician.
PR UNKNOWN, hs, line, oval, pub 1784, NPG.

WRAY, Daniel (1701-1783) antiquary.
P NATHANIEL DANCE, 1769?, hs, Queen's College, Cambridge.
PR LONGMATE, after silhouette by M.Wray, wl in profile, aquatint, for Nichols's *Literary Illustrations*, 1817, BM, NPG.

WREY or WRAY, Sir Bourchier (1714-1784) dilettante.
P GEORGE KNAPTON, 1744(?), hl, Society of Dilettanti, Brooks's

Club, London.

WRIGHT, Ichabod Charles (1795-1871) translator of Dante.
D UNKNOWN, ink, Castle Art Gallery, Nottingham.
PR C.TURNER, after E.U.Eddis, hs, mezz, BM, NPG.

WRIGHT, John Wesley (1769-1805) naval commander.
PR T.BLOOD, hs, stipple, for *Naval Chronicle*, 1815, BM, NPG.

WRIGHT, Joseph (of Derby) (1734-1797) painter.
P Self-portrait (?), *c*1770, wearing hat, Derby Museum and Art Gallery. Self-portrait, hs, NPG 4090. Self-portrait, hl wearing turban, National Gallery of Canada, Ottawa.
D Self-portrait, *c*1758, hs in oval, pencil, Fitzwilliam Museum, Cambridge. Self-portrait, *c*1767–70, in fur cap, charcoal, Derby Museum and Art Gallery.
G JOSEPH WRIGHT, 'A Philosopher giving a lecture on the Orrery', oil, (sitter on the extreme right of the group), Derby Museum and Art Gallery.

WRIGHT, Mrs Patience (1725-1786) wax-modeller.
PR UNKNOWN, wl, with wax model, line, for *London Mag*, 1775, BM, NPG.

WRIGHT, Thomas (1711-1786) mathematician and astronomer.
PR T.FRYE, hl seated with diagrams, mezz, 1737, BM, NPG. UNKNOWN, hs, line, for *Gent Mag*, 1793, BM, NPG.

WRIGHT, Thomas (1789-1875) prison philanthropist.
D G.F.WATTS, *c*1850-1, head, chalk, NPG 1016.

WRIGHT, Waller Rodwell (*d*1826) consul for the Ionian islands.
PR C.KNIGHT, after E.Scott, hl with masonic orders, stipple, pub 1813, BM, NPG.

WRIXON-BECHER, Eliza, Lady (1791-1872) née O'Neill, actress.
P J.J.MASQUERIER, *c*1815, hl, NPG 445. A.W.DEVIS, 1816, 'as Belvidera' in Otway's *Venice Preserved*, Wolverhampton Art Gallery. T.C.THOMPSON, NGI 604. G.F.JOSEPH, 'as the tragic muse', Garrick Club, London.
M SIR W.J.NEWTON, NGI.
PR T.BLOOD, after S.Drummond, hl, stipple, for *European Mag*, 1814, BM, NPG. H.DAWE, as Juliet in *Romeo and Juliet*, wl, mezz, BM.

WROTTESLEY, Sir John Wrottesley, 1st Baron (1771-1841) politician.
G SIR G.HAYTER, 'The House of Commons, 1833', oil, NPG 54.

WROUGHTON, Richard (1748-1822) actor and theatrical manager.
D SAMUEL DE WILDE, 1815, as Sir John Restless in *All in the Wrong*, w/c, Garrick Club, London. JAMES ROBERTS, as Edward in Shirley's *Edward the Black Prince*, wl in armour, BM.
PR Various theatrical prints, BM, NPG.

WYATT, Benjamin Dean (1775-1850?) architect.
PR T.BLOOD, after S.Drummond, hl, stipple, for *European Mag*, 1812, BM, NPG.

WYATT, James (1746-1813) architect.
P SIR WILLIAM BEECHEY, hl, Royal Academy, London. JOHN

OPIE, RIBA, London.
D GEORGE DANCE, 1795, hl, Royal Academy.
SC J.C.F.ROSSI, bronze bust, NPG 344. UNKNOWN, Wedgwood medallion, Brooklyn Museum, USA.
PR C.TURNER, after M.C.Wyatt, hl, mezz, pub 1809, BM, NPG. J.SINGLETON, after O.Humphry, hl, stipple, BM, NPG.

WYATT, Richard James (1795-1850) sculptor.
D JOHN PARTRIDGE, 1825, hs, pencil, NPG 3944 (19), woodcut after it for *Illustrated London News*, 1850, NPG.
SC JOHN GIBSON, *c*1850, medallion, Wyatt's grave, Protestant Cemetery, Rome.
PR UNKNOWN, after S.Pearce, for *Art Journal*, 1850, BM, NPG.

WYATVILLE, Sir Jeffry (1766-1840) architect.
D SIR FRANCIS CHANTREY, hs pencil sketches, NPG 316a (147–149).
SC SIR FRANCIS CHANTREY, 1837, marble bust, Royal Coll.
PR H.ROBINSON, after R.Evans, nearly wl with compasses and plans, stipple, pub 1834, BM, NPG.

WYNCH, Florentina, see Lady Sale.

WYNDHAM, Sir Charles, see 2nd Earl of Egremont.

WYNDHAM, Sir George O'Brien, see 3rd Earl of Egremont.

WYNFORD, William Draper Best, 1st Baron (1767-1845) chief justice of the common pleas.
P H.W.PICKERSGILL, tql in judges robes, Bridport Town Hall, Dorset. JOHN PARTRIDGE, *c*1826, tql seated in robes, Middle Temple, London. UNKNOWN, tql seated, Wadham College, Oxford.
PR W.SAY, after H.Pickersgill, tql seated in robes, mezz, pub 1815, BM, NPG. F.HALPIN, after T.Lawrence, hl, line, BM.
C JOHN DOYLE, 'A Constitutional Tilt', 1832, pen and pencil, BM.

WYNN, Charles Watkin Williams (1775-1850) politician.
P SIR M.A.SHEE, hl, Christ Church, Oxford, engr W.J.Ward, mezz, pub 1835, BM, NPG.
G SIR G.HAYTER, 'The House of Commons, 1833', oil, NPG 54.

WYON, William (1795-1851) chief engraver at the royal mint.
D CARL VOGEL, 1837, hs, Küpferstichkabinett, Staatliche Kunstsammlungen, Dresden. C.H.LEAR, *c*1845, hs, chalk, NPG 1456(21). WILLIAM BROCKEDON, 1825, hs, pencil and chalk, NPG 2515(8).
SC L.C.WYON, bronze medallion, for the Art Union, BM, NPG.
PR W.DRUMMOND, after E.U.Eddis, hl, lith, for *Athenaeum Portraits*, 1835, BM, NPG. J.KIRKWOOD, after L.C.Wyon, 1842, hl, for Sainthill's *Olla Podrida*, BM, NPG.

WYSE, Sir Thomas (1791-1862) politician and diplomatist.
P JOHN PARTRIDGE, hl, NGI 140.
G JOHN PARTRIDGE, 'The Fine Arts Commissioners, 1846', NPG 342, 343.
SC COSSOS and BRONTOS, marble, NGI 8185.
PR E.SCRIVEN, after B.E.Duppa, hl in cloak, stipple, for Saunders's *Political Reformers*, 1841, BM, NPG.

WYVILL, Christopher (1740-1822) advocate for parliamentary reform.
PR H.MEYER, after J.Hoppner, hl, mezz, BM, NPG.

Y

YARMOUTH, Amalie Sophie Marianne Wallmoden, Countess of (1704-1765) mistress of George II.
PR G. DE KÖNING, after Peter van Hoogh, hl, mezz, NPG.

YARRELL, William (1784-1856) zoologist.
PR F.A.HEATH, after a photograph by Maull and Polyblank, hl, stipple and line, pub 1859, NPG. M.GAUCI, after E.U.Eddis, hl, lith, BM. T.H.MAGUIRE, tql, lith, for *Ipswich Museum Portraits*, BM, NPG.

YATES, Mrs Elizabeth (1799-1860) actress.
PR T.WOOLNOTH, after T.Wageman, as Grace Huntley, wl, stipple, for Cumberland's *British Theatre*, 1833, BM.

YATES, Frederick Henry (1797-1842) actor.
P JAMES LONSDALE, hl seated, Garrick Club, London, engr W.Say, mezz, pub 1826, BM. UNKNOWN, hs, oval, Garrick Club.
PR R.CRUIKSHANK, as M.Grimacier in *Cozening*, wl, coloured etch, BM.

YATES, Mrs Mary Ann (1728-1787) actress.
P FRANCIS COTES, tql, holding book, Garrick Club, London.
M SAMUEL COTES, 1769, as Electra in Voltaire's *Orestes*, on ivory, V & A.
PR Various theatrical prints, BM, NPG.

YATES, Richard (1706?-1796) comedian.
D JAMES ROBERTS, 1781, wl, Garrick Club, London.
PR Various theatrical prints, BM, NPG.

YATES, Richard (1769-1834) divine and antiquary.
PR H.MEYER, after S.Drummond, hs, stipple, for *European Mag*, 1818, BM, NPG.

YEARSLEY, Mrs Ann (1756-1806) poet.
PR J.GROZER, after S.Shiells, nearly wl seated, mezz, pub 1787, BM, NPG. W.LOWRY, hl in hat, line, pub 1787, BM, NPG.

YELLOWLEES, William (1796-c1859) artist.
P Self-portrait, 1814, hs, SNPG 1247.
SC WILLIAM EWING, 1818, ivory medallion, SNPG 1859.

YELVERTON, Barry, see 1st Viscount Avonmore.

YEO, Sir James Lucas (1782-1818) commodore.
PR H.R.COOK, after A.Buck, hs in uniform, for *Naval Chronicle*, 1810, BM, NPG.

YEO, Richard (d1779) medallist.
D CHARLES GRIGNION, jun, hs, chalk, BM.
G JOHAN ZOFFANY, 'Royal Academicians, 1772', oil, Royal Coll.
PR UNKNOWN, hl, mezz, NPG.

YONGE, Sir George, 5th Bart (1731-1812) Governor of the Cape of Good Hope.
PR E.SCOTT, after M.Brown, hl, stipple, pub 1790, BM, NPG. P.RAJON, after J.Reynolds, hl, etch, for *Gazette des Beaux Arts*, 2 Per, vol 7, p 407, BM.

YORK, Cardinal Henry Benedict Maria Clement Stuart (1725-1807) second son of the Old Pretender and brother of Bonnie Prince Charlie.
P ANTONIO DAVID, 1732, hl, SNPG 888; version, NPG 435. LOUIS GABRIEL BLANCHET, 1738, tql, Royal Coll. After DOMENICO CORVI, (type of c1748), SNPG 624. After POMPEO BATONI (?), hl, NPG 129.

D Attrib H.D.HAMILTON, c1786, hs in robes, pastel, NPG 378.
SC GIOACCHIMO HAMERANI, 1788, silver medal, NPG 2784.

YORK and ALBANY, Edward Augustus, Duke of (1739-1767) son of Frederick, Prince of Wales.
P RICHARD WILSON, c1751, with his brother, Later George III and his tutor Dr Ayscough, NPG 1165. SIR JOSHUA REYNOLDS, 1758-59, hl in uniform, Royal Coll. NATHANIEL DANCE, 1764, wl in Garter robes, Royal Coll. SIR JOSHUA REYNOLDS, 1766, hs with horsewhip, Royal Coll.
D J.E.LIOTARD, hl with Garter star, Royal Coll.
G RICHARD BROMPTON, 'Edward Duke of York and his friends', oil, Royal Coll.
SC JOSEPH NOLLEKENS, 1766, bust, Royal Coll.

YORK and ALBANY, Frederick Augustus, Duke of (1763-1827) second son of George III, commander in chief of the army.
P JOHAN ZOFFANY, c1700, wl as a child, Royal Coll. SIR JOSHUA REYNOLDS, c1788, wl in Garter robes, Royal Coll. SIR DAVID WILKIE, 1823, wl seated, NPG 2936. SIR THOMAS LAWRENCE, RA 1816, wl, Royal Coll. SIR WILLIAM BEECHEY, wl in uniform, Waddesdon Manor (NT), Bucks. After JOHN JACKSON, hs, NPG 1615.
M JEREMIAH MEYER, c1767, hl, oval, Royal Coll. JEREMIAH MEYER, as a young man, oval, Royal Coll. RICHARD COSWAY, as a young man, ivory, oval, Royal Coll.
SL UNKNOWN, wl, with George IV, NPG 1691a.
G JOHAN ZOFFANY, 'George III and family', oil, 1770, Royal Coll. SIR GEORGE HAYTER, 'The Trial of Queen Caroline, 1820', oil, NPG 999.
SC CHARLES LOCHÉE, 1787, Wedgwood medallion, Nottingham City Art Gallery and Museum. J.C.LOCHÉE, c1787, marble bust, Royal Coll. JOSEPH NOLLEKENS, 1813, marble bust, Royal Coll. THOMAS CAMPBELL, marble bust, Hopetoun House, Lothian region, Scotland. Attrib I.FRANCIS, bust, Royal Coll. ISAAC PARKES, silver medal, National Museum of Ireland. JOHN DE VEAUX, wax medallion, NPG 2921.

YORKE, Charles (1722-1770) lord chancellor.
PR BOVI, after wax by I.Gosset in 1766, stipple, pub 1796, NPG. UNKNOWN, hs, profile, in wig and gown, stipple, BM. S.FREEMAN, copy of above, stipple, for *European Mag*, 1803, BM.

YORKE, Sir Charles (1790-1880) field-marshal.
PH UNKNOWN, hl, in uniform, NPG.

YORKE, Charles Philip (1799-1873), see 4th Earl of Hardwicke.

YORKE, Henry Redhead (1772-1813) publicist.
PR J.WARD, after W.Hay, hl in uniform, mezz, pub 1796, BM, NPG. S.W.REYNOLDS, after J.R.Smith, tql, mezz, pub 1796, BM.

YORKE, Sir James (1799-1871), see Scarlett.

YORKE, Joseph, Baron Dover, see Dover.

YORKE, Sir Joseph Sydney (1768-1831) admiral.
P UNKNOWN, c1793-5, hl in naval uniform, NMM, Greenwich.
PR V.GREEN, after C.Read, as a child of three, tql with dog, oval, mezz, pub 1772, BM, NPG.

YORKE, Philip (1720-1790), see 2nd Earl of Hardwicke.

YORKE, Philip (1743-1804) politician and author.
PR E.SCRIVEN, after T.Gainsborough, tql, stipple, BM, NPG.

YORKE, Philip (1757-1834), see 3rd Earl of Hardwicke.

YOUNG, Arthur (1741-1820) agriculturist, traveller and writer.
D GEORGE DANCE, 1794, hl, profile, NPG 1162.
G JAMES BARRY, 'The Society for the Encouragement of Arts', oil, Royal Society of Arts, London.
SC GEORGE GARRARD, 1804, marble bust, Petworth (NT), West Sussex.
PR W.HINTON, after J.Rising, hl, stipple, for *European Mag*, 1795, BM, NPG.

YOUNG, Sir Charles George (1795-1869) garter king-of-arms.
PR G.J.BLACK, hl, lith, NPG.

YOUNG, Charles Mayne (1777-1856) actor and comedian.
P GEORGE CLINT, with Miss Phillis Glover in *Hamlet*, V & A. G.H.HARLOW, hs, Garrick Club, London. SIR EDWIN LANDSEER, hs, as King John, Garrick Club.
D JOHN LINNELL, hl profile, chalk, NPG 1814. G.H.HARLOW, head, pencil and sanguine, Garrick Club. Various w/cs in character by SAMUEL DE WILDE, Garrick Club.
G SIR G.HAYTER, 'The Trial of Queen Caroline, 1820', oil, NPG 999.

PR Large number of theatrical prints, BM, NPG.

YOUNG, Sir George (1732-1810) admiral.
M JOHN SMART, 1805, V & A.

YOUNG, Matthew (1750-1800) bishop of Clonfert.
P UNKNOWN, hl in robes, Trinity College, Dublin.
SC THOMAS KIRK, 1827, marble bust, Trinity College, Dublin.

YOUNG, Thomas (1773-1829) physician, physicist and egyptologist.
P H.P.BRIGGS, after Sir Thomas Lawrence, hl, The Royal Society, London.
G J.F.SKILL, J.GILBERT, W. and E.WALKER, 'Men of Science Living in 1807–08', pencil and wash, NPG 1075.
SC SIR FRANCIS CHANTREY, medallion portrait on memorial tablet, Westminster Abbey, London.

YOUNG, Sir William, 2nd Bart (1749-1815) politician and writer.
P SIR BENJAMIN WEST, 1767, hl, a leaving portrait, Eton College, Berks.
PR T.HOLLOWAY, hs, line, oval, for *European Mag*, 1787, BM, NPG. J.COLLYER, after J.Brown (1788), tql, circle, stipple, BM, NPG. W.SAY, after W.Beechey, tql, mezz, pub 1805, BM.

YOUNG, Sir William (1751-1821) admiral.
C R.DIGHTON, wl, etch, pub 1809, NPG.

Z

ZOFFANY, Johan (1733-1810) painter.
P Self-portrait, *c*1759, hl with palette, Mainfränkisches Museum, Würzburg. Two self-portraits: 1775, hl with dog; 1776, hl with hour glass and skull, Uffizi Gallery, Florence. Self-portrait, 1776, hl with palette, Accademia Etrusca, Cortona.
D Self-portrait, *c*1775, hs, chalk, BM. Self-portrait, 1782, hs, Ashmolean Museum, Oxford. GEORGE DANCE, 1793, hs profile, Royal Academy, London. Self-portrait, *c*1795, hs, NPG 2536.

M UNKNOWN, hs, V & A.
G JOHAN ZOFFANY, with companions in his studio, oil, Uffizi Gallery, Florence. JOHAN ZOFFANY, 'Royal Academicians, 1772', oil, Royal Coll.

ZUCCARELLI, Francesco (1702-1788) lancscape painter.
P RICHARD WILSON, 1751, hs, TATE 3727.
G JOHAN ZOFFANY, 'Royal Academicians 1772', oil, Royal Coll.

ZUYLESTEIN, William Henry, see 4th Earl of Rochford.